A LIGHT IN DARKNESS

VOLUME ONE

Seven Messages
to the Seven Churches

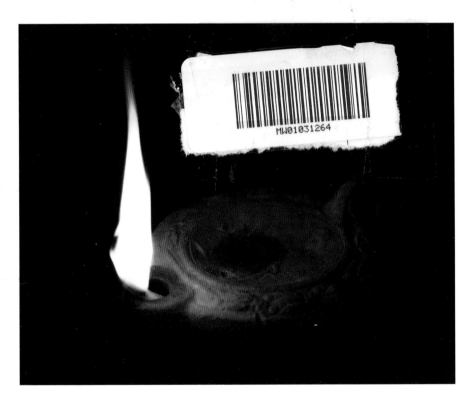

PUBLISHED IN PARTNERSHIP

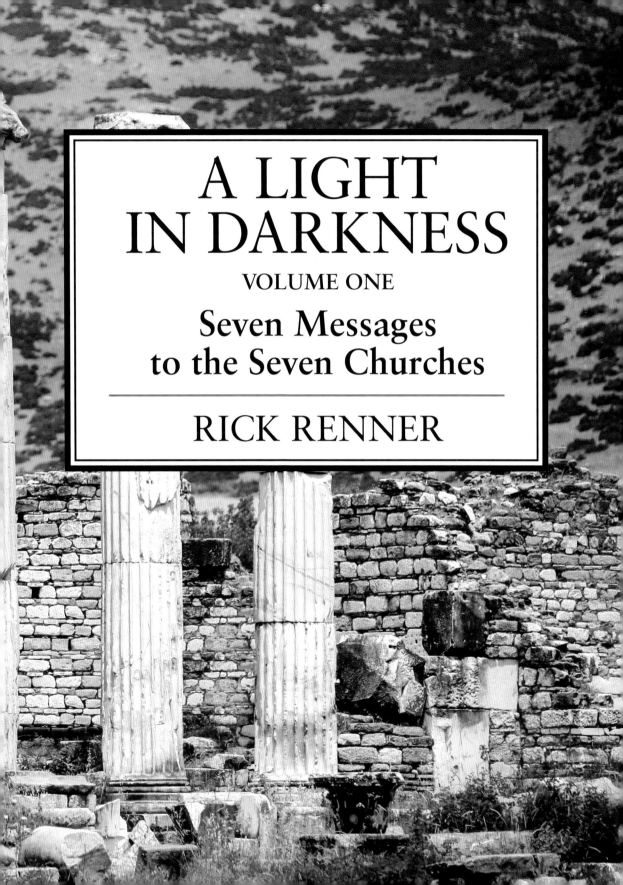

A LIGHT IN DARKNESS

VOLUME ONE

Seven Messages to the Seven Churches

RICK RENNER

ENDORSEMENTS

The following endorsements were written by archeologists, museum directors, historians, Classical Greek scholars, theologians, Bible teachers, pastors, and best-selling authors. All are held in the utmost esteem by those who have benefited from their significant contributions in their respective fields. I am both honored and thankful that each of these individuals took the time to examine this manuscript and to share their expert conclusions about this work.

Rick Renner

As I have shown in my own book (*Guide to the Seven Churches*), the great cities of Ephesus, Smyrna, Pergamum, Thyatira, Sardis, Philadelphia, and Laodicea were historically very significant in both the Greek and Roman worlds and were homes to the early Christian Church. Researching these cities and the development of the churches in this territory is a lifelong occupation. Renner has done an outstanding job of documenting and presenting the evidence about these cities and churches. This book would be a great addition to any serious student's library.

Fatih Cimok
- Turkish Scholar of Biblical Literature
- Author of many books, including: *Biblical Anatolia*; *Guide to the Seven Churches*; *Journeys of Paul*; *Antioch Mosaics*; *Cappadocia*; *Antioch on the Orontes*; *Saint Sophia*; *Saint Saviour in Chora*; *Saint Paul in Anatolia and Cyprus*; and *Pergamum*.

My shelves are filled with historical works on the subjects of the seven churches of Revelation, but not one of them compares to this volume of *Seven Messages to the Seven Churches*. It is set in a category of its own because of its pages and pages of researched material and the vast amount of photos, art, and illustrations included that assist in showing what life was like in the ancient world. This book is too big for my shelves, so I'll make sure to put it in a visible place where I can refer to it often. Renner has done us an outstanding service by putting all of this on paper.

Because so many books on this subject have already been written, I didn't expect to discover a new book filled with such marvelous graphics and information about these ancient sites. I was quite surprised to see the enormity of this book and the obvious in-depth research that Renner did to produce such a large volume. It may be the most thorough book I've ever seen on this subject. The written material is no less excellent than the beautiful photos and art that cover each page of the book.

Cengiz İçten
- Former Director and Chief Archeologist of the Ephesus Museum in Selçuk, Turkey
- Led the primary excavations of the ancient city of Ephesus for 40 years
- Escort and professional guide for heads of state during official visits to Turkey

---

For many years, I have been working as a professor and instructor of expert historical guides for Turkey. I have personally taught and prepared more than 5,000 of these guides, and my specialty has always been to teach guides who take groups to the sites of the seven churches from the book of Revelation. I am very familiar with the subject, so it is hard to surprise or impress me. But I can honestly say that I was deeply impressed with Renner's book. Renner did an excellent job of studying and discovering hidden truths and facts. I am so confident in his book that I will recommend it to my students and to future historical guides for Turkey. Renner's book will definitely help my students, as well as anyone who wants to learn more about the seven churches of Revelation. In fact, as soon as I read his book, I requested that a copy would be delivered to me for my personal library and another copy to the library of Izmir's Yaşar University.

Dr. Şadan Gökovali
- Masters and Doctorate Degree in Communications in Tourism and Public Relations
- Formerly Professor at Aegean University and Dokuz Eylul University; currently Professor at Yaşar University, all located in Izmir (ancient Smyrna)
- Professor of Mythology and the History of Anatolian Religions
- Instructor of Professional National Tour Guides for Turkey
- Collaborated with Azra Erhat, the famous Turkish author of the classic work, *Dictionary of Mythology*
- Author of such books as *Ephesus*, *Izmir*, *Pergamum*, and *Istanbul*

The first volume of Rick Renner's projected four-volume work dealing with the seven churches of Revelation contributes greatly to the reader's understanding of the conditions that existed in the Eastern Mediterranean world of the late First and early Second Centuries AD. In highly readable prose, Renner introduces us to the geography, history, and daily life of that milieu. Indeed, one of the strengths of the book is the way the author has presented a great deal of scholarly research and information in such a brief and interesting — one might almost say entertaining — way. Indeed, the reader continually runs the risk of overlooking the book's solid scholarship, just because it is so highly readable and its narrative moves along so smoothly and rapidly. If, as the Roman poet Horace said, the secret of great writing is "art concealing art," one cannot but agree that Rick Renner has admirably succeeded in this respect.

Renner has also done a marvelous job of integrating Scripture and historical background. Because I am not a biblical scholar or theologian, many of the more challenging religious aspects of this volume of *Seven Messages to the Seven Churches* lie beyond my sphere of scholarly expertise. But as one who has taught about the Mediterranean world for almost half a century, I am familiar with the historical circumstances that prevailed at this time. And I can say without hesitation that Rick Renner has done an outstanding job — not only of mastering and interpreting an extensive and controversial body of scholarly research, but also of presenting it in such a way that even non-scholarly readers, who are largely unfamiliar with these matters, will have no trouble following the author through this often-difficult maze. In fact, the author seems very aware of these readers as he patiently and skillfully explains many difficult points without digressing and damaging the flow of his narrative.

I highly recommend this first volume of *Seven Messages to the Seven Churches* — both to scholars for the new light it sheds on an old subject, as well as to lay readers who are interested in learning about this fascinating and — as Renner notes in his Introduction — seminal epoch in the evolution of Christianity.

Dr. John S. Catlin
Professor Emeritus of Classics and Letters
University of Oklahoma

———————————

When reading this book, I unconsciously remember back to the years of persecution against Christians in the Soviet Union that I experienced as a young Christian man. This book helps me appreciate the feat of faith accomplished by God's people who have gone the way of suffering and selfless devotion before us. As I read its pages, my faith is strengthened. I learn to be steadfast in trials and yet thankful to the Lord for the freedom He has granted us today to believe and proclaim the Gospel.

Time and time again, Rick Renner has presented quality research work in his books, which contain many captivating historical facts unknown to most contemporary Christians. However, this book is in a class of its own. It will carry the reader into the atmosphere of the First Century AD and help him or her perceive in a deeper way the price paid by the Early Church to get established and carry the message on to posterity.

Sergei V. Ryakhovskiy, Ph.D.
Bishop, Chairman of the Russian Union of Pentecostal Faith Christians
Member of National Public Chamber Under the President of Russian Federation
Moscow, Russia

An author must have outstanding writing skills and be the master of his language to be able to express deep spiritual truths in plain, simple words and thus ensure that the contents of his book are both intriguing and captivating to his reader. This is one reason Rick Renner's first volume of *Seven Messages to the Seven Churches* is, without exaggeration, exceptional — lavishly illustrated with historical materials presented in a skillful manner that vividly and intricately interweaves the Gospel narrative with numerous historical scenes.

One can be certain that this work will be welcomed with due attention by both believers and non-Christians. The book will prove itself profitable not only in offering rich teaching for personal spiritual growth, but also in providing comprehensive study material for seminaries and Bible schools, Bible study groups, youth and adult home groups, and for many other settings.

This first volume of *Seven Messages to the Seven Churches* is written very skillfully, conveying the spirit and life of the New Testament. I believe it will arouse genuine interest amongst a broad reading audience. I gladly recommend this book and expect its publication to be a significant event for the Russian-speaking Christian community.

Vladimir Obrovets, Ph.D.
Vice-President of the Russian-American Institute
Senior Pastor, Second Baptist Church
Moscow, Russia

Rick Renner's brilliantly executed work, *A Light in Darkness, Volume One*, is an exquisitely balanced collection of photographs and prose. This book offers a carefully guided tour of the life experience of First Century believers, as well as an authentic exposé of the challenges they faced — challenges not unlike our own. How rare to find in one volume such depth of knowledge and truth relevant to the apostle John's apocalyptic message to the end-times Church. Contemporary disciples of Yeshua (Jesus) will rejoice over Renner's stellar achievement. His meticulous research is a gift to all who embrace biblical history with pleasure!

Messianic Rabbi Jonathan Bernis
President and CEO
Jewish Voice Ministries International
Phoenix, Arizona

Rick Renner's first volume of *A Light in Darkness* is a unique and comprehensive work dealing with the messages of Christ to the seven churches in the book of Revelation. With vast knowledge and rich usage of historical, geographical, cultural, and linguistic contexts, Rick makes this ancient biblical message freshly alive for today. Prepare yourself to hear what the Spirit is saying to the Church — and to *you* — as you journey through this gold mine of revelation!

Joyce Meyer
Bible Teacher
New York Times Best-Selling Author
Joyce Meyer Ministries
Fenton, Missouri

I believe that God has given me a very special and personal spiritual blessing in being asked to endorse *A Light in Darkness, Volume One,* by Rick Renner. As I looked through its pages and read portions of its text, I was humbled by the Spirit of God. Tears came to my eyes. This was God's gift to me — in part an answer to my prayer that He would take whatever years I have left and use them to prepare me to meet Him face to face. I so long to hear Jesus speak to me those words, "Well done." What, then, could be more appropriate than to enlighten my soul with this truly magnificent jewel that totally illumines the student's understanding (for a student is what you will become as you read this book), revealing every facet of truth regarding Jesus' appearance to John on the isle of Patmos and His messages to the churches of Ephesus and Smyrna?

This book is a treasure! I've been to the sites of these ancient churches and taught God's Word there. Yet never have I possessed in one book the wealth of information about these places as I find in *A Light in Darkness, Volume One*. My teaching will take on an entirely new dimension because of Rick's extensive study and research.

This volume of *Seven Messages to the Seven Churches* will baptize its readers, immersing them in the totality of all they can glean from every contextual aspect so they can fully experience a deeper understanding of and identification with Jesus' messages to His Church. Surely careful study will bring to all those who study this book the cleansing of the water of God's Word and the determination to live fully as an overcomer.

Oh, how I pray that this book series will truly become a light to the Church that helps prepare believers for the days to come!

Kay Arthur
Author and Bible Teacher
Precepts Ministries International

Within the covers of this first volume are profound prayer instructions needed for today's Church as we prepare for the return of our Messiah. I am grateful for Rick Renner's detailed research that has produced this in-depth study of the message to the seven churches by our Lord Jesus Christ. My scriptural foundation for prayer has been reinforced through this work. St. Teresa of Avila wrote: "The more the Lord favors you in prayer, the more necessary it will be that your prayer and good works have a good foundation." This encyclopedia of truth captures my imagination and reinforces my intense desire to see those of us in the modern-day Church repent and return to our first love.

While on tour in North Africa, I walked the Roman Road and reverently toured coliseums where Christians were martyred. Now through the pages of this first volume of *Seven Messages to the Seven Churches*, I have again walked with the fathers and mothers of our faith. Along with my brother, Rick Renner, I salute those who have gone before, and I pray I will always follow them as they followed Jesus Christ.

Germaine Copeland
Bible Teacher
Author of the *Prayers That Avail Much* Book Series
Word Ministries, Inc.

The quality and content of this book is equal to or better than any textbook I have used on this subject. Yet to that quality Rick adds a passion that makes the cities and churches of the First Century come alive to readers in the Twenty-First Century.

As you read and study this volume, you will experience what life was like on the streets and in the stadiums and marketplaces of the cities of Asia Minor. Rick doesn't just tell you about these seven cities — he puts you there. The more you read, the more you will agree: This first volume of *Seven Messages to the Seven Churches* is one of a kind.

Bob Yandian
Author and Bible Teacher
Bob Yandian Ministries
Tulsa, Oklahoma

———————————

The Early Church — with all of its glories and victories, its defeats and character deficiencies — is superbly documented on the pages of this book. Over the years in my search for truth, I have read volumes to get what just one page of this expertly whittled printed work offers its readers. *A Light in Darkness* grants its students a fresh look at the churches and regions of the early New Testament. It is a profoundly valuable resource for every serious student and curious learner.

Dr. Robb Thompson
Author, Motivational Speaker, and Bible Instructor
Robb Thompson International
Tinley Park, Illinois

———————————

Rick Renner has made a contribution of inestimable value by writing this first volume of *Seven Messages to the Seven Churches*. This book is unparalleled in its depth, detail, and scope, and I believe it will be both an instant and enduring classic. It is a feast for the heart, the mind, and the eyes.

Scripture was not written in a vacuum; it was penned in the context of history, culture, politics, personalities, and ideologies. When readers are unaware of these contextual factors, many nuances and understandings of Scripture are left undiscovered. In this outstanding work, Rick has bridged the gap between Scripture itself and the framework in which it was written. As a result, readers will be able to see Scripture more clearly as they grasp its three-dimensional, living-color context.

As you read *A Light in Darkness, Volume One*, you will journey with Rick back to the world of the First Century and experience it firsthand. This is a book that I and countless others will cherish for a lifetime.

Tony Cooke
Author, Bible Teacher, and Conference Speaker
Tony Cooke Ministries
Tulsa, Oklahoma

———————————————

Every believer and seeker of truth would be well-served to read this volume of *Seven Messages to the Seven Churches*. Within its pages, Rick Renner uncovers a wealth of biblical inspiration and historical truth. His dedication to producing such a high-impact book attests to his love for God, His Word, and His people.

James Robison
Author, Bible Teacher, and Host of *Life Today*
LIFE Outreach International
Fort Worth, Texas

———————————————

Thorough and engaging, Renner's work leaps off the page to bring us face-to-face with the historical context of Scripture. I was impressed. Highly recommended!

Dave Stotts
Historian
Host of the *Drive Thru History* Series

DEDICATION

At this moment, more Christians are being persecuted for their faith in Jesus Christ than in the entire 2,000 years of Church history combined. Although the Western Church lives in relative comfort and peace, millions of believers around the world are suffering right now for their faith.

Persecution is not a relic of the past, nor is it simply an intellectual lesson in Church history. It is a present-day reality for millions of people who have committed their lives to Christ. Since the birth of the Church, there have always been those willing to answer God's call to go where no preacher has yet gone and to shine the light of the Gospel where it has never shone before. Yet God has always required a sacrificial price to be paid by those who carry the light into darkness.

My heart is filled with thanksgiving for those in the past, those in the present, and those in the future who will carry the light of truth into this lost and dying world. A great price has been paid by those who preceded us. That price continues to be paid today in many parts of the world, and it will continue to be paid in the future by those who are willing to go forth in God's power and grace to shine a light in the darkness, no matter the cost.

This book is dedicated to every one of those faithful believers.

TABLE OF CONTENTS

PATMOS:
JOHN'S VISION
OF THE EXALTED
CHRIST

Note: Titles in italics denote more in-depth articles pertaining to related subject matter.

EPHESUS: FULFILLING A DIVINE MANDATE IN ASIA

SMYRNA: HOLDING FAST IN THE MIDST OF TRIBULATION

CONCLUSION   667

ACKNOWLEDGMENTS

To publish a book with this much content and design requires the combined efforts of many people. I want to take this opportunity to acknowledge the team members who participated in this mammoth project and who demonstrated an impressive level of dedication and commitment throughout this complex process. I extend my heartfelt thanks to the following:

- My executive assistant, *Maxim Myasnikov*, who assisted me in so many practical and logistical ways throughout the production of this book and whose expertise helped ensure that every aspect of the multiple research trips ran smoothly.

- Our able on-site historian and guide, *Asil Tunçer*, who provided a wealth of expert information from his own scholarly research and enabled us to gain admittance to rarely accessed areas during our series of research trips to the sites of the seven ancient churches in Turkey — and who became our dear Turkish friend.

- My editor, *Cindy Hansen*, who was the chief editor on this book project. Cindy has worked side by side with Denise and me on many book projects, and we've found her to be not only a top-notch editor dedicated to excellence, but also one who possesses the gift of "spiritual common sense" — a quality that has helped us present truth on the printed page in a way that is most helpful to our readers.

- *Andrell Corbin*, a key member of our editorial team, who provided valuable insight and offered her wonderful, God-given gift to choose just the right words for any given purpose whenever she was called upon for assistance.

- *Eric Hansen*, our editorial assistant for the Turkey team, who stayed by my side with unflagging energy and a sharp, analytical mind through the long hours of on-site exploration — taking notes, calculating statistical data, and assisting in every practical way he could to help make the research trips successful.

- *Mica Kilstrom*, our research assistant, who spent long hours in footnote research in the determined effort to provide accurate documentation of facts wherever needed.

- *Dougal Hansen*, who worked as an editorial assistant and proofreader through each stage of the editorial process, building the book's comprehensive index and reading every word contained within the pages of this volume multiple times in the pursuit of making the text error-free.

- *Debbie Pullman*, the talented graphic artist in our design team who worked hundreds of hours on this project, willingly and patiently offering her creative skills to help me design this book in all its intricate detail, both inside and out. Every page of this book reflects her professional touch.

- *Danyelle Wilson*, our design assistant, who was always ready to step in when called upon and assist in the often-complicated process of finding and acquiring the myriad of photos and graphics needed for the development of the book's design.

- *Oleg Kharitonov*, our Moscow graphic designer, who spent many long hours meticulously preparing hundreds of photos taken during our research trips for possible publication.

- *Becky Gilbert*, whose attention to detail greatly assisted us in proofreading the text-designed manuscript.

- Our Moscow staff photographer, *Alexander Gladilov*, whose artistic eye helped capture a wealth of amazing photographs from the sites of the ancient cities we explored during our research trips to Turkey.

Every person who participated in this project did an outstanding job, but I want to especially acknowledge Maxim Myasnikov, (my executive assistant); Cindy Hansen (my editor); Debbie Pullman (graphic artist and text designer); and Alexander Gladilov (Moscow staff photographer). These dedicated workers invested hundreds of hours into this project, and my wife Denise and I are thankful for the excellent attitude they demonstrated and for the hard work they put forth to produce this first in a series of four volumes. Ten extensive research trips were made to Turkey with several of the team members listed above, and one even made a trip to Moscow to work with our staff photographer and Moscow designer. This required time away from their families, and Denise and I want to express our gratitude for their willingness to do whatever was required to produce this series with diligence and a devotion to excellence.

In addition to the people listed above, I especially want to say thanks to Wally and June Blume — God-given friends and ministry partners who have become so very dear to Denise and me. It was their contributions that enabled us to move forward with so many aspects of this undertaking. I also want to express my deepest thanks to Robb Thompson and Tony Cooke, two friends who demonstrated unfailing love, care, and devotion as Denise and I walked through one of the most life-altering phases of our own spiritual journey during the many months it took to complete this book.

I also want to thank the staff and members of the Moscow Good News Church for permitting their pastor the time needed to research and write a book of this size.

Denise and I are so thankful that God has called us to the Russian-speaking people and that our congregation is so supportive of us. We count it both an honor and a privilege to serve them.

Of course, our sons are a vital part of our executive team, and I have witnessed their commitment to fulfill their respective roles in helping Denise and me in the ministry as never before. I simply don't have words to express my gratitude to them or my love for each of them and their families. After Denise, I consider our sons and their wives the most important partners in our ministry.

Lastly, but most importantly, I want to thank Denise for her deep commitment to the Lord, for her devotion to our marriage, and for steadfastly loving me with the *agape* love of Jesus Christ. Throughout the time I worked on this enormous project, Denise walked with me, stood by me, prayed with me, and grew closer to me than ever before. She has read every word of this book, making comments and suggestions that I both appreciated and needed to hear. Denise has been a priceless partner from the very beginning of our marriage, and she remains the most important person in my life. Above all others, I thank her for her dedication to me, to our family, and to our ministry — and specifically for being such an encouragement to me as I wrote this first volume of *Seven Messages to the Seven Churches*.

Rick Renner

FOREWORD

by Dr. Bill Bennett

It is beyond the capacity of my vocabulary to adequately evaluate this volume of *Seven Messages to the Seven Churches* — Brother Rick Renner's treatment of the seven ancient churches of Asia. I simply don't have the verbal dexterity to do justice to such a profoundly instructive volume. I have not encountered a book on this subject that is so beautifully written, so graphically designed, and so replete with truth. I am deeply humbled and honored to be asked to write the foreword, and I do so with alacrity because I believe this book is the most extensive and insightful treatment ever written on the subject.

I mentored Rick in his earlier years and, of course, rejoice to see what God has wrought in the lives of this man and his incredibly godly wife, Denise. Both have been totally surrendered in sharing the redeeming Gospel to the ends of the earth, no matter the cost. This first volume of *Seven Messages to the Seven Churches* is just another proof of the price Rick and Denise are willing to pay in spreading the Good News to all humankind.

A Light in Darkness is absolutely unprecedented both in its length and in the value of its contents. Rick not only provides in-depth biblical discussion regarding the seven churches of Revelation, but he also supplies scintillating historical facts surrounding those congregations. His writings greatly elucidate our understanding of Jesus' messages to those ancient churches — as well as to all churches of all generations — and reveal the relevance of those messages to us today. In fact, I believe I am well within the bounds of accuracy when I say that this four-volume series called *Seven Messages to the Seven Churches* will be the masterpiece in print on this subject. I believe this series is what scholars would call Rick's "*tome*" — his greatest work among the more than 30 books he has written to date.

This volume is extraordinarily valuable because it sheds light — not to be found elsewhere in one book — on many areas of Christian interest. Permit me to list some of the obvious areas:

1. <u>Christology</u> — It exalts the glory of Christ to the highest.

2. <u>Theology</u> — It presents God as the Lord of eternity and time and as the ultimate Ruler of the universe.

3. <u>Pneumatology</u> — It shows the indispensable role of the Holy Spirit in both Christian theology and experience.

4. <u>Soteriology</u> — Jesus' word to all mankind is "repent or perish," and this *tome* sounds this warning strong and clear.

5. <u>Sanctification</u> — The redeemed life is not only pardoned but delivered from the power and practice of sin, and so declares *A Light in Darkness*.

6. <u>History</u> — Much history, not found in any other book on this subject I have read, is related to make Jesus' messages to the seven churches profoundly more meaningful.

7. <u>Archeology</u> — Archeology is used to confirm facts already recorded in the Bible and to uncover truths hidden until unearthed by the spade of the archeologist. Many examples of these invaluable insights are found in this book.

8. <u>Art</u> — Not only is *A Light in Darkness* a written record of past history, but this history is made refreshingly delightful through pictures depicting the events narrated.

9. <u>Homiletics</u> — No preacher would want to preach on the seven churches of Revelation without consulting this book series. I have expounded on the seven churches many times and will do so again. The next time I do, my messages will be greatly inspired by the material in this volume.

10. <u>Ecclesiology</u> — *A Light in Darkness* portrays the Church of Jesus Christ throughout the ages. Anyone reading this book can see his own church described, whether for good or for bad.

11. <u>Devotion</u> — The book of Revelation is the Apocalypse (*Apocalupsis* in Greek), meaning *the unveiling of Christ to the whole world*. So moving is the picture of Jesus Christ in this book that any believer reading it will be profoundly touched in his heart, resulting in joyful praise to the once-crucified but now risen, reigning, redeeming, and soon-returning Lord Jesus Christ.

12. <u>Didactics</u> — The book of Revelation is a treasure trove for the teacher. I predict that no knowledgeable teacher of the seven churches will fail to use the material in *A Light in Darkness*. Teachers of the seven churches owe their students the insights in this book, which are not found anywhere else in one treatise.

13. <u>Evangelism</u> — The value of lost souls and their salvation through the only Savior is stressed throughout this volume.

14. <u>Missions</u> — The urgency to share the Gospel to the ends of the earth, in obedience to Christ's Great Commission, has always been the heartbeat of this author. This urgency is pressed into the hearts of all those who read the words contained in this volume.

15. <u>Angelology</u> — A masterful word is given on the role and limitations of angels in divine revelation and human experience.

16. <u>Apostleship</u> — This volume includes an insightful treatise on the meaning and the manifestation of biblical apostleship.

17. <u>Prophecy</u> — Prophecy is presented in this book as both the *forth-telling* and the *foretelling* of God's message — the two essentials of authentic biblical prophecy.

18. <u>The Persecuted Church</u> — While the Western Church lives in relative comfort, Christians throughout the world today are being persecuted as never before throughout some 2,000 years of Church history. This volume is a salute to all those who have paid the supreme price in the past to carry the light of the Gospel into the darkness of a lost world. It is also a tribute to those who will continue to shine God's light in the darkness, even if it costs them their lives.

19. <u>The Living Christ, Ruler of History</u> — History is *"His Story"* — a truth that this book brilliantly confirms.

I possess a library of some 11,000-plus volumes, scores of which treat the seven churches of Asia, such as Dr. Vance Havner's remarkable classic, *Repent or Perish*. However, I have no book so filled with enlightening, in-depth truth on the seven churches as this volume of *Seven Messages to the Seven Churches*.

Some books are to be carelessly thumbed through and discarded. Others are to be read and studied and then placed on the shelf, scarcely to be opened again. Then there are a few that are to be read and studied and contemplated and digested — and then used and applied and quoted all our lives. Such is this volume of *Seven Messages to the Seven Churches*. I am placing it close at hand so I can refer to it often (just as I have done with Rick's *Sparkling Gems From the Greek 1* devotional).

I urge you to read and study this book carefully. Chew it, digest it, and then apply it to your own life. After you have done so, share it with others. Recommend this book to your friends, and continue to pray that God will use its truth to the ends of the earth until Jesus comes.

Dr. Bill Bennett

Founder-President of Mentoring Men for the Master International
Chaplain, Southeastern Baptist Theological Seminary, Wake Forest, NC
General Chairman of Trustees of Alpha Ministries of India
Phi Beta Kappa, *Summa Cum Laude* graduate,
Wake Forest and Duke Universities, North Carolina
Pastor of churches ranging from 85 to 8,000 members for half a century

FOREWORD
by Mr. Asil S. Tunçer

I have been fortunate to be involved with this project from the early stages of the research Mr. Renner conducted as he pursued the writing of this in-depth work. I remember well the day I first met him. I was scheduled to guide him and his team on an extensive research expedition through the city of Ephesus. As soon as I shook his hand, I was immediately drawn by his authentic, friendly approach toward me and the confident manner in which he carried himself as he discussed the history of the ancient sites we were about to visit. There was an instant connection of respect and trust between us. As the days of research continued, I pondered this huge coincidence — that two men with a similar lifelong interest in the historical study of these ancient cities would meet and experience such a connection. From the beginning, it seemed clear that I was the right person to aid him in the research for his book and that he was also the right person for me to know as a friend and fellow colleague.

When I first started working with Mr. Renner, I knew only that he was conducting research for a book he was writing. Even as I watched him and his assistants take pages of notes and his photographer snap thousands of pictures, I had little idea regarding the extent of the project that was being pursued.

Later Mr. Renner sent me a sample of the text-designed manuscript, which included many illustrations and photographs. At that moment, I realized I was witnessing a far more serious book project in the making than I had first comprehended — one that was a candidate for being known as a peerless work among the many books that have been written on this subject. The more I came to understand the serious nature of this project, the more I tried to improve my own knowledge so I could be of the best assistance possible to Mr. Renner as he endeavored to compile all that was needed to complete the book. I was also able to gain entry into certain rarely accessed areas of the sites for the team by obtaining permissions from the management staff of various museums so that the most detailed and accurate historical information possible could be gathered.

A few years before meeting Mr. Renner, I had written my own book manuscript on the city of Ephesus after many years of personal research and study. As I embarked on this journey of assisting him with the research for his project, I decided to set aside my pursuit of getting my book published in order to focus on helping Mr. Renner complete his work. Today I am very glad I made that decision. Through my interaction and association with this good man, I have learned much more as I researched on his behalf regarding this subject that is our mutual passion. As a result, my own book has become better.

Serving as the guide for the multiple research trips conducted by Mr. Renner with his team was a uniquely rewarding experience. I thoroughly enjoyed our in-depth discussions about the history of each city as we walked through the ruins together. I was impressed with Mr. Renner's passion to discover the answers to the minutest historical details. I watched as his team members would pull out their tape measures to take measurements wherever we went — whether calculating the number of columns that once lined an elegant street or the number of shops that once stood in an ancient marketplace. Keeping a meticulous record of their findings, the team worked diligently to glean every possible bit of information that would help them understand precisely what a given location looked like 2,000 years ago. Mr. Renner's pursuit of such details also filled in gaps of information that I needed for my own scholarly pursuits and challenged me to search out even more knowledge in the subject of my expertise.

If Mr. Renner asked me a question I didn't know as we explored an ancient site, I would conduct more research, studying as long as necessary until I determined I had found the correct answer. The next day, we would discuss the matter, reviewing our notes and studying the actual ruins themselves until we both agreed that we were on the right track and had come to the best possible conclusion on that particular matter. It was that kind of mutual support that I so appreciated about my relationship with Mr. Renner as I assisted him in his research. Today we call each other "brother" with the utmost level of mutual respect and esteem.

I consider it an honor that I was able to be of assistance in the completion of this outstanding book project. This first volume that you hold in your hands will take you on a unique journey, transporting you to ancient Roman times. It will enrich your understanding of the historical importance of Ephesus and Smyrna, both of which played such significant roles in the Roman Empire, especially in the First Century. This volume should be added to the library of anyone who is a student of this region's history of early Christianity.

This subject matter is my own life's passion, so it means a great deal to me that I am able to say with conviction that Mr. Renner successfully captured the heart of what once existed in ancient Ephesus and Smyrna. His explanations and illustrations adeptly place these cities within their biblical, historical, and archaeological context, reflecting their strategic importance from each of these perspectives. Thus, this volume serves as an invaluable aid in the study of these ancient sites. The next three volumes of the *Seven Messages to the Seven Churches* series will certainly fulfill the same purpose regarding the study of the other five cities found in the book of Revelation.

I consider Mr. Renner's book an excellent research source from which to begin studying the history of the seven churches. He rivets your attention as he takes you on a ride back through the centuries to the Roman Empire of New Testament times. Whether or not you have ever visited the sites of these ancient cities, this book will open its doors wide and allow you unparalleled access through its outstanding descriptions.

There is no doubt in my mind that there is currently no other book in this field that can surpass this first volume of *Seven Messages to the Seven Churches*.

Mr. Asil S. Tunçer

Historian and Professional Tour Guide
Izmir, Turkey

PREFACE

In 1985, my wife Denise and I were just beginning to pursue the dream God had planted in our hearts to teach His Word to the nations of the world. We were committed to that call, and we surrendered everything to see that dream come to pass. God's grace was on Denise and me, and we watched in amazement as He unfolded a marvelous plan that has taken our family around the world. When we first started, we had no idea that the Lord would eventually relocate our family to Russia according to His purposes or that I would become the author of dozens of books, several of which would become bestsellers. As we look back at our lives through the years since that time, we can only express our gratitude to God for placing His hand on us and for using my books to touch a worldwide audience of people who desire to know Jesus Christ more intimately.

From the very onset of this supernatural journey in God, Denise and I began to talk about the possibility of my writing a book on the subject of Jesus' messages to the seven churches in the book of Revelation. Denise will attest to the fact that my attention has always been drawn to Jesus' words to the pastors of those seven churches. Both of us vividly recall those early days of ministry in the 1980s when we traveled with our young sons by automobile, teaching seminars in local churches throughout the United States. In the early morning hours, I'd grab my satchel of study books and kiss Denise goodbye. Then I'd leave the hotel room, where our children still slept, to head to any nearby coffee shop that would allow me to sit and study for hours with a steady refill of coffee. When it was time to take Denise and the boys to breakfast, I'd pack my books into my satchel and head back to the hotel room. However, the next morning I'd be right back at that coffee shop again to resume my studying.

For hundreds — perhaps even thousands — of hours, I studied my Greek New Testament, along with my faithful study books and well-worn commentaries written by some of the greatest theological minds of the last century. However, when it came to Jesus' messages to the seven churches, the deep desire to understand what He was endeavoring to communicate never left me. Gradually I began to teach more and more about those seven messages, compelled by a strong inner desire to do so.

More than 30 years have passed since those earliest days of study, and my love for Jesus' messages to the seven churches has never changed. To understand this subject as thoroughly as possible, I've made multiple trips to conduct research at the ancient sites of the seven cities mentioned in the book of Revelation. I've also visited museums all over the world to study relics from these cities. Over the years, I've researched countless writings of ancient authors on this subject and have read multiple commentaries and books by contemporary authors who have also written about Jesus' seven messages. And as I write the final words to this first volume, I remain convinced that these seven messages of Christ are just as needed today as they were when first penned by the apostle John almost 2,000 years ago.

Information regarding these seven historical cities in the Roman province of Asia is constantly being updated; therefore, this book has gone through a rigorous verification process to confirm that facts, dates, and other historical information are as accurate as possible. Should you desire further study in this area, a list of important resource material has been included in the back matter of this book.

My goal in writing *Seven Messages to the Seven Churches* is threefold: to teach regarding the meaning and significance of Christ's words to the seven churches in Asia; to introduce readers to the realities that early believers faced in the First Century; and to discuss how these two factors pertain to the present-day challenges faced by the modern Church in this hour. To the best of my ability, I have written this first volume of the series carefully, accurately, and with a spirit attuned to the heart of God. As a human being, I fall very short of perfection, but I have done my best to give Jesus my all in the writing of this book. My prayer is that it will be a blessing to you and to people in future generations who love the Word of God and who desire to hold fast to their faith in Jesus Christ to the end.

Rick Renner

INTRODUCTION

When the apostle John received the book of Revelation, he was living as an exiled prisoner, banished to the rocky island of Patmos — the remote and secluded island prison where the Roman government sent those deemed to be its most dangerous political offenders. John had been arrested, judged by the Roman legal system, and sent with a shipload of other criminals to languish and die on a forsaken island.

During John's time on Patmos, he encountered the risen Lord as no one had ever seen Him before. In one split second, the spirit realm suddenly opened, and John found himself standing in another dimension where he heard and saw things almost beyond description — a panoramic vision both of things present and of things yet to come, all of which John later recorded in the book of Revelation. For almost 2,000 years, believers and scholars have been captivated by the sights and sounds the apostle John described in the 22 chapters of this apocalyptic book.

When John received this vision, the First Century was coming to an end. The Church of Jesus Christ was only decades old, yet it was already gripped with serious challenges from within and without. In the first three chapters of Revelation, Christ addressed those challenges and the problems facing the Church at that time.

It has been 20 centuries since Jesus first spoke those words to the seven early churches. However, as we study these age-old messages and compare them to the current status of the Church, it is evident that the challenges and problems facing the Body of Christ today are precisely the same ones Jesus addressed nearly 2,000 years ago. What Jesus Christ said to His Church then is what He is still saying to the Church now.

Jesus' messages in Revelation chapters 2 and 3 were written to seven pastors who presided over congregations located in seven cities in the Roman province of Asia. These particular cities form the backdrop to the seven messages Christ spoke; therefore, a great deal of attention has been focused in this book series on informing you, the reader, about the geographical, sociological, historical, religious, and political backgrounds of each respective city, all of which had great influence on the seven churches.

In this first of four volumes, we will take an in-depth look at John's vision of the risen Christ and the historical background leading up to that vision (Chapter One and Two). We will also delve into the messages Jesus gave in the vision to the pastors of the churches in Ephesus and Smyrna. There is a deliberate order to this discussion, designed to assist you in understanding the general environments in which these spiritual events took place. Detailed "guided tours" of Ephesus and Smyrna are provided (Chapters Three and Six) preceding Christ's messages to the congregations of these ancient cities (Chapters Five and Seven, highlighted on parchment pages). These tour chapters explicitly explain the social and historical settings in which these early believers lived and the problems they confronted in their respective settings. In addition, a scripturally based historical account of Paul's ministry in Ephesus is included in Chapter Four. I urge you to carefully read these important historical chapters to discover the enormity both of the challenges these believers faced and of the ultimate outcome those who remained faithful were able to achieve.

Thus, we come to the reason this book is entitled *A Light in Darkness*. In John 1:5, the apostle John wrote, "And the light shineth in darkness; and the darkness comprehended it not." The word "comprehended" is the Greek word *katalambano*, which is a compound of the words *kata* and *lambano*. The word *kata* implies the idea of *a force that is conquering, dominating, or subjugating*, whereas the word *lambano* means *to seize, to take, or to firmly grasp*. But when these two are combined into one word, the new word means *to firmly seize something, to pull it down, to tackle it, to conquer it, to subdue it*, or *to take something under one's dominating control*. Thus, let me suggest that an expanded translation of John 1:5 in today's modern language could read this way: "*And the light shined in darkness, but the darkness simply didn't have the ability to overcome it, take it down, subdue it, or dominate it.*"

In the following pages, our journey will twist and turn through various aspects of Early Church history, proving that regardless of the kind or the frequency of attacks against God's people, darkness simply doesn't have the power to overcome the light. No matter how intense the pressure or the attack waged against the Church, the fiery truth of God's Word and the influence of His people will continue to blaze, sending forth a powerful, far-reaching light — even in the darkest spiritual environments — that simply cannot be extinguished.

That is the central message of this volume, as well as the three volumes that follow in the *Seven Messages to the Seven Churches* series. This project is the result of many years of study and of a decision I made decades ago to thoroughly prepare for its writing. Multiple research trips over the years have been a part of this required preparation — trips that involved exploring ancient ruins, studying relics in museums, and delving into historical archives. The staff photographer who accompanied me on several trips to these ancient cities also took thousands of on-site photographs, from which hundreds were selected for this four-volume series. This investment of time and effort has provided a wealth of background information that is vital to understanding more fully the reasons Jesus said what He did to the pastors of these seven ancient churches.

In our research, we have been unable to find another commentary as comprehensive or thorough as this book is in covering the subject of these seven ancient churches — specifically the churches of Ephesus and Smyrna. And as you read this book, you'll discover that this is much more than a commentary. It is also an in-depth compilation of information about the Early Church that will awaken you as never before to the pertinence of the New Testament in this modern-day world you live in. Reading a book with so much information and in-depth teaching may seem daunting to some, but I encourage you to accept the challenge and allow the truth it contains to enrich your life and deepen your relationship with God.

The Body of Christ is confronted with many serious challenges and problems in these last days before Jesus returns. Never has it been more important to understand what the Spirit is saying to the Church. Although these seven messages were first spoken approximately 2,000 years ago, they are just as relevant today as when they were first given. It is therefore time to more fully understand what Jesus is saying to His people in this hour — and, specifically, what He is saying to you.

Rick Renner

And the light shined in darkness,
but the darkness simply didn't have the ability
to overcome it, take it down,
subdue it, or dominate it.
— John 1:5

PATMOS: JOHN'S VISION OF THE EXALTED CHRIST

Situated in the sapphire waters of the Aegean Sea, the desolate island of Patmos was an open-air prison for the most dangerous of Roman prisoners. Categorized as either common criminals or political offenders, prisoners were dispersed to different parts of the island according to their classification. A cave on this hostile, forsaken island became the temporary home of the apostle John after he was arrested for his faith and banished to Patmos by decree of the Emperor Domitian. It was here that the elderly apostle's isolation was unexpectedly invaded when he was caught up into the realm of the Spirit to behold the exalted Christ manifested in all His splendor. In this vision, Jesus delivered to John seven messages to seven churches of Asia — messages that still apply to His Church today.

Pictured here is the 60-mile waterway between the mainland of Asia Minor and the ancient island of Patmos. Prisoners were regularly transported by ship from the western shores of Asia Minor to this remote and notorious island prison that can be seen in the distance in this photograph. The apostle John was carried by ship across this waterway to be incarcerated on Patmos for 18 months during the rule of the Emperor Domitian.

Chapter One

THE ISLAND OF PATMOS

In the year 95 AD, a sailing vessel filled with prisoners slowly glided into the port on the island of Patmos. On board was the elderly apostle John, one of the newest prisoners to be delivered to this forbidding fragment of rugged land jutting out of the Aegean's blue waters in the region known as the Icarian Sea.

Designated as a prison where many of Rome's worst enemies and criminals were incarcerated, this small, desolate island belonged to a group of islands known as the Sporades. It was located 24 miles off the coastline of Asia Minor (modern-day Turkey), approximately 60 miles from the ancient city of Ephesus.

Ships arriving at the port of Patmos were filled with Roman prisoners who were considered the scum of society and the absolute worst of all humankind. Murderers, thieves, rapists, insurrectionists, and perpetrators of other heinous crimes were all carried by boat to this remote volcanic island — the "Alcatraz" of the First Century.

As this particular ship drew closer to shore, the rowers shoved their oars into the water to slow its pace. Little by little the vessel slowed as it approached the dock, passing the rocky crags that descended dramatically into the crashing waves of the sea along the coast of Patmos.

Many prisoners who tried to escape Patmos had been crushed on these sharp rocks by the strong currents that carried them to their deaths. As the ship glided past these jagged cliffs en route to the port, the prisoners on board must have contemplated the fate of those hapless prisoners, as well as the impossible prospect of their own escape from this open-air prison in the middle of the Icarian Sea.

As the ship docked, soldiers on board yelled at the men fettered in chains, barking out commands for the prisoners to get up and start moving toward the plank that led to the dock. The crack of whips, the screams of the Roman soldiers, and the complaints of the captives could all be heard as the prisoners were herded like cattle off the ship. Down the plank

were often transferred there so soldiers, wardens, and interrogators could treat them with a level of brutality that wouldn't have been tolerated elsewhere.

COMMON CRIMINALS VS. POLITICAL OFFENDERS

When the prisoners disembarked from the ship, they were divided into two groups: *common criminals* and *political offenders*. Then each group was transferred to different parts of the island.

Common criminals were scourged as a part of their official welcome to the island. This scourging was designed to serve as a warning that poor behavior would be dealt with swiftly and harshly.[2] Criminals incarcerated on Patmos worked under the constant gaze of Roman soldiers, who watched their every movement and punished them ferociously for the least offense. Some early Christian writers recorded that prisoners on Patmos worked in mine quarries; however, archeologists have found no evidence on the island to support these claims.

Political offenders were treated with a greater degree of respect than common criminals on Patmos and were allowed to freely roam the barren island.[3] However, this type of prison sentence didn't bode well for political prisoners, for they were not provided any clothes, food, water, or medical services and were responsible for their own survival in the harsh conditions of the island. As a result, many died of starvation, disease, a lack of clean water, or exposure.

the soldiers led their human cargo, handing them over to the merciless prison guards who awaited them on the dock. These guards would be the prisoners' hard taskmasters as long as the ill-fated captives were detained on the island. When the prisoners didn't move fast enough, the guards would lash their backs with whips and beat them with clubs to forcibly keep them moving toward the desired destination.

Roman society had a high tolerance for human abuse. Yet even Roman law demanded fair treatment of prisoners, especially if they were Roman citizens. In fact, Roman law didn't permit abusive treatment of prisoners. However, since Patmos was isolated, desolate, and mostly forsaken, what transpired there wasn't visible to the public eye. As a result, laws that guaranteed the good treatment of prisoners could be, and often *were*, ignored.[1] Thus, the Roman government considered Patmos to be an ideal place for especially dangerous criminals, who

Above and Below: *The photo above shows the actual harbor where ancient ships ported at Patmos. The graphic below depicts how the harbor may have looked at the time the ship carrying the apostle John arrived at the island. Both common criminals and political offenders were exiled to Patmos. John was sent to this desolate island as a political offender because of his refusal to worship the Emperor Domitian as deity.*

Above: This photo shows the ruins of the Church of St. Mary in the city of Ephesus. This was the first official church structure ever constructed in honor of the Virgin Mary and was so named in memory of Mary's residency in the city of Ephesus. The Third Ecumenical Council was held in this building in the year 431 AD.

Political offenders sometimes formed communities to create a better chance of survival in such a hostile environment. At the time the apostle John arrived on Patmos in 95 AD, it's known that several communities already existed, populated by people — and even entire families — who had been exiled to the island as political prisoners of the Roman Empire.

How did John, the sole survivor of the original 12 disciples by 95 AD, become an exiled prisoner on Patmos? The answer to this question is vital to this book. We must therefore pause to recall the remarkable account of John's life in the years leading up to his exile on this forsaken island.

JOHN AND MARY'S RESIDENCY IN EPHESUS

The role of the apostle John was uniquely different from the other apostles because Jesus had given John the responsibility to care for His mother Mary. As John wrote his own gospel, he vividly remembered when Jesus entrusted the care of Mary to him. In his own words, John related that moment:

> Now there stood by the cross of Jesus His mother, and His mother's sister, Mary the wife of Clopas, and Mary Magdalene. When Jesus therefore saw His mother, and the disciple whom He loved standing by, He said to His mother, "Woman, behold your son!" Then He said to the disciple, "Behold your mother!" *and from that hour that disciple took her to his own home.*
> John 19:25-27 NKJV

Early Church history confirms that John cared for Mary to the end of her life. When he and the other apostles left Jerusalem between 37-44 AD, John ministered in various parts of Asia, probably settling in Ephesus with Mary later, sometime around the year 67 AD.

(Continued on page 12)

MARY'S RESIDENCE IN EPHESUS

In addition to the many historical documents that substantiate John's residence in Ephesus, there is solid archeological evidence that indicates Mary also resided in this city.

Some early traditions claim that Mary lived and died in Jerusalem. However, it must be noted that when Helene, the Emperor Constantine's mother, went to Jerusalem early in the Fourth Century to locate all the holy sites and returned claiming she'd found nearly every one imaginable, she never once declared to have found the grave of Mary.[4] At that time, there was a religious law stating that church buildings should be constructed on sites where New Testament figures had lived or were buried. If Christians at that time had known of such evidence, Helene surely would have identified Mary's grave and begun the construction of a church over its site. The fact that no such church was built strongly indicates that the believers living in Jerusalem at the time of Helene's arrival possessed no evidence that Mary had been buried in their city. It was another century before the Church of the Sepulchre of Mary would be built near Gethsemane, on the spot

10

Right: The stones below the darkened line on this wall are original stones from the First Century house that many scholars assert was Mary's hilltop home during her residency in Ephesus. Today this ancient home is used as a place of worship.

where Catholic tradition claims Mary was buried by the apostles before her subsequent Assumption into Heaven.

When Early Church historian Jerome (347-420 AD) wrote his historical piece documenting all the holy sites in Jerusalem — one of the most well-written geographical documents concerning this ancient city — he did not include Mary's tomb. This is another strong indication that in the Fourth Century, no knowledge existed of Mary's grave in Jerusalem. In fact, the only church constructed in Mary's name existing at that time was the Church of St. Mary in Ephesus, lending strong support to the belief that she lived the final days of her life not in Jerusalem, but in the city of Ephesus.

In 431 AD, one of the most important Church Councils to be held in 2,000 years of Church history was conducted in the Church of St. Mary in Ephesus.[5] At that famous doctrinal meeting, the Council debated Jesus' divinity — and Mary's role in Jesus' birth was a key component of their conversation. One byproduct of this famous Council was a specific statement commemorating the residences of both John and Mary in Ephesus. That statement in 431 AD is a part of Church history that cannot be ignored or denied, and it clearly states that Mary moved to Ephesus with the apostle John.

Today above the ancient city of Ephesus on the slopes of what was once called Mt. Koresos, one can visit a small, three-room chapel constructed on the ancient ruins of a church that dates back to the Fourth Century. Excavations have revealed that this old church was built on top of a modest First Century house, which many scholars claim was the very house where Mary resided during the final years she lived in Ephesus. The location of this house — on top of a hill and outside the Ephesian city limits —

Left: The marble fragments in this photo are the original tiles that the resident of this house walked on nearly 2,000 years ago. If this was the home of Mary, as many claim, it is likely that Mary walked on these very marble tiles that once beautifully decorated the floor.

would have provided a safe haven for Mary. Yet this ancient house was still near enough to Ephesus for visitors to travel up the hill for a brief stay.

Original stones are still visible from both the First Century house and the Fourth Century church that was later built on the house's foundation. A red line on the outside of the building and a blackened line on the inside of the chapel distinguish the newer stones from the original stones below the line. The room to the right of the main chapel is the oldest section, built directly on top of the original foundation that still exists from the First Century house.

When excavations were first carried out from 1891-1894, archeologists learned that members of a distant mountain village had revered these four-walled, roofless ruins for centuries. These villagers claim to be descendants of the Ephesian Christians who took refuge in the mountains during the early persecutions. Believing it was at this site that Mary had died, many generations of these villagers made the five-hour pilgrimage every year over rugged mountain paths to the place they called Panaya Kapulu ("Chapel of the Most Holy").

The archeologists also discovered marble fragments from the original floor of the First Century dwelling. Today these 2,000-year-old marble fragments are carefully laid together and concealed under the carpet that visitors walk across in the small room to the right of the chapel. If this is indeed the home where Mary lived in Ephesus, as many scholars believe it to be, it is likely that these small marble fragments are pieces of the very floor Mary walked on when she lived in Ephesus. It is also certain that until the time the mother of Jesus went home to Heaven, she received many visitors who had traveled from afar to see this humble woman of God.

Above: This ancient walkway leads to the site where the apostle John once lived and was buried. Below: These ruins are all that remain of the Temple of Artemis, which stood just below the hill where the apostle John resided.

Below: These four pillars mark the actual burial site of the apostle John. For more than 30 years, John oversaw the churches of Asia and wrote the gospel of John and his three epistles from this relatively remote location outside of Ephesus.

There is an array of historical sources confirming that Mary, the mother of Jesus, moved to Ephesus with John. Perhaps the most significant evidence that attests to Mary's residency in this city are the ruins of the ancient church building located in Ephesus that was named in Mary's memory — the *first* church building in the entire world to be named in her honor. Since churches were built in honor of local saints at that time, it is reasonable to conclude that Mary was once a local resident and that the church was therefore named in her honor.

John's residency in Ephesus is a fact established by many early writers, including Eusebius, the earliest historian of the Church. A Second Century bishop of Ephesus named Polycrates, who was born approximately 30 years after John's death, wrote that John's tomb was in the city of Ephesus and that he was the most beloved disciple.[6] In 180 AD, a bishop of Lyons named Irenaeus, a contemporary of Polycrates, recorded that John lived in Ephesus and wrote his gospel at his home there.[7] Irenaeus personally knew Polycarp, the famous bishop of Smyrna, and wrote that Polycarp had personally known John while he was still alive in Ephesus.[8] All of these historical records, and others too numerous to include in this text, are sufficient to show that the apostle John lived and ministered in Ephesus during the latter part of his life.

John lived in a community located on a hill on the outskirts of Ephesus, known today as Mount Ayasuluk.[9] This small Christian community was situated high above the Temple of Artemis, just beyond the notice of Roman authorities.

Above and Below: The model above depicts how the Church of St. John looked when it was constructed during the rule of the Emperor Justinian. According to historical records, it was built directly over the former residence of the apostle John and on the exact site of his burial place. Below is a photo of the same site as it looks today. Having suffered damage over the centuries, the ancient church now lies in ruins.

Above: The view from the hilltop where John lived. The Stadium of Ephesus was located on the lower hill in the distance, and it is likely that John could hear the roar of the crowds as fellow believers were forced into the stadium to fight gladiators and wild beasts. In the lower left are the ruins of the great Temple of Artemis.

A higher level of toleration was often extended to people living outside the city limits because their refusal to conform to local standards wasn't as obvious. Therefore, John, along with the small community of believers, lived on top of the nearby hill where they could avoid the constant pagan pressures that existed inside the city of Ephesus. These early believers had learned through hard experience that the authorities were more concerned with in-town residents who violated Roman law or the emperor's edicts for all to worship him.

Perhaps the most important reason John resided outside the city limits of Ephesus was that he gave oversight to all the churches of Asia and therefore had to meet with leaders who traveled from across the entire region to see him. If John had lived directly within Ephesus, these visits would have been much more complicated

and dangerous. But because John lived in a not-so-noticeable residence on top of a hill behind the Temple of Artemis, he could meet more easily with visiting leaders who were concerned about being arrested in Ephesus. On the other hand, Timothy was serving as pastor of the church of Ephesus at this time (1 Timothy 1:3,4) and probably resided within the city itself, since that was where most of his congregation lived.[10]

As early as 381 AD, John's residence in Ephesus was so well documented that Christian pilgrims were already coming to Ephesus to visit his home and to honor his burial place. An early church was also built on the site of John's tomb. Later the Emperor Justinian built a magnificent church on this same site. It was the second most magnificent church building ever constructed in Asia Minor — second only in size to Hagia Sophia in the Eastern

Empire's capital city of Constantinople (the modern-day city of Istanbul, Turkey). Of these ancient structures, Procopius, a court historian of the Emperor Justinian, wrote:

> There chanced to be a certain place before the city of Ephesus, lying on a steep hill that is bare of soil and incapable of producing crops... On that site the locals had built a church in early times in memory of the Apostle John. This apostle has been named the Theologian because the nature of God was described by him in a manner beyond the unaided power of man. This church, which was small and in a ruined condition because of its great age, the Emperor Justinian tore down and replaced with a church so large and beautiful, that, to speak briefly, it resembles closely in all respects, and is a rival to, the church which he dedicated to all the Apostles in the imperial city.[11]

THE EMPEROR BEHIND JOHN'S ARREST IN EPHESUS

After the apostle Paul was beheaded in Rome in the year 67 AD, the apostle John's leadership role in Asia became significantly more visible to the local churches of that region. For approximately 27 more years, John guided the churches from his hilltop home. But near the age of 90, John experienced the unexpected: *He was arrested, shackled, and transferred to Rome to stand trial before the Emperor Domitian as a political offender.*[12]

Early Church leaders such as Irenaeus, Eusebius, Jerome, and others wrote that

John was banished from Ephesus and exiled to the island of Patmos during the Emperor Domitian's fourteenth year of rule.[13] This would place John's arrival on Patmos in the year 95 AD. However, the actual date of his arrest was some time earlier, possibly as early as the year 93 AD.

Before we discuss what is known about John's arrest, let's first consider the role the Emperor Domitian played in Asia — and especially in the city of Ephesus — at that time.

Domitian was born in 51 AD, the son of the Emperor Vespasian and the younger brother of Titus, who ruled the Roman Empire for two short years after the death of his father Vespasian. In 81 AD, Titus became strangely ill. As he lay dying, his younger and jealous brother Domitian demanded that the Praetorian Guard hastily name *him* the new emperor. Domitian was quickly given the title "Augustus" — and upon Titus' death, he became the sole ruler of the Roman Empire. Domitian's strategy to have himself so swiftly proclaimed emperor, even as his brother was taking his last breath, placed a lasting umbrella of suspicion over Domitian's rule. Speculation persisted that Domitian played a role in the strange sickness that abruptly claimed his brother's life and ended Titus' short, two-year reign of the Roman Empire.

At first, Domitian appeared to be benevolent, and people had high hopes that he would be a kind ruler. He demonstrated skills that proved he could be an able manager; he exhibited an understanding of economics; and he was deeply immersed in pagan idolatry — all qualities that pleased the

Roman population. During his rule, Domitian also proved to be a fabulous builder. In fact, some of the most marvelous and massive architectural structures ever constructed in the Roman Empire were completed during his rule. Initially, Domitian seemed to display the leadership abilities Rome needed and appeared to genuinely care for the welfare of the empire. But as time passed, this emperor began to show his true nature, emerging as one of the most wicked and merciless tyrants in human history.

Although other emperors also involved themselves in civil affairs, Domitian pushed his way into the people's civic life in a manner unmatched by any previous ruler. Convinced it was his sole responsibility to set the proper moral code for the empire, Domitian declared himself *censor perpetuus* — a Latin phrase meaning "Perpetual Censor." This gave him the legal right to reset the moral code of Rome according to what he believed was morally right and wrong.[14] It also gave him the right to *censor* or *eliminate* any part of the society he deemed offensive or unnecessary — and any person or group who stood in opposition to his ideals. The emperor's self-appointed role of *censor perpetuus* was not well accepted by the upper echelon of Roman society. They viewed the emperor's establishment of a new moral code as grossly hypocritical, since rumors abounded regarding his own acts of incest and of homosexual relations with young boys.

Once the *censor perpetuus* had been granted, the Emperor Domitian possessed a powerful new weapon that he could use to censor, silence, eliminate, or

Right: Pictured here is a bronze statue of the Emperor Domitian seated on a horse. Scholars believe this magnificent statue was used as part of the imperial cult worship of Domitian.

purge any public or private person who spoke disparagingly of him or who opposed his commands. He quickly began taking advantage of this new tool to secretly arrest and imprison those whom he disliked or distrusted. What began in secret soon became public as scores of people began to be arrested, shackled, imprisoned, forced to fight gladiators and beasts in the arena, or slain with the sword. The torturous acts carried out during this time were horrific. One writer tells us that Domitian's men delighted in "inserting fire through [victims'] private parts" to elicit false confessions and to be entertained by others' pain.[15]

about this time that he declared himself *dominus et deus*, a Latin phrase meaning *lord and god*. Other emperors had been deified after death, but Domitian wanted more. He wanted to receive worship as a god while he *lived*.[17]

When Domitian made his declaration of godhood, temples began to be constructed in his honor and a new order of priesthood was created that was dedicated to serve people who dropped to their knees to worship the emperor. In every part of the far-flung empire, people dipped their heads in deference as they passed Domitian's image, bowed their knees before his temples, or burned incense at temple altars to acknowledge his divinity. Those who refused to comply were *censored* — that is, they were *arrested, imprisoned, exiled,* or *killed.*

The tragedy Domitian created for so many caused even his close confidants to realize that he was a monster who needed to be eliminated. In what would be the last moments of his life in 96 AD, he retired to his bedroom for a nap. A close associate named Stephanos came to Domitian's chamber, pretending to bring the emperor written proof of a plot to murder him. As Domitian read the document, Stephanos pulled out a hidden knife and began to repeatedly stab the emperor. However, Stephanos' blows were not hard enough to kill him, and Domitian fought back until the two were locked in a death match on the floor. Domitian tried to gain control of the knife, even attempting to gouge out his attacker's eyes. But Stephanos' co-conspirators then entered

The historian Pliny the Younger recalled the drama this created for many of his personal friends when he wrote, "...I stood amidst the flames of thunderbolts dropping all around me, and there were certain clear indications to make me suppose a like end was awaiting me."[16]

By the year 93 AD, Domitian's madness had reached an all-time high. It was the room to assist him in the murder, and together they hacked the emperor to death.[18]

Domitian's 15-year rule was marked with such horrendous atrocities that upon his death, the Senate issued its *damnatio memotiae* — an official edict that damned the evil emperor's rule and called for an eradication of his memory, including the demolition of temples, buildings, and statues that had been constructed in his honor.

A MIRACULOUS DELIVERANCE FROM BOILING OIL

A few years prior to Domitian's assassination, the elderly John was dispatched to Rome, where he stood trial before the cruel Roman emperor. At that point, John had lived in his hilltop home for many years. From his lofty vantage point, he could look out and see the blue waters of Ephesus' manmade harbor. He could hear the roar of the crowds coming from the Great Stadium, where so many of his personal friends had been forced to fight wild beasts to the death. He could also look down upon the legendary Temple of Artemis that stood in the valley below. Years later when John was approaching a natural death as an old man, he would request to be buried near this hilltop residence where he had lived out his last years on this earth.

One day at this home, possibly in the year 93 AD, Roman soldiers made a surprise appearance and arrested John. The elderly apostle was then forcibly taken from his beloved home, chained and shackled as a dangerous criminal, and put on a ship that carried him to

Rome to stand trial before the Emperor Domitian.

Soon after arriving in Rome, John was escorted down a long hallway into a throne room, where he was forced to stand before the tyrannical emperor. Domitian ordered the apostle to burn pagan incense to save his own life, but John refused.

The early Christian apologist Tertullian gives an amazing account of what happened when John refused to bow to imperial pressure. Domitian became furious and ordered John to be thrown into a vat of boiling oil. Observers waited for John to die in the boiling oil, but instead,

Left: This ancient fresco from the monastery on Patmos is an early depiction of the apostle John being transported by ship as a prisoner to the island. To his right is his faithful ministry assistant, Prochorus — who, according to many early writers, accompanied John during his 18-month exile.

regarding John's subsequent journey to Patmos and his time spent in exile there, the full sphere of legends will be shared that have been related about this apostle through the centuries. However, this record of John's miraculous escape from boiling oil does *not* fall into the category of legend; rather, it should be looked upon as an actual miracle in which John experienced the delivering power of God.

After his audience before Domitian, John was loaded onto another ship that would transport him to the island of Patmos. This was truly an amazing series of events that John could have never predicted or anticipated. For 29 years, he had served the churches of Asia with no known legal squabbles or arrest. The last of the original 12 apostles, he had lived quietly in his hilltop home, loved and deeply respected by all who knew him. Then suddenly, soldiers invaded his world of solace and arrested him, bound him, put him on a ship, and sent him to Rome — the Babylon of the First Century — to stand trial before one of the world's worst monsters. And after being supernaturally delivered unscathed from a horrendous death in boiling oil, John found himself on a ship filled with criminals, sailing to the worst island prison in the entire known world at that time.

they watched as John then got out of the vat — unharmed! When the emperor saw John emerge from the boiling oil unscathed, he was terrified. Domitian then gave the order for John to be forever taken away from his presence and exiled to Patmos to suffer the fate of hardened criminals.[19]

Tertullian, who was known for his accuracy, recorded John's survival from boiling oil as a historical fact. Other early Christian writers also recorded this supernatural event. This particular account should therefore be regarded seriously as a *true* event that happened in the apostle John's life when he was arrested and dispatched to the city of Rome. As our discussion continues

Above: This cave has been called the Cave of the Revelation for 1,600 years. It is reputed to be the cave where John lived on Patmos and where he supernaturally received the book of Revelation.

JOHN FINDS ANOTHER HILLTOP HOME ON PATMOS

When John's ship first docked at the port of Patmos, we may assume that he took his place among the other prisoners and obediently walked down the plank that led to the deck. Common criminals were then entrusted into the hands of guards, while John and the other political prisoners were abandoned with no directions, no help, and no guidance — left to roam an unfamiliar island that was nearly devoid of food and fresh water. It was up

to each individual political prisoner to find a way to survive in this hostile environment. This would have been a difficult feat for even a young man to accomplish. Imagine, therefore, how challenging the prospect of survival on Patmos must have been for John in his old age.

At some point, John located an abandoned cave about halfway up the slope that led to the top of the island's acropolis — a cave that he apparently used as his home while he lived on Patmos. The cave still exists today with a small chapel built within its stone walls. It is located directly in the side of the mountain and originally had one open side, thus allowing for a spectacular view of the valley below and the sea in the distance. The ceiling is so low that it can easily be touched without reaching very high. The cave is divided into three natural rooms that are separated by a large, single column of stone in the very center of the rooms. The view from the open side is one of the most beautiful vistas on the island of Patmos, and the protruding rock that covered the open side provided protection from both harsh sunlight and foul weather.

In one corner of the cave near the floor is a natural niche where, according to Early Church writers, John laid his head as he slept.[20] A few feet higher and to the right in the cave wall is a second niche, perfectly suited as a handhold to help pull oneself up from the floor. Early chroniclers recorded that John used this second niche to pull himself up from the ground after sleeping at night. Although it cannot be proven that John used either of these niches, it is quite easy to see that they would have been ideal for these purposes for anyone who lived in

Above: If John lived here, as many historical records state, this was the view he saw from the mouth of his island cave.

this cave in times past. Even today the cave is dry and warm, indicating that it would have served as suitable living quarters for someone seeking a place of habitation on the rugged and desolate island. And for nearly 1,600 years, this cave has been identified as the very place where John lived during his exile on the island of Patmos.

Today local monks relate the oral history about this cave to visitors. The corner of the cave where he slept, they say, is the very place where John was lying when he was suddenly surprised by a vision of the exalted Jesus, who appeared to John and revealed the details recorded in the 22 chapters of the book of Revelation. For this very reason, this cave has been called the *Cave of the Revelation* for nearly 1,600 years, and there is no logical or historical reason to dispute this ancient claim.

So on this abandoned, forsaken island where the apostle John had been exiled by the emperor of the Roman Empire, Jesus Christ Himself paid a visit to the lonely cave that John had made his temporary home. Domitian had sent John to Patmos with the intention of keeping him isolated from those he loved. But on that day, the One who calls Himself the *King of kings* and *Lord of lords* (Revelation 19:16) stepped into that hole in the earth

(Continued on page 25)

PROCHORUS, JOHN'S DISCIPLE

There is an early Christian tradition *not* recorded in the New Testament that is categorically asserted by ancient writings and upheld by many people who live on the island of Patmos today. According to this tradition, John did not live alone in his isolated cave on Patmos; rather, he lived there with a disciple named *Prochorus*.[21]

Above: This icon depicts John with his disciple Prochorus at his side in the Cave of the Revelation, where both men are reputed to have lived during John's exile on the island.

Prochorus is first mentioned in Acts 6:5, where the Bible tells us he was among the first seven men chosen to be deacons: "And the saying pleased the whole multitude: and they chose Stephen, a man full of faith and of the Holy Ghost, and Philip, and *Prochorus*, and Nicanor, and Timon, and Parmenas, and Nicolas, a proselyte of Antioch."

Every one of these men began as a deacon. However, it's clear that after they proved themselves faithful, at least three of them moved into more visible positions in the Early Church.

- Stephen became an evangelist whose ministry was accompanied by great signs and wonders (*see* Acts 6:8).

- Philip also became a powerful evangelist (*see* Acts 21:8).

- Nicolas became a teacher with significant influence, which later enabled him to lead people into serious doctrinal error.

- Irenaeus later wrote that it was this same Nicolas who became the father of the Nicolaitans — a sect of immoral believers.[22] In Revelation 2:6 and 15, Jesus declared that He *hated* the influence of the Nicolaitans. Another Early Church father, Hippolytus of Rome, stated that this Nicolas was one of the original seven deacons and was rebuked by the apostles for encouraging followers to yield to the sinful desires of the flesh.[23]

These examples make it obvious that at least three of the original seven men gained a higher level of visibility beyond their original roles as deacons. Therefore, it is very possible that the other four deacons, including Prochorus, also later moved into other positions of ministry.

Another very early tradition asserts that Prochorus first ministered with the apostle Peter in Judea but was later ordained by the apostles as the bishop of Nicomedia,[24] a city in northwest Asia Minor. Afterward, Prochorus joined the apostle John in the province of Asia, where he served as John's helper. Tradition further states that Prochorus helped the elderly apostle write the gospel of John, later accompanying him into exile to Patmos and penning the book of Revelation as John dictated it to him.

These traditions concerning Prochorus have been shared from generation to generation for 1,600 years. There is no specific mention in the New Testament about Prochorus being present with John on Patmos. However, it is a historical fact that many high-ranking individuals had special helpers and assistants. A case in point was the apostle Paul.

Luke was Paul's special assistant who traveled with the apostle everywhere he went. When Paul wrote his last epistle from prison, he stated, "Only Luke is with me..." (*see* 2 Timothy 4:11). Luke never left Paul's side.

In fact, the reason we have explicit details about Paul's ministry is that Luke — the writer of the book of Acts — witnessed it all. Therefore, Luke could vividly recall every detail he recorded in the book of Acts from personal experience, *especially* concerning Paul's journeys. This is one reason why the Holy Spirit chose Luke to record the events of the New Testament in the book of Acts. As Paul's assistant and constant companion, Luke was a firsthand witness of the *acts of the apostles.*

The Catholic, Orthodox, and Armenian churches embrace the account of Prochorus'accompanying the apostle John during his exile on Patmos. Because this story of Prochorus has been told for so many centuries, a great measure of credibility is lent to the possibility that some elements of these accounts are true. There is no doubt that residents of modern Patmos believe the story is true and count Prochorus' presence on the island with the apostle John as a part of the island's significant history.

This 1,600-year-old Patmos tradition states that when John saw into the Spirit — simultaneously *hearing* and *seeing* the book of Revelation — he was so overwhelmed by the power of God and by the events he saw that he was unable to write. In Revelation 1:17, John himself testified that he was overwhelmed with the presence of the glorified Jesus. He wrote, "And when I saw him, I fell at his feet as dead...." According to tradition, John's physical senses were suspended during this experience, rendering him unable to write. Therefore, Prochorus listened as John uttered the words of the Revelation, writing down what he heard word for word as John dictated what he was seeing and experiencing.

Early tradition also states that when John was released from the island of Patmos, his disciple Prochorus accompanied him back to Ephesus. There Prochorus continued to assist the elderly apostle, helping him pen the epistles of First John, Second John, and Third John. After John's death, Prochorus is believed to have returned to his position as the bishop of Nicomedia. Later while Prochorus was preaching to pagans in Antioch with great success, he was attacked by a mob and died a martyr's death.

Above: *Early records state that while John was on Patmos, he evangelized much of the population and started the first church on the island. In this fresco from the ancient monastery on Patmos, John is pictured leading a group of converts who have come to Christ.*

to reveal Himself to John as no one had ever seen Him before.

AMNESTY GRANTED, JOHN RETURNS HOME

After the death of Domitian in 96 AD, amnesty was granted to those who had been wrongfully imprisoned during the evil emperor's rule. The apostle John was one of the political prisoners who received a pardon, and he was released to return to his hilltop home just outside of Ephesus.

Whether true or not, many traditions have persisted over the centuries regarding John's time on the island of Patmos. Some of the earliest traditions include:[25]

1. Miracles performed by the apostle.

2. A contest of powers that occurred between John and an island sorcerer, very similar to Paul's conflict with a sorcerer in Acts 13:6-12.

3. John's establishment of a church on Patmos with the help of his disciple Prochorus — who, tradition says, voluntarily went into exile in order to serve the elderly apostle. The same tradition clearly states that when the people of the

Above: After John's release from Patmos, he returned to Ephesus to continue his ministry. This well-preserved fresco from the monastery on Patmos depicts the burial of the apostle John at the site of his hilltop home in Ephesus.

island heard that John was returning to Ephesus, they gathered at the shore and cried as they bade him farewell.

In his final remarks on the subject of the apostle John, Irenaeus wrote that John returned to Ephesus after the death of Domitian.[26] Most sources agree that the elderly apostle lived until the year 100 AD, although other sources state he may have lived until 104 AD. This would mean that John lived to be approximately 100 years old. He was the only one of the original 12 apostles to die a natural death, even though he suffered at least one attempt on his life and 18 months of exile on the island of Patmos.

'I, JOHN'

As John began the book of Revelation, he first introduced himself to his readers. In Revelation 1:9, he wrote, "I, John, who also am your brother and companion in tribulation, and in the kingdom and patience of Jesus Christ, was in the isle that is called Patmos, for the word of God and the testimony of Jesus Christ."

Notice that John began by saying, "I, *John....*"

(Continued on page 28)

EMPERORS OF THE ROMAN EMPIRE THROUGH CONSTANTINE

Julio-Claudian Dynasty

Augustus	27 BC–14 AD
Tiberius	14–37 AD
Caligula	37–41 AD
Claudius	41–54 AD
Nero	54–68 AD

Short-lived Emperors

Galba	68–69 AD
Otho	69 AD
Vitellius	69 AD

Flavian Dynasty

Vespasian	69–79 AD
Titus	79–81 AD
Domitian	81–96 AD

Nervan / Antonine Dynasty

Nerva	96–98 AD
Trajan	98–117 AD
Hadrian	117–138 AD
Antoninus Pius	138–161 AD
Marcus Aurelius	161–180 AD
Lucius Verus	161–169 AD
Commodus	180–192 AD

Civil War Emperors

Pertinax	193 AD
Didius Julianus	193 AD

The Severan Dynasty

Septimius Severus	193–211 AD
Caracalla	211–217 AD
Geta	209–211 AD
Macrinus	217–218 AD
Elagabulus	218–222 AD
Alexander Severus	222–235 AD

Emperors During Anarchy

Maximinus Thrax	235–238 AD
Gordian I	238 AD
Gordian II	238 AD
Pupienus and Balbinus	238 AD
Gordian III	238–244 AD
Philip the Arab	244–249 AD
Decius	249–251 AD
Trebonianus Gallus	251–253 AD
Volusianus	251–253 AD
Aemilius Aemiianus	253 AD
Valerian	253–260 AD
Gallienus	253–268 AD
Saloninus	260 AD
Claudius II	268–270 AD
Quintillus	270 AD
Aurelian	270–275 AD
Tacitus	275–276 AD
Florianus	276 AD
Probus	276–282 AD
Carus	282–284 AD
Numerian	283–284 AD
Carinus	283–285 AD

Renewed Empire (Tetrarchy)

Diocletian	284–305 AD
Maximian	286–305 AD
Constantius I	305–306 AD
Galerius	305–311 AD
Severus II	306–307 AD
Maximian	307–308 AD
Maxentius	306–312 AD
Constantine	307–337 AD

By the time the final strokes on the book of Revelation were penned, John was again residing in his hilltop home on the outskirts of Ephesus. Although the empire had known peace in the two years since Domitian's death, that peace abruptly ended as a brand-new scourge of persecution began that no one had anticipated. It is important to understand the sequence of events that led to this new wave of persecution against Christians.

After Domitian's death in 96 AD, the Emperor Nerva came to power. By Roman standards, Nerva was already an old man of 61 years when he became emperor. He was also in bad health and was often ill, too physically weak to rule ruthlessly. Because Nerva wanted to overcome the atrocities of his predecessor, he made an oath not to kill senators and proceeded to develop urban programs that made him popular with the masses. It was said that under Domitian, no one could do anything because control was so strict. Nerva's rule represented a short, two-year period when society became a "free-for-all" where there was very little control and people could do whatever they wished.

But this situation abruptly changed when the Praetorian Guard decided to take matters into their own hands in 97 AD. They arrested the Emperor Nerva, held him prisoner in his own palace, and demanded that the emperor issue the order for the conspirators in Domitian's death to be executed. Nerva refused, so the soldiers took it upon themselves to find the conspirators and put them to death. Because the people of Rome loved Nerva, he survived the horrible ordeal;

(Continued on page 30)

EMPEROR NERVA

The Emperor Nerva was born in 35 AD, the son of a rich Roman lawyer. As the nephew of the Emperor Tiberius' great-granddaughter, Nerva was distantly related to the Julio-Claudian dynasty. Nerva served several emperors — including Nero, who sought his help to suppress a conspiracy, and Vespasian, who chose him to be a consul in 71 AD. Domitian also selected Nerva to serve as his consul in the year 90 AD. In 96 AD when Domitian was assassinated, the Senate quickly declared Nerva emperor, thus ending a reign of violence, intense fear, terror, and massacre.

The Senate then issued its *damnatio memotiae* — an official edict that damned Domitian's rule and called for an eradication of his memory, including the demolition of temples, buildings, and statues that had been constructed in his honor. The situation quickly got out of control all over the Roman Empire. Countless buildings were destroyed and imperial temples burned where Domitian had been worshiped. Many former informants were put to death. Pardons were issued to many who had been wrongly imprisoned, including a pardon given to the apostle John that resulted in his release from the island of Patmos.

To overcome the atrocities of his predecessor, Nerva made an oath not to kill senators and proceeded to develop urban programs that would make him popular with the masses. However, these actions didn't satisfy the army that remembered Domitian as the emperor who gave them a pay raise.

Unrest in the empire erupted in 97 AD when the Praetorian Guard arrested the Emperor Nerva and held him prisoner in his own palace. Several conspirators in Domitian's death were still imprisoned, and the Praetorian Guard demanded their release so they could be executed. Nerva refused to surrender these prisoners, so the soldiers found the conspirators

themselves and put them to death. Nerva remained untouched, but he knew his authority had diminished in the eyes of the military, so he proceeded to select a successor for his position as emperor. In the end, he chose a highly respected governor with many legions of soldiers under his command — Marcus Ulpius Traianus, who later came to be known as the Emperor Trajan.

In October of 97 AD, Trajan was officially adopted as the son of the Emperor Nerva and thereby became official inheritor of the throne. In the year 98 AD, Nerva was overcome with fever and died soon afterward. He was so loved by the Roman people that in death, he was quickly deified by the Senate and his ashes were placed inside the Mausoleum of Augustus with members of the ruling Julio-Claudian dynasty. Nerva ruled the Roman Empire from 96-98 AD.

however, his authority was badly damaged, and he knew he had lost the respect of the military. Therefore, he began to search for a successor to replace him.[27]

Nerva had no child of his own, so instead he chose as his successor a highly respected governor who was a successful commander of many legions of soldiers. The name of that governor was Marcus Ulpius Traianus, who later came to be known simply as the Emperor Trajan.

In October of 97 AD, Nerva adopted Trajan as his son, and Trajan thereby became the official heir to the throne. One year later, Nerva became ill and died. Because he was viewed as a kind, benevolent, grandfatherly-type ruler and was deeply loved by the Roman people, the Senate quickly deified him and his burnt ashes were placed inside the Mausoleum of Augustus with members of the ruling Julio-Claudian dynasty. Nerva ruled the Roman Empire from 96-98 AD.

Trajan was then proclaimed emperor, and the period of peace that believers had enjoyed for two years came to a grinding halt as Trajan reactivated persecution against Christians. This persecution was especially intense in Asia where the apostle John lived and directed the churches of the region.

In a letter from Pliny the Younger, the Roman governor of Bithynia, to Trajan and confirmed by Trajan's letter back to Pliny, it is clear that it was the policy of the Roman government to apply great pressure on believers in order to force them to renounce Christ, abandon their newfound faith, and return to the ancient pagan religions.[28] (*See* "Pliny the Younger's Questions About Christians

and Trajan's Reply" on pages 33-35.) The two-year reprieve that believers had experienced during Nerva's reign was replaced with one of the worst periods of Roman persecution — and that dark period was just beginning about the time John was writing the book of Revelation. As a result of this renewed persecution, believers were suffering terribly and were confronted with new concerns about their future.

This leads us back to Revelation 1:9 and the reason it was so important for John to identify himself to his readers. In the first chapter, John mentioned his name *three* times, which was very unusual. In verse 1, he stated, "The Revelation of Jesus Christ, which God gave unto him, to shew unto his servants things which must shortly come to pass; and he sent and signified it by his angel *unto his servant John*." Then in verse 4, he wrote, "*John* to the seven churches which are in Asia…."

But in verse 9, John stated his identity even *stronger* than the first two times. He said, "*I, John…*" with an emphasis on the word "I," as if he was trying to draw special attention to himself. After telling the readers twice already that he was the author of this message, John then told them a *third* time. But this time, he used the word "I" — the Greek word *ego* — almost as if to raise the volume of his voice to make sure his readers understood that he really was the one writing. John was telling them, "This is John writing to you. It's really me — *John*!"

No name had more authority than John's throughout all the churches of Asia. Paul, Peter, Philip, and Bartholomew

(Continued on page 35)

EMPEROR TRAJAN

The Emperor Trajan was born in 53 AD, the son of a military commander of non-Italian descent. Due to his astonishing military career, Trajan rose to high ranks in the Roman army and assisted Domitian in putting down the rebellion of Antonius Saturninus in Upper Germany. In 85 AD, Trajan was chosen by Domitian to become praetor, and in 91 AD, Domitian rewarded Trajan with a consulship.

When Nerva was declared Roman Emperor in 96 AD, Trajan was sent to assume the position of governor of upper Germany. The following year, Nerva suffered embarrassment in Rome and began to look for an heir to the Roman throne. Nerva's choice of Trajan was a shrewd one, given Trajan's popularity with the Roman military, and the emperor promptly adopted Trajan as his legal son and heir.

When Nerva died in 98 AD, Trajan was officially declared Roman Emperor, but he didn't return to Rome to assume his office until the summer of 99 AD. As he entered the city, the streets of Rome were lined with people who jubilantly rejoiced at the arrival of their new emperor. Trajan walked the streets, talked to people, hugged senators, and connected his leadership to the hearts of the upper-, middle-, and lower-class populations.

In the following years, Trajan proved to be a good administrator, a wise manager, and a brilliant politician. Modest in his lifestyle and a firm believer in the pagan gods, Trajan was married to Pompeia Plotina, a woman also known for modesty and humility. The early medical writer, Galen, wrote that Trajan restored the road system, built bridges, and provided for the poor.[29] All of these actions made Trajan one of the most popular men to ever rule the Roman Empire.

Trajan was also a masterful military commander who was deeply loved by his troops. During his rule, three wars were fought against a kingdom north of the Danube River in what is known today as Romania. In 101 AD, Trajan led his troops a second time across the Danube to vanquish the foes in that region. When he returned to Rome, he was received in a great triumphal parade as the masses filled the city in celebration. But the victory didn't last long. In 105 AD, Trajan once again led his troops across the Danube to wage a final war against the kingdom in the north. This victory was so decisive that the foreign king committed suicide. The kingdom's treasures were seized and transferred to Rome, and by 106 AD, that kingdom was incorporated into the Roman Empire. The record of this remarkable victory is included in the bas relief that adorns Trajan's Column in the city of Rome.

The years 107-113 AD were peaceful years marked with frequent celebrations in the city of Rome. The Roman Coliseum was regularly packed with cheering crowds attending gladiator fights, which were among the most extravagant games in the history of the Roman Empire. During those years, the astonishing number of 10,000 gladiators killed a total of 11,000 wild animals imported from Africa! Also during that time period, massive building projects commenced; the enormous complex known as the Trajan Forum was dedicated in Rome; and a great harbor was constructed at the mouth of the Tiber River, allowing ships to dock there and ship their cargo by barge up the Tiber to Rome.

But in 114 AD, peacetime ended when Trajan returned to war in a fight against Parthia, a kingdom encompassing parts of modern-day Iran and Iraq. It was a battle that was swiftly won. Then in 115 AD, Trajan traveled south with his troops into Mesopotamia and quickly conquered the entire region. However, this victory was short-lived. In 116 AD, the conquered foes in Mesopotamia attacked Trajan's army with vigor. In 117 AD, an arrow that was aimed at Trajan missed the emperor but killed one of his bodyguards. After prolonged fighting, the opposing forces retreated and Trajan ordered his troops to withdraw. Roman historian Cassius Dio recorded that Trajan's health began to deteriorate at this point, and his declining health was affected even more by further rebellions in Cyrenaica (modern-day eastern Libya) and Syria.[30]

Cassius Dio also recorded that in August of 117 AD, after suffering a stroke that left him partially paralyzed, Emperor Trajan "suddenly expired, after reigning 19 years, 6 months and 15 days."[31] The emperor's body was transported back to the city of Rome, and his ashes were placed in a golden vase at the base of Trajan's Column, which bears record of his victories against the kingdom north of the Danube.

In life, Trajan was viewed as divine and was worshiped in imperial temples built in his honor in the major cities of the Roman Empire. During his rule, persecution continued against Christians and was especially intense in Asia Minor. Historians remember Trajan as one of the greatest rulers of the Roman Empire, who cared for the welfare of citizens, embellished the empire with the construction of roads and bridges, and waged successful military campaigns. Nonetheless, Trajan is also known for ruthlessly persecuting and martyring Christians. He ruled the Roman Empire from 98-117 AD.

PLINY THE YOUNGER'S QUESTIONS

(**Author's Note:** Pliny the Younger was governor of the Roman province of Bithynia in northwest Asia Minor from 111-113 AD. He exchanged many letters with the Emperor Trajan on a variety of administrative, political, and religious matters. Below are two letters, one from Pliny to the Emperor Trajan, in which he asks Trajan if he is taking the appropriate measures to force believers away from Christianity and back to paganism. The second letter is Trajan's response to Pliny.[32])

Pliny to the Emperor Trajan: It is my practice, my lord, to refer to you all matters concerning which I am in doubt. For who can better give guidance to my hesitation or inform my ignorance? I have never participated in trials of Christians. I therefore do not know what offenses it is the practice to punish or investigate, and to what extent. And I have been not a little hesitant as to whether there should be any distinction on account of age or no difference between the very young and the more mature; whether pardon is to be granted for repentance, or, if a man has once been a Christian, it does him no good to have ceased to be one; whether the name itself, even without offenses, or only the offenses associated with the name are to be punished.

Meanwhile, in the case of those who were denounced to me as Christians, I have observed the following procedure: I interrogated these as to whether they were Christians; those who confessed I interrogated a second and a third time, threatening them with punishment; those who persisted I ordered executed. For I had no doubt that, whatever the nature of their creed, stubbornness and inflexible obstinacy surely deserve to be punished. There were others possessed of the same folly; but because they were Roman citizens, I signed an order for them to be transferred to Rome.

Soon accusations spread, as usually happens, because of the proceedings going on, and several incidents occurred. An anonymous document was published containing the names of many persons. Those who denied that they were or had been Christians, when they invoked the gods in words dictated by me, offered prayer with incense and wine to your image, which I had ordered to be brought for this purpose together with statues of the gods, and moreover cursed Christ — none of which those who are really Christians, it is said, can be forced to do — these I thought should be discharged. Others named by the informer declared that they were Christians, but then denied it, asserting that they had been but had ceased to be, some three years before, others many years, some as much as 25 years. They all worshiped your image and the statues of the gods and cursed Christ. They asserted, however, that the sum and substance of their fault or error had been that they were accustomed to meet on a fixed day before

dawn and sing responsively a hymn to Christ as to a god, and to bind themselves by oath — not to some crime, not to commit fraud, theft, or adultery, not to falsify their trust, nor to refuse to return a trust when called upon to do so. When this was over, it was their custom to depart and to assemble again to partake of food — but ordinary and innocent food. Even this, they affirmed, they had ceased to do after my edict by which, in accordance with your instructions, I had forbidden political associations. Accordingly, I judged it all the more necessary to find out what the truth was by torturing two female slaves who were called deaconesses. But I discovered nothing else but depraved, excessive superstition.

I therefore postponed the investigation and hastened to consult you. For the matter seemed to me to warrant consulting you, especially because of the number involved. For many persons of every age, every rank, and also of both sexes are and will be endangered. For the contagion of this superstition has spread not only to the cities but also to the villages and farms. But it seems possible to check and cure it. It is certainly quite clear that the temples, which had been almost deserted, have begun to be frequented, that the established religious rites, long neglected, are being resumed, and that from everywhere sacrificial animals are coming, for which until now very few purchasers could be found. Hence it is easy to imagine what a multitude of people can be reformed if an opportunity for repentance is afforded.

Trajan to Pliny: You observed proper procedure, my dear Pliny, in sifting the cases of those who had been denounced to you as Christians. For it is not possible to lay down any general rule to serve as a kind of fixed standard. They are not to be sought out; if they are denounced and proved guilty, they are to be punished, with this reservation, that whoever denies that he is a Christian and really proves it — that is, by worshiping our gods — even though he was under suspicion in the past, shall obtain pardon through repentance. But anonymously posted accusations ought to have no place in any prosecution. For this is both a dangerous kind of precedent and out of keeping with the spirit of our age.

had all ministered in Asia, but by the time John wrote the book of Revelation, all these other apostles were already martyred and their voices silenced (*see* "What Happened to the Other Apostles?" on pages 48-55). Paul started the church in Ephesus and had great apostolic authority throughout Asia. But in 67 AD, Paul was beheaded in Rome during the rule of Nero. By the time the apostle John wrote the book of Revelation, Paul's voice had been silent for almost 30 years, except for the scriptures he had written.

Paul had appointed Timothy as pastor of the church of Ephesus (*see* 1 Timothy 1:3), a fact that is confirmed by the ancient writings of Polycrates. According to Polycrates, Timothy worked for many years in conjunction with the apostle John after the death of Paul.[33] Timothy served as pastor until his death at age 80 when he was attacked by a pagan mob on the streets of Ephesus. The apostle John had even outlived Timothy.

By the time John wrote the book of Revelation, he was the last survivor of the original 12 apostles and had provided oversight to the churches of Asia for almost 30 years. Consequently, his voice carried more weight than anyone else in the region — and, in fact, in the entire Christian world. Thus, when John wrote to his readers, he made use of his name and the authority that belonged only to him. His readers were suffering terribly, and John knew they needed to hear from *him* at that moment. That is why he identified himself as the author three times, and the last time said in essence, "This is *John* writing to you. It's really me — *John*!"

'YOUR BROTHER'

John knew that no one carried more apostolic authority than he. But when he introduced himself in the book of Revelation, notice that he didn't say, "I, John, the last of Jesus' first 12 apostles," or "I, John, the sole surviving charter member of Jesus' original team," or "I, John, the most important apostolic voice in the Church." Instead, he writes, "I, John, *your brother*...."

As noted earlier, at the time of this writing, the Church was once again facing great persecution. The two-year reprieve experienced during the short reign of the Emperor Nerva had ended when the Emperor Trajan came to power. Once again, believers were subjected to governmental pressure to abandon Christ and return to the pagan temples. As a result, believers all over the Roman Empire were suffering as they stood firm in the face of opposition.

These were hard times when the Church needed encouragement, and no one had more authority or respect than John. Thus, when John said, "I, John, your brother," those words "your brother" must have meant so much to his readers, communicating a vital message to strengthen them in that moment of desperate need.

Today we tend to freely use the word "brother," especially in Christian circles. But in New Testament times, this word had great significance and was not used loosely. It comes from the Greek word *adelphos*, which in its very oldest sense was used by the medical world to describe *two people who were born from the same womb*. So when ancient Greeks greeted each other as "brothers," they meant to convey the idea: "*You and I are brothers! We came out of the same womb of humanity. We have the same feelings; we have similar emotions; and we deal with the same problems in life. In every respect, we are brothers!*"

By using this terminology, John came down to the level of his readers to identify with their position in life, as well as with their personal struggles and victories. He was truly their brother — born from the womb of God, related by the blood of Jesus Christ, a member of the same spiritual family. Although John was a great apostle, he used the word "brother" to let them know he understood their predicaments. He was their "brother" in the tribulations they were facing in life.

But in New Testament times, the word "brother" carried another very significant meaning that doesn't exist in our world today. This word "brother" was also a special term used during the time of Alexander the Great to describe *faithful soldiers*. These fighting men were true *brothers*, *comrades*, and *partners* who united together to fight the same battles, handle the same weapons, and win the same wars.

From time to time, Alexander the Great would hold huge public ceremonies where he would give awards to soldiers who had gone the extra mile in battle. When the most coveted awards were given, Alexander would beckon the most faithful soldiers on stage to stand next to him. Before an audience of adoring soldiers, he would embrace each faithful soldier and publicly declare, "Alexander the Great is proud to be the brother of this soldier!"

The word "brother" used by Alexander the Great in these great ceremonies was this same Greek word *adelphos*, which referred to men who were *brothers in battle*. This was the highest and greatest compliment that could be given to a soldier during the time of this great general.

To be a "brother" also meant that a person was a *true comrade*. These *soldiers* had stood together through the thick of many battles and had thereby achieved a special level of *brotherhood* — a bond known only by those who stay united together in the heat of the fray. This meaning was also a part of what John had in mind when he called himself a "brother" to his reading audience.

Consider what it must have meant to those early believers who read John's words when he called himself their "brother." They were struggling greatly due to the many political pressures that were mounting against them. By identifying himself as their brother, John came down to their level as one who was facing similar circumstances and feeling the same emotions — but who, like them, was still in the fight and pushing forward. With

ALEXANDER THE GREAT

Alexander the Great was one of the most important figures in human history. Although this man lived a short life (356-323 BC), his achievements were remarkable. The son of Philip II of Macedonia, Alexander was taught by the great Greek philosopher Aristotle. He was only 20 years old when his father died and he inherited the Macedonian kingdom.

Over the next 13 years of his short life, Alexander established the great Greek Empire for which he was so famous, was proclaimed the Pharaoh of Egypt, and spread the Greek language and culture across all the lands he controlled. Alexander's influence had a guiding hand in every aspect of life and cultural development, and he is still revered by many as the greatest military leader in human history.

Above: This view of the rugged, desolate shoreline of Patmos is similar to what the apostle John would have seen as the ship that carried him into exile neared its destination. Almost devoid of natural water sources or food supplies, Patmos offered little hope of sustenance and survival to the prisoners sentenced to live on this barren, isolated island in the Aegean Sea. Another view of Patmos is shown on the following page.

this one word of encouragement and identification, it must have almost felt as if John had put his arm around their shoulders and said, "I completely understand what you're going through." Although these early believers were struggling, they hadn't given up the fight. They were still on the spiritual frontlines — faithfully trudging along, one step at a time, holding fast to truth no matter the cost. So when John identified himself as their "brother," it was the equivalent of saying it was an honor to be their *comrade*. No matter how well or how badly these believers were doing in the midst of their fight, at least they were *still fighting*!

It is evident from certain ancient documents that some early Christians didn't fare so well in the face of these intense pressures. At the insistence of pagan interrogators, some believers *did* curse Christ and return to the pagan temples in order to save their lives. But by using the word "brother" to identify himself with the early believers of these seven congregations, John let them know that *they* were exceptionally fine Christian soldiers and that he was proud to be their "brother."

'COMPANION IN TRIBULATION'

John didn't stop with calling himself the brother of his reading audience. He went on to say in Revelation 1:9 that he was their "companion in tribulation." The word "companion" is the Greek word *sunkoinonos*, a compound of the words *sun* and *koinonia*. The first part of the word is *sun*, a word that carries the idea of *partnership*

or *cooperation*. This was also a very important concept John wanted to convey as he reached out to encourage his readers.

An example of the word *sun* can be found in Second Corinthians 6:1, where Paul wrote that we are "coworkers" together with God. The word "coworkers" is the Greek word *sunergos*, which is a compound of the words *sun* and *ergos*. The word *sun*, as indicated above, gives the impression of something done in *partnership* or *cooperation* with someone else.

The second part of the word "coworkers" is the Greek word *ergos*, a word that can depict either *work* or a *worker*. When the words *sun* and *ergos* are joined to form the word *sunergos*, as in Second Corinthians 6:1, the new word takes on the meaning of *two or more workers who are joined together for a common cause or project*. It is no longer the image of what one worker does by himself, but rather of what he accomplishes in *partnership* or *cooperation* with others.

In Revelation 1:9, John used the word *sun* to describe a *partnership* and a *kinship* that he felt with his readers. However, he joined the word *sun* to the Greek word *koinonia*, a word that means *to fellowship*; *to share something together*; or *to have a commonality in experience*. But when the words *sun* and *koinonia* are joined to form the word *sunkoinonos*, the new word carries twice the impact. It means to be *co-joined as partners in a common experience*. It is the equivalent of saying, "*What you are experiencing is precisely what I am experiencing. We are real partners in this experience. I'm right here with you, because I am going through the same things you are going through right now.*"

John's use of this term *sunkoinonos* must have been another source of great encouragement to the believers who read his message. It would have been a natural temptation for them to wonder why they

were struggling or to wonder if there was something defective or blemished in their faith that allowed these circumstances to arise against them. To hear this one word from John — and for him to tell them that he was facing the same ordeals they were facing — must have brought a sense of relief and inner strength to their souls. They were not alone in their predicament, for even the greatest leader of the day was facing difficult times.

There are moments when the most powerful thing a Christian leader can do is to come down and meet his congregation right on the level of their struggles. Rather than condescend to their people and make them feel guilty for experiencing difficult times, a good leader crawls down in the ditch to join those under his care who are struggling. He not only calls himself their "brother," but he also takes it a step further: He becomes transparent before them, letting them know he is experiencing exactly the same things *they* are experiencing.

John did this for his readers. Not only did he call himself their brother, but he also identified himself as their partner and companion in tribulation. Of course, he *was*! He had spent 18 months on the desolate island of Patmos, exiled there as an elderly man. If anyone understood hardship and tribulation, it was John. He had faced and survived great trials and persecution. This gave him the right to speak on the subject of suffering from personal experience, which must have helped open the hearts of his readers.

When John stated that he was their "companion in tribulation," he used the Greek word *thlipsis* for "tribulation." This word doesn't simply mean *hardship* or

difficulties; rather, it describes *the most excruciating type of stress and pressure*. By using this word, John informed his readers that he had been subjected to an extreme level of *crushing* and *debilitating* pressure because of his faith.

In Paul's epistles, when he described stressful, agonizing, or life-threatening situations that he and others faced during the course of their ministries, he often used the word *thlipsis* to describe these events. Historically, this word is interesting, as it was first used to depict an act of *torture*. The victim would be bound tightly and then laid flat on his back with a huge stone or boulder suspended on a rope above him. The torturers would demand that the victim confess his crime. If he refused, the stone was lowered closer and closer to his prostrate body. If the victim continually refused to confess his crime, the stone was eventually lowered so close that the victim could not move and could scarcely breathe. At that point, he was *trapped* — *pinned in place* and *unable to move*. Finally, the rope was cut and the stone with all its weight fell upon the victim, *crushing* him to death.

Therefore, when the word *thlipsis* is used to describe difficult circumstances, it is meant to depict *events that make one feel trapped, pinned to the wall, and unable to move or negotiate a way out of that circumstance*. The person feels *smothered*, *suffocated*, or *crushed* by a devastating experience. This was the word John used to describe the events he had faced in his own ministry as a result of persecution.

Try to imagine how John must have felt when he realized he was going to be placed on a ship carrying criminals and deposited on one of the worst island prisons in the world. On that day when he disembarked from the ship and was left to wander around the rugged island with no food, clothes, shelter, or help whatsoever, he must have been tempted to feel *trapped* and *unable to negotiate his way out of that circumstance.* If anyone understood what it meant to be pinned against a wall and unable to escape a situation, it certainly would have been the apostle John!

But John victoriously survived and endured his experience on Patmos against all odds. Who would have imagined that a man in his mid-90s would return from spending 18 months in such a hostile environment to continue his ministry? The fact that John faced and overcame the worst kind of situation earned him the right to speak to others who were also facing terrible ordeals.

'THE KINGDOM AND PATIENCE OF JESUS CHRIST'

The apostle John went on to write to his readers that he was their companion not only in tribulation, but also in "the kingdom and patience of Jesus Christ."

The word "kingdom" is the Greek word *basileia*, a word that depicts *a ruler, a ruling power*, or *a kingdom.* Some buildings in Roman periods were called *basilicas* because they were places where ruling decisions were carried out by authorities. As time progressed, large cathedrals were often referred to as basilicas because they were important church buildings where spiritual authorities provided oversight to entire regions and where the most important decisions were decided.

As John listed the shared experiences he'd had with his readers, he was careful to note that he and his readers had also been partners in experiencing the Kingdom of God and the reality of God's ruling power. Even though hard times were certainly pressing upon these early believers, it was also a fact that the city of Ephesus, where John resided, and all of Asia had seen a remarkable advance of the Kingdom of God in their generation.

This entire region had experienced mighty demonstrations of God's miraculous power as the first Gospel preachers carried the truth of Jesus Christ into gross pagan darkness. The book of Acts is filled with records of healings, miracles, demonic deliverances, and large numbers of people who repented and who burned their occult scrolls and charms after receiving Christ as their Savior. In the midst of great evil, the Church of Jesus Christ was born in the

Left: Pictured are the ruins of Curetes Street, which marked the center of the beautiful ancient city of Ephesus where the first Christian church in Asia was established by the apostle Paul and his team in 52 AD. Despite the grossly pagan environment of Ephesus and the periods of intense persecution against Christians in the years that followed, the Ephesian church flourished and grew, becoming the largest body of believers in the entire region.

power of the Holy Spirit — and, to a great measure, the Church had risen with power and spiritual authority. So as John wrote about the various ways in which he had shared mutual experiences with his readers, he reminded them that not only had they suffered hardships together — they had also mutually shared in *the Kingdom of God* and all of its mighty power.

A lesson is to be learned from Revelation 1:9. As John identified with the suffering believers, he knew it was important to recall not only the hard times, but also the good times. Although they were experiencing difficulties at that moment in their lives, they had also known many glorious moments of victory. It was important that they didn't lose sight of the great things God had already done simply because they were facing monumental problems at the moment. The same Kingdom power that had worked

on their behalf in the past was still present to work in the future.

John reminded his readers that they *knew* Kingdom power and that it was just as much a part of their mutual experience as were the sufferings they were presently facing. Their proven experience with the Kingdom of God and all of its mighty power was a fact to which they needed to hold fast during this difficult time. Therefore, John included *the Kingdom* in his list of things he and these early believers had shared together.

But the apostle John also pointed out that they had been co-sharers in the "patience of Jesus Christ." This is very important, for a sustained ruling of God's Kingdom *requires* patience. But what does the word "patience" mean in this context, and why is it necessary to experience the sustained ruling power of the Kingdom of God?

The word "patience" in this verse comes from the Greek word *hupomene*, which is a compound of the Greek words *hupo* and *meno*. The word *hupo* in this case means *under*, whereas the word *meno* means *to abide* or *to stay*, such as when referring to a resolute decision about which one will not move from his position or stance. However, when the words *hupo* and *meno* are compounded into one word, the picture changes dramatically. The word *hupo* in this case portrays a person who is under some type of heavy load or circumstance that would normally cause a person to bend, to break, or to change his position in order to escape troublesome pressures.

But the second part of the word is the Greek word *meno*, which means *to abide*. As used in this word "patience" (*hupomene*), it portrays a person absolutely committed to what he believes and to the position he holds to be true and dear. Regardless of how heavy the pressure seems to be or how much trouble mounts against him, he refuses to move or to surrender. He *sticks* to his position; he *abides by* what he believes; and he *stays put*, no matter what tries to come upon him.

A more accurate translation of the Greek word *hupomene* would be *endurance*, thereby depicting one's ability to *outlast* hard times. This is precisely the reason one scholar translates the word *hupomene* as *staying power* or *hang-in-there power*. When *hupomene* is working in a person's life, it gives him *the supernatural ability to remain steadfast and to never surrender his position or beliefs, even in the face of insurmountable challenges and stress.*

The leaders of the Early Church often referred to *hupomene* as "the Queen of all virtues."[34] They asserted that those who possessed this virtue would eventually outlast the hard times that caused them much suffering and would be heralded as champions. When *hupomene* is working in people's hearts and souls, it gives them the *inward fortitude to stay put and to never give up or surrender their position.* Then when hard times eventually pass, those who have endured and remained steadfast are lauded, honored, and recognized as victors in the fight of faith. This is the reason early believers called this quality the Queen of all virtues.

The intense resistance that came against the Early Church made it necessary for believers to possess this kind of *endurance* and *resolve* in order to keep furthering God's Kingdom on the earth. To survive through periods of persecution, including the renewed persecution they were currently facing, the believers needed *hupomene* — the inward fortitude to stay put and to never give up or surrender their position. This is always needful, especially in parts of the world where the Gospel light is shining into darkness for the first time. Evil may try to overcome the light, but if the light-bearers will stay put and endure to the end, eventually the darkness will crumble as the glorious light of Jesus Christ pushes it out of the way. But "patience" — in actuality, *endurance* — is required of believers in every age if they are to overcome the many difficulties that try to assail them.

'WAS IN THE ISLE THAT IS CALLED PATMOS'

Of course, one of John's own personal difficulties was his experience on the island of Patmos. In fact, when he wrote about his experience on that island, he communicated the sense of *surprise* he felt when these events were taking place. He wrote, "I, John, who also am your brother and

Above: This painting by Eugenio Landesio, entitled, "Saint John on the Island of Patmos," depicts the apostle John in front of the cave where he lived while exiled on the Isle of Patmos. Many believe it was here that John fell into a suspended state while Jesus appeared to him and gave him the message contained in the book of Revelation.

companion in tribulation, and in the kingdom and patience of Jesus Christ, was in the isle that is called Patmos" (Revelation 1:9).

Notice particularly where John wrote that he "...*was in* the isle that is called Patmos." The word "was" comes from the Greek word *ginomai*, which conveys a sense of *shock* and *surprise*, *something that happens unexpectedly* or *something that catches one off guard*. John used the Greek word *ginomai* in this case to describe to his readers how he felt when all these events were unfolding in his life. Because John never could have predicted the events that brought him to the island of Patmos, he used this word *ginomai* to convey the idea, "*In a way I never could*

have expected, predicted, or anticipated, I came to find myself on the island of Patmos."

When John's readers saw the word "Patmos," it must have sent shivers down their spines because Patmos was *one of the most dreaded places* on the entire planet during the First Century. The island was windy, hot, and desolate. It was 10 miles long, 6 miles wide, and approximately 50 square miles in size. Its coastline of 37 miles was covered with the dangerous rocky crags that John and other prisoners had seen as their ship made its way to the port.

Patmos was a notorious island that had first been settled by Dorians, one of three major tribes of ancient Greece. Later Ionians, another of the three major tribes, populated the island, and Patmos flourished with a population of approximately 15,000 people. During the Sixth and Seventh Centuries BC, the residents were busy constructing an array of temples on its acropolis. There were ancient pagan temples to *Zeus, Apollo, Artemis, Dionysus,* and a host of other Greek gods. But because the island was difficult to reach and had an insufficient water supply to sustain its population, the people began deserting the island. Eventually it was altogether abandoned — but not before its forests and trees had been completely harvested and depleted. By the time the island had been stripped, very little was left in terms of natural vegetation. Even animals had a hard time surviving on Patmos because

so little natural food existed to provide them sustenance. What had begun as a beautiful, flourishing island had become a large, remote rock in the middle of the sea.

This is precisely what made Patmos a perfect place of exile — it was *remote, deserted, harsh,* and *hard to reach.* The island was ideally suited for prisoners whom Rome wanted to move off the mainland and make inaccessible to the main population. And because it lay on the exact route from Rome to Asia Minor, it was ideally positioned for ships carrying prisoners to stop and unload their human cargo.

As stated earlier, common criminals imprisoned on Patmos were forced into hard labor of some sort and kept under a watchful eye, whereas political offenders were granted a higher level of freedom. The latter category of prisoners was allowed to freely roam about the island; however, these prisoners were given nothing in terms of food or clothes needed for human survival. Thus, political offenders frequently perished from lack of food, drinking water, medical attention, and even sufficient clothing to give protection from the hot sun that cooked the rocks of the volcanic island. For all these reasons, John's mention of the name "Patmos" would have evoked strong emotions from his readers, who understood the severity of a sentence of exile to that forbidding place.

Left: The carved pillars that adorn the front of this cathedral — built centuries ago on a hilltop in Patmos in honor of the apostle John — originally were decorative columns used in the ancient Temple of Diana that once stood on the exact spot where the monastery stands today.

'FOR THE WORD OF GOD AND TESTIMONY OF JESUS CHRIST'

Why was this sole survivor of Jesus' original apostles arrested in his old age in Ephesus? A probable answer can be found in the writings of the Roman historian Cassius Dio, who described what happened to exiled political prisoners after Domitian's death: "[Emperor] Nerva also released all who were on trial for *maiestas* [high treason] and restored the exiles."[35]

Eusebius also wrote about this development: "The sentences of Domitian were annulled, and the Roman Senate decreed the return of those who had been unjustly banished and the restoration of their property." The Apostle John, after his banishment to the island, took up his abode at Ephesus.[36] This charge of "high treason" against the apostle John would have included such specific charges as rebellion against state authorities, propagating false religion, undermining state religion, and refusal to worship the emperor.

Because John refused to worship the emperor, he was therefore judged as undermining state religion. And because he preached the Lordship and Kingship of Jesus Christ, he faced the accusation of propagating a false religion and encouraging allegiance to another king. The combination of these offenses made John's crimes grievous in the minds of Roman authorities, especially in the mind of the evil Roman Emperor Domitian.

John was also the last surviving member of Jesus' first 12 apostles. Domitian had long hated Christians for their refusal to worship him. So when he discovered John was the last member of those original

Above: Today modern Patmos boasts a small Greek population, but it is easy to imagine how difficult it was for prisoners of Rome to survive on the remote, barren island. Even today, natural water sources are in short supply on Patmos, requiring local residents to import most of their water from the mainland.

12 apostles, it may have provided another incentive for Domitian to attack an old man like John. This was the ultimate *censorship* — the opportunity to arrest, imprison, or kill John and thereby deal a final deathblow to the memory of that Jewish upstart, Jesus of Nazareth.

'I WAS IN THE SPIRIT ON THE LORD'S DAY'

The first commentary about the book of Revelation was written in the Third Century by the Early Church writer Victorinus. In that commentary, Victorinus stated that John worked as a prisoner in the mine quarries of Patmos.[37] However,

(Continued on page 56)

WHAT HAPPENED
TO THE OTHER APOSTLES?

In spite of hard times, the apostles remained in Jerusalem for several years before journeying elsewhere in obedience to Jesus' command in Acts 1:8 to take the Gospel first to Jerusalem, then to Judea and Samaria, and finally to "the uttermost parts of the earth." Sometime after 44 AD, the 11 remaining apostles, along with Matthias (chosen in Acts 1:15-26 to fill the vacant place created by Judas' death), began traveling to take the Gospel message to the ends of the earth in accordance with Jesus' Great Commission.

Considering the difficulties associated with travel in the ancient world — where people primarily journeyed either by foot, by ship, or on the back of an animal — it is simply remarkable to see how far the apostles took the life-changing message of the Gospel. As discussed earlier, John ministered in Ephesus after leaving Jerusalem. The following is a historical recounting of where the other 11 apostles went, where they preached, and how each one met death as a result of his divine assignment.

JAMES,
BROTHER OF JOHN

In 44 AD, the apostle *James*, the brother of John, was beheaded during the time of Herod Agrippa I (*see* Acts 12:1,2). Herod Agrippa I was the grandson of Herod the Great and reigned as king over an area even larger than the region ruled by his grandfather. In 44 AD, Herod Agrippa I began a vicious persecution of the Church in order to satisfy the Jewish leadership in Jerusalem. James' visibility as a Christian leader in Jerusalem may have been the reason he was chosen as Agrippa's first victim. According to the Early Church historian Eusebius, the man who led James to his judgment was so moved by James' unwavering confession of faith that he himself became a believer and was beheaded together with James.[38]

ANDREW

Besides the information provided by the Early Church theologian Origen, Eusebius is our other primary source that tells us *Andrew* went to Scythia to preach the Gospel[39] — a region that included:

- Kazakhstan, Russia, and eastern Ukraine (inhabited by Scythians since at least the Eighth Century BC).
- The northern Caucasus area, including Azerbaijan and Georgia.
- Ukraine, Belarus, and Poland up to Oceanus Sarmaticus, known also as the Baltic region.
- Southern Ukraine with the lower Danube River area and Bulgaria, also known as Scythia Minor.

The tradition of Andrew ministering in this part of the world is so ingrained in Church history that he is even recognized as a patron saint of the Orthodox Church in Ukraine and Russia. In addition, the following historians of the Early Church record Andrew's missionary journeys:

- Gregory of Nazianzus reported that Andrew went to Epirus[40] (a region straddling modern-day Greece and Albania).
- Jerome states that Andrew took the Gospel message to Achaia[41] (south-central Greece).
- Theodoret wrote that Andrew took the Gospel to Greece.[42]

The truth is, it is likely that all of these ancient historians are correct. The Byzantine historian Nicephorus included all of these as a part of Andrew's travels, writing that the apostle took the Gospel to Cappadocia, Galatia, Bithynia, Byzantium, Macedonia, Thessaly, Achaia, and Scythia.[43] Scholars generally agree that Andrew was crucified at the order of a Roman governor in the city of Patras, located in Achaia. Andrew was bound with ropes to an X-shaped cross, known as a *decussate* cross, where he hung for a very long time and suffered a prolonged death. Andrew's martyrdom took place during the rule of Nero near the year 60 AD.

BARTHOLOMEW

Tradition says that *Bartholomew*, who was also known as Nathanael, took the Gospel to the region known today as Armenia. According to Eusebius, Pantaneus (who was Origen's spiritual mentor), reported that Bartholomew had made disciples in India and that he'd given his converts the gospel of Matthew.[44] "India" was a term that encompassed a large region, including Arabia Felix (modern-day Yemen). Other early accounts state that Bartholomew preached in Mesopotamia, Persia, Egypt, Laconia (a southern region of Greece), Phrygia (a kingdom in central Asia Minor), on the shores of the Black Sea, and in Armenia. The tradition of Bartholomew preaching the Gospel in Armenia is so well established that he is recognized as the patron saint of that nation.

According to a very early tradition, Bartholomew was martyred in Albanopolis, an ancient city in Armenia. Some early traditions present him as being beheaded, crucified, flayed with a knife, or skinned alive, suffering a miserable death at the hands of pagans. Some assert that he was killed in India; however, the earlier tradition of martyrdom in Albanopolis is more likely.

JAMES, SON OF ALPHAEUS

James was also known as *the son of Alphaeus* and was not the same James who was beheaded in Acts 12:1,2. According to a strong early tradition, James preached throughout Israel before traveling to minister to pagans in Egypt, where tradition states he was martyred as a result of pagan opposition.

JUDE

Tradition holds that *Jude*, who was also known as Thaddaeus, traveled to preach the Gospel in Judea, Samaria, Idumaea, Syria, Mesopotamia (modern-day Iraq), and Libya — often accompanied by Simon the Zealot. The two also traveled to Persia, known in today's world as the country of Iran, to preach the Gospel. Jude is believed to have been bludgeoned to death by local pagans who opposed his ministry in either Syria or Persia in 65 AD.

MATTHEW

According to early traditions passed down to us primarily through Early Church theologians Irenaeus and Clement of Alexandria, *Matthew* (also known as Levi the tax collector) preached the Gospel among the Jews for 15 years. Eusebius reports that before Matthew took the Gospel to other nations, he first wrote his gospel in the Hebrew language for Hebrew-speaking people.[45] Other early sources indicate that Matthew then took the Gospel to the region of Ethiopia on the Caspian Sea (*not* the country of Ethiopia in Africa), then on to Persia, Macedonia, and Syria.

Although very little is known about Matthew's martyrdom, it is strongly suggested that his death occurred in Ethiopia, and one tradition states that Matthew was killed on the orders of the king of Ethiopia while the apostle was worshiping at church. Other scholars believe that Matthew was either burned, stoned, or beheaded. Matthew is most remembered for his contribution of writing the gospel of Matthew.

MATTHIAS

Although *Matthias* was chosen as a disciple after the death of Judas Iscariot (*see* Acts 1:26), he was recognized by the other 11 apostles as a legitimate apostle and is therefore included here in this discussion. According to early documents written by Nicephorus,[46] Matthias first ministered in Judea and then to the barbarians and cannibals in the interior of Ethiopia in Africa. One tradition says Matthias was killed in Sebastopolis (a city in the northeastern region of Asia Minor) and was buried there. Other traditions place his martyrdom in Jerusalem. However, the strongest evidence points to his martyrdom in Ethiopia.

PETER

Paul referred to *Peter* as an apostle to the Jews, and Peter's life certainly demonstrated that he had a special grace for ministry to the Jewish people. Eventually Peter traveled to Rome, where early tradition states he served as bishop of the church in Rome.

Peter's first epistle was written from Rome. In it, he wrote, "The church that is at Babylon, elected together with you, saluteth you; and so doth Marcus my son" (1 Peter 5:13). This name Babylon referred to Rome and its pagan influences, because the real Babylon on the Euphrates was already abandoned and in ruins. Scholars believe that this "Babylon" comment was Peter's way of describing the city of Rome and identifying Rome as the place where he wrote his first epistle.

Notice Peter also specifically stated that Mark was with him at the time he wrote his first epistle, the book of First Peter. From the writings of Bishop

Papias of Hierapolis and Clement of Alexandria, it is known that Mark wrote the gospel of Mark while he was living in Rome because Christians in Rome wanted him to write a clear presentation of the doctrines Peter had preached to them.[47] Irenaeus confirms this information,[48] and Early Church leader Clement of Rome, in his epistle to the Corinthians that he wrote sometime between 95-97 AD, places *both* Peter and Paul in Rome.[49] The following Early Church writers also confirm that Peter and Paul were martyred in Rome: Bishop Ignatius of Antioch, in a document written before 117 AD;[50] Bishop Dionysus of Corinth, in a letter written between 165-174 AD;[51] and Tertullian.[52]

Between 198-217 AD, Caius, one of Rome's Early Church leaders, wrote these words (recorded in Eusebius' *Church History*): "But I can show the trophies of the Apostles. If you care to go to the Vatican or to the road to Ostia, thou shalt find the trophies of those who have founded this Church [referring to the Roman church]."[53]

Scholars believe that Caius' use of the word "trophies" was a specific reference to the graves of Peter and Paul in Rome. This lets us know that both apostles' burial sites were known between the years 198-217 AD. According to strong early traditions, Peter was crucified upside down near the present-day Vatican either in the year 67 or 68 AD. Under St. Peter's Basilica in Rome is an ancient necropolis (cemetery), which, according to the Catholic Church, contains the burial place of Peter. This claim is most likely factual. Eusebius writes about "the inscription of the names of Peter and Paul, which have been preserved to the present day on their burial-places there."[54]

Peter's and Paul's deaths occurred somewhere around the fourteenth year of Nero's reign, probably in the year 67 AD, a date accepted by scholars and attested to by both Eusebius and Jerome. In his writings, Jerome states that Peter came to Rome during the rule of the Emperor Claudius in the year 42 AD, and it is believed that this apostle ministered in Rome approximately 25 years before suffering martyrdom.[55] From Rome, the apostle Peter wrote the epistles that came to be known as First and Second Peter. In his lifetime, Peter's apostolic authority was widely recognized, and he was viewed as a leader among the apostles.

PHILIP

When *Philip* began his traveling ministry, he took the Gospel to Phrygia, a region located in what is known today as central Turkey. Philip's martyrdom in Hierapolis is a well-established fact in church tradition. It is interesting to note that many early documents claim that Philip the deacon (who later became Philip the evangelist) and Philip the apostle may both be buried in Hierapolis. Today visitors to the ancient city of Hierapolis can view the ruins of an ancient church building built on top of Philip's gravesite.

THOMAS

Today India recognizes *Thomas* as the apostle to India because of a long-held tradition that Thomas brought the Gospel to the Kerala area of India, a territory located near the Indian west coast. This tradition is confirmed in the writings of Ephraem, Syrus, Ambrose, Paulinus, Jerome, and Gregory of Tours, as well as other Early Church writers. Afterward, Thomas traveled further eastward to bring the Gospel to the eastern coast of India. There tradition says that Thomas was killed near the city of Madras — speared to death by pagans who opposed his ministry. In that region today, there remains a bas relief dating to the Seventh Century that states Thomas laid down his life in that area. It is believed that at some point, perhaps during Thomas' journey to India, he preached the Gospel in what is known today as Iraq and Iran.

SIMON

Simon was known also as *Simon the Zealot* because he was so politically zealous for Israel before Jesus called him into the ministry. Early Church fathers wrote that Simon was later compelled by that same zeal to take the Gospel to pagans along the Black Sea and in Egypt, northern Africa, and even Britain. Later Simon joined Jude in carrying the Gospel message to Persia and to ancient Armenia (a region that today is part of modern-day Iraq and Georgia), where both Simon and Jude were martyred.

Two early traditions state that Simon was sawn in half at Suanir, Persia, or in Colchis, an ancient kingdom in the Caucasus region of modern-day Georgia. The ancient Armenian historian Moses of Chorene wrote that Simon was martyred at Weriosphora in Caucasian Iberia, also a part of modern-day Georgia.[56] Simon's place of burial is unknown.

since there is no evidence that mine quarries ever existed on Patmos, some doubt is cast on this particular piece of information.

Early tradition from the island of Patmos specifically states that John was in the cave he had made his temporary home at the time he was caught into another realm and received the book of Revelation (thus, the reason that the cave is referred to as the *Cave of the Revelation*). But regardless of *where* this supernatural experience occurred, John gave us insight into how it took place when he said, "I was in the Spirit on the Lord's day..." (Revelation 1:10).

The word "was" is the Greek word *ginomai*, the same word discussed on page 45. As noted earlier, the word *ginomai* in this case describes *something that happens unexpectedly* or *something that catches one off guard*. This tells us that John was not expecting this divine encounter. When it occurred, it took him completely by surprise and caught him off guard. In a way he never could have predicted, he suddenly found himself "in the spirit."

This word "spirit" is capitalized in the *King James Version*, but in the original Greek, it is not. Actually, the phrase "in the Spirit" is a translation of the Greek words *en pneumatic*. This phrase lacks a definite article and should therefore be translated, "*In a way I never could have planned, predicted, or anticipated, I suddenly found myself IN SPIRIT on the Lord's day.*" This phrase "in spirit" is a term to describe *another realm, another dimension,* or *a spiritual realm far different from the natural world* that surrounded John.

When the phrase "in spirit" is combined with the preceding usage of the word *ginomai*, which depicts an element of *surprise*, the new phrase gives a clear picture of what John experienced and how he felt when it occurred. Whether he was located in a mine quarry or in his cave is not absolutely clear. But it *is* clear that when John experienced this divine encounter, he did *not* know it was about to happen. The apostle was going about his business, when suddenly — *out of nowhere, taking him completely off guard and by surprise* — he abruptly found himself no longer in the same physical place but standing in *another dimension.* He had somehow passed from the natural realm into the realm of the spirit and was now "in spirit," or in a totally different realm.

John related that this happened on "the Lord's day." Casual readers take this to mean "Sunday," but it actually has nothing to do with Sunday at all. The phrase "the Lord's day" is a translation of the Greek word *kuriakos*, a specific word that was used primarily to describe the *Emperor's Day*. It has been proven from ancient inscriptions that the word *kuriakos* was a common word for anything *imperial* and that the first day of each month was designated as an *imperial day* when the ruling emperor was especially celebrated. That day was referred to as *kuriakos* or the *Emperor's Day*.[57]

This means Jesus Christ chose to reveal Himself as the *King of kings* and *Lord of lords* on the very day that the entire Roman Empire was specially celebrating the supposed deity of the wicked Emperor Domitian. It must have struck John that on the same day when the whole world was

THE ISLAND OF PATMOS 57

worshiping a fraudulent, evil human ruler, the *True Ruler* stepped into the forsaken place where John was exiled and revealed Himself in all of His glory to him.

'AND HEARD BEHIND ME A GREAT VOICE, LIKE AS A TRUMPET'

All of a sudden, John "heard" a great voice, like as a trumpet, coming from behind him in the spirit realm. The word "heard" is the Greek word *akouo*, which simply means *to hear*. This is the same word from which the word *acoustics* is derived. John wrote that it was a "*great* voice." The word "great" is the word *mega*, meaning *huge*, and the word "voice" is *phone*, simply the word for *a voice*. When the two words are used together, the phrase describes not merely *a voice*, but *a great, huge, gigantic voice*.

The voice John heard was so loud that he said it was "like as a trumpet." The word "trumpet" is the Greek word *salpignos*, and the tense used indicates that the sound of the voice was as loud and clear as the blast of a trumpet. Just as a trumpet blast gets the attention of those who hear it, the sound of Jesus' voice spoke forth so loudly and clearly that John was captured by its force and knew immediately he was to submit to the authority of the One speaking.

'SAYING, I AM ALPHA AND OMEGA, THE FIRST AND THE LAST'

With John's attention captured, Jesus then announced Himself to the elderly apostle, saying, "... I am Alpha and Omega, the first and the last..." (Revelation 1:11).

Alpha is the first letter of the Greek alphabet, and *omega* is the last letter. Thus, Jesus further explained that just like *alpha* and *omega*, He is "the first and the last." However, this phrase in Greek refers to much more than merely the beginning and ending of an alphabet. It was an ancient formula used to convey *eternity* and *timelessness*. By using this well-known formula when speaking to John, Jesus was in essence declaring, "*I am eternal and timeless.*"

But in addition to this self-declaration of *timelessness* and *eternity*, Jesus also conveyed to John that He is both the *beginning* of everything and the *conclusion* to everything. And not only is Jesus the *beginning* and the *end*, but He embraces *everything in between* as well. He is all in all, and nothing in the universe and no part of human history has been exempt from His presence. He is literally the beginning, the end, and everything in between. Because He is ever-present, there is nothing that has or ever will escape His attention and knowledge. Because He is the Alpha and Omega, the beginning and the end, He knows the *past*, the *present*, and the *future*.

'WHAT THOU SEEST WRITE IN A BOOK'

Jesus went on to say, "...What thou seest, write in a book, and send it unto the seven churches which are in Asia; unto Ephesus, and unto Smyrna, and unto Pergamos, and unto Thyatira, and unto Sardis, and unto Philadelphia, and unto Laodicea" (v. 11). Jesus commanded John to write in a book all that was about to be shown to him. Then John was to send this divine message to the seven churches that were in Asia.

It must be noted that there were approximately 1,000 cities in Asia Minor at that time; however, the seven cities Jesus listed were the largest and most pagan cities in the region. Due to their significant populations, these particular seven cities had the largest congregations and the greatest influence on other churches in Asia.

Sending the book of the Revelation to the seven churches in these cities was easily achievable because all seven cities were connected to each other by a series of roads. The location of the cities on these interconnected roads and John's own residence in Ephesus makes it likely that the Revelation was first delivered to the church in *Ephesus*, then on to *Smyrna*, then to *Pergamum*, then to *Thyatira*, then to *Sardis*, then to *Philadelphia*, and finally to *Laodicea*. In other words, the delivery of the messages to the seven churches most likely occurred in the exact order in which Jesus spoke specific messages to the churches in Revelation chapters 1-3.

To each of these seven churches, Jesus said, "I know thy works...." As He delivered to John His messages for these seven churches, it was apparent that Jesus was very familiar with each of these churches. He used allegories that drew on the cities' unique histories, describing specific problems and challenges that each church faced. Jesus even called out a particular church member's name and described a problem that one pastor had with his manipulative wife. Although no one had

ever seen Jesus in any of these churches, it was apparent that He had walked among each congregation and was very familiar with the spiritual condition of each church.

But before Jesus spoke forth these messages to each respective church, He first continued to reveal Himself to John — *the disciple whom He loved*. This was truly a new "revelation of Jesus Christ" — a revelation so powerful that John fell at his feet as dead and had to be quickened to consciousness by the resuscitating touch of Jesus' hand.

John said in Revelation 1:12, "And I turned to see the voice that spake with me...." What the apostle beheld when he turned around and what then transpired during this supernatural visitation will be the next focus in our discussion. In this small cave on the isolated isle of Patmos, Jesus was about to reveal His heart to John regarding the seven major churches of Asia. Contained in these seven messages would be divine insight, warning, and instruction — not only for the seven ancient churches, but for the Church at large to heed and obey in the ages to come.

Right: *Grikos Beach — Patmos, Greece*

Revelation 1:12-20

12 And I turned to see the voice that spake with me. And being turned, I saw seven golden candlesticks;

13 And in the midst of the seven candlesticks one like unto the Son of man, clothed with a garment down to the foot, and girt about the paps with a golden girdle.

14 His head and his hairs were white like wool, as white as snow; and his eyes were as a flame of fire;

15 And his feet like unto fine brass, as if they burned in a furnace; and his voice as the sound of many waters.

16 And he had in his right hand seven stars: and out of his mouth went a sharp twoedged sword: and his countenance was as the sun shineth in his strength.

17 And when I saw him, I fell at his feet as dead. And he laid his right hand upon me, saying unto me, Fear not; I am the first and the last:

18 I am he that liveth, and was dead; and, behold, I am alive for evermore, Amen; and have the keys of hell and of death.

19 Write the things which thou hast seen, and the things which are, and the things which shall be hereafter;

20 The mystery of the seven stars which thou sawest in my right hand, and the seven golden candlesticks. The seven stars are the angels of the seven churches: and the seven candlesticks which thou sawest are the seven churches.

Chapter Two

'THE VOICE
THAT SPAKE WITH ME'

At some point while John was imprisoned on the island of Patmos, God abruptly invaded his solitary world of exile and drew John into the realm of the spirit, where He revealed to the elderly apostle mighty truths about things present and things yet to come. Ancient historical records kept on the island of Patmos assert that this event occurred in John's cave home and that he shared that cave with Prochorus, his disciple and assistant. Other early Christian writers stated that John received the vision in a mine quarry on Patmos. However, no mine quarries have ever been discovered on the island, and there is no evidence to support this claim. It is therefore most likely this supernatural event occurred in the cave that became John's home in exile, as stated in the ancient records of Patmos.

As noted on pages 45 and 56, this spiritual experience took John completely off guard and by surprise. We know this because the apostle wrote, "*I was in the Spirit* on the Lord's day…" (Revelation 1:10). The word "was" is the Greek word *ginomai*, which in this case describes *something that happens unexpectedly or something that catches one off guard*. The phrase "in the spirit" is a translation of the Greek words *en pneumatic*. In the Greek, this phrase lacks a definite article and would literally be translated "*in spirit*," which describes *another realm, another dimension*, or *a spiritual realm far different from the natural world* that surrounded John.

When the words *ginomai* and *en pneumatic* are used together, as in this verse, the meaning is clear: John did *not* know this experience was about to happen. Suddenly — *being taken completely off guard and by surprise* — John found himself in *another dimension*, a totally different realm. He was "in spirit," having passed from the natural realm into the spirit realm. Thus, John's words in this verse convey the following idea: "*In a way I never could have planned, predicted, or anticipated, I suddenly found myself in the spirit realm….*"

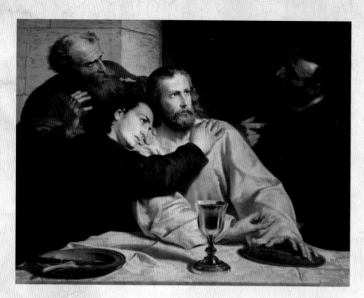

Left: This Nineteenth Century painting portrays the close relationship John enjoyed with his beloved Master during the three and a half years of Jesus' earthly ministry. It is entitled, "Jesus and St. John at Last Supper" and is today displayed in St. Michaels Church in Leuven, Belgium.

As soon as John found himself in the realm of the spirit, he heard behind him "…a great voice, as of a trumpet, saying, I am Alpha and Omega, the first and the last: and, What thou seest, write in a book, and send it unto the seven churches which are in Asia; unto *Ephesus*, and unto *Smyrna*, and unto *Pergamos*, and unto *Thyatira*, and unto *Sardis*, and unto *Philadelphia*, and unto Laodicea" (Revelation 1:10,11). When John heard that voice behind him, he instantly knew it was the voice of Jesus. After all, how could he ever forget *that* voice?

In Revelation 1:12, the apostle described his immediate response to that beloved sound, so long unheard: "And I turned to see the voice that spake with me…."

The voice came from behind John, so he turned to see the source of the sound. The word "turned" is from the Greek word *epistrepho*, which means to *completely turn around*. The use of this word tells us John's vision was experienced both in the realm of the spirit and in the natural realm. John had to *physically turn completely around* "to see the voice" that was speaking to him.

This phrase "see the voice" is without parallel in the New Testament. It is unusual, of course, because it is impossible to "see" a voice. The word "voice" comes from the Greek word *phone*, a word that simply describes *a voice*. But there was something about *this* voice that caused John to quickly turn to "see" it. The word "see" is the Greek word *blepo*, which means *to see, to watch, to look at, to give attention to, to pay heed to*, or *to perceive*. When John heard this voice, he perceived something so special and familiar about the sound that he eagerly turned to see *who* was speaking.

John hadn't heard Jesus speak for approximately 60 years, but he had never forgotten the sound of his Master's voice. As a younger man, John had listened to that voice for three and a half years as one of Jesus' disciples. Throughout the years since he had last seen Jesus, John had carried the sound of that beloved voice in his heart.

Although John was an old man, he was still deeply touched by the love he had received from Jesus. His vivid memories of walking with Jesus during His earthly ministry are apparent in what he wrote to his readers in First John 1:1-3:

> That which was from the beginning, which *we have heard*, which *we have seen with our eyes*, which *we have looked upon*, and *our hands have handled*, of the Word of life; (for the life was manifested, and *we have seen it*, and bear witness, and shew unto you that eternal life, which was with the Father, and *was manifested unto us*;) that which we have seen and heard declare we unto you, that ye also may have fellowship with us: and truly our fellowship is with the Father, and with his Son Jesus Christ.

John could still remember the touch of Jesus' hands and the loving look in His eyes. And John's words "we have heard" let us know that he could still hear the sound of Jesus' voice in his heart and soul. For 60 years, John had held those precious memories close to his heart, looking forward to the day when he would once again see the Lord.

So when the apostle John heard the voice that was speaking to him, he immediately recognized it. He knew it was the voice of Jesus! His response would be similar to yours if you hadn't spoken to a well-loved relative for many years and then suddenly you heard that relative's voice behind you. Once you perceived it was the voice of one you deeply loved and missed, it would be natural for you to joyfully turn around to see if it really was that person!

When John turned around to follow the sound of that voice, the barrier between the natural world and the realm of the spirit was suddenly removed, like window curtains that are pulled apart to reveal the view outside. At that moment, John did indeed see Jesus — but the Person he saw was nothing like the memories he had carried in his heart for those 60 years. The voice was the same tender, compassionate one John remembered so well, but the physical appearance of Jesus was dramatically transformed. John beheld Jesus *not* as he had known Him during His earthly walk, but in His exalted and present-day role as *King* and *Priest*.

WHY SEVEN GOLDEN CANDLESTICKS?

In verses 12 and 13, John began to express what his eyes beheld as he turned around to see the One speaking to him. But before John described Jesus in His exalted state, he first mentioned the "seven golden candlesticks" he saw — and the fact that Jesus was standing in the midst of them.

...And being turned, I saw seven golden candlesticks; and in the midst of the seven candlesticks one like unto the Son of man....

At that moment, John didn't understand the significance of the seven candlesticks, although Jesus would soon explain their symbolic meaning to the

EPHESUS

SMYRNA

PERGAMUM

THYATIRA

SARDIS

PHILADELPHIA

LAODICEA

apostle, telling him, "...The seven candlesticks which thou sawest are the seven churches" (Revelation 1:20). Those "seven churches" were the same churches Jesus had referred to earlier in Revelation 1:11: *Ephesus, Smyrna, Pergamum, Thyatira, Sardis, Philadelphia,* and *Laodicea.*

However, the question still remains: Why these seven churches? New Testament scholars speculate that hundreds of congregations had been established in the region of Asia by the time John penned the book of Revelation in the latter years of the First Century. During the apostle Paul's three-year stay in Ephesus that began in 52 AD, Paul had dispatched apostolic teams throughout Asia. As a result, churches were started in many parts of that province — and this was only the beginning. These churches were located in such cities as *Assos, Colossae, Derbe, Didyma, Hierapolis, Iconium, Lystra, Antioch in Pisidia, Melitus, Perga,* and *Troas* and were specifically mentioned in various New Testament books, indicating their strategic value to the advancement of the Gospel.

Although the population of the region was mostly pagan, the Gospel had made a remarkable impact in the few short years since Paul had arrived in Asia, more than 40 years before John's vision on the island of Patmos. The number of churches already established throughout Asia was a testimony to how mightily the Holy Spirit's power had worked through those who dared to challenge the darkness that ruled over that province.

But when Jesus addressed *these* seven churches, He was directing His attention to seven of the oldest and most prestigious churches in the province. The churches in Ephesus, Smyrna, Pergamum, and Laodicea were started during the time Paul lived in Ephesus, and their beginnings are directly connected to Paul's influence and ministry. Many scholars believe that Thyatira, Sardis, and Philadelphia also date to this same period. If this is true, these churches had likely been functioning for nearly 40 *years* when Jesus spoke His message to the apostle John on Patmos.

This may seem like a relatively short period of time, but the entire Christian movement in Asia was only about 40 years old. Thus, in terms of time and organization, these seven churches were among the most mature of the region. Moreover, since these churches were most likely founded during the time of Paul's ministry in Ephesus, they almost certainly held a prominent position among the other churches in the region.

But if there were hundreds of churches in that region, why did Jesus choose to speak to these particular churches? Their connection to Paul's ministry couldn't have been the only reason. Other large and well-known churches, such as the congregations in Colossae and Hierapolis, had also been established in the same region as a result of Paul's ministry in Ephesus but were not included among the churches Jesus addressed.

After Paul was beheaded in Rome in 67 AD, the apostle John served as overseer for the local churches of Asia. For approximately 27 years, John guided the churches from his hilltop home located on the outskirts of Ephesus. John was familiar with hundreds of churches and many leaders from the province. So why were these specific churches chosen to be the recipients of Jesus' messages? Did Jesus randomly select them, or was there a specific reason He addressed these churches and not others?

WHY THESE SEVEN CHURCHES?

As noted earlier in Chapter One, the seven cities where these churches were located were the largest and most pagan cities in the province of Asia. As a result, these seven churches may have had the largest congregations and exerted the greatest influence on other churches of the region. Although it cannot be confirmed by early writings, some church historians actually theorize that Asia was divided into church districts, with the seven churches named in the book of Revelation serving as overseeing bodies for each district.[1] This is indeed an interesting hypothesis that is worthy of consideration, although New Testament records alone cannot support it.

However, the New Testament does give us examples of churches that were

Above: The church of Laodicea was closely connected to the churches in the neighboring cities of Hierapolis (left) and Colossae (right). Today the ruins of Hierapolis still echo the once-elegant beauty of the city's structures and hot mineral pools for which it was so famous. As for Colossae, its ruins lie hidden and unexcavated under a hilltop near the mountains from which cool, fresh waters flowed to satisfy the needs of the ancient city's population.

closely related to each other and that worked side by side in close partnership. For instance, the churches of Laodicea, Hierapolis, and Colossae were all just a day's walk from each other. Paul's writings make it very clear that these three churches were closely connected and provided spiritual support to each other.

In Colossians 1:7, we read that while based in Ephesus, Paul sent Epaphras back to his own hometown of Colossae to start a church. Then in Colossians 4:12 and 13, Paul indicated that Epaphras also provided guidance to and had spiritual responsibility for the nearby churches in Laodicea and Hierapolis. In fact, it is likely that the churches in Laodicea

and Hierapolis were started as a result of Epaphras' work in Colossae, carried out under Paul's authority and direction. The connection between the churches in these three cities was so strong that when Paul wrote to the Colossian believers, he presumed the congregations in Laodicea and Hierapolis would also be recipients of the same letter (*see* Colossians 4:16). The same would have been conversely true if Paul wrote a letter to either Laodicea or Hierapolis.

Some scholars speculate that this close relationship between the churches of Colossae, Laodicea, and Hierapolis may be an example of how the region was divided into church districts.[2] The city of Laodicea was the administrative center for the Lycus Valley region and had the largest population of any city in that part of Asia. As a result, the Laodicean church had become the largest and most influential church in that region. Those who theorize that the province of Asia was divided into seven districts propose that the church in Laodicea was the spiritual head for one of those districts. If this was the case, it would be logical to infer that the churches in Ephesus, Smyrna, Pergamum, Thyatira, Sardis, and Philadelphia also served as leading churches for the other districts.

Whether this is true or not, the close relationship that existed between the congregations of Colossae, Laodicea, and Hierapolis remains worth noting. The example of these three sister churches working side by side while maintaining a permanent connection to the "mother church" in Ephesus reveals the spirit of partnership and cooperation that existed among many New Testament churches. Unlike the lack of connection that often exists between churches of the various "camps" within the modern Church, New Testament churches were spiritually related by apostolic relationships and looked to each other for guidance, help, and support. So as we consider the possibility that Asia was divided into seven church districts and that these particular seven churches were the spiritual overseeing bodies for those districts, we can also surmise that each of these seven prominent churches would have represented hundreds of churches in its district. In that case, each message Jesus gave these seven churches would actually

have been intended for an entire group of churches.

Certainly the problems in these seven churches were representative of the problems faced by churches throughout the entire Roman Empire at that time. Even if the seven churches Jesus specifically addressed weren't district heads, as some suppose, they *were* microcosms of the Church at large during the First Century. Early believers lived in a world of widespread paganism, ungodly morals, and intense persecution. Consequently, churches throughout Asia Minor and the rest of the Roman Empire were grappling with horrible persecution, a temptation to commit immorality, and the gradual invasion of false apostles and teachers bringing damnable doctrines that endorsed compromise. Jesus addressed these universal problems in His messages to the seven churches, thus making it clear that these seven churches were representative of the Church at large at the end of the First Century.

This is in fact why Jesus addressed *seven* churches and not six, eight, or some other number. The number seven was not coincidental. In Scripture, *seven* represents *completion* or *perfection*. The fact that Jesus addressed seven churches and the challenges they faced implies that He was addressing the *complete picture* emerging in the churches of that time and that His seven messages comprised the *complete answer* they needed.

Alternately, many Bible teachers propose that these seven churches represent *seven different eras within the Church Age*. This interesting theory teaches that Jesus gave John a prophetic preview of what would develop in the Church between the time John received the vision until the conclusion of the Church Age. This idea is based on Revelation 1:19, which says, "Write the things which thou hast seen, and the things which are, and the things which shall be hereafter."

Based on this teaching, Jesus was directing His messages both to churches that existed at that time ("the things which are") and to churches that would emerge in the ages to follow ("and the things which shall be hereafter"). Those who teach this verse from that perspective have developed a near-science to explain the division of Church history as categorized by Jesus' messages to the seven churches. For instance, they contend that His message to Ephesus symbolizes the apostolic age; His message to Smyrna symbolizes the age of persecution; and His message to Thyatira symbolizes the age of false doctrine. Proponents of this teaching continue to connect the other churches addressed in the book of Revelation to the various phases of Church history, all the way to the end of the Church Age.

A number of problems arise with this type of interpretation. For instance, there is no historical interpretation in Church history to affirm this approach — except for those who have attempted to interpret it as such in more recent times. Those who teach from this point of view generally divide the seven churches into the following prophetic time frames and categories (with some variation):

Ephesus: *The Apostolic Age* — Pentecost to 170 AD

Smyrna: *The Age of Persecution* — 170-312 AD

Pergamum: *The Age of False Doctrine* — 312-606 AD

Thyatira: *The Age of Darkness* — 606-1520 AD

Sardis: *The Age of Reformation* — 1520-1750 AD

Philadelphia: *The Age of Missions* — 1750-1906 AD

Laodicea: *The Age of Apostasy* — 1906 to the present

This approach to the seven churches is entertaining, but any serious student of history would be hard-pressed to support these divisions because they simply do not

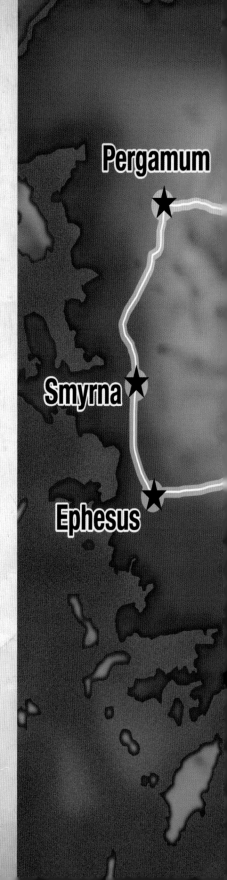

Thyatira

★ Sardis

hiladelphia ★

★

Laodicea

correspond accurately with actual historical facts. In fact, to make the theory work, one must leave huge gaps in the historical record. Furthermore, this approach to the seven churches would mean that the Church will be weak, powerless, and conquered by materialism and apostasy at the end of the Church Age. This in no way corresponds to the outpouring of the Holy Spirit that God promised in the last days or the powerful Church that Scripture foretells will emerge in the latter days.

The truth is that although all seven of these churches were real local churches that existed in the First Century, they also represent the types of local bodies that have existed throughout the centuries. If Jesus' messages to these churches were pertinent only for certain time frames of the past, they could be discounted as having no application to us today. But because the problems identified in these seven churches are the same problems the Church has grappled with ever since, Jesus' messages to these churches become a microcosm of the *entire* Church until the end of the Church Age.

Although these messages are almost 2,000 years old, they are as relevant and applicable today as they were in the First Century when they were first given. Jesus has never ceased to speak to His Body through each message spoken to the apostle John in Revelation chapters 1-3. The Head of the Church still cries out: "He that hath an ear, let him hear what the Spirit saith unto the churches" (*see* Revelation 2:7; 2:11; 2:17; 2:29; 3:6; 3:13; 3:22).

One of the only factors that explains with some certainty why Jesus addressed these particular seven churches was their physical location. Sending the book of the Revelation to the local churches in these seven cities would have been easily achievable because they were all connected by a series of roads — primarily by the great circular road that wound throughout that region of Asia, beginning and ending at Ephesus.

Travel between these particular cities was reasonably trouble-free by First Century standards. If someone started on that road from Ephesus and traveled north, he would eventually arrive in Smyrna. If he continued traveling that road, he would reach Pergamum and then move on to Thyatira, Sardis, Philadelphia, and Laodicea before arriving back in Ephesus.

With this in mind, it is reasonable to assume that the book of Revelation was probably delivered first to the church of Ephesus, because John lived near the city and based his oversight of churches from his hilltop home behind the Temple of Artemis. Then after copies of this book were made in Ephesus, the books would have been delivered to the other churches — most likely in the exact order that Jesus addressed the churches in Revelation chapters 1-3.

Many other theories have been offered over the years in an attempt to explain why Jesus addressed the seven churches mentioned in the book of Revelation. However, the most likely explanation centers around their two greatest common factors: 1) the role Ephesus played in each of them, and 2) the circular road that connected them. By addressing the problems these seven churches faced, Jesus addressed the common problems faced by local bodies throughout all ages.

WHY 'GOLDEN' CANDLESTICKS?

John went on to say in Revelation 1:12 and 13, "...And being turned, I saw seven *golden* candlesticks; and in the midst of the seven candlesticks one like unto the Son of man...."

The word "golden" is from the Greek word *chrusos* — the word for *gold* used in both the Septuagint (the Greek version of the Old Testament) and the Greek New Testament. This particular word is used throughout ancient literature to describe the purest form of gold.

Just as is true today, the most sought-after and expensive gold in the ancient world was the gold that was *absolutely pure*. Other forms of this precious metal were less valuable because they were mixed with silver, producing a lower and less desirable grade of gold.

John writes in verse 12 that the seven candlesticks he saw were "golden." Because he uses the word *chrusos*, we know there was nothing inferior, low-grade, or undesirable about those candlesticks. In God's eyes, they were *pure gold*, fashioned out of the most high-grade, desirable material.

Although gold can be found as solid nuggets, the majority of gold is located in rock that must be mined from the earth, and the process of extracting it has always been long and expensive. First, the rock must be removed from the earth and then crushed into dust. Once the rock is crushed, tons of water wash away the lighter rock and dirt, leaving behind the heavier raw gold. The exposed gold is then gathered and placed into a furnace with blazing hot temperatures that melt the precious metal into liquid form. As the molten gold bubbles under the heat of the blaze, impurities with a lower density than gold (called "slag" or "dross") begin to rise to the surface — impurities that would have otherwise gone unnoticed. The worthless black slag is then scraped off by the gold worker using a special instrument. This process is repeated again and again, each time with a hotter furnace, until all impurities have been exposed and scraped off and the only substance left is *pure* gold.

This refining process is long and laborious, and the heat that must be endured by the gold worker is furiously intense. From beginning to end, the process is tedious, expensive, uncomfortable, and complicated — but it is the only way to produce the *purest gold*. Eliminating the impurities in gold without fire is impossible. And although these blemishes are invisible to the naked eye, they will weaken any object made from a batch of gold from which they are *not* removed. On the other hand, once this process has been fully completed, a soft, pliable, pure form of gold is produced that the artisan can then shape into an exquisite object.

Because of the high cost required to produce this grade of pure, refined gold, it became *the* metal associated with royalty or nobility. In the ancient world, only pure gold was fitting for magnificently wealthy, powerful kings or nobility and was therefore used to make their cups, bowls, plates, saucers, and platters, as well as many other items. When ambassadors or the head of a foreign state came to visit a king, they came with gifts. To bring a gift crafted of gold (*chrusos*) was a way of showing the highest respect and honor. Gold was also the preferred metal used to fashion all the instruments for the holiest part of God's temple.

Just as is true today, silver was also a precious metal in ancient times, although not as desirable as gold. Silver tarnishes, whereas gold doesn't rust, tarnish, corrode, or corrupt with time. Gold coins

Above: The purification of gold was an expensive process that involved extracting the precious metal from rock using a blazing hot fire. The intense heat caused the impurities to rise to the surface, where they could then be removed from the molten metal. This process was repeated until all impurities had been eliminated and nothing was left except pure gold.

can lay buried in the earth or under the sea for hundreds or even thousands of years and still retain their brilliance. Thus, pure gold was also a symbol of *glory that never fades*. There was simply nothing more valuable than pure gold at the time the book of Revelation was written. It is therefore very significant that this word was used to symbolize the seven churches.

The use of the word "golden" in Revelation 1:12 conveys the *immense value* that Jesus Christ places on His Church. In His sight, the Church is so precious that even silver isn't good enough to portray it. Especially in our modern age when so much criticism is leveled against the Body of Christ and so many people focus on its failures and weaknesses, it is good for us to remember that Jesus gave His own blood to purchase His Church and that it is *valuable* and *precious* to Him.

The Church is still in the process of purification and refinement, but regardless of its imperfections, Jesus still sees the Church as *pure gold*. So whenever you're tempted to focus on the imperfections of God's people, think back to the gold worker in the midst of the refining process, scraping impurities off the surface of the hot molten gold. The Church's refining process is still in progress, and the Holy Spirit's fire is working to expose all blemishes in order to bring the Church to a higher level of purification.

You may sometimes feel disheartened by what you see or know about the Church. You may feel discouraged at times because of your experiences with a local body. You may even be tempted to think that the modern Church is in such an irreversibly sad condition that it will never turn around for the better. But whenever your mind is bombarded by such thoughts, it is vital to remember that Jesus loves His Church, that He bought it with His own blood, and that the Holy Spirit is still actively working to purify it.

As believers, not one of us is exempt from that purifying process. Each of us must allow the Holy Spirit's fire to expose our weaknesses, impurities, and defects so Jesus can scrape them away. This removal

process is painful, and we don't enjoy the fire that burns up the chaff in our lives. And just when we think the task is finished, the Holy Spirit turns up the blaze another notch, and the process is started all over again! But the heat of the refining fire is essential for us to be purified and strengthened to fulfill the Master's will.

The Church's imperfections are nothing new, and as long as the Church awaits the coming of Jesus, this refining process will never end. Jesus Christ — the Head of the Church and our Great Refiner — desires His Church to reach the highest possible state of purity, holiness, and spiritual maturity. Ephesians 5:26,27 confirms this truth:

> **That he [Jesus] might sanctify and cleanse it [the Church] with the washing of water by the word, that he might present it to himself a glorious church, not having spot, or wrinkle, or any such thing; but that it should be holy and without blemish.**

Jesus isn't blind to the defects in the Church. But even with all the glaring problems that have existed throughout the past 2,000 years of Church history, Jesus has never abandoned His people. With great patience, He has overseen the purifying and refining process ever since the outpouring of the Holy Spirit on the Day of Pentecost, and He will continue to do so until the Church reaches the glorious state of maturity He desires.

When we see Jesus face to face, we will all finally be transformed into His image, free from all imperfections just as He is. But until then, Jesus will keep working as the Great Refiner, washing us with the water of His Word and allowing the

Holy Spirit's fire to burn away the dross and make us the light He has called us to be in this world.

WHY CANDLESTICKS?

> John went on to say in Revelation 1:12, "And I turned to see the voice that spake with me. And being turned, I saw seven golden *candlesticks*."

The word "candlesticks" gives us a mental impression of wax candles such as we use today. However, in the First Century, there were no wax candles because such candles weren't invented until many years later.

The word "candlesticks" used in Revelation 1:12 is the Greek word *luchnos*. This word could only refer to *an oil-burning lamp* — the primary source of manmade light used in New Testament times. This type of lamp was hand-fashioned from clay and was small enough to be carried in the palm of one's hand. It was designed to hold oil and had a long wick that, once saturated, could be ignited to illuminate darkness. Consequently, the *luchnos* was a very important part of daily life in the First Century.

Every First Century building, from the smallest house to the greatest palace, depended on oil-burning lamps to provide light. Every house, every apartment, every store, and every place of business in the ancient world had at least one — and often *many* — oil-burning lamps. This is one reason these ancient lamps are often discovered in great numbers in archeological excavations in the Middle East.

Because these oil-burning lamps were made of clay, they were very fragile. Often they were so brittle that they could be broken by the mere squeeze of a hand. Therefore, anyone carrying one of these lamps had to be careful not to break it, spill the oil, and lose the light that the lamp provided.

It is clear why God used these lamps to symbolically depict the Church of Jesus Christ. The Church is comprised of fragile, imperfect human beings. Considering man's human frailties, it is a miracle that Jesus still sees His people as "golden." Who would have ever imagined that God would put His Spirit in a vessel so fragile as a human body, or in a Church made up of human beings who are so imperfect! But that is precisely

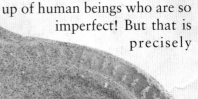

what He did. God chose the Church as His primary instrument for giving His light to a dark world.

These earthen lamps contained *oil* — a symbol of the Holy Spirit in both the Old and New Testaments. Just as these oil-burning lamps contained oil, the Church is the container of the Holy Spirit in this world. Although it is true that the weaknesses of God's people are readily evident, it is even more true that He has graciously chosen to deposit the oil of the Holy Spirit within them — and that He has provided a sufficient measure of that divine oil for His Church to extend His life-giving light to the very ends of the earth.

However, for the oil in these ancient lamps to provide light, a wick was required. The wick was inserted into the mouth of the lamp and ran deep into its base, where it became saturated with oil. When the wick was then lit, it would burn and give light for many hours or even days before the lamp needed to be refilled again.

Likewise, the Church contains a reservoir of the Holy Spirit's oil, but each believer must allow his or her heart to become *soaked* in that oil before the

Church can shine God's light into this world as He intended it to do. Just as an empty oil-burning lamp has no ability to produce light, believers cannot produce enduring light when they are empty of the Holy Spirit's oil. One infilling of God's Spirit may last for a while, but soon they must be replenished with a fresh infilling. This can only happen as believers allow the Holy Spirit to drench their spirits in times of private fellowship with the Lord and then to set them ablaze with His fire. This is the way God has designed the Church to shine forth His light, penetrate a world of darkness, and set people free.

It is also significant to note that light was produced at the *mouth* of this oil-burning lamp. Similarly, a believer's mouth is the outlet for the Holy Spirit's fire and light to pour forth through the preaching of the Gospel. As dark as this world is today, it is difficult to imagine how much darker it would be if there were no faith-filled believers using their mouths to proclaim the life-giving truth of Jesus Christ.

Regarding the image John saw and described as "seven golden candlesticks," many have speculated that it may have in fact been the seven-branched golden candlestick used in certain aspects of Old Testament worship (*see* Exodus 25:31-40). This lamp was a fabulous

Right: This First Century lamp is typical of those used throughout Asia Minor. Notice the wick that extends from the mouth of the lamp. Once the wick was saturated with oil, it could be lit and allowed to burn for hours or even days, depending on the amount of oil it contained. The details seen on the body of the lamp are typical of lamps made in Asia Minor during this time period.

Above: Some suggest that the lamps in John's vision were symbolic of the seven-branched candelabra used in the Temple during Old Testament times. However, this doesn't agree with the Greek text, which portrays the image of seven distinct lamps — representing the seven individual churches, each with unique characteristics and a distinct identity. © Mary Evans Picture Library

creation comprised of seven oil-burning lamps joined on a single stand. However, this seven-branched lamp could not be what John saw in his vision, for his words indicate he saw seven distinct and separate lamps. Each lamp was independent of the other; each was filled with its own oil; each had its own stand; and each provided its own light.

These seven distinct lamps provide a marvelous portrayal not only of the seven churches in the book of Revelation, but also of all local churches throughout the Church Age. Every church has its own separate identity; each is independent geographically; each is responsible for remaining filled with the oil of the Holy Spirit; and each is held accountable for

fulfilling its unique role in shining forth the light of the Gospel into the surrounding community and the world beyond.

WHAT JESUS SAID ABOUT OIL LAMPS

In Matthew 5:15, Jesus referred to these same type of oil-burning lamps when He said, "Neither do men light a candle, and put it under a bushel, but on a candlestick; and it giveth light unto all that are in the house."

Right: This circular-shaped oil lamp is typical of a style referred to as Herodian because most were made during the reign of King Herod the Great. As seen with this example, the majority of lamps were decorated with different symbols or types of reliefs.

The word "candle" in this verse is again an unfortunate translation of the Greek word *luchnos*, which refers to an *oil lamp* precisely like the ones described earlier in Revelation 1:12. Thus, Matthew 5:15 could be literally translated: "Neither do men light an *oil lamp*, and put it under a bushel...." But what did Jesus mean when He spoke about putting a lamp under a "bushel"? What is a "bushel," and what is its significance to the symbolic meaning of the "seven golden candlesticks" John saw in his vision?

The word "bushel" comes from the Greek word *modios*, which refers to *a jar or container used to measure grain*. If an oil-burning lamp were placed under this type of container, the lack of oxygen would suffocate and snuff out its light. By using this example, Jesus admonishes us that the Church must keep the Gospel out in the open where it can be seen and heard, thus providing light to those who live in darkness.

Jesus went on to say, "Neither do men light a candle, and put it under a bushel, but on a *candlestick*...." The Greek word used for "candlestick" is the word *luchnia*, which describes *an elevated stand* on which a lamp was placed so it could provide the maximum amount of light.

Throughout the Roman Empire during New Testament times, it was customary to place oil-burning lamps on elevated pedestals to provide a superior light that would illuminate the entire surrounding area. The higher the lamp was placed, the brighter the light that was produced.

Thus, in Matthew 5:15, Jesus was stating that the light of the Gospel must be lifted as high as possible so it can produce its maximum effect. Once elevated, the light becomes so great that "...it giveth light unto all that are in the house."

If you place a lamp on a table, you'll illuminate the people sitting around the table. But if you elevate that same lamp by putting it on a pedestal, the light that previously only illuminated a handful of people will begin to impact everyone in the room. The amount of light produced is the same, but the elevated position of the lamp makes the light much more effective.

Likewise, if the Church is going to shine its light as God intended, believers must dare to lift the message of the Gospel up high — to elevate it and put it on a pedestal according to His purposes. God is calling believers to extend their sphere of influence so they can make an eternal impact on an ever-increasing number of people who are lost and without hope.

Although the Church is comprised of imperfect human beings, Jesus has never abandoned it, and He has never forgotten the price He paid for it. Even with all its defects, the Church is still as precious as pure gold to Him. Jesus longs for His people to allow Him to saturate their hearts with the oil of the Holy Spirit and then set them ablaze with His fire so the light of truth can shine forth to a lost and dying world.

Try to imagine how encouraging the Lord's symbolic use of these oil-burning lamps must have been to the seven churches in Asia. The believers in these congregations would have understood God's intended meaning.

Each of these churches had its own identity and purpose. Each

was facing unique and serious problems. Each was situated in the midst of paganism and gross spiritual darkness. And each had endured horrible seasons of persecution at the hands of the Roman government. Yet rather than instructing His people to hide from the hostile world that surrounded them, Jesus did the opposite. By depicting them as "seven golden candlesticks," He was calling His people to be repeatedly refilled with the oil of the Holy Spirit and to lift the light of the Gospel higher and higher so more and more people could be given the eternal life He had died to purchase for them.

'IN THE MIDST OF THE SEVEN GOLDEN CANDLESTICKS'

John went on to relate what he saw in the vision: "...And being turned, I saw seven golden candlesticks; and in the midst of the seven candlesticks one like unto the Son of man..." (Revelation 1:12,13).

The word "midst" is the Greek word mesos, which can be translated as in the midst, in the middle, or in the center. Thus, this word portrays Jesus standing right in the very center of these seven golden candlesticks.

As discussed earlier, the seven churches mentioned here were most likely the leading congregations of Asia. Yet despite their prominent status, these local bodies had problems — some of which were

of a very serious nature. Nevertheless, Jesus didn't distance Himself from these churches. Regardless of their imperfections and problems, He stood right in the very midst of them.

This close proximity infers that Jesus is not ashamed of His Church, even though it is comprised of flawed human beings. In fact, having purchased their redemption through His death and resurrection, Jesus is now delighted to abide in the midst of His blood-bought people, whom He values as *pure gold*.

In the vision, John saw Jesus standing like a Great Overseer in the *midst* of the seven golden candlesticks, His eyes focused on them. This explains Jesus' intimate knowledge about each of these seven congregations and the reason He would later say to each of them, "I *know*

thy works" (*see* Revelation 2:2; 2:9; 2:13; 2:19; 3:1; 3:8; 3:15).

This word "know," which appears in all these verses, is the Greek word *oida*. This word appears more than 300 times in the New Testament and comes from a Greek root that means to *see*. Thus, the word *oida* in these verses describes what Jesus had *seen personally*, not what He had obtained from an outside source. This was *knowledge* based on *personal observation*. By standing in the midst of the seven golden candlesticks, Jesus was in a position *to see* everything that happened in these churches, both good and bad.

This should be taken as both an encouragement and a warning to the Church of every age. As the Head of the Church, Jesus stands in the midst of His people, lovingly overseeing everything that transpires, both positive and negative. He knows from personal observation every victory won, every misstep taken, every challenge faced, and every demonic attack withstood.

- Regarding the congregation in Ephesus, Jesus could see (*oida*) their labor, patience, and intolerance for false doctrine — but He could also see that they had lost their first love.

- Regarding the congregation in Smyrna, Jesus could see (*oida*) their tribulation and poverty — but He could also see that they were struggling with a fear of future calamity.

- Regarding the congregation in Pergamum, Jesus could see (*oida*) the paganism and demonic activity the believers confronted on a daily basis, as well as the price many of them were paying to remain firm in the face of opposition. But He could also see that the damnable doctrine of the Nicolaitans was trying to influence the church and lead its people astray.

- Regarding the congregation in Thyatira, Jesus could see (*oida*) that they were hardworking, that they were dedicated to works of charity and to serving people in need, and that they demonstrated patience and excellence in whatever they undertook to do for the Lord. But He could also see that a woman named Jezebel was seducing God's people with damnable doctrines that endorsed loose living and ungodly morals.

- Regarding the congregation in Sardis, Jesus could see (*oida*) that they had enjoyed a strong beginning in their faith, but He could also see that their steadfastness was slipping and that they were in danger of dying spiritually.

- Regarding the congregation in Philadelphia, Jesus could see (*oida*) that they had rare opportunities and open doors to declare the Gospel, but He could also see that they needed to hold fast during challenging times.

- Regarding the congregation in Laodicea, Jesus could see (*oida*) nothing positive. He saw that they

were neither hot nor cold, rebuked them for their self-sufficiency, and pleaded with them to open the door and allow Him back inside their church once more.

Likewise, Jesus stands in the midst of His people today, overseeing all the activities that transpire among them. He sees both the *good* and the *bad*. He sees their love, faith, patience, and commitment. He also sees the actions that are out of line with His character and His plan for the Church.

When we are tempted to feel dismayed about the carnality and powerlessness that sometimes seem so pervasive in the contemporary Body of Christ, it is important for us to remember that Jesus paid the highest price of all for the Church, that He loves His people, and that He still remains in the *midst* of them. As has been true throughout the centuries, if believers will listen, they will still hear the voice of Jesus, urging them to hear what He is saying to His Church and to repent wherever repentance is needed.

'ONE LIKE UNTO THE SON OF MAN'

As John continued relating his vision, he said, "...And being turned, I saw seven golden candlesticks; and in the midst of the seven candlesticks *one like unto the Son of man*..." (Revelation 1:12,13).

Jesus in His full glory both as God and glorified Man united eternally — our great King and High Priest.

In the phrase, "like unto the Son of man," the words "like unto" are a translation of the Greek word *homoios*, which describes a *resemblance*, *similarity*, or *likeness*. Jesus' physical appearance had been transformed from the way John remembered Jesus in His humanity. The Person who stood before the apostle was a vision of the glorified Christ in His kingly and priestly attire. The One standing in the midst of the seven golden candlesticks had a *likeness*, *resemblance*, or *similarity* to the way John remembered Jesus, yet He was also very different.

The manner of *likeness* John was referring to in this verse isn't stated. He may have been referring to a physical attribute such as Jesus' facial features, height, or weight. But the word *homoios* is sufficient to convey that something about the image John beheld was *similar* to his memory of the Master — enough for him to immediately recognize that the One he was seeing was Jesus Himself.

Some scholars suggest that John's description of Jesus in the vision is an allusion to Daniel 7:13, where the prophet Daniel describes "one like the Son of

As noted earlier, when John turned to follow the sound of the voice he heard behind him, he did indeed see Jesus. However, John did not see Jesus as He had appeared during His earthly walk, but rather in His exalted and present-day role as *King* and *Priest*. As the apostle focused his eyes on the dazzling countenance of the Person who stood before him, this Person looked "like unto the Son of man."

The Greek text actually has no definite article before the words "Son of man." This means that the phrase doesn't necessarily refer to Jesus in His role as the Son of Man; rather, it portrays the humanity of Jesus that John so clearly remembered from nearly 60 years earlier. Scholar Albert Barnes wrote, "Indeed, the costume in which he [Jesus] appeared was so unlike that in which John had been accustomed to see the Lord Jesus in the days of his flesh...."[3] Thus, John beheld man" coming with the clouds of Heaven.[4] The similarity between these two texts, written more than 600 years apart, is certainly remarkable. It is likely that Daniel and John did indeed see exactly the same image — Jesus Christ revealed as One given everlasting dominion and glory and a Kingdom that will never be destroyed.

> I saw in the night visions, and, behold, one like the Son of man came with the clouds of heaven, and came to the Ancient of days, and they brought him near before him. And there was given him dominion, and glory, and a kingdom, that all people, nations, and languages, should serve him: his dominion is an everlasting dominion, which shall not pass away, and his kingdom that which shall not be destroyed.
>
> Daniel 7:13,14

Consider what it was like for John to see Jesus as the Heavenly King whose Kingdom will never end. This would have been an especially significant message to the elderly apostle, who was suffering imprisonment on Patmos at the hands of the wicked and demented Emperor Domitian. In fact, this image of Jesus would have served as a source of strength and courage for all believers at the end of the First Century who were suffering as a result of Domitian's cruel reign. The message of the vision was clear: Human kings and kingdoms would eventually fade with the passing of time, but the *true* King and His Kingdom will *never* pass away.

Domitian was not the only Roman Emperor to resist the Gospel. Persecution of believers may have begun as early as the rule of the Emperor Claudius (41-54

AD) and continued routinely for nearly 300 years, until restrictions on Christian worship were formally rescinded during the rule of the Emperor Constantine (307-337 AD). Throughout history, many kings and rulers have put forth their best effort to extinguish the light of the Gospel and obliterate the Church. But no one will ever have the power or authority to successfully resist the King of kings and Head of the Church, Jesus Christ.

In John's introductory remarks to the book of Revelation, he had already written that the Giver of the book of Revelation was Jesus Christ, "the prince of the kings of the earth" (*see* Revelation 1:5). The word "prince" is the word *archon*, a Greek word that denotes *one who holds the highest and most exalted position*. The verse goes on to say that Jesus is Prince over "the kings of the earth." The word "kings" is a form of the Greek word *basileuo*, which means *to rule* or *to reign*. However, the form of the word used in Revelation 1:5 not only refers to human *kings* or *rulers*, but also to *kingdoms* or *governments*. Finally, the word "earth" describes *the earth or an earthly sphere*.

It is significant that John made this statement in his introduction. By doing so, he proclaimed from the very beginning of the book that Jesus is *the most highly exalted King* and that *He possesses supreme power and authority* — more than any *ruler* or *government* that will ever exist in the earthly sphere.

The apostle Paul marvelously described Jesus' exalted and kingly position when he wrote that the Father set Jesus at His own right hand "...in the heavenly places, far above all principality, and power, and might, and dominion, and every name that is named, not only in this world, but also in that which is to come" (Ephesians 1:20,21). Paul also proclaimed the exalted position of Christ in Philippians 2:9-11:

> **Wherefore God also hath highly exalted him, and given him a name which is above every name: that at the name of Jesus every knee should bow, of things in heaven, and things in earth; and things under the earth; and that every tongue should confess that Jesus Christ is Lord, to the glory of God the Father.**

The powers of darkness may try to overcome the light, but the risen Christ transcends them all. This is why John wrote in his gospel: "And the light shineth in darkness; and the darkness comprehended it not" (John 1:5). In light of the distress the Early Church was suffering, this verse is worth noting, for it also conveyed a powerful message to believers who were suffering because of the testimony of Jesus Christ.

The word "comprehended" in John 1:5 is the Greek word *katalambano*, which is a compound of the words *kata* and *lambano*. The word *kata* carries the force of something that is *dominating* or *subjugating*. The word *lambano* means *to seize* or *to grab hold of*. When the two words are compounded, the new word means *to seize, to pull down, to tackle, to conquer,* or *to hold under one's power*. Therefore, this verse could be translated, *"Darkness does not have the ability to suppress or to hold the light under its domain."*

Even in what seems to be the darkest or bleakest situation, the efforts of evil will always be thwarted by the prevailing power of God's light. Almost 2,000 years of Church history have proven beyond a shadow of a doubt that darkness does not have the power or authority to silence the voice or permanently put out the light of Jesus Christ and His Church.

The appearance of Jesus in John's vision as the risen and exalted Christ signaled a powerful message to the early believers. They were suffering so much agony, tribulation, and unabating persecution. Thus, Jesus' glorified appearance, possibly alluding to Daniel's vision of the Lord more than 600 years earlier, shouted to the Early Church that Jesus is *the* King of kings. He holds the highest seat of power; He possesses dominion over all; and His Kingdom will never cease. Other kings and governments will come and go throughout the ages, but Jesus' Kingdom is everlasting and supersedes all others. A time will come when opposition will cease and all people, tribes, and nations will bow before Christ *the* King.

'CLOTHED WITH A GARMENT DOWN TO THE FOOT'

> John continued to declare, "...And in the midst of the seven candlesticks one like unto the Son of man, *clothed with a garment down to the foot...*" (Revelation 1:13).

The word "clothed" is derived from the Greek word *enduo*, a term that referred to *the act of putting on clothes*

or one who is dressed in a garment. It should be noted that this is the same word used in Luke 24:49 when Jesus told His disciples, "And, behold, I send the promise of my Father upon you: but tarry ye in the city of Jerusalem, until ye be *endued* with power from on high." The word "endued" in this verse is also derived from the word *enduo* but is used figuratively to describe the moment when the disciples were filled with the Holy Spirit on the Day of Pentecost and thereby *clothed* with power (*see* Acts 2:1-4). On the Day of Pentecost, the 120 disciples present in the Upper Room were *endued* or *invested* with power as the Holy Spirit was graciously *conferred upon* them in fulfillment of prophecy.

It must also be noted that the Greek tense used with the word *enduo* in Revelation 1:13 implies that this particular garment was conferred upon Christ *once and for all*. He was given this garment by the Father and will be thus clothed forevermore. The Greek tense literally means Jesus *was* clothed, He is clothed, and He

Left: This icon from Greece represents Christ dressed in the richly colored and ornamented high priestly garments that were designed for Aaron and his sons in Exodus 28. Although John's vision doesn't explicitly state the color or design of Jesus' garments in his vision, it seems that Jesus was clothed in a way that represented Him as both King and Great High Priest. In this icon, Christ is crowned to show His rule over the affairs of the universe, although John made no mention of a crown when relating his vision in Revelation 1.

will always be clothed with this particular garment that reaches "down to the foot."

The phrase "down to the foot" is a translation of *poderes*, a Greek word used only this one time in the entire New Testament. It describes a robe that *flows all the way down to the ankles but leaves the feet exposed*, which explains why John could later describe Jesus' feet in verse 15. The word poderes is used seven times in the Greek Septuagint to describe *the attire of the high priest.*

Perhaps the best example of this word *poderes* is found in Exodus 28, where God told Moses how to make "holy garments" for Aaron and his sons, who would serve as priests. The priestly garment was to be made of gold, blue, purple, and scarlet thread and fine woven linen. It was to reach down to the ankles, exactly like the robe Christ was wearing in John's vision. For this reason, it is suggested that one symbolic meaning of the garment Jesus wore in John's vision was to portray Him in His role as the Great High Priest.

- Hebrews 3:1 (*NKJV*) declares that Jesus is the "High Priest of our confession."

- Hebrews 4:15,16 describes Jesus Christ as the High Priest who can be touched with the feelings of our infirmities, a truth that has been a comfort to believers throughout the centuries. In these verses, God calls each of us to come boldly before the throne of grace to obtain mercy and to find help in our time of need from Jesus, our High Priest.

- Hebrews 5:5,6 reveals that the office of High Priest was conferred upon Jesus and that His priesthood will remain "forever" after the order of Melchizedec.

- Hebrews 7:24 tells us that Jesus' role as our Great High Priest is "unchangeable."

The ministry of Jesus Christ as our High Priest is one of the most important themes of the New Testament. Jesus *was* clothed with priestly garments; He *is* clothed with priestly garments; and He *will always be* clothed with priestly garments — because He is *forever* the High Priest of our confession.

The way Jesus was clothed when He appeared to John sent an extremely important message to the apostle and to the Church at large. John was about to receive Jesus' messages for the seven churches, some of which would contain correction and stern yet loving rebukes from Christ in response to wrong beliefs and behaviors that were emerging in the churches. However, by appearing to John as High Priest, Jesus' intercessory ministry was the prominent feature the apostle noticed before anything else.

We already saw in Revelation 1:5 that Jesus revealed Himself *first* and *foremost* as the Prince and Supreme Sovereign of the kings of the earth. Then in Revelation 1:13, Christ appeared as High Priest, thus affirming that He was standing in His priestly role, interceding for the churches He was about to discipline and correct. As we will see in the next section, verse 13 also provides another glimpse of Jesus as the Supreme Sovereign. And a few verses

Right: Pictured here is a solid gold royal belt of Phoenician origin from the Fifth Century BC, similar to the royal belt worn by Christ in John's vision. This fabulous piece is displayed in the Museo Arquelogogico Nacional in Madrid, Spain.

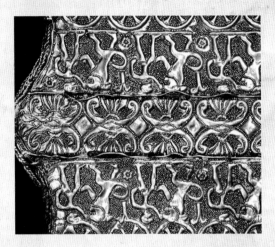

later, Jesus is seen as Judge to those who disregard His commandments and refuse to heed His instruction.

But regarding John's description of Jesus' "garment down to the foot," John portrayed the intercessory ministry of Jesus, which will never change as long as the Church is in the world. This is an office that was once and for all conferred upon Christ and is *unchangeable*. Jesus *was*, *is*, and *will always be* interceding on behalf of the Church that He purchased with His own blood.

'GIRT ABOUT THE PAPS WITH A GOLDEN GIRDLE'

In John's description of Jesus' appearance, he went on to write, "And in the midst of the seven candlesticks one like unto the Son of man, clothed with a garment down to the foot, *and girt about the paps with a golden girdle*" (Revelation 1:13).

The word "girt" is a translation of the Greek word *peridzunnumi* — a compound of the word *peri*, which means *around*, and the word *zuni*, which describes *a wide belt*. When the two words are compounded,

the new word portrays *a wide belt that is wrapped around oneself*. But John tells us that this belt was worn not around the waist, but around the "paps" — an obsolete term translated from the Greek word *mastos*, which describes the *mid-* to *upper-chest* or *breasts*. Thus, this broad belt, which John calls a "golden girdle," was noticeably wrapped around Jesus' mid-chest.

In the ancient world, belts were often worn around the waist to tightly hold long, flowing garments together. However, it was customary for kings in the East to wear large belts fashioned of gold and positioned high up on their chests.[5] Thus clothed, a king's splendid gown would flow downward with greater freedom of movement, and as he walked, the gown would sweep along in a grand manner that was glorious to behold. This wide royal belt was fashioned of gold and served as a symbol of *power*, *majesty*, *dignity*, and *authority*. Worn on the king's mid-chest, this "golden girdle" was impossible to miss and designed to impress those who beheld it. In biblical times, there was no higher status symbol.

Kings of lesser wealth and power wore belts on their mid-chest as well; however,

Above: This belt is made of gold and silver and was taken from the mummy of Sosphenq II in Egypt. Although this belt is a rich treasure, it in no way compares to the solid gold belt Christ wore around His mid-chest in John's vision on the island of Patmos.

their belts were made of strands of gold woven together with other, less valuable materials. The cost was simply too high for a lesser king to own a belt made of pure gold. Thus, when a king displayed a belt of pure gold on his upper body, onlookers would know that this was a king with immense wealth, power, and authority.

It is therefore no surprise that the apostle John saw Jesus with a golden belt wrapped around His mid-chest, for as mentioned earlier, Jesus was revealed in verse 5 as "the prince of the kings of the earth." Displaying His *power, majesty, dignity, authority,* and *vast resources,* Jesus was attired in a splendid robe that flowed downward from the golden belt that encircled His chest. With a grandeur and majesty far greater than any earthly king of the East, Jesus' magnificent kingly garments moved in a sweeping fashion as He walked among the seven golden candlesticks and approached John to give

him messages to the seven churches. What an awesome sight this must have been to behold. Never had an earthly king come close in power and majesty to the risen Christ, who alone conquered every enemy, including death itself.

Some suggest that the belt described here was a reference to the golden sash worn by the Levitical priests of the Old Testament. However, priestly belts were not made of pure gold. This golden girdle portrayed Jesus not in the role of a *priest* but in that of a *King* possessing unimaginable greatness. This was a very significant image for the apostle John and the early believers who were suffering such intense opposition for the sake of the Gospel. For Jesus to appear with a belt of pure gold around His upper mid-chest reminded all First Century believers that He holds ultimate power over all the affairs of the earth — including human rulers, governments, and the Church — over which He rules as King and Lord.

'HIS HEAD AND HIS HAIRS WERE WHITE LIKE WOOL, AS WHITE AS SNOW'

> As John continued to describe the appearance of the risen Lord, he stated, "His head and *his hairs were white like wool,* as white as snow…" (v. 14).

John's words immediately bring to mind the prophet Daniel's vision of "the Ancient of Days." In Daniel 7:9, Daniel related, "I beheld till the thrones were cast down, and the Ancient of days did sit, *whose garment was white as snow, and the hair of his head like the pure wool….*"

Similarities between the visions of Daniel and John lead many serious scholars to conclude that Daniel and the apostle John saw and experienced the same Person in their respective visions. Some suggest that Daniel's vision presented a divine preview of Christ exalted as King hundreds of years *before* His resurrection, whereas John saw the glorified King of kings *after* His resurrection. Others have theorized that Daniel's description of the Ancient of Days was Christ as He looked before manifesting in human form; however, this theory is difficult to support with Scripture. It is more likely that Daniel did indeed see the exalted Christ more than 600 years in advance of His resurrection.

But there is an often-missed and intriguing feature of Daniel's vision that is worth noting here — one that is very similar to other New Testament teachings about Christ, yet different from John's

vision. Before Daniel described the garments worn by the One he called "the Ancient of Days," he first stated, "I beheld till the thrones were cast down, and the Ancient of days did *sit…*" (Daniel 7:9).

In this verse, the Ancient of Days is pictured *seated* on a throne above all other thrones, which corresponds with other teachings in the New Testament that describe Jesus as *seated at the right hand of the Father* (*see* Ephesians 1:20-23; Colossians 3:1; Hebrews 1:3, 10:12, 12:2).

This "seated" position figuratively speaks of *rest* and *completion.* Thus, the picture of Jesus being "seated" in the heavenlies implies that His work of redemption is finished and that He now *rests* after accomplishing His divine assignment. This is very similar to Daniel's vision of the Ancient of Days, who was also *seated.* However, to understand the significance of this common element, we must first answer the question: *What is the symbolic meaning of Christ being seated at the "right hand" of the Father?*

The "right hand" was used symbolically in the Old Testament to mean a number of things:

- It was used to impart *special blessings* (*see* Genesis 48:14-18; Psalm 16:11).

- It conveyed *power* (*see* Exodus 15:6,12; Isaiah 63:12).

- It spoke of *a position of authority* (*see* 1 Kings 2:19; 1 Chronicles 6:39; Psalm 45:9).

- It depicted *protection, safety,* and *favor* (*see* Psalm 16:8, 17:7, 18:35, 20:6, 21:8, 44:3, 60:5,

63:8, 73:23, 77:10, 78:54, 89:13, 98:1, 108:6, 121:5, 138:7; 139:10; Isaiah 41:10,13).

- It carried the ideas of *strength* and *victory* (*see* Psalm 98:1, 110:1, 118:15; Isaiah 62:8).

In addition, a person who sat at the right hand of a great ruler in New Testament times was viewed as one who had been given great power and authority. All these facets of symbolic meaning help us better understand the scriptural claim that Jesus is seated at the "right hand" of the Father (*see* Matthew 26:64; Mark 14:62, 16:19; Luke 22:69; Acts 2:33, 5:31; Romans 8:34; Ephesians 1:20; 1 Peter 3:22). These verses do not describe a mere seating arrangement. Rather, they declare something very similar to Daniel's description of the "Ancient of Days" in Daniel 7:9. Just as the Ancient of Days sat down after kings, thrones, and powers were defeated, so did Jesus sit down at the right hand of the Father after His work of redemption was finished. Jesus Christ is *the* Possessor of *authority*, *blessings*, *favor*, *power*, *protection*, *safety*, *strength*, and *victory*.

This leads us to a significant difference between the visions of Daniel and John. In Daniel's vision, the "Ancient of Days" was seated; however, in John's vision, Jesus was seen *standing* and *walking*. Something had occurred that caused Christ to rise from His seat of power.

The position of "standing" in Scripture often represents a person who is so *uneasy*, *disturbed*, and *unsettled* by something he has seen or something he knows that it has caused him to rise from his resting position to take action. The fact that Christ was standing in the vision signaled a clear message to the Church: Jesus had seen something in the seven churches that deeply concerned Him — so much so that He stood to take notice of it. Later in Revelation 2:1, John wrote that Jesus was *walking* in the midst of the seven candlesticks. This indicates that He was moving in *a purposeful direction* to deal with the issues that had roused Him from His rest.

This picture of Christ "standing" in Heaven only appears *twice* in the New Testament and is therefore a noteworthy event. The first instance is found in Acts 7:54-56, which relates the stoning of Stephen:

> When they heard these things, they were cut to the heart, and they gnashed on him with their teeth. But he, being full of the Holy Ghost, looked up stedfastly into heaven, and saw the glory of God, and Jesus standing on the right hand of God, and said, Behold, I see the heavens opened, and the Son of man standing on the right hand of God.

Stephen was chosen to be one of the first seven deacons (Acts 6:5) and then later became a powerful preacher whose ministry was accompanied with signs and wonders (Acts 6:8). He was also the *first* Christian to be martyred for his faith. When Jesus saw Stephen being stoned to death, it so roused the Lord that He rose from His seated, resting position at the right hand of the Father and took note of what was occurring. Like a general who stands to honor a fellow soldier, Jesus stood up from His throne when Stephen gave his life for

Above: The stoning of Stephen is illustrated in this wood engraving by Schnorr von Carolsfeld (1794-1874). According to early Christian tradition, Stephen was stoned outside the Lion's Gate in the city of Jerusalem and became the first Christian martyr.

his faith. Many believe that whenever Christians are martyred for their faith, Jesus still stands to attention.

The only other time Jesus is seen standing in the New Testament is in the first three chapters of Revelation, where John saw Him risen from His place of rest because of the events occurring in the seven churches that disturbed and concerned Him. Jesus could not sit by and watch these events take place without

addressing them. Although the work of redemption is finished, the work of purifying the Church is *not*. Christ was therefore standing and walking among the candlesticks to take a scrutinizing look at the churches and know their true condition. His intention was to strengthen the churches that were suffering and in need of encouragement and to correct and rebuke those that needed correction and reproof. Thus, both persecution *against* the churches and problems *inside* the churches had roused Jesus from His throne.

As John goes on to describe Jesus' appearance in Revelation 1:14, he says, "His head and his hairs were white like wool, as white as snow...." The word "white" is the Greek word *leukos*, which can be translated *white* but can also mean *light*, *bright*, *shining*, *brilliant*, or *resplendent*. It is probable that when John described Jesus' head and hair as being *leukos*, his intended meaning was that Jesus' head and hair *shone brightly with resplendent light*. Similar words are used in Daniel 7:9 to describe the outward appearance of the Ancient of Days: "...The Ancient of days did sit, whose garment was white as snow, and the hair of his head like the pure wool...." These words clearly describe the glory that radiated from Jesus' presence, so dazzling and luminous that His entire being was absorbed in the light.

The word translated "white" in Revelation 1:14 is the same Greek word used in Matthew 17:2 to describe the *intense glory* seen at the Transfiguration of Jesus on Mount Tabor: "And [Jesus] was transfigured before them: and his face did shine as the sun, and his raiment was white as the light." The word "shine" in Greek carries the idea of an intense bright light that beams forth brilliantly. Matthew wrote that Jesus' face shone "as the sun," which tells us this was an almost blinding light.

And not only did Jesus' face shine brilliantly, but His raiment was also as "white" as the light. The word "white" is *leukos*, which is the same Greek word the John used in Revelation 1:14 to describe Jesus' head and hair. This word translated "white" is also used in Matthew 28:3 to describe the countenance of the angel at the garden tomb on the morning of Jesus' resurrection. According to Matthew's account, Mary Magdalene and the other Mary came to the garden to see Jesus' tomb. When they arrived, the stone was removed, the tomb was empty, and Jesus was already resurrected; however, the angel who had rolled away the stone was still in the garden. Matthew described in verse 3 what the women saw: "His countenance was like lightning, and his raiment white as snow."

The word "lightning" in this verse describes what one sees and feels when a brilliant flash of lightning fills the sky with millions of volts of electricity. In a split second, a dark night can be completely illuminated by a single lightning bolt. But unlike a flash of lightning that lasts only seconds, the light that radiated from the angel's face didn't quickly dissipate but rather shone continuously.

In addition to the brightness of the angel's face, Matthew described the angel's garment as "...raiment white as snow." Again, the word "white" is the Greek word *leukos* — the same word used in Matthew 17:2 to denote the shining brilliance that radiated from Jesus' clothes when He was transfigured on Mount Tabor. It is also the same word used by John to illustrate the *white* or *resplendent* light radiating from Jesus' head and hair in Revelation 1:14. In fact, the words "white as snow" are translated from the identical Greek phrase in both Matthew 28:3 and Revelation 1:14.

Above: Artist Giovanni Battista Paggi (1554-1627) painted this depiction of the shining radiance of Jesus' transfiguration on Mount Tabor.

John had already written that Jesus' head and hair were "white like wool," but these words were not sufficient to describe how *white* this particular "white" really was. Some speculate that Christ's head and hair were white to represent His age-less purity and holiness — and certainly no one has ever possessed more purity or holiness than Jesus. It is more likely, however, that John described Jesus' head and hair being "white as snow" because the dazzling light that shone forth from Him reminded the apostle of bright sunlight reflecting off pure white snow. John was doing his best to describe a truly indescribable sight — the supernaturally brilliant radiance of God's glory shining forth from the countenance of the exalted King of kings.

'HIS EYES WERE AS A FLAME OF FIRE'

> As John tried to focus his eyes on the brilliant image before him, one can only imagine how he might have strained to see through the bright light to the Person behind it. In Revelation 1:14, the apostle went on to describe the powerful moment when he finally gazed into the eyes of the risen Lord: "…His eyes were *as a flame of fire*."

The words "his eyes" are a translation of the Greek phrase *ophthalmoi autou*. The word *ophthalmoi* is the plural Greek word for *eyes* and is where we get the word *ophthamalogy*. The word *autou* means *of him*. When the two words are used together as one phrase, they carry a sense of wonder, as if to mean there was something about *Jesus'* eyes that was *unique* and *different* from the eyes of all others. The Greek structure should literally be translated "the eyes of him" — emphasizing

the fact that Jesus' eyes were unequaled, unsurpassed, unmatched, and unlike anyone else's eyes.

John says that when he looked into *those* eyes, they were "as a flame of fire." The Greek word for "flame" is *phloz* — which describes *swirling, whirling, flickering flames that bend, twist, turn, and arch upward*. The word translated "fire" is *puros*, the Greek word for *a burning fire*. Thus, the phrase "flame of fire" depicts *a brightly burning fire with flames swirling, whirling, flickering, twisting, turning, and arching upward toward the sky*. This, then, is not a depiction of *heat* but of the *character* of fire.

Many readers misread this phrase and conclude that Jesus had real fire *in* His eyes. But John didn't say that. He said that Jesus' eyes were "as" a flame of fire. That word "as" means *like, similar to*, or *with the same effect as* fire. To understand what John was trying to communicate here, it is necessary to stop and think about the effect a campfire or a fire in a fireplace has upon a person who stares at it for any length of time. The longer a person looks into a fire, the more the flickering flames have a *magnetic, mesmerizing* effect on his eyes, mind, and senses. Soon the person gazing into the fire gets lost in the swirling, turning, twisting flames that flicker back and forth as the wood crackles and pops and the flames reach upward and disappear out of sight. The fire has its own character, both captivating and sedating, drawing people near to watch the dance of its flames as it gives out its warmth.

These seem to be the qualities of fire that John was thinking of when he peered into Jesus' eyes and became *transfixed* by

what he saw. Although he had looked into those eyes thousands of times nearly 60 years earlier, something was different about *these* eyes. In the vision, Jesus' eyes were *compelling, irresistible, riveting,* and *gripping*. They exuded intelligence and magnetism. Like the flickering flames of a fire, those eyes drew John closer and *captivated* him completely. John must have been drawn by the warmth and love pouring forth from Jesus' eyes. Yet that wasn't all John saw, for Jesus' eyes also burned with a searching gaze, looking intently into each of the seven churches to see and address their specific needs and problems.

"Fire" is an important symbol in Scripture and frequently represents *purification* and *judgment*. Which effect of divine fire we experience depends wholly on our response to God. If we as individuals, or as the Church at large, submit to the pleadings of the Holy Spirit and "hear what the Spirit saith unto the churches," we will experience the *first* type of fire — a holy fire intended to purify and to make us more like Christ. The first fire is unavoidable for a Church that is submitted to the Lordship of Christ and to the dealings of the Holy Spirit; however, cooperating with this fire does not result in severe discipline.

On the other hand, if we resist the pleadings of the Holy Spirit and stubbornly continue to act in ways that are contrary to Christ's character, there is a *second* type of fire that burns up chaff and consumes everything that stands opposed to God. Of course, God is merciful, and even this kind of fire is an act of His love and mercy. Consuming everything that is wrong and displeasing to Christ, this fire clears the way for genuine repentance so individuals or churches can rebuild with proper methods and behaviors that are compatible with Jesus' nature.

Jesus' intense, searching eyes, which seemed "as" a flame of fire, captivated John's attention, signaling to the apostle that the Head of the Church was

Above: *This is an artist's rendering of the brazen altar that was located in front of the entrance of the Old Testament tabernacle. The altar was made out of bronze, which was symbolic of both judgment and cleansing. Thus, the brazen altar was a place where sacrifices were offered and sin was judged for the cleansing of God's people.* © Mary Evans Picture Library

examining the churches and preparing to deliver a potent message. Some of the churches were about to be encouraged by the words of Christ — such as the churches of Smyrna and Philadelphia, which received *no* correction at all. The other five churches — Ephesus, Pergamum, Thyatira, Sardis, and Laodicea — were about to be warned of impending judgment if they didn't repent. As King and Head of the Church, Christ had every right to search the churches and require them to change.

This may explain why Jesus appeared to the apostle John first as King (Revelation 1:5) and second as the Great High Priest (Revelation 1:13). Five of the seven churches were on the verge of judgment,

and Jesus, their Great High Priest, was interceding for them. The very fact that He came to warn them meant He did not want to judge them. If they were willing to hear the Holy Spirit's voice and repent, they could avoid the fires that bring judgment. What happened next would depend on whether or not the churches chose to hear the Savior's pleading and submit to His commands.

- The church of Ephesus would be told to repent, or else they would completely jeopardize their position of leadership (*see* Revelation 2:5).

- The church of Pergamum would be told to repent, or Jesus Himself would wage war against them with the sword of His mouth (*see* Revelation 2:16).

- The church of Thyatira would be told that some of them had already been given an opportunity to turn from their error and had not; therefore, judgment was coming unless they heeded Jesus' urgent call to repent (*see* Revelation 2:21,22).

- The church of Sardis would be told to repent of their complacency, or judgment would come upon them suddenly (*see* Revelation 3:2,3).

- The church of Laodicea would be told to repent of their pride and arrogance and to allow Jesus back into their midst again (*see* Revelation 3:19,20).

The type of fire these churches experienced would depend on their response — but the fire of God *was* coming. It *was* and *is* unavoidable for every believer, every local church, and for the Church at large in every age.

'HIS FEET WERE LIKE UNTO FINE BRASS'

In Revelation 1:15, John wrote that his eyes caught a glimpse of Jesus' feet. John describes them as follows: "And *his feet like unto fine brass*, as if they burned in a furnace...."

The long, flowing robe stopped at Jesus' ankles, which allowed John to see His feet. The word "feet" is *podes*, which is used in the plural to denote *both feet*. There is no mention that Jesus was wearing shoes, so the implication is given that He was shoeless in this vision.

It is likely that the Levitical priesthood ministered in the sanctuary barefooted, for there is no mention of any foot coverings when Moses wrote about all the other parts of the priestly garments. Shoes were viewed as carrying the contamination of the world and were therefore to be removed when one entered a holy place. The earliest scriptural example of this is found in Exodus 3:5, where God instructed Moses to "...put off thy shoes from off thy feet; for the place whereon thou standest is holy ground." Thus, the image of a barefooted Christ portrays Him as One who is completely pure from the contamination of the world.

When John saw Jesus' feet, he described them as "like unto fine brass." This word for "brass" is used only twice in the New Testament — in this verse and in Revelation 2:18. It is the Greek word *chalkolibanon*, a very unusual compound of two Greek words that is formed from the words *chalkos* and *libanos*. The word *chalkos* describes *an alloy of copper, mixed with either tin (bronze) or zinc (brass)* and is used frequently in ancient writings. The word *libanos* is the Greek word for *the frankincense tree and the gum derived from it*. Since the golden gum of the frankincense tree was not used as an alloy in metal, this compound word should be taken to mean *brass or bronze that possessed the deep, rich golden hue of frankincense*.

First, let's look at the biblical meaning of the words "brass" and "bronze," because these metals had a very important significance in the Old Testament.

Genesis 4:22 is the first time the word "brass" or "bronze" — the Greek word *chalkos* — is found in the Old Testament. In this verse, it is used to describe the metal out of which *cutting instruments* were made by Tubal-Cain, who made tools for farming purposes. In the centuries that followed, however, it was discovered that *chalkos* was also an ideal material for making stronger weapons. As a result, bronze was used to make helmets, axes, swords, knives, spearheads, and other pieces of weaponry used in warfare. Later it was also used to make important parts of chariots because it was so durable and difficult to break. For several thousand years, including the First Century, *chalkos* was the foremost metal used to make weapons of war.

The Septuagint uses the word *chalkos* again in the book of Exodus to describe the material used to build certain crucial parts of the tabernacle. First, Moses ordered the altar in the tabernacle to be covered with "brass" or "bronze" (*see* Exodus 27:1-8; 38:1-7) This altar is referred to as the "brazen altar" (*see* Exodus 39:39). He also ordered that a laver be made of "brass" or "bronze." This is referred to as the "laver of brass" (*see* Exodus 30:17-21; 38:8). The "brazen altar" represented a place of *judgment* and *cleansing*, and the "laver of brass" also typified these two aspects of God's character.

Thus, biblical literature is known to use "brass" or "bronze" in connection with judgment. This symbolic meaning has great consequence to the vision of the exalted Christ in Revelation 1:15.

As noted above, the second part of the compound word used in Revelation 1:15 is *libanos*, the Greek word for the *frankincense tree and the gum derived from it*. Once the gum dries, it becomes brittle, is bitter to the taste, and produces a powerful, aromatic fragrance when burned. Frankincense was the chief fragrance used in temple worship in Jerusalem. It was considered to be such a holy substance that Hebrew merchants were strictly forbidden to sell it to pagans.[6]

Frankincense became such an integral part of temple worship, rituals, and services that some scholars estimate an annual use of 700 pounds of this precious substance to fulfill temple requirements.[7] Because the frankincense tree didn't grow in Israel, frankincense was imported from Arabia and Sheba (*see* Isaiah 60:6; Jeremiah 6:20), which made it *very* expensive. Although its primary use was for priestly ministry, it was also the preferred fragrance of kings.

It is significant that at Christ's *first* appearance in the New Testament, He was associated with frankincense, which foretold His high priestly ministry. Matthew 2:11 records the visit of the Magi, who came bearing gifts for the Jesus at the beginning of His life: "And when they [the Magi] were come into the house, they saw the young child with Mary his mother, and fell down, and worshipped him: and when they had opened their treasures, they presented unto him gifts; gold, *frankincense*, and *myrrh*."

The gifts the Magi brought to Jesus were both symbolic and extremely

Above: *The frankincense tree, technically called the Boderllis Sacra, grows in the Middle East. The bark is sliced, allowing the frankincense resin to leak out. The resin was collected, dried, and burned as incense in the Old Testament tabernacle and later in the temple.*

Above: *It is estimated that 700 pounds of dried frankincense was used annually in temple worship. This aromatic incense was considered to be so holy that Jewish merchants were forbidden to sell it to pagans.*

valuable. *Gold* was a gift for a *king*. Frankincense was associated with a *priest* or *priestly functions*. Myrrh was a component in perfume used for the embalming of bodies (*see* John 19:39). Therefore, the gifts of the Magi were all prophetic, foretelling the role this Child would eventually have as *King* and *High Priest* and *Savior* of mankind through His death and resurrection.

Revelation 1:15 reveals Christ in His *last* appearance in the New Testament — and once again, He is associated with frankincense. However, this time the word for "frankincense" is linked to the word for "brass" or "bronze." Since frankincense wasn't an alloy that was mixed with metal, it can be surmised that the words "like unto fine brass" provide an allegorical message about Christ to the

seven churches and to the Church at large throughout the ages — combining the symbolic meanings of both *brass* and *frankincense* to paint a picture of *stability*, *judgment*, *holiness*, and *prayer*.

Because brass or bronze was an important symbol of judgment in the Old Testament, this image of Jesus with feet "like unto fine brass" also tells us that Christ is prepared to bring judgment when it is necessary. Those who resist Jesus' commands will soon discover that He will ultimately trample down every plan and purpose of man that stands against the character of God. However, brass or bronze is heavy, and it is difficult to quickly move an object made of this metal. The fact that the appearance of Jesus' feet was like brass or bronze clearly sends the message that when Christ moves to bring judgment,

Right: This photo shows the rugged shores of Patmos, which can be fiercely beaten during a storm. When a storm is raging, the sound of the waves crashing against the rocks can be heard at locations all over the remote island. Some scholars say John likened the voice of the exalted Jesus in the vision to the sound of these roaring waves, which he could probably hear from his cave home on the island.

He does so slowly to provide "space to repent" (*see* Revelation 2:21).

John further wrote that Jesus' feet looked "as if they burned in a furnace." This tells us the metal had not yet set; in other words, the decision-making process was still being "forged in the crucible." The metal had been heated and poured forth, but because it still glowed brightly, we know that the hardening process was not yet complete.

Although Christ was surely moving toward the seven churches to bring rebuke, correction, or even judgment, the decision had not yet been reached. It was still in the crucible. Slowly lifting one foot at a time, Jesus wasn't rushing to judgment; rather, He was moving slowly enough to give each person or church an opportunity to avoid judgment by repenting before suffering the consequences of continued error or sin.

The use of *libanos* — the word meaning *frankincense* — in connection with the Greek word for "brass" or "bronze" in this verse is certainly intentional and must be considered. Perhaps Jesus' feet were doused in the incense of the heavenly Holy of Holies, where He ever lives to make intercession for those who come to Him (*see* Hebrews 7:25). Or perhaps Christ's feet that are "like unto fine brass" carry the golden hue of frankincense because He lives in the atmosphere of prayer, where He continually intercedes as the Great High Priest for every person He has ever washed in His blood. Although He is poised with potential judgment if necessary, Jesus is, *has been*, and *always will be* interceding in prayer for the Church, pleading for His people to hear Him and repent before He arrives with judgment.

The word "voice" is the Greek word *phone*, which simply means *a voice*. But John was so overwhelmed by the power of *this* voice that he likens it to "the sound of many waters." John had already recorded that Jesus' voice sounded like "a great trumpet" (v. 12). Then in verse 15, John used the illustration of "many waters" to tell us that the voice of the exalted Christ was so powerful, it swept across the apostle's entire being like the roaring waves of the sea, drowning out everything until nothing else could be heard.

Some believe that God used this expression because of John's residence on the island of Patmos and his proximity to the sea. Especially during storms, Patmos could be fiercely beaten by the waves. It is quite possible that John could hear the waves crashing against the island's shores during a storm. The roar of the waves pounding against rugged rock would have reverberated up the side of the mountain and into John's cave residence, making it difficult for him to hear any other sound until the storm subsided.

However, this same expression is used multiple times in Scripture to describe the awe-inspiring voice of God (*see* Ezekiel 1:24; 43:2; Daniel 10:6; Revelation 14:2; 19:6). All of these verses liken the voice of God to the sound of many waters.

When Christ speaks, all other voices are silent, all arguments cease, and no one else is able to utter a sound. Christ — and Christ alone — is heard when He speaks as the King of kings and the Head of the Church. In this verse, John experienced the majestic, commanding voice that no force or power on earth can resist. When *this* voice speaks, *everyone* listens.

'HIS VOICE AS THE SOUND OF MANY WATERS'

John went on in verse 15 to describe the voice of Jesus as he heard it during the vision: "And his feet like unto fine brass, as if they burned in a furnace; *and his voice as the sound of many waters.*"

'HE HAD IN HIS RIGHT HAND SEVEN STARS'

> In Revelation 1:16, John continued to describe the image of the exalted Christ who stood before him in the vision: "And he had in his right hand *seven stars*...."

The word "stars" comes from the Greek word *asteras*, which simply means *stars*. The symbolic meaning of these stars is found in Jesus' words in Revelation 1:20, where He stated that "...the seven stars are the *angels* of the seven churches...."

What does the word "angel" mean in this context? The word "angel" is the Greek word *angelos*, which is most often translated *angel* in the New Testament. However, this Greek word has additional meanings *besides* the word "angel." It is also translated *messenger* (*see* Luke 7:24, 9:52; James 2:25). Some authors suggest that this word "angel" infers that a specific angel was assigned to each of these seven churches in Asia. Although this suggestion is interesting, it is also problematic for a number of reasons.

Jesus referred to these particular "angels" again in Revelation 2:1, 2:12, 2:18, 3:1, 3:7, and 3:14, where He charged them with the responsibility of presenting the words of the exalted Christ to the seven churches. It would be the responsibility of these "angels" to bring either encouragement or correction to the seven

churches — yet nowhere does the New Testament teach that heavenly angels are involved in church leadership or that they teach or deliver messages to local congregations. Furthermore, these so-called "angels" were called to *repent* along with the members of the seven churches. This means that the "angels" Jesus addressed in this vision were guilty of committing sin. Therefore, although churches may indeed have angels who watch over and protect them, it is highly unlikely that this word "angel" — the Greek word *angelos* — could refer to *heavenly angels* in these particular verses.

It seems more likely that these "angels" were the *human messengers* of the seven churches — in other words, the

Left: It is estimated that the universe holds 10 billion trillion stars, each of which is different in composition, color, size, and luminosity. In Revelation 1:16, Jesus likened the "angels" of the seven churches to "seven stars" — a reference to the seven spiritual overseers or pastors of the churches He was addressing.

angels but to the pastors who presided over the churches in Ephesus, Smyrna, Pergamum, Thyatira, Sardis, Philadelphia, and Laodicea.

John also wrote that Christ "had in his right hand seven stars." The word "had" is the Greek word *echo*, which means *to hold tightly or to hold in one's firm grasp*. The tense used in this verse is in the progressive form, which literally means that Christ *was holding* these seven stars and *would be constantly holding* them in His masterful grip. They were in His hand; they were under His protection; and He was holding them tightly with a firm grasp. This lets us know that these seven stars were in Jesus' *absolute power* and *control*.

The position of these seven pastors — held firmly in Christ's right hand and under His custodial care — strongly implies that they would be *answerable* and *accountable* to Jesus for delivering His message to the churches under their oversight. Jesus was calling the seven churches to heed His message, but He would hold the *messengers* or the *pastors* accountable for delivering the messages accurately on His behalf. They were to be the *vocal instruments* through which He, as Head of the Church, could speak to His seven churches in Asia.

individuals who held a position of oversight in each congregation. This most notably would refer to the *pastors* of the seven churches.

By delivering the messages to the pastors *first*, Jesus demonstrated that He honors the structure of authority He has established in the local church and does not bypass His appointed leaders even to deliver a message to His people. Before the congregation hears the message, Jesus makes sure the pastor hears what He has to say *first*. Then it becomes the pastor's God-given responsibility to deliver that divine message to the congregation under his oversight. Therefore, it is most likely that the word "angels" in Revelation 1:20 did not refer to supernatural

But let's pause for a moment to consider why Jesus used "stars" to describe the pastors of these seven churches. What was the symbolic significance, and what does the scriptural use of this metaphor say about pastoral ministry?

When we look up at the sky on a clear night, at least 3,000 stars are visible without binoculars or a telescope. But consider these facts about stars and the vast universe we live in:[8]

☆ It is estimated that our Milky Way galaxy has 100 billion stars.

☆ Beyond our Milky Way galaxy are an additional 100 billion galaxies in the universe.

☆ Based on recent scientific research, astronomers now believe there are *10 billion trillion* stars in the total universe. That is 10,000,000,000,000,000,000,000 stars — an unfathomable number for the human mind to comprehend.

☆ The study of stars began in 2,500 BC, when Sumerian priests, astronomers, and astrologists studied stars for the purposes of *religion, worship, science, navigation*, and *determining seasons*.

☆ Greeks and Romans believed the stars were heavenly representations of their gods; thus, the planets (which shone like bright stars in the night sky) were named *Mercury, Venus, Mars, Jupiter, Saturn, Uranus*, and *Neptune* — all Roman names of Greek gods.

☆ When something out of the ordinary occurred in a constellation of stars, it was usually viewed in the ancient world as a heavenly declaration of favor or of coming judgment. Stars were studied very seriously and were used to determine future destinies of individuals, kings, nations, and empires.

☆ Like human beings, each star has a beginning and an end, a birth and a death. After its birth, a star lives through several cycles of growth, but eventually it begins to cast off its outer layers in preparation for death. Every star is destined to die as its time runs out; thus, *there is no such thing as a permanent star.*

Left: This image from the NASA/ESA Hubble Space Telescope shows a compact star-forming region in the constellation Cygnus (The Swan). A newly formed star called S106 IR is shrouded in dust at the center of the image and is responsible for the surrounding gas cloud's hourglass-like shape and the turbulence visible within. Nearly 2,000 light-years from earth, the nebula measures several light-years in length and appears in a relatively isolated region of the Milky Way galaxy. © Hubble view of star-forming region S106 / NASA & ESA

☆ The lifespan of a star is determined by the amount of fuel it has *at its core* and the rate at which it uses that fuel.

☆ Massive stars have shorter life spans because they experience *greater pressure* at their cores, which causes them to burn energy more rapidly.

☆ Smaller stars burn less brilliantly, but because they experience *less pressure* at their core than massive stars do, the smaller stars usually burn longer.

☆ As is true with human beings, the behavior of young stars and older stars are very different. Younger stars are known to rotate rapidly and have high levels of "surface activity." As stars mature and grow older, they slow down and their surface activity begins to diminish.

☆ Although older stars rotate more slowly and have less surface activity, it is in their mature years that they produce the strongest and most stable light.

☆ Like human beings, no two stars are alike. Out of the 10 billion trillion stars in the universe, each one is unique in its physical characteristics and size. Furthermore, each star gives off its own unique level of luminosity and hue based on surface temperatures. A star can be shades of red, yellow, blue, or white, depending on a variety of factors.

☆ Although stars may cross the orbits of other stars, each star has a specific, predetermined orbit from which it veers very little, even over a time span of thousands of years. This explains why the signs in the heavens haven't changed over the course of history.

Now let's consider how these facts about stars help explain in part why these seven "angels" — or, most likely, seven *pastors* — were represented by seven "stars" in Jesus' right hand.

Right: The Antennae Galaxies, once believed to be two sedate spiral galaxies similar to the Milky Way, are said to be in a state of starbust — a dynamic period in which all of the gas within the galaxies is being used to form stars, causing stars to be literally ripped from their host galaxies to form a streaming arc between the two. These far-flung stars and streamers of gas stretch out into space, creating long tidal tails reminiscent of antennae, from which the two galaxies inherit their name. © Antennae Galaxies reloaded, ESA/Hubble & NASA

☆ These pastors were intended to shine like stars in the spiritual darkness that permeated Asia Minor in the First Century and to be guiding lights to the churches. The seven churches themselves had been likened to oil lamps. But the pastors of these seven churches were called to shine like stars in order to give *guidance* to people in darkness; help *navigate* lost people to Christ; assist believers in *worship*; and teach the Word of God so people would learn how to recognize the *seasons of life* and how to effectively sow and reap in each respective season.

If these seven pastors fulfilled these responsibilities, they would indeed become God's *guiding lights* in their generation, impacting the *future* and *destiny* of the people under their charge, their churches, their cities, and even the regions where they served.

☆ Like the stars in the heavens, even the most bright and shining pastoral ministry is *temporary* and *fading*. Although a pastor may serve in one location for many years, there is no such thing as a permanent pastor. Eventually a time comes when his light begins to fade so a new "star" can be born. In time, each pastor begins to wind down and prepare for another pastor to take his place and become a guiding light for that church and community.

☆ The lifespan of a pastor's ministry may be short or long, depending on several factors. One key factor is the amount of spiritual fuel and endurance he has *at his core*, as well as the rate at which he expends that fuel in running his race.

Very often pastors of larger churches have ministries with shorter life spans because they experience such great pressure at their core, which causes them to burn out more quickly. And although it may seem as if pastors with smaller congregations burn less brilliantly or have less impact, they may shine their light longer because they experience less pressure at the core. The amount of spiritual fuel resident within a pastor, his use of that fuel, and his ability to endure pressure at his core are all critical factors in determining the longevity of his ministry.

☆ Like massive stars, those pastors who have larger congregations run the risk of experiencing pressure *at their core* if they burn too fast and furiously. Pastors who lead smaller congregations may not shine as brightly in terms of prominence or fame, but they may burn longer because they're not subjected to the incessant pressure at their core that pastors of larger churches experience.

Left: Known as the Monkey Head Nebula, this colorful region, 6,400 light-years from earth in the constellation of Orion (The Hunter), is filled with young stars embedded with bright wisps of cosmic gas and dust. © New Hubble image of NGC 2174, NASA, ESA, and the Hubble Heritage Team (STScI/AURA)

What transpires *at the core* of a pastor's life is what determines his or her *brevity* or *longevity* in the ministry.

☆ Like stars, younger pastors are much more involved in "surface activity" and spin much faster in terms of schedule. Constant movement and a fixation on what impresses flesh is often the fruit of younger "stars" in the ministry. But as they grow older and more consistent in their walk with God, pastors often come to the conclusion that "surface activity" is not a mark of maturity.

As a result, the strongest and best years of ministry for pastors usually occur as they grow more mature and come to know Jesus Christ in a deeper way. Pastors who survive the pressure at their core and use their Spirit-given fuel wisely find that their latter years of ministry are their strongest years, because they are able to provide a steady and stable source of light for their churches and communities.

☆ Like the 10 billion trillion stars in the universe, no two pastors are exactly alike. God calls some pastors to lead massive churches, others to lead medium-sized churches, and still others to lead smaller churches. Some pastors are called to be bright lights — "stars" — who are well known to the masses, whereas others are called to have less visibility in smaller churches or communities. Regardless of the size of their congregations or ministries, however, pastors are called to shine their light in a way that is consistent with their own unique calling.

☆ Like stars, each pastor will be different from every other pastor in his specific characteristics, luminosity, and hue. Each person has his own unique experiences to draw from and his own "spiritual temperature" in God. Pastors shine with different hues, yet all represent various facets of God's character.

☆ Just as stars have an appointed orbit, God has a predetermined course — an "orbit," if you will — for each pastor to follow. This would include the details that make a pastor's call to minister the Gospel distinct and unique, such as where he is called to serve, what culture he is called to touch, and which people he is called to minister to. Just as stars cross the paths of other stars, each pastor's course will cross the paths of other pastors so he can fellowship with and be influenced by them. Nonetheless, a pastor must be careful not to veer from his own divine call so his light can shine in the area or the "orbit" God has ordained for *him*.

Right: *This image shows the cluster Westerlund 2 and the surrounding region — 20,000 light years from earth. © Westerlund 2 — Hubble's 25th anniversary image, NASA, ESA, the Hubble Heritage Team (STScI/AURA), A. Nota (ESA/STScI), and the Westerlund 2 Science Team*

Right: In 83 AD, Domitian ordered this particular coin to be minted to commemorate the deification of his young son, who had recently died. Domitian's intention in minting such a coin was to build a widespread public perception of himself as a divine and almighty god. Above is one side of the coin, which depicted the emperor's head. The other side of the coin is shown on the opposite page.

But is there further insight to glean on the symbolic meaning of the phrase "seven stars" in Revelation 1:16? So far no symbolism in this vision of Christ has been accidental, and it *must* be assumed that the image of Christ holding "seven stars in his right hand" had a special significance to the apostle John and to the other First Century believers who read John's words.

Indeed, historical evidence suggests that the "seven stars in the right hand" of Christ was an image taken directly from the worship of *Domitian*. This symbolism would have been especially significant to John and other believers who were suffering as a result of the intense persecution against Christians instigated under Domitian's rule.[9]

The Emperor Domitian asserted that he and his Flavian family were descended directly from the gods. Because no god was more powerful than the god *Jupiter* (the Roman name for the Greek god *Zeus*), he was obsessed with the idea that the Flavian family could trace their ancestry to this god. This explains why Domitian authorized a massive undertaking to restore and enlarge the *Temple of Jupiter* located on Capitoline Hill in Rome.[10] It

also explains why he built small, private temples to Jupiter in several of his private residences. These architectural endeavors were designed to create the public perception that the Flavian family had descended from Jupiter.

But in 93 AD, Domitian's preoccupation with his descendency from Jupiter became full-blown when he pressured the Roman Senate to proclaim him *dominus et deus*, an official title that meant Domitian was *lord* and *god* (*see* page 17). He was no longer to be viewed only as a *descendent* of deity — now he was officially declared to be completely divine himself. As a result, a new religion emerged, complete with temples to Domitian constructed all over the Roman Empire and a priesthood dedicated to the worship of the emperor. This marked a new low in the pagan culture of the empire, for although it was not unusual for an emperor to be deified

Left: *This side of the coin portrayed Domitian's son sitting on top of a heavenly globe, playing with seven stars. The inscription reads "The Divine Caesar, Son of the Emperor Domitian." The purpose of this coin's design was to promote the idea that Domitian's son was baby Jupiter and that as his father, Domitian was an even greater god than Jupiter himself.*

of the coin was to promote the public's perception of their emperor as one who was on the same level as Jupiter — the god who they believed possessed the greatest power over the world.

There were hundreds of variations of these coins depicting the divine status of Domitian. But the image imprinted on one particular coin was especially significant. Once we understand the background behind this image, we may better explain another symbolic meaning for the "seven stars in the right hand" of the exalted Christ.

In 73 AD, Domitian's wife had given birth to a son, who later died in 82 AD of unknown causes.[13] At the time of his young son's death, Domitian ordered him to be deified. In commemoration of the dead boy's deification, a coin was minted in 83 AD that portrayed the emperor's dead son as an infant, sitting on a heavenly globe with his arms stretched out toward the heavens and playing with seven stars. The coin had an inscription that read: DIVI CAESAR IMP DOMITIANI F — which means: *The Divine Caesar, Son of the Emperor Domitian.*[14]

When historian Ethelbert Stauffer describes this particular coin, he writes

after death, it was the first time a religion had been created for public worship of an emperor while he still lived.

In 96 AD, Domitian was murdered and the Senate issued a decree commanding all temples, statues, and idols of the hated emperor to be obliterated.[11] However, coins proclaiming the dead emperor's divine status had already been minted all over the Roman Empire, and it was impossible to fully eradicate them. As a result, vast numbers of these coins survived even to this present moment — archeological evidence that demonstrates how widespread the worship of Domitian was by the end of his rule in the First Century.

One classic example of these coins was minted in 84 AD — years before the official declaration of Domitian's deity. It bears the head of Domitian on one side and, on the reverse side, Jupiter holding a thunderbolt and spear.[12] The purpose that the imagery on the coin was especially crafted to picture the emperor's dead son as an infant "…sitting on the globe of heaven, playing with the stars. The legend runs *divus caesar imp domitiani f* — the divine Caesar, son of the Emperor Domitian. The seven stars indicate the seven planets, a symbol of heavenly dominion over the world."[15]

Dr. Ernest Janzen of Toronto University affirms: "The infant is depicted as baby Jupiter, and the globe represents world dominion and power…the infant depicted on the globe was the son of [a] god and that infant was conqueror of the world."[16]

Domitian's dead son was pictured as *baby* Jupiter on the coin — the son of a god and therefore the conqueror of the world. By implication, then, the child's father was *God Almighty* and Domitian must possess a rank even *greater* than Jupiter.

Such was the intended message of the coin design. No one was greater than Domitian. Even Jupiter was a baby compared to the almighty Domitian, who possessed and exercised power over *áll* the affairs of the heavens and earth.

This leads us directly to the image of Christ holding "seven stars" in Revelation 1:16 — an image that John and all the believers living in Ephesus and other parts of Asia had probably seen very often.

The city of Ephesus was chosen to be the home of the largest temple dedicated to Domitian in all of Asia. This massive, multi-level temple was located in Domitian Square on Curetes Street in the most prestigious part of Ephesus (*see* pages 234-237). Its location in the heart of the city emphasizes the central role that this religion played in Ephesus during Domitian's rule.

In fact, it has been suggested that the apostle John was arrested because he refused to enter this temple or to burn incense before an idol of Domitian. Although this cannot be confirmed as a historical fact, it is a fact that many Christians were imprisoned and martyred because they would not burn incense to idols of Domitian or call him *lord* and *god*.

Because the city of Ephesus was the largest center for Domitian worship in Asia, there is little doubt that these idolatrous coins were used in great quantities in the city. It is probable that every coin bag in Ephesus held coins that bore the divine image of Domitian.

Due to a change in financial policies at that time, the official amount of silver in a denarius was increased to 12 percent during the Emperor Domitian's rule.[17] This meant that many freshly made coins were minted during this period — including *this* coin that pictured Domitian's dead son playing with stars and exercising spiritual power over the heavens and earth.

Nearly every coin in the city bore some type of image that proclaimed the emperor as *god* in the flesh. These coins were so abundant that it would have been difficult for anyone in the city to do business without using one of them.

So when John saw the "seven stars" in the right hand of the exalted Christ, it is likely that he had seen this image many times before he was exiled to Patmos. As a resident of Ephesus, the apostle had probably carried similar coins in his own coin bag and used them to make purchases.

At the time of John's vision of the exalted Christ, Domitian seemed to be the one exercising ultimate authority and power over a vast portion of the earth. But John would have known what those seven stars in the right hand of Jesus meant: that Christ is the One who *really* possesses power, authority, and control over Heaven and earth, *not* Domitian or his dead son. No matter what Domitian may have declared about himself, the fact remained that only *One* truly possesses ultimate authority and power. The future did not lie in the hands of the emperor but in the hands of the King of kings Himself — the *true* Emperor of the universe.

It is significant to note that the "seven stars" were in the "right hand" of Christ. Because the right hand speaks of *ruling power*, this symbolism may indicate that Jesus would *first* express His rule through the representation He had placed in each local church. Before each congregation heard the message Jesus had for that particular church, their pastor would hear it. If Christ had words of encouragement for them, the pastor who answered to Him would hear His encouragement first. If a church was to be rebuked, the local pastor who answered to Christ would be the first to hear and to digest the divine rebuke.

This is a clear reminder that the Head of the Church does not bypass the authority that He Himself has set in place. He holds in His right hand those whom He has authorized and anointed to lead His people. Invested with the power to act as His representatives and to speak as His prophetic voice, these shining "stars" are especially accountable to the One who has appointed them as His overseers for the Church.

'OUT OF HIS MOUTH WENT A SHARP TWOEDGED SWORD'

In Revelation 1:16, John continued to describe Jesus as he beheld Him in the vision: "And he had in his right hand seven stars: *and out of his mouth went a sharp twoedged sword....*"

This image of a "sharp two-edged sword" coming from the mouth of Christ may at first seem to represent some kind of brutal attack. However, Jesus loves the Church. Even when He brings painful correction to His people, He does so to help them, not to attack or to kill them. The concept of brutality has no place in the character of Christ, nor does it have a place in this text. Hence, it is essential to explore the Greek words used in this phrase more deeply to discover the purpose and function of this "sharp two-edged sword."

First, the word "sharp" is a form of the Greek word *oxus*, which was used to describe *sour wine, sour vinegar,* or *a medical solution used to anesthetize people experiencing severe pain.* It could also include the meaning of *bitter.*

This is the same type of solution offered to Jesus when He hung on the Cross (*see* Mark 15:36). In daily life, this solution was also used regularly *to cleanse disease and infection* or *to cleanse dirty*

Right: The Greek word for the sharp, "two-edged sword" that came out of Jesus' mouth in John's vision is rhomphaia — *a long, two-edged blade that was slightly curved and so razor sharp that it could cut through most armor.*

wounds. It was given to people who were sick with fevers or stomach problems. The solution might have been bitter to the taste, but after attacking infection and disease, it produced a subsequent *healing effect.*

The word *oxus* can also carry the secondary meaning of *sharp.* Most translations of this verse render this word as "sharp" because of its connection with Christ's sword, but *oxus* is rarely translated that way. The most common New Testament usage of this word suggests that it refers to *the sanitizing effect of a medicinal cleanser; an astringent intended to attack infection and remove disease; or an anesthetizing wine given to patients who were suffering with excruciating pain.* This was precisely the solution given to a patient to anesthetize and numb him before a painful surgical procedure.

The use of the word *oxus* in this text suggests that because compromise with the world was spreading like a disease in some of these Asia churches, Jesus was preparing to perform a radical and potentially painful procedure to remove it. The sword was therefore positioned and ready to slice into the Body of Christ to extricate the disease.

No matter how carefully or how slowly Jesus proceeds in correcting His Church, there is no way to avoid the painful effects of judgment against sin or erring leadership. Correction is always a painful procedure, and often it is bitter

to the taste. But to reveal Jesus' compassionate heart and His desire to alleviate His people's pain during this ordeal, His sword is shown as carrying the *anesthesia* of the Holy Spirit to numb the pain of the procedure. The purpose of divine judgment is not to wound but to cleanse and heal the Church, restoring individuals who would otherwise be destroyed because they are infected with disease that is ravaging them from within.

In Revelation 2:6 and 15, we read that the doctrine of the Nicolaitans was attempting to gain a foothold in the Asia

The instrument of removal was the "two-edged sword." It is significant to note that this sword proceeded from Jesus' mouth — or from His *words*. The words of Jesus contain sanitizing characteristics that purge and purify, as described in Ephesians 5:25-27 regarding His loving relationship with the Church:

> ...Christ also loved the church, and gave himself for it; that he might sanctify and cleanse it with the washing of water by the word, that he might present it to himself a glorious church, not having spot, or wrinkle, or any such thing; but that it should be holy and without blemish.

But these words that proceed from the mouth of the exalted Christ not only purify — they also purge or extract by cutting or severing, as would a sword. We find this description of the Word operating as a sword in Hebrews 4:12. The text defines the specific and intricate cutting or dividing that is accomplished by the sword, or the word, of the Lord:

> For the word of God is quick, and powerful, and sharper than any twoedged sword, piercing even to the dividing asunder of soul and spirit, and of the joints and marrow, and is a discerner of the thoughts and intents of the heart.

The use of the word "two-edged" sword is significant in this passage because it indicates the serious intent of the one who wields it and the severity of the cut such a sword inflicts. The Greek word for a "two-edged sword" is the word *rhomphaia*, which describes one of the most fearsome weapons of the ancient world.

churches. This doctrine had been resisted by the church of Ephesus (v. 6), but it was spreading very quickly in the church of Pergamum (v. 15).

In Revelation 2:12, Jesus addressed the church of Pergamum with a two-edged sword in His mouth, which implies He was coming to extract this spiritual disease *before* the church became entirely infected with it. However, Jesus also came with a merciful application of spiritual anesthetic to ease the pain of the procedure and to apply what was needed to bring healing once the extraction was complete.

Above: *The* rhomphaia *was an effective weapon when a soldier needed to thrash or hack his way through a densely populated enemy line. Romans dreaded this two-edged sword, even adapting their armor with new mountings to protect themselves from its lethal slicing motion.*

Romans had a sundry of swords, but no sword was more feared than the *rhomphaia*. This was a sword that had been developed by Thracians, who were among the most aggressive fighters of the First Century. Thracian fighters used many weapons, which included a sword like that of the Romans, a sickle, a polearm, and a *rhomphaia* — the same word that is translated as a "two-edged sword" coming from Christ's mouth in Revelation 1:16.

The *rhomphaia* was a long-bladed weapon attached to a long pole. Its extraordinary length gave a fighter superior striking power so that, if needed, it could replace the spear. A fighter with a *rhomphaia* was able to deal a deadly, slicing blow to an enemy with a wide swing from a relatively safe distance, and its two-edged blade was so razor sharp that it could cut through most armor.

The blade of a *rhomphaia* was usually slightly curved and therefore ideal for *thrashing*, *slicing*, and *hacking* one's way through a densely populated enemy line. Its iron blade was sharpened on both sides to give it the most superior cutting action. If the slender curve of the blade was wrapped around an opponent's midsection and pulled, this sword could easily slice an enemy's body in half. Romans dreaded this weapon so much that they adapted their armor with new mountings to protect themselves from the slicing and hacking motion of the *rhomphaia*.

When needed, the outer rounded edge of this sword was ideal for *decapitation*, which is a very important point we will return to when we study Jesus' message to the church of Pergamum in Volume Two. As you will see in that discussion, the Roman proconsul who ruled from Pergamum had the privilege to decide who lived and who died. If he ruled against a person and gave the order for someone to be executed, the victim would be decapitated by the outer rounded edge of a *rhomphaia*.

It is interesting that this is the same word used in Luke 2:34,35 when Simeon came into the temple in Jerusalem at the time of the infant Jesus' dedication: "And Simeon blessed them, and said unto

Mary his mother, Behold, this child is set for the fall and rising again of many in Israel; and for a sign which shall be spoken against; (Yea, a sword [*rhomphaia*] shall pierce through thy own soul also,) that the thoughts of many hearts may be revealed." The word *rhomphaia* in verse 35 gives us a graphic picture of the pain Mary would feel as she beheld her Son on the Cross and saw the agony He was suffering for the sins of mankind. That hideous sight would "tear up" Mary's soul as surely as a two-edged sword can rip through a human body.

With all this in mind, let's consider Revelation 1:16, where John saw the exalted Christ with a *rhomphaia* proceeding from His mouth. Since Jesus was preparing to address these seven churches in Asia, the image of the two-edged sword suggests that there were hostile opponents in those churches who were resisting God and His Word.

In this chapter, Jesus is portrayed as King and the Great High Priest who intercedes for the Church. But He doesn't leave correction to happenstance. Taking one purposeful step at a time with His feet of brass, Jesus moved in the direction of the seven churches. He moved slowly enough to give the churches time to repent, but He kept moving in their direction to bring correction if they did not repent. Those who refused to hear what the Holy Spirit was saying to the churches would soon learn that Jesus will act in mercy and compassion to attack spiritual disease and cleanse it from the Church. Christ loves the Church so much that, *if* necessary, He will remove those who resist Him and eradicate any false doctrine or worldly compromise that has spread like a disease so His churches can once again be healthy.

'HIS COUNTENANCE WAS AS THE SUN'

> In Revelation 1:16, John went on to say, "And he had in his right hand seven stars: and out of his mouth went a sharp twoedged sword: *and his countenance was as the sun shineth in his strength*."

The word "countenance" is the Greek word *opsis*, which can refer to the *face*. However, in this context it seems that John used opsis to refer to Jesus' overall *outward appearance*. The word *opsis* is also used in other New Testament scriptures to describe one's entire outward appearance, which is almost certainly the meaning here.

John said that Jesus' outward appearance was "as the sun shineth in his strength." The word "sun" is *helios*, the Greek word for the *sun* itself. The word "shineth" means *an outraying of glory* and describes the absolute splendor John beheld as he looked upon the exalted Christ. In the previous verses, John described what he was seeing in the vision detail by detail. John then made this statement to summarize the image of Jesus in His exalted state. Christ's image was glorious beyond description, and the only way the apostle knew to describe what he saw was to say that Jesus' countenance was "as the sun shineth in his strength."

The word "strength" is the Greek word *dunamis*, which describes a sight *explosively* bright beyond imagination — like the sun shining at the height of its power. Of course, the light of the sun is so bright that a person can't look at it continuously without causing permanent damage to his eyes. John's use of this simile therefore tells us that the sight of the exalted Christ was so brilliant and dazzling that he could hardly gaze upon Him. John's eyes had never seen such glory.

This brings to remembrance the experience of the apostle Paul, then called Saul of Tarsus, when he was on the road to Damascus and witnessed the exalted Christ for the first time. Acts 9:3 states, "And as he journeyed, he came near Damascus: and suddenly there shined around about him a light from heaven." The phrase "shined around" is the Greek word *periastrapto*, which is a compound of the words *peri* and *astrapto*. The word *peri* means *around*, and the word *astrapto*

Above: On the road to Damascus, Saul was blinded by a dazzling light from Heaven.

means *lightning*. Thus, when that supernatural light "shined around" Paul, it was as if unending flashes of brilliant lightning suddenly and completely surrounded him.

The verse goes on to describe this brilliant flash as a "light" from Heaven. The word "light" is *phos*, which expresses the idea that Paul was completely engulfed by the most dazzling *light* he had ever witnessed. This light from Heaven was so great, it blinded Paul for three days until Ananias came and laid hands on him by the direction of the Lord (*see* Acts 9:8-18). The fact that Paul's physical eyes were so affected tells us this wasn't a vision of the spiritual or mental realm; rather, Paul actually saw the vision with his physical eyes.

When Paul recounted his story to King Agrippa in Acts 26:13, he told the king, "At midday, O king, I saw in the way a light from heaven, above the brightness of the sun, shining round about me and them which journeyed with me." Using words similar to John's words in Revelation 1:16, Paul told Agrippa that the light he had seen was "above the brightness of the sun."

Years later on the island of Patmos, the apostle John was a witness to the same glory of Jesus Christ. John was so overtaken by the divine light radiating from the risen Christ that his physical senses could take no more. Like Paul on the road to Damascus, and like many others who had seen the glory of God in times past, John *collapsed* to the ground. Lying on the ground, John was simultaneously *engulfed by* and *bathed in* the glorious rays that emanated from Christ's presence and flooded every part of his spirit and soul.

'WHEN I SAW HIM'

Then in Revelation 1:17, John continued, "And when I *saw* him...."

The word "saw" is from the root *horao*, a Greek word that encompasses several ideas, including *to see*, *to perceive*, *to grasp*, or *to recognize*. The various nuances of meaning are important in this text. The use of this word reveals that John did more than just *see* Jesus. As this divine experience continued to unfold, John began to *comprehend* what he was seeing. Although his mind had been stunned by the glory and power of this vision, at last his mind began to *grasp* the meaning of the image he saw before him and to *recognize* its significance.

Others before John had experienced visions of the exalted Christ. Stephen saw the exalted Christ as he was being stoned to death (*see* Acts 7:55). The apostle Paul saw the exalted Christ on the road to Damascus (*see* Acts 9:3; 26:13). Paul later wrote that he knew a man who was taken into the third heaven and who heard and saw things he wasn't permitted to speak of, leaving the impression that he was writing of himself (*see* 2 Corinthians 12:1-4). This may have been a vision the apostle experienced when he was stoned and left for dead in the city of Lystra (*see* Acts 14:19,20). However, no one ever had a vision that compared with the one shown to John on the island of Patmos. It is by far the most detailed New Testament vision of the exalted Christ ever recorded.

Revelation 1:12-16 seems to suggest that what John was seeing in the vision was so breathtaking that his eyes and his mind couldn't take it in all at once, so he absorbed the vision one feature at a time.

- First, John's eyes focused on the seven golden candlesticks.

- Second, his eyes saw Christ standing among the golden candlesticks.

- Third, he saw the kingly and priestly garments that draped from Jesus' shoulders all the way down to His feet.

- Fourth, John's eyes were captured by the dazzling belt of gold around Jesus' mid-chest, designating power and authority.

- Fifth, his eyes focused on the white, resplendent light gleaming from Christ's head and hair.

- Sixth, John's eyes were transfixed by Jesus' eyes that were as a flame of fire.

- Seventh, he saw Jesus' feet, which were like golden brass.

- Eighth, John heard the voice of Christ, which was as the sound of many waters.

- Ninth, his eyes rested on the seven stars in Jesus' right hand.

- Tenth, John focused on the sword proceeding from the mouth of Christ.

- *Finally*, John wrote that Jesus' overall countenance was as the sun shining in its greatest power.

It was only *after* John wrote about all these various features he had seen that he used the Greek word *horao*, which means *to see, to perceive, to grasp,* or *to recognize.* We don't know the quantity of time involved in the opening part of the vision. However, the word *horao* tells us that a moment came when all of these images came together in John's mind. At that moment, the apostle truly understood who was standing before him and what all these features of the image were intended to mean. Perhaps his senses were so stunned and he was so taken aback that he couldn't immediately draw conclusions from the various details he initially focused on. But a moment came when John began to *comprehend* and *perceive* what he was seeing. He finally *realized* that he was looking

glory too much for his body to endure. Suddenly the apostle's physical strength departed from him, and he fell limp at the feet of Jesus "as dead." This description is important, for it reveals the suddenness and the speed with which John fell. The word "dead" is *nekros* — the same word used for *a corpse or dead body*. Thus, we know that the apostle's physical strength left him so quickly that it must have felt as if life itself was abruptly drained from him. His legs buckled under him, and he literally *collapsed* in a heap at Jesus' feet as one who is dead.

The Old Testament tells of many who were overwhelmed by the glory of God and fell down on their faces as a result.

- Genesis 17:3 records that *Abram* fell on his face when God spoke with him.

- Joshua 5:14,15 tells us that *Joshua* fell on his face when he experienced the strong presence of the Lord.

- Ezekiel 1:28 and 3:23 relate that *Ezekiel* fell flat on his face when the glory of the Lord appeared to him.

- Daniel 8:17 and 10:15 state that *Daniel* collapsed on the ground when he encountered the glory of God.

- Matthew 17:6 records that when God's glory was manifested to

upon Jesus Christ — the *King of kings* and *Lord of lords*, the *Great High Priest*, and the *Head of the Church*.

'I FELL AT HIS FEET AS DEAD'

> The apostle John went on to relate, "...When I saw him, *I fell at his feet as dead*..." (Revelation 1:17).

The words "I fell" come from the Greek word *pipto*, a word that means to fall. As it is used in this verse, *pipto* carries the idea of one who *falls hard* or one who *physically collapses*. The sheer weight of this experience was too much for John's mind to fathom, the intense

Peter, *James*, and *John*, they were so overwhelmed that they fell to the ground.

- Acts 9:3 and 26:13 reveal that *Paul* fell hard to the earth when he saw the exalted Christ on the road to Damascus.

- Revelation 19:10 relates that the apostle *John* fell once again at the feet of Jesus at the conclusion of his vision on the island of Patmos.

In addition, it is normal for people to fall on their faces in the presence of Almighty God as a gesture of honor, worship, and humility. Philippians 2:10,11 promises that a day is coming when every knee will bow before Jesus Christ and every tongue will confess that He is Lord. Revelation 4:10 says the 24 elders around the throne in Heaven are even now bowing before Jesus and casting their crowns at His feet as a part of their honor, respect, and worship. And a day is coming in the near future when all those who have been washed in the blood of the Lamb will join around that majestic throne to worship and give honor to Jesus Christ. It will be every believer's *duty* and *privilege*.

So in most cases where the Bible tells of people who were eyewitnesses of God's glory, their response was to involuntarily fall to the ground as their legs buckled under them and the strength was drained from their bodies. Stunned and overwhelmed by God's glory, they were engulfed in His presence and rendered *paralyzed*, *speechless*, and *dumbfounded* by His awesome power.

This is precisely what happened when John began to comprehend the full impact of the image he saw before him. Stunned by the divine power that had surged through his being and knocked him from his feet, the apostle lay limp and lifeless, like a dead man, at the feet of the exalted Christ — the King of kings and the Lord of lords.

'AND HE LAID HIS RIGHT HAND UPON ME'

At that precise moment, Jesus reached out in all His glory to lay His right hand on John, rousing him from his spiritual stupor. Suddenly John was summoned to his senses by the touch of Christ's hand — that same familiar touch he remembered so well from almost 60 years earlier. John wrote about this moment in Revelation 1:17: "And when I saw him, I fell at his feet as dead. *And he laid his right hand upon me*...."

When John felt the touch of *that* hand as he lay prostrate on the ground, there is no doubt that he recognized that unforgettable touch. During the three and a half years John walked with Jesus in His earthly ministry, he had seen the Master lay His hands on thousands of people who suffered or needed a compassionate, healing touch. Although Jesus' physical characteristics were different from those John recalled from his earlier association with Him, at that moment John knew that Jesus' tender, loving touch was exactly the same as what he had carried in his memories for 60 years.

Try to imagine the scene. The risen Lord was revealed to John in His kingly and priestly attire, His countenance shining as bright as the sun in all of its power. Collapsing under the weight of the glory, John lay at Jesus' feet, so dazed by what he was witnessing that he was speechless and as immovable as a dead man.

In that exact moment, Jesus reached down from His position of power to touch John and give comfort and strength to him. Jesus Christ — the King of kings and Lord of lords, the Great High Priest, and the Head of the Church — didn't consider Himself too high in His exalted position to reach down to touch and reassure His beloved disciple. This was a demonstration of the humility of Christ, as the apostle Paul described in Philippians 2:6-8: "Who [Jesus], being in the form of God, thought it not robbery to be equal with God: but made himself of no reputation, and took upon him the form of a servant, and was made in the likeness of men: and being found in fashion as a man, he humbled himself, and became obedient unto death, even the death of the cross."

It was out of the question in the First Century for mighty kings to associate with lowly subjects; however, humility is a divine characteristic and one of the chief features of Jesus Christ's character. Consider Paul's words in Philippians 2:6-8. These are probably the strongest verses about humility in the New Testament, and they demonstrate that Christ's behavior has always been marked by humility.

When Paul wrote that Jesus always existed in the "form" of God, he used the Greek word *morphe*. This word *morphe* describes *an outward form* — meaning that in Jesus' preexistence, He looked just like God. Jesus wasn't just a component of God, nor was He a symbol of God. In reality, He *was* God. As the eternal God Himself, Jesus Christ possessed the very shape and outward appearance of God — a form that included great splendor, glory, power, and a divine presence so strong that no flesh could endure it.

But Paul said that Jesus "made himself of no reputation" (Philippians 2:7). This phrase comes from the Greek word *kenos*, which means *to make empty*, *to evacuate*, *to vacate*, *to deprive*, *to divest*, or *to relinquish*. The only way Jesus could make this limited appearance on earth as a Man was to willfully, deliberately, and temporarily let go of all the outward attributes of His deity. For 33 years on this earth, God divested Himself of all His heavenly glory and "took upon him the form of a servant."

The phrase "took upon him" perfectly describes that marvelous moment when God laid hold of human flesh and took that form upon Himself so He might appear as a Man on the earth. The words "took upon him" are a translation of the Greek word *lambano*, which means *to take*, *to seize*, *to catch*, *to latch on to*, *to clutch*, or *to grasp*. This word reveals the wonderful truth that God literally reached out from His eternal existence into the material world He had created and took human flesh upon Himself in "the form of a servant."

The word "form" in this phrase is exactly the same word that describes Jesus being in the form of God. It is the Greek

Above: James Jacques Joseph Tissot (1836-1902) painted "The First Nail," his version of Jesus' ultimate act of humility, when He willingly "...humbled himself and became obedient unto death, even the death of a cross" (Philippians 2:8).

word *morphe*. This means that just as Jesus in His preexistent form had all the outward appearance of God, He also existed in the exact form of a Man — appearing and living on this earth in the same way as any other man. For a brief time in His eternal existence, Jesus emptied Himself of outward divine attributes and literally became like a Man in every way.

Paul then said that Jesus took upon Himself the form of a "servant." This is the Greek word *doulos*, which refers to *a slave*. Paul used this word to picture the *vast difference* between Jesus' preexistent state and His earthly life.

Out of His deep love for you and me, Jesus was willing to leave His majestic realms of glory to enter the world of humanity — coming down to our level so He could become an effective High Priest on our behalf. Shedding all His visible attributes of deity that were too much for man's flesh to endure, Jesus clothed Himself in human flesh and was manifested as a Man on the earth.

All of this required the greatest *humility* ever witnessed since the creation of the world. But Philippians 2:8 reveals that even more humility was required: "And being found in fashion as a man, he humbled himself, and became obedient unto death, even the death of the cross." That word "fashion" is the Greek word *schema*. This is extremely important, for this was the word used in ancient times to depict *a king who exchanged his kingly garments for the clothing of a beggar for a brief period of time.*

This is precisely what occurred when Jesus left the majestic realms of Heaven. It is the true story of a King who traded His royal garments and took upon Himself the clothing of a servant. But the story doesn't stop there. Jesus loved us so much that He "...humbled himself, and became obedient unto death, even the death of the cross" (v. 8).

The word "humbled" is the Greek word tapeinao, and it means *to be humble, to be lowly,* and *to be willing to stoop to any measure that is needed.* Think of the humility that would be required for God to shed His magnificent glory and lower Himself to become like a member of His own creation! Consider the greatness of God's love that drove Him to divest Himself of all His splendor and become like a man. This is an amazing truth, particularly when we think of how much the flesh recoils at the thought of being humble or preferring someone else above itself. Yet Jesus humbled Himself "...and became obedient unto death, even the death of the cross."

When this verse says that Jesus humbled Himself "...unto death, even the death of the cross," the word "unto" is from the Greek word *mechri*, which means *to such an extent.* The word *mechri* is sufficient in itself to dramatize the point that this level of humility was shocking; however, the verse goes on to say that Jesus so humbled Himself that He was willing to suffer "...even the death of the cross." The word "even" is the Greek word *de*, which *emphatically* means *even.* The Greek carries this idea: "*Can you imagine it! Jesus humbled Himself to such a lowly position and became so obedient that He even stooped low enough to die a miserable death on the Cross!*"

It is truly an awesome concept for our human minds to grasp. The Almighty God, clothed in radiant glory from eternities past, came to this earth for one purpose: so He could one day humble Himself to the point of dying a horrible death on the Cross, thereby purchasing our eternal salvation. All of this required *humility* on a level far beyond anything we could ever comprehend or that has ever been requested of any of us — yet this was the very reason Jesus came.

Although Jesus is now exalted — sitting at the Father's right hand and arrayed in splendor beyond human imagination — His humility still remains intact, consistent, and unchanged. It is one of the chief characteristics of His nature. He *was* humble, He *is* humble, and He *will always be* humble, just as Hebrews 13:8 says, "Jesus Christ the same yesterday, and to day, and for ever."

Thus, it was in pure humility that the exalted Christ — the King of kings and

the Lord of lords — reached down to lay His hand on His beloved apostle who lay prostrate on the ground before Him. No earthly king would pay such heed to or dare to touch a lowly servant. But Jesus reached out to assist John, just as He does for all who belong to Him.

In Revelation 1:17, John says Christ "laid" His hand on him. The word "laid" comes from the Greek word *tithimi*, which means *to place* or *to lay*, and it depicts Christ lovingly *placing His hand* on John, exactly as John had seen Him do for so many people throughout His earthly ministry:

- "And Jesus *put forth his hand, and touched him*, saying, I will; be thou clean. And immediately his leprosy was cleansed" (Matthew 8:3).

- "And immediately Jesus *stretched forth his hand, and caught him* [Peter], and said unto him, O thou of little faith, wherefore didst thou doubt?" (Matthew 14:31).

- "And they bring unto him one that was deaf, and had an impediment in his speech; and they beseech him [Jesus] to *put his hand upon him*. And he took him aside from the multitude, and put his fingers into his ears, and he spit, and touched his tongue…. And straightway his ears were opened, and the string of his tongue was loosed, and he spake plain" (Mark 7:32,33,35).

- "And he [Jesus] took the blind man by the hand, and led him out of the town; and when he had spit on

his eyes, and *put his hands upon him*, he asked him if he saw ought. And he looked up, and said, I see men as trees, walking. After that he put his hands again upon his eyes, and made him look up: and he was restored, and saw every man clearly" (Mark 8:23-25).

This same familiar touch of the Master's hand was what John suddenly felt as he lay prostrate on the ground, overcome by all he was witnessing. And with that loving touch, John regained strength to arise and receive further revelation from Jesus.

'SAYING, FEAR NOT; I AM THE FIRST AND THE LAST'

> As John continued to relate his vision of the exalted Christ, he stated, "And when I saw him, I fell at his feet as dead. And he laid his right hand upon me, *saying unto me, Fear not; I am the first and the last*" (Revelation 1:17).

It is important to note John's wording here. He said that Jesus was "…saying unto me, Fear not…." The Greek tense for "saying" conveys the idea of *redundancy*, implying that John was stating, "*Christ kept on saying unto me.*" Because John's physical senses were affected, it seems that he didn't respond the first time Jesus spoke to him. So just as a father or mother awakens a child, Jesus gently shook John, nudging the apostle back to his senses as

Above: This 1875 engraving by Gustave Dore depicts Jesus laying His hand on a sick boy to heal him — an act of divine compassion that reoccurred countless times during His earthly ministry. As John lay prostrate before the exalted Christ on the island of Patmos, the apostle recognized that same compassionate touch of the Master's hand, giving him strength to arise and receive the divine revelation that was still to come forth.

He said over and over again, "*Fear not, fear not, fear not...*"

Just as John recognized the touch of that hand, he must have also recognized this command. The words "fear not" were a common command that Jesus spoke to His disciples during His earthly ministry.

For example, in Matthew 14:27, He miraculously appeared to the disciples in the middle of a storm and told them, "...Be of good cheer; it is I; *be not afraid.*"

The words "fear not" are actually an order to *stop* something that is already in progress. Christ gave this command because John was feeling fear as a result of this supernatural experience. Although it was normal for John to respond in respect and honor to the vision he was witnessing of the risen Lord, Jesus wanted to reassure John that there was no need for fear and that He hadn't revealed Himself in His glory in order to terrify His disciple. John had to stop fearing so he could receive and comprehend the rest of the vision that was about to be revealed to him.

After quickening John from a state of altered consciousness, Jesus then told the apostle, "I am the first and the last." The words "I am" are from the Greek phrase *ego eimi*. This phrase appears 24 times in the gospel of John and more than a dozen times in the other gospels; however, the most notable example is found in John 18.

After Jesus received Judas' kiss of betrayal in the Garden of Gethsemane, He stepped forward and asked the crowd of soldiers, "...Whom seek ye? They answered him, Jesus of Nazareth. Jesus saith unto them, I *am* he.... As soon then as he had said unto them, I *am* he, they went backward, and fell to the ground" (*see* John 18:4-6). Notice that Jesus told them, "I am *he*." The word *he* is italicized in the *King James Version*, which means it doesn't appear in the original Greek. The Greek simply says *ego eimi* — which could be translated, "*I AM!*"

When the soldiers asked Jesus, "Who are You?" they probably expected Him to answer, "Jesus of Nazareth" — but instead, He answered, "I AM!" John 18:6 relates, "As soon then as he had said unto them, I am he, they went backward, and fell to the ground." A more accurate rendering would read this way: "*As soon then as he said unto them, I AM, they went backward and fell to the ground.*"

The verse says the soldiers went backward and "fell to the ground" upon hearing Jesus' answer. Once again, the word "fell" is the Greek word *pipto*, which means *to fall* and, in this context, carries the idea of one who *falls hard* or who *physically collapses*. The words "to the ground" are taken from the Greek word chamai, which depicts these soldiers falling *abruptly* and then *forcefully* hitting the ground. Some force suddenly and unexpectedly knocked these troops and temple guards flat to the ground.

Roman soldiers and a large number of trained temple guards had all come with weapons, swords, and clubs to capture Jesus. But when Jesus answered them with the words, "I AM" — thus identifying Himself as the "I AM" of the Old Testament — a great blast of God's power was unleashed. The force of that divine power was so strong that it literally thrust the troops and temple police backward, causing them to stagger and stumble as they hit the ground hard.

What a shock it must have been for those soldiers to discover that the mere words of Jesus were enough to overwhelm and overpower them. Absolutely *no* force in this universe is strong enough to resist the power of Jesus Christ! When the great "I AM" opens His mouth and speaks, every power that attempts to defy Him or His Word is pushed backward and shaken until it staggers, stumbles, and falls to the ground.

Jesus also used the words *ego eimi* in John 8:58 to declare His divinity. He said, "...Verily, verily, I say unto you, Before

Above: *This ancient fresco by Italian artist Giotto di Bondone (dated 1305) depicts Judas betraying Jesus with a kiss. Immediately following this moment in the Garden of Geth-semane, the soldiers who had come to arrest Jesus were all knocked down by the force of God's power when Jesus declared His deity with two simple words: "I AM" (John 18:6).*

Abraham was, *I am*." Those final words in the verse are the Greek words *ego eimi* and should be translated, "*I AM!*"

Then in John 13:19, Jesus said, "Now I tell you before it come, that, when it is come to pass, ye may believe that I am he." Once again, the word "he" in this verse is italicized in the *King James Version*, which means it was supplied by the translators and is not found in the original Greek. The Greek words used are *ego eimi*, meaning that Jesus was simply saying, "*...ye may believe that I AM!*"

Jesus used this phrase multiple times to strongly and boldly affirm that He is the great "I AM" of the Old Testament. There is no doubt that those who heard Jesus say those words *ego eimi* immediately recognized their significance. These were the very same words God used to identify Himself when He spoke to Moses on Mount Horeb in Exodus 3:14.

Thus, when Jesus used the words *ego eimi* in Revelation 1:17 and told John, "*...I am* the first and the last," it emphatically reminded John that Jesus Christ is the great "I AM." But Jesus also declared that He is "*the first and the last*" — a phrase very similar to Jesus' declaration in Revelation 1:8 when He said, "I am Alpha and Omega, the beginning and the ending...."

It is important to point out that the phrase "the first" in Revelation 1:17 has a definite article in front of it. In other words, Jesus isn't just *a* beginning; rather, He is *the* beginning. Everything started with Him, and He is *the* first of everything that exists. This agrees with Colossians 1:17, which says, "And he is before all things, and by him all things consist."

But Jesus isn't just "*the first*" — Revelation 1:17 also says He is "*the last*." The Greek phrase translated "the last" also uses a definite article, which means that Jesus is not just *an* ending; He is *the* last. The Greek word for "last" is masculine rather than neuter, indicating that the end of all things is *Jesus Christ Himself*.

By making this self-pronouncement, Christ reassured the apostle John that everything was under His control and that nothing occurring in the world had taken Him by surprise. He is the Alpha and Omega, the beginning and the end, the first and the last — and He is everything in between. Nothing exists without Him; all things are held together by Him; and

Left: "Adoration of the Shepherds," by Gerard van Honthorst (1622), depicts the shepherds worshiping the infant Messiah, born in a humble stable in Bethlehem. Although this was the beginning of Jesus' life on this earth, Christ had coexisted with the Father and the Holy Spirit for eternities past as the preincarnate Son of God.

'I AM HE THAT LIVETH, AND WAS DEAD, AND, BEHOLD, I AM ALIVE FOR EVERMORE'

> Many believers were being martyred for their faith at the end of the First Century, making Jesus' next words very significant: "I am he that liveth, and was dead; and, behold, *I am alive for evermore*, Amen…" (Revelation 1:18).

nothing transpires that He isn't aware of. That certainly included the tragic suffering and martyrdom that was being carried out with a vengeance against believers throughout Asia Minor and the Roman Empire at that time. Jesus was also well aware of His people's tendency to compromise to avoid conflicts with a pagan world.

Just as the soldiers couldn't resist Jesus Christ in the Garden of Gethsemane, no human force can successfully stop the work of His Church. Jesus Christ will ultimately be revealed not only as *the first*, but also as *the last*. All of history began with Him; history has been sustained by Him; and history will ultimately be summed up in Him.

The existence of Jesus Christ did *not* begin at His birth in Bethlehem. Rather, His birth simply initiated His temporary manifestation in the earthly realm — one that lasted for 33 years. Before that, the preincarnate Christ eternally coexisted with the Father and the Holy Spirit. When the apostle Paul wrote about this truth, he called it a *great mystery*: "And without controversy great is the mystery of godliness: God was manifest in the flesh…" (1 Timothy 3:16). Christ descended from His heavenly throne to offer Himself as a spotless Lamb and to wash us from our sins in His own blood (*see* Revelation 1:5). But the fact is that Jesus always *was*, always *is*, and always *will be* — a

Above: This Nineteenth Century illustration by James Jacques Joseph is entitled, "The Rich Man in Hell," and depicts the rich man in Hades asking Abraham to send the beggar Lazarus to him with water to cool his parched tongue (see Luke 16:19-31). Hades describes a temporary state or place of death. Many scholars believe it refers to spiritual death.

recurrent theme in John's revelation of the exalted Christ.

Revelation 1:18 says that Christ now "liveth." The word "liveth" in Greek means that Jesus Christ now lives *forever* — *perpetually* and *continuously*. His life is *an unending life* that will never see death again. Jesus once visited death in the past, which is why He says that He "was dead." The word "was" is the word *ginomai*, which in this context clearly means that Christ *temporarily became* dead. Death had no power to hold Him in the grave; it was nothing but a *brief interruption* to His endless life.

In fact, Hebrews 2:9 states that Jesus tasted death once and for all for every man. Indeed, the Lord Jesus Christ was once dead, but now He *lives perpetually*. Death is already permanently behind Him, and He lives forevermore.

Victory over death was the greatest victory ever won. It was the victory that permanently settled the score and placed Jesus back on the throne as Lord of all who are in Heaven, on the earth, and under the earth (*see* Philippians 2:10). With Jesus' resurrection, the price for redemption was paid and the powers of darkness crushed. That is why Paul declared in Colossians 2:14,15: "Blotting out the handwriting of ordinances that was against us, which was contrary to us, and took it out of the way, nailing it to his [Jesus'] cross; and having spoiled principalities and powers, he made a shew of them openly, triumphing over them in it."

That is also why Jesus jubilantly proclaims in Revelation 1:18, "I am he that liveth, and was dead; and, behold, I am alive for evermore, Amen...." The word "behold" is very difficult to translate, for it is an emotional word packed with explosive feelings of shock and wonder. It could be taken to mean, "*Wow — imagine it!*" or "*Isn't it amazing!*" This clearly tells us that even though Jesus Christ is exalted and has crushed all the powers of darkness, He is actually *thrilled* by the mere thought of the great victory over death He has won — so much so that He Himself exclaims, "*Amen!*"

This was a powerful message to early believers, many of whom were suffering martyrdom for their faith. They were reminded that because Jesus had defeated death by His resurrection, they could, if needed, face death with courage. Just as Christ's death was nothing more than a brief interruption, believers could be reassured that their death would also be temporary and that they would live in glory with Him forever.

'THE KEYS OF HELL AND OF DEATH'

In Revelation 1:18, Jesus went on to say, "I am he that liveth, and was dead; and, behold, I am alive for evermore, Amen; and have *the keys of hell and of death.*"

The word "keys" is the Greek word *kleis*, a word used in Greek literature to describe *a key that unlocks or locks the gate to Heaven* or *a key that unlocks or locks the gate of the underworld.* In ancient times,

Above: This 1914 painting, entitled, "Destroying the Wicked," depicts people being judged and sent to hell, which is also the Hebrew word Gehenna *and refers to a place of eternal anguish, torment, and separation from God. © Mary Evans Picture Library*

keys to huge gates were extremely large and had to be carried either on one's belt or on a chain draped over one's shoulder. Although the key could be used from the inside to lock others out, it could also lock a door from the outside to keep people in. Only the possessor of a key had the power to open and close the massive gate. Even in modern times, officials honor people by giving them a "key to the city." Keys denote authority — the ability to lock and unlock and to bind and release.

The word rendered "hell" is the Greek word *Hades*, which refers to the *underworld*. In both classical Greek and biblical literature, Hades is a term that was used to describe the abode or realm of the dead, and, in some cases, even the grave. Many people believed that Hades was a gloomy place located within the earth, and Scripture itself indicates that one had to descend in order to enter it (*see* Matthew 11:23; Luke 16:23). It is likened to a prison that is locked or unlocked with keys (*see* Matthew 16:18). According to Revelation 1:18, Christ alone is Possessor of the key to Hades.

The word Hades does not refer to the eternal or ultimate destination of the wicked, which is called *Gehenna* in the Bible and is a place of eternal anguish and torment. *Gehenna* was associated with a valley outside of Jerusalem where garbage and unclean animal carcasses were disposed of. The word also referred to a place of eternal judgment in the lake of fire (*see* Revelation 20:11-15).

On the other hand, *Hades* describes a temporary state or place of death, and many scholars believe it refers to *spiritual death*. Hades seems to have various

chambers that held all of mankind under the Old Covenant, because all are sinners (Romans 3:23) and the price of redemption had yet to be paid. Even the Old Testament saints would have been captive in Hades, awaiting the promise of Christ's triumph over sin, death, and the grave. After His resurrection, Jesus led captivity captive (Ephesians 4:8) — liberating by His victory those who had lived by faith but were subject to the penalties of sin and death. Eventually a day of judgment will come when the grave gives up the dead and Jesus Christ throws Hades into the lake of everlasting fire (*see* Revelation 20:14). He is the One who has conquered death, and He alone has the right to possess the key controlling spiritual death and the grave.

Revelation 1:18 also declares that Christ possesses the *keys of death*. The word translated "death" here is the Greek word *thanatos*, which refers primarily to *physical* death. When Christ came forth from the grave, He broke the power of death itself for all those who come to Him in repentance. The writer of Hebrews declared in Hebrews 2:14,15: "Forasmuch then as the children are partakers of flesh and blood, he [Jesus] also himself likewise took part of the same; that through death he might destroy him that had the power of death, that is, the devil; and deliver them who through fear of death were all their lifetime subject to bondage."

The book of Revelation reveals Jesus as the Conqueror of death, hell, and the grave. Even the holiest among us are sinners and subject to the penalties of sin; none of us can deliver ourselves from death by our own power or holiness. But it is critical to note that the entire book of Revelation centers around the exalted Christ, risen in victory and possessing all authority. Holding the keys of death and Hades and the keys of the abyss, Jesus is firmly in charge. He alone can loose the seven seals. He alone can order the trumpets of judgment to sound. He alone can order the vials of judgment poured forth. He alone can return and, with but a word from His mouth, utterly destroy all the armies of the world in opposition to God's purposes. Although every force of hell would seek to undo His Kingdom, in the end, evil will accomplish only what Christ permits. All authority is subject to Him, even death and Hades, which He will ultimately cast into the eternal lake of fire.

THE COMMAND TO WRITE

In Revelation 1:19, John then related the direct order he received from Christ: "Write the things which thou hast seen, and the things which are, and the things which shall be hereafter."

In the original Greek, there is a sense of *urgency* in this command, indicating that this was something that had to be done quickly. Jesus was slowly moving forward to bring judgment to some of the churches, so the sooner they heard His warnings, the more time they would have to repent before it is too late.

Above: *Jesus Christ rose from the dead in triumph and now holds the keys of authority over death and the grave. © Mary Evans / Classic Stock / H. Armstrong Roberts*

Jesus Christ is our Champion and Victor. He has won the victory for us. He is the Possessor of the keys that represent power and authority over death and the grave. Jesus has arisen as our triumphant Lord, King, Priest, and Savior.

It is beyond the scope of this book to plumb the depths of this theme that is found throughout Revelation. However,

- First, Jesus commanded John to write "the things which thou has seen," a reference to the magnificent vision of the exalted Christ recorded in Revelation 1:12-18.

- Second, He commanded John to write about "the things which are," a reference to the condition of the seven churches that are in Asia, as is recorded in Revelation 2:1-3:22.

- Third, Jesus commanded John to write about "the things which shall be hereafter," a reference to Revelation chapters 4 to 22 — chapters relating endtime events that will occur in the future.

THE MYSTERIES EXPLAINED

Jesus then explained the meanings of the "seven stars" and "seven golden candlesticks" (Revelation 1:20): "The mystery of the seven stars which thou sawcst in my right hand, and the seven golden candlesticks. The seven stars are the angels of the seven churches: and the seven candlesticks are the seven churches." Thus, we know that the "seven stars" were the "angels" of the seven churches, and the "seven candlesticks" were representative of the seven Asia churches Jesus was about to address.

In the next two chapters of Revelation, John will relate the specific message Christ directed to the *angel* of each church. For example, Jesus

began by saying, "Unto the angel of the church of Ephesus write…" (Revelation 2:1); then He continued to address each of the other six churches in the same manner.

As we will discuss in depth in Chapter Five, the word "angel" as Jesus used it here referred to the designated leaders or pastors of each of these seven churches. Nowhere does the New Testament teach that heavenly angels lead or pastor churches, nor is there even a hint that heavenly angels are charged with teaching the Word of God. The Greek word for "angel" is *angelos*, which can also be translated *messenger*. The primary function of a "messenger" is to deliver a message. Thus, these seven pastors were God's messengers to their respective congregations. As such, each pastor would hear the words of Christ before his congregation heard them. The pastor would then be charged with the task of spiritually digesting Jesus' message and then delivering it with power and accuracy to the church under his care.

These messages, although directed to specific First Century congregations, nevertheless remain profoundly pertinent to the Church at large in every age — including and especially the modern Church of this hour. But before the seven pastors could convey Jesus' messages to their congregations — and before future generations of believers could benefit from the truths found in these timeless messages — John first had to receive the fullness of the divine vision that was unfolding before him. Only then would the elderly apostle be able to obey Jesus' command to "write the things which thou hast seen, and the things which are, and the things which shall be hereafter" (Revelation 1:19) — providing us with a divine written record that has spoken through the centuries to a Church commissioned to proclaim the Gospel to a lost world until Jesus' return.

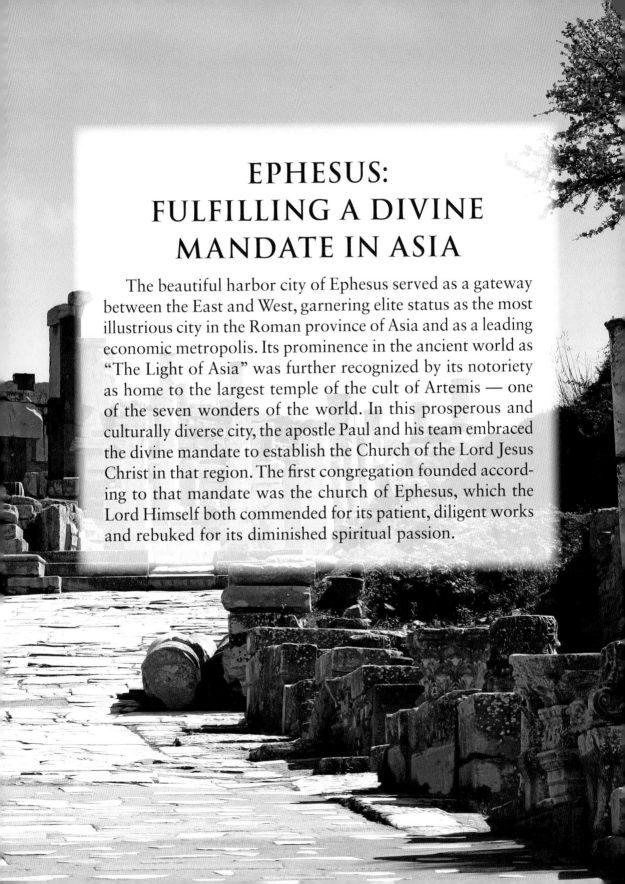

EPHESUS:
FULFILLING A DIVINE
MANDATE IN ASIA

The beautiful harbor city of Ephesus served as a gateway between the East and West, garnering elite status as the most illustrious city in the Roman province of Asia and as a leading economic metropolis. Its prominence in the ancient world as "The Light of Asia" was further recognized by its notoriety as home to the largest temple of the cult of Artemis — one of the seven wonders of the world. In this prosperous and culturally diverse city, the apostle Paul and his team embraced the divine mandate to establish the Church of the Lord Jesus Christ in that region. The first congregation founded according to that mandate was the church of Ephesus, which the Lord Himself both commended for its patient, diligent works and rebuked for its diminished spiritual passion.

Chapter Three

THE CITY OF EPHESUS

In the year 52 AD, a ship appeared on the horizon of the Aegean Sea outside the immense manmade harbor at the legendary city of Ephesus. From outward appearances, no one could have ever known that this ship, which originally set sail from the lovely port city of Cenchrea in Greece, carried three passengers whose presence in Ephesus would eventually impact the entire region of Asia. It seemed to be just another of the thousands of ships that annually docked at this key port of the ancient world, but it most assuredly was *not* just another ship. The apostle Paul and the husband-wife team of Aquila and Priscilla were on board, and they were preparing to come ashore at Ephesus to inaugurate the most successful and notable phase of their ministries.

After sailing for many days, the moment had finally come for the apostle Paul and his team to arrive in Ephesus, one of the most sophisticated and pagan cities in the world at that time. This was a groundbreaking experience and a landmark moment in their ministries, for it seems that as yet, no church had been established in this illustrious city. This was apostolic ministry in the truest sense of the word, for these three God-sent ministers were entering a region where no one had gone before to establish the Church (*see* 2 Corinthians 10:14-16).

ARRIVAL AT THE GREAT HARBOR OF EPHESUS

From the Aegean Sea, the ship sailed five miles up the Cayster River to reach the Harbor of Ephesus. ❶ As it entered the harbor, the ship

Left: This ancient mosaic depicts cargo ships that traveled to major ports in seaside cities of the Roman Empire. When the apostle Paul, Aquila, and Priscilla came to Ephesus in 52 AD, they arrived in a similar Roman ship that had carried them from the port city of Cenchrea in Greece. Disembarking at the famous Harbor of Ephesus, the apostolic team then made their way past the Harbor Bathhouse and Harbor Marketplace, through the Harbor Gate, and onto the dazzling white marble boulevard that led them to the heart of the city.

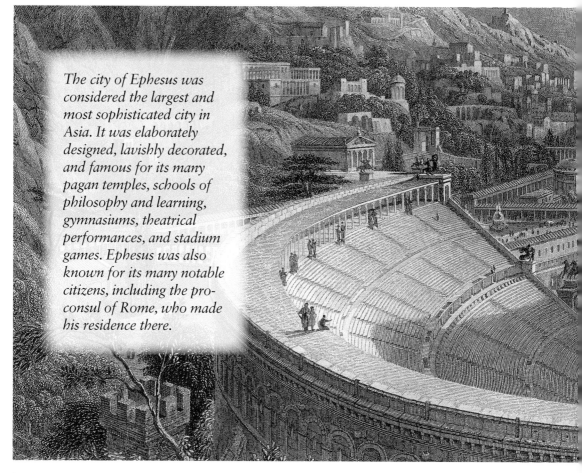

The city of Ephesus was considered the largest and most sophisticated city in Asia. It was elaborately designed, lavishly decorated, and famous for its many pagan temples, schools of philosophy and learning, gymnasiums, theatrical performances, and stadium games. Ephesus was also known for its many notable citizens, including the pro-consul of Rome, who made his residence there.

began to slow its speed in preparation for docking. It is likely that Paul, Aquila, and Priscilla stood on the deck and looked toward the distant city in anticipation of their arrival.

From the deck, Paul could look up and see the Hellenistic Barracks, **2** located on the mountaintop to the right of the harbor. These ancient barracks were built in the Third Century BC and were used as a monitoring post to regulate the incoming and outgoing ships. Paul and his team may have been as amazed as tourists are today to see how close the barracks sit to the rim of the mountain.

Some scholars assert that Paul himself was later incarcerated in those Hellenistic Barracks.[1] If that is true, Paul certainly didn't realize as he first gazed upon the sight that one day in the not-so-distant future, he himself would be held there as a prisoner for the Gospel.

The ship drew closer and closer to the port, making it possible for the team to make out the faint outline of the Great Theater of Ephesus, spreading out like a mighty fan across the hill at the top of the marble harbor boulevard. It would have been natural for Paul, Aquila, and Priscilla to feel excitement as they anticipated their

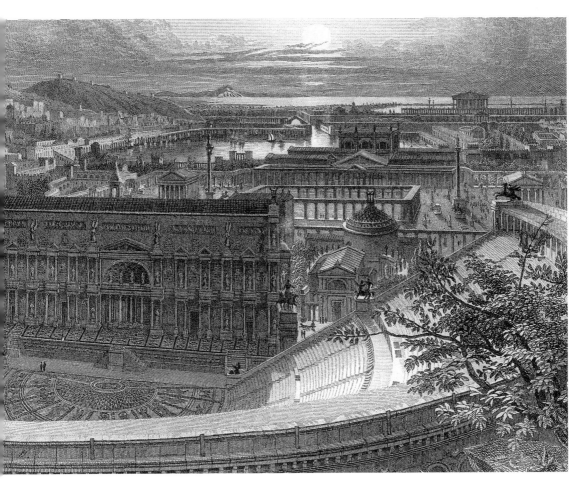

imminent arrival to the city. So many challenges and momentous victories awaited Paul in Ephesus — most of which were unknown to him as he arrived to start his ministry there.

'THE GATEWAY TO ASIA'

The enormous Harbor of Ephesus was known far and wide throughout the Roman Empire. Because it was a manmade harbor, it was renowned as a great achievement of human engineering. Nearly 800 years earlier, this entire area had been a natural bay for the Aegean Sea. But the bay had filled up over many centuries of silting, leaving the Cayster River as the only natural outlet to the Aegean Sea.[2]

During the Third and Second Century BC, several rulers of Asia Minor, including Lysimachus,[3] Eumenes II, and Attalus II,[4] each played their roles in deepening the Harbor of Ephesus and widening the Cayster River to make way for multiple ships to forge their way from the Aegean Sea to Ephesus' port. At one point the far inland end of the river was massively widened to approximately 1,500 feet so that more than 100 ships could be docked at the port at one time.

Right: Roman ships served various functions. Some were used for warfare in the Roman naval forces; others were used primarily as cargo ships; and other smaller and lighter ships were used for the transport of passengers. Although cargo ships transported goods to other cities throughout the Roman Empire, passengers could also travel on cargo ships that were destined for their desired port. This illustration depicts a Roman merchant ship (left) sailing past a Roman warship. The shape of the warship and the multiple tiers of rowers allowed it to move at amazing rates of speed. This ship has two tiers of rowers; later versions of this type of ship were larger and had additional tiers. It is very possible that when Paul and his team sailed to Ephesus, they traveled on a ship similar to one of the ships pictured here.

Once completed, the Harbor of Ephesus proved to be one of the most profitable harbors in the entire Roman Empire. Because of the unending flow of ships that docked at this port with goods from abroad, Ephesus became known as "The Gateway to Asia"[5] — the largest trading center and one of the biggest cities in Asia.

On that landmark day in 52 AD when a particular ship arrived carrying an apostolic team ready to launch their God-ordained mission in Asia, the famous Harbor of Ephesus was literally filled with large sailing vessels. Approximately 30 years before Paul's team arrived at Ephesus, Strabo, the famous Roman geographer and historian, recorded that the artificial Harbor of Ephesus was beginning to fill up with silt and sediment that poured into it from upstream, making navigation into the harbor increasingly difficult.[6] However, at the time Paul arrived in Ephesus, ships were still forging their way to the port to unload goods for the markets of this busy commercial center.

PREPARING TO DISEMBARK

At long last, the ship docked at Ephesus' port, and Paul, Aquila, and Priscilla began to experience the sights, sounds, and smells that were so typical of ports of the day. Sailors unloaded cargo — boxes, huge clay vessels, nets, etc. — piling everything in heaps on the pavement just beyond their ship. Paul and his companions lined up with the rest of the passengers and crew as they prepared to disembark.

the long walk up the marble harbor boulevard, which would take them into one of the most splendid cities in all of Asia. At long last, they were going to see this remarkable city as a ministry team on assignment for the Kingdom of God.

A MASS CONVERGENCE OF CULTURES

No cultural lesson could have ever prepared Paul and his companions for the sights they were about to behold. Paul was from the university town of Tarsus — a very rich and sophisticated city in its own right. But in those first moments when Paul and his team stepped off the ship and began to experience the famed city of Ephesus, they would have beheld sights that literally overwhelmed both their physical senses and their minds as the magnitude of their divine assignment began to dawn on them.

All around the port, the three would have seen ships from every imaginable part of the Roman Empire, flying flags of different colors and displaying various insignias on the tall masts. This was a common sight in Ephesus, for ships sailed into the port every day around the clock from every part of the far-flung empire — Rome, Crete, Palestine, Carthage, Spain, Alexandria, Greece, and so on. The bulk of the ships were loaded with valuable cargo that would be transported to other cities on the well-constructed roads that led from Ephesus to other cities throughout Asia.

Because of this amazing port and the city's excellent road system, Ephesus had emerged as the biggest business center of the region, a place where money was

During the First Century AD, people came to Ephesus for various reasons. Some came to see friends and family. Others traveled to the city for trade and business. Still others came to worship in the pagan shrines or to study in the various schools of philosophy. Then there were those who came to make appeals in the legal courts of Ephesus, one of the foremost court systems in Asia. But Paul, Aquila, and Priscilla were there for *other* reasons. The Holy Spirit had led them to Ephesus to establish a ministry base that would dramatically impact the entire region with the message of the Gospel.

Excitement must have raced through the hearts and minds of these three as they gathered their belongings and prepared to exit the ship. They were about to start easily made.[7] Transportation of goods and the accessibility to other cities were two reasons Ephesus had earned its title as "The Gateway to Asia." These were also major contributing factors to the immense wealth and prosperity that had come to this city and the reason it boasted the highest standard of living in all of Asia.

Paul and his team were about to see this plush treasure trove themselves for the first time. Not only would they see Ephesus' physical wealth, but they were also about to experience a rich collage of different nationalities, cultures, and languages — probably far more diversity than they had encountered in any other single place.

Once off the ship, the three merged with the crowd as people bumped and jostled each other in a common effort to forge their way to the Harbor Gate. Paul, Aquila, and Priscilla could hear people speaking a wide variety of languages — Latin, Aramaic, Hebrew, Greek, and Egyptian, just to mention a few. Paul, who was a master of languages, probably heard languages and dialects he had never encountered and didn't recognize. The three team members would have been immediately struck with the reality that they had just stepped into a place where the entire civilized world seemed to converge in one spot.

'THE LIGHT OF ASIA'

In New Testament times, Ephesus was the fourth greatest city in the world. The first was *Rome*; the second was *Alexandria*; the third was *Antioch*;

(Continued on page 150)

AUGUSTUS CAESAR

The Emperor Augustus was born in 63 BC with the given name of Gaius Octavius. His mother was the daughter of Julia, who was the sister of Julius Caesar. When Octavius was four years old, his father died. In the years that followed, Octavius became a special interest of his great-uncle Julius Caesar.

Young Octavius took his first step toward assuming power in Rome after the vicious murder of Julius Caesar in 44 BC by members of the Roman Senate. Mark Antony, Caesar's right-hand man, tried to seize the moment to take power into his own hands. However, when Julius Caesar's will was read, it was revealed that Octavius had been chosen as Caesar's heir. A chaotic struggle for power ensued over the next several years. Octavius (hereafter called Octavian) and Antony eventually agreed to form a three-man military dictatorship, called the Second Triumvirate, with a third Caesarian named Lepidus. Each of the three men controlled specific territories of the Roman Empire.

While Octavian consolidated his power in the Western Empire, Mark Antony illegally wed the Egyptian Queen Cleopatra in an attempt to strengthen his hold on the Eastern Empire. In 32 BC, Mark Antony made his famous political statement called the *Donations of Alexandria*, a proclamation that willed his various territories in the Roman Empire to his children borne by Cleopatra and that also made Caesarion, Julius Caesar's son by Cleopatra, Caesar's legitimate son and heir. Upon hearing of this proclamation, the Roman Senate was enraged, stripping Antony of his powers and declaring war on Cleopatra and her forces. This proclamation also caused an irreparable breach between Octavian and Mark Antony. Civil war erupted, and Octavian was ultimately victorious when his ships and troops defeated Antony's army at the Battle of Actium. To avoid capture,

Mark Antony fled to Egypt — but one year later Octavian waged war against Egypt, and the capital city of Alexandria was conquered. To avoid public humiliation as prisoners of war, Mark Antony and Cleopatra both committed suicide. Thus ended the rule of the Egyptian Ptolemies, and Octavian became the indisputable leader of the Roman Empire. In 27 BC, the Senate gave him the official title of Augustus, meaning *exalted one*, and he became the first official Roman emperor.

After a long and prosperous reign, Augustus fell sick and died in 14 AD at the age of 75. It is said that while dying, he called for a mirror, combed his hair, freshened his face, and requested that his friends applaud him as he departed this life because he had played his role in life so well.

Augustus is known as the Caesar who gave a decree for all the world to be taxed at the time of the birth of Jesus Christ (*see* Luke 2:1). Because Augustus and his wife Livia produced no heir, a son by Livia's first marriage named Tiberius was chosen to succeed Augustus as the next Roman emperor. Augustus Caesar ruled the Roman Empire from 27 BC to 14 AD.

and the fourth was *Ephesus*.[8] Prosperous and sophisticated, Ephesus was considered one of the most precious jewels in the crown of the Roman Empire.

The official capital of Asia was Pergamum. However, Emperor Augustus was so captivated by the grandeur, sophistication, and intellectual atmosphere of Ephesus that he made it the official residence for the proconsul of Rome. Ephesus' influence was also demonstrated by the Roman law that required a new governor to disembark and enter the province of Asia from the Ephesian port when he came to take up office.[9] On the day Paul's team arrived, the crowd didn't realize three God-anointed preachers with great spiritual authority were arriving at that same port to take up office in Ephesus and inaugurate the rule of God's Kingdom in the region.

Ephesus was referred to as "The Light of Asia"[10] because it was known as a city of tolerance and a place of enlightenment where new ideas were birthed. This may

be another reason the Holy Spirit chose Ephesus as the base for Paul and his team.

However, this apostolic team was bringing the *true* light to Asia. In the days and years to come, demonized rulers would exert all their power to suffocate the light of the Gospel in Ephesus. But in the end, darkness would not have the power to overcome it (*see* John 1:5).

THE POPULATION BOOM OF ANCIENT EPHESUS

As Paul, Aquila, and Priscilla embarked on their tour of Ephesus, they observed all kinds of people — those with light skin, dark skin, and every other shade in between. The Greeks, Romans, and Egyptians had all formed particularly large communities in the city. Egyptians especially felt at home in Ephesus because there were so many pagan temples, and the luxurious lifestyle satisfied their taste for opulent living.

Even Antony and Cleopatra had spent the winter in Ephesus in 33 BC.[11] In fact,

Above: *Illustration of ancient Ephesus, referred to as "The Light of Asia."*

Above: Legend says that Mark Antony immediately fell in love with Cleopatra when they first met aboard her ship on the river Cnidus. However, it may have been the Egyptian queen's vast wealth that drew Antony to her. He needed riches to support his military ambitions, and Cleopatra needed Antony to achieve her political aspirations. In the end, they both committed suicide and are remembered as one of history's most famous love affairs.

some believe that the first Egyptian-style Temple of Serapis in Ephesus, which was later replaced with a larger temple, was originally built at the order of Cleopatra.

Right: The lifestyle of Mark Antony and Cleopatra was notorious for luxury and extravagance. While living together in Alexandria, they enjoyed excessively lavish living in an environment of decadence. The painting here depicts one of their banquets, where they were known to dissolve pearls in cups of wine. Because Ephesus had a large Egyptian community, Mark Antony and Cleopatra spent the winter there in the year 33 BC.

Left: The well-organized Roman army was the most ferocious fighting machine the world had ever witnessed. Soldiers typically were equipped with a loin belt, breastplate, lance, shield, sword, helmet, and a pair of greaves (to protect their legs). The relief shown here portrays the Praetorian Guard, an elite group of soldiers who were originally formed to serve as bodyguards for Augustus. The Praetorian Guard later emerged as the main military force to control the Roman capital. In addition to serving Roman emperors, these elite soldiers also protected regional governors in faraway provinces.

As the apostolic team kept walking toward the Harbor Gate, they couldn't help but notice a huge number of sailors. This was no surprise, since a harbor of such enormous size would require a multitude of sailors to maintain and sail the ships. However, the team members also couldn't help but notice the large number of Roman soldiers intermingled in the crowd everywhere they turned.

Because Ephesus was the residence of the proconsul of Rome — the highest official in all of Asia and the personal representative of the Roman emperor and the Senate — an especially large attachment of soldiers was stationed there to maintain order and defend the city. Ephesus was already known as a great city of business, intellect, and state-of-the-art innovation. However, the Roman proconsul's presence and residence in Ephesus also made it one of the empire's most important military strongholds in First Century Asia.

In most major Roman cities where large communities of sailors and soldiers were located, a large prostitution industry also flourished, and Ephesus was no exception. Present-day evidence in the ruins of the ancient city demonstrates how prevalent the Ephesian prostitution business was

Right: This is an engraved foot-print in the pavement of Marble Street, which some scholars assert is an ancient Roman advertisement to direct potential customers to the Central Brothel of Ephesus. As in most Roman cities, the prostitution business in Ephesus was both large and a significant contributor to the economy.

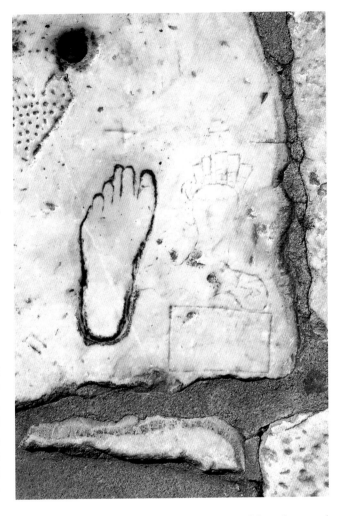

during New Testament times. In the pavement on the central Marble Street, a set of engraved footprints can be seen. Next to one of these footprints is the engraving of a stylish woman's face. Some suggest that this was an advertisement, informing potential clients that if they followed the footprints engraved in the pavement, the footprints would lead them to the Central Brothel, the city's primary place of prostitution, where sexual pleasure could be obtained for a price.[12]

First Century Ephesus also had a growing population of foreign laborers. The city was developing so quickly that there weren't enough local laborers to do manual construction. A large portion of the Ephesian population lived luxurious lives and therefore weren't given to hard labor, so they looked elsewhere for workers. As a result, immigrants came from far and wide to work on the city's monumental construction projects.

Another part of the growing population was the slave community of Ephesus.

As people had become wealthy, the need for more slaves had increased. So in addition to the common workers who flooded the city, the slave population had also swelled over the years.

All these factors contributed to the population boom that was occurring in Ephesus in 52 AD. By the time Paul, Aquila, and Priscilla arrived to fulfill their divine assignment for God's Kingdom, the city was "bursting at the seams."

(Continued on page 164)

SLAVERY IN THE GREEK AND ROMAN WORLD

Slavery was a common practice both in ancient Greek culture and later in the Roman Empire. In order to understand Greek slavery, one must first consider the form of slavery that existed in Athens, for this ancient city set the standard for slavery in all Greek-speaking lands.

In the Fifth Century BC, Athens had approximately 100,000 slaves, which was between one-third to one-half of the Athenian population. It was common for most Athenians to own at least one slave, except in the case of the very poor.[13] Slavery played such a significant role in ancient Greek societies that up to 20 percent of the entire population were slaves, the majority of which were women.[14]

Because slavery played such a vital part in Athenian society, it was generally believed that slaves should be treated with respect. It was rare for slaves to be beaten and even rarer for them to be executed by their owners. Slaves didn't only perform menial tasks; they could also be granted positions that included a high level of authority. For example, a slave could direct the business of a local shop on behalf of his owner, with the profits going to the owner. Slaves were often paid a minimal wage and were granted certain legal rights, including the right to take their masters into a court of law to request higher wages.[15]

Most Athenian slaves were born into slavery. However, if they performed faithfully for many years and were able to save enough money, they could purchase their freedom and gain the status of a "freed" person. To obtain this status was a difficult and lengthy process — and once it was granted, it came with fewer privileges than a person who had been born naturally free enjoyed. A newly freed person was given a status similar to an alien resident. Freed people were also forbidden to serve in governmental positions. Thus, foreign slaves who had been obtained as a result of war were prevented from holding positions of influence in matters of government,

Above: This ancient painting from a Greek plate depicts a slave carrying two vessels.

even if they earned their freedom at a later time. However, children born to a freed person were considered free from the moment of birth and were treated with the same honor that belonged to any natural-born citizen.[16]

The Greek philosopher Aristotle (384-322 BC) wrote briefly about slavery and about his convictions regarding people who were born into slavery in his influential book *Politics*, as well as in his other works. Aristotle suggested that those born as slaves had inferior intellects and were biologically designed to be slaves; therefore, it was best for them to live contented lives in their natural subservient condition.

The following quotes from Aristotle's works reveal his convictions about what has been termed "natural slavery":

"From the hour of their birth, some are marked out for subjugation, others for rule."[17]

"One who is a human being belonging by nature not to himself but to another is by nature a slave; and a person is a human being belonging to another if being a man he is an article of property, and an article of property is an instrument for action separable from its owner."[18]

"For he is by nature a slave who is capable of belonging to another (and that is why he does so belong), and who participates in reason so far as to apprehend it but not to possess it; for the animals other than man are subservient not to reason, by apprehending it, but to feelings." [19]

"Hence there are by nature various classes of rulers and ruled. For the free rules the slave, the male the female, and the man the child in a different way. And all possess the various parts of the soul, but possess them in different ways; for the slave has not got the deliberative part at all, and the female has it, but without full authority, while the child has it, but in an undeveloped form."[20]

Other schools of Greek philosophy disagreed with Aristotle and rejected the notion that men born into slavery were inferior. They did, however, believe that if one *was* a slave, his happiness depended on how well he or she performed in that capacity. They fiercely asserted that even if a slave physically and legally belonged to someone else, his soul remained free and could never become the property of a master. They adamantly wrote that slaves should be treated with respect and that their masters should care well for them.

Slavery in the Roman Empire found its roots in Greek slavery but was different in many ways. First, many more slaves existed in the Roman Empire than in earlier Greek times. Particularly during the time of the Emperor Augustus at the beginning of the First Century, the slave population escalated dramatically in the Roman Empire. The city of Rome alone had a slave population of between 300,000 and 350,000 during this time period. Since the entire population of Rome was approximately 1,000,000 people, this meant that slaves made up nearly 35 percent of the city's population. In all of Italy, there were approximately 2,000,000 slaves out of a total national population of 5,500,000 people.[21]

Wealthy Romans loathed physical labor of any kind and therefore became dependent on their slaves for even the most simple tasks. Getting dressed, holding a towel while a master washed his hands, pouring bath water to prepare for a master's bath, cooking and setting dishes on the table — *all* of these tasks were done for the wealthy class by slaves.

Whereas the majority of slaves among Greeks were women, in the Roman Empire, the majority of slaves were male.[22] There were also two different categories of slaves in the Roman world — *public slaves* and *private slaves*. Public slaves were owned by the state and were used in great numbers to assist in the massive building projects that were being constructed all over the empire. In addition, they were used as gladiators in public games and as chariot drivers for the chariots that traveled in great numbers on Roman roads. Public slaves also maintained city premises, served as caretakers for public buildings, were assistants to magistrates and priests, and performed dangerous or undesirable jobs such as working as firemen, jailers, and executioners.[23]

Private slaves were owned by private individuals or by private families and generally possessed less freedom than public slaves. If a person or a family privately owned a group of three or more slaves, those slaves were known as *familia*. Slaves who worked in a master's home or private villa in the countryside were referred to as *familia urbana*, and those who performed agricultural jobs were called *familia rustica*. According to a Roman writer named Gaius, "Slaves were in the power of their masters; in all nations the masters had the power of life and death over the slaves."[24]

Slavery was such an integral part of Roman society that slaves could be found in almost every realm of life, although they were forbidden to participate in the military or to hold governmental positions. Slaves were often very educated, and their gifts and talents were highly valued. Slaves of wealthy masters often held such trusted positions as household or palace stewards, secretaries, or financial managers — managing vast fortunes on behalf of their masters.

Highly educated slaves were frequently given the task of educating the children of rich Roman families.

Slaves were also assigned menial tasks that Romans considered too low for them to do themselves, especially tasks that included manual labor, which Romans despised. For slaves involved in manual labor, the average life expectancy was only 20 years.[25]

Similar to the Greek idea of slavery, Romans slaves were either *born* into slavery or *became* slaves due to a variety of circumstances. But unlike Greece, where only foreigners and people born into slavery could be slaves, even Roman citizens could become slaves under certain circumstances. Nevertheless, the primary source for new slaves in the Roman Empire was *not* children born into slavery, but foreigners who were captured in Rome's many military campaigns. These military conquests brought a constant stream of new slaves to stand on the auction blocks of Roman slave markets.[26] Such was the case for the slave market in Ephesus — one of the largest in the entire Roman Empire during the First Century.

Most Roman slave markets were disgusting and deplorable places, where human beings were paraded in front of potential buyers and then put on auction blocks to be sold to the highest bidder. But before this buying, selling, and trading of human beings commenced, prospective buyers were

Above: This stone engraving from the First Century depicts four slaves preparing their owner's hair. Slaves performed many functions, including personal assistance in their owners' private matters.

permitted to "inspect the merchandise."

For instance, a slave's value was largely determined by the condition of his teeth. If he had good teeth, he was probably in decent physical condition and therefore more expensive. If his teeth were rotten, he could be purchased for a lesser price. Therefore, a potential buyer would usually shove back a slave's head, force open his mouth, and inspect his teeth to see if they were decayed or in fairly good shape.

If a slave was going to be used in menial work requiring a great deal of physical abuse, potential buyers were allowed to spit in the slaves' faces, slap them, and even curse at them to see how much abuse the slave could endure. If a slave could swallow his pride, grit his teeth, and hold his temper during this humiliating abuse, it was assumed that he could be used for hard manual labor without giving his new owner a lot of trouble.

Physically, slaves looked so much like the rest of the population that at one point, the Roman Senate considered mandating that slaves wear special clothes to identify them as slaves. The only slaves that showed a difference in their appearance were those from the eastern regions of the empire, whose ears were pierced as a sign of their servitude.

However, each slave on the auction block wore a scroll around his neck that gave his name, his nationality, his character, and a written guarantee that he was free of disease and would not steal or run away. If a buyer purchased a slave who later proved defective, he could return the slave up to six months later and receive a refund of his purchase price.[27] Also, before the purchase was finalized, Roman law required that the slave be medically inspected to make sure he had no disease that could infect the purchaser's family or other slaves.[28]

Slaves could be purchased for a variety of prices — for as little as 500 denarii or for as much as 875,000

denarii — depending on their physical conditions and skills. A simple slave girl could be bought for 1,800 denarii, whereas a more beautiful slave girl could cost as much as 6,000 denarii.[29] Male slaves with a good physique, special skills, and higher education could cost enormous sums. Romans preferred male slaves to female slaves because men were physically able to do more tasks than women.

were considered a master's property, the master could also sell them, lend them to friends, or even rent them out to others.

Unlike Greeks who treated slaves with a measure of respect, slaves in the Roman Empire were often whipped and treated with cruelty. Roman philosopher Seneca tried to encourage the humane treatment of slaves, writing to masters: "It is strange that we should think it a good thing to send a poor unfortunate slave to prison. Why are we so anxious to beat him at once and break his legs? We should wait until our anger has cooled off before fixing a punishment.... For we punish by sword and execution, chains, imprisonment, and starvation a crime that deserves only a light beating."[30]

Roman slaves did have one unique legal right, although it was difficult to enforce: the right to practice their own religion. For example, if a master worshiped one god and his slave worshiped another god, the slave had the legal right to worship as he wished. This was particularly important for the growing Christian Church, which was, at least in the early years, primarily comprised of people from local slave populations.

This law allowed Christians to practice their own faith; however, problems nonetheless arose because

Once a slave had been purchased — or once a person had surrendered himself to become a slave in order to escape criminal prosecution or to repay a debt — he was thenceforth considered the legal property of his master. In the Roman world, a slave owner could do anything he wished with his slaves: He could also abuse them, molest them, or even kill them if he wished to do so. Since slaves

Above: This mosaic from Carthage depicts a slave carrying food on a large platter to a banquet. If slaves proved themselves talented and faithful, they could be assigned to great positions of authority in a home. On the other hand, if found inferior, they were assigned to manual work. Some slaves were highly educated and served as secretaries, household stewards, or financial managers for their owners. Rich homes could afford many slaves.

everyone in the Roman Empire was required to worship the emperor. Although slaves had the right to privately worship as they wished, they still were required to publicly recognize the divinity of the emperor, or their disobedience to Roman law would eventually result in persecution. Hence, their supposed right to worship as they wished wasn't entirely real.

As mentioned earlier, it was possible for a person to sell himself into a life of slavery in order to escape punishment for criminal activities. And if a man was in debt and unable to pay his bills, he could also pay the debt by surrendering himself as a slave to his creditor. This practice was never legally validated, but it still occurred with some regularity in Roman society.

By law, slaves were not permitted to own anything. Even the clothes they wore didn't legally belong to them. However, they *were* permitted to earn a small wage that they were legally allowed to save.[31] If a slave was able to save a sufficient amount of money, he could attempt to purchase his freedom and thereby become a "freedman" — if his master agreed to allow it. This was the case with the two famous servants *Mazeus* and *Mithridates*, two freedmen who constructed the great Mazeus and Mithridates Gate in the center of Ephesus as a dedication to their former owners who had allowed them to purchase their freedom (for further information, *see* pages 210-212).

Because of their regular close contact, relationships between masters and their domestic slaves were often more reciprocal than other master-slave relationships. It wasn't even uncommon for close friendships to develop between household slaves and their masters over a period of years. Although it's true that Romans often treated their slaves harshly, it's also true that many Romans frequently granted freedom to slaves who were growing older and had served faithfully for many years. This possibility that their masters might eventually grant them freedom encouraged slaves to remain obedient and to prove themselves faithful.

If a master freed his slave, this gave the former slave a measure of liberty but did not guarantee him Roman citizenship. On the other hand, freedom that was granted by a city magistrate did provide a freedman with full Roman citizenship. However, even as Roman citizens, freedmen were still not allowed to hold public office, nor were their children allowed this right.

It has been suggested that the slave population in Asia was greater in numbers than in any other part of the Roman Empire. For instance, it is believed that out of Pergamum's entire population, up to 40 percent of the local residents were slaves![32] Since Pergamum was the capital of Asia, it is quite possible that this assessment is fairly accurate, for it certainly would have required a huge

Above: This detailed relief depicts a slave bowed low in servitude, but then standing upright and shaking the hand of his former master who has granted his freedom from slavery. When slaves were freed, they were called freedmen. They often remained bound to their former owners out of gratitude for their freedom, demonstrating that gratitude by taking their former owners' names.

slave population to maintain and care for the vast number of public and imperial buildings that filled the capital city.

THE CHALLENGE OF SLAVERY IN THE CHRISTIAN COMMUNITY

The subject of slavery is addressed frequently in the New Testament, especially in Paul's and Peter's epistles (*see* Ephesians 6:5-9; Colossians 3:22, 4:1; 1 Timothy 6:1,2; Titus 2:9,10; 1 Peter 2:18-22). The abundance of verses in the New Testament that deal with the issue of slaves and masters tells us that both slaves and slave owners were believers and members of early local churches.

You can imagine the daunting challenges Early Church pastors faced as they endeavored to spiritually lead both masters and slaves in a single congregation. Normally masters and slaves would never co-mingle in a social context. However, in the local church, all class distinctions disappeared. This is the reason Paul wrote that in Christ, there is "neither bond nor free" (*see* Galatians 3:28; Colossians 3:11).

Although it seems there were many slave owners *and* slaves among the early believers, it is also clear that these class distinctions didn't exist within the framework of the Church. At home, the slave owner was the master and his slave was a slave, and this distinction maintained a measure of separation between the two groups of people. But in the local church, this distinction was

so obliterated that Acts 13:1 mentions two men that most theologians believe were slaves — "Simeon, called Niger, and Lucius, or Cyrene" — who publicly served right alongside Barnabas. It also mentions Manean, a wealthy Roman who had been raised with the tetrarch Herod, and Saul, who would later be called the apostle Paul.

It was revolutionary to think that men of this high caliber would publicly serve in the same group as slaves. However, in Christ these distinctions

Left: Slavery was an accepted part of life in the Roman Empire of biblical times. This First Century fresco depicts a slave combing her young mistress's hair.

but Paul pled for mercy for the new convert. Paul told Philemon, "For perhaps he therefore departed for a season, that thou shouldest receive him for ever; not now as a servant, but above a servant, a brother beloved, specially to me, but how much more unto thee, both in the flesh, and in the Lord" (Philemon 1:15,16).

Although New Testament Scripture doesn't condone slavery, the verses that deal with the issue of slave owners and slaves never once encourage believing slaves to rebel against their masters or to demand their freedom. Rather, slaves are exhorted to perform their tasks as unto the Lord, while believing slave owners are commanded to treat their slaves with kindness and not to forget that their own Master — the Lord in Heaven — is watching to see how well they do so.

All of these scriptures gave guidance to early pastors and their congregations and helped slave owners and slaves learn to live together in a faith community. This was a very needed message in the Roman world of the First Century, where up to 30 percent of the population was comprised of slaves.

were erased, even if they continued to be recognized outside the local church. In the world, such fellowship between free men and slaves was rare indeed — but in Christ and in His Church, all men are equal before God.

The book of Philemon is entirely dedicated to instructing a believing slave owner named Philemon on how to respond to a runaway slave named Onesimus, who repented and came to faith in Christ. Legally Philemon had the right to severely punish Onesimus,

This illustration gives an indication of what the Harbor Gate, surrounded by the city of Ephesus may have originally looked like in the First and Second Century AD. Serving as the port entrance to the city, this ancient gate was an architectural wonder that caused newcomers to stand and gaze upon it in awe.

Above: This photo shows the western end of the marble boulevard called the Arcadiane, which began where the Harbor Gate once stood and led to the base of the Great Theater. Today overgrown trees and shrubs now stand where people once passed under the arches of this monumental gate.

BUILDINGS AT THE HARBOR

As Paul and his team disembarked from the ship and began observing their immediate surroundings, they could see an early marketplace that was later replaced in approximately 150 AD. This was officially called the Harbor *Agora*, which means the Harbor Marketplace. ❸

There were three official marketplaces in the city:

- One located at the harbor, known for the buying and selling of slaves.

- One near the Great Theater, which was the marketplace for the central city where bulk supplies could be purchased at discount prices.

- One in the upper part of the city, which was filled with specialty goods and services primarily for the extremely wealthy class of Ephesus.

The Harbor Marketplace was the one Paul and his team observed as they walked toward the Harbor Gate. This marketplace wasn't only a place of commerce; it was also one of the largest slave markets in the entire civilized world at that time. The business of buying and selling slaves was considered too dirty to be conducted in the middle of a great city and was therefore carried out on the outskirts near the harbor. In this particular Harbor *Agora*, countless slaves had been put on display and sold in the years preceding the arrival of Paul and his team.

The New Testament word for "redemption" comes from the Greek word *agoridzo*, which evolved from the word *agora*, the Greek word for *the marketplace where slaves were purchased*. At the time Paul arrived in Ephesus, this city was noted as one of the largest centers of slave trade in the First Century. Therefore, when Ephesian believers later read Paul's epistle to them and saw the word "redemption" — the Greek word *agoridzo* — it was a term they would have particularly understood.

The abundance of slaves in Ephesus also sheds light on the reason Paul addressed "masters" and "servants" in Ephesians 6:5. He said, "Servants, be obedient to them that are your masters according to the flesh, with fear and trembling, in singleness of your heart, as unto Christ." When the church was birthed and began to grow in Ephesus, many of the first believers were slaves who had been bought and sold in the very marketplace that Paul, Aquila, and Priscilla walked past upon their arrival in the city. It probably didn't occur to the three at that moment, but many of their future church members would come from this dreadful place.

This would also hold true in the churches that would later be birthed throughout Asia. A substantial number of the first Christians were slaves, and many of these members of the Early Church remained slaves even after they became believers.

THE HARBOR GATE

Past the Harbor Marketplace, Paul, Aquila, and Priscilla approached the great Harbor Gate, ❹ which was the official entrance to Ephesus from the port. It was an arched gate with massive columns crafted of beautifully carved stone. Impressive structures such as this one were often placed at entry points to an ancient city for the purpose of instilling a sense of awe in newcomers as they entered the city.

The Harbor Gate that existed at the time of Paul's arrival was eventually replaced by an even greater structure, possibly constructed during the reign of Septimus Severus (193-211 AD). Nevertheless, the gate that Paul and his team walked through was a marvelous sight to see. Those who passed through this highly decorated arched entry to Ephesus were awestruck by the detail, workmanship, and variety of historical figures and events carved in its relief sculptures.

As the three visitors walked through the Harbor Gate, the grandeur of Ephesus must have taken their breath away. Their eyes fell upon the immense white marble boulevard that lay before them, lined with covered colonnades and supported with magnificent columns. In the distance at the far end of the boulevard, they could see the famous Great Theater of Ephesus spread out across the mountain slope. They had seen the theater from a distance when their ship was approaching, but now that they were much closer, they could begin to comprehend its massive dimensions. The whole scene that was spread before these three companions must have dazzled them.

THE ARCADIANE

This spectacular white marble boulevard was 1,800 feet in length, 35 feet wide, and lined with approximately 200 columns fashioned from marble. From where Paul, Aquila, and Priscilla stood, the boulevard must have looked endless, going all the way from the Harbor Gate to the steps that led up to the Great Theater.

As Paul stood on that marble boulevard, he must have gazed in amazement at the Great Theater in front of him. He didn't know that in three years, thousands of idol worshipers would gather in that same theater to raise their voices against him and his companions in the ministry (*see* Acts 19:24-41). In those first moments in the city, Paul gazed at the theater as an admirable architectural feat, not as the place where he'd one day be challenged and ultimately driven from the city.

Eventually the boulevard became known as the Arcadiane ❺ because it was restored by the order of Emperor Arcadius (395-408 AD) and was subsequently renamed in his honor.[33] But when Paul, Aquila, and Priscilla arrived in 52 AD, the long boulevard, made of pure white marble, was still in its stunning original state.

The decorations along this pristine marble boulevard were lavish — letting newcomers know they had entered a city of great wealth and power. It must have been mind-boggling for Paul's team as they walked up this boulevard for the first time. Both sides of the street were lined with a long row of *stoas* — long, covered colonnades ❻ that followed the entire length of the Arcadiane on both sides — all the way from where it began at the Harbor Gate to where it ended at the base of

the Great Theater. The colonnade roof was covered with terracotta tiles laid atop heavy beams. The beams came at a downward angle from the colonnade's upper back wall, resting on hand-carved capitals that crowned 200 magnificent pillars.

Modern excavations of these covered colonnades attest to the wealth that

Left: This glorious marble avenue became known as the Arcadiane after its restoration was ordered by the Emperor Arcadius (395-408 AD). Its wide array of shops, columns, mosaic sidewalks, and statues that lined each side of the boulevard gave the impression of great wealth to people entering Ephesus for the first time. After Paul and his team disembarked from the ship that had brought them from Cenchrea, they walked on this harbor boulevard as they entered the city. The Arcadiane was flanked on both sides with approximately 200 columns fashioned of granite and marble, and it concluded at the steps that led up to the Great Theater of Ephesus.

It must have been astonishing to Paul, Aquila, and Priscilla to see this kind of exquisite craftsmanship on the floors of a side-street market!

The colonnades were filled with people shopping in specialty shops that carried exquisite products and goods brought to the city on ships from abroad. Souvenirs, miniature idols, amulets, magic inscriptions written on scrolls, and a wealth of other goods could be purchased in the shops. Interspersed between the shops were statues of Greek and Roman leaders, historians, poets, writers, and musicians. Elegance and graceful adornments abounded everywhere the human eye could see. And because of an inscription unearthed by an archeological excavation near the Great Theater, we know that this marvelous marble boulevard was even lighted at night with two rows of torches.

existed in the ancient city of Ephesus. The floors of these colonnades have been unearthed, revealing fabulous mosaics of a quality rivaling works of art found in grand palaces. Yet Ephesus was so lavish that these incredible mosaics were *part of the pavement* for those who shopped under the roofs of the covered colonnades.

Above: *These majestic bulls with garlands adorned altars that were stationed at the entrance of Domitian's Harbor Bathhouse, located alongside the Arcadiane in the city of Ephesus.*

THE HARBOR BATHHOUSE

As Paul and his companions walked up the Arcadiane, they would have noticed a beautiful gate that led to the Harbor Bathhouse. ❼ This huge complex preceded an even larger bathhouse that would later be built by the Emperor Domitian. The ruins of Domitian's Harbor Bathhouse, the dimensions of which were 480 feet by 510 feet, bear witness that the massive structure was fabulous almost beyond belief. Nevertheless, the earlier Harbor Bathhouse Paul and his team observed that day was located right on the edge of the harbor and was very important for health reasons.

It was customary for people arriving at the city by ship to immediately go to the Harbor Bathhouse to cleanse themselves. Because people had a general awareness of a connection between cleanliness and sickness, this rule was applied as a way of making sure no diseases were carried into the city of Ephesus. Therefore, it is likely that Paul and his team, along with all other passengers, went directly to this bathhouse to cleanse themselves before entering this city where a large proportion of the population was lavishly dressed and adorned.

MARBLE STREET AND THE PLATEIA IN CORESSUS

Although the Arcadiane came to a dead end at the base of the Great Theater, it was also at that juncture where it actually intersected with a new street. Now the pedestrian had three choices: 1) He could walk up the steps to the entrance of the Great Theater; 2) he could turn right and walk on a road officially named

Above: The Harbor Bathhouse was impressive both in magnitude and in elegance. The ruins that remain today are of a huge bathhouse built during the rule of the Emperor Domitian. This larger complex was built on the site of an even more ancient bathhouse that stood when Paul and his team arrived in Ephesus. Domitian's Harbor Bathhouse was famous throughout Asia Minor because of its immense size, its lavish decorations, and its exquisite pieces of sculpture and art.

Right: This is an artist's rendering of how the interior of Domitian's Harbor Bathhouse probably looked, based on bathhouses that were built in other cities of the Roman Empire.

Marble Street, ❽ which led to a school of philosophy built on the site where the Celsus Library stands today; or 3) he could turn left and follow the street called the Plateia in Coressus, ❾ which led to the Stadium of Ephesus and eventually to the Temple of Artemis. This crossroad gave every pedestrian the choice of *entertainment* in the Great Theater, *education* at the school of philosophy, or *bloodshed* in the stadium.

Regardless of which direction a person chose to take, both Marble Street and the Plateia in Coressus Street were generously adorned with columns. The columns were 33 feet high, fashioned of marble or granite, and crowned with hand-carved Corinthian and Ionian capitals that rested on their tops like graceful tiaras. These columns symmetrically lined both sides of the street, and at sporadic intervals between the columns were both idols and statues of honored citizens. In fact, the number of idols and statues on display would have seemed too numerous for the three visitors to count as they gazed down these streets in both directions.

Idols and statues were carved from white marble and sculpted to precisely replicate human form in every detail. On display in our modern museums, these statues show only white marble. But at the time Paul, Aquila, and Priscilla arrived in Ephesus, they were painted to give them a lifelike impression. Hair was painted to look real — so real that a viewer might feel

Left: These steps lead up to the Great Theater of Ephesus, where approximately 24,000 people could be accommodated at public events.

like he could actually reach out and run his fingers through it. The flesh was perfectly painted to give the impression of real flesh instead of stone. If idols and statues were adorned with clothes, those clothes were painted in rich detail to look just like actual clothing made out of fabric.

Especially in the part of the world dominated by Greek society, the naked human body was often portrayed in art. The walls of palaces and temples all over ancient Greek lands were adorned with reliefs depicting naked men and women. If women were portrayed in sculpture, they were usually clothed statues of honored women, such as wives of emperors; half-dressed statues of Amazons (legendary women warriors reputed to have founded Ephesus' first ancient settlement); or goddesses, many of whom were portrayed half-dressed or naked.

Certainly some men were portrayed in Greek art with elements of clothing, but Greeks particularly loved to display men from every level of life in nudity, representing them with excellent physiques because the human body had virtually become an object of worship. In fact, during classical Greek times, the rule was that men should always be depicted as muscular and strong. For this reason, nearly all sculptures of men from that period depict naked men with ideal, perfect physiques.

For Paul, Aquila, and Priscilla, the Greeks' artistic display of nakedness must have been deplorable and disturbing. As Jews, these three had been instructed from childhood that the human body was holy and that public nudity was an offense to God. And since these images still retained the original paint, one can imagine how

174

objectionable the sight must have been to Paul and his companions.

For the Gospel preachers, these idols and statues must have been deeply offensive. The sight must have given Paul and his team a deeper revelation of the rampant depravity in the city, as well as the enormous challenge set before them: to convert pagans to Christ and then to teach them to withdraw from the wicked lifestyle to which they were accustomed so they could begin living a life of holiness that pleased God.

When Paul and his team reached the crossroad at the base of the Great Theater, they could have looked both directions and seen hundreds of these flesh-colored statues and idolatrous monuments lining the street to their right and to their left.

The team had come to Ephesus knowing that the city was spiritually dark. Nonetheless, they also knew that God had called them there and that His grace mightily abounds where sin and wickedness has previously ruled (*see* Romans 5:20). In the years following the historic arrival of this apostolic team, God's grace would indeed abound mightily in this place where wickedness had reigned since the city's inception thousands of years earlier.

Below: Romans admired sculptures chiseled by ancient Greek masters who had perfected the human body in stone, so they made new copies of Greek statues and displayed them in pivotal locations throughout the Roman Empire. The Lancelotti Discobolous *pictured here represents the kinds of statues that once adorned the now-vacant pedestals on the Arcadiane and the Plateia in Coressus in the city of Ephesus.*

Left: The Plateia in Coressus was a beautiful road paved with marble and lined with 33-foot-tall columns fashioned of marble and granite. Interspersed between the columns were pedestals on which stood statues of honored residents, emperors, and gods. The Plateia in Coressus started at the top of the Arcadiane and meandered to the entrance of the Great Stadium — a massive complex where public games were performed before nearly 30,000 spectators.

Above: This photo shows the back wall of the Stadium of Ephesus — a stadium so huge that its arena was approximately eight square acres in size. It may be that the apostle Paul fought wild beasts in this very stadium, as indicated in First Corinthians 15:32.

Above: These are the original seats in the Stadium of Ephesus. Thousands of spectators regularly gathered in this massive stadium and sat on these very seats to watch a variety of games and to cheer as human beings were slaughtered for the sake of entertainment.

THE STADIUM OF EPHESUS

Standing at the end of the Arcadiane, Paul, Aquila, and Priscilla could have turned right onto Marble Street that led to the school of philosophy or turned left onto the Plateia in Coressus Street that would lead them to the Great Stadium of Ephesus. ⓾ If they walked the long road to the stadium, they would have passed pillars, statues, idols,

Left: Main entrance to the Great Stadium of Ephesus

Below: Gladiators, animals, and victims all entered the arena from this entrance. Gladiators who were killed during the games were afterward carried through this same entrance to be buried in mass graves located a short distance from the Stadium of Ephesus.

Below: When gladiators died in the Stadium of Ephesus, their bodies were carried behind the east end of the arena to be buried in gladiator graves. In recent years, these mass graves were excavated, revealing new insights about the lives and deaths of Roman gladiators, including information about the physical wounds they suffered because of their profession.

Above: All Roman stadiums had the same basic elements. This sketch depicts the tunnels, underground passageways, and trapdoors in the floor of the Roman Coliseum's arena. The Coliseum had 76 entrances through which spectators could quickly enter and exit the five tiers of seats, which were covered with a massive canopy designed to protect patrons from the harsh, hot sunlight. When the Roman emperor attended events, he proceeded into the Coliseum through a highly ornamented, beautifully painted entrance and took his seat in the Emperor's Box near the center of the stadium.

monuments, and shops that sat just behind the sidewalks on both sides of the street.

The Stadium of Ephesus was an impressive structure by any measure. Built in the Third Century BC, it had already served the people of Ephesus for nearly 300 years. Just a few years after Paul's arrival in Ephesus, the Emperor Nero gave the order to have this stadium enlarged to accommodate 30,000 spectators.[34] The deep impression where the stadium arena was once located encompasses eight square acres, providing us with an idea of the stadium's massive size at the height of its glory.

Spectators regularly filled the seats of the Stadium of Ephesus to watch chariot races, to shout and cheer at the blood-splattering gladiatorial fights, or to watch aggressive wild beasts attack and devour human beings. The sound of many thousands of spectators lifting their voices and thunderously shouting — combined with the reverberating noise of the crowd's feet stomping and pounding on the stadium's stone floors — would echo loudly across

Right: Every stadium had a special entrance for notable public figures to use. This entrance to the Coliseum was designed to receive emperors and dignitaries. Its vaulted ceiling was covered with beautifully carved and painted relief sculptures.

the marble streets and bounce off the stone structures of the city. Even people on ships in the harbor who were still far from land would be able to hear the raucous noise of the stadium crowds.

Chariot racing was extremely exciting and considered to be one of the greatest sports of the First Century. All over the Roman Empire, stadiums filled to capacity on the days of chariot races. It was big business and attracted enormous crowds. The deafening roars of the crowd would become louder and louder as people cheered, yelled, and furiously screamed at the chariots racing around the track.

Gladiatorial fights were also conducted in the Stadium of Ephesus, although they were usually conducted at the east end of the arena, where approximately 10,000 people could gather to watch the fights. If such fights were taking place when Paul and his companions entered the city, they surely would have heard sounds familiar to the citizens of Ephesus: thousands of people gasping in horror, falling silent, and then suddenly erupting with shouts of elation as gladiators sunk their weapons into their victims' bodies, causing more blood to spill onto the floor of the arena.

Such gladiatorial fights were especially popular in cities that had large communities of soldiers or veterans. Since Ephesus had a significant soldier population, this may explain why these fights were so popular in that city.

Gladiatorial fights amounted to cold-blooded butchery — a bloodbath that left carnage in piles on the arena floor. Like sportsmen hunting prey, these gladiators marched into the ring to slaughter prisoners, kill slaves, and murder victims who had fallen out of favor with local authorities. When a day of fighting was finished and the crowd rose to go home, the sand on the arena floor was literally soaked with the blood of the dead. During Paul's time — as well as during the seasons of Roman persecution that occurred at intervals throughout the next few centuries — it is believed that precious believers were dragged into this arena to die at the hands of such gladiators.

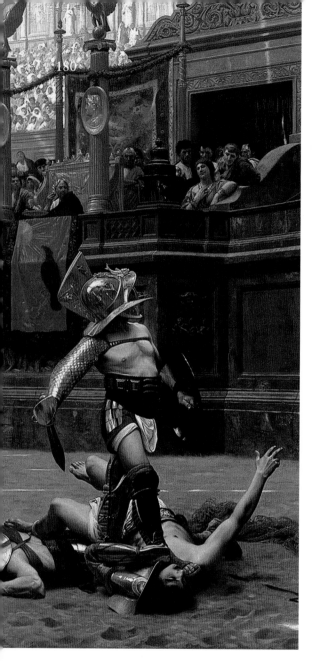

180

Dressed in helmets, armor, and shields, gladiators used axes, spears, swords, tridents, and nets to horrifically attack the defenseless unarmed men and women who stood before them. It was brutal, but the crowds loved it — and whatever the crowds of the Roman Empire loved, the emperor made sure they got it. Games were conducted frequently to quench the bloodthirsty hunger of the masses. Since local authorities were entrusted with the job of executing condemned criminals, they used gladiator games as the public instrument to carry out executions, thereby turning the killing of the condemned into entertainment. Especially during the reigns of Nero and Domitian, blood flowed freely in the Stadium of Ephesus and in stadiums throughout the empire.

The pagan crowds also loved to watch wild beasts pounce on defenseless victims to maul and eat them alive. The crowds were thrilled when hidden doors on the floor of the arena suddenly opened and dangerous animals rushed into the stadium from unexpected directions to take victims by surprise. Lions, tigers, leopards, bears, boars, and wild dogs attacked, mutilated, and devoured people's flesh right before the eyes of the ticket-purchasing crowd.

Did Paul, Aquila, and Priscilla arrive just in time to hear the eruptions of the roaring crowd as it reacted to the sight of blood and gore being spilled onto the arena floor? Is it possible that they watched slaves carry the dead bodies of gladiators out of the arena on stretchers, to be thrown like garbage into the mass graves ⓫ located just beyond the back wall of the stadium? It certainly *is* possible that these things were happening at the very moment the apostolic team arrived in Ephesus on that historic day.

181

Above: Horrendous forms of torture and death were inflicted on believers during Nero's reign, including forcing them into stadium arenas to face gladiators, throwing them to wild animals to be eaten alive, or crucifying them. Many Christians were dipped in pitch, tied to stakes, and then set on fire.

In Asia, there were stadiums in Ephesus, Smyrna, Laodicea, and Hierapolis, as well as in other Asia cities — and in each of these stadiums, such games took a high toll on human life. During the reigns of Nero (54-68 AD) and Domitian (81-96 AD), persecution against Christians was at an all-time high. Faithful believers were forced into the stadiums to face gladiators or to fight wild beasts. And at each event, crowds rose to their feet and shouted with great enthusiasm at the sight of the Christians' blood.

Roman historian Tacitus wrote of the persecution that befell believers during Nero's reign, saying, "...They [Christian believers] were covered with wild beasts' skins and torn to death by dogs; or they were fastened on crosses, and when daylight failed were burned to serve as lamps by night."[35]

In First Corinthians 15:32 (*NASB*), Paul told his readers that he "...fought with wild beasts at Ephesus." Some scholars assert that this reference to fighting wild beasts was allegorical language only, since no record of such a fight exists in the book of Acts. They also contend that a literal interpretation is unlikely because it was considered unlawful for a Roman citizen to be put in the arena with wild beasts. These scholars assert that Paul was referring to betrayers, deceivers, or even Judiazers when he wrote about "wild beasts."

However, although Paul was a Roman citizen, it is a fact that he was forced on several occasions to endure situations a Roman citizen wouldn't normally have

Above: Pictured here is a rendering of gladiators and victims facing wild animals in a public stadium. Criminals condemned to die by execution — a category that often included Christians — were frequently hurled into the arena to face mutilation and a horrible death by savage beasts. This provided entertainment for the masses and spared the government the effort and expense of executing criminals another way.

been required to endure. Most importantly, the Greek word Paul used in this verse referred to an actual fight with wild beasts.

While Paul was yet alive, believers did suffer many different types of terrible persecutions, which included fighting wild beasts so crowds could be entertained. And believers did face wild beasts in the Stadium of Ephesus. Therefore, some believe it is probable that at some point during his years of residency in the city, Paul was escorted into the stadium to face wild beasts as other believers had done.

It seems unlikely that Paul would use such terminology only in an allegorical fashion when this was a stark reality for many of his readers who had lost friends and relatives to wild beasts in stadiums. The language Paul used in First Corinthians 15:32 describes a real event that many believers endured all over the Roman Empire, including believers who were serving Christ in the city of Ephesus. Paul stated that he fought wild beasts in Ephesus. That statement should be evidence enough to substantiate the belief that the stadium Paul observed when he first arrived in Ephesus would one day be the arena where he would face ferocious animals and ultimately survive the experience.

(Continued on page 197)

ROMAN CHARIOT RACING IN PAUL'S DAY

Chariot racing was extremely popular and considered one of the greatest sports of the First Century. The sport began with the Greeks, probably before the Olympic Games were initiated.[36] Roman historian Livy recorded that chariot racing began in Rome as early as the Sixth Century BC,[37] and it had become eminently popular with Romans by 70 BC. The sport remained popular even after the seat of the Roman Empire was shifted to Constantinople after Rome fell in the Fifth Century AD. Chariot racing began to decline through the Seventh Century but continued in a lesser form at least until the Crusaders sacked Constantinople in 1204.[38]

During New Testament times, however, chariot racing was in its heyday, an immensely popular sport in cities scattered all over the Roman Empire.

Above: This beautiful mosaic depicts the intense excitement generated by a Roman chariot race.

Left: A stone relief sculpture of a Greek charioteer from the Sixth Century BC.

Great masses of people turned out for these exciting racing events, and Roman stadiums were filled to capacity on the days when chariot races were scheduled. To the Romans, chariot racing meant intense competition and big business.

Charioteers belonged to specific chariot teams and wore colors and uniforms that indicated to which team they belonged. The four major colors were green, red, white, and blue, although the Roman historian Suetonius tells us that the Emperor Domitian added gold and purple uniforms during his reign, making a total of six colors for competing teams.[39] In addition to their colorful uniforms, the charioteers wore special equipment to protect them in case of an accident during a race. A helmet, kneepads, and shin pads were standard parts of a charioteer's equipment, as was a knife attached to his waist, kept on hand in case of a crash in which he had to liberate himself from the crushing weight of a chariot or horse.

An abundance of mosaics from that period depicting the sport of chariot racing reveal that charioteers wore fashionable hairstyles, usually long curls pulled to one side, and that their horses were handsomely adorned with special decorations. Some mosaics show horses with pearls and strands of gold woven into their manes. Most often, the charioteer is depicted holding the reins of the horses in his left hand, a method used to control the left horse, which seemed to serve as the pilot for the other horses in the team. The charioteer's right hand usually holds a whip, used to drive the horses faster and faster around the track.

Chariots utilized the most advanced technology of that day. These ancient vehicles were not only constructed to move at a high rate of speed, but they were also finely crafted pieces of art

Right: This stone relief depicts a charioteer racing around a stadium in a chariot typical of the First Century.

on wheels. Depending on the size of the chariot and the type of race, chariots were pulled by two, three, four, six, seven, or even ten horses. If a team of two horses pulled a chariot, it was called a *bigae*. A chariot with a team of three horses was called a *trigae*, and one with four horses was called a *quadrigae*. A chariot pulled by a team of six horses was called a *sejuges*; and one with a team of seven horses was called a *septemjuges*. Finally, a chariot pulled by a team of ten horses was called a *decemjuges*.

Pliny the Elder wrote that some of the finest horses were bred in Africa and Spain.[40] At times, these horses were used for up to 20 years before being retired to reproduce more w i n n i n g horses. If a team of horses won many races, they could gain a level of notoriety and fame surpassing that of the charioteer himself.

Each team had its own professional personnel, such as doctors to treat the athletes; coaches and trainers to sharpen the charioteers' skills; blacksmiths trained to repair their chariots and fix broken equipment; veterinarians to treat the horses; and workers of pagan magic to perform sacrifices and speak incantations on behalf of the team before the contest commenced. Charioteers were usually from the lowest social classes and were often slaves. However, if they obtained a winning record at the games, their success made them famous, causing them to rise from obscurity and attain celebrity status.

On the day of the races, people eagerly packed the stadium for the special event. The anticipation of the crowds grew as they waited for the moment when the trumpet would

Left: This famous pavement mosaic discovered in Rome represents a typical depiction of a circus charioteer of the Albata (white) faction with one of his horses.

phrase meaning *fury and passion of the games*) — the state of highly charged emotions within an excited crowd of chariot-racing devotees.[41] Sometimes the furor of the crowd became so intense that it would erupt into a riot where fans fought other fans.[42] The worst of these riots occurred in the Byzantine capital of Constantinople in 532 AD. By then, chariot racing had become a much more politically charged sport, leading to the "Nika riots," which ultimately resulted in the deaths of 30,000 people and caused the Emperor Justinian to temporarily suspend the sport for several years.[43]

sound to announce that it was time for the games to begin. The governor of the race would arise from his special viewing box to step forward and drop a napkin. This was the official signal that the gates were to be opened so the teams of horses could charge forward at full speed, pulling their highly decorated chariots and charioteers around the track. Dust from the track billowed into the sky as the charioteers whipped their teams of horses into a frenzy. As chariots raced around the track, the deafening roar of the crowd got louder and louder as people cheered, yelled, and feverishly screamed.

Just as people are given to emotionalism at today's sporting events, such as football or soccer, fans at the ancient chariot races were known to be quite emotional about the chariot races. This state of emotionalism was actually referred to as *furor circensis* (Latin

In the Roman world, men and women were mostly separated at public events, but chariot races provided one social event where men and women could mingle and sit side by side. As a result, stadiums were packed with both male and female spectators.

Those in charge of the chariot races packed as many as 24 games into

Right: This Third Century pavement mosaic shows a circus charioteer of the Veneta (blue) faction with one of his horses.

one day,[44] and up to 12 chariots could participate in a single race.[45] A race could prove fatal to the charioteer if he didn't retain tight control over his team of horses as they raced around the curve of the track. Because of the speed of the horses, the tight curve at each end of the track, and all the competitors fighting for space with their own teams of horses, chariots often crashed with devastating consequences, causing the spectators to shout with enthusiasm. Between the races were novelty races, such as trick riding, foot races, and other kinds of special exhibitions.

A particular chariot team that enjoyed continual success became so famous that other cities would invite them on tour to compete with their teams. Much like sports teams that travel from city to city today, successful chariot teams traveled the empire and filled stadiums everywhere to capacity with shouting crowds who purchased tickets for an afternoon of entertainment.

At the conclusion of the day, the winners received their prizes — crowns made of olive leaves, victors' palm leaves, and chains or crowns made of gold. But in addition to these symbolic prizes, there was a huge monetary reward for chariot-race winners. Although most charioteers were conscripted from the slave population, those who repeatedly won races could amass enough fortune to purchase their freedom from slavery. One charioteer named Scorpus, who won more than 2,000 races in his lifetime, was able in only one hour of racing to accumulate 15 heavy bags of gold pieces, thrown at him by approving spectators.[46] Although legally a slave, Scorpus became fabulously rich, as was the case for many of the charioteers who won multiple races.

GLADIATORS IN PAUL'S DAY

It is generally believed that the earliest gladiatorial fights occurred among the Etruscans.[47] However, because no funeral steles from that period have been found that depict gladiators, historians have assigned the origin of gladiatorial fighting to the Romans in the year 264 BC.[48]

Above: This mosaic depicts a scene of fighting gladiators. In the earlier years of gladiatorial fighting, it was considered too low for status-conscious Roman citizens to fight in the arena. Therefore, slaves, criminals, and individuals who had fallen out of favor with the government were conscripted to become gladiators and forced to fight. As the atmosphere of the Roman Empire changed and the bloodlust of the crowds increased, gladiatorial fights became more popular and many men volunteered to be gladiators to fight for fame and money. Gladiatorial fights were carried out in massive stadiums and amphitheaters in every province of the empire. Gladiators trained in special gladiatorial schools; they were members of gladiatorial teams; and the contests were highly organized events attended by thousands of spectators.

At first, these barbarous fights were included as a part of the funerary process for deceased wealthy Roman citizens. The Early Christian writer Tertullian wrote about this at the end of the Second Century AD when gladiatorial fights were still popular, stating that according to ancient Roman belief, "...the souls of the departed were appeased by human blood...."[49]

In other words, to satisfy the souls of the dead, Romans thought it necessary to shed human blood as a form of spiritual propitiation. For this cause, prisoners, slaves, and people who had fallen out of good favor with society were sacrificed or killed by gladiators at funerals. For instance, it is recorded that 6,000 gladiators fought during the funerary celebrations in honor of the deceased Emperor Sulla in 78 BC.[50]

Almost 150 years later, the religious significance of gladiatorial fights to appease the dead had nearly disappeared, and the games' primary purpose had become to provide entertainment for the blood-thirsty masses who attended these horrifically barbaric events. In 29 BC, the first amphitheater in Rome designed solely for gladiatorial fights was constructed.[51] Years earlier, a school specializing in the training of gladiators, called a *ludus*, had been established in the city.

Slaves, prisoners of war, and condemned criminals were often conscripted to be gladiators, although a Roman citizen could willfully choose to become a professional gladiator or to fight as a hobby. Senators, noblemen, and even emperors were known to fight in the arena as gladiators.[52] Those who did it for sport were honored. In earlier years, those who abandoned normal life to enter the gladiatorial games purely for monetary gain were often ostracized and required to forfeit all

Right: This marble statue of a dying gladiator is found today in the Louvre Museum in Paris. The extensive training that gladiators endured was designed to fulfill one ultimate purpose: They were to fight valiantly to the death in a way that not only entertained the masses, but that also reflected the pride and glory of Rome.

citizenship rights. But this situation had changed by the latter years of the Roman Empire. As the taste for blood continued to grow among the masses and gladiatorial fights became more and more popular, many men volunteered to be gladiators and fought for fame and money.[53]

The word "gladiator" comes from the Latin word *gladius*, which means *sword*. Although gladiators fought with many types of weapons, the *gladius* was the primary weapon they used. Before being sent into the arena to fight, new recruits were sent to a special gladiatoral school, called a *ludus* in Latin, where trained killers taught them how to fight with the sword. The most famous

of these schools was the Ludus Magnus, the largest of the four gladiatorial schools founded near the Coliseum by the Emperor Domitian in Rome.[54]

Because the *ludus* instructors didn't want young recruits to be maimed in practice, the recruits practiced with wooden swords against wooden posts. New gladiators didn't use real weapons with sharp blades until the day of their first actual contest. If a recruit survived his first contest, his status was elevated to *veteranus*, the Latin term meaning *veteran*, which gave him a higher rank than the new recruits who were continually arriving at the *ludus*.[55]

Physical training was the chief purpose of the *ludus*. Recruits were

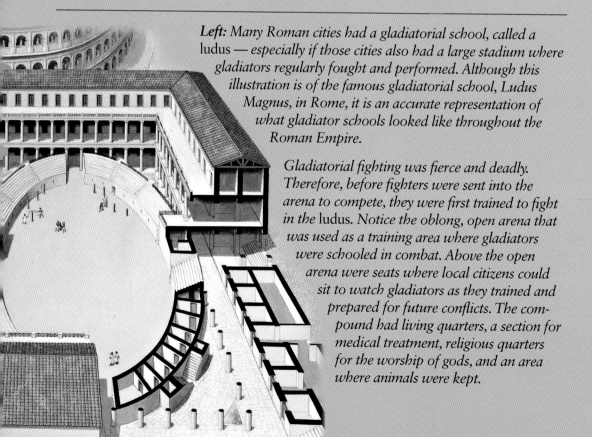

Left: Many Roman cities had a gladiatorial school, called a ludus — especially if those cities also had a large stadium where gladiators regularly fought and performed. Although this illustration is of the famous gladiatorial school, Ludus Magnus, in Rome, it is an accurate representation of what gladiator schools looked like throughout the Roman Empire.

Gladiatorial fighting was fierce and deadly. Therefore, before fighters were sent into the arena to compete, they were first trained to fight in the ludus. Notice the oblong, open arena that was used as a training area where gladiators were schooled in combat. Above the open arena were seats where local citizens could sit to watch gladiators as they trained and prepared for future conflicts. The compound had living quarters, a section for medical treatment, religious quarters for the worship of gods, and an area where animals were kept.

Above: This sketch illustrates a gladiatorial fight in a Roman stadium. On days when such fights took place, the events could last all day long, and by the end of the day, the floor of the arena would be soaked with blood. In the morning, the games would usually commence with fights between wild beasts that had been released into the arena to hunt and kill each other. Then "animal hunts" would be conducted in which men with weapons were pitted against wild beasts in a fight to the death. Lions, tigers, leopards, bears, wild dogs, and even rhinoceroses and elephants were used in these stadium events to fight each other or humans while the crowds looked on, shouting with bloodthirsty jubilation.

physically and mentally pushed to their limits to steel them for the fights that lay ahead in their future.

In the arena, gladiators would face fierce fighters who challenged them with both light and heavy weaponry. The gladiators would wear metal helmets, wield deadly swords, bear giant shields of various shapes, and carry terribly dangerous tridents and large nets. Because the conflict in the arena was so horrifically brutal, fighters went through intense training in order to win and survive the fight. They performed physical exercises

for hours each day, ran laps around the courtyard of the *ludus*, wrestled each other, and fought in mock competitions with other recruits.

In addition to this strenuous regimen of physical training, the *ludus* also provided a medical facility where gladiators were cared for with the highest quality of medical attention. The physical condition of gladiators was vital for success in the arena, so each gladiator was assigned a doctor and masseur to tend to his personal care.[56]

All this mental and physical training taught gladiators to fight to the

SABATI
IS

Above: The writer Cassius Dio recorded that 9,000 animals were slaughtered during the 100 days of games that marked the opening of the Coliseum.[57] There were countless wild animal hunts and gladiatorial fights during this time — and for a special celebration, the floor of the Coliseum was flooded with water so ships could conduct a naval battle for the excited spectators.

death and to do it in a fashion that entertained the masses who came to see a demonstration of their physical powers. Thus, gladiators weren't just killers; they were also entertainers who killed with flair to appease the thunderous shouts of adoring fans who packed the stadium seats. These fans came not only to witness the shedding of blood, but also to see it done with excellence and style.

To the crowd seated in the stadium, gladiatorial games meant more than a day of bloody sport. The gladiators symbolized the people of the Roman Empire, and the victorious gladiator represented Rome's conquering might over its foes. Each time a victim succumbed to death, the

Right: When Mount Vesuvius erupted in 79 AD, the ash buried the city of Pompeii. In 1860, the volcanic ash was removed from the ruins of the city, and this near-perfect gladiator helmet was discovered. This type of helmet was part of the equipment used by gladiators fighting in stadiums throughout the Roman Empire.

Above: Some of the most brutal and popular contests were battles that occurred between gladiators and wild beasts. Secret doors constructed on the floors of stadiums were covered with sand to conceal their location. Then at key moments, the doors sprang open to release ferocious animals into the arena to fight the armed gladiators to the death. The scenes that ensued were gruesome, horrific, and grisly — and it was all done for the entertainment of the stadium crowd.

shouting crowds viewed it as a symbolic moment when Rome once again proved its supremacy over its enemies. In time, this sport became so popular in Asia that it was performed in Ephesus, Smyrna, Laodicea, Hierapolis, and other large cities throughout the region.

In addition to bloody gladiatorial fights, the shows in the Roman stadiums included gladiators hunting and fighting lions, tigers, leopards, bears, wild dogs, boars, hippopotamuses, elephants, and other exotic wild beasts. Gladiatorial shows also included the execution of condemned criminals.

On a typical day of contests, the first events were *venationes* — the fighting of wild animals in the arena. The purpose of the *venationes* was to demonstrate man's ability to prevail over nature.[58] When Paul wrote that he "...fought with wild beasts at Ephesus..." (1 Corinthians 15:32 *NAS*), it is likely that he was talking about one of these *venationes* events during a day of gladiatorial contests when he was forced into the Stadium of Ephesus to face wild animals.

Near the middle of the day, the *venationes* ended so the *noxii* and *cruciarii* could commence. The *noxii*

and *cruciarii* referred to the death and execution of common criminals. During this part of the day, condemned people and criminals were torn to pieces, flayed with knives, crucified, mutilated, eaten alive by wild animals, or burned alive.[59] Decapitation was considered the least painful form of death, so beheading was reserved for people of higher class whom society did not believe deserved a large degree of pain as they were executed.

Later in the afternoon, the gladiatorial fights finally commenced and lasted the rest of the day. There was no grading system to the games, so gladiators fought until an opponent died or was too physically wounded to continue or until both were too exhausted to fight any longer. If a fighter fell with wounds so grave that he couldn't regain the strength to fight, only the organizer of the event retained the right to determine whether the wounded gladiator would live or die.[60] The organizer would appeal to the crowd for their decision on the matter. If the crowd cried out *"Igula!"* (*"Put the lance through him!"*), the organizer would give the signal for the standing gladiator to finish off the wounded fighter by thrusting a lance or sword through him.

Most gladiators died during the first year of their career. The following

information was taken from tomb inscriptions for gladiators. The list, now displayed in the Museum of Ephesus in Selçuk, Turkey, reveals the history of 11 gladiators, stating such facts as each gladiator's age, the amount of time he spent training, how many victories he won, and, in some cases, when he died.[61]

▶ 21 years, 4 years training, died during his fifth fight

▶ 22 years, 13 victories

▶ 23 years, survived 8 fights, died during his ninth fight

▶ 25 years, survived 20 fights, 9 victories

▶ 27 years, survived 15 fights, died during his sixteenth fight

▶ 30 years, survived 34 fights, 21 victories, 9 draws, 4 defeats (always pardoned)

▶ 35 years, 20 victories

▶ 38 years, 18 victories

▶ 48 years, 19 victories, 20 years of service

▶ 60 years, freed and pensioned gladiator

▶ 99 years, freed and pensioned gladiator

The first gladiatorial contests recorded in Ephesus occurred in the year 69 BC and were organized by a Roman commander named Lucullus. After the Stadium of Ephesus was expanded during the Emperor Nero's reign (54-68 AD), the huge structure held approximately 30,000 spectators for special events.[62] However, to accommodate the regular schedule of gladiatorial fights, the eastern end of the stadium was sectioned off and turned into a gladiatorial arena where human beings were regularly mutilated and slaughtered in the name of sport.

Left and Right: When excavations were conducted in the ancient ruins of Ephesus, many gravestones were discovered that depict gladiators as they were originally armed with their weapons. These gravestones are now displayed in the Museum of Ephesus in Selçuk, Turkey.

communities of soldiers or veterans were located. Ephesus boasted a large attachment of soldiers, which may explain the unusually large size of its stadium.

One can still see the sectioned-off eastern portion of the stadium used for gladiatorial fights. A special entrance still exists in that part of the stadium through which gladiators, wild animals, and human victims entered the arena to fight and to face death. A short walk 900 feet east of the stadium takes a visitor to a large graveyard where the remains of ancient gladiators still lie buried today.

As one of the most significant sites for gladiatorial fights in Asia Minor, Ephesus also had a very large *ludus* where new recruits were transformed into trained killers. The Ephesian school included barracks to serve as living quarters for the fighters and eating facilities where excellent meals were provided for them. As in all gladiatorial schools, fighters were put on high-calorie diets to increase their body weight, thus adding natural physical padding for protection against the blows of an enemy's weapon.[63]

Gladiatorial fights were popular everywhere, but they were especially loved in cities where large

Because massive crowds attended gladiatorial events, no cost was spared to adorn Roman stadiums with intricate stone-carved decorations depicting gladiator fights, wild-beast hunts, chariot races, and other sporting events that transpired within their arenas. The Stadium of Ephesus was no exception. Its construction was so advanced that it even included a huge awning made of canvas sails from ships. The canvas material was stretched around the perimeter of the stadium, utilizing ropes and winches normally used as gear for ships, to provide protection from the sun for spectators. The operation of this awning was so sophisticated that it required the assistance of professional sailors to operate it correctly.

An entire host of victims — including many Christians — were massacred in the Stadium of Ephesus and in the stadiums and arenas throughout the Roman Empire. The gladiatorial fights were so popular in Ephesus, and were thought so reasonable that they even occurred on the stage of the Great Theater where drama and musical events normally took place.

Above: These are the well-preserved ruins of the Great Theater of Ephesus, which accommodated approximately 24,000 people at various public events, including dramatic performances, theatrical shows, comedies, musical productions, public speeches, and at times even gladiatorial fights.

THE GREAT THEATER

If Paul and his team visited the stadium, afterward they would have returned to the top of the marble boulevard, later known as the Arcadiane, to resume their tour. At that point, they would have stood at the base of giant steps that led up to the entrance of the Great Theater. **12**

Tilting their heads to look up, the three would have seen rows upon rows of seats in the massive amphitheater that rose into the sky above their heads. They may have even walked up the steps to enter the theater so they could see this amazing edifice up close. If a show was in progress, they'd have been prohibited to enter. Nonetheless, they would have heard thousands of people laughing at the comical performances being carried out on stage.

This Great Theater was built by the Emperor Claudius (41-54 AD) and was one of the largest theaters in the ancient world. During the reign of Nero (54-68 AD), the Theater of Ephesus was expanded to add an additional 1,000 seats, thus accommodating 25,000 people at single events. The final touches were added to the theater during the reign of Trajan (98-117 AD).[64]

Nero's expansion of the Great Theater occurred during Paul's tenure in Ephesus, which was the early period of Nero's reign. As a patron of the arts, Nero contributed vast resources for the development and expansion of theaters across the Empire. As a result of this brief benevolent period in his rule of madness, Nero's first years as emperor are called his "Golden Years."

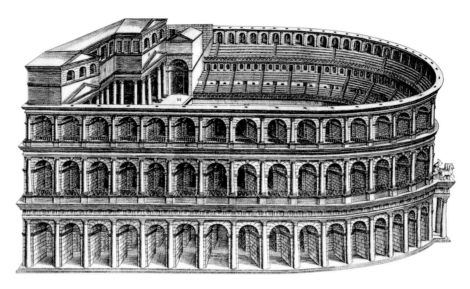

Above and Below: These sketches illustrate the design and décor of a typical Roman amphitheater. The seating area was circular and often built on the slopes of hills and mountains. If it was a stand-alone amphitheater, its circular seating was supported with mighty arches that served as entrances or covered walkways. The backstage wall was sometimes constructed of highly decorated stone and therefore permanent, but its wall could also be constructed of wood to make it removable. The central entrance in the backstage wall was used by leading actors, and the two side doors were used by supporting cast members. On days when the weather was extremely hot, a giant canopy made from ship sails could be extended across the top of the theater to give theater patrons protection from the sun.

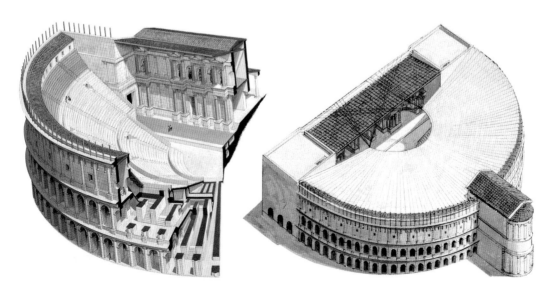

Above: This illustration depicts First Century reliefs of actors' masks used in tragedies and comedic performances. By this time, the beautiful and classical plays of the Greeks had fallen out of favor with Romans, who preferred lewd performances filled with sexual innuendoes, mockery, gags, and dirty jokes. As time progressed, classical Greek performances were primarily conducted in private theaters or reading rooms for the elite, whereas the public stage was used to put on crude comedic and satirical shows to satisfy the degenerating appetite of the Roman masses.

The physical additions Nero added to the Great Theater of Ephesus are an example of the munificence of this madman during the few good years of his reign.

In classical times, an earlier theater stood on the same place where the present theater stands, but as people's morals slipped and the empire degenerated, a new type of entertainment dominated the stage. Mobs packed the theater to watch repulsively vulgar shows. Comedies were foul and rude — further evidence of how badly the Roman world was sinking deeper into depravity. During the time of Paul's three-year stay in Ephesus, the performances were steadily growing more indecent and revolting. By this time, serious theater, such as dramatic performances by Euripides, were performed on private stages in large homes or before smaller, more intelligent audiences.

As if the trashy public shows were not already offensive enough, a tone of mockery also emerged in comedic performances.

Publicly insulting dignitaries with the foulest of language became fashionable, and sexual innuendoes and situations were carried out on stage to make crowds laugh. Lowbrow shows that insulted one's intelligence were provided for the public's increasingly base instincts. The theater changed to suit the rapidly changing tastes of the crowd. Soon the theater had been reduced to little more than an outdoor amphitheater with performances designed to publicly disgrace, dishonor, and humiliate.

Historical records depict believers literally being dragged on stage in crude costumes that pagans forced them to wear, where actors then subjected them to lewd acts that violated their conscience.[65] These degrading acts in the theater were done deliberately to humiliate believers and to poke fun at their faith.

This may be the exact picture Paul had in mind when he wrote from Ephesus and said, "…We are made a *spectacle* unto the world…" (1 Corinthians 4:9). The word "spectacle" is *theatron*, the Greek word that describes a *theater* or *a performance carried out on stage*. A literal translation would be "…We are made a *theater* to the world.…"

By using the word *theatron* — drawn from the world of theater where rude, ill-mannered theater crowds reveled in irreverent, disrespectful mockery — Paul meant to tell us that he and his companions felt as if they were ideal objects of mockery for the pagan world. Although Ephesus was widely acclaimed as "The Light of Asia" because it was intellectually open to new ideas, unbelievers and idol worshipers ridiculed the light of Christianity. So when Paul wrote that they were a "spectacle to the world," he was saying that the unsaved world considered them to be a joke and an object of mockery.

If Paul and his team had been allowed to roam around the interior of the theater and explore this mighty architectural edifice where dramas, comedies, and musical

events transpired, they would have seen multiple rows of handmade marble seats, a fabulous stage backdrop, and a rounded orchestra pit. The Great Theater of Ephesus was truly an amazing sight to behold.

However, the day Paul first viewed the Great Theater, he had no idea what a profound personal drama would unfold in that very place three years later. In Acts 19:29, we find the biblical account of Paul's friends — Gaius and Aristarchus — being hauled into the Great Theater of Ephesus to be harassed by an unbelieving crowd. Thousands of idol worshipers would gather that day in protest of Paul's ministry, creating a crisis so severe that he'd be forced to flee the city and eventually turn over the church to Timothy's leadership (*see* Acts 20:1; 1 Timothy 1:3).

THE CENTRAL MARKETPLACE

As the team began walking up Marble Street — a road that led to the legendary Curetes Street — they would have encountered the hustle and bustle of a large marketplace on the right side of the road. The market was teeming with activity as masses of people continually went in and out of its gates carrying fruit, baskets, home products, wine, and incense for sacrificial offerings to idols. This was the Central Marketplace of Ephesus. ⓭

Although originally constructed in ancient Greek times, the Central

Left: This richly colored Roman mosaic shows two actors' masks. Masks were used in Roman theaters for various types of performances, such as tragedy, comedy, and satire.

Above: Acts 19:23-41 records that these same seats in the Great Theater of Ephesus were once filled with angry idol-makers who gathered there to protest Paul's preaching. Their grievance concerned the power in Paul's message to change lives, for it was negatively affecting the sales of Artemis idols in their business. According to Acts 19:28, from these very seats in the Great Theater, the angry idol-makers raised their voices in unison and shouted, "Great is Artemis of the Ephesians!"

Marketplace that the apostolic team observed that day had been reconstructed and expanded during the First Century.[66] The dimensions of this place of commerce were 330 feet by 330 feet, making it a considerably large marketplace for the ancient world. It was surrounded with covered colonnades on all four sides, and approximately 300 massive columns of marble and granite supported the heavy stone cornices that ran perpendicular to the length of the market. From the courtyard, four steps that extended along the entire length of each side led up to the covered colonnades where more than 100 shops held a wide variety of products for customers to purchase.

Food, home supplies, manufactured goods, and a sundry of other products were bought and sold in this vast ancient "shopping mall," including many specialty goods imported from Egypt. Egypt was the wealthiest country in the world during the First Century, and Egyptians had

money to spend, so the market was filled with these imported goods to cater to the needs of the local Egyptian population. In addition, customers knew they could come to the Central Marketplace of Ephesus to purchase bulk supplies of needed goods — another reason this city was known as one of the most prominent commercial centers in the entire Roman Empire.

The Central Marketplace was also a center for political debate, and new ideas were frequently being introduced for discussion and deliberation. This explains why Paul debated in a similar marketplace in Athens (*see* Acts 17:17).

In 43 AD, an imposing statue of the Emperor Claudius was erected in the center of the Central Marketplace. Claudius was later poisoned by his wife Agrippina, the mother of Nero, so her son could assume the throne and be declared the new Roman Emperor.[67] But when Paul and his team first arrived in Ephesus, Claudius was still emperor and his likeness towered over the Central Market courtyard.

(Continued on page 204)

Left: Ephesus had three marketplaces — one at the harbor, one at the very center of the city, and a third in the upper part of the city. This is a photo of the Central Marketplace that was situated in the very heart of Ephesus near the Arcadiane, the Great Theater, Marble Street, and Philosophers' Square. It had more than 100 shops, 300 columns made of granite and marble, a large, circular building called a tolos *in the center of the market, and a southwest gate used primarily by male worshipers on their way to the Temple of Serapis.*

EMPEROR CLAUDIUS

The Roman Emperor Claudius was born in 10 BC. He was the son of Antonia, (who was the daughter of Mark Antony) and the uncle of the Emperor Caligula (37-41 AD). By 41 AD, Caligula's cruelty had become so excessive and depraved that the Praetorian Guard conspired to assassinate him at the Palatine Games, conducted in an auditorium not far from the imperial palace. As Caligula exited the auditorium through a private passageway, an attacker stabbed him in the chest. As the emperor fell to the ground, more assassins ruthlessly stabbed him, delivering more than 30 blows to his writhing body.

After the murder of the Emperor Caligula, the Praetorian Guards found Claudius, the deceased emperor's uncle, hiding behind a curtain in the imperial palace. They quickly took him to a camp where he was declared Emperor of the Roman Empire. Although mentally astute, Claudius had been concealed from public view since an early age because he had little control of his bodily movements and suffered from a speech impediment so severe that it was considered an embarrassment to the family. Claudius was so despised that his grandmother Livia said he was "a monster of a man." For these and other reasons, the Senate wasn't keen about the idea of Claudius becoming emperor; however, the senators had little choice because the army was in his favor.

Claudius ruthlessly executed Caligula's assassins and took preventative measures to guard against his own assassination. Nevertheless, several attempts were made on Claudius' life. Because of a constant fear of death and his continual suspicion regarding

possible conspiracies planned against him, Claudius executed 35 senators and 300 Roman knights. He also ordered the expulsion of Jews from Rome, which is the reason Aquila and Priscilla left Rome in 49 AD (*see* Acts 18:2). There is little doubt that this environment of fear and the barbarous acts of the Emperor Claudius adversely affected his adopted son, Lucius Domitus, who later became known as the Emperor Nero.

Emperor Claudius married four times: *first* to Plautina Urgulanilla; *second* to Aelia Paetina; and *third* to Messalina, who bore him a son named Britannicus and a daughter named Octavia. The Emperor Claudius gave Octavia in marriage to his adopted son, Lucius Domitus, who would later become the Emperor Nero. Claudius' third wife was charged with infidelity and was executed in 48 AD. In the year 49 AD, Claudius married his *fourth* wife, Agrippina, who was the sister of the Emperor Caligula and mother of the Emperor Nero. In October 54 AD, Agrippina killed Claudius with the help of a poisoner (a professional alchemist and poison-maker), and Nero ascended the throne to become the new Roman emperor. Claudius ruled the Roman Empire from 41-54 AD.

Surely Aquila and Priscilla were quick to recognize the identity of that statue, for Claudius had wreaked havoc in their lives. Originally from the city of Rome, the two had been driven out when the emperor ordered the expulsion of Jews from Rome in 49 AD (*see* Acts 18:2).

Looking up at the imposing statue of Claudius must have brought back certain painful memories for Aquila and Priscilla. That event had only occurred a few years earlier and was probably still very fresh in their memories. Imagine the grief they

Above: *This photo shows a wide view of the ruins of the Central Marketplace of Ephesus. In the center a cluster of trees now grows where a large, circular building called a* tolos *once stood. Each morning before business commenced, local merchants could visit the* tolos *to offer sacrifices and petition the gods for their blessing on that day's business transactions.*

must have felt as they were forced to pack up all their belongings, say farewell to their friends, and leave behind their lives in Rome against their will.

That had indeed been a tragic event in the lives of Aquila and Priscilla. But it also proved the truth Paul wrote in Romans 8:28: "And we know that all things work together for good to them that love God, to them who are the called according to his purpose." After their heartbreaking expulsion from Rome, it looked like all was lost for this couple — but not in God's eyes. That eviction put them on the

Above: These three stone engravings depict common scenes in a First Century Roman marketplace such as the Central Marketplace of Ephesus. The first engraving shows a man selling his goods at a shop; the second depicts a cutlery shop; and the third shows a banker doing business with a customer. A wide variety of goods could be purchased in Roman markets, including grains, foods, wines, home supplies, and fine fabrics. Marketplaces were usually very large and had many shops under the roofs of its covered colonnades.

road to Corinth, where they met Paul and started the most brilliant phase of their ministry — a phase that outshone anything they had left behind in Rome.

What began as a tragedy became the very means by which a new team was created that would propel the Gospel into new lands. Aquila and Priscilla entered the city of Ephesus as part of one of the

Below: These are the ruins of some of the 100 shops that once operated in the bustling Central Marketplace of Ephesus.

greatest apostolic teams in history, working side by side with the apostle Paul to give birth to the church of Ephesus — a church destined to lead the establishment of the Church throughout Asia.

In addition to Claudius' daunting image, the team was probably horrified to see all the statues of Greek and Roman gods that literally covered the courtyard. A large, circular building called a *tolos* ⑭ was constructed right in the center of the marketplace. Every morning before business hours began, sellers and workers made their way into this structure to offer sacrifices and to burn incense in hope of gaining favor from the gods for that particular day's business transactions. In addition, many sacrificial monuments on pedestals were also scattered throughout the market to make it convenient for shoppers to stop at any moment to burn incense or give offerings to the gods. These altars gave silent witness to the extent that idolatry was interwoven into the fabric of Ephesian life, where idols, incense, and shopping were all strangely mingled together.

In addition to the statues of idols, dozens of beautifully carved, painted statues dedicated to imperial dignitaries and outstanding citizens of Ephesus were also displayed in key parts of the market. As the apostle Paul strolled on the grounds of this massive, open-air mall and found himself completely

Right: The Hall of Nero was a long, covered colonnade dedicated to the goddess Artemis, to Nero's mother Agrippina, and to Nero himself. This elegantly designed, two-story building was located on the west side of Marble Street overlooking the Central Marketplace.

surrounded on every side by images, statues, figures, and sacrificial monuments, it would have become very clear to him just how pagan this illustrious city really was.

THE HALL OF NERO

Just above the market and to the right of Marble Street was a long, two-story building built in honor of Artemis, Ephesus' Mother Goddess of fertility. From this site, a spectator had a panoramic view of the entire marketplace below. When Paul and his team arrived in Ephesus in 52 AD while Claudius was still emperor, this temple was in its original state. But only two years later, Claudius was dead and Nero had assumed the

Right: The Temple of Serapis was the largest temple in Ephesus after the Temple of Artemis. It was constructed of monumental marble blocks, and eight massive columns adorned the front of the temple, each weighing approximately 114 tons (including the base, column, and capital). This temple was deliberately positioned behind the back wall of the Central Marketplace to hide it from public view and to conceal its dark, supernatural activities, including male-dominated religious services that involved ritualistic orgies.

throne. Not long after Nero became emperor, he ordered this temple to be expanded and embellished.

As noted earlier, Claudius was poisoned by his wife Agrippina, who was also Nero's mother. So when the enhanced temple was complete, Nero ordered an inscription to be engraved in its walls declaring its threefold dedication: first to *Artemis*, goddess of the city; second to *Agrippina*, whose role in Claudius' death gave rise to Nero's rule; and third to *Nero* himself.

The inscription of Nero's name on this temple is the reason archeologists refer to it as the Hall of Nero, ⑮ even though it was actually a temple to the goddess Artemis. It sat right above the marketplace on the east, with its primary entrance situated on Marble Street. The impressive facade of this two-story temple lured worshipers to stop and offer incense or offerings as they proceeded toward Curetes Street. However, when Paul first walked around the open space of the Central Marketplace, he saw the earlier temple dedicated to Artemis, not the embellished version that was to be built a few years later.

THE TEMPLE OF SERAPIS

The Central Marketplace had three mighty gates:

- The North Gate, ⑯ which opened onto what was later called the Arcadiane.

- The South Gate, ⑰ known as the Gate of Mazeus and Mithridates, which opened onto Philosophers' Square (*see* pages 210-212).

- The Southwest Gate, ⑱ through which worshipers could enter the dark and mysterious Temple of Serapis. ⑲ This religion primarily

the pieces, Isis reassembled them and then assisted in raising Serapis back to life. Legend stated that Serapis was then seated on a mighty throne, from which he would judge every soul in the afterlife according to the weight of each person's works. For the Egyptians, Serapis was the lord of life and master over death.

This cult was notorious for its supernatural activity. People who were drawn to know the secrets of the dark underworld were especially attracted to the Temple of Serapis. The priests of Serapis intruded into the spirit realm and conducted shadowy activities in the temple day and night. Because many Egyptians lived in Ephesus, this temple was continually busy with worshipers. However, only converts were permitted inside the Temple of Serapis because the practices were considered "secrets," not to be viewed by outsiders.

Ruins that exist at that site today are from a second temple built in the Second Century, but an earlier temple on the same site may have been constructed at the order of Cleopatra when she and Antony wintered in Ephesus in the year 33 BC. If true, then that earlier Temple of Serapis existed when Paul, Aquila, and Priscilla arrived in Ephesus. The ruins that exist today are colossal in proportion — more mammoth than any other temple in Ephesus, with the exception of the Great Temple of Artemis. Along the upper front of the temple were eight enormous columns, weighing approximately 114 tons *each*, including base, column, and capital.

The supernatural activity and dark religious practices in the Temple of Serapis were so notorious that the apostolic team would have recoiled at the very thought of

attracted men and was known for deviant sexual activities as part of its religious rituals.

Serapis was the Egyptian god of heaven, of the underworld, of fertility, and of medicine, and he was husband to the goddess Isis. According to Egyptian legend, Serapis was killed and cut to pieces by his brother Set, the Egyptian god of the powers of darkness. Legend then said that Set scattered the dismembered pieces of Serapis into the sea. When Isis, Serapis' wife, heard of the tragedy, she sailed the seas searching for the dismembered parts of her husband's body. After gathering

Right: This photo shows the Gate of Mazeus and Mithridates. These two servants constructed this magnificent gate between the Central Marketplace and Philosophers' Square, and upon its completion in 3 BC, they dedicated it to their former masters who had granted them freedom from slavery. Inscriptions on the top of the gate inform us that Mazeus and Mithridates had formerly belonged to the Emperor Augustus and his wife Livia. The pavement directly in front of the gate is all that remains of the Philosophers' Square that existed when Paul and his team arrived in 52 AD.

entering it. In most places where this vile religion was practiced, its temples were spiritual cesspools — virtual breeding grounds of demonic activity.

THE GATE OF MAZEUS AND MITHRIDATES

On their way to Curetes Street from the Central Marketplace, Paul and his companions may have passed through the Gate of Mazeus and Mithridates, a huge gate on the south side of the Central Marketplace that had been erected by two famous freed slaves. This astounding gate was built like a triumphal arch, but it had three arches instead of one.

The freedmen who built the gate had become fabulously rich as a result of formerly serving as slaves in the imperial household. Later the two men built the three-arched gate to honor the imperial family and demonstrate gratitude for their freedom. After construction was completed in 3 BC, the two freedmen dedicated the gate to the imperial family: to the Emperor Augustus and the Empress Livia, and to their daughter Julia and son-in-law Agrippa.

When Paul, Aquila, and Priscilla walked through the arches of this spectacular gate, they probably stopped to

read the many inscriptions that covered its walls concerning public decrees, laws, and historical events, just as many other newcomers to Ephesus did. They also could have read the following dedication, written in Latin:

This gate was built by Mazeus in honor of his patrons the emperor Augustus, son of the divinized Caesar, the high priest, twelve times consul, twenty times tribune, and Livia, the spouse of Caesar Augustus; and by

Mithridates, in honor of his patrons, Marcus Agrippa, the son of Lucius, three times consul, emperor, six times tribune, and Julia, the daughter of Augustus Caesar.[68]

Those who looked upon this gate for the first time marveled at the history represented in its inscriptions and intricate carvings depicting historical figures and events. People still marvel at the sight of these engravings today, so one can just imagine the wonder this impressive gate inspired when Paul and his companions walked through it on their first tour of Ephesus.

The Gate of Mazeus and Mithridates had four niches in the interior of the arches. In these niches stood attractive statues of the Emperor Augustus and his imperial family to remind those who walked through the gate in whose honor it had been constructed. In addition, two tombs sat at both ends of the gate for the two slaves who built this magnificent structure.

PHILOSOPHERS' SQUARE, THE SCHOOL OF TYRANNUS, AND THE LIBRARY

Once through the Gate of Mazeus and Mithridates, Paul and his team entered a marvelous courtyard referred to as Philosophers' Square. ㉙ This was the center of learning in the city of Ephesus and was famous throughout Asia for its noteworthy philosophers who were trained in the School of Plato in Athens. Students from the lands surrounding

Above: The construction of the Celsus Library was finished in the year 117 AD on the exact site of the former school of philosophy in Ephesus. This library didn't exist at the time of Paul's arrival in Ephesus in 52 AD but was later constructed during the reign of Trajan, a period when many Christians suffered martyrdom. This photo shows the first floor of the library facade with the statues of four lovely women gracing the entrance — each respectively representing wisdom, understanding, virtue, and science.

Right: Acts 19:9 says the apostle Paul was seen "...disputing daily in the school of one Tyrannus." Some scholars assert that the School of Tyrannus was located at the top of the steps shown in this photo. It was situated on the edge of Philosophers' Square, a popular gathering point for Jews who lived in Ephesus.

the Aegean Sea and beyond traveled to Ephesus to sit at the feet of these learned thinkers. The sarcophagus that held the remains of a famous sophist philosopher named Dionysus still sits on these ancient grounds. **21** This grave serves as a visible reminder to visitors of the many philosophers who once congregated on this very site and of the influence that teachers, educators, and philosophers once held in this district of the city.

In the year 110 AD, construction began on the large Celsus Library **22** that eventually occupied Philosophers' Square. The library was finally completed in 117 AD. The world's largest library of that time was located in Alexandria, and the second largest library was in Pergamum. But the Celsus Library of Ephesus ranked third in size[69] and included storage space for at least 12,000 volumes.[70]

The library's architecture and construction was simply breathtaking. Its tall facade had multiple porticoes and elegant columns. Four exquisite statues of women were erected in niches on the front of the building with large inscriptions on their bases indicating what each represented: *wisdom*, *understanding*, *virtue*, and *science*. These statues bore silent testimony to the fact that the Ephesian population cherished learning. Indeed, the entire

beautiful structure of the Celsus Library was intended to communicate the message that learning and education was highly valued in the city of Ephesus.

But in 52 AD when Paul, Aquila, and Priscilla arrived in Ephesus, the library was not yet built and Philosophers' Square was still a frequent meeting place for those who desired to engage in philosophical debate and discussion, including the city's Jewish community. For this reason, a well-known local schoolmaster

named Tyrannus (whether a Jew or a Gentile is uncertain) operated a school of learning at Philosophers' Square. Just to the side of the square, and still visible today, was a rather large set of steps that some scholars believe led from the square to the entrance of Tyrannus' school. ㉓ According to these scholars, this is the location of the same School of Tyrannus mentioned in Acts 19:9, where the Bible says, "But when divers were hardened, and believed not, but spake evil of that way before the multitude, he [Paul] departed from them, and separated the disciples, disputing daily in the school of one Tyrannus."

When Paul and his team walked through this legendary part of the city, Paul probably had no inkling that he would be teaching classes at this notable school. Yet a day would soon come when Paul taught freely from the Word of God on these very premises. Paul's education had perfectly equipped him to stand alongside pagan educators, philosophers, and orators and to teach as an instructor at Tyrannus' school. Acts 19:20 tells us that the Word of God "mightily grew" in Ephesus during the months and years following the apostolic team's initial arrival in the city. Paul's instruction at this school was undoubtedly a powerful factor in that growth. Paul's eloquent teaching appealed to Jews who congregated in this place of discussion and learning, as well as to pagans who found no fulfillment in their vain religion and rituals. But when Paul, Aquila, and Priscilla first strolled into this area of the city, they didn't yet realize the eternal impact they would have in the school situated on a raised area just south of Philosophers' Square.

THE CENTRAL BROTHEL OF EPHESUS

It may seem strange that the Central Brothel of Ephesus **24** would be located so near to a center of education, but in the Greek world, sexual activities of all types were not considered taboo. Although Ephesus was a Roman city by this time, its history was largely Greek. As a result, Greek thought and culture dominated not only Ephesus but all of Asia as well — including an extremely liberal attitude concerning sexual activities. This brothel was located in the heart of the city, which indicates how deeply the Greek way of thinking about these matters was entrenched in the Ephesian population.

The Central Brothel of Ephesus was a huge, two-story complex just a few steps away from Philosophers' Square. The facility was so large that it had approximately 30 rooms on the first floor alone,

Above: This photo shows the walkway that led to the entrance of the Central Brothel of Ephesus. This brothel was located across the street from Philosophers' Square and near the Central Marketplace, which made it easily accessible for customers to regularly visit for sexual services. The Central Brothel had two floors and more than 30 rooms where prostitutes served clients.

in addition to the many rooms on its second level. Beautiful frescoes covered the walls; the floors were intricately decorated with marvelous mosaics; and several fountains graced the inner décor of the brothel complex. The building was difficult to ignore, but Paul and his companions would have thoroughly shunned this house of ill repute. It was a place of moral filth, filled with vulgarities and acts of debauchery that violated every law of God that Paul and his team carried in their hearts and souls. However, as they walked from Philosophers' Square toward the famous Curetes Street, they had no choice but to pass the brothel as they turned east to start up the street toward the Heroon and the Tomb of Arsinoe.

THE HEROON AND TOMB OF ARSINOE

As the team moved up Curetes Street, they would have seen to their right a small but important Heroon. **25** A "heroon" referred to a sacred building where people could stop to honor city founders, city fathers, and heroes, as well as to worship gods who were not important enough to have entire temples dedicated to their honor. In this cult building, local residents gave homage to the past or offered sacrifices and burned sacred incense to the gods to help secure for themselves a good future.

As the three visitors walked past the Heroon, looking right and left at both sides of Curetes Street, they must have once again been struck by the vast number of pillars, columns, statues, and idols that lined the street. Then as they looked to the right, their gaze would have focused next on the large Tomb of Arsinoe **26** — the grave of Queen Cleopatra's younger sister.

During the years when Cleopatra was at war with her two siblings as they vied for the Egyptian throne, her sister Arsinoe was taken captive by Julius Caesar, who was allied with Cleopatra. Although Arsinoe was forced to march as a captured prisoner during Caesar's triumphal march in Rome, afterward he granted the young princess sanctuary in Ephesus, which was known to be a safe haven for Egyptians. The fact that Caesar chose Ephesus as Arsinoe's place of refuge bears witness to the vast numbers of Egyptians who lived in Ephesus at that time — sufficient numbers to help Arsinoe feel at home in this foreign city.

But Arsinoe still wasn't safe. For several years, she took up residency in the Temple of Artemis, seeking the protection of the patron goddess. However, in 41 BC Arsinoe was executed on the steps of the temple by order of Mark Antony and at the instigation of her sister, Queen Cleopatra.[71]

It is unusual that an Egyptian of such rank would be buried outside of Alexandria. But over the years, Arsinoe's life had become so intertwined with her adopted city that after her death, she was buried in a large tomb right in the heart of Ephesus at the beginning of Curetes Street, not too far from Philosophers' Square.

Being a lover of history, Paul may have stood and stared at the tomb of such a historically eminent person. He may have taken a moment to ponder the fates of Julius Caesar, Mark Antony, and Arsinoe, as well as the scheming of Cleopatra that dramatically affected each of these lives.

Everywhere Paul and his team looked in this ancient city, they must have felt surrounded by a deep sense of history. But this was still only the beginning of Curetes Street. There was so much more to see further up the road.

CURETES STREET

As Paul and his companions strolled up the legendary Curetes Street, ㉗ they were about to enter one of the city's oldest sections and come face to face with the worst display of idolatry and paganism in the central part of Ephesus. The only scenes worse than what the three likely encountered on Curetes Street were the events that regularly occurred in the Temple of Artemis on the outskirts of the city.

The Temple of Artemis notwithstanding, there was plenty of debauchery to be seen on Curetes Street. The apostolic team not only beheld a plethora of idols and statues of gods, but it is almost certain that the three also observed so-called Curetes priests dancing wildly up and down the street. In these ritualistic dances, the priests would work themselves up in a religious frenzy, hurling their bodies one way and then another in a trance-like state to the

accompaniment of musical instruments and the furious banging of drums.

According to mythology, Zeus impregnated the goddess Leto. As Leto was nearing the moment of giving birth to the twins Apollo and Artemis, Leto asked six demigods to conceal the birth of her twins from Hera, the jealous wife of Zeus. Leto feared that Hera would surely kill the children if she discovered their birth.

Above: Curetes Street was lined with fabulous terraced homes, idols, statues of honored residents and heroes, monuments of educators and doctors, shops, restaurants with exquisite mosaic floors, public baths and toilets, and the Tomb of Arsinoe, the famous sister of Queen Cleopatra who was murdered on the steps of the Temple of Artemis in 41 BC. Curetes Street meandered up the hill to the city's upper district, where the local council ruled the affairs of Ephesus.

To conceal the birth of Leto's children, the demigods — called Curetes — incessantly banged swords, shields, and musical instruments, attempting to make enough noise to conceal the crying of the newborn twins. The noise was loud enough to hide the infants' cries and therefore protected the twins from the wrath of Hera. As a result of this legend, a class of priests emerged that were called Curetes, whose primary function was to serve as guardians of the goddess Artemis.[72]

Frenzied music and riotous noise played a significant role in the myth of the first Curetes demigods; therefore, the priests of Curetes in Ephesus perpetuated the belief that loud, annoying, nearly ear-deafening noise provided protection for the goddess Artemis and safeguarded local citizens from evil forces. During Paul's day, a significant part of the priests' functions included their hypnotic dancing in a trance-like state up and down the street to the incessant, wild beating of drums, the clanging of cymbals, and the playing of high-pitched flutes. It is very likely that this raucous priestly activity was occurring on the very day Paul, Aquila, and Priscilla first walked up Curetes Street.

HERA

The sight must have been repulsive to Paul as pagan priests whirled in circles and jerked back and forth, flinging their bodies in seizure-like fits. The sight was annoying even to the people of Ephesus, but it was tolerated because people believed that the bizarre behavior of these priests provided supernatural protection. The entire atmosphere on this street was permeated with sexually-oriented dances and rituals in order to satisfy the appetites of the gods.

The constant activity of the Curetes priests on this street is one reason it was called Curetes Street. But there was yet another reason. It was also called Curetes Street because it was used as a sacred processional road leading to the Temple of Artemis. Because Curetes priests were associated with Artemis, they frequently led the way when pagan worshipers

Above: The illustration above is an artist's rendering of the original "Marble Room," a large room in one of the terrace homes on the south side of Curetes Street in the city of Ephesus. A fountain was in the center of the room; its doors were bronze; and the walls were paneled in blue, green, red, brown, and white marble panels. Many fragments of these marble panels and other parts of these fabulous homes still exist in the archeological excavations in Ephesus today and are displayed on the following pages.

walked from Ephesus to the Temple of Artemis in parades and processionals.

Tradition states that Timothy, having overcome a spirit of fear that tried to control him at an earlier age (*see* 2 Timothy 1:7), became very bold for the Lord in the latter years of his life. Early Church writings record that at the age of 80, Timothy entered one of the main streets of Ephesus to reprimand a pagan crowd for their wild and idolatrous activities. According to tradition, the riotous crowd beat Timothy to death with rods they were carrying, the tops of which displayed images of various gods. Some scholars believe it was on Curetes Street that Timothy's martyrdom occurred during a pagan processional that got out of control amidst the frenzied dancing and celebrating of priests and pagan worshipers.[73] If this is true, little did Paul know as he walked on Curetes Street with Aquila and Priscilla that tragic events would transpire one day on that very street involving his dearest spiritual son.

Above: The photo shows the hand-painted walls in the terrace houses of Ephesus that have survived from the First Century. Frescoes on walls portrayed mythological characters, gods, heroes, poets, musicians, warriors, and honored leaders. Rooms were large, elegant, and intricately decorated.

TERRACE HOMES IN CENTRAL EPHESUS

Curetes Street represented the most exclusive section of the city, with palatial residences blanketing the upward slope of the hill that towered over Ephesus. Paul and his team must have stopped for a moment to gaze at those magnificent

Left: Wealthy homes in Ephesus, such as the one shown here, had many large rooms, including bedrooms, theater rooms for entertaining guests, courtyards, kitchens, and living quarters for servants. These luxurious residences also had running water, indoor toilets, and ventilation systems.

homes — opulent enough to capture the attention of anyone seeing them for the first time.

These terrace homes 28 located near Curetes Street were the most prestigious in the city. No one lived in this high-class neighborhood except the wealthy.

Perhaps nothing demonstrates this abundance of wealth better than the remains of these lavish residences in Ephesus that have survived from the time of Augustus (27 BC-14 AD). The fact that they can be dated to the time of Augustus means these were the same terrace houses Paul and his team gazed upon in 52 AD. By studying what remains of these residences, we are able to clearly see how affluently the wealthy class lived at the time Paul and his team made their residence in Ephesus. The people who lived in these homes were not ordinary citizens, but rather people of great fortune.

As Paul and his companions stood on Curetes Street and looked to their right, they would have first seen the massive, red terracotta tile roofs and the third-floor windows of these luxurious residences. A closer look would have then revealed narrow lanes meandering between the rows of houses, with elegant stairs leading from one terrace to the next. Flanking these lanes on both sides were countless statues, idols, and columns crowned with intricately carved capitals. It would have been a stunning sight for the apostolic team to behold.

Nevertheless, what these three visitors could observe from the street paled in comparison to the ornate decorations that adorned the interiors of these First Century mansions, where every imaginable convenience of comfort and luxury existed. In fact, the terrace houses of Ephesus represented some of the finest homes in the entire Roman Empire.

Fabulous hand-painted frescoes adorned the walls of these ancient mansions — even in the rooms where indoor toilets were installed. But these homes

Left: Restaurants were an integral part of Roman life, although they were primarily frequented by men and occasionally by women of ill-repute. First Century restaurants were laid out much like restaurants today — with a large seating area, display counters, and concealed kitchens where food was prepared for servers, who would then carry the food to the patrons' tables. This photo is of an ancient restaurant in Rome, but it is similar to restaurants that were found throughout the Roman Empire.

Above: *This photo shows the fabulous mosaics that covered the sidewalks directly in front of the shops, cafes, and restaurants that were on the legendary Curetes Street. Such mosaics were common in Ephesus — so common that they adorned sidewalks in nearly every street-side colonnade in the city.*

Right: *This is an artist's rendering of how the restaurant on page 226 may have originally looked nearly 2,000 years ago when it was filled with patrons. The walls were decorated with faux marble, frescoes, vaulted ceilings, and floors inlaid with small tiles. Romans were particularly fond of stews, soups, and casseroles. They were keen on spices and used pepper in nearly every recipe. Popular meat dishes included venison, boar, lamb, beef, pork, crane, pheasant, partridge, fish, shellfish, oysters, and mussels.*

Above: Toilets were very public places where people sat side by side and talked freely with one another. Although many wealthy homes had private toilets that were quite nice, every city had large public toilet structures that could be used by common people, visitors to the city, and slaves. Men and women used the same toilets with no dividers and no embarrassment, as this was the custom of the day.

were decorated with more than beautiful frescoes. Other rooms were finished from top to bottom with beautiful inlaid marble slabs, and some rooms were decked with exquisite ivory friezes. Decorating both the floors and ceilings of indoor cupolas (small domes resting on pillars with a circular or polygonal base) were intricate mosaics depicting Roman emperors, Greek and Roman philosophers, and Greek and Roman gods such as Aphrodite, Dionysus, Poseidon, and Eros.

These multi-leveled, massive homes included staircases, courtyards, marble and granite columns that supported the courtyard roof, and atrium-style windows that permitted daylight into the courtyard. The homes also boasted kitchens, bedrooms, living rooms, reception rooms, baths, indoor toilets, and in-home theaters. They were so sophisticated that they even had ventilation systems to allow cool air to circulate throughout the interior in the summer and a central heating system to provide warmth in the winter. These palatial residences were simply remarkable, and the extraordinary number of them built near the upper part of Curetes Street testifies to the enormous wealth of ancient Ephesus.

Built directly between these luxurious homes and Curetes

Street was a roofed colonnade **㉙** that included shops, restaurants, taverns, and places of business. The floors of these shops and the pavement of the colonnade sidewalk were pure works of art. However, for this high-class neighborhood, these outstanding artistic masterpieces were simply part of the pavement people walked on as they strolled through the colonnade along Curetes Street.

PUBLIC TOILETS AND CENTRAL BATHHOUSE

As Paul, Aquila, and Priscilla stood next to the colonnade on Curetes Street, they would have seen a large stone structure on the opposite side of the street. This building held the Public Toilets **㉚** of central Ephesus. More than likely, the team would have witnessed slaves hurrying in and out of the door that led to the Public Toilets as they carried out a practice that was commonplace all over the Roman Empire. If wealthy residents needed to relieve themselves while visiting the city, they used the Public Toilets like everyone else. However, these toilets were fashioned of marble and were cold. Therefore, before they arrived to use the facilities, the rich would send their slaves ahead to sit on the cold marble seats to warm them for their arrival.

Such a practice seems unthinkable to us today, but at that time a visit to the Public Toilets was not such a private affair. In fact, there were no partitions between each toilet to provide privacy because the Public Toilets were viewed as a place for social interaction and business negotiations.[74] To the modern mind, this whole picture seems incongruous with the elegant and sophisticated culture of

Above: Unlike today's public bathrooms that have dividers to provide for modesty and privacy, Roman public toilets had no such dividers. It was customary for people to sit side by side as they used the facilities. Like the public baths, public toilets were places where people socially interacted with others. A groove with running water ran perpendicular to the marble toilet seats, which people used to cleanse themselves. A sponge attached to the end of a stick was dipped into the running water and used as an ancient version of toilet paper.

Ephesus. However, interaction at the Public Toilets was commonplace and accepted by Ephesian society. It wasn't even deemed inappropriate or impolite for men and women to sit side by side.

Above: These columns were situated in the interior of the Central Bathhouse in the city of Ephesus. The bathhouse was immense, large enough to accommodate many patrons at one time. Men bathed in the mornings and evenings, while women primarily used the bathhouse in the afternoon while men were conducting business in other parts of the city. The décor and accommodations of the Central Bathhouse of Ephesus were extremely luxurious, as was true in most bathhouses in the Roman Empire.

Next to the Public Toilets was another facility where some of the Ephesians' most significant public interaction occurred. This was the Central Bathhouse **31** of the city.

In the ancient world, bathhouses were palaces of leisure and relaxation. Afternoon was the time when women were allowed to use the bathhouse; mornings and evenings were reserved for men. Musicians played soft, soothing music while patrons bathed in pools and relaxed in the comfortable, steamy atmosphere. The bathhouse experience was one to be enjoyed and prolonged as long as possible — an event that could last for many hours.

When people came to the bathhouse, their stay would include visits to the *caldarium* (the hot room), the *tepidarium* (the mild room), and the *frigidarium* (the cold room). Special rooms in the bathhouse were also provided where clients could obtain sexual pleasure for a price.

In bathhouses throughout the Roman Empire, men came to read, converse with each other, or hold business meetings.

Right: The painter Lawrence Alma-Tadema tried to recreate the luxurious atmosphere that existed in Roman bathhouses. Illicit activities were rampant in bathhouses across the sprawling Roman Empire; therefore, the imperial baths were shunned by Christian leaders and believers. Men and women were not allowed to bathe together, so this painting depicts women separated from men, who can be seen in the background.

Bottom: The Central Bathhouse of Ephesus stood next to the Public Toilets on Curetes Street, conveniently located for use by both local residents and visitors to the city of Ephesus. The bathhouse had many rooms, lavish decorations, and musicians who played relaxing music. Like other bathhouses in the Roman Empire, the Central Bathhouse of Ephesus was designed to be a palace of relaxation and pleasure where decadent activities were commonplace.

Left: This illustration conveys the opulence of Roman baths and demonstrates the important role these baths played in Roman society. The Bathhouse of Diocletian (pictured here) was possibly the most lavish bathhouse ever constructed and could accommodate thousands of people at one time. It was decorated with inlaid marble floors, painted ceilings, arches, domes, glass windows, and multiple statues of leaders and pagan gods. Although the bathhouses of Ephesus are in complete ruins today, these structures would have been very luxurious, given the significant wealth of the city.

They also came to have sexual encounters with prostitutes who specifically served clients in the bathhouse or to engage in perverse activities with other men spending time there.

The Romans' acceptance of homosexuality as a normal practice came over a process of time. At first, Romans were offended with the Greeks' tendency toward homosexuality and even referred to it as "the Greek vice."[75] But as time passed, Romans' disgust with homosexuality slowly evaporated, and Roman society gradually became open-minded toward and accepting of the practice.

As a result, bathhouses were places of moral depravity in the Roman Empire. It is likely that the Central Bathhouse, located very near the Central Brothel of Ephesus, was one place where such deeds occurred. This was true not only of Ephesus, but of bathhouses throughout the Roman Empire.

Above: This artist's illustration depicts what the Baths of Caracalla in Rome may have looked like at the peak of their popularity. The bathhouse was surrounded by a tall wall that had covered colonnades in the interior section, as well as lush gardens, statues, fountains, and pathways for visitors to use as they strolled through the large grounds. The inside of the baths had floors covered with extraordinary mosaics, painted columns that supported balconies, domed ceilings with intricate decorations, pools, waterfalls, fountains, massage rooms, and libraries.

The bathhouse ruins that remain in Ephesus today are from the expanded structure built in the Second Century. But when Paul, Aquila, and Priscilla relocated to the city of Ephesus, a substantial bathhouse already existed in this same spot.

As the apostolic team resumed their walk up the sloping incline of Curetes Street, it's very possible that they encountered men with wet hair coming out of the main entrance of the Central Bathhouse onto the main streets of the city. If so, the irony of that moment is worth considering. Although those emerging from the bathhouse had just washed their bodies, their souls were still caked with the filth of the perversions they had likely participated in within the walls of that place. Little did they know that the three strangers with whom they'd just crossed paths were on divine assignment — sent to Ephesus to proclaim Good News that would wash their pagan souls with the cleansing waters of God's Word.

234

Left: These were the central steps that led to the second-floor sanctuary of the Temple of Domitian, located in the center of Domitian Square. The temple was constructed to honor the Emperor Vespasian and the Emperor Titus. But after Titus suddenly died, Domitian ascended the throne and declared his own divinity, demanding that the citizens of the Roman Empire worship him. As a result, this structure was transformed into a temple to the emperor where residents of Ephesus could worship Domitian as deity.

THE TEMPLE OF DOMITIAN AND THE FOUNTAIN OF DOMITIAN

As Paul and his team journeyed onward, they would have passed many temples along the way. To their right, they passed the future site of the Temple of Domitian, **32** which would be built approximately 40 years later.

Although this temple didn't exist in 52 AD when Paul first arrived in Ephesus, it's necessary to mention it because of its significance to Church history. The Roman Emperor Domitian built this temple while the apostle John and Timothy were both ministering in Ephesus. Domitian's ruthless reign played a major role in John's writing of the book of Revelation. As mentioned in Chapter One, this was the emperor who exiled John to the island of Patmos, located in the Aegean Sea just off the coast of Asia. It was on this island

Above and Right: In the center of Domitian Square was the magnificent Temple of Domitian that included a variety of altars adorned with garlanded bulls, typical of architectural ornaments during the reign of the Emperor Domitian (81-96 AD). Also in the square was the Fountain of Domitian, originally called the Fountain of Pollio, named after the man who constructed it in the year 93 AD. The fountain was a complex structure with a great arch that included a statue of Zeus, as well as other Greek and Roman gods.

that John received the book of Revelation, including Jesus' seven messages to the seven churches of Asia.

The Emperor Domitian ascended to the throne in the year 81 AD. His initial behavior as emperor gave the impression that he would be an honest ruler and wise administrator — but it soon became evident to all that Domitian would find his place among the most cruel and tyrannical rulers in human history.

In 89 or 90 AD, Domitian gave the order for a large temple to be constructed on a place that came to be known as Domitian Square. 33 It was a splendid, two-story building boasting of majestic columns crowned with elaborate capitals and a fabulous facade. A host of statues adorned the facade, including impressive sculptures of muscular barbarians, and a large staircase led to the second floor where the primary sanctuary of worship was located.

Domitian ordered the construction of the temple to honor his father (the Emperor Vespasian) and himself and to pay homage to his brother Titus. It was a temple built in honor of emperors, and particularly in honor of the Flavian Dynasty. But shortly after the temple was finished, Domitian's behavior took a new twist as he proclaimed his own divinity and adopted the title *dominus et deus* — the Latin phrase meaning *lord and god*. Afterward, the temple became known as the Temple of Domitian and a cult religion was established — complete with priests, priestesses, and a decorative altar on which worshipers regularly offered sacrifices and offerings as an act of homage to the Emperor Domitian.

The temple measured 150 feet by 300 feet and was nestled among a myriad of statues of gods and goddesses in the very center of Ephesus. Its unusual location tells us how massive emperor worship had become and what an immense influence the worship of Domitian exerted in the social, political, economic, and religious life of Ephesus. Its calculated setting among all the gods and goddesses of Greece and Rome was intended to be a silent proclamation that Domitian was no ordinary emperor but had joined the ranks of the divine even while yet alive.

Throughout the empire, it was compulsory for people to declare that Domitian was *dominus et deus*, which meant Domitian was *lord and god* of the Roman Empire. Anyone who refused to make this confession was viewed as a traitor to the

Left: Ruins of the Temple of Domitian in ancient Ephesus.

Left: This sculpted head and arm of the Emperor Domitian are exhibited in the Museum of Ephesus — the only remaining fragments of a colossal statue of the emperor that once stood in the Temple of Domitian in Ephesus. This gigantic and imposing statue originally stood 27 feet tall. The arm alone displayed in this photo is approximately seven feet in height.

Below: The altar displayed below is the actual altar that was once in the inner sanctuary of the Temple of Domitian, located in the heart of Ephesus.

emperor and was therefore subjected to some of the most severe persecution that ever transpired in the course of history.

As noted in Chapter One, the apostle John became a target of Domitian's demented cruelty when John refused to acknowledge that Domitian was *dominus et deus,* and the emperor ordered John to be brought to Rome and executed.

Church fathers record that the emperor had John thrown into a cauldron of boiling oil, but God miraculously delivered the apostle unharmed. It was only when John's execution failed that the emperor resorted to exiling John to the isle of Patmos in 95 AD.[76]

Then in the year 96 AD, Domitian was assassinated, and the Senate issued

Right: *Statues of muscular barbarians adorned the tops of columns on the front facade of the Temple of Domitian. Very little of the original facade remains today, but pictured to the right is one of the many original barbarian statues that was once displayed on the facade of this notorious temple. The dimensions of this structure were 150 feet by 300 feet — making it one of the largest in the central section of Ephesus. Its deliberate placement among other temples and gods was intended to remind residents that Domitian possessed divine status.*

its *damnatio memotiae* — an official edict that *damned* Domitian's rule and called for the eradication of his memory.[77] This purge included the obliteration of temples, buildings, and statues that had been constructed in the emperor's honor. However, local city authorities prevented the destruction of the fabulous Temple of Domitian, located in the heart of Ephesus, by rededicating the temple in honor of Vespasian and Titus.

Facing the Temple of Domitian was an arched fountain known as the Fountain of Domitian, **34** often referred to as the Fountain of Pollio in honor of the man who constructed the first fountain on this site in 93 AD. The original fountain was an enormous edifice with dazzling

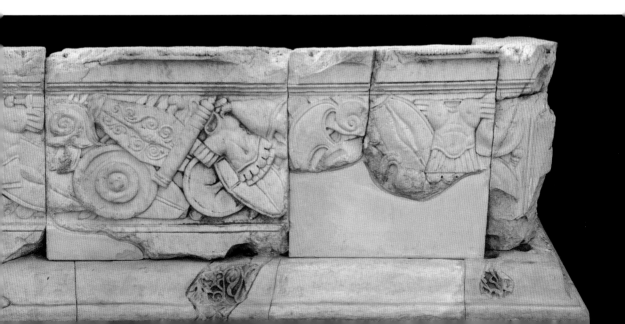

Corinthian columns; a statue group depicting the giant Polyphemus' mythological attempt on Odysseus' life; and an imposing idol of Zeus. What remains today of the water and drainage pipes reveals that this fountain was quite a complicated construction project for the First Century. Because this square was consecrated to the worship and honor of Domitian, no expense was spared in constructing both the temple and the fountain.

THE BASILICA

As Paul, Aquila, and Priscilla continued to meander up Curetes Street, they may have slowly zigzagged from one side of the street to the other, inspecting all the historical elements that symmetrically flanked the lengthy marble road — beautiful columns and a host of statues depicting gods, citizens, athletes, musicians, poets, philosophers, historians, and city fathers. If they followed this road to its conclusion, they would have found themselves at the entrance to the upper portion of the city — the Administrative District.

In this privileged section of the city, the local Council assembled in the Bouleterion, Ephesus' place of government, and the wealthy class shopped in the Upper Marketplace. Specially privileged citizens

Left: The Basilica was 495 feet long, and the inside of its central section had 134 majestic Ionic columns, each topped with the horned heads of two projecting bulls. The Basilica was used as a public forum, as a center of philosophy, as a place where ideas were exchanged, and as an art gallery dedicated to deceased and living members of the Julio-Claudian dynasty.

Above: This is one of the well-preserved bullhead capitals that sat atop the 134 columns in the Basilica in the upper district of Ephesus. The bull was a religious symbol that represented power and fertility and was an important emblem in the worship of the pagan goddess Artemis.

bathed in exclusive baths, and the affluent and influential exercised in the elite Upper Gymnasium. It was also home to the Temple of Isis, the Prytaneum, the Temple of Dea Roma, and the Magnesia Gate.

If Paul and his team entered the upper Administrative District of the city, they would have immediately walked into the Basilica ㉟ — one of the most magnificent buildings in Ephesus. Built in 11 AD, this majestic 495-foot-long building was expanded by Nero and graced with additional columns crowned with Corinthian capitals, giving a cathedral-like appearance to its interior.

As visitors entered the building, they immediately saw two impressive rows of 67 Ionic columns. These columns supported the weight of the Basilica roof and divided the three arched aisles that ran the length of the entire building. A total of 134 columns topped with two projecting bulls on either side gave the impression that great power was required to support the roof of the mighty structure. But the bull was also an important emblem in cult worship, symbolizing both power

and fertility. Thus, the vast number and strategic location of these 268 bulls also conveyed the message that the Basilica was used for this purpose.

To an outside observer, it would have been immediately clear that this was an elite part of the city. People who strolled through the 134 columns were dressed in garments embroidered with gold, signifying their high social status. Women's faces were enhanced with cosmetics — a very expensive product in the First Century — and their hair was elaborately braided, with strands of pure gold interwoven in the locks of their hair. Earrings, rings, arm bracelets, and jewelry worn on these wealthy women's ankles and feet were fashioned of gold and silver, making it very apparent that they were accustomed to a life of luxury.

In the Basilica and Administrative District, it would have been evident that the men were also accustomed to a higher lifestyle. These men wore expensive, flowing garments as they strolled through the arched aisles, exchanging ideas about business and politics.

The Basilica was not only an architectural wonder and a remarkable work of art — it was also a public forum, a center of idea exchange, a cathedral of philosophy, and a center of idol worship. This massive edifice served as a gathering place for poets, philosophers, politicians, wealthy businessmen, and luxuriously gowned women. Here the elite could socialize, voice their support and objections to ideas, or listen to their educated acquaintances who also lived in the upper district of Ephesus.

Left: The Greeks used vases to chronicle nearly every aspect of life. This is a detail taken from an ancient Greek vase that depicts the various kinds of clothing worn by women in Greek lands. Women generally were clothed in tunics that reached to their feet. The woman at the top is pictured in a Doric tunic; the women below her are clothed in lighter tunics; and the four women at the bottom are dressed in more elaborate clothing that had sleeves and was gathered with belts at the hips and waists. Although Asia was a Roman province, its customs and styles were influenced by an illustrious Greek past. Therefore, this is the type of clothing that would have been indicative of that region in Roman times.

Right: The customary clothing for a Greek man was a tunic covered with a large woolen cloth that was wrapped around the body. In cold weather, the woolen cloth could also be pulled over the head and used like a hood. In this detail from an ancient Greek vase, the man on the top is shown wearing an expensive tunic, and the man just below him demonstrates how the tunic could be folded back in warmer weather. The three figures in the middle are shown wearing the large woolen cloak, and the man at the bottom is wearing an expensive tunic with a cloak to give a sense of grandeur.

Statues of the Emperor Augustus and Empress Livia were erected on large podiums in the east annex, and the walls of the Basilica were lined with portraits and inscriptions of the Julio-Claudian dynasty. Thus, the Basilica not only had the appearance of a temple, but it also resembled an imperial gallery, dedicated to the memory of both deceased and living imperial family members.

When Paul, Aquila, and Priscilla saw this building for the first time, its incredible beauty must have stunned them. Like any other newcomers, they would have walked the length of the Basilica to inspect its art, gaze upon its monuments, and read the inscriptions carved in its columns and walls. They would have also seen the large, open door located near the center of the building, through which residents and visitors could walk into the most historical marketplace of Ephesus.

THE UPPER MARKETPLACE AND NECROPOLIS

After seeing the Harbor Marketplace and the Central Marketplace near Marble Street, Paul and his team would have been immediately struck by the elegance of the Upper Marketplace **36** in Ephesus' upper city. Without a doubt, this marketplace, which measured 480 feet by 168 feet, was the most impressive one in Ephesus.

This ancient market was exceptional in every way — superbly designed, exquisitely decorated, and rich in history. Paul had walked through marketplaces in Tarsus, Antioch, Jerusalem, Athens, Corinth, and Cenchrea, but what he and his companions were about to see was different from any market they'd ever seen before.

Above: The Upper Marketplace of Ephesus was primarily used by the rich upper class who lived and worked in this more exclusive section of the city. Three sides of the market were flanked with 150 marvelous marble columns. Statues of famous citizens, politicians, educators, philosophers, emperors, and gods stood high on pedestals throughout the Upper Marketplace.

This magnificent marketplace was constructed during the reign of the Emperor Augustus (27 BC-14 AD), and it was largely expanded during the reign of the Emperor Claudius (41-54 AD), who was still ruling as emperor when this apostolic team arrived in Ephesus.[78]

The massive Upper Marketplace was truly remarkable. Three sides of this ancient square were lined with 150 marble columns, each capped with an intricately crafted capital. Most impressive were the many graves and crypts scattered throughout the marketplace. These were not tombs of mere commoners, but of well-known citizens — some dating more than 700 years before the birth of Christ.

If Paul stopped to read the names inscribed on these gravesites, he would have been taken aback. Many were legendary figures of Greek and Roman history — people he had probably heard about since childhood. It was obvious that this wasn't just a shopping center; it was a necropolis, an ancient cemetery, designed to honor the illustrious dead of Ephesus.

Imagine how surprised Paul must have been to see shoppers leisurely meandering in and out of shops that were interspersed among the graves of historical giants from the past — including scholars, historians, writers, poets, philosophers, politicians, and statesmen. But for those who lived in the upper district of Ephesus, this was a common sight. History abounded on every side in their city, but especially throughout the Upper Marketplace of Ephesus.

Above: When Paul and his team arrived in 52 AD, a significant temple to the goddess Isis stood near the entrance of the Upper Marketplace. Remnants of the reddish granite columns are still scattered on the grounds of this marketplace — columns that were once transported from Egypt to adorn the exterior of this pagan temple. Not much remains of the Temple of Isis except for its foundation stones, seen in this photo.

THE TEMPLE OF ISIS

Located near the center of the Upper Marketplace was the great Egyptian Temple of Isis. **37** High walls surrounded the temple's exterior, erected to keep the curious eyes of the outside world from viewing the secret rites that transpired deep inside the inner part of this dark, mysterious sanctuary. Just as the cult of Serapis attracted men, the worship of Isis especially attracted women. Because women were generally restricted from entering public markets in the Roman Empire, the Temple of Isis was located near the market entrance to provide access for women who wanted to worship there. The highly visible, central location of the Temple of Isis provides evidence of the enormous popularity this cult had gained in the city of Ephesus. It would have been impossible for Paul and his team to miss the Temple of Isis as they surveyed the Upper Marketplace.

The door was first opened for Egyptian cults to be carried to distant lands after Alexander the Great was declared Pharaoh of Egypt in 332 BC[79] (*see* pages 511-519 for more information on Alexander the Great). At that time, Egyptians carried the husband-and-wife cult of Serapis and Isis to Ephesus and on into Asia, where their religion began to play a major role in many parts of the province. The impact of this cult on the city of Ephesus was substantial, as worshipers paid homage to the god Serapis near the Central Marketplace and to Serapis' wife, the goddess Isis, at the temple in the elegant Upper Marketplace.

The cult of Isis particularly appealed to people of education and wealth. Perhaps this was the result of Cleopatra's influence on the Greeks and Egyptians who lived in Ephesus. Cleopatra's fierce dedication to the goddess Isis was widely known throughout the Roman Empire. Cleopatra adorned herself as the high priestess of Isis, even wearing a headdress and priestly clothing to make her appear as the goddess Isis. As noted earlier, Cleopatra and Antony wintered in Ephesus in the year 33 BC, and some scholars suggest that the Egyptian temples of Isis and Serapis in Ephesus were erected as a result of Cleopatra's visit to Ephesus and her influence in that city.

The Temple of Isis had 16 tall columns. Exotic music played ceaselessly as incense billowed into the air from the altars where worshipers gathered to show reverence to the gods.

Worshipers of the goddess Isis would hold a huge festival each year in March to remember the time Isis sailed the seas in search of the scattered remains of her husband Serapis, who had been killed and dismembered by his brother Set, the Egyptian god of darkness.[80] This colorful festival was filled with pageantry, merriment, dancing, and singing. Costumed worshipers packed the streets, parading down Curetes Street to Marble Street, then to the Arcadiane, and finally ending at the Harbor of Ephesus, where a ceremonial ship awaited the ritual blessing of priests in memory of Isis sailing the seas.

Each year in October, a second celebration in honor of Isis was also conducted, involving thousands of participants.[81] Multitudes again took to the streets in costumes, this time to

reenact the dramatic moment when the god Serapis was raised from the dead after Isis found and reassembled his scattered remains. For days prior to this October celebration, Egyptians and Greeks alike would lament over the slaying of Serapis. But then the grievous mourning would conclude as multitudes began rejoicing in the streets to mark Serapis' "resurrection."

Unlike other temples in Ephesus where people could freely walk in from the street to offer incense or view the proceedings, the activities in the Temple of Isis were hidden from public view. The temple was a place where dark, secret rites were conducted behind its tall walls using

Left: The temple pictured here is a religious complex similar to the Temple of Isis in Ephesus, with tall exterior walls to conceal its secret rituals from the public. Such temples were highly ornamented, richly colored, and filled with the smoke of sacrifices and incense.

fire, water, incense, and other elements associated with occult practices.

If Paul and his team walked around the perimeter of the Temple of Isis, they would have seen Greek and Egyptian inscriptions on the outside of the tall compound walls. From behind the walls, the sounds of the priestesses' exotic music and clacking castanets could be heard. The team would have also smelled the aromatic smoke of sacrificial incense as it seeped over the walls of that hidden and secret shrine.

Only a few details about the dark cult of Isis are known. For instance, people could convert to this cult only if the goddess personally summoned them through dreams and visions. Also, to become an adherent, one had to pass through intensive rites of purification, followed by rituals that replicated the story of Isis traveling the seas to collect the dismembered parts of her husband. In every way, the cults of Isis and Serapis were mysterious, dark, and demonic.

THE WATER PALACE

The Water Palace 38 didn't exist at the time of Paul's arrival, because it was another monumental structure constructed near the beginning of the Emperor Domitian's rule. However, because Domitian is central to the book of Revelation, the Water Palace is mentioned here. This great fountain stood on the southwest edge of the Upper Marketplace just a few steps east of the Temple of Domitian and Domitian Square.

The Water Palace fountain was enormous in its dimensions. It had two floors and multiple niches that were each constructed like small temples. Each temple-niche held statues of various Greek and Roman gods, and water sprayed magnificently from the statues and idols on every level. It was truly an elaborate work of art that must have amazed visitors who gazed upon the intricate workmanship represented in the structure.

Above: The Prytaneum was one of the oldest buildings in the upper district of Ephesus. Because it was the headquarters of Curetes priests in Ephesus, a large idol of Artemis was placed in a highly visible position. The Prytaneum was one of the oldest and most beautiful buildings in all of upper Ephesus.

THE PRYTANEUM

Once the team had seen enough of the Upper Marketplace, they would have reentered the Basilica. Perhaps they tilted their heads back to look upward at the great vaulted ceilings or looked to the left and right at the hand-chiseled idols and statues scattered throughout the huge structure.

Finally, the three may have noticed a marvelous structure on the opposite side of the Basilica. Walking over to explore further, they would have discovered an elegant and very significant building known as the Prytaneum.

The Prytaneum ❸❾ was an ancient old public building that had been constructed approximately 300 years earlier.[82] The gorgeous structure the three visitors beheld still looked much the same as it had throughout the reign of the Emperor Augustus. The Prytaneum may have been old, but in 52 AD, it still retained elements of its glory from the past.

The function of this building was similar to a town hall, but it was also used for receptions held to honor individuals and for banquets associated with religious festivals. The floors were sumptuously decorated with exquisite mosaics, and the walls were paneled with elegant marble. A statue of Artemis was placed in a significantly visible location — an important feature since this was the headquarters of the Curetes priests of Ephesus. In the center of the largest room was a sacred hearth, where gods were honored with

Above: *The Temple of Dea Roma, the official goddess of Rome, stood adjacent to the Prytaneum. In 29 BC, the Emperor Augustus ordered the construction of the temple, which was specially dedicated to the emperor's memory.*

incense and offerings. Adjoining rooms of the Prytaneum connected it to the Temple of Hestia, ⓴ where priests continually burned sacred fire to the goddess Hestia. Because of the Curetes priests' influence in Ephesus, this was likely considered the second most holy site in the ancient city of Ephesus after the Temple of Artemis.

From the Prytaneum in the upper district of the city, the Curetes priests would carry on religious rituals in Ephesus that were connected to the goddess Artemis. As mentioned earlier, the Curetes priests would parade up and down the main street of Ephesus on a regular basis, performing their wild and raucous ritualistic dances. This is the primary reason Ephesus' main street later became known as "Curetes Street."

TEMPLE OF DEA ROMA

As the team continued up the street, their eyes would have been drawn to the Temple of Dea Roma, ⓴ located just a few steps beyond the Prytaneum. At the time of Julius Caesar, the Roman conquerors felt a need to unify the various lands, languages, and cultures of the empire. They therefore searched for some concept or entity around which people could find common ground, regardless of language, nationality, culture, or class distinction. The answer was the creation of a new god — *Dea Roma*, the goddess of the Roman Empire.

The Roman government declared that every person in the empire had to unify around this goddess that epitomized the spirit of Rome. However, over time it became a commonly accepted belief that

Right: This small amphitheater was referred to as the Bouleterion, a name derived from the Greek word boule, *meaning to counsel. It was the official meeting place of the city council. At night the amphitheater was transformed into the Odeion, used for theatrical and musical performances catering to the wealthier residents of Ephesus who lived and worked in the city's upper district. The Bouleterion that exists today was built in the year 150 AD on the site of an amphitheater dating back to a much earlier time in Greek history.*

the goddess Dea Roma actually resided in the Roman emperor — whoever was currently ruling at the moment. Thus, the Roman emperor wasn't only revered as a human lord; he was also worshiped as divine — the human vessel containing the spirit of the goddess Dea Roma.[83]

When Paul and his team came to Ephesus in 52 AD, this cult of Dea Roma was already well established in the city. The Temple of Dea Roma, towering over the heads of the apostolic team as they walked up the street toward the Bouleterion, represented one of the most significant temples dedicated to this Roman goddess. This particular temple was dedicated to the Emperor Augustus, who had authorized its construction during a visit he made to Ephesus in 29 BC. It possessed a unique Asian characteristic in that it included a special chamber for another goddess — the goddess Artemis.

It is significant that Artemis, the ruling goddess of the region, had been given a place in a temple dedicated to the goddess of Rome. This signaled a message to the citizens of Ephesus that Artemis and the goddess of Rome worked together as spiritual forces to guide the decisions being made by the city senators, who gathered for council meetings in the adjacent Bouleterion.

THE BOULETERION

The Bouleterion **42** was a government structure for the city of Ephesus. The building visible today is the result of an expansion carried out in 150 AD, which enlarged and embellished the earlier Bouleterion that Paul, Aquila, and Priscilla saw when they came to Ephesus.

The word "Bouleterion" comes from the Greek word *boule*, which means *to counsel* — and, indeed, this structure was the meeting place where the local city council conducted matters of business.

This amphitheater could hold approximately 2,000 people and was used for multiple purposes. During the day, it was the location where city council (or city senate) meetings convened. These senators were selected from high-ranking, distinguished families, and each was required to earn a higher education and to effectively use his influence to help rule and govern life in Ephesus.

But in the evenings, this building was transformed into a marvelous concert hall called the *Odeion*. The general population of Ephesus attended shows in the Great Theater, located at the top of the Arcadiane, but the richer class stayed closer to the upper part of the city. Therefore, the Odeion was used to hold musical, theatrical, and dramatic performances designed specifically for the upper-class population that rarely attended events in the Great Theater.

Right: This huge edifice was once the Upper Bathhouse and Gymnasium in the upper district of Ephesus. It had four massive rooms with floors covered with mosaics and walls paneled in richly colored marbles.

The Odeion consisted of three main sections: the auditorium, the orchestra, and a two-storied marble backdrop for the stage, which was decorated with elegant statues and intricate carvings. A section of seats was constructed on the slopes of a hill, and other sections were built on vaulted arches. Patrons reached their seats by climbing multiple sets of stairs.

The Odeion Theater also had a permanent roof that protected patrons, senators, and council members from the sun or foul weather. This is most likely the reason that no drains have been located in the surrounding area. This building was truly a remarkable work of art.

THE UPPER BATHHOUSE AND GYMNASIUM

The splendidly decorated bathhouses of the upper city were constructed to service the needs of the wealthy, the educated, and the city's politicians. The Upper Bathhouse ⓭ had four bathing rooms, multiple bathing basins, and many windows to let in the sunlight. A large latrine was connected with other smaller rooms used for multiple purposes, including commercial transactions and the providing of sexual services. The floors were covered with beautiful mosaics and the walls paneled in sumptuous marbles.

People in this region of the city were committed to physical exercise, athletic competition, the development of their physiques, and the attainment of physical beauty. Consequently, a large Upper Gymnasium was constructed as an annex to the Upper Bathhouse, where clients could leisurely stroll, relax, or engage in physical exercise.

The Upper Bathhouse and Gymnasium ruins in upper Ephesus today actually date from the Second Century. However, excavations have revealed that a bathhouse and gymnasium existed in this same location as early as the Hellenistic age.[84] This means Paul, Aquila, and Priscilla would have seen a similar Upper Bathhouse and

Gymnasium in this same spot when they inspected the upper city in 52 AD.

THE SOUTH ROAD AND MAGNESIA GATE

Along the entire length of the Upper Marketplace was the South Road, **44** which led to the upper entrance of the city. Like other streets in the Ephesus, this road was lined with covered colonnades that offered a wide variety of shops. It was also highly decorated with statues, idols, and pagan gods — all of which were intricately and colorfully painted to make their appearance seem lifelike to observers.

If Paul walked the length of the South Road, they would have eventually reached the Magnesia Gate, **45** which was the departure point to the city of Magnesia on the Cayster River. However, the South Road also connected the upper part of Ephesus to the road that was often filled with worshipers traveling to the Temple of Artemis in order to participate in its cult rituals.

The Magnesia Gate that Paul, Aquila, and Priscilla saw was built during the First Century BC. Massive friezes of various weapons and large marble lions served as furnishings for the gate. On either side of its central arch were two towers, embellished with carvings and decorative moldings. From the Magnesia Gate, city walls extended in both directions, encircling most of the city.

If the apostolic team walked all the way to the Magnesia Gate, this would have completed their tour of Ephesus. Beyond the gate, the road led to the Great Temple of Artemis, cutting through mountainous areas and circling around the actual base of a mountain along the way.

All along this road were reliefs carved from stone that depicted the goddess Artemis in her various roles, including her role as protector of the dead. During special holidays, worshipers traveled from all over the Roman Empire to participate in the activities of Artemis worship. On such holidays, a large cart carrying a statue of the goddess would be followed by hundreds, perhaps even thousands, of worshipers, singing and chanting magical phrases to invoke her blessing. This cart and its procession would start in the city

of Ephesus and continue onward past the Magnesia Gate, all the way to the Great Temple of Artemis, located approximately one and a half miles from the city. When Paul, Aquila, and Priscilla arrived in Ephesus, this tradition was still deeply embedded in the lives of the Ephesian people.

If Paul and his team traveled this road, they would have walked past all those stone reliefs until they eventually reached the Temple of Artemis, one of the most famous temples of ancient times and named one of the Seven Wonders of the World.

(Continued on page 263)

Left: The South Road turned to the right of Curetes Street and led past the eastern side of the Temple of Domitian, eventually turning to run parallel to the south side of the Upper Marketplace. This was a significant road in the ancient world because it led through Ephesus' upper district and on to the eastern entrance of the city at the Gate of Magnesia.

Below: The Magnesia Gate served as the official entrance to Ephesus from the upper district of the city. It was called the Magnesia Gate because it led from Ephesus to the city of Magnesia on the Cayster River. However, this gate was also important to Artemis worshipers because the South Road on which it was located led to the legendary Temple of Artemis on the outskirts of the city.

PAUL'S PREVIOUS EXPERIENCE WITH IDOLATRY

Before Paul came to Ephesus, he had lived in Corinth, where the world's largest Temple of Aphrodite was located. Paul had also personally seen the Acropolis in Athens and viewed the many idols in that Greek city. Experience with idolatry and occultism wasn't new to Paul, but what he was about to experience in Ephesus was beyond anything he'd ever witnessed, for Ephesus and the other cities of Asia were possibly among the most pagan cities in human history. One of Paul's most notable encounters with idolatry and paganism occurred when he first entered Athens. What he witnessed was so

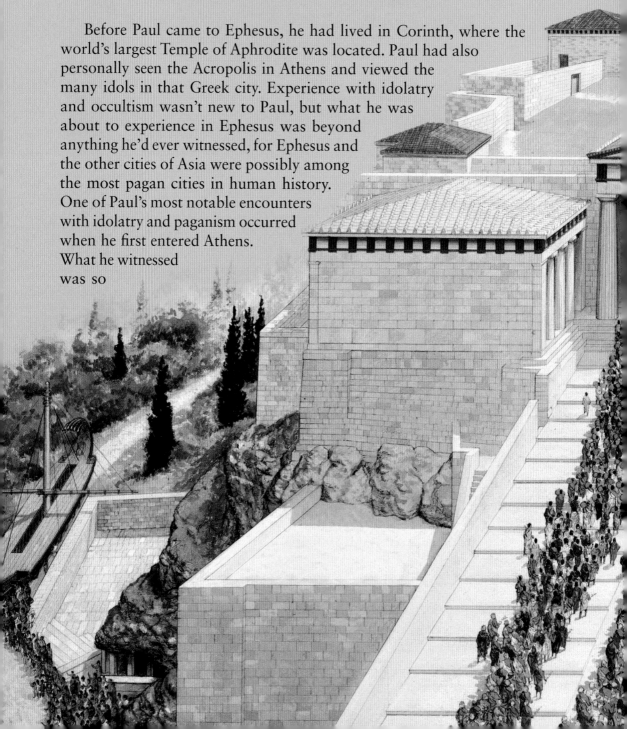

This illustration shows the Acropolis of Athens, which housed the great Temple of Athena, along with many other pagan temples. When certain philosophers heard Paul preach, they brought him to the Areopagus — the high court of the city — to speak to a group of distinguished city leaders who desired to know what new doctrine he had brought to the city. Historical records show that the city of Athens had more than 30,000 idols, which explains why Acts 17:16 states that Paul's "...spirit was stirred in him, when he saw the city wholly given to idolatry."

appalling that the Bible says "...his spirit was stirred in him, when he saw the city wholly given to idolatry" (Acts 17:16).

In the Greek text, the word "stirred" is the Greek word *paroxuneto*, which is derived from the word *paraxusmos*, a compound of the words *para* and *xusmos*. The word *para* means *alongside* and carries the idea of *being close*. The second part of the word is the Greek word *xusmos*, which describes *something sharp*, such as a knife, and normally indicates *a very sharp situation*. When the two words are joined together, the compound word describes *someone who has taken something so close to the heart that it has become a sharply felt agitation to him.*

This word carries such a sense of agitation that the word *paraxusmos* has been translated *to call into combat*. This is a particularly apt translation, because it tells us Paul didn't retreat or run in fear when he saw the darkness of the city. Instead, the word *paraxumos* implies that he charged full-steam ahead to wage warfare against the evil forces of the city.

Left and Above: *The Temple of Artemis in Ephesus, noted as one of the Seven Wonders of the World, was highly decorated and beautifully painted. Although it no longer exists in Ephesus today, its exterior would have been similarly decorated to the Temple of Athena in Athens (pictured above). The illustration on the left depicts how a portion of the relief sculptures from the front facade of the Temple of Athena look today compared to how they may have looked when they were intricately painted more than 2,000 years ago. The relief of the horsemen is stunning and shows remarkable workmanship even in white marble. But when paint is applied to the sculptures (shown in the illustrations both on the left and right), as was true in their original form, one can see how gorgeous these reliefs were when they adorned a still-active temple. Even the fabric was painted in great detail to give the people depicted in the sculptures a realistic, lifelike appearance.*

Preaching God's Word is the highest form of spiritual warfare, for the mighty two-edged sword that is the Word of God has the greatest power available in this life to banish the forces of darkness from any environment. Based on multiple uses of this word in the New Testament (*see* Acts 15:39; Hebrews 10:24), we know that the word *paraxusmos* also means *to irritate, to incite (whether to good or to evil), to anger, to inflame,* or *to enrage.* From this, we can easily ascertain that Paul was deeply troubled and ready to wield the sword of the Spirit to combat the wickedness he saw all around him in Athens.

The verse goes on to tell us exactly what disturbed Paul so deeply: "…when he saw the city wholly given to idolatry." The word "saw" is the Greek word *theoreo,* which means *to gaze at* or *to look upon.* From this same root we derive the word *theater.* The usage of this word is important in this context, for it reveals that idolatry was so visible in Athens, Paul perceived the whole city to be like a huge stage set for its practice. When the verse says Paul "saw" the idolatry, the Greek uses a participle. This means it could be translated that Paul "…saw and continually kept on seeing…."

Everywhere Paul looked, he saw idols, for they could be found on every street and corner in the city of Athens. He found himself surrounded with thousands of marble statues of Greek gods and deities. As noted in the

paragraphs above, there were so many idols in Athens that the original Greek could literally be translated, "*He saw and continually kept on seeing that the city was wholly given to idols.*"

Left: This is an artist's rendering of how the goddess Athena may have looked in the Temple of Athena on top of the acropolis in ancient Athens. The idol was made of wood, covered with ivory for skin, and draped in material that included 220 pounds of pure gold. Athena held a massive shield made of bronze, and the statue of Nike in her right hand was life-sized. The statue's base was adorned with marvelous gilded relief, and a reflective pool in front of Athena provided an awe-inspiring view of the idol to worshipers as they entered the door of the temple.

The phrase "wholly given to idolatry" is from the word *kateidoolos*, a compound of the words *kata* and *doulos*. The word *kata* carries the idea of *domination* or *subjugation*. The word *doulos* is the word for *a slave who is sold to his owner*. This slave completely belongs to his master and lives to fulfill the wishes and desires of his master. When the words *kata* and *doulos* are compounded, the new word is *kateidoolos*, which is used in Acts 17:16. It means *to be completely dominated by, subject to, and sold out to the rule of idols*. In other words, the idols were the masters, and the people of Athens were the slaves. The entire city was dominated by idols, and the people lived their lives under the rule and dominion of idolatry. The worship of idols and multiple gods was so woven into the fabric of Athens that it literally dominated every part of the inhabitants' public and private lives.

One expositor says that the word *kateidoolos* can be translated *sunk in idolatry*, *rife with idolatry*, or *gross idolatry*. This makes sense, for archeological findings and historical records show that at least 30,000 idols were on public display in the city — and that doesn't even take into account the thousands of miniature idols that were kept in people's private residences.[85] There were so many "gods" in this city that one Roman satirist of the First Century wrote that it was "easier to find a god than to find a man" in Athens.[86] Another historian stated that a day in Athens without taking account of the gods and their temples would be a day spent with one's eyes half-closed![87]

Idols were on every street, at every street crossing, and at every prominent location in the city. The briefest stroll through the city would expose a visitor to countless gods. And none of this takes into account the diminutive temples built at the entrance of every house, where family members would place their own preferred idol and make sacrifices to it every day as a part of their daily routine.

It was into this environment that Paul entered in Acts 17. With the sword of the Spirit — the Word of God — the apostle began to preach and wage warfare against the evil forces of darkness that had long ruled Athens.

But as pervasive as the idolatry and paganism was in Athens, the spiritual atmosphere in cities that lay ahead in Paul's future were perhaps even more diabolical. What Paul saw in Athens didn't compare to the breeding ground of occultism he was about to experience in Ephesus, Smyrna, Pergamum, Thyatira, Sardis, Philadelphia, and Laodicea. Because Athens was a center of learning, its form of paganism was developed and refined. In contrast, the paganism of Asia was dark, exotic, mysterious, and bizarre. When Paul and his apostolic team entered Ephesus and the other Asia cities, they encountered people engrossed in mystery religions that celebrated deviant sexual religious practices; engaged in dark, secret rituals and supernatural activities; and used amulets, charms, emblems, secret occult writings, and codes.

Although the apostle Paul had already experienced paganism in other cities, all of these factors created a feverish occult environment in Ephesus beyond anything he had ever seen or experienced before. Pagan worship permeated every arena of life for the city's inhabitants. And because Ephesus was the largest city in the region and possessed excellent roads that connected it to all the other cities, its idolatry and pagan worship had reached its long tentacles into all of Asia. It has been argued that the paganism and idolatry in Athens paled in comparison to the widespread paganism in Ephesus and other Asia Minor cities.

The day Paul, Aquila, and Priscilla arrived at the Ephesian port, they entered a city composed of a strange mix of elegance, wealth, business, government, culture, learning, education, and vile wickedness. Paul had been greatly disturbed by what he encountered in Athens, so we can only begin to imagine how troubled and ill at ease he must felt upon his arrival in Ephesus. Everywhere he and his team looked, they were surrounded by everything the Gospel stood against — including *idolatry, immorality,* and *occultism,* and the list went on and on. To Paul and his team, the entire city must have appeared demonized and in dire need of deliverance.

Seeing the challenge before them in Ephesus, the apostolic team could have rushed back to the port and purchased three tickets on the next ship to get them out of that place. But Paul and his companions knew that the Holy Spirit had orchestrated their divine mandate to this virulently pagan city. Asia Minor was ripe for harvest, and they had an assignment to complete. Regardless of what they saw or experienced, they would not budge from the mission God had sent them to fulfill. Because of the steadfast determination and the divine power that enabled this apostolic team, the forces of darkness would be pushed out of the way and the church of Ephesus birthed. And from this historic ministry base, God's Word would eventually spread throughout all of Asia Minor and beyond.

THE TEMPLE OF ARTEMIS: ITS ORIGIN, ITS RELIGIOUS PRACTICES, AND ITS ROLE IN THE CITY OF EPHESUS

Paul's team must have been very aware that they were physically and spiritually entering the territory of Artemis worship — a religion that so dominated the city of Ephesus, it had become the world center of this abominable, demonic cult. The city was proudly called the official "Warden of the Temple of Artemis" because it had the largest Temple of Artemis **46** in the entire ancient world.[88]

Legend states that the Amazons — renowned ancient female warriors — founded the earliest settlement of Ephesus as early as 3,000 BC.[89] Many serious scholars have proposed that the name "Ephesus" could possibly be a derivative of the word "Apasas," meaning *the city of the Mother Goddess* — a name borrowed from a city in the ancient kingdom of Arzawa, which existed in that region in the latter part of the second millennium BC.[90]

This name ascribed to the ancient settlement of Ephesus indicates that a special connection existed between its early settlers and the worship of Cybele, the multi-breasted Mother Goddess of fertility.

The original inhabitants of the settlement were driven out by Ionian Greek

Left: Pictured here is a statue of the goddess Artemis from the Museum of Ephesus in Selçuk, Turkey. Hundreds of similar terracotta images of Artemis have been excavated in the ancient city of Ephesus, indicating how popular the worship of this goddess was in Asia Minor during Roman times.

Right: This painting by Adolf Pirsh (1885) shows a front view of the Temple of Artemis with the apostle Paul preaching to pagans outside the temple complex. The painting portrays the elaborate external reliefs and the massive columns that were an integral part of the temple décor.

settlers around the year 1,000 BC. When the new inhabitants arrived, they assimilated the local religion of Cybele with the Greek worship of Artemis.[91] Thus, a unique version of Artemis worship was created, different than that which existed in other Greek-dominated lands.

Scholars say it is likely that a meteor once fell from the heavens and crashed to earth near the outskirts of Ephesus.[92] However, over the years, a legend developed around this event. The legend claimed it was a perfect image of Artemis — as depicted by ancient statues viewed in museums today — that fell from the heavens, and this myth eventually became entrenched in the minds of the local people. In Acts 19:35, the town clerk — one of the highest and most honored governmental positions in Ephesus at the time — referred to this legend when he declared, "...Ye men of Ephesus, what man is there that knoweth not how that the city of the Ephesians is a worshipper of the great goddess Artemis, and *of the image which fell down from Jupiter?*"

Notice the town clerk didn't say *individuals* in Ephesus worshiped Artemis. Rather, he said "...the *city* of the Ephesians is a worshipper of the great goddess Artemis...." This was *citywide* worship.

The Greek word for "worshiper" in Acts 19:35 is *neokoros*, a word that involves more than just the concept of *worship*. It also depicts *a temple guardian, a warden, a protector,* or *a maintainer of a temple*. This word describes those who were entrusted with the charge to maintain, administrate, and protect temple facilities.

Because this word *neokoros* is used in this verse by a high official of the city, we know that by the time Paul and his team arrived, the entire city of Ephesus believed it was their responsibility to be *guardian, warden, protector,* and *maintainer* of the Temple of Artemis. This statement in the book of Acts is one of the clear signs revealing the depth to which this dark religion had subdued and consumed the people in Ephesus.

The city of Ephesus was so entirely built around the worship of Artemis that the month of the spring equinox was named after Artemis. Throughout that month, the city celebrated a long festival in honor of the goddess.[93]

Several temples built on this same spot had been destroyed or burned over the centuries, including a substantial temple that burned down the night Alexander the Great was born (estimated by scholars to be July 20 or 21, 356 BC). When asked why the goddess didn't protect her temple from fire, the priests and priestesses would answer that she was away from the temple at the time the fire occurred because she wanted to observe the birth of Alexander the Great in Macedonia.[94]

After the fire that destroyed their Temple of Artemis, the Ephesians simply began to construct another temple. The new structure was more elaborate than the previous one and took 220 years to build. This was the Great Temple of Artemis that existed when Paul and his team arrived in 52 AD.

The Temple of Artemis was located at a vantage point where passengers on ships could see it as their ship approached the harbor. It must have been an impressive sight to people who saw it for the first time. Elated worshipers arriving on ships were told the goddess was watching their arrival. They would see the massive image of Artemis facing them from the temple grounds, growing larger and larger as the ship approached the port. This sight must have created a great sense of anticipation in the pagan throngs who journeyed to Ephesus for the sole purpose of worshiping the idol of Artemis.

The Temple of Artemis was built just outside of Ephesus — on the very spot where her image had reputedly fallen from Jupiter — and was a major source of income for the city. Every year, crowds thronged to the multiple festivals that were conducted in honor of the goddess. Throughout the province of Asia and the entire Roman Empire, people would travel to Ephesus for this purpose. Many would arrive on ships from around the world to worship Artemis on these special festival days. Some scholars estimate that at such times, the city would swell from its normal population of 250,000 to more than 1,000,000 people.

THE TEMPLE OF ARTEMIS

The Temple of Artemis was such a wonder in the ancient world that writers of that time recorded a great deal of information about its architectural design, its exterior facade, and its lavish interior. Because the foundation for the giant idol of Artemis still exists today in Ephesus on the site of the temple grounds, it is known exactly where the idol of Artemis stood inside the temple. Based on various sources of information, this artistic rendering shows what the Temple of Artemis probably looked like in 52 AD when Paul and his team arrived in Ephesus.

Above: The Temple of Artemis that existed at the time of Paul's arrival in 52 AD was considered one of the Seven Wonders of the World. Today only one column and scattered stones remain, as much of the material from the temple was later harvested and used in the construction of other local buildings.

The temple's ornate facade directly faced the harbor, framed beautifully by the mountains that loomed behind the enormous marble structure. The temple was 425 feet long and 220 feet wide, and it had 127 marble columns, each of which was 60 feet high. For those who walked the length of the temple, it must have seemed as if they were walking through a forest of marble.

Whether people approached the Temple of Artemis from the harbor along the Plateia in Coressus Street or on foot along the upper South Road leading from Ephesus, they would have seen this imposing structure long before they ever stood in its presence. From a distance, visitors could begin to see the details of this magnificent temple: those marvelous columns of marble lining the temple; the statues of lions and bulls guarding the doorways; the Gorgons (mythological female monsters that served as protective deities) standing on either side of Artemis on the temple pediment; and the winged female messengers of stone that looked as if they were ready to fly away at any moment.

The colossal image of Artemis depicted a woman wearing a turret-shaped crown on her head, marking her both as a goddess and as the official Protectress of Ephesus. Each of her arms rested on a twisted column, and she was served on either side by eunuch priests or lions whose role was to defend and minister to her. Her torso

Right: A massive statue of Artemis, similar to the one pictured here, stood on a pedestal inside the Temple of Artemis and faced the ancient Harbor of Ephesus.

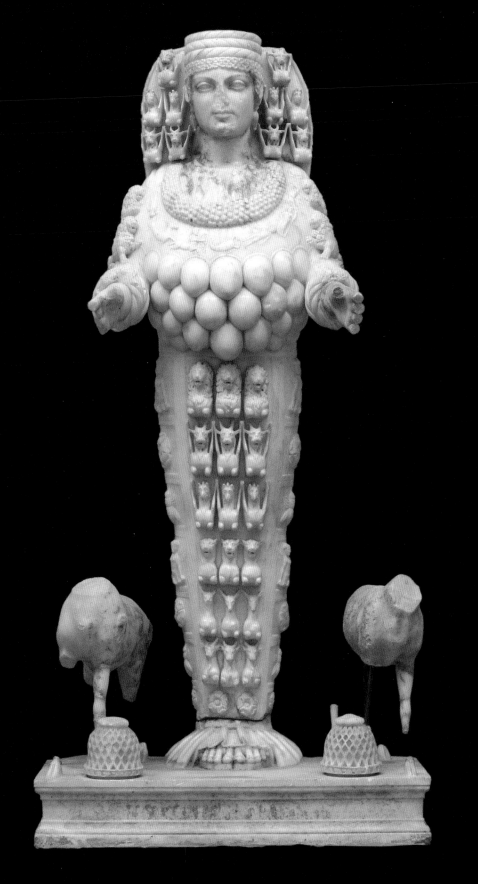

was lined with multiple rows of bulls' testes, which were regularly sacrificed to her because semen from bulls was considered holy, especially in regard to her role as the goddess of fertility. The 268 massive bull capitals that topped 134 marble columns in the Basilica of the upper district were emblems associated with the worship of Artemis. From her waist down, her lower body was covered with sculpted rows of lions, rams, and bulls.

Archibald Henry Sayce, a notable historian, wrote that the worship of "the Mother Goddess" (named Artemis in Ephesus and worshiped under other names in various parts of the region) required up to 6,000 priestesses to serve the goddess in one temple alone.[95] Indeed, there were *thousands* of priests and priestesses serving at the Temple of Artemis. Eunuch priests served under the direction of a high priest. Three classes of priestesses — Mellierae, Hierae, and Parierae — also served in the temple.

Some scholars suggest that the priestesses of Artemis were called *Melissae*, the Greek word for *bees*. This may point to early myths connecting the bee to the Ephesian goddess, as well as to earlier versions of the Mother Goddess of fertility in other ancient cultures of that region.[96] It may also be the reason that the image of a bee is a frequent symbol on the coins found in the ruins of Ephesus. In addition, this term may have referred to the way large numbers of priestesses swarmed like bees throughout the grounds of the Temple of Artemis as they performed their religious rituals.

This evil temple was breathtaking to look upon. When the Greek poet and historian Antipater of Sidon compiled his list of the "Seven Wonders of the World," he included the Temple of Artemis. He wrote: "I have set eyes on the wall of lofty Babylon on which is a road for chariots, and the statue of Zeus by the Alpheus, and the hanging gardens, and the colossus of the Sun, and the huge labor of the high pyramids, and the vast tomb of Mausolus; but when I saw the house of Artemis that mounted to the clouds, those other marvels lost their brilliancy, and I said, 'Lo, apart from Olympus, the Sun never looked on aught so grand.'"[97]

When the Greek writer Philon of Byzantium recorded his thoughts about the Temple of Artemis, he wrote similar words: "I have seen the walls and Hanging Gardens of ancient Babylon, the statue of Olympian Zeus, the Colossus of Rhodes, the mighty work of the high Pyramids and the tomb of Mausolus. But when I saw the temple at Ephesus rising to the clouds, all these other wonders were put in the shade."[98]

All of this religious activity on special holidays brought a great deal of business and money to Ephesus. It attracted thousands of visitors who needed a place to sleep and food to eat while staying in the city. It also meant the prostitution business would flourish; the bathhouses would be filled with clients paying for their services; and huge amounts of money would be spent on items purchased by visitors in the shops along the main streets of the city and in its large marketplaces.

Revenues would also soar at the Great Theater as visitors bought tickets to the shows. The stadium would be packed with blood-hungry spectators. In addition, worshipers would spend vast sums of money on silver, bronze, and terra-cotta images of the goddess Artemis to take home after the holidays concluded, as well as amulets, charms, occult scrolls, and religious services performed on their behalf by priests and priestess in local pagan shrines. Visitors were also frequently tattooed before leaving to have a permanent memory of their visit to this holy city, where the gods felt comfortable enough to dwell among men in the temples.

A CENTER OF OCCULTISM AND PAGANISM IN ASIA

Ephesus was steeped in witchcraft, sorcery, idol worship, and other forms of paganism. This occult atmosphere drew many people to migrate there in order to test new religious ideas. Whatever new idea or religion proved a "hit" in Ephesus would be more likely to make its way into other Asia cities. The excellent road system that led from Ephesus to these other cities made it easy for a new idea or new religion to spread outward from Ephesus to other places.

As a result, Ephesus was not only a primary center of commerce for that region of the world, but also of occultism. New forms of paganism were constantly

Above: Divine strategy was evident in choosing Ephesus as the ministry base for the apostle Paul and his team. Known as "The Gateway to Asia," Ephesus was considered the most influential city in the First Century Roman province of Asia. Broad Roman roads led from Ephesus to the other cities named in the book of Revelation, providing an effective means of transportation and communication so Paul and his ministry team could travel forth to proclaim the Gospel and establish churches in each of the region's major cities.

being introduced to "test the market" and thereby gain a foothold in Asia. By the time Paul and his team walked the streets of Ephesus in 52 AD, the city was comprised of a mammoth community of pagans and a small community of approximately 10,000 Jews.

Upon arriving in Ephesus, Paul and his companions discovered a city that was fully immersed in spiritual darkness and occultism of the highest order. Almost the entire population was consumed with superstitions and magic, including many in the Jewish community who had also been affected by the widespread use of occultism. People expressed ardent faith in their amulets, charms, and secret emblems that supposedly had the power to chase away evil spirits and protect them from danger.

Scrolls known as "Ephesian Letters" were a particularly popular item in Ephesus. People came from around the world to purchase these scrolls, upon which were inscribed mystical, magical writings and incantations that reputedly held the power to remedy illness, make the infertile fertile, and guarantee success for nearly every endeavor in life, love, or business.[99]

Although Paul had certainly encountered blatant displays of paganism in his previous travels, the people's pervasive and active devotion to idolatry and false gods he and his team witnessed in Ephesus was at a level beyond anything he had ever seen. Paul had lived in Corinth where the world's most revered Temple of Aphrodite was located. He had visited Athens and viewed such a vast number of idols in the city that "...his spirit was stirred in him, when he saw the city wholly given to idolatry" (Acts 17:16). Idolatry was nothing new to Paul, but the magnitude of the paganism on display in Ephesus was above and beyond anything he could have anticipated. Nevertheless, this powerful city, which was in itself a pagan headquarters, was the place to which the Holy Spirit had led him and his team to establish a ministry headquarters that would eventually transform the spiritual atmosphere of the province of Asia.

Daring to enter Ephesus and establish a ministry base in that city was a great act of courage on the part of Paul and his team. In fact, it almost seemed fanciful to believe a church could be established in the midst of such perverse darkness. Yet divine strategy can be seen in the choice of this unlikely city as the place to start the first church in Asia. The accomplishment of this assignment would let believers everywhere know that if such a feat could be done there, it could be done anywhere.

The spiritual and natural forces of evil that ruled Ephesus and all of Asia didn't know it yet, but they were about to be confronted by the mighty power of God packaged in these three willing vessels. In one of the worst spiritual environments in the entire world, one of the strongest churches of the New Testament was about to be born in the power of the Spirit. Through the obedience of these three early believers and their willingness to tackle what seemed impossible to the natural mind, the forces of hell would soon be forced to move out of the way so the great church of Ephesus could be born. From there, the glorious light of the Gospel would begin to blaze throughout all of Asia and the greater peninsula of Asia Minor.

(Continued on page 277)

Above: This well-preserved Roman road is one of the best examples of the fine roads built by the ancient Romans throughout the empire. Sewage pipes usually ran under the central part of the streets of Roman cities, concealed underneath large street stones. Often the streets were dirty from animal waste and the litter of heavy traffic. Consequently, stepping stones (see pages 274-275) were constructed at key locations for people to use when crossing the street.

A MINISTRY BASE IN ASIA

The seven ancient cities mentioned in the book of Revelation — *Ephesus, Smyrna, Pergamum, Thyatira, Sardis, Philadelphia,* and *Laodicea* — were among the most pagan cities in the Roman province of Asia during Paul's day. Although the proconsul of Rome officially ruled Asia from Pergamum, Ephesus was the largest of these cities and the actual place of residence for the proconsul.[100] As such, Ephesus set the standard for idolatry and paganism, and all of Asia followed suit.

A primary factor that placed Ephesus in such a central role was the network of roads that connected this key port to other Asia cities. Romans were famous for their ability to construct excellent roads, and it was said that all Roman roads eventually led to Rome. But in Asia, all roads led to the city of Ephesus.

From Ephesus, every major Roman city and town in the region could be reached by traveling these well-constructed roads, which were used both to transport commercial goods and to export paganism to the other cities of Asia. Roads from Ephesus had to be excellent because the city was the home of Rome's proconsul, and he would often travel from Ephesus to neighboring cities. In addition, Ephesus was one of the primary cities in Asia where criminal and civil trials occurred,[101] so roads were essential for people traveling back and forth from their cities to Ephesus for legal business.

The city of Ephesus lay at the intersection of two ancient major overland routes: 1) the coastal road that ran north through Smyrna and Pergamum to Troas (near ancient Troy), and 2) the western route to Colossae, Hierapolis, Laodicea, regions of Phrygia, and beyond. Ephesus was also the starting point for a special postal route that connected all seven cities mentioned in the book of Revelation.[102]

For example, if a person traveled the postal road north from Ephesus, it would lead him directly to the city of Smyrna. From Smyrna, the road led onward to Pergamum. From Pergamum, one could take that road to Thyatira and then travel on to Sardis. From Sardis, the postal road led to Philadelphia. From Philadelphia, it continued on to Laodicea. And if one kept following the postal road from Laodicea, he would eventually return to the city of Ephesus. In addition, roads from the cities of Colossae,

Hierapolis, Melitus, and other important Asia cities, as well as from the Macedonian city of Philippi, also provided easy access to the city of Ephesus.

Today these Roman roads still exist in many parts of the former Roman Empire — ancient testaments to the vast amount of labor and money Romans invested to develop this part of their infrastructure. But when the builders of these marvelous roads were busy constructing them for the expansion of the empire, they had no idea that these same ancient highways would one day facilitate Gospel preachers as they traveled to cities throughout the empire to preach the Gospel and to establish the Church in each location.

Left: Most Roman cities had streets that were slightly raised so that water would drain off into gutters on either side of the street. Chariot and cart traffic was so heavy on city roads that ruts were carved into the stone pavement. Note the stone curbs of this marble road and the ruts formed as a result of all the chariots and carts that traveled the street for hundreds of years. Such ruts are still visible today on ancient Roman roads all over the former territory of the Roman Empire.

Because Ephesus was so vital to the region and well connected to other cities, it was an ideal location from which to launch a mighty apostolic mission into Asia. No city would have served more effectively than Ephesus as the base of operation. It had a port to receive visitors and preachers from abroad; facilities to host Christian guests in need of accommodations; schools of learning and education; and marvelous roads that could be utilized to plant churches in nearby cities.

These were most assuredly some of the reasons the Holy Spirit selected Ephesus to become the hub for mission activities in the region. Paul and his team arrived in 52 AD to challenge the forces of darkness in the city and

to lay the foundation for what would become the largest church of the First Century and one of the most successful mission campaigns in all of Church history. Just as paganism had spread from this city to other Asia cities across these roads, so Paul and his team could now take the message of the Cross of Christ to other cities in the region from a ministry base in Ephesus.

There's a very important lesson to be learned from the strategy carried out by Paul and his team as they established the Church in Asia. People often search endlessly for complex strategies and new methods to spread the Gospel when the best plan is often a simple one. For Paul and his team, the plan was extremely simple: Start a church in Ephesus; get it established; then follow the road to the next city and do it all over again.

Although it cannot be said with absolute certainty, most scholars believe that the churches in Smyrna, Pergamum, Thyatira, Sardis, Philadelphia,

and Laodicea were all started during Paul's tenure in Ephesus.[103] The mother church was located in the city of Ephesus. From that ministry base, many other churches were birthed under the leadership of the apostle Paul and the team he developed during his three-year stay in that city.

It's logical to conclude that because Paul couldn't be in all places at all times and do everything himself, he sent team members from Ephesus to travel those amazing Roman roads to other cities and establish churches. A good example of this can be seen in the way the Colossian church was established.

Colossae wasn't so far from Ephesus, but evidently Paul didn't go there himself. In Colossians 1:7, the apostle writes that he sent an emissary — a dearly loved brother named Epaphras — to that city on his behalf to preach the Gospel and to give birth to the church at Colossae. It is clear from the book of Colossians that this church maintained an ongoing relationship with the church of Ephesus and even looked to the Ephesian church and to the apostle Paul for relationship, leadership, instruction, and spiritual covering.

When God calls us to do something new and potentially magnificent, we shouldn't always seek complex strategies that overcomplicate the matter. If we will listen, the Holy Spirit can give us simple strategies that can impact our lives, our families, our neighborhoods, our cities, our nation, and even other nations of the world.

The best strategies are often the ones that are simple to implement and hard to confuse — not those that seem difficult to understand. Such was the case for the Early Church. It may not sound very deep or profound, but the best strategy for spreading the Gospel in First Century Asia was simply to follow the road.

THE CITY OF EPHESUS
AS IT EXISTED IN 52 AD

The following numbered list corresponds to the route and sights described in this chapter. There are many other ruins in ancient Ephesus that were built in later centuries. However, in this chapter we have dealt mainly with buildings, monuments, and religious structures that existed at the time Paul, Aquila, and Priscilla entered the city in 52 AD — with a few exceptions.

Included in this tour of ancient Ephesus were the Temple of Domitian and the Fountain of Domitian, constructed in the years 89-93 AD, as well as the Water Palace, which was constructed in 80 AD. Because the Emperor Domitian plays such a significant role in our discussion of Jesus' messages to the seven churches in the book of Revelation, these three structures are included in this list. Also mentioned is the Celsus Library, built later in the Second Century in the area of Philosophers' Square.

---

1. Harbor of Ephesus
2. Hellenistic Barracks
3. Harbor Marketplace (*Agora*)
4. Harbor Gate
5. The Arcadiane
6. Covered colonnades on the Arcadiane
7. Harbor Bathhouse
8. Marble Street
9. Plateia in Coressus Street
10. Stadium of Ephesus
11. Mass graves of gladiators
12. Great Theater of Ephesus
13. Central Marketplace (*Agora*)
14. Tolos
15. Hall of Nero
16. North Gate of the Central Marketplace
17. Gate of Mazeus and Mithridates
18. Southwest Gate of the Central Marketplace
19. Temple of Serapis
20. Philosophers' Square
21. Sarcophagus of sophist philosopher, Dionysus
22. Celsus Library
23. School of Tyrannus

24. Central Brothel of Ephesus
25. Heroon
26. Tomb of Arsinoe
27. Curetes Street
28. Terrace Homes
29. Covered colonnade on Curetes Street
30. Public Toilets
31. Central Bathhouse
32. Temple of Domitian
33. Domitian Square
34. Fountain of Domitian
35. Basilica
36. Upper Marketplace (*Agora*)
37. Temple of Isis
38. Water Palace
39. Prytaneum
40. Temple of Hestia
41. Temple of Dea Roma
42. Bouleterion and Odeion
43. Upper Bathhouse and Gymnasium
44. South Road
45. Magnesia Gate
46. Temple of Artemis

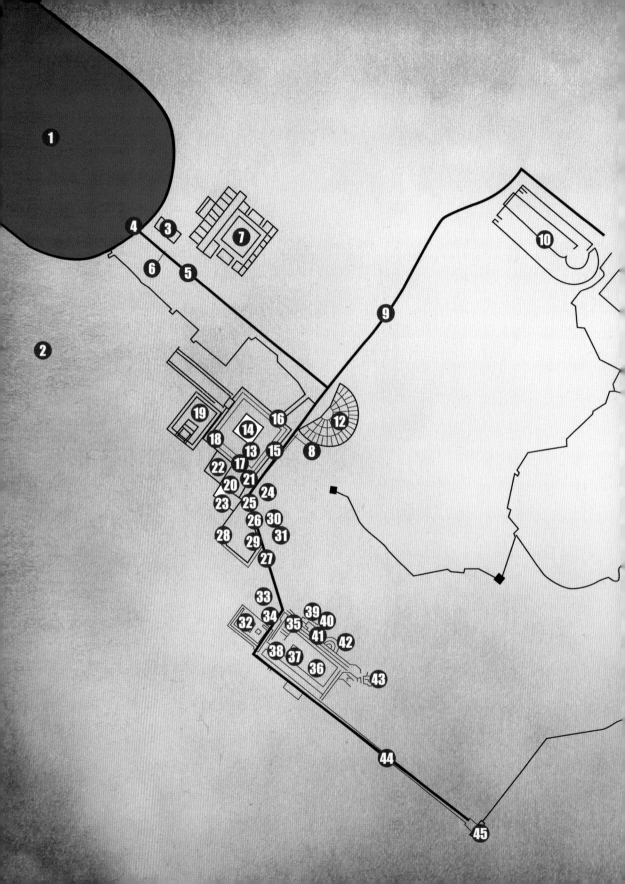

Map of Ancient Ephesus

⑪

46

Chapter Four

ESTABLISHING A MINISTRY HEADQUARTERS IN EPHESUS

The church in Ephesus was the largest in the province of Asia and served as a ministry headquarters throughout the region. It would be difficult to overestimate the significance of this work, for the Ephesian congregation was to become the central church for all others established in Asia.

The events pertaining to Paul's ministry in the city of Ephesus are vividly recorded between Acts 18:19 and Acts 20:1. To understand the extreme challenges that were inherent in the ministry assignment God gave Paul and his team, it's very important that we study the dramatic events that unfolded along the streets of this strategic pagan city soon after their arrival.

Acts 18:19 relates that soon after Paul arrived and got settled into Ephesus, he made his way to the local synagogue to share the message of Christ with the leaders of the Jewish community. Throughout the Roman Empire, synagogues were places where Jews met together for spiritual, intellectual, and social purposes; therefore, Paul knew it was the place to go if he wanted to reach the Ephesian Jews with the message of the Gospel.

The Jews who lived in Ephesus were reputed to be intelligent, gifted, and educated, and many scholarly and intellectual Jewish leaders would congregate at Philosophers' Square. Located at the western end of Curetes Street, this large public square regularly attracted the local intelligentsia, who would gather to discuss and debate issues and ideas with each other (*see* pages 213-216).

Especially in the foreign lands where Jews had been scattered, synagogues provided vital meeting places for people of the Jewish faith.

Left: Pictured are the ruins of Curetes Street, Ephesus' legendary central road that was lined with covered colonnades, marble columns, statues, and idols. Curetes Street led from the wealthy upper district down to the central district, where people conducted business and the intellectual crowd congregated in Philosophers' Square.

Left and Right: Some scholars suggest that the Jewish synagogue of Ephesus was located just behind Philosophers' Square at the western end of Curetes Street — west of the site where the Celsus Library was later built in the Second Century. (Left: Ruins of the library exterior. Right: An artistic drawing of the interior.) If this is accurate, the Jewish community enjoyed a prime location for their meeting place right in the heart of the city, implying an unusual level of favor with Ephesus' pagan leadership for at least a significant period of time during the Roman Empire's Imperial period.

However, the exact site of the Ephesian synagogue has never been determined with certainty. Some archeological research suggests there may have been a synagogue located directly behind Philosophers' Square, just west of the site where the Celsus Library was later built. Other evidence indicates there may have been a synagogue north of the Great Theater.

The monotheistic Jewish faith was diametrically opposed to the pagan religions. Because pagans espoused belief in many gods, they considered the concept of giving homage to only one God repulsive. So if Jews were permitted to build a synagogue in a pagan city, the land allocated for these structures was usually located in out-of-the-way, less visible locations. Because of pagan opposition, many Jewish communities didn't even have actual buildings for synagogues. However, since the only requirement for an official synagogue was an assembly of ten Jews, the community would simply gather under the open sky in some cases.

An exact location for the synagogue in Ephesus has never been determined; therefore, some scholars suggest that the Ephesian Jews gathered in an open-air meeting place. However, the idea that a physical synagogue building existed somewhere in Ephesus is supported by the wording in Acts 18:19, which says that Paul "entered *into* the synagogue." The word "into" is the Greek word *eis*, which literally means *to the inside of*, as in the act of walking *into* a building. This strongly implies that the Jewish community in Ephesus met in an actual structure located somewhere in the city.

Because the synagogue was the primary place where Jews gathered for

worship and for the public reading and teaching of Scripture, it was the center of their social lives. As the four gospels relate, even Jesus habitually went to the synagogue on the Sabbath for the public reading of Scripture (*see* Luke 4:16). Thus, when Paul entered the Ephesian synagogue, he was stepping into the customs, the culture, and the very heart of the local Jewish community.

As Paul approached that synagogue for the first time, he may have reflected on the mixed reactions he had experienced in other cities when he had entered synagogues to proclaim the Gospel to Jewish audiences. What reaction would he encounter this time as he stood before

the sophisticated Jewish crowd of Ephesus? Would they receive him, or would they reject his message as Jews had done on most occasions? Paul had reason to wonder about this, given the opposition from Jews he had previously faced in Paphos (Acts 13:6-8), Antioch in Pisidia (Acts 13:45-50), Iconium (Acts 14:2-5), Thessalonica (Acts 17:5-9), Berea (Acts 17:13), and Corinth (Acts 18:6,12-17).

Yet Paul never lost sight of the fact that the Gospel was "to the Jew first" (Romans 1:16), even though he was indisputably the apostle to the Gentiles (*see* Ephesians 3:1-8). Biblical record reveals that he consistently attempted to preach to Jews first when he entered a new city or territory and that this was the case when he and his team first arrived in Ephesus. One exception to this practice occurred in Lystra (*see* Acts 14:6-18). There Paul preached to a Gentile audience first, perhaps because the Jewish community in Lystra was small or nonexistent.

Like metal is drawn to a magnet, Paul was drawn to the synagogues of the cities to which he traveled, where he could meet others who shared his religious heritage and nationality. Most of his ministry was conducted in the pagan world — but even when Jews disagreed with him, tried to ruin his reputation, or attempted to kill him, Paul never forgot they were his kinsmen according to the flesh (Romans 9:3). He knew the Jewish people — how they thought, how they felt, what they believed, and how they reasoned among themselves. He felt comfortable with those who gathered in synagogues, because they were his distant relatives. Thus, wherever he traveled, Paul always tried to give the Jewish community the first opportunity to hear the Good News, even though his principal call was to the Gentile world, and his efforts with the Jews were primarily futile.

It is therefore reasonable to wonder what was going through Paul's mind as he stepped into the synagogue of Ephesus to share the message of the Gospel with a new group of Jews. And these weren't just any Jews — they were Ephesian Jews, which meant they were members of a highly educated and learned community.

Acts 18:19 relates that as soon as Paul entered the Ephesian synagogue, he "reasoned with the Jews." The word "reasoned" comes from the Greek word *dialegomai*, which means *to reason, to argue,*

to dispute, or *to convince*. In other words, Paul's immediate strategy was to try to convince his listeners that the Old Testament Messianic scriptures were fulfilled in the death, burial, and resurrection of Jesus Christ.

During this first short trip to Ephesus, Paul had an unusually delightful experience with the leading Jews of the city. Instead of being met with the customary opposition and hatred, he encountered open-minded people who wanted to hear his message. However, Paul's visit was cut short because of a Nazarite vow he had made in Cenchrea (*see* Acts 18:18),

Left: These are the ruins of the ancient Aegean Harbor of Cenchrea, from which Paul and his team sailed to Ephesus in 52 AD. Cenchrea was a rich seaport seven miles east of Corinth. In Romans 16:1, Paul mentions Phoebe, a deaconess from the Cenchrean church, which was likely started during Paul's 18-month stay in Corinth.

shortly before he crossed the Aegean Sea to Ephesus.[1] This ceremonial vow to abstain from strong drink and from cutting one's hair had great moral and religious significance to the Jews; therefore, some scholars believe that Paul may have made this vow to commend himself to the Jews for the purpose of winning some to Christ (*see* 1 Corinthians 9:20).

According to Jewish law, once a Nazarite vow was made, only 30 days were allowed for the fulfillment of all the rituals connected to the vow, and a portion of those rituals could only be fulfilled at the temple in Jerusalem. This meant that Paul had to leave Ephesus and arrive in Jerusalem before the 30 days were completed.

Apparently Paul's ministry impacted the Jews of Ephesus so greatly that they didn't want him to leave so soon. That's why Acts 18:20 states that "...they desired him to tarry longer time with them...."

The word "desired" is the Greek word *erotao*, which means *to strongly request*. The Greek tense implies that they asked Paul *repeatedly* to remain with them. They were so intrigued by his message that they *pleaded with him and implored him again and again* to extend his stay. But Paul was committed to keeping his vow, so he "...bade them farewell, saying, I must by all means keep this feast that cometh in Jerusalem: but I will return again unto you, if God will. And he sailed from Ephesus" (Acts 18:21).

Paul's first visit to Ephesus was brief, but during that short visit, he diligently sowed seeds of truth among Jewish listeners. When he departed, Aquila and Priscilla stayed behind to continue the work, going to the synagogue day after day to mingle with the Jewish community and to proclaim Christ to the open-minded Jewish listeners who assembled there. It was during one of these visits to the synagogue that they heard of a man named *Apollos*.

APOLLOS OF ALEXANDRIA

We don't know how Aquila and Priscilla first met Apollos, although it is likely that they approached him after hearing him lecture in the local synagogue. Acts 18:26 relates that the first time the couple heard Apollos speak publicly, they were so impressed by what they heard that they drew him aside to fully explain the whole Gospel message to him. Not long after that, Apollos became a part of the apostolic team in Ephesus.

Acts 18:24-26 provides significant insight into this man Apollos:

> **And a certain Jew named Apollos, born at Alexandria, an eloquent man, and mighty in scriptures, came to Ephesus. This man was instructed in the way of the Lord; and being fervent in the spirit, he spake and taught diligently the things of the Lord, knowing only the baptism of John. And he began to speak boldly in the synagogue: whom when Aquila and Priscilla had heard, they took him unto them, and expounded unto him the way of God more perfectly.**

Let's begin looking at Apollos by considering the city where he had spent most of his life — the legendary city of Alexandria. In 332 BC, Alexander the Great established the city of Alexandria as the new Egyptian capital on the banks of the Mediterranean Sea. In size, this ancient city was second only to Rome. It was named Alexandria in honor of Alexander the Great, who had "resolved to build a large and populous Greek city, and give it his name."²

In time, the city of Alexandria became the most plush and luxuriant city in the

world. It was home to kings, queens, diplomats, and generals, as well as to many of the greatest scholars and brightest educators of the day. The famous Egyptian queen, Cleopatra, ruled from Alexandria, and because she loved the city, she spared no expense to embellish it. At the time of her death in 30 BC, and well into the second half of the First Century, the city was

known as one of the most resplendent cities in the world, second only to Rome.[3]

Alexandria had many remarkable features that set it apart as one of the most outstanding cities of its time. It boasted two harbors, one smaller and one larger, and a great lighthouse[4] — which was listed as one of the Seven Wonders of the World.[5] The streets of central Alexandria were adorned

Above: The Great Lighthouse at Alexandria was the first lighthouse ever built and was named one of the Seven Wonders of the World. Built during the Third Century BC, it stood as a symbol of Alexandria's greatness and guided trade ships into the city's busy harbor for approximately 1,500 years.

with beautiful temples, massive statues, memorials, governmental buildings, a large monument dedicated to the memory of Alexander the Great, and tombs for Egyptian kings and queens. In addition, royal quarters had been constructed on a long pier that extended into the Mediterranean Sea, where Queen Cleopatra lived in opulent style. The city was also famous for its universities and schools of higher education — institutions that offered the finest education available in the world at that time. However, the most important feature of the city was the Great Library of Alexandria. First established by the Egyptian king Ptolemy II (283-246 BC), this structure was the largest and most splendid library of the ancient world.

When construction of the library was first announced, Ptolemy II declared that his goal was "to collect, if he could, all the books in the inhabited world, and, if he heard of, or saw, any book worthy of study, he would buy it."[6] As a result of this monumental endeavor, the Great Library of Alexandria became the largest library in the world, followed by the library in Pergamum and then by the library in Ephesus. Ancient Alexandrian scholars collected scrolls and books from all over the world in great quantities — to the extent that, according to the Jewish historian Josephus, no less than 500,000 documents were kept in the Great Library of Alexandria. In fact, the library contained the largest collection of ancient documents — including the most extensive collection of Jewish literature amassed outside of Israel — in the entire ancient world.

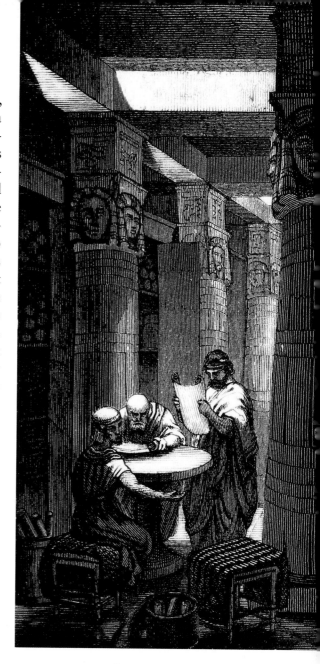

Demetrius of Phalerum, the first chief librarian, was so earnest in his desire to collect "all the books of the inhabited world" that he even gave the order for the Old Testament Hebrew Scriptures to be translated into the Greek language so they could be read by the Greek-speaking world. This massive undertaking produced a Greek version of the Old Testament

Left: The Great Library of Alexandria was renowned worldwide. Its elaborate halls, filled with exquisite Egyptian reliefs, held the largest collection of scrolls and documents in the ancient world — more than 500,000 in all.

the surrounding region. If this calculation is accurate, Alexandria had the largest Jewish community in the ancient world outside of Israel.

With such a large Jewish population, it is no wonder that the Jews exerted a significant intellectual and financial influence in this ancient city. Because of their massive numbers, Jews in Alexandria were granted freedoms not found in other cities. The Jewish community had synagogues, schools of theology, and numerous distinguished scholars. This helps explain why the Great Library of Alexandria held some of the most ancient Jewish writings that existed in the world at that time.[8]

Alexandrian scholars were noted for their intelligence and sophistication; however, none excelled more in intellectual brilliance or in education regarding matters of theology, history, geography, philosophy, and finance than the Jewish scholars of this great city. This was the environment in which Apollos was raised. It was here that he received his education and where his views of world history and theology were developed. Alexandrian Jewish scholars were famous for their careful interpretation of Old Testament Scriptures. It is therefore very likely that Apollos' religious views had been shaped by the pervading theological beliefs held by the Jews of this city where he had spent most of his life.

called the Septuagint, considered to be one of the Alexandrian scholars' greatest achievements.[7] The name Septuagint is derived from the Greek word meaning *seventy* in honor of the 70 Jewish scholars who translated it from the Hebrew language into Greek.

Some historians estimate that nearly one million Jews lived in Alexandria and

ELOQUENT AND MIGHTY IN SCRIPTURES

Apollos' high level of education and his personal dedication to the careful interpretation of Old Testament Scripture is made clear in Acts 18:24, which states that he was "...an eloquent man, and mighty in the scriptures...."

The Greek word for "eloquent" reveals Apollos' advanced level of education. It is the word *logios*, which explicitly describes a person who is learned or *educated*. In fact, this word denotes *one who has become distinguished by his study and education*. The use of the word *logios* to describe Apollos indicates that this man's educational pedigree was impressive.

It must be noted, however, that *logios* could also describe *one who has mastered the art of public speech*. Early records written by historians of the Church affirm that Apollos was a gifted orator and an eloquent, convincing public speaker.[9] Because he was so educated and his vocabulary was so large, Apollos was highly skilled in speaking authoritatively and persuasively. When people heard him speak and sensed his spiritual passion, they knew they were in the presence of a brilliant man who was passionately committed to studying and proclaiming the truths of God's Word. This was the quality that captured the attention of Aquila and Priscilla on the day they first heard him speak in the Ephesian synagogue.

Acts 18:24 also states that Apollos was "mighty in the scriptures." The word "mighty" is the Greek word *dunatos*, which means *powerful*. But as used here, the word *dunatos* carries the idea of one who has a *masterful grip* on something.

In the context of this verse, it refers to Apollos' *masterful grip* on Old Testament Scripture. Only a person who was serious about theological study and reflection would possess such an extensive command of the Scriptures. This suggests that Apollos may have been a student in the Jewish theological schools of Alexandria — an impressive educational background indeed.

There is more we can determine about Apollos by dissecting the Greek words contained in the next verse. Acts 18:25

Left: In the First Century, Philosophers' Square was located where these ruins of the Celsus Library now stand. This was the area where the Ephesian intellectual crowd would gather to debate and listen to new ideas. Thus, it is very possible that Apollos taught curious onlookers from the Scriptures at this location.

states, "This man was instructed in the way of the Lord; and being fervent in the spirit, he spake and taught diligently the things of the Lord, knowing only the baptism of John."

First, it must be noted that the word "instructed" in this verse comes from the Greek word *katecheo* and denotes *one who has advanced knowledge in comparison to others and is highly educated in a certain subject*. The use of this word "instructed" indicates that Apollos was a serious student of the Old Testament. He possessed expert knowledge about this subject that had been passed on to him in the synagogue by rabbis or in the classrooms of Alexandrian schools of theology.

Furthermore, it is important to note that the Greek tense for "instructed" is continuous, which means that Apollos wasn't an ordinary student who simply wanted to graduate and receive a diploma. Rather, he was thoroughly committed to the Word of God and had proven it by giving himself to continuous study and instruction over the years.

The effect of God's Word on Apollos' life is made plain in Acts 18:25, which states that Apollos was "fervent in the spirit." The word "fervent" means *to be full of enthusiasm*. Thus, we know that Apollos was *enthusiastically bubbling over* with love for the Word — and when Aquila and Priscilla heard him speak, they were struck by this man's deep passion for the things of God.

Yet despite Apollos' theological pursuits and intense spiritual fervor, Aquila and Priscilla discerned that his knowledge about Jesus was incomplete. Acts 18:25 tells us that Apollos knew "...only the baptism of John."

This phrase reveals something significant about Apollos' understanding of Jesus at the time Aquila and Priscilla first heard him speak. It implies that Apollos either heard John the Baptist preaching at the Jordan River or that he had been influenced by the preaching of John's disciples, who may have traveled to the city of Alexandria. With nearly one million Jews in the vicinity of Alexandria, it is quite possible that some of John's disciples traveled to Alexandria and that their message had been heard and entertained in theological circles that included Apollos.

Bible scholar A. T. Robertson writes the likely scenario:

> Apollos knew only what the Baptist knew when he died, that John had preached the coming of the Messiah, had baptized him, had identified him as the Son of God, had proclaimed the baptism of the Holy Spirit, but [John] had not seen the Cross, the Resurrection of Jesus, or the great Day of Pentecost.[10]

Acts 18:25 says Apollos "...taught diligently the things of the Lord...," but the word "Lord" is an incorrect translation. The Greek actually states that he "...taught diligently the things of *Jesus....*"

Some take this phrase to imply that Apollos was already a full-fledged New Testament believer by this time. But further insight into the phrase "the things of Jesus" in Greek is important at this juncture. It is translated from the words *ta peri tou Iesou* — which in no way refer to a personal, saving knowledge of Jesus Christ. This phrase affirms only that Apollos knew certain things about Jesus.

The fact that Apollos spoke publicly concerning the "things" he knew about Jesus means he placed some confidence

in the possibility that Jesus was the long-awaited Messiah. However, it also seems to confirm A. T. Robertson's position that Apollos' knowledge of Jesus was limited to facts, details, and Messianic prophecies or to what he had heard others say about Jesus.

Apollos had a solid grasp of Old Testament Scripture and may have even believed Jesus was the Messiah. Nevertheless, something was incomplete in

Left: Marble Street in Ephesus started at the base of the Great Theater and ended at Curetes Street. Philosophers' Square was located at the juncture of these two ancient roads, where some scholars suggest Priscilla and Aquila first met their future team member, Apollos.

take it into one's own arms. This undoubtedly means Aquila and Priscilla made an arrangement to meet privately with Apollos so they could lead him further along in his faith. They drew him to themselves as a friend, became his spiritual mentors, and "...*expounded* unto him the way of God more perfectly."

The word "expounded" supports the view that Apollos had never heard the full story of Jesus, for the Greek word denotes *a full and complete explanation.* Recognizing this man's hungry heart and open mind, Aquila and Priscilla seized the opportunity to fully inform him about Jesus' death and resurrection and the events that transpired after the outpouring of the Holy Spirit on the Day of Pentecost.

Verse 26 goes on to say that Aquila and Priscilla "...expounded unto him *the way* of God more perfectly." The phrase "the way" was a New Testament expression referring to the way and truth of Jesus Christ. The use of this phrase "the way" at this point affirms again that Aquila and Priscilla presented to Apollos a full explanation of the Gospel, which he had probably never completely heard. Bible commentator William Barclay says that after they presented the full message of Jesus to him, "Apollos, who already knew Jesus as a figure in history, came also to know Him as a living presence."[11]

Apollos' presentation, causing Aquila and Priscilla to draw him aside privately to fill in the gaps. As Acts 18:26 states, "...They took him unto them, and expounded unto him the way of God more perfectly."

The phrase "they took him unto them" is a translation of the Greek word *proselabonto.* It is a compound of the words *pros* and *lambano. Pros* means *toward,* and *lambano* means *to take,* as in *to personally draw something toward oneself and*

Above: *Pictured are the ruins of a central road that ran through the ancient city of Corinth, where Paul ministered for 18 months before traveling on to Ephesus. The huge Temple of Aphrodite used to stand on top of the mountain pictured in the background.*

When this husband-and-wife team decided to focus their time and attention on Apollos, they didn't know what a pivotal role he would play in the Church of the First Century. They had no idea that the man they were ministering to would one day become the able leader of the Corinthian church and a comrade of Paul and other apostles or that his name would eventually find a place in various chapters of the New Testament.

This serves as a reminder that when we take the time to help someone, we are often unaware of whose life we are touching. Because Aquila and Priscilla gave attention to this intelligent, God-loving Alexandrian, Apollos obtained a more complete knowledge of Jesus Christ, eventually joined the ministry team in Ephesus, and later became a key leader in the Early Church.

It's uncertain how much time elapsed between the events related in Acts 18:24-28, but the space of time was adequate for this new Alexandrian brother to emerge as a leader in the newly developing church of Ephesus. In fact, Apollos became so established and respected that Acts 18:27,28 states, "…When he was disposed to pass into Achaia, the brethren wrote, exhorting the disciples to receive him: who, when he was come, helped them much which had believed through grace: for he mightily convinced the Jews, and that publickly, shewing by the scriptures that Jesus was Christ."

When Paul and his team arrived in 52 AD, there was no mention of any "brethren" in Ephesus, so this reference to "brethren" in Acts 18:27 is worth consideration. While Paul was in Jerusalem, the team members he left behind were not simply waiting idly for him to return. They were busy preaching, teaching, and establishing the new congregation.

Back in Corinth, Aquila and Priscilla had worked side by side with Paul for almost two years, so they knew exactly how to proceed even in his absence. As a result, the church of Ephesus was growing daily — and by the time Apollos departed for Achaia, it was already so mature that the "brethren" of the Ephesian church wrote a letter to introduce and endorse Apollos to the churches of that Greek province. Thus, we know that when Paul finally returned to Ephesus, a thriving congregation was waiting to greet him.

Why Apollos elected to relocate to Corinth in Achaia is not specifically stated in the New Testament. However, an addition in the Codex Bezae (an ancient Greek-Latin translation of the text) suggests that some Corinthian believers heard Apollos preach in Ephesus and asked him to travel with them to Corinth.[12] Certainly Apollos' breadth of education and mastery of language would have been seen as fitting qualities for the one who would pastor the Corinthian church. Apollos' command of Scripture, his ability to exegete, his expertise in Hebrew and Greek, and his oratorical abilities would have been extremely helpful to anyone who served as overseer of the large Corinthian church.

In First Corinthians 1-3, Paul states that Apollos eventually became one of the key leaders of the Corinthian congregation and made a significant contribution to the churches throughout Achaia. Paul told the Corinthians, "I have planted, Apollos watered…" (1 Corinthians 3:6).

Acts 18:27 says that when Apollos arrived in Achaia, he "…helped them much which had believed through grace." The phrase "which had believed" probably refers to the believers who were saved during Paul's previous residency in Corinth. But in addition to affirming and instructing these Corinthian believers, Apollos also utilized his past studies and his in-depth knowledge of the Old Testament to evangelize the Jewish community in Corinth. Acts 18:28 goes on to say that he "…mightily convinced the Jews, and that publicly, shewing by the scriptures that Jesus was Christ."

PAUL RETURNS TO EPHESUS AND FINDS 12 UNUSUAL DISCIPLES

After fulfilling his vow in Jerusalem, the apostle Paul returned to Ephesus to rejoin the team he had left behind. In his absence, the church he had established with his team had been growing; Aquila and Priscilla had formed a relationship with Apollos; and Apollos had been dispatched to Corinth to provide pastoral leadership for the church in that city. But after a long and arduous journey from Jerusalem, Paul was finally reentering Ephesus to begin what would be the longest residency and the most glorious phase of ministry that he would experience in any city. Consider just a few of the things Paul and his team would accomplish during his three years in Ephesus:

- Evil forces would be challenged.

- Demons would be cast out.

- Pagan worshipers would repent and burn their occult items.

- Thousands of angry idolmakers would gather in the Great Theater of Ephesus to raise their voices against Paul and his team in an attempt to stop their preaching that had resulted in so many coming to Christ in the city.

- A ministry headquarters would be established from which numerous churches would be started in Smyrna, Pergamum, Thyatira, Sardis, Philadelphia, Laodicea, and other cities throughout Asia.

Acts 19:2-7 tells of an intriguing incident that occurred when Paul first reentered Ephesus and encountered an unusual group of disciples. Upon meeting these disciples, Paul was curious about their faith.

> He [Paul] **said unto them, Have ye received the Holy Ghost since ye believed? And they said unto him, We have not so much as heard whether there be any Holy Ghost. And he said unto them, Unto what then were ye baptized? And they said, Unto John's baptism. Then said Paul, John verily baptized with the baptism of repentance, saying unto the people, that they should believe on him which should come after him, that is, on Christ Jesus. When they heard this, they were baptized in the name of the Lord Jesus. And when Paul had laid his hands on them, the Holy Ghost came on them; and they spake with tongues, and prophesied. And all the men were about twelve.**

It seems that these disciples were in the same spiritual state that Apollos was in at the time he met Aquila and Priscilla. Just as Apollos had known only the baptism of John, these disciples knew and believed in John's baptism unto repentance — but that was all they knew. As Paul spoke to the group, he sensed that something was amiss and that their faith was incomplete. So he delved deeper in his conversation with the 12 disciples, asking them, "...Have ye received the Holy Ghost since ye believed?..." (Acts 19:2).

They answered, "...We have not so much as heard whether there be any Holy Ghost" (v. 2).

This was a confirmation to Paul that something was missing in the faith of these god-fearing Jews. Therefore, he asked further, "...Unto what then were ye baptized? And they said, Unto John's baptism" (Acts 19:3).

Because Ephesus was a very large city with many districts, it is possible that these particular 12 disciples had never been in the right place at the right time to encounter Aquila and Priscilla. Like Apollos, these men had heard of Jesus and the mighty works He had done, and they may have even believed that Jesus was the Messiah. But they had never heard the complete Gospel message and therefore were not yet genuine New Testament believers.

In Romans 8:9, Paul wrote, "...Now if any man have not the Spirit of Christ, he is none of his." When Paul recognized their total ignorance about the Holy Spirit, it became crystal clear to him that

Right: Italian painter Bassamo del Grappa painted this 1560 painting, entitled, "The Sermon of the Apostle Paul." The scene provides the artist's perception of Paul as the apostle preaches a fiery message from the steps of a marble structure that looks much like the buildings of ancient Ephesus.

these 12 disciples were stuck in a time warp. It would be Paul's privilege to bring them out of the past so they could repent, make Jesus Christ the Lord of their lives, get water-baptized, and receive the infilling of the Holy Spirit.

These 12 disciples remind me of the story of four Japanese soldiers who fled into the mountainous regions of the Philippines in 1944 during World War II to avoid being captured by Allied forces. Year after year, *for 30 years*, these four soldiers continued to hide from the enemy, struggling to survive and living in total isolation to remain faithful to their commanding officer and avoid capture. Thirty years later, one had surrendered and two had died — but one faithful soldier remained in the dense Philippine jungles, still unaware that the war had ended.

In 1974, a group of historical researchers began a search for this final soldier. The researchers recognized the soldier's intense determination to be faithful to his commander's last orders. They knew that even if they found him, he wouldn't emerge from the jungle unless he had a direct order from his World War II commander.

Finally, when it was discovered where this lonely soldier was hiding, the researchers brought the soldier's former commander, still living in Japan, to the Philippines to give the order for the soldier

to surrender. When the soldier emerged from the jungle and heard the news that all combat activity had ceased 30 years earlier, he was stunned. He had been fighting a battle that had ended long ago because no one had ever told him the war was over!

When Paul encountered these disciples in Ephesus, he must have been shocked to discover an entire group of men who were still waiting for the Messiah to come. How could they not know? But like those four Japanese soldiers, these 12 men lived in a remote region, and no one had ever informed them that the Son of God had come to earth, died for mankind's sins, and been raised from the dead. Living in Ephesus, far from Christian activity, these men were still anticipating the coming of the Messiah.

Just like Apollos, these God-fearing disciples had heard and believed in John the Baptist's message and were awaiting the fulfillment of Scripture that the Messiah would come. Unaware that this event had already occurred, they were simply faithfully waiting.

But God hadn't forgotten these men. He knew exactly where they were, and He made sure to send someone across their path to help them complete their faith. That someone was the apostle Paul. Imagine how glad these 12 disciples were when Paul revealed the good news that the Messiah had indeed come and been raised from the dead — and then went on to relate all the powerful events that had occurred since the Day of Pentecost!

Paul told them, "…John verily baptized with the baptism of repentance, saying unto the people, that they should believe on him which should come after him…" (Acts 19:4). This was exactly the message they had held on to during those years in Ephesus. But then Paul took it one step further and gladly told them that all these prophecies had already been fulfilled in the Person of Christ Jesus.

Acts 19:5 goes on to tell us, "When they heard this [Paul's explanation that the Messiah had come in the Person of Jesus Christ], they were baptized in the name of the Lord Jesus."

If they had already been saved and baptized by New Testament standards, Paul would have never re-baptized them, for no teaching in the New Testament advocates re-baptism. This is the strongest evidence that Paul's encounter with these 12 men led to the very moment that they were actually born again.

But Paul didn't stop there. Acts 19:6,7 goes on to tell us, "And when Paul had laid his hands upon them, the Holy Ghost came upon them; and they spake with tongues and prophesied. And all the men were about twelve."

In these verses, we find the New Testament pattern for new believers. Paul led the 12 disciples to Christ and then wasted no time in baptizing them in water. Then immediately afterward, he laid hands on them to receive the infilling of the Holy Spirit. In other words, once the men were born again, there was no need for them to wait to be baptized in water or filled with the Holy Spirit. Paul recognized the importance of leading the men into the fullness of their salvation and therefore made sure he didn't leave them before these three acts were completed.

It is tragic that when people are led to Christ today, water baptism is often delayed or never carried out at all, and the infilling of the Holy Spirit is presented as an optional experience. The New Testament pattern shows that all three should be implemented as quickly as possible in a new believer.

As for this group of 12 disciples, it seems odd that they had never received a full understanding of Jesus, especially since Aquila, Priscilla, and others were very actively ministering in the city. But as mentioned earlier, Ephesus was a very large metropolis, and it is probable that there were sizable sections of the city's population who had never heard of Aquila and Priscilla or the other team members. This would have especially been true during this early phase of ministry when the Church was small and the Gospel message was still relatively new. It seems that this was the case with the 12 men whom Paul

Left: This painting by Spanish artist El Greco (1541-1614) depicts the moment the Holy Spirit first powerfully filled the infant Church as believers prayed in the Upper Room on the Day of Pentecost (see Acts 2:1-5).

encountered as he reentered Ephesus to rejoin his team.

What was the "chance" that the apostle Paul would accidentally bump into this group of 12 disciples in a city this large? There was nothing accidental or coincidental about this event.

When those 12 disciples first believed many years earlier, God saw their expression of faith and He never forgot. At the right time, He supernaturally directed Paul across their path so they would have the knowledge they needed to fulfill their yet-incomplete commitment to the Messiah.

We must never forget that when a person has expressed true, heartfelt faith to God, it is up to the Lord to ensure that someone crosses his path to bring his faith to completion. Of course, it is also up to the believer whom the Lord sends to discern and obey the Holy Spirit's leading. Otherwise, God will have to look elsewhere for a willing vessel to use to answer that person's heartfelt response of faith.

We are all called to be willing vessels, always available for the Lord's use on a moment's notice. Therefore, we must continually ask ourselves: *Am I the person God wants to use to bring someone to a more complete knowledge of Jesus Christ today?*

SUCCESS AND CONFLICT IN THE LOCAL SYNAGOGUE

After Paul resettled into Ephesus, he once again went directly to the synagogue to pick up where he had left off.

> And he [Paul] went into the synagogue, and spake boldly for the space of three months, disputing and persuading the things concerning the kingdom of God. But when divers were hardened, and believed not, but spake evil of that way before the multitude, he departed from them, and separated the disciples, disputing daily in the school of one Tyrannus.
> **Acts 19:8,9**

Verse 8 says that Paul entered the synagogue and "...spake boldly for the space of three months, disputing and persuading the things concerning the kingdom of God." The words "spake boldly" are from the Greek word *parresiadzomai*, which literally means *to speak freely*, *to speak boldly*, *to speak unashamedly*, or *to speak fearlessly*. For the first three months of his return to Ephesus, Paul focused on the Jewish leadership who gathered in the local synagogue, fearlessly and boldly proclaiming the message of Christ to them.

It is remarkable that Paul was allowed to speak in the synagogue for three months. Certainly it is the longest recorded period of time Paul was allowed to preach Christ in a synagogue. This provides a clue regarding the effectiveness of Paul's preaching to this particular Jewish audience. The open-minded, intellectual Jews of Ephesus must have truly been intrigued by the apostle's message.

Acts 19:8 says that during those three months, Paul was "disputing" with his listeners and "persuading" them concerning the many truths of God's Kingdom. The word "disputing" is the Greek word *dialegomai*, which means he *argued* and *debated* with the leaders of the Jewish community.

The verse goes on to state that Paul was "persuading" the Jews who gathered to listen to him. This is very important, for it once again reveals Paul's effectiveness in this synagogue. The word "persuading" is the Greek word *peitho*. It means *to convince*, *to persuade*, *to influence*, *to sway*, or *to bring someone around to understand and agree with your point of view*. In this verse, it indicates that Paul's manner of *debating* was so compelling that many Jewish leaders who heard him were *convinced* and *won over* by the message they heard him preach. In other words, they repented of their sin and received Jesus Christ as the Messiah.

Yet despite Paul's success with some of his Jewish listeners, he didn't have this same effect on all who heard him (*see* Acts 19:9). Religion is tolerant as long as it isn't threatened. But when it begins to perceive that a foe has entered its territory to convert its followers, religion can become ugly and perverse.

That is precisely what happened in Ephesus. For approximately 90 days, Paul's message regarding Jesus Christ remained interesting, intriguing, and tolerable to the larger Jewish community that resided in Ephesus. But when many leading Jews began converting to Jesus Christ, the religious spirits that ruled the synagogue felt threatened and the hospitable atmosphere quickly evaporated. Acts 19:9 says, "But when divers were hardened, and

Above: *The stately Hall of Nero stood along Marble Street on the way to Philosophers' Square. Some scholars suggest that the local synagogue where Paul preached was located in this busy section of the city.*

believed not, but spake evil of that way before the multitude, he departed from them, and separated the disciples, disputing daily in the school of one Tyrannus."

This verse states that some Jews were "hardened." This is the Greek word *skleruno*, and it means to be *hardened*, *stubborn*, *obstinate*, or *difficult*. It indicates *harshness*, *intolerance*, or *nastiness* toward a person or a particular subject.

In other words, these listeners became very angry and made a strong decision to reject Paul's message outright. The Greek word indicates that they were *intolerant* and *nasty* and that they deliberately *refused* to believe. Although they had heard the message, they made a strong decision to *reject* it.

How people respond to the Gospel determines the outcome of their heart condition. If a person receives the Gospel message, his response creates a *soft* heart. But if he deliberately refuses to repent, his decision causes his heart to become *hardened*. And if he continues to reject the Gospel, eventually this person will become so hardened that the very mention of the Gospel will cause him to act with *negativity*, *harshness*, *intolerance*, *nastiness*, and *antagonism*.

This was the case with those in the synagogue of Ephesus who took a stand against Jesus Christ. Their hardened hearts caused them to become antagonistic — so much so that they "spake evil of that way" (v. 9).

The phrase "spake evil" comes from the Greek word *kakolegeo*, which is a compound of the words *kakos* and *logos*. The word *kakos* describes something *evil, harmful, injurious, malevolent, malicious, spiteful,* or *mean.* The word *logos* simply means *words.* But when compounded into one word, they form the word *kakologeo*, which describes *malicious words that are deliberately devised and spoken to produce harm, hurt, and injury.*

Thus, these were not simply words of disagreement; rather, they were cleverly designed words and preplanned statements intended to damage Paul's reputation and ruin the impact of his message and ministry. These hostile Jews were spewing out premeditated, sinister, and villainous allegations in hopes of shutting Paul down. And, unfortunately, they did it publicly! That is why the verse goes on to say they spoke these words "before the multitude." The word "multitude" probably refers to those in the synagogue, which explains why Paul made the decision to leave the synagogue at the end of that three-month period.

When the opposition from unbelieving Jews became intense, Paul knew his effectiveness in the synagogue had ceased. Every time he tried to raise his voice to speak to the crowd, the opposing Jews were so vocal, loud, and nasty that he was unable to successfully carry on his ministry.

It is significant to note that Paul had the maturity to recognize when he had lost his effectiveness and it was no longer profitable to debate with his Jewish audience. Had he stayed and fought longer or harder, it wouldn't have produced anything of lasting quality and may have created an even worse situation.

If we will listen to the Holy Spirit, He will show us when to speak and when to be quiet — when to stay and when to move on. We must learn to be sensitive to the voice of the Holy Spirit in every situation. Then we can know when we are to remain in the battle or when it is wiser for us to withdraw, break camp, and relocate to new territory where greater victories will be won. The Holy Spirit will lead us — *if* we will quiet our hearts and listen for His voice.

THE SCHOOL OF TYRANNUS

When Paul realized that the battle in the Ephesian synagogue was counter-productive and no longer worth the effort, "…he departed from them, and separated the disciples, disputing daily in the school of one Tyrannus" (Acts 19:9).

The word "departed" is a derivative of the Greek word *aphistemi*, which describes not merely a physical departure, but *a complete withdrawal from one place to relocate to another*. Thus, we know that when Paul finally left the Ephesian synagogue, he withdrew with no intention of returning. This suggests that the opposition of unbelieving Jews became so intense that Paul had no desire to return to that battlefield again. Figuratively speaking, he shook the dust from his feet and walked out the door. But as Paul departed from the synagogue, he didn't leave empty-handed, for

Left: As today's visitors of Ephesus' ruins walk down Marble Street toward Curetes Street, they eventually reach the ancient stairs pictured here, located next to the area called Philosophers' Square during Paul's residence in the city. Some scholars believe that the School of Tyrannus — where Paul taught during his three-year stay in Ephesus — was located near the top of these stairs.

many had already been convinced of the truths he had preached concerning the Kingdom of God.

Acts 19:9 says Paul "separated the disciples." The "disciples" were those who believed his message — and when he left the synagogue, he took them with him. The Greek word for "separated" is *aphoridzo* — a word so severe that it is used to describe *the act of excommunication*. This strongly suggests that when these disciples walked away from the synagogue, it was a pivotal moment in their lives — a point of no return when they took a stand for Christ.

Every so often, occasions like this come in life — landmark moments when Christ calls us to leave the past behind. At such times, we must choose to make a break with everything we have known and loved in order to move into the new place where He is calling us. Such moments are difficult to experience because the flesh always screams in fear when it is forced to leave behind the familiar and the comfortable.

However, just beyond our common struggle of self-surrender is where we discover the greatest power of God. Getting there can be grueling. But once we put our flesh under and surrender to the Holy Spirit, resurrection power is soon released in our lives. We can see this spiritual principle in operation in Acts 19:9, for it was only *after* Paul and the new Jewish believers left the synagogue that God unleashed miracles in the city of Ephesus.

We don't know how Paul felt when he left the synagogue. Initially he may have had high hopes that the positive response he first received from this Jewish

community would last. As he gathered his disciples together and they walked away from the synagogue to begin fresh in a new place, it is possible that Paul felt heartbroken over the souls he had to leave behind. Perhaps he was tempted to feel discouraged or as if he had lost an important battle. But regardless of how Paul may have felt, Acts 19:9 relates that

Left: These intricately carved capitals once graced elegant marble columns in the city of Ephesus, providing a vivid glimpse into the architectural beauty that surrounded Paul as he daily set forth his case for the Gospel in the School of Tyrannus.

moments when it looks like all is lost, we must remind ourselves that when a door closes, God is already behind the scenes, working to open another door. In Paul's case, the door God opened was a place the Bible calls "the school of one Tyrannus."

The word "school" is the Greek word *schole* and most likely refers to *a lecture hall* or perhaps even one of the many halls used for trade guilds in the city of Ephesus. Some scholars even suggest that the ancient steps that still lead upward from Philosophers' Square to the foundation of a building long gone may have been the very steps leading to the School of Tyrannus referred to in this text (*see* pages 213-216).

The question, "Who was Tyrannus?" has long been a subject of debate, and there is no definitive answer. Some speculate that Tyrannus was a Jewish philosopher who owned and operated a school, whereas others propose that Tyrannus was a governmental leader in whose honor this school of learning was named. Still other historians theorize that this was a pagan educator who was sympathetic to Paul and his message and therefore allowed Paul to use his lecture hall in hours when it wasn't otherwise in use. It is worth observing that the name Tyrannus has been found in many First Century inscriptions among the ruins of Ephesus, supporting the New Testament claim that this school existed in Paul's time.[13]

he found an effective venue to continue preaching the Gospel as he "...disputed daily in the school of one Tyrannus."

Although it looked as if an important door for the Gospel was closing, God had already prepared another, more effective place for Paul and his group of disciples to meet in the city. The same thing happens in our lives as we seek to obey God's will. In

Above: The ruins of the once-beautiful Celsus Library, situated in the strategic heart of Ephesus. The Library was not yet built during the years Paul taught in the nearby School of Tyrannus.

The Western text (the Old Latin translation of the original Greek) of Acts 19:9 adds that Paul "...argued daily in the hall of Tyrannus from the fifth hour to the tenth." If this is true, it means Paul spoke in this lecture hall every day from 11 a.m. to 4 p.m.[14] This is a fascinating insight, especially since work hours in ancient Asia began very early and finished by 11 a.m. to avoid the heat of the midday sun. Most schools in that region concluded daily operations by 10 a.m.[15]

During the hottest hours of the day, the city's population retreated to homes, bathhouses, and other places where they could find shelter from the afternoon heat. If businesses commenced again later in the day, they generally reopened at approximately 4 p.m. Ephesians were so strict in keeping these hours that most of the city retired for an afternoon nap by 1 p.m.[16]

The added phrase in the Western version of Acts 19:9 suggests that Paul may have waited until normal classes concluded and then used this hall during after-school hours. As students filed out of the building at 10 a.m., Paul and his team entered the hall. Those who were hungry for the truth Paul offered would skip their afternoon nap and make their way to the hall of Tyrannus where they could hear Paul deliver his messages for five hours each day.

Paul's entire stay in Ephesus lasted approximately three years.[17] But regarding Paul's teaching ministry in the School of Tyrannus, Acts 19:10 states that the apostle "…continued by the space of two years; so that all they which dwelt in Asia heard the word of the Lord Jesus, both Jews and Greeks." If Paul literally taught every day from 11 a.m. to 4 p.m., he accumulated approximately 3,000 hours of teaching during those two years. Hour after hour, revelation and insight poured forth from the apostle for anyone who wished to listen. In fact, the verse goes on to say Paul's teaching became so well-known that "all they which dwelt in Asia" heard of it.

Of course, it was humanly impossible for Paul to personally preach to "all they which dwelt in Asia." But his influence in Ephesus grew as he taught every day during those two years.

If some archeologists are correct, the steps that once led to the School of Tyrannus are located right at the juncture of Marble Street and Curetes Street — the most strategic location in the city. This means the apostle Paul taught God's Word for two years not in some out-of-the-way place, but in the heart of the most historic and prestigious neighborhood in Ephesus and in one of the most visible locations in the entire city.

At the same time, those who heard Paul's daily teaching were passing it along to others, Paul's fellow team members were also being dispatched to start churches in other regions. As a result, the population of Asia was exposed to the Gospel in a very short period of time.

It is conceivable that all seven churches referred to in Revelation chapters 2 and 3 were birthed during this two-year time frame, either by Paul himself or by those he sent from the ministry headquarters in Ephesus.

OUT-OF-THE-ORDINARY MIRACLES!

God's strategic wisdom was powerfully demonstrated in the events that transpired during the apostle Paul's three years of ministry in Ephesus. In this wicked city — so obsessed with the mystical, magical realm of the occult and with all kinds of dark, supernatural activities — God unleashed miracles unlike any Paul had ever experienced. These were the most extraordinary miracles of his ministry, necessary in order to ignite the interest of a crowd so accustomed to the supernatural. Normal miracles would never have been enough to grab hold of and keep the attention of the population. Therefore, God unleashed His power and "…wrought *special* miracles by the hands of Paul" (Acts 19:11).

Of course, all miracles are special in that they reveal God's power to supersede natural laws. However, the miracles God performed through the apostle Paul in Ephesus were so unusual and rare, so above and beyond the level of the miraculous he had previously experienced, that the *King James* translators specifically called them "*special* miracles." These miracles were truly out of the ordinary. They were unique, extraordinary, and incomparable works of God.

The word "wrought" in Acts 19:11 deserves special attention. It is the Greek

308

word *poieo*, a word often used to denote *creativity*. Because the word *poieo* is used here, it suggests that the mighty works Paul performed in Ephesus were *miracles of a creative nature*. That is why the translators used the phrase "special miracles." The word *poieo* strongly suggests that these were creative miracles — such as the sudden, miraculous replacement of limbs or body parts. Certainly that kind of supernatural demonstration is above and beyond normal healing power and would fall into the category of "special miracles"!

In addition, the Greek tense used in this verse presents the idea of *continuous action*. In other words, when these uncommon miracles began to occur, it wasn't just a matter of an occasional miracle happening now and then. Rather, there was *an unending flow of miracles that continued with no interruption*. The Bible doesn't tell us how long this season of extraordinary miracles lasted. However, the Greek tense makes it clear that when it started, it continued without a pause until that particular season finally concluded.

Although God performed a great number of miracles through Paul in different phases of his ministry, not all of them were miracles of *this* magnitude. These types of spectacular miracles were rare. In fact, this is the only occasion in the book of Acts where it refers to "special miracles."

The word "miracles" is actually the Greek word *dunamis*, which refers to *explosive, dynamic power*. This immediately tells us that *phenomenal amounts of supernatural, explosive power* were flowing through Paul's hands. In fact, a better

rendering of the phrase "special miracles" would be *"mighty, exceptional, out-of-the-ordinary demonstrations of power."*

This kind of power was so extraordinary that another Greek word in the phrase translated "special miracles" implies that even Paul was taken aback by it. That word is *tugchano*, an old word meaning *to hit upon, to happen upon*, or *to fall into*. It seems to imply that Paul literally *hit upon, happened upon*, or *fell into* a level of God's power that was without equal in his experience and beyond his wildest expectation. Even he was startled by the exceptional assortment of profound miracles occurring through his own hands during this particular season.

Left: In this 1693 painting by French artist Jean Restout, entitled, "Miracles of St. Paul at Ephesus," the artist depicts how the sick and diseased would flock to Paul to be healed and delivered of evil spirits. Note the person next to the apostle offering a cloth for Paul to touch so God's power could be transferred and released when the cloth was laid upon the sick.

THE ROLE OF HANDKERCHIEFS AND APRONS

As this season of special miracles continued in Paul's ministry at the School of Tyrannus, these signs and wonders weren't just occurring through the apostle's hands. God's power was even being released through articles of his clothing when they were laid upon the sick and upon those oppressed by evil spirits. Acts 19:12 refers to this supernatural phenomenon: "So that from his body were brought unto the sick *handkerchiefs* or *aprons*, and the diseases departed from them, and the evil spirits went out of them."

The words "handkerchiefs" and "aprons" don't accurately convey the meaning of the Greek text; therefore, a more in-depth study of the Greek words is warranted to see what can be learned. The Greek word for "handkerchief" is *soudarion*, a word that could be used to describe either *a sweat rag of a common laborer* or *a garment that is wrapped about one's head*, such as the head garments men in the Middle East wear today.

In the First Century, it was customary for men to wear long and beautifully patterned pieces of material around their heads, especially if temperatures were hot. The head garment provided protection from the sun, kept the head cool in hot weather, and soaked up sweat that would otherwise stream down the brow and face. The word "handkerchief" in Acts 19:12 probably refers to Paul's headpiece, since that was the way this particular Greek word was most commonly used.

The word "apron" is *simikinthion* — a word that could be used to depict either *a decorative garment worn around the waist for wealthy, educated, and sophisticated men* or *an apron worn around the waist of a common laborer*. This Greek word was used for both scenarios.

Acts 18:3 explicitly states that Paul was familiar with the tentmaking business: "And because he [Paul] was of the

Above: *In the foreground of this drawing by artist Christoph Weigel, a person places a cloth touched by Paul on someone who is infirmed. Acts 19:12 tells us that when this was done, divine power was released into the person's sick body to heal and deliver.*

same craft, he abode with them [Aquila and Priscilla] and wrought: for by their occupation they were tentmakers." Consequently, many have speculated that the words translated "handkerchiefs" and "aprons" could refer to a common laborer's attire.

We know from Paul's epistles that he occasionally worked outside the ministry to pay his own bills so he wouldn't burden the churches he was serving (*see* 1 Corinthians 4:12; 9:6; 1 Thessalonians 2:9; 2 Thessalonians 3:8). But it is important for the serious student of the Word to understand the meaning of *skenopoios*, the Greek word for "tentmakers." This word referred to a wide range of activities that included *the profession of making cloaks, curtains, shoes, or any products made from leather*. Although Acts 18:3 translates it as "tentmakers," it is frequently translated as a *leatherworker* in other literature from that same period.

Therefore, one must recognize that although the manual profession Paul learned as a young man could have included tentmaking skills, it probably entailed much more. In author and historian Fatih Cimok's book *Journeys of Paul*, Cimok correctly noted that it is unfeasible that Paul worked in the actual making of tents, because the profession of making tents required "...looms and materials for weaving which would not have been convenient to carry for a person like Paul who was usually on the move...."[18]

If Paul did work manually in Ephesus in the early morning hours, as some have suggested, it would not have been out of character for him to do so, since this had often been his practice in other locations. The possibility that the words "handkerchiefs" and "aprons" describe a common worker's attire has led some to suggest that Paul worked in the leather industry in the early-morning hours before he arrived daily at the School of Tyrannus.[19] This could indicate that the apostle came straight from the workplace still dressed in the clothing of a common laborer, including the laborer's "handkerchief" and "apron."

However, there is a *second view* that may be more worthy of consideration. Those who gathered near the School of Tyrannus were usually rich, sophisticated intellectuals who congregated to show off, to prove their wealth, to communicate new ideas and concepts, and to share new philosophical hypotheses with others of the same sociological status. This was *not* a place where common workers in sweat rags and workers' aprons would be found mingling with the intellectual crowd.

The people who gathered in this section of the city were from the upper crust of society and were dressed appropriately for their rank. In hot temperatures, the majority of these men wore stylish headdresses with brightly colored patterns and elegant wraps around their waists. This type of clothing was a *status symbol* for the rich and sophisticated who lived in Asia during the First Century.

It is highly improbable that a teacher of this distinguished school would dress in the attire of a common laborer. It would have been out of place and completely unbefitting for Paul to come to such a prestigious school dressed in such a manner. Even if he did work in the leather industry or the tentmaking business, it

is more probable that he would have changed his clothing before arriving at the school and dressed suitably in an expensive headpiece with an elegant wrap tied about his waist. Although this second view is also based on speculation, it falls more in line with the customs and standards of the vicinity where the School of Tyrannus was probably located.

What *is* known about these garments — whatever kind of garments they were — is that they were *saturated* with the anointing of God. These articles of clothing, infused with divine power, were taken from Paul's body to be laid upon people too ill to make the journey to where the apostle was ministering. Although the text doesn't explicitly state the details, it seems logical to assume that these articles of clothing were cut into smaller pieces so they could be taken to larger numbers of sick, diseased, and demon-possessed people who lived throughout the city of Ephesus.

It is interesting to note that this is the only time an occurrence of transferring the anointing through articles of clothing is found in the book of Acts. This type of supernatural manifestation would have been especially well received by the population of Ephesus, which had a preoccupation and fascination with spiritual *fetishes* (objects regarded with awe as being the

Left: This is a relief of a First Century pagan procession on its way to sacrifice a bull to the gods. The man with his right hand extended toward the altar is the one charged with officiating the ceremony. Notice his elegant toga and head-wrap, which were commonly worn by men of high rank during New Testament times. Although some scholars speculate that the words "handkerchiefs" and "aprons" in Acts 19:12 refer to a common laborer's clothing, it is more likely that Paul wore this kind of elegant head-piece and wrap about his waist, which was considered appropriate attire for men who gathered in prestigious districts of Roman cities.

habitation of a potent spirit or as having magical power).

People in Ephesus wore amulets around their necks and carried small pieces of "Ephesian Letters" in their pockets for good luck (*see* pages 316-317, 330, 337-339 for more information). It was also common for people to "take home a piece of the power" by purchasing a myriad of fetishes at their local pagan temples. They believed these objects carried spiritual power and would bring blessing to their homes and businesses.[20]

Although this religious practice could be found all over the pagan world of the First Century, it was especially prevalent in Ephesus, and it seems that God met these pagans at the point of their faith. Because they believed that material objects could transmit power, they were able to release their faith in the anointing that was resident in articles of Paul's clothing. Consequently, these pieces of clothing were laid on the sick and diseased with outstanding results, with many being miraculously healed and delivered as evil spirits went out of them.

THE SICK, THE DISEASED, AND THOSE WITH EVIL SPIRITS

Acts 19:12 also provides a specific record regarding the various categories of people who were healed and delivered as a result of the divine invasion of power that accompanied Paul's ministry in Ephesus. It says, "So that from his body were brought unto the *sick* handkerchiefs or aprons, and the *diseases* departed from them, and the *evil spirits* went out of them."

Right: A nighttime festival with its bull sacrifice is shown underway at the great Temple of Artemis in Ephesus. Pagan worship flourished in this ancient city, causing it to be a fertile breeding ground for every manner of demonic activity.

To gain a better understanding of these three categories of people, let's consider the Greek words in this verse for "sick," "diseases," and "evil spirits." In the Greek text, these are three very different words that tell very different stories about the various categories of infirmed people.

First, Acts 19:12 refers to the "sick." This is the Greek word *astheneo*, which is a word that generally describes *a person who is frail in health*. This word *astheneo* commonly referred to *people who were so physically weak that they were unable to travel* — in this case, to the location where Paul was teaching the Word of God. It carried the idea of those who were *feeble, fragile, faint, incapacitated, disabled*, or simply in such *poor health* that it would be unthinkable to transport them. Their condition was so delicate that they would most likely be *shut-ins* or *homebound*.

Second, the word "diseases" is used, translated from a Greek word that has a very different meaning than the one translated "sick." Actually, the word translated "diseases" can actually be considered an amplification of the word "sick" (*astheneo*) — providing even greater insight into the frail condition of these people who were homebound because of their conditions. That Greek word translated "diseases" is *nosos*, an old word with a long and interesting history.

In ancient Greek literature, the word *nosos* was specifically used to describe sicknesses caused by *invisible entities*, such as *demons*. In fact, nearly every time the word *nosos* was used in connection with illness, it was understood that the sickness was *spirit-inflicted*. The word portrayed *people who were tormented physically or mentally; people who were afflicted by an unseen entity;* or *those who were vexed with lunacy or madness*. The ancient view was that these individuals had been ruthlessly subjected to cruel

treatment by spirits and were therefore "*dis*-eased" people.

The word *nosos* was also used to describe *plagues* that were attributed to demonically inspired disasters or *physical terminal illnesses* for which medical science had no known remedy. If it was a *nosos* plague sent to an entire city or region, the ancients believed it was a scourge of demon spirits that simply had to run its course because none of their natural efforts would stop it. Medical attempts to treat a *nosos* illness were considered futile because

nosos was a type of sickness or demonic attack beyond help and recovery.

Whether the manifestation of *nosos* was terminal cancer, some other deadly illness, or a spirit-inflicted mental madness, people of that day assumed that someone with a *nosos* disease had no hope of recuperation. Every time the word *nosos* was used, it described what the ancient Greeks believed to be *an unalterable, irreversible, incurable, permanent condition.*

Due to the multiplicity of dark pagan religions that flourished in Ephesus, the

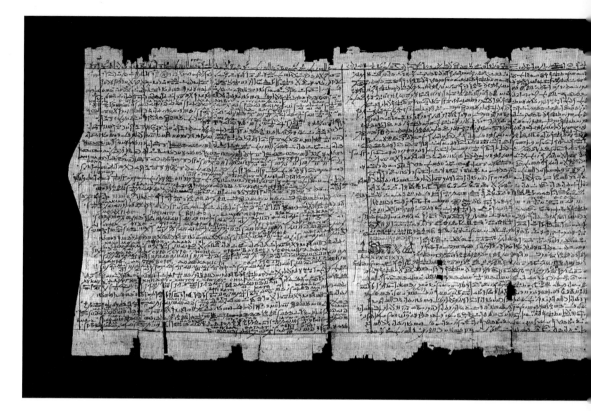

city was a fertile breeding ground for demonic activity. The religion of Artemis, the supreme goddess of the city, as well as the many other alternative forms of pagan worship, all involved worshipers in occult rituals and supernatural activities that could have caused people to fall under the influence of evil spirits. It should therefore come as no surprise that many people in this city were tormented with untreatable, spirit-inflicted sicknesses that came upon them as a result of curses, spells, and magic.

But in addition to the pagan religions mentioned above, Ephesus was also noted throughout the Roman Empire in the First Century for its "Ephesian Letters." This term is not a reference to Paul's letter to the Ephesians. Rather, it refers to a strange concoction of *magic words* and *codes* written on small scrolls or pieces of papyrus, which were then tucked into amulets that people carried or wore around their necks. Pagans believed that these Ephesian Letters had magical power to bless and prosper, to curse, or to vex.

These magical words and spells held great sway in the lives of the Ephesian citizens. In fact, many writers of that time referred to them in historical records, poetry, and theatrical performances. Even ancient medical books refer to the supernatural power of these magical phrases and codes.

These magical incantations were used by local citizens to conjur up spirits for a sundry of reasons. No doubt this is one reason some in Ephesus suffered from spirit-inflicted illnesses that medical science could

not help. However, as we read in Acts 19:12, when Paul's garments were laid on them, "...the diseases departed from them, and the evil spirits went out of them."

The wording in Acts 19:12 makes it clear that the elimination of these diseases was linked to the departure of evil spirits. The moment victims were freed of evil spirits, they were also freed of the sicknesses the evil spirits had caused, confirming that the diseases were spirit-induced. The verse says that the diseases "departed" — translated from the Greek word *apallasso*, which means *to be set free, to be changed, to be radically transformed*, or *to be liberated or unfettered from something*.

It is significant that the word *apallasso* is used in this verse, because it was actually a First Century medical term

Above: Ephesus was noted in the First Century for Ephesian Letters. These were a strange concoction of magic words and codes written on small scrolls of parchment or pieces of papyrus, which were then tucked into amulets that people carried or wore around their necks. Pictured here is the "London Magical Papyrus" from the British Museum archives, an ancient document filled with spells, recipes, and magic words — the kind of words represented on these smaller scrolls, which people believed to hold magical power to bless and prosper, to curse, or to vex.

that described people who had been *completely cured of a disease*. This term never denoted a temporary cure — only a permanent one. Thus, we know that when

the divine power resident within Paul's clothing touched these afflicted people, they were permanently freed of the sickness and oppression that had relentlessly tormented them.

Acts 19:12 also tells us the diseases left when "the evil spirits went out" of them. To understand the significance of this statement, we must first take a closer look at the word "evil" in connection with "evil spirits." The word "evil" is the word *poneros*, a well-known word that describes something that is *foul, vile, malicious, malevolent, malignant, hostile,* and *vicious.* In the Bible, it is often used to depict actions, laws, or people whose behavior is opposed to the righteous nature of God. For example, God's nature is *righteous, good, holy,* and *pure,* but the word *poneros* would depict something that is *unrighteous, wicked, unholy,* and *impure.*

When the Greek word *poneros* is used in connection with *animals,* it often depicts animals that are *savage, wild, vicious,* and *dangerous.* Such beasts are so dangerous that they pose a risk of life to those near them. Similarly, when the word *poneros* is connected to the word *spirits* to form the phrase "evil spirits," as is found in Acts 19:12, we know that these spirits created *havoc* and *destruction,* were *malicious* to those in whom they dwelt, and brought *harm* and *danger* to anyone nearby. This may explain why severe demoniacs lived far from population centers, such as the two demon-possessed men in Matthew 8:28 who lived in a remote region of the Gadarenes.

Acts 19:12 goes on to say that when Paul's garments touched the diseased, the evil spirits "went out" of them. The words "went out" comes from the Greek word *ekporeuomai,* a compound of the words *ek* and *poreuomai.* The word *ek* means *out,* as in *to go out, to leave,* or *to go away.* The word *poreuomai* means *to journey,* as in *to leave one place and go to another.* When the two words are compounded, the new word *ekporeuomai* implies an even stronger meaning. It gives the impression that when Paul's garments touched those who had "evil spirits," the anointing transmitted from his garments to them caused the evil spirits so much anguish and torment that they swiftly *went out* of the afflicted like those who are *evicted, ousted, thrown out,* or *forcibly removed.*

God's power came in and the evil spirits swiftly went out — and when they departed, the physical and mental afflictions caused by those spirits left with them. The evil spirits were literally *ejected* or *evicted,* just as an unwanted person would be ejected or evicted from a house. One expositor states that the word *ekporeuomai* actually gives the impression that these evil spirits *escaped* from the anointing in Paul's clothes. And when they left, the cure was permanent. Once touched by Paul's garments, the sick and diseased were *liberated* and *set free.*

One may not conclude from this text that all sickness and disease are spirit-induced. However, it leaves open the possibility that some who are tormented with agonizing physical and mental conditions that medical science cannot help may be suffering from afflictions that are not natural but rather are the result of an evil spiritual entity.

VAGABOND JEWISH EXORCISTS

Paul's miraculous ministry was so prominent that it even attracted the attention of seven local exorcists. These exorcists observed Paul long enough to recognize that he had exceptional authority over evil spirits. They must have gawked in amazement at the way demons immediately responded to his authority. Soon these seven exorcists unsuccessfully attempted to use the name of "Jesus whom Paul preacheth" as part of a new magic formula to drive demons out of the possessed. Acts 19:13-17 relates this account:

Then certain of the vagabond Jews, exorcists, took upon them to call over them which had evil spirits the name of the Lord Jesus, saying, We adjure thee by Jesus whom Paul preacheth. And there were seven sons of one Sceva, a Jew, and chief of the priests, which did so. And the evil spirit answered and said, Jesus I know, and Paul I know; but who are ye? And the man in whom the evil spirit was leaped on them, and overcame them, and prevailed against them, so that they fled out of that house naked and wounded. And this was known to all the Jews and Greeks also dwelling at Ephesus; and fear fell on them all, and the name of the Lord Jesus was magnified.

Verse 13 states that these were "vagabond" Jews. The word "vagabond" is a Greek word that simply means those who

Below: An incantation bowl — also known as a demon bowl, devil trap bowl, or magic bowl — was widely used in the ancient Middle East as a form of protection against evil spirits. They were similar in purpose to the Ephesian letters (magic words written on small parchment scrolls, tucked into amulets). Such bowls usually inscribed

words in a spiral, beginning at the rim and moving toward the center. Commonly placed under the threshold, courtyards, homes, and graveyards, the bowls were buried face down to capture demons. There was a widely held belief that once the name of a deity was known, a written incantation using that name would obligate the god or goddess to carry out the wishes of the magician. This provides insight into the reason the name of Jesus generated such interest among the seven sons of Sceva.

*Above Left: A clay magic bowl with Aramaic writing, from the National Archaeological Museum in Athens, Greece. **Above Right:** This incantation bowl was excavated in Nippur, Mesopotamia. The Aramaic inscription spirals toward the center depiction of a demon. Such bowls were considered "demon traps" — capable of ensnaring the demon by the power of the inscripted magic spell. Most homes excavated in Nippur's Jewish settlement had these bowls buried in them.*

wandered or *traveled*. These were men whose profession was to wander throughout the city, from home to home and from place to place, to conduct exorcisms for those who hired them for their services. They used spells, charms, incantations, magic formulas, and other occult rituals in their attempts to expel demons.

It is significant to note that these were *Jewish* exorcists. Historical literature tells of a group of Jews who practiced occult rituals that were forbidden by God (*see* Deuteronomy 18:9-12). The profession of exorcism was practiced among Jews even during the time of Solomon and became well established over many centuries. Jewish practitioners of magic were very highly regarded among the Jews because they were believed to possess special power over demon spirits.[21] It is possible that these men

were simply Jewish exorcists. However, a second hypothesis suggested by some scholars is that these particular exorcists were apostate Jews who fell into paganism and practiced it along with their father Sceva.

As mentioned earlier, there were unusually large numbers of demonized people during the First Century as a result of the supernatural activities in pagan temples and the population's total immersion in occult activities. This gave rise to a thriving exorcism business, a well-respected profession among pagans. The people believed that certain "gifted" individuals had the power to liberate those infested with evil spirits by using the right incantations, spells, or magical names that demons would respect and obey. These individuals would at times even invoke the names of angels in their attempts to control and cast out demon spirits. Professional exorcists were serious students of rituals, and they demanded huge sums of money for their services.

Acts 19:13 specifically uses the word "exorcists," derived from the Greek word *exorkidzo*, which simply means *to adjure, to beg*, or *to implore*. This is the only time the word is used in the New Testament. In Acts 19:13, this word is used to depict those who *adjured*, *implored*, and *begged* demon spirits to obey. With no real authority over the spirits, they resorted to their spells, charms, incantations, and magical names to try to coax evil spirits to cooperate with them. Pagan exorcisms of this type could go on for days and weeks — which explains why exorcists could demand very high payments for their services.

The exorcists referred to in Acts 19:13 tried to use the name of Jesus, but they clearly didn't know Him experientially. Instead, they attempted to use Jesus' name as they would any other magical name. This is clear by the fact that they said, "…We adjure you by Jesus whom Paul preacheth." They knew nothing of Jesus Himself, except that they had heard Paul use this special name to successfully expel demons from those who were possessed. These exorcists must have believed they had discovered a powerful, new magical name that they could incorporate into their other spells and incantations in the act of pagan exorcism.

WHO IS 'SCEVA'?

Acts 19:14 goes on to relate, "And there were seven sons of one Sceva, a Jew, and chief of the priests, which did so." Before we proceed to the dramatic events

that unfolded between the seven sons of Sceva and a demon-possessed man in Acts 19:14-16, let's first look at this name "Sceva," referred to in verse 14. Over the years, the question "Who was Sceva?" has been a subject of great debate among biblical scholars. For possible answers to this question, let's consider the authoritative opinions of two respected theologians and historians: F. F. Bruce and J. A. Alexander.

F. F. Bruce states, "It is conceivable that Sceva was related to one of the Jewish high-priestly families; more probably, however, [the word 'chief'] is to be

Left: This is one artist's depiction of the ancient city of Ephesus. Magnificent in its physical beauty, the city that became the ministry base for the Church in Asia was spiritually oppressive and teeming with demonic activity. In 52 AD, that spiritual darkness began to be dispelled as Paul and his team arrived to proclaim the truth of Jesus Christ and set people free.

regarded as an advertisement…. [Luke] was merely giving Sceva's own account of himself."[22] So according to Bruce, it is unlikely that Sceva was an actual chief of Jewish priests; rather, he may have used the title "chief" to bestow a sense of importance upon himself.

This idea is carried even further by J. A. Alexander in his work on the book of Acts. He states, "A *chief priest*, resident at Ephesus, is something strange, and has been variously explained according to the different senses of the Greek word. It is not impossible that a member of the sacerdotal race, entitled to be thus distinguished, may have been residing there. But it is also possible that *chief priest* here has reference to the worship of Diana [Artemis], and that this Sceva was a renegade or apostate Jew. This is the less improbable because the Greek word [for chief priest] was not only in general use among the heathen, but occurs repeatedly on coins and in other inscriptions relating to the worship of Diana at Ephesus."[23]

Making all of this even more interesting is the fact that the name "Sceva" isn't Jewish in origin. It is a Hellenized version of a Latin name that means *left-handed*, which in the vernacular of the First Century was slang that referred to someone who was *untrustworthy, perverse, reprobate, a wretch,* or *a scoundrel.* If this "Sceva" was one of the chief priests in the worship of Artemis (Diana), as J. A. Alexander suggests, it is entirely possible that the name "Sceva" wasn't even this man's real name. It may have been a fictitious name inserted by Luke to express his opinion of this local apostate Jew who converted to paganism and practiced it with his seven sons.

If these suggestions are true, the text would then convey the following idea: *"And there were seven sons of one Sceva,*

a Jew — a wretched, reprobate scoundrel who advertised himself as being great and who served as one of the high-ranking priests in the worship of Artemis — a man known for practicing pagan exorcism with his seven sons."

The answer to who Sceva was cannot be given with certainty, but the previous opinions provide explanations worthy of consideration. It is possible that this Jewish man named Sceva converted to paganism and practiced occult rituals forbidden by the Old Testament — and then led his seven sons into the same practice.

A DEMONIC CONFRONTATION WITH THE SEVEN SONS OF SCEVA

Acts 19:15 continues to relate that a demonic confrontation occurred between a demon-possessed man and the seven sons of Sceva who boasted to be professional exorcists. As noted earlier, these local exorcists saw Paul successfully using the name of Jesus to exercise authority over demons. Hoping to expel demons from a severely demonized man in Ephesus, they added the name of Jesus to their list of magical names to use.

But according to Acts 19:15, their attempt was futile. In fact, the verse says

---

Left: This 1695 line drawing by Christoph Weigel, entitled, "The Sons of Sceva," effectively portrays the violence of the scene related in Acts 19:13-16. According to this passage of Scripture, seven Ephesian exorcists unsuccessfully attempted to expel evil spirits from a demon-possessed man and were brutally attacked by the demoniac as a result.

that the demon indwelling the man challenged them: "And the evil spirit answered and said, Jesus I know, and Paul I know; but who are ye?"

The actual structure of the Greek text says, "And *answering*, the evil spirit said...." The Greek tense tells us this was *not a single answer*; rather, the demon spirit that possessed the man was continually responding to each attempt made to drive him out. Thus, the spirit was *answering* each time they tried to use a new magical name, spell, or incantation to drive him out. This, of course, means that evil spirits have *intelligence* and the ability *to speak* and even *to converse*.

This ability of evil spirits to speak is evident in the four gospels and in the book of Acts. A study of the Scriptures makes it clear that demon spirits are capable of these abilities:

- They can possess specific information about things, places, or people.

- They can know the names of people.

- They have the ability to indwell a human being and engage that person's vocal apparatus to terrorize others, to blaspheme, to challenge, to make requests, and to scream, shriek, and cry out.

Vivid examples of evil spirits possessing both intelligence and the ability to speak can be found in Matthew 8:29 and Mark 5:7-12, where we read about the demoniac of Gadara. This tortured man was indwelt by a legion of demons that demonstrated both intelligence and the ability to speak when they were confronted by the power of Jesus Christ. Mark 1:23-25 relates another example of this phenomenon. In this instance, evil spirits in a man spoke so freely that Jesus had to command them to stop talking and be silent.

Then in Mark 1:34, we are told that many sick people and those possessed with demons gathered to be healed and delivered by Jesus. The evil spirits referred to in this verse were so informed and fluid in speech that Jesus actually had to forbid them to speak so they wouldn't reveal who He was before the time. These are just a few New Testament examples demonstrating that demons have both intelligence and the ability to use the vocal organs of the person in whom they dwell.

Going back to Acts 19:15, we read that this man had an "evil spirit." All demons are evil, but it is worthwhile to take note of the word "evil" in this context. It is the word *poneros* — the same word discussed earlier regarding Acts 19:13. As previously noted, when used in connection with animals, the word *poneros* depicts *ferocious*, *savage*, and *dangerous* beasts. Likewise, when this Greek word is used to describe *spirits* that indwell people, these spirits are *ferocious*, *savage*, *dangerous*, and *malicious* to those in whom they dwell and bring *harm* and *danger* to those who are in close proximity to them.

First, the evil spirits are dangerous to the person they indwell, often creating harmful and self-injuring behavior. The New Testament has many examples of such savage, spirit-induced behavior. One example is found in Luke 9:37-39, where Luke tells us of a boy who periodically experienced demonic attacks that were injurious to his health. Luke describes it like this: "And, lo, a spirit taketh him, and he suddenly crieth out; and it teareth him that he foameth again, and bruising him hardly departeth from him" (v. 39). Matthew relates the same account in Matthew 17:14 and 15, adding that the evil spirit would hurl the boy into fire and water. This was *ferocious, savage, dangerous,* and *malicious* treatment by the demon spirit against the one it possessed.

Another example is found in Mark 5:5, where we find the demoniac of Gadara, who was continually wandering in the mountains and among the tombs, crying out and "cutting himself with stones." What a miserable picture of this man! He continually wandered around that isolated region, crying out in pain and agony while slicing his body with sharp stones — and it was all the result of the "evil spirits" that indwelt him. It is no wonder that these spirits are called *poneros* in the Greek, for they truly are *evil*.

In Acts 19:15, the evil spirit responded to the seven exorcists: "...Jesus I know, and Paul I know; but who are ye?" The words translated "know" in the two phrases — "Jesus *I know*" and "Paul *I know*" — are two distinctly different words in the Greek text.

In the phrase, "Jesus *I know*," the word "know" is the Greek word *ginosko*. The word *ginosko* has a wide range of

Right: This drawing, entitled, "Jesus Healing the Lunatic," shows why the demon confronting the seven sons of Sceva declared, "Jesus I know." No one understood Jesus' authority more than the demons that were forced to obey Him.

meanings, depending on the context in which it is used. In the Classical Greek period and in New Testament times, the foremost meaning of *ginosko* was *to recognize a person or a thing, to acknowledge*, or *to have a full comprehension about the person or thing being acknowledged*. There is no question that the use of the word *ginosko* here means the wicked spirit that inhabited this man *admitted, conceded*, and *affirmed* that the name "Jesus" was *well known* to it. Like all evil spirits, this demon *was familiar* with Jesus, *fully comprehended* and *acknowledged* who Jesus was, and had possessed this knowledge for a long time. So when the evil spirit said, "Jesus I know," it was saying in effect, "...*Jesus I know and fully comprehend with absolute certainty....*"

On the other hand, in the phrase, "and Paul *I know*," the word "know" is translated from a completely different Greek word. It is the word *epistamai*, which describes *a knowledge obtained by outward observation*. In other words, Paul's reputation was growing as one who had authority over demons, and it had captured the attention of the spirit world. Demons were "tuning in" to observe Paul's activities.

The word *epistamai* implicitly reveals that the dark spirit world in Ephesus had recently become familiar with Paul's ministry. The apostle's activities were a great threat to the demonic forces over that city,

---

Left: Jesus was well known by the kingdom of darkness as He went about doing good and healing all who were oppressed of the devil (see Acts 10:38).

and they were taken aback by his spiritual power. Therefore, the evil spirits of the territory were *scrutinizing* this newcomer and *carefully watching* him move through each situation as one who possessed great authority. This word *epistamai* also implies that these demonic spirits were *spying* and *conducting surveillance* on this newcomer who had invaded their dark stronghold so they could stay aware of what Paul was doing and look for ways to oppose him. The word epistamai therefore carries the idea: "...*and Paul I know because I have recently become familiar with him by carefully following and observing his activities....*"

But then the evil spirit asked the seven sons of Sceva an interesting question: "But who are ye?" This question should be understood in the context of the entire verse. The reader should understand the text to mean: "*Jesus I know and fully comprehend with absolute certainty, and Paul I know because I have recently become familiar with him by carefully following and observing his activities — but I have no idea who you are! In fact, we know nothing about you! You've never done anything to get our attention or to make us spy on your activities. We don't recognize you or your authority at all!*"

One would think that demonic forces would recognize pagan exorcists who regularly delved into occult practices; however, the evil spirit in the man didn't recognize these exorcists at all.

This is a clear example of how the devil uses people but has no regard for them. The evil spirit in this man was inflamed by the seven exorcists' feeble and ineffective attempt to cast him out. First, it

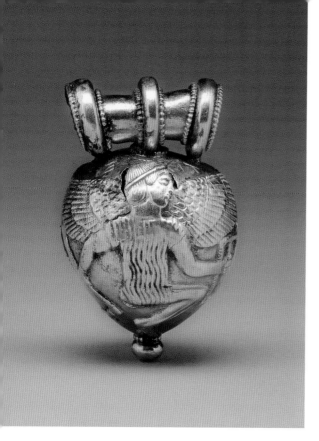

The word "overcame" is a translation of the word *katakurieuo*, a compound of the words *kata* and *kurios*. The word *kata* carries the idea of a force that is *dominating* or *subjugating*, and the word *kurios* is the Greek word for a *lord* or *master*. When compounded into one word, the new word means *to completely conquer*, *to master*, *to quash*, *to crush*, *to subdue*, *to defeat*, *to force into a humiliating submission*, or *to bring one to his knees in surrender*.

The word *katakurieuo* leaves no room for misunderstanding — this was a *humiliating* rout for these seven exorcists. Their defeat was so complete that the evil spirit *"prevailed* against them." The word "prevail" is a translation of the Greek word *ischuos*, which describes a *mighty* individual, such as a man with such muscular strength or physical power that he could defeat any opponent.

It is indisputably clear that evil spirits have the ability to supernaturally energize those in whom they dwell. When they do, the demonized individuals may exhibit inexplicable physical strength.

One of the best examples of this is found in Mark 5:3,4. Here we read again about the demoniac of Gadara, who was so supernaturally energized that no one could bind him, not even with fetters and chains. If people were successful enough to attach the fetters and chains around this

verbally demeaned and humiliated them. Then the evil spirit unexpectedly seized the full use of the possessed man's body to physically attack and injure them. Acts 19:16 tells us, "And the man in whom the evil spirit was *leaped* on them, and *overcame* them, and *prevailed* against them, so that they fled out of that house naked and wounded."

When the text says the man "leaped" on them, it is the Greek word *ephallomai*, which means *to leap upon*, *to jump upon*, or *to pounce upon*, as a panther leaps on a weak and defenseless animal. This word carries the idea of abruptly taking a victim by surprise, which means these professional exorcists were completely taken off guard by this attack. Not only did the demon-possessed man leap on them, but the verse also says that he "...overcame them, and prevailed against them...."

man, he was so empowered by demons that he could tear those heavy iron chains to pieces and get free almost without effort. Absolutely no one could tame him or bring him under control — *except* for Jesus.

The demons that inhabited this man were violent beyond any human's ability to control. It must be noted that ancient Greek literature used the word *daimonian* — the word "demon" — to portray a person who is *mad* or *insane*. But this is not only the Classical Greek view. The New Testament also shows that those who were possessed with evil spirits were *mad* and often afflicted with *physical sicknesses*. This is why Matthew 4:24 says, "…They brought unto him [Jesus] all sick people that were taken with divers diseases and torments, and those which were possessed with devils, and those which were lunatick, and those that had the palsy; and he healed them."

Jesus has authority over evil spirits and has given authority to those who trust in Him to cast out demons in His name. This was the secret of Paul's success. But these seven sons of Sceva were *not* believers; they were simply pagan exorcists trying a new formula against evil forces. However, they soon discovered they were no match for the demons that indwelt the demoniac at Ephesus!

As the seven exorcists commanded the evil spirit to leave the man, suddenly the demon wearied of the harassment. In a split second, the entire scene changed. As the evil spirit seized the man's body and demonically energized it, the man surged forward like a fierce wild animal and pounced upon them. After being severely beaten and battered, they fled the scene in fear. Verse 16 says, "…they fled out of that house naked and wounded."

The word "fled" in Greek is *ekpheugo*. This word is a compound of the word *ek* — meaning *out*, as to *exit* or to *leave* a place — and the word *pheugo*, which means *to flee* or *to run swiftly*. When these two words are compounded, the new word conveys the idea that those seven sons of Sceva *got out* of that house *as quickly as they possibly could*, making a mad dash for *a fast exit*. And no wonder they wanted to get out so quickly — they had been injured and had even lost their clothes in the attack!

The verse says the seven men fled out of "that house," referring to the house where the demoniac was kept. The wording of this phrase implies that this was a well-known house. It wasn't just *a* house; it was *the* house where this savage man lived. It was the house everyone avoided and stayed far from, for too much fear was associated with it and with the violent activities that took place there. And at that moment, it was the exorcists themselves who were escaping from "that house" in such great haste!

When the men ran out of the house, Acts 19:16 says they were "naked and wounded." The word "naked" is *gumnos*, an often-used Greek word that simply means *naked*. The word "wounded" is *traumatidzo*, which means *to cause injury or harm* and is where we get the words *trauma* and *traumatized*.

We don't know the exact details of this demonic attack, how long it lasted, or how badly these seven sons of Sceva suffered. We do know, however, that by the time they exited the house, they were *naked*, *physically wounded*, and *traumatized*.

When people heard that these particular exorcists had miserably failed to exorcise the demon, it was big news in Ephesus. Everyone heard how the evil spirit acknowledged the name and authority of Jesus and even knew the name of Paul, Christ's servant — yet did *not* recognize these professional pagan exorcists. In this worst-case demonic scenario, it was only Jesus Christ's name and His servant's authority that were respected by the demon world.

Because pagans in Ephesus were preoccupied with the magical power of secret names, spells, and incantations, the fact that this demon knew the names of Jesus and Paul would have seemed very significant to the Ephesian citizens. No one else had ever been able to help this demon-possessed man. But this spirit-possessed man, who was apparently well known in Ephesus, actually *spoke* and *admitted* to knowing both the names of Jesus and Paul. This would have signaled to the pagan population that the name of Jesus contained great power. And the fact that the evil spirit even acknowledged Paul would have given the apostle a higher level of authority in the eyes of the people.

As a result of this event, a new preeminence was immediately given to the name of Jesus in Ephesus, and Paul's influence increased. Acts 19:17 describes the impact this incident had on those who heard about it: "And this was known to all the Jews and Greeks also dwelling at Ephesus; and fear fell on them all, and the name of the Lord Jesus was magnified."

News of this event quickly reached both the Jewish and Greek communities in Ephesus; however, the Bible doesn't specify how. Perhaps there were eyewitnesses of the event who told others about it. Or perhaps those who had hired the seven sons of Sceva reported this event to friends, who then spread the news to others. Maybe there were witnesses who heard the screams of the exorcists and saw them running naked from the house.

One possibility exists that isn't recorded and cannot be proven: Some scholars believe that when Paul heard of this event, he may have stepped into the picture and cast the demon out of the man, finishing what the exorcists had been powerless to do.

Regardless of how the news was spread, it made a significant impression on both Jews and pagan Greeks. Both groups were impressed that the name of Jesus was known by the evil spirit that inhabited this man. As a result, this verse says, "…*Fear* fell on them all…" (v. 17).

The Greek word for "fear" is *phobos*, which in this case describes a *reverential fear*, *hush*, or *amazement* that literally *fell* on the residents of the city. It brought a speechlessness to the entire community — and a new awareness of the name of Jesus. This is why the verse goes on to say, "…And the name of the Lord Jesus was magnified."

It must be noted that Luke refers here to the "*Lord* Jesus," not just to "Jesus." The word "Lord" is the Greek word *kurios*, meaning *lord* or *supreme master*. This violent episode between the demon and the seven sons of Sceva had demonstrated that Jesus alone has the power and might to demand respect of evil spiritual forces. By calling him "Lord Jesus" in this context, Luke tells us that Jesus came out of the ordeal as the Champion and that as a result, His name was

Above: Pictured here are two bullas. These hollow pendants contained protective charms or perfume and were worn as amulets, especially by children. A stopper at the top, held in place by a chain or cord, secured the contents.

"magnified" — *enlarged*, *expanded*, and *maximized* — throughout the city.

Thus, the failed attempt of the seven exorcists was an event used by God to bring attention to the name of Jesus and to escalate the pace of the Gospel work in Ephesus. Large numbers of conversions took place as people turned from occult deeds with genuine acts of repentance. There is no question that the power of God was being unleashed in the heart of this dark pagan city and that its foundation — which had been established on the bedrock of idolatry and paganism — was being shaken to its very core. Life in Ephesus was being eternally impacted by the power of the Gospel, and many who lived in the region would never be the same again.

PAGANS PUBLICLY CONFESS CHRIST'S LORDSHIP

Acts 19:18 goes on to relate a significant event that occurred in Ephesus during this time: "And many that believed came, and confessed, and shewed their deeds." The verse specifically tells us three things about this event that must be considered to grasp the full picture. It says that many who believed in Jesus: 1) "came," 2) "confessed," and 3) "showed their deeds." We must ponder each of these points because they reveal a great deal of vital information about a public repentance that dramatically affected the city of Ephesus and accelerated the growth of the Ephesian church.

First, this verse states that those who believed "came." The Greek tense used here with this word is very important because it speaks of *repeated action*. It therefore carries the idea that when people started coming to Christ, it wasn't a one-time event; *they just kept on coming*. Thus, the language strongly depicts an event that was far-reaching and long-lasting. Streams of people were coming to faith in Christ. The verse doesn't say exactly how many came to Christ at this time; however, the use of the word "many," translated from the Greek word *polloi*, assures us that it was an enormous number of people. This word describes a *great quantity*, *a great magnitude*, or *a great multitude* and can actually be translated *masses*. By using this word, the verse informs us that *masses of people* publicly repented and committed their lives to Jesus Christ. This was no small affair; it was a citywide event that permanently affected the atmosphere of Ephesus.

Second, Acts 19:18 states that when they came, they "confessed." The word "confessed" comes from the Greek word *exomologeo*, which is a compound of the words *ek* and *homologeo*. The word *ek* means *out*, and the word *homologeo* means *to confess*. But when these two words are compounded into one word, the new word means *to outwardly confess*, *to loudly declare*, *to shout out*, *to blurt out*, *to publicly agree*, or even *to loudly announce*.

Perhaps the best example of *exomologeo* in the New Testament is found in Philippians 2:10 and 11, where Paul declares that a day is coming when every knee will bow and every tongue will "confess" (*exomologeo*) that Jesus Christ is Lord. Thus, this verse unequivocally describes a day when every created being in Heaven, in earth, and in hell will all join together in one universe-wide proclamation as they *loudly yell*, *shout*, *blurt out*, and *publicly agree* that Jesus Christ is Lord. Even those in hell with no opportunity to repent will publicly *shout out* with the full strength of their voices that Jesus is Lord.

What a sad prospect that is to consider. Those who rejected Jesus Christ and refused to acknowledge Him in this life will finally fall to their knees and *shout forth* their acknowledgment of His Lordship. However, their confession will come too late to reverse their eternal condition.

Regarding the powerful time of public repentance in Ephesus, there was nothing quiet about that event. The declaration of Jesus' Lordship that these former pagans made was done openly, overtly, and brazenly. Just as they had previously lived solely for fleshly indulgences, at that moment they gave themselves completely to Jesus. And as they came to Him, they came with a *vocal proclamation* of faith that let everyone know they were serious about their commitment to His Lordship. Their verbal confession was *public, loud, clear,* and *unmistakable*.

This is in agreement with Romans 10:9, which says, "That if thou shalt confess with thy mouth the Lord Jesus, and shalt believe in thine heart that God hath raised him from the dead, thou shalt be saved." The word "confess" in this verse is translated from the Greek word *homologeo*, the second part of the word *exomologeo* used in Acts 19:18. It means *to proclaim*, *to confess*, or *to agree* and was often used in a judicial context to denote a person who is legally bound by a public statement.

In Romans 10:9, Paul makes it clear that private, unspoken belief is not enough for genuine repentance when a person first comes to Christ. In addition to heartfelt faith, God requires a declaration of Jesus' Lordship that is done *publicly* and *openly*.

Nothing was private or silent about this event in Ephesus as the masses came to repent and receive Christ. As they came, they were all declaring out loud that Jesus is Lord. Their vocal proclamation was done so *loudly* and *openly* that everyone who heard it understood the commitment they were making to Jesus. This was a radical, total break from paganism and a complete turning over of their lives to the living God.

Then Acts 19:18 informs us that they "showed their deeds." This phrase is important in this context because it reveals the integrity of the people's decision for God. Their actions demonstrated the trustworthiness of their repentance. The word translated "showed" is key in proving the sincerity of their confession of sin and their submission to Christ. It is the Greek word *anaggello*, which means *to reveal*, *to show*, or *to display*. As used in this context, the word means that these new believers gave up everything, laying it all on the altar and holding nothing back as they yielded themselves completely to Jesus and to His Lordship. The word *anaggello* plainly means they *acknowledged* their sin, *confessed* that they were sinners, *admitted* their sinful guilt before God, and *conceded* their need to repent. And as a result, they were completely cleansed by the blood of Jesus as they came with sincere hearts to the Lord.

The word "deeds" shows what the people gave up *first* as they came to the Lord. Because they had previously been immersed in occult activities and these practices had ruled them spiritually, this was the first area of their lives they surrendered as they turned to Christ. The word "deeds" is actually the Greek word *periergos* — a purely pagan word that refers to *the rituals and practices of sorcery, magic, black arts, paranormal activity, spells, incantations, secret mystical formulas, and everything else connected to idol worship and occult practices.*

The word *periergos* is a simple compound of the Greek words *peri* and *ergos*. The word *peri* means *around*, and the word *ergos* means *works*. But when compounded into one word, they become a word that is nearly always used in an occult context. The word *periergos* denotes *one who is completely engaged, engrossed, or preoccupied in occult practices*. It depicts a person or group of people who are *absorbed* in the rituals of the occult. This word vividly depicted the Ephesians, for all the inhabitants of Ephesus — except Jews and Christians — were idolaters who had been reared in the world of paganism.

What we view as *occult* and *dark* was a way of life to pagans in the Roman Empire. From the cradle to the grave, paganism was the only religion that was known to the vast majority. The influence of paganism and its practices affected people's personal lives, relationships, families, businesses,

Above: *Gustave Dore's 1865 drawing, entitled, "Paul in Ephesus," depicts the dramatic scene Paul witnessed one day on the streets of Ephesus when a multitude of new believers openly declared their complete break from idolatry and their allegiance to Jesus Christ. The apostle looks on as the crowd burns the books and articles of pagan worship that had defined their former lives.*

societies, politics, and the administration of government. *Occult rituals, practices, and deeds were woven into the very fabric of life itself in the Roman Empire.* And First Century Ephesus — as well as the entire region of Asia — was home to some of the darkest and most abominable paganism in the world.

The Ephesian population was so consumed with the occult that one could assert they ate, drank, and breathed magic the way the people of Athens ate, drank, and breathed philosophy. This fact highlights the significance of that day of public repentance on the streets of Ephesus. As these former pagans proclaimed Jesus the Lord and Master of their lives, they lay all elements of their pagan past on the altar, publicly confessing and renouncing their sin.

A GREAT FIRE TO BURN EVERYTHING CONNECTED TO THE PAST

The dramatic actions of these new believers in Ephesus provided additional evidence that their repentance was genuine.

> Many of them also which used curious arts brought their books together, and burned them before all men: and they counted the price of them, and found it fifty thousand pieces of silver. So mightily grew the word of God and prevailed.
> — Acts 19:19,20

The phrase "curious arts" is again the word *periergos*, the word that describes *the rituals and practices of sorcery, magic, black arts, paranormal activity, spells, incantations, secret mystical formulas,* and *everything else connected to idol worship and occult practices.* Pagans often used fetishes, such as emblems, wands, circles, squares, hexagons, and other geometric shapes that they believed held secret power. The words "curious arts" includes all types of occult rituals and practices that were used in an attempt to connect with and obtain help from the spirit realm.

But the verse specifically says that there were many who "used" curious arts. The word "used" is the Greek word for *a practitioner.* This is important, because it affirms that a large number of those confessing Christ were not novices in occult practices. Rather, many of them had been diligent disciples of magic, sorcery, spells, incantations, and mystical formulas. Before the Gospel penetrated Ephesus, the practice of paganism was all they knew. As a result, many of them had practiced magic and regularly participated in occult rituals connected to idol worship in every sphere of their lives.

The pagans who lived in Ephesus were particularly committed to living their lives according to special magical writings contained in scrolls or on pieces of papyrus tucked away in amulets or carried elsewhere on their bodies. As noted on page 272, Ephesus was very famous for a particular type of magical writings called Ephesian Letters. Most scholars believe that this is what Acts 19:19 is referring to when it says that the people "…brought their books together, and burned them before all men…."

These Ephesian Letters were mystical writings that contained secret combinations of numbers or letters. It is recorded that the earliest known Ephesian Letters

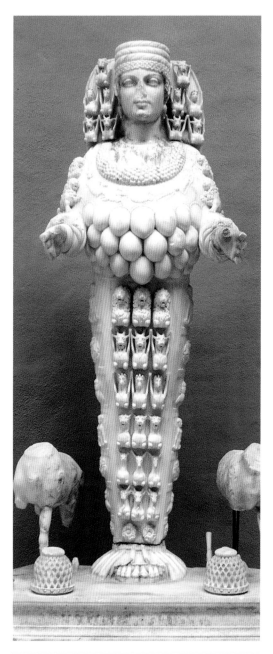

Above: This statue of Artemis from the Ephesus Museum is the same image sculpted countless times by the very idolmakers who felt threatened by the message preached by Paul and his team.

were inscribed into the base of the giant statue of Artemis that stood in the Temple of Artemis at Ephesus.[24] It was believed that these "secret sayings" contained power to heal illnesses, remedy infertility, and bring success to nearly any endeavor. In time, the temple workers produced similar "magical sayings" on other articles and made them available to the population for a price. To an outsider's eyes, these writings looked like pure nonsense, but pagans nonetheless asserted that these mystical writings contained special power. Thus, Ephesus was filled with people who believed in the power of these Ephesian Letters.

Bible scholar F. F. Bruce wrote, "A number of such magical scrolls have survived to our day.... The special connection of Ephesus with magic is reflected in the use of the term 'Ephesian scripts' [i.e., Ephesian Letters] for such magical scrolls. The spells which they contain are the merest gibberish, a rigmarole of words and names considered to be unusually potent, arranged sometimes in patterns which were part of the essence of the spell, but they fetched high prices."[25] The more powerful charms were circulated among exorcists and were sold for a very high fee.

But Acts 19:19 specifically says that the people "...brought their *books* together...." The word "books" is the word *biblios*. This word can be translated *books*, but it doesn't refer to books as we think of them today. Bound books didn't exist at that time. Rather, as noted by F. F. Bruce, these were scrolls or sometimes small parchments of paper that had magical codes or numbers written on them. But when the pagan crowd in Ephesus turned from idolatry, repented of sin,

Above: It is recorded that the earliest known Ephesian Letters were inscribed into the base of the giant statue of Artemis that stood in the Temple of Artemis at Ephesus. The "London Magical Papyrus" (above) includes magical words similar to what may have been in those ancient inscriptions.

and confessed Jesus Christ as Lord, they "…*burned* them before all men…."

The word "burned" is the Greek word *katakaio*, which means *to burn up* or *to completely consume with fire*. The intention of these former pagans was to *obliterate*, *eliminate*, *wipe out*, and *completely eradicate* these articles from the past so they could never turn to them again. It was literally a point of no return for these new believers.

This verse also says that the people carried out this act of repentance "*before all men.*" The word "before" is *enopion*, a Greek word that means they did it *within the eyesight of everyone who was close enough to watch them*. Such an enormous burning event must have gotten the attention of the entire city, for what they were doing was shocking to a pagan population. In the minds of pagans, these were

holy, revered articles. So when these new believers publicly burned these items, it was evident to all that they were categorically renouncing them and declaring their connection to paganism and all occult practices permanently severed. And this powerful act of repentance was done *publicly* and *unashamedly* so that onlookers understood it represented a complete *termination* with the past.

When God calls people to repent, He frequently requires a complete amputation of past friendships, deeds, and practices. Many believers throughout Christian history could testify that God required a separation from places and people that their souls once deemed precious and familiar. Although such a radical requirement can be intensely painful to the flesh and soul, God knows that a person's willingness to sever himself from past sinful actions is confirmation that his repentance is genuine.

Thus, when God requires such drastic actions in cooperation with repentance, it is always for good reason. He wants to ensure that every connection to the past is broken and that the person separates himself completely from all emotions and habits linked to past destructive behavior. This greatly reduces the possibility that the person will revert to past sinful patterns, nor will he be likely to act on the occasional yearning to return to old relationships or to an old way of living that is no longer compatible with who he has become in Jesus Christ.

This is the type of radical repentance God required of pagans who came to Christ in Ephesus. Their connection to past occult practices had been entrenched in and intertwined through every area of their past lives. Therefore, if they had retained occult items in their homes after repenting of their sin and receiving Christ — even if those items were kept stored away and out of sight — there would have been a strong likelihood that these new believers might resort to using those pagan articles again when facing difficult times.

Many of these parchments no doubt had been handed down from generation to generation and had sentimental value, and the monetary value of the texts themselves was quite high. For all these reasons, it was important for these new believers to burn these items and put an end once and for all to the temptation to turn to them for "help" at a future time.

In the words of John the Baptist, the "axe was laid to the root" (*see* Matthew 3:10) the day these books went up

in smoke. With the parchments gone, it meant that there was no returning to past pagan ties for these Ephesian believers. From that moment on, they could freely move forward in their spiritual walk. Their willingness to burn these pagan articles from their former lives confirmed to all who witnessed their act of repentance just how serious they were about following Jesus Christ.

Acts 19:19 tells us that the combined value of these "books" was "fifty thousand pieces of silver." This is an enormous amount of money by First Century standards. Indeed, the fact that these new believers had so many of these "books" shows how widespread the use of Ephesian Letters was in the city of Ephesus. One piece of silver — which was most likely a *drachma* — was estimated to be the equivalent of a full day's wage. Estimates of what 50,000 silver drachmas would be worth today is somewhere between *four million* and *eight million dollars.*

The cost of repentance was very high for Ephesians who came to Christ, but not higher than the price they might have paid by retaining an unhealthy connection to their former lives. That great bonfire in Ephesus — where they severed every connection to their pagan past — was no doubt a difficult moment. They watched as what was once so dear to them burned before their very eyes. Yet that public act of repentance was a necessary and liberating decision — a step of faith that paved the path for them to walk away completely free.

Acts 19:20 describes the aftermath of this event: "So mightily grew the word

of God and prevailed." When people embrace God's Word and forsake their sin, they create an atmosphere in which the Spirit of God can move in great power and the work of God can be supernaturally accelerated. After the Ephesian believers' public burning of pagan books, their city was prepared for

Above: This drawing by Christoph Weigel provides a sense of the drama that this defining moment in Ephesus provided when new believers burned their pagan scrolls. As these new believers threw every trace of their pagan past into the flames, the boldness of their public act of repentance surely captured the attention of the Ephesian populace.

Above: This sprawling view of the Great Theater of Ephesus provides a broad perspective of the setting where Gaius and Aristarchus were taken on the day of the riot recounted in Acts 19. On that day, these ancient theater seats were filled with thousands of screaming, enraged idolmakers and pagans — all intent on defending the city's patron goddess, Artemis, from the new Christian sect.

a mighty move of God's Spirit. From that point forward, Paul and his team began to move at an even faster rate of speed to establish the Church in that region.

Assisted by a mighty display of divine power through signs, wonders, and miracles, God's work was put on a fast track. As a result, the church of Ephesus would eventually become the largest church in the First Century. From this headquarters, other churches would be planted in Smyrna, Pergamum, Thyatira, Sardis, Laodicea, Philadelphia, and in scores of cities throughout Asia.

THE RIOT AT EPHESUS

At the conclusion of Paul's three years of ministry in Ephesus, a great riot occurred in the Great Theater of Ephesus. The circumstances of this riot are recorded in Acts 19:23-27.

> And the same time there arose no small stir about that way. For a certain man named Demetrius, a silversmith, which made silver shrines for Diana [Artemis], brought no small gain unto the craftsman. Whom he called together with the workmen of like occupation, and said, Sirs, ye know that by this craft we have our wealth. Moreover ye see and hear,

Above: This aerial view of the ruins of the Great Theater of Ephesus provides a sense of the structure's beauty during biblical times.

that not alone at Ephesus, but almost throughout all Asia, this Paul hath persuaded and turned away much people, saying that they be no gods, which are made with hands: So that not only this our craft is in danger to be set at nought; but also that the temple of the great goddess Diana should be despised, and her magnificence should be destroyed, whom all Asia and the world worshippeth.

A closer look at this passage reveals how intense this situation was for Paul and his ministry team. Verse 23 says, "And the same time there arose no small stir about that way." The word "small" is *oligos*, which describes something *small*. But in this verse, it is used with a negative to let us know that this event was

not small; rather, it was a *huge* event that impacted the entire city of Ephesus.

The word "stir" is the Greek word *tarachos*, an old word that described *an uproar*, *a disturbance*, or *trouble*. In some literature, this word was used to depict *civil disorder and civil unrest*. The use of these two words *oligos* and *tarachos* — "no small stir" — indicates that this event constituted a *huge uproar*. It was a *disturbance* that *upset* the entire population of Ephesus.

The phrase "about that way" is an expression used in similar forms two other times in Acts to describe the new movement of Christianity (*see* Acts 9:2; 18:26). Following Jesus truly represented a new way of life for those who received

Him — as well as an entirely new way of thinking for the Jews and pagans who didn't believe in Him.

So what was the cause of the huge uproar that occurred in Ephesus at that time? By then, Paul had lived in Ephesus for a number of years, and the message of Christ had made a huge impact on the city of Ephesus. In fact, it is believed that thousands of pagans had turned to Christ. These widespread conversions had a negative financial repercussion for temples and for those who sold pagan religious paraphernalia, such as miniature idols, amulets, magic formulas, and other items. But in addition to affecting sales of religious merchandise, pagan families were feeling threatened as they watched family members and friends convert to a new faith that was completely foreign to them. As the message of Christ spread like wildfire throughout the city and the church grew, fearful pagans began to feel under siege, threatened by the invasion of an alien religion.

As the days, weeks, and months went by, the number of converts continued to increase — and idolmakers in the city became increasingly angry. These men made their living by selling idols and other pagan religious merchandise; however, the sale of their merchandise was rapidly declining because large numbers of people were converting to Christ and were therefore no longer in need of their wares.

Although it is true that the idolmakers may have also been upset because pagans were abandoning their age-old religion, it is evident that they were most disturbed by the decline of idol sales. Soon their discontent erupted into a demonstration

that made the city potentially vulnerable to Roman disciplinary action.

The Roman Empire was massive, and keeping it intact and at peace was a challenging task that required contingents of soldiers posted in every region. The possibility of the empire unraveling was a continual concern of the Roman government, so the official policy provided no tolerance for civil unrest. Roman officials were known to severely discipline cities where public outbursts or demonstrations broke out, such as the riot described in Acts 19. They were aware that if such riots were permitted and left unpunished, unrest could spread to other parts of the empire. Therefore, when such disturbances occurred, the cities where they took place suffered *extreme* disciplinary action. Those who instigated such events were often brutally punished or executed.

DEMETRIUS, INSTIGATOR OF THE RIOT

In Acts 19:24, the Bible states that this massive riot was instigated by a man named Demetrius. Scripture doesn't related exactly who this Demetrius is, but it does suggest that he was the leader of the guild responsible for making shrines, statues, and idols of the goddess Diana (the Roman name for Artemis). In addition to making idols of Artemis, these guild members made fetishes, amulets, and jewelry of a pagan nature. Acts 19:24 tells us, "For a certain man named Demetrius, a silversmith, which made silver shrines for Diana, brought no small gain unto the craftsmen."

Notice that the verse emphasizes that Demetrius "…brought no small gain unto

Above: This painting by artist Matthew Frey (b. 1974) depicts Demetrius inciting a riot among the craftsmen of Ephesus against Paul and his companions.

the craftsmen." Through Demetrius' leadership and marketing skills, the silversmiths (or idolmakers) in Ephesus had become very prosperous. Along with other craftsmen who made miniature idols of Artemis from marble or terracotta materials, the chief occupation of the silversmiths was to make idols for the vast numbers of worshipers and tourists who annually traveled to Ephesus to participate in the cult rituals conducted at the Great Temple of Artemis. Serving as silent witnesses to these idolmakers are the scores of miniature Artemis idols that have been unearthed in the ruins of ancient Ephesus — the work of ancient pagan craftsmen.

Acts 19:25,26 indicates these idolmakers and artisans had become wealthy as a result of their trade. However, Paul's successful ministry in Ephesus was threatening their financial success. These verses relate what Demetrius said to the other craftsmen.

> Whom he [Demetrius] **called together with the workmen of like occupation, and said, Sirs, ye know that by this craft we have our wealth. Moreover ye see and hear, that not alone at Ephesus, but almost throughout**

all Asia, this Paul hath persuaded and turned away much people, saying that they be no gods, which are made with hands.

The word "wealth" is the primary indicator that reveals the level of prosperity the idolmakers of Ephesus had attained. It is the Greek word *euporia*, the word for *success*. It can be translated *wealth*, *affluence*, or *abundance*. This word affirms that the Ephesian idolmakers had become quite affluent as a result of their business.

After summoning an unknown number of idolmakers and silversmiths into the Great Theater of Ephesus, Demetrius began to venomously rant against Paul and his ministry team. As noted on page 197, the Great Theater of Ephesus seated approximately 24,000 people. It was the largest venue in the city besides the stadium. There was no need to use such a large venue for a small crowd, especially since Ephesus had many smaller meeting places to accommodate lesser crowds.

Some assert that because this prestigious theater was used for such a meeting, there were probably *thousands* of idolmakers and members of this particular guild in Ephesus. Artemis was the patron goddess of Ephesus, and her temple was one of the Seven Wonders of the World. It is therefore logical to conclude that the guild responsible for crafting merchandise in her honor would have been one of the largest and most respected guilds in Ephesus. A small venue never would have accommodated such a large number of people. This may be why Demetrius summoned the idolmakers to the Great Theater. It was the only place that could accommodate such a massive gathering of artisans.

Left: A huge, riotous crowd of idolmakers and silversmiths gathered in the Great Theater of Ephesus, ranting against Paul and his ministry team for damaging the success of their pagan industry.

Try to imagine how the scene appeared that day. The seats of the Great Theater of Ephesus were teeming with angry, seething idolmakers, upset because a foreign preacher had settled into their city and was putting their wealth and influence at risk. As these rich artisans sat in the theater — adorned with necklaces, rings, bracelets, amulets, and other jewelry of an occult nature — they listened intently as Demetrius' words incited a growing sense of hostility against Paul and his companions. Their incomes had been drastically reduced as a result of the apostle's ministry, so it wouldn't have taken much coaxing from Demetrius to inflame this crowd. As he stood on the stage before them, he angrily told them, "…This Paul hath persuaded and turned away much people, saying that they be no gods, which are made with hands" (Acts 19:26).

The word "persuaded" is from the Greek word *peitho*, which means *to convince, to allure, to influence,* or *to persuade.* Demetrius' words make it clear that Paul's preaching had been extremely effective. People all over Asia were being *persuaded* to believe the Gospel. The pagan listeners were being thoroughly convinced of the trustworthiness of Paul's message and relied on it to be true. Converts to Christ were being made all over Asia — which is the reason Demetrius and the other idolmakers were so troubled.

The phrase "much people" is used in verse 26 to depict the number of people coming to faith in Christ. The Greek phrase means *a considerable multitude* and confirms that *very large* numbers of people were repenting of sin and turning to Christ.

The word *peitho* is immediately followed by the word *methistimi*, translated as the phrase "and turned away." In many Bible versions, this word isn't even included in the translation — which is unfortunate, given its importance in revealing the intensity and permanence of the pagans' repentance. The word *methistimi* is a compound of *meta* and *istimi*. The word *meta* means *to change*, and the word *istimi* describes *a position*. When the two are compounded to form one word, the new word means *to change positions*.

This word *methistimi* would only be used to mean that those who believed were *completely turning* from their former gods and *changing their position* from paganism to faith in the Gospel. Thus, Paul's preaching was so effective that it *convinced* and *persuaded* massive numbers of people to completely forsake their former pagan beliefs and make a radical change to faith in Jesus Christ.

This is the reason the idolmakers and artisans feared that their idol-making business would continue to deteriorate and that the worship of Artemis was in jeopardy. Demetrius confirmed that fear as he passionately pleaded with the idolmakers, "So that not only this our craft is in danger to be set at nought; but also that the temple of the great goddess Diana [Artemis] should be despised, and her magnificence should be destroyed, whom all Asia and the world worshippeth" (Acts 19:27).

THE GOSPEL: THE ULTIMATE RISK TO ARTEMIS AND HER TEMPLE

In Demetrius' view, their craft and the Temple of Artemis itself were in "danger" of being "set at nought." The word "danger" means *to be at risk, to be at peril,* or *to face a serious threat.* Demetrius' words make it clear that the idolmakers' business was *at peril.* For these artisans, the Gospel message created a *dangerous situation* that *risked* their good fortune. If pagans continued converting to Christ at this rate, income would continue to decline. Demetrius was so troubled about this possibility that he argued, "...Our craft is in danger to be set at *nought*; but

Above: *This model of the Temple of Artemis from the Museum of Ephesus gives us a glimpse into the grandeur of the magnificent structure. The temple would ultimately be destroyed by paganism's greatest threat: a people's rejection of idolatry in favor of the truth of Jesus Christ.*

also that the temple of the great goddess Diana [Artemis]…" (v. 27).

The word "nought" is *apelegmos,* which is often translated *disrepute.* But the word *apelegmos* means much more than *disrepute.* For example, if a consumer went to the market to purchase a product, he was allowed to closely examine the product he was purchasing before paying for it. If the product was found to be defective after examination, the buyer had the right to reject it. The word *apelegmos*

is the exact word that would have been used in this situation and literally means *to reject after examination.*

It was evident to Demetrius that Paul's preaching was causing pagans to closely examine what they really believed and to rethink what they had formerly believed to be true. After hearing Paul's proclamation that there were no gods made with hands, many were awakening to the revelation of this truth and were rejecting idolatry and paganism. As a result, the

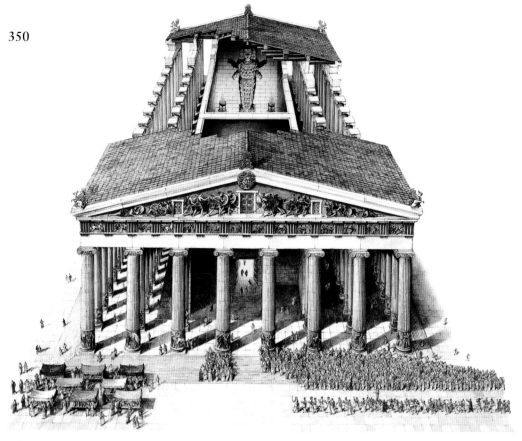

Above: *Aptly named one of the Seven Wonders of the World, the Great Temple of Artemis was a magnificent structure at the time Paul and his team ministered in Ephesus. Every year several hundred thousand visitors would throng to the temple from throughout Asia Minor to pay homage to the Mother Goddess at her most renowned place of pagan worship.*

worship of Artemis was being adversely affected. Demetrius knew that as people were taught to think more deeply, even greater numbers would reject the old ways. That is why he voiced his worries: If this mass rejection of paganism wasn't stopped, it was possible that "...the temple of the great goddess Diana [Artemis] should be *despised* and her magnificence should be destroyed...."

The word "despised" is the word *ouden*, which amazingly means *nothing*. Although the worship of Artemis had ruled this region for many centuries,

Demetrius knew that something had to be done to stop this massive departure from paganism; otherwise, even the worship of their patron goddess Artemis would eventually be reduced to nothing with "...her *magnificence* destroyed..." (v. 27 *NKJV*).

The word "magnificence" is *megaleiotes*, which portrays something that is *majestic, impressive, resplendent,* or *awe-inspiring.* Four times larger than the Parthenon in Athens, the Great Temple of Artemis, which stood at the outskirts of Ephesus during the First Century, truly was a resplendent and awe-inspiring architectural structure. As for the giant statue of Artemis that stood in the temple's inner sanctuary, Pliny the Elder wrote about its ancient splendor, stating that the magnificent statue was sculpted exactly the same way each of the seven times the temple was rebuilt.[26] (*See* pages 263-271 for more information about the Great Temple of Artemis in Ephesus.)

Demetrius was obviously apprehensive that the goddess Artemis and her temple would ultimately suffer destruction. The word "destroyed" in verse 27 comes from the Greek word *kathaireo.* This word means *to tear down* or *to pull down,* like a wrecking crew destroying a building — *taking it down, dissembling it,* and *reducing it to ruins.* This was the ultimate outcome Demetrius feared for both the Great Temple of Artemis and the worship of the goddess. He realized that the enormous success of this new sect could cause the huge influx of visitors who came annually to worship at the Temple of Artemis to eventually dry up. If the people no longer came or if Artemis' reputation was ruined, Demetrius knew that the local idol-making business would be totally destroyed.

So although Demetrius appeared to be a religious defender of Artemis, the bottom line for him was a practical one.

Below: Nothing is left but the ruins of the marble platform where the mighty statue of Artemis once stood in the Great Temple of Artemis. The temple was ultimately destroyed by those who had forsaken paganism and embraced Christianity as truth.

The Gospel message Paul preached was creating a serious loss of money for him and the other artisans who dealt in pagan idols, fetishes, charms, amulets, and other forms of pagan-oriented jewelry.

In the end, the fears expressed by Demetrius were prophetic. The worship of Artemis was eventually abandoned in the Fourth Century as paganism became more and more widely rejected.[27] Nearly 400 years after Demetrius gathered the assembly of artisans in the Great Theater of Ephesus, the magnificent Temple of Artemis was completely dissembled as Christians gladly followed imperial edicts authorizing them to do so — ensuring that no one would ever return to the wicked worship of the pagan goddess.[28] The columns and pieces of carved marble were transported to other cities in Asia, where they were incorporated into the construction of church buildings. Nothing remained of the once-resplendent temple except for a few scattered and broken stones that had no value.

The ignominious end of this foul, dark religion is even more remarkable when one considers how many centuries it had completely dominated the region. As Demetrius declared, "...All Asia and the world worshippeth" the goddess Artemis (v. 27). The word "Asia" referred to the western region of Asia Minor (modern-day Turkey). However, Demetrius boasted that "the world" also worshiped the goddess Artemis. That Greek word for "world" embraced a region far larger than Asia Minor. It is actually the word *oikoumene*, and it specifically referred to *the inhabited world*. In the First Century, this meant the entirety of the Greek and Roman worlds.

The Great Temple of Artemis in Ephesus was the largest of all such temples, but it wasn't the only temple to Artemis — or Diana, as she was known in the Roman world. Temples to this goddess had been erected all over the Greek and Roman Empire. It was a worldwide religion in the First Century.

Acts 19:28 says, "And when they heard these sayings, they were full of wrath, and cried out, saying, Great is Diana of the Ephesians." The word "wrath" is the word *thumos*, a word that depicts *explosive anger*. When used to depict human anger, it expresses *a sudden outburst of anger, rage, or fury*. In the New Testament, it is usually translated as *wrath* and depicts a wrath that leads to damnation and judgment. Acts 19:28 states that these artisans were "full" of wrath after hearing Demetrius, indicating that they were *overtaken with intense anger* and *totally enraged*. The crowd's emotions were violently roused, and they were ready to damn anyone who dared to harm the reputation of Artemis.

In that moment of emotion, this multitude of idolmakers "...cried out, saying, Great is Diana of the Ephesians." The Greek word translated "cried out" is *kradzo*, which means *to scream, to shriek, to yell, to shout*, or *to bellow as loudly as possible*. But the Greek tense used indicates that the people cried out continuously. Thus, we know that the crowd gathered in the Ephesian theater was engaged in *incessant screaming, yelling, and shouting* that went on for at least two hours (v. 34). In fact, the noise from inside the Great Theater of Ephesus swelled so uproariously that, as Acts

Above: The seats of the Great Theater of Ephesus held up to 24,000 spectators and were likely filled to capacity on the day of the riot, when angry idolmakers gathered to deal with the threat that Paul and his team posed to their businesses connected with the production of pagan fetishes.

19:29 says, "...the whole city was filled with confusion...."

Several factors contributed to the city-wide disturbance created by the unceasing clamor of the crowd in the Great Theater of Ephesus that day. There was the architectural design of the theater itself; the location of the city nestled between two mountains; an abundance of sound-resonating marble throughout the city; and a harbor filled with water that reflected sound. Thus, the incessant roar of the crowd — simultaneously bouncing off mountains, marble, and water — reverberated to every corner of the city.

The noise was so deafening that people streamed out of their homes and businesses into every street to find out what was happening. Public outbursts were rare, so it wasn't long before the entire city was thrown into a state of turmoil as the noise continued without abate. The situation in the theater was raging out of control, causing confusion to run rampant throughout the streets of the city.

GAIUS AND ARISTARCHUS

Soon the great city of Ephesus — with its widespread reputation for sophistication, education, and elegance — was overtaken by a mob running down the streets toward the source of the commotion. Meanwhile, the word went out for Paul and his associates to be apprehended and brought into the theater. Acts 19:29 relates what happened next: "...And having caught Gaius and Aristarchus, men of Macedonia, Paul's companions in travel, they rushed with one accord into the theatre" to join the thousands of

screaming idolmakers who were already gathered there.

The word "caught" is the word *sunarpadzo*, which means *to snatch*, *to clutch*, *to abduct*, or *to take by force*. Thus, the Ephesian mob *abducted and took by force to the theater* two members of Paul's ministry team named Gaius and Aristarchus, who were "…men of Macedonia, Paul's companions in travel…."

The names *Gaius* and *Aristarchus* appear several times in Paul's writings, providing us with some information about these men. For example, when Paul resided at Corinth, he wrote at the end of his letter to the Romans, "Gaius mine host, and of the whole church, saluteth you…" (Romans 16:23). It is most likely that Gaius was a wealthy Corinthian who owned a house large enough to accommodate Paul and to meet all the apostle's needs while he resided in Corinth. And although Paul was not known for baptizing a great number of people, Gaius was among those whom Paul said he had baptized (*see* 1 Corinthians 1:14). Many

Left: The view in this photo shows the floor and stage of the Great Theater of Ephesus, where Gaius and Aristarchus were dragged after Demetrius stirred up his fellow idolmakers with dire warnings about the loss of business because of this new Christian sect. One can only imagine what the two Gospel preachers felt as they stared up at the throng of idolmakers who filled the theater seats and screamed angry accusations at them.

Aristarchus listed as one of Paul's traveling companions is in Acts 19:29. Some scholars suggest that Aristarchus had traveled with Paul since his conversion, although this can't be said with certainty. Colossians 4:10 lets us know that Aristarchus was with Paul when he was imprisoned in Rome. Paul wrote, "Aristarchus my fellowprisoner saluteth you...." Then in Philemon 1:24, Paul included Aristarchus in a list of his fellow laborers, along with Marcus, Demas, and Lucas. Regardless of where he first encountered Aristarchus, this man was Paul's traveling companion and associate who worked in the ministry with him for many years.

Both Gaius and Aristarchus were with Paul in Ephesus and were widely recognized as Paul's companions; consequently, they were targets whom the mob sought out on the day of the great riot. It isn't known if the angry pagan throng searched for Paul, but Scripture does say that they seized Gaius and Aristarchus, dragged them up the steps into the theater, and shoved them onto the stage or the theater floor.

It's difficult to comprehend what Paul's associates felt as they stood looking into the hostile, angry faces of the

years later when the apostle John wrote his third epistle, he addressed it to a man named Gaius, and many scholars speculate that this refers to the same Gaius mentioned in Romans 16.

Aristarchus was a convert from Thessalonica and most likely came to Christ at the same time that others repented during Paul's ministry in Thessalonica. It isn't exactly clear how long he remained in Thessalonica after his conversion or when he actually began to accompany Paul in his travels. The first time we see

Above: *This Gustave Dore engraving, entitled, "St. Paul Rescued From the Multitude," depicts one of the many times the apostle had to be protected from an angry mob during his years of ministry. This type of violent scene is the very thing the disciples and Ephesian officials sought to avoid by preventing Paul from entering the theater on the day of the riot.*

enormous crowd stacked high in the theater seats before them. Behind the two men rose the huge, marble backdrop wall, protruding high into the sky overhead and decorated with multi-colored stone columns and with intricately carved statues and idols. Stationed along the top of the back wall were fully equipped Roman soldiers whose job was to keep watch and make sure no foreign army ever tried to attack the city during festive events conducted in the theater. The high-rise seats of the theater were filled not only with the crowd of idolmakers, but with the mob who had rushed in to take part in the commotion. Paul's two associates were surrounded on every side.

On the same stage where public performances normally occurred, these men were about to become the biggest show in town. One would have to study the mockery that regularly transpired on such stages (*see* page 199) to comprehend the possible mistreatment Gaius and Aristarchus may have endured that afternoon. How long the two men suffered humiliation before the hostile crowd is uncertain. But when Paul discovered what was happening, he attempted to go to the theater to join his associates — despite the risk to his own personal safety.

THE INFLUENCE OF PAUL'S DISCIPLES AND POWERFUL FRIENDS

Acts 19:30,31 says, "And when Paul would have entered in unto the people, the disciples suffered him not. And certain of the chief of Asia, which were his friends, sent unto him, desiring him that he would not adventure himself into the theatre."

Verse 30 states that Paul "...*would* have entered in unto the people...." The word "would" here is a translation of the Greek word *boulemai*, a Greek word that means *to counsel*, *to advise*, or *to exercise one's will* about something. In this context, it means that after thinking through all the consequences of his decision, Paul had *counseled* himself and *made up his mind* to enter the theater. Fully realizing that it could place his life in jeopardy, Paul concluded that he should join his friends in their plight.

Verse 30 goes on to say that Paul "...would have entered in unto the *people*...." The word "people" is the Greek word *demos*, a word that could refer either to *the ruling body of a Greek city-state* or simply to *a large public assembly*. It isn't likely that the word *demos* in this verse described the Ephesian senators, since meetings of the city leaders occurred in the upper part of the city in a building called the Bouleterion (*see* pages 250-252). In this context, the word *demos* most likely refers to *a mass of public citizens*. Two hours of nonstop screaming and shouting had reverberated throughout the entire city, attracting people from every quarter of Ephesus to run toward the source of the disturbance to see what was happening. By that time, the theater was packed.

Acts 19:30 tells us that as Paul himself began to make his way toward the theater, "...the disciples suffered him not." The word "disciples" is the Greek word *mathetes*, a well-known New Testament word that describes *a student who is bound by commitment to a teacher in order to attain that teacher's knowledge*. This word would never describe a casual listener or a mere attendee. On the contrary, the word

Above: *On a peak overlooking what was once the Harbor of Ephesus stands the ruins of the Hellenistic Barracks, where tradition says Paul was detained at some point during his stay in Ephesus. It is possible that the apostle was held in custody within the walls of this ancient tower on the day of the riot as a means of protection from the mob.*

mathetes portrays *a person who is bound by a free-will commitment to a teacher.* This is not a legal term; rather, it is a word that describes a person who has *willfully* and *deliberately* positioned himself under a leader and has *inwardly resolved* to be *a faithful, loyal, dedicated follower* of that leader. The person possesses an *allegiance* with the one to whom he has submitted himself and will follow and obey that leader at all costs. By this definition, there are very few genuine disciples.

So when Acts 19:30 states that the *disciples* prohibited Paul from entering the Great Theater of Ephesus, it is referring to *ardent* followers — serious students who believed in Paul and felt a strong allegiance to him and to his ministry.

Therefore, when they saw that the apostle had determined to enter the theater, they took action to stop him.

It is natural that Paul wanted to join his ministry associates who were potentially facing trouble in the theater. But although this act of courage may at first appear heroic, it must also be seen as a decision that could have resulted in Paul's premature death and the end of his ministry. If he had done as he planned and suffered death as a result, the loss of his ministry would have been a devastating blow to the work of God's Kingdom.

These verses provide a vivid example of how God often uses friends and disciples to stop us from making mistakes that may have devastating consequences.

Paul's desire to enter the theater may have seemed like the right thing to do at that moment. But the apostle had much more work to do, and those who were committed to him and his ministry stepped forward — possibly against his will — to stop him from making a mistake that could have had life-threatening ramifications.

And it wasn't only committed disciples who tried to stop Paul from entering the theater. Even high-ranking pagan unbelievers who respected the apostle knew that this wasn't the right thing for him to do. Acts 19:31 says, "And certain of the chief of Asia, which were his friends, sent unto him, desiring him that he would not adventure himself into the theatre."

The "certain of the chief of Asia" is a translation of the word *Asiarch*, which is a title derived from the word Asia and *archos*. The word Asia, of course, referred to that region of the world. The word *archos* is the Greek word that describes *someone of a high rank or position*. When the two words were compounded, the new word was a particular title given to ten high-ranking men throughout Asia Minor.

These ten men were representatives of Rome who resided in ten different cities in Asia Minor and served as officials in the cult of Rome and the worship of the Roman emperor. The Asiarchs were responsible for overseeing opening games

Above: This artist's rendering depicts a shop similar to the many places of business in Ephesus where silver or terracotta idols of Artemis could be purchased by pagan worshipers.

in the stadiums, for officiating at public ceremonies, and for acting as a liaison between the populace and the emperor.[29]

This is a very important point because it reveals that Paul's ministry had not only impacted the lower classes, but it had also permeated the most lofty classes of society. Just as Jesus had been a Friend to sinners and tax collectors, Paul was a friend to the Asiarch — a pagan unbeliever serving in the religion of the emperor. Yet this man had been sufficiently exposed to Paul to develop a strong respect for him. So when the Asiarch suddenly became aware of Paul's intention to enter the theater, he and his high-ranking associates took action to prevent him from being personally injured as a result of such a rash action.

Paul was a spiritual man, but as God often does with His people, He used others to redirect Paul's steps and to prohibit him from a detrimental course of action. In this case, the Lord came from every direction, using both believing disciples and high-ranking pagans, to stop Paul from taking a step that could have resulted in tragedy.

Acts 19 doesn't tell us whether or not Paul agreed with those who protested his intention to enter the theater. Regardless of how the apostle felt about the situation, however, it remains a fact that their actions stopped the apostle from acting on a decision he had already made.

Although the book of Acts doesn't state it, there is a longstanding tradition claiming that Paul was taken into protective custody during this time in order to protect his life. The ruins of an ancient tower sit atop of one of the peaks outside the ancient city of Ephesus, and for nearly 2,000 years people have referred to it as the prison of the apostle Paul. It is actually an army barrack that dates back to Hellenistic times and was situated inside the ancient city wall; however, it is possible that it could have served as a place of custody or detention during the First Century. There are no definitive records that prove Paul's imprisonment there, but this aspect of the story has been consistently passed down through the ages and is therefore worthy of consideration.[30]

A CROWD RAGING OUT OF CONTROL

As the tumultuous scene at the theater continued to evolve, it eventually became little more than a massive shouting match. Acts 19:32 says, "Some therefore cried one thing, and some another: for the assembly was confused; and the more part knew not wherefore they were come together."

People had come running to the theater from every quarter of the city to find out what the noise was all about. What started with Demetrius and a large group of artisans had become a theater packed to overflowing with people — many of whom didn't even know why they were there! The majority of the crowd only knew that a demonstration was taking place, and they wanted to find out what was happening.

One can understand why the people would be so intrigued by a disturbance of this nature since such an event was so rare in the Roman Empire. In this volatile atmosphere, people's passionate emotions were like a bomb ready to be detonated at any moment. This was a very unusual occurrence in an environment that was normally very regulated and controlled.

Verse 33 tells us what happened next. Without warning, Jews from the local synagogue who had long been offended with Paul moved into action: "And they drew Alexander out of the multitude, the Jews putting him forward. And Alexander beckoned with the hand, and would have made his defence unto the people."

No one knows for certain why the Jews put this Alexander forward. The Bible doesn't tell us which Alexander this was or what happened to him after this incident. He could have been recruited to bring a defense for the Jews and to make it clear that Jesus Christ and the synagogue were not related. Or perhaps he was a Jew who had converted from Judaism to Christianity, so the Jewish leaders decided to use this angry mob to punish him. Anything written about this man named Alexander beyond what is stated in Scripture is speculation.

Once Alexander was standing before the crowd, he "beckoned with the hand" in an attempt to get the attention of the people and calm them down. But every attempt to calm the crowd was futile.

As mentioned earlier, the opposition of unbelieving Jews in Ephesus had been strong against Paul and his team. In fact, their hostility had been so intense that Paul had found it impossible to continue his ministry in the synagogue and decided to move elsewhere. When Paul found a new location where he could teach about Jesus at the School of Tyrannus, certain Jewish converts followed him — a fact that the Ephesian Jews had never forgotten.

Despite Jewish opposition to Paul's ministry, however, the pagan community viewed the newly emerging Christian faith merely as a new form of Judaism. Paul himself was Jewish, and his ministry in Ephesus started in the Jewish community. To pagans who had never really heard the message of the Gospel, it seemed logical to

Below: These marble fragments are remnants of the back stage that once stood in the Great Theater of Ephesus. This magnificent theater was still in its heyday at the time of the great riot that was instigated by Ephesian idolmakers who opposed the Gospel message (see Acts 19).

conclude that Christianity was little more than a new twist to an old Jewish message. So when pagans began to convert to Christ in Ephesus, many pagans believed it was the Jews' doing — a misperception that produced a growing antagonism toward the Jewish community in the city.

This explains why the pagan audience erupted in anger when they discovered this man Alexander was of Jewish descent: "But when they knew that he was a Jew, all with one voice about the space of two hours cried out, Great is Diana [Artemis] of the Ephesians" (Acts 19:34).

THE TOWN CLERK OF EPHESUS

Acts 19:35 says, "And when the town clerk had appeased the people, he said, Ye men of Ephesus, what man is there that knoweth not how that the city of the Ephesians is a worshipper of the great goddess Diana, and of the image which fell down from Jupiter?"

The term "town clerk" is translated from the Greek word *grammateus*, which can also be translated *scribe*. But in the context of a local Roman government, the word *grammateus* was a technical term that described one of the highest public officials. Romans occupied most public offices in Roman provinces, but the post of *grammateus* was held by a local Ephesian citizen and was the highest position held by any local citizen. It was this official's responsibility to make sure that citizens lived in compliance with Roman law and that order was maintained in the city. He was both an interpreter and enforcer of law.[31]

During this disturbance in Ephesus, the town clerk moved very quickly to "appease" or to *calm down* the crowd.

When the people saw who it was, they understood the power of this man's office. So as he stood on the stage before them, his presence brought a soothing calm to a very turbulent situation.

Once the crowd was quieted, the public official put them at ease by reminding his listeners that Ephesus was "...a worshipper of the great goddess Diana...." As noted on page 264, the word "worshiper" is the Greek word *neokoros*, a word that depicts *a temple guardian, a warden, a protector,* or *a maintainer of a temple.* Pagan Ephesian citizens firmly believed it was *their* collective responsibility to be *guardian, warden,*

Left: These are the ruins of the road called the Plateia in Coressus, which people used to travel from the center of Ephesus to the Great Stadium and onward to the Temple of Artemis. It was one of the most important roads in Ephesus, leaving no doubt that Paul and his team walked on it frequently as they moved about the city.

protector, and *maintainer* of the Temple of Artemis. The town clerk reminded the crowd that this was indeed their role and that they were being unnecessarily moved by emotion in this situation.

It is remarkable to note that this official didn't use this opportunity to condemn Paul or his associates. In fact, he spoke respectfully and tolerantly of the Christians, saying, "Seeing then that these things cannot be spoken again, ye ought to be quiet, and to do nothing rashly. For ye have brought hither these men, which are neither robbers of churches, nor yet blasphemers of your goddess" (Acts 19:36,37).

The phrase "robbers of churches" is a poor translation and should be translated "a desecrator of temples." Although the rituals of paganism were offensive and repulsive to the Gospel preachers, they didn't use their pulpits to insult, offend, or speak rudely of those who belonged to other religions. For instance, when Paul was in Athens and spoke to the crowd gathered in the Areopagus, he spoke very respectfully of them and their beliefs, even though he knew their religion was ungodly. Paul's example in the book of Acts demonstrates that he could express respect even when speaking to those of differing beliefs. Paul had far greater difficulty dealing with rebellious leaders in the church than he did getting along with pagans. In fact, Acts 19:31 shows that Paul had pagan friends in high places who seemed to care deeply for him.

The town clerk went on to tell the crowd that Paul and his associates were not known to be "blasphemers of your goddess." Even though the preachers detested the religion of Artemis and wanted to see people delivered from its deception, they were not known for insulting that religion or those who adhered to it. These ministers had practiced verbal restraint and expressed respect toward those who were spiritually lost — and as a result, they received mercy in return from the town clerk on that turbulent day in Ephesus.

Finally, the town clerk ended the debate. He declared:

> Wherefore if Demetrius, and the craftsmen which are with him, have a matter against any man, the law is open, and there are deputies: let them implead one another. But if ye inquire any thing concerning other matters, it shall be determined in a lawful assembly. For we are in danger to be called in question for this day's uproar, there being no cause whereby we may give an account of this concourse."
>
> Acts 19:38-40

The town clerk knew the severe consequences of such a public display, so "…when he had thus spoken, he dismissed the assembly" (v. 41).

With the riot over, the crowd got up from their seats and poured out of the theater onto the streets. Although humiliated, Gaius and Aristarchus were released unharmed, and it appears that Alexander, whoever he was, went free as well. Acts 20:1 relates what happened next: "After the uproar was ceased, Paul called unto him his disciples, and embraced them, and departed for to go into Macedonia."

A BASE FOR THE WORK IN ASIA

Acts 19:21 tells us that Paul had long sensed the Holy Spirit leading him to depart from Ephesus. It was in his heart to travel to Macedonia and Achaia, then on to Jerusalem, and eventually to preach in Rome itself. Paul was certain that the Holy Spirit was leading him to do this even

before the riot occurred in Ephesus. In fact, Acts 19:22 tells us that Paul had already sent Timothy and Erastus on to Macedonia and that they were waiting for him there.

When Paul departed from Ephesus, he said goodbye to one of the most glorious phases of his ministry. In three short years, the church of Ephesus had been birthed; the sick had been miraculously healed; demons had been expelled; the Word of God had become magnified throughout all of Asia; and Paul had survived a riot that could have resulted in his death. From Ephesus, Paul or his disciples had also begun establishing other churches in Smyrna, Pergamum, Thyatira, Sardis, Philadelphia, and Laodicea — as well as in other cities of that region, such as Colossae, Hierapolis, and Melitus. But throughout the First Century, the Ephesian church would remain the largest church in all of Asia.

When it was time for Paul to leave Ephesus, he "…called unto him the disciples, and embraced them, and departed…" (Acts 20:1). But this wasn't the end of his relationship with Ephesus. In the not-so-distant future, Paul would dispatch Timothy to serve as the senior pastor of the Ephesian church (*see* 1 Timothy 1:3). Because of his close relationship with Timothy and the Ephesian believers, Paul also later wrote an epistle to the church of Ephesus, which gave us the book of Ephesians.

Early Church historians record that Timothy served the church of Ephesus for many years and died at approximately 80 years old (*see* page 35 for more about Timothy's death in Ephesus). As discussed in Chapter One, the apostle John relocated to Ephesus after Paul's martyrdom. There

Above: These columns were part of the colonnade that once lined all four sides of the Central Marketplace in Ephesus. This massive market was just a few minutes' walk from the Great Theater where Paul's companions, Gaius and Aristarchus, were forced to face a raging mob of pagans.

John became the overseer of the churches of Asia while living for many years on the hilltop directly behind the Great Temple of Artemis. After the Emperor Domitian's assassination, John was released from the island of Patmos and returned to Ephesus, where he continued his ministry until he died a natural death.

For 2,000 years, believers have read about the events that occurred in Ephesus and have been enriched by Paul's letter to the Ephesian church. However, Paul's ministry in Ephesus wasn't always glorious. In Second Corinthians 1:8 and 9 (*NKJV*), the apostle tells us that in addition to a host of victories, he experienced many low moments as well. He wrote, "For we do not want you to be ignorant, brethren, of our trouble which came to us in Asia: that we were burdened beyond measure, above strength, so that we despaired even of life. Yes, we had the sentence of death in ourselves...."

Yet through all the challenges Paul and his team faced, they stood firm on the Word of God, and the light of the Gospel came shining through the darkness. Evil was pushed back; the love and power of Jesus Christ brought transformation to countless people's lives; and a ministry base was established in Asia that we are still talking about today.

Revelation 2:1-7

1 Unto the angel of the church of Ephesus write; These things saith he that holdeth the seven stars in his right hand, who walketh in the midst of the seven golden candlesticks;

2 I know thy works, and thy labour, and thy patience, and how thou canst not bear them which are evil: and thou hast tried them which say they are apostles, and are not, and hast found them liars:

3 And hast borne, and hast patience, and for my names sake hast laboured, and hast not fainted.

4 Nevertheless I have somewhat against thee, because thou hast left thy first love.

5 Remember therefore from whence thou art fallen, and repent, and do the first works; or else I will come unto thee quickly, and will remove thy candlestick out of his place, except thou repent.

6 But this thou hast, that thou hatest the deeds of the Nicolaitans, which I also hate.

7 He that hath an ear, let him hear what the Spirit saith unto the churches; To him that overcometh will I give to eat of the tree of life, which is in the midst of the paradise of God.

Chapter Five

JESUS' MESSAGE
TO THE CHURCH OF EPHESUS

Although the churches at Jerusalem, Antioch, and Corinth all had a tremendous influence on the development of the Early Church, it seems that none had an impact as significant as the church of Ephesus. Because of its unique beginning, strategic location, and enormous size, the Ephesian church had a monumental level of influence on churches throughout Asia. In addition, the repercussions of spiritual events that occurred in Ephesus rippled out to churches in every part of the Roman Empire. Many of these events were recorded in the book of Acts — events so numerous that an entire book could be written on that subject alone. The following is a brief recap of some of the significant events that took place in Ephesus and were covered in previous chapters.

- The church of Ephesus was started as a result of the apostle Paul and his ministerial partnership with his colaborers Aquila and Priscilla (*see* pages 206-207).

- One of the first people to be converted in Ephesus was Apollos of Alexandria (*see* page 286). Apollos eventually became the pastor of the Corinthian church, which resulted in an ongoing relationship between the churches at Ephesus and Corinth that lasted for many years.

- Special miracles and significant deliverance from demon powers occurred as a result of Paul's ministry, which caused the name of Jesus to be known and magnified throughout all of Asia (*see* pages 307-319).

- After Paul departed from Ephesus, he asked Timothy to serve as pastor of the Ephesian church, a position the younger minister accepted (*see* 1 Timothy 1:3). Early writers tell us that Timothy eventually died a martyr's death in Ephesus (*see* page 223).

- The apostle Paul was beheaded in Rome during the rule of the Emperor Nero.[1] After Paul's death, a new overseer was needed for Asia, so the apostle John relocated to Ephesus. John became overseer of all the Asia churches, guiding them for many years from his home on the hilltop located directly behind the Temple of Artemis near the city of Ephesus (*see* pages 14-15).

- When John first moved to the city of Ephesus, he brought Mary, the mother of Jesus, along with him. At the time of Jesus' crucifixion, He had entrusted His mother into John's care (*see* John 19:25-27). Historical records seem to affirm that John cared for Mary until her death (*see* page 8).

- The apostle John was arrested in Ephesus during the reign of the Emperor Domitian and was subsequently exiled to the island of Patmos, where he lived until Domitian died. When amnesty was granted to many people who had been wrongly imprisoned during Domitian's reign, John was also released. Returning to his hilltop home near Ephesus, John continued to give apostolic oversight to the churches of Asia (*see* page 25).

- The gospel of John and the epistles of First John, Second John, and Third John were all written during the time of John's residency in Ephesus (*see* page 12).

In addition, evidence suggests that the earliest circulation of the book of Revelation coincides with the time John lived in Ephesus after his release from Patmos.

- John died in Ephesus at a very old age. According to his wishes, he was buried near his hilltop home. A large basilica was later constructed on the site of John's grave by the Emperor Justinian as a memorial of the apostle's residency in Ephesus (*see* pages 12-15).

Left: This photo shows what was long considered by many to be the tomb of St. Luke. Although it is now known that this was not Luke's tomb, the very fact that it was long associated with Luke confirms a common belief among scholars that he had a long-term association with the city of Ephesus.

Luke's tomb for centuries undergirds the common belief that he was a frequent visitor to the city. Luke was one of Paul's traveling companions, so it is reasonable to assume that he was in Ephesus with Paul on multiple occasions. Some historians suggest that Luke was even a long-term resident of Ephesus at some point in his life and that he was buried in this city in an unknown location. However, more reliable records indicate that Luke died at the age of 74 and was buried in Bithynia (which may, in fact, be a copyist's error for the Greek region of Boeotia).[2]

It is also reasonable to conclude that the presence of Jesus' mother was a special attraction in Ephesus during the First Century and that many Christian leaders — including apostles who had known Mary since Jesus' earthly ministry — made visits to Ephesus in order to see her. In fact, certain historical records indicate that as Mary approached her own death, she called for the surviving original apostles to come to her.[3] In all likelihood, this event took place at her home near Ephesus; however, some early traditions assert that it occurred in Jerusalem, where Mary may have traveled for one last visit before she departed this world.[4]

These are just some of the reasons the church of Ephesus held a unique place in early Christian history, unequaled by any other First Century church.

In addition to these extraordinary events, the Christian community in Ephesus served as "host" to many well-known Christians traveling between Jerusalem and Rome or throughout Asia. For example, an ancient monument in the ruins of Ephesus is often referred to as St. Luke's tomb. Although it is now known that this monument has no connection to Luke at all, the fact that it was referred to as St.

Historical writings reveal that Ephesus was also home to many later Christian leaders, such as Polycrates, a Second Century bishop of Ephesus,[5] and Justin Martyr. This latter Church leader was a philosopher who converted to Christ in 130 AD and spent the rest of his life defending the Christian faith, particularly in Asia Minor. Justin died the death of a martyr in 165 AD in the city of Rome.[6]

The Christian community in Ephesus eventually became so large that the city was officially declared a "Christian city." However, at the time of John's exile on the island of Patmos, the Ephesian Christians

Right and Below: The Early Church associated Ephesus with Mary, the mother of Jesus, who resided near the city in her latter years. This close connection is demonstrated by the fact that an early cathedral (the ruins of which are pictured here) was named in her honor. The Church Council of 431 AD was held at this site to conduct scriptural debates regarding the relationship between Jesus' deity and humanity and the doctrine of original sin.

were undergoing severe persecution at the hands of Domitian's government.

It is during this period of adversity that the spirit realm opened before John and he saw things no human eyes had ever witnessed.

'UNTO THE ANGEL'

After John described the vision he beheld of the exalted Christ in all of His splendor and glory (*see* Chapter Two), he began to relate the message Jesus delivered to each of "the angels of the seven churches" (Revelation 1:20). As John listened, Jesus directed His first message "unto *the angel* of the church of Ephesus..." (Revelation 2:1).

The word "angel" is the Greek word *angelos*, which is most often translated *angel* in the New Testament but is also at times translated *messenger* (*see* Luke 7:24; James 2:25). Although local churches may

have angels that watch over and protect them, it is unlikely that this word "angel" refers to *heavenly messengers* in these verses. As mentioned in Chapter Two (*see* page 139), Jesus was addressing the *human messengers* of the seven churches — the individuals, most notably the *pastors*, who had oversight of each congregation.

Along with many other noted theologians, John Walvoord concluded that the word *angelos* in the context of Revelation 2 and 3 refers to human messengers who represented Jesus Christ to the local congregations. Walvoord wrote that the word *angelos* not only refers to heavenly angels in the Bible, but it is "...often used also of men in Greek literature as a whole, and in several instances this word referred to human messengers in the Bible (Matthew 11:10; Mark 1:2; Luke 7:24,27; 9:52). It is properly understood here [in Revelation 2 and 3] to be human messengers to these churches. These messengers were probably the pastors of the churches...."[7]

Walvoord's conclusion is based soundly in the teachings of Scripture. There is no biblical reason to conclude that Jesus gave messages to John so the apostle could then give those divine instructions to heavenly angels. According to Scripture, angels receive their instructions directly from God Himself, not from human sources (*see* Psalm 103:20). They would therefore have no need of written messages from a man, such as those written by John to the seven churches. Finally, and most importantly, not a single instance is recorded in the New Testament in which angels teach, rebuke, correct, or preach to the Church of Jesus Christ. Thus, to interpret the word "angel" — the

Greek word *angelos* — as a *heavenly angel* in Revelation 2 and 3 creates serious theological inconsistencies.

In light of what Scripture reveals about the various roles angels fulfill, few serious scholars conclude that the "angels" of the seven churches in Revelation 2 and 3 were heavenly angels. (*See* the following section, entitled, "Scriptural Roles of Heavenly Angels," for further discussion on this subject.) Most theologians agree that the "angels" whom Jesus addressed were in fact human messengers — the *seven pastors who each oversaw one of those local churches*. By delivering the messages to the pastors *first*, Jesus demonstrated that He honors and does not bypass the authority He has set in the local church. Before the church heard His message, Jesus wanted the pastor to hear it. It then became the local pastor's God-given responsibility to deliver that divine message to the congregation that was under his oversight.

THE CHURCH AT EPHESUS

In Revelation 2:1, Jesus continued to address His message "unto the angel of the *church* of Ephesus...."

The word "church" is the Greek word *ekklesia*, a compound of the words *ek* and *kaleo*. The word *ek* is one of the most frequently used words in both Classical and New Testament Greek. Its meaning can be

(Continued on page 388)

SCRIPTURAL ROLES
OF HEAVENLY ANGELS

In the New Testament, angels are entrusted with the care of the elect — the heirs of salvation (*see* Hebrews 1:14). There is no record in the Bible of angels assisting evil people, although there are multiple references of angels releasing judgment *against* the wicked. The primary assignments of Heaven-sent angels are in respect to *the elect*. God sends angels to meet His people's needs; to strengthen the weary; to give believers supernatural guidance (which, in the New Testament, most frequently occurs in dreams or visions); to provide protection and deliverance from harm; to carry out superhuman feats; to make special announcements; and to release divine judgment. The Bible never explicitly states how many angels God created, but Hebrews 12:22 says that the heavenly hosts of angels are "innumerable."

The apostle Paul strongly warned against a preoccupation with angels (*see* Colossians 2:18). So-called angelic preaching and teaching was viewed as one of the primary sources of false doctrine in the Early Church (*see* Galatians 1:8). During the First Century, much of the false teaching Paul combated was due to so-called "revelations" that purportedly came directly from angels. For instance, the doctrinal problems that were emerging in the church at Colossae and other churches in the Lycus Valley could be traced to claims that angels had appeared with new teachings and revelations.[8] Hence, it is no surprise that many cults and sects in existence today were also formed on the basis of alleged angelic revelations and teachings.

Following is a New Testament list of activities that angels perform. As you carefully read this information, note that there isn't a single record anywhere in the New Testament that encourages or endorses the concept that angels are charged with preaching or teaching God's Word. There is also not one instance in which God sends angels to bring correction or rebuke to a local congregation of believers.

In addition, angels are not redeemed; they have no personal experience with the indwelling Holy Spirit, as believers do. Therefore, although the roles of angels are varied and vital, they do *not* include preaching or teaching about redemption. These responsibilities are assigned to human messengers — specifically to the five-fold ministry gifts (apostles, prophets, evangelists, pastors, and teachers) — who are anointed by God's Spirit to speak on behalf of Jesus Christ to His Church. In fact, angels watch preachers to hear what they say (*see* 1 Peter 1:12).

Finally, please keep in mind that this section is about what angels do *today*. In the future, they will have additional roles, such as separating the righteous from the lost (Matthew 13:41,42,49,50), accompanying Jesus at His Second Coming

"Angels Minister to Christ" by artist Bernardino Passeri

(2 Thessalonians 1:7,8), and so on. But for the purposes of this discussion, we will focus on the roles of angels in this present Church Age.

ANGELS MEET PHYSICAL NEEDS

Matthew 4:11 and Mark 1:13 state that when Jesus concluded His 40-day fast in the wilderness, angels appeared to Him and ministered to Him, thereby *meeting Jesus' physical needs*.

"Jesus in the Garden" by artist Gustave Doré

1:13 relate that angels "ministered" to Jesus, this means that they took on the role of servants and ministered to Jesus' physical and tangible needs after His 40 days of fasting and being tempted by the devil in the wilderness.

ANGELS GIVE STRENGTH

The Bible provides many examples of angels strengthening the weary; however, the best New Testament example is found in Luke 22:43, where an angel strengthened Jesus in the Garden of Gethsemane during the most difficult time of His earthly life. This verse says, "And there appeared an angel unto him from heaven, strengthening him."

When Jesus could find no one else to stand with Him in His hour of need, God provided supernatural assistance in the form of an angel to "strengthen" Jesus. This word "strengthen" comes from the Greek word *enischuo*, a compound of the words *en* and *ischuos*. The word *en* means *in*, and the word *ischuos* is the Greek word for *might* or *strength*. In New Testament times, the word *ischuos* denoted men with *great*

In both of these verses, the word translated "ministered" comes from the Greek word *diakonos*. Wherever this word is used in the New Testament, it depicts *a servant whose chief occupation is to meet some kind of physical or tangible need*. The word *diakonos* is most notably used in Acts 6:2, where it is translated as "serve," referring to the role of the men who were chosen to meet the physical needs of widows in the church at Jerusalem. So when Matthew 4:11 and Mark

An Angel Warns Joseph in a Dream (Matthew 2:13)

muscular abilities, such as champions or heroes. But when these two words *en* and *ischuos* are compounded, the new word means *to impart strength*; *to empower someone*; *to fill a person with physical vigor*; or *to give someone a renewed vitality*. In essence, it describes a person who may have been feeling exhausted and depleted but then suddenly receives a robust blast of energy that instantly *recharges* him.

This means that when Jesus' disciples and friends couldn't be depended on in His hour of need, God provided an angel who *empowered*, *recharged*, and *imparted strength to* Jesus, thus *renewing His vitality* so He could victoriously face the most difficult hour

of His life. Thus, Luke 22:43 provides a vivid New Testament example of how angels *strengthen the weary*.

ANGELS GIVE SUPERNATURAL GUIDANCE

Examples of how angels provide *supernatural guidance* are abundant in the New Testament. In Matthew 2:13, an angel appeared to Joseph in a dream and told him to quickly take Mary and the young Christ Child into Egypt because Herod would seek to kill Jesus. When Herod died, an angel appeared in a dream to Joseph in Egypt, informing him that Herod was dead and that he and his family could now return to Israel. In both of these instances, the supernatural angelic guidance occurred in dreams.

In Acts 8:26, an angel spoke to Philip the evangelist and told him to turn south from Jerusalem toward Gaza. Whether or not the angel told Philip the reason for that divine command, he was quick to obey. Following the guidance provided by this angel, Philip turned south and soon met a powerful Ethiopian eunuch who served under Queen Candice of Ethiopia. At that precise moment, this influential man was reading the book of Isaiah and longing for someone to explain the Scriptures to him.

God had heard the heart cry of the eunuch and sent an angel to tell Philip to turn south. If Philip had disobeyed or had second-guessed the angel's guidance, the eunuch's questions would have remained unanswered. But because Philip listened and obeyed, the eunuch was saved and then baptized in water — and his story became one of the most famous conversions in the book of Acts. This landmark event came to pass because of supernatural angelic guidance.

In Acts 10, we find a powerful example of angelic guidance that changed the course of history. In this passage, an angel appeared in a vision to an Italian centurion named Cornelius who lived in Caesarea. Although Cornelius was unsaved at that moment, he was also divinely chosen. God heard this man's prayers and saw the alms he had

given to the poor, so He intervened on Cornelius' behalf by providing angelic guidance. The angel who appeared to Cornelius instructed him to send his servants to Joppa to summon Peter and his companions to come to him. When Peter arrived at Cornelius' residence, the apostle preached the Gospel to those who were present. All who heard Peter repented and were filled with the Holy Spirit. At that historic moment, the door to salvation was opened to the Gentiles, and the Gospel message began to go forth into the Gentile world.

The apostle Paul also experienced supernatural angelic guidance when he was on a ship in the midst of a raging storm at sea. After the ship's crew had fought the storm for many days, Paul came forward and boldly declared, "And now I exhort you to be of good cheer: for there shall be no loss of any man's life among you, but of the ship. For there stood by me this night the angel of God, whose I am, and whom I serve, saying, Fear not, Paul; thou must be brought before Caesar: and, lo, God hath given thee all them that sail with thee" (Acts 27:22-24).

Although the storm still raged for many more days, the message that the angel spoke to Paul came to pass exactly as it has been said. The ship was lost, but not a single soul perished in that destructive storm. When Paul and the other men were tempted to fear for their lives, God sent an angel to calm the inner storm that was raging in their

© Mary Evans Picture Library

Above: Peter and John are released from prison by an angel (Acts 5:19,20).

minds and souls. And because Paul believed the word of the Lord spoken through the angel, everyone on board survived. This ordeal, which could have ended so horribly, resulted instead in a great revival on the island of Melita, where they were stranded after the ship was lost at sea (*see* Acts 28:1-9).

ANGELS PROVIDE PROTECTION AND DELIVERANCE

The Old Testament is filled with clear evidence that God assigns angels to guard and protect His people. For instance, Psalm 34:7 says that angels encamp around those who fear the Lord to deliver them. Psalm 91:11 promises that God will give His angels charge over His people to keep them in all their ways.

We see an example of how angels guard and protect God's people in Acts 5:17-20. In this account, the high priest rose up against the apostles and had them arrested and thrown into prison. Then Acts 5:19,20 says, "But the angel of the Lord by night opened the prison doors, and brought them forth, and said, Go, stand and speak in the temple to the people all the words of this life."

That night an angel intervened to protect the apostles and set them free. In an instant, they were delivered from harm. However, it must be noted that the *angel* told the *apostles* to go preach and teach. If it were possible for an angel to preach and teach, *this* was that moment. Imagine how powerful the effect would have been if an angel had appeared in splendor to preach the Gospel on the temple grounds. But angels can't do this because they are never assigned the duty of preaching or teaching — even though they often provide supernatural strength, support, protection, and, if needed, deliverance for believers who do preach and teach.

A few chapters later in Acts 12 is the account of Peter's arrest and imprisonment — one of the best illustrations of how angels protect and deliver God's people. After Herod ordered the beheading of James (*see* Acts 12:1,2), he saw that many Jews approved of his action. Therefore, in order to garner

An angel rescues Peter from prison (Acts 12:7-9).

more support and popularity with the angry mob of Christian-haters, Herod gave the order for the apostle Peter to be arrested next. The authorities may have recalled the previous time when the group of apostles miraculously escaped from prison, because this time Peter was delivered to "four quaternions of soldiers" (Acts 12:4).

A "quaternion" referred to *a group of four Roman soldiers*. So four quaternions (i.e., four different groups containing four soldiers each) successively took turns guarding Peter throughout the four watches of the night — one quaternion for each watch. In total, 16 heavily armed Roman soldiers were assigned to guard Peter that night.

However, Peter had an invisible guard that was far more powerful than all 16 Roman soldiers combined!

Acts 12:6 states that Peter was sleeping between two prison guards while two other guards stood watch at the prison door. *Suddenly* the angel of the Lord came into the prison cell and awoke Peter from his sleep, telling him to rise up quickly and leave the prison. Instantly the chains that held Peter loosened and fell to the ground. The angel then told the apostle to put on his shoes and follow him — and Peter obeyed.

Not only did the angel of the Lord set Peter free from the chains that held him, but apparently the angel also temporarily blinded the guards so they were unaware of what was happening. Peter followed the angel through the first and second ward until he came to an iron gate, which supernaturally opened in front of him without anyone touching it. Perhaps Peter didn't realize he wasn't dreaming until he actually stood on the street outside the prison — *free.* An angel had just delivered the apostle from the horrible fate that awaited him at the hands of Herod (vv. 7-11).

There are many more examples in both the Old and New Testaments of angels providing the elect with supernatural protection and deliverance from harm. This is an essential part of the ministry God has assigned to His heavenly hosts.

ANGELS MAKE DIVINE ANNOUNCEMENTS

Although angels do make announcements, their vocal role in the affairs of mankind is not the same as that of human preachers and teachers. Ministers who preach and teach must study, pray, and prepare to teach the Word of God. Once their preparation is complete, ministers then depend on the anointing and inspiration of the Holy Spirit as they speak from their spirits and souls — elaborating, processing, and using human experience to convey what God has shown them in the Scriptures.

Angels don't need to study, pray, or prepare. They listen and speak verbatim what God has instructed them to

speak. They are *repeaters*, not *preachers*. Once an angel has delivered the message to someone exactly as God dictated it, he disappears as quickly as he initially appeared.

Thus, angels are God-sent heavenly messengers who make word-for-word announcements. Only twice in the entire New Testament is there a record of an angel ever conversing with a person — in the cases of Zacharias, the father of John the Baptist, and of Mary, the mother of Jesus.

In Mary's case, the angel Gabriel appeared to this young virgin and made the announcement that she would give birth to Jesus. Mary asked the angel, "…How shall this be, seeing I know not a man?" (Luke 1:34). Gabriel answered her question and clarified that this would be a miraculous birth (v. 35). As God's angelic messenger, Gabriel was only permitted to speak information that was spoken to him — so once Gabriel's mission was complete, he disappeared. Although he was an archangel, Gabriel's function was to repeat the exact message God had entrusted to him and nothing more.

As humans, we are commanded to preach the Gospel and teach God's Word. It is our lifelong responsibility — especially if we are called to the ministry — to study, preach, teach, expose error, rebuke, correct, and instruct

Left: The Angel Gabriel Announces the Birth of the Savior (Luke 1: 26-38).

(*see* 2 Timothy 3:14-4:2). In fact, for all their supernatural abilities, angels cannot even grasp the full glory of our redemption in Christ. As Peter wrote: "Unto whom it was revealed, that not unto themselves, but unto us they did minister the things, which are now reported unto you by them that have preached the gospel unto you with the Holy Ghost sent down from heaven; which things the angels desire to look into" (1 Peter 1:12).

In this verse, the apostle Peter described the great privilege human beings possess to preach and teach God's Word by the power of the Holy Spirit. In fact, angels are so fascinated by this divine privilege that they watch in amazement as men and women preach the Gospel. Angels observe believers as they preach and teach, and they supernaturally assist believers by orchestrating circumstances to eliminate any hindrance to the preaching of the Gospel. But angels are *spectators* — never participants — when it comes to preaching and teaching.

The Bible is replete with illustrations of angels being sent from Heaven to repeat word-for-word announcements from God.

- Luke 1:11-17 relates that an angel *announced* to Zacharias that his wife would give birth to a son — John the Baptist.

- Luke 1:26-33 states that Gabriel *announced* the birth of Jesus to Mary.

- Luke 2:9-14 records that a multitude of heavenly angels *announced* the birth of Jesus to the shepherds.

- Three gospel accounts — Matthew 28:5-7; Mark 16:6,7; and Luke 24:5-7 — testify that angels *announced* Jesus' resurrection.

- Acts 1:11 says two angels appeared to the apostles at the time of Jesus' ascension and *announced* that Jesus would return in the same manner as they saw Him go into Heaven.

- First Thessalonians 4:16,17 foretells that the voice of the archangel will *announce* that moment when believers will be caught up together, along with those who are resurrected to meet the Lord in the air.

- The book of Revelation is filled with *angelic announcements* that initiate judgments upon the earth and its unbelieving inhabitants.

- The one instance in the Bible that seems to refer to an angel preaching is found in Revelation 14:6,7. It says, "And I saw another angel fly in the midst of heaven, having the everlasting gospel to preach unto them that dwell on the earth, and to every nation, and kindred, and tongue, and people, saying with a loud voice, Fear God, and give glory to him; for the hour of his judgment is come: and worship him that made heaven, and earth, and the sea, and the fountains of waters." However, the word "preach" in this context would more properly be translated "proclaim" or "announce." As in other instances throughout the Scriptures, the angel in these verses had been sent from Heaven to announce a word-for-word message directly from God.

The seven "angels" referred to in Revelation chapters 2 and 3 are charged with the responsibility to speak messages to the local congregations. This previous discussion explains why Jesus could be referring only to human messengers — the pastors of those local congregations. The role of angels as heavenly messengers is to repeat verbatim the specific, limited message God sends them to deliver — not to teach, rebuke, correct, or preach to the Church of Jesus Christ.

ANGELS PERFORM SUPERHUMAN FEATS

There are multiple examples in the Old Testament of angels performing superhuman feats. But the New Testament also portrays angels in this way. Perhaps the best example is when the angels rolled away the massive stone that lay before Jesus' garden tomb. Matthew 28:2 says, "...The angel of the Lord descended from heaven, and came and rolled back the stone from the door, and sat upon it."

The word "stone" is the Greek word *lithos*, which simply means *a stone*. It is known, however, that the stones placed in front of such tombs were very large — impossible for a human being to move without the assistance of several people. It must also be noted that the word "sat" in this verse is the Greek word *kathemai*, which means *to sit down*. Some have suggested that the angel's ability to sit on top of such a huge stone as if it were a chair may indicate the gigantic size of the angel himself. However, regardless of this heavenly angel's size as he appeared to those who gazed upon him, the removal of this immense, heavy stone in front of Jesus' tomb would have been a simple feat for such a supernatural being.

A remarkable example of an angel's superhuman strength is recorded in Revelation 20:1-3, where John writes: "And I saw an angel come down from heaven, having the key of the bottomless pit and a great chain in his hand. And he laid hold on the dragon, that old serpent, which is the Devil, and Satan, and bound him a thousand years, and cast him into the bottomless pit, and shut him up, and set a seal upon him, that he should deceive the nations no more, till the thousand years should be fulfilled: and after that he must be loosed a little season."

At the appointed time, an unnamed angel will seize Satan, bind him with a great chain, shut him up in the bottomless pit, and then seal it so he cannot escape. No natural human being would ever be able to perform such a feat, but this passage of Scripture

clearly states that a day is coming when an angel will single-handedly accomplish this task — scriptural proof of the great power heavenly angels possess.

ANGELS WORSHIP

Revelation 5:11,12 says, "And I beheld, and I heard the voice of many angels round about the throne and the beasts and the elders: and the number of them was ten thousand times ten thousand, and thousands of thousands; saying with a loud voice, Worthy is the Lamb that was slain to receive power, and riches, and wisdom, and strength, and honour, and glory, and blessing."

Notice in these verses that the angels declared praises to the Lamb, but it doesn't say they sang to Him. Since singing is a primary feature of worship, most theologians believe that

angels do sing, but there is actually no record in Scripture to support this proposition. However, there are many scriptural instances where angels worship by making declarations about the character and greatness of God (*see* Isaiah 6:2-4).

One of the most famous passages is found in Luke 2:13,14: "And suddenly there was with the angel a multitude of the heavenly host praising God, and saying, Glory to God in the highest, and on earth peace, good will toward men." Most people mistake this text to mean that the angels were singing when they appeared to the shepherds, but these verses state that these heavenly hosts were praising God and *saying*, "Glory to God in the highest...." Nonetheless, based on everything the Bible teaches about worship, it would be logical to conclude that besides making declarations in worship of God, angels also worship God with music, both instrumental and vocal, that is beyond the human imagination to conceive.

ANGELS RELEASE GOD'S JUDGMENT

Many New Testament scriptures portray the ability of angels to release God's judgment. One of the clearest examples is found in Acts 12:22 and 23, where it states that people began to worship Herod as a god. Rather than protest against the praise of men, Herod seemed to encourage it. Verse 23

says, "And immediately the angel of the Lord smote him, because he gave not God the glory: and he was eaten of worms, and gave up the ghost." Herod's death as a result of worms is a fact well established in historical records.[9] However, this event as it is recorded in Acts 12:23 makes it clear that Herod's miserable death was the result of a judgment released against him by an angel.

Nowhere in the Bible is the remarkable power of angels to release judgment better demonstrated than in the book of Revelation.

- In Revelation 7:1, four angels are sent to release judgment upon the earth and sea.

- In Revelation chapters 8 through 11, seven angels sound seven trumpets that release seven judgments into the earth.

- In Revelation 14:17-20, an angel swings a sharp sickle on the earth that releases great wrath.

- In Revelation chapters 15 and 16, seven angels pour judgment out of seven bowls onto the earth and its inhabitants.

All the angelic roles listed in this section are recorded in God's Word, giving us a clear picture of what angels do and don't do. It is vital for us to understand these scriptural parameters of angelic responsibilities in order to rightly divide the Word when considering Jesus' messages to the angels of the seven churches in the book of Revelation. Because angels are never instructed in Scripture to lead local churches, we can conclude that the "angels" Jesus addressed in John's vision on the island of Patmos were human messengers — most likely the pastors of each respective church — and not supernatural angels.

slightly altered, depending on the context in which it is used, but the word *ek* primarily means *out*. It can signify an *exit*, such as when a person *leaves* one room to relocate to another room. It can also convey the idea of *separation*, a point that is important in the context of a "church."

The second part of the compound word *ekklesia* is the word *kaleo*. The basic meaning of *kaleo* is *to beckon*, *to call*, *to invite*, or *to summon*. When the words *ek* and *kaleo* are compounded, the new word *ekklesia* literally means *those who are called out*.

Studying the New Testament usage of the Greek word *kaleo* provides further insight into the meaning of the compound word *ekklesia* as it pertains to the local church. Although the word *kaleo* can simply mean *to call*, it is often used to convey the idea of an *invitation* that isn't made available to everyone else. Because everyone isn't invited, those who *are* should view the invitation as a privilege and a prestigious honor to be appreciated, treasured, prized, and revered.

The New Testament abounds with 148 examples of this word *kaleo*. Two notable examples are found in Matthew 22:2-10 and Luke 14:17-24. In Matthew 22, the word *kaleo* is used in Jesus' parable to describe a special invitation extended by a king who was asking people to attend a great marriage feast. Such royal events were closed to the public; a person couldn't attend without being *called* or *invited*. Receiving an invitation to attend this type of special occasion was therefore considered an honor.

Then in Luke 14:7-24, Jesus taught two parables in which various forms of the word *kaleo* are used 12 times to denote invitations given to people to attend a wedding and a great feast. Both parables in this passage of Scripture emphatically convey the idea of the great *honor* and *privilege* bestowed on a person who was called or invited to such an event.

The apostle Paul used the Greek word *kaleo* and its various forms 49 times in his epistles. For instance, he used this word *kaleo* to describe God's call to repent — to be set free from spiritual darkness and the world of sin and to become a part of His family. This divine call comes to each person when God opens his or her spiritual ears to hear the Gospel's invitation to salvation. Without the Lord's participation, no sinner will ever enter the Kingdom of God, for entrance is by invitation only. When the Holy Spirit opens a person's spiritual ears to truly hear the Gospel message, that is precisely when God's invitation is extended to him or her. To be a recipient of this invitation is both an *honor* and a *privilege*.

This explains why the apostle John wrote, "Behold, what manner of love the Father hath bestowed upon us, that we should be *called* the sons of God..." (1 John 3:1). It should be noted that the entire New Testament plainly teaches this concept. Those of us who are children of God have been *called* or *invited* to this honored and privileged position — a position we never could have attained unless God had extended the invitation (*see* Romans 1:6,7; 8:28,30; 9:24; 1 Corinthians 1:2,9,24,26; 7:18,20,21,22,24; Galatians 1:6; Ephesians 4:1,4; Colossians 3:15; 1 Thessalonians 2:12; 4:7; 2 Thessalonians 2:14; 1 Timothy 6:12;

Right: Nicolas-Bernard Lepicie's 1767 painting, entitled, "The Conversion of St. Paul," depicts the moment when Jesus appeared to Paul and he received the kaleo of God, separating him from the world and giving him the special honor of preaching the Gospel of Jesus Christ.

2 Timothy 1:9; Hebrews 9:15; James 2:7; 1 Peter 1:15; 2:9,21; 5:10; 2 Peter 1:3; 1 John 3:1; Jude 1:1).

Paul also used the word *kaleo* in First Corinthians 1:9 to state that God has invited us all into fellowship with His Son: "God is faithful, by whom ye were called unto the fellowship of his Son Jesus Christ our Lord." The door to this intimate fellowship with Christ is open to those whom God has called. Like the king in Jesus' parable (Matthew 22:1-10), God has invited us to His banqueting table, where we are honored to fellowship with Christ. Once again, this invitation is extended only to the called; therefore, it should be held in high esteem.

But in a much more personal way, the apostle Paul used the word *kaleo* and its various forms to describe his own *call* to be an apostle (*see* Romans 1:1; 1 Corinthians 1:1; 15:9). In Galatians 1:15, Paul also used *kaleo* to describe God's call on his life. He wrote, "But when it pleased God, who separated me from my mother's womb, and *called* me by his grace." It is significant that Paul would use this word to describe his own separation from his mother's womb and his call to be an apostle. This lets us know that Paul never lost sight of the fact that his position as an apostle wasn't a result of his own efforts. He recognized he had received a rare opportunity to participate in a divine purpose not extended to many others (*see* 1 Corinthians 12:29). This call — this *kaleo* — was both an honor and a privilege.

Hebrews 11:8 is an exceptional example of the word *kaleo*, describing the divine call that Abraham received. This divine invitation to Abraham was completely unique, setting him apart in a special category. Until that moment in history, no one had ever received such an invitation. Abraham's call was an honor and a privilege extended to no one else. Once again, the concepts of *honor* and *privilege* are integrally linked to the Greek word *kaleo*.

THE EKKLESIA

> As noted before, the word *ek* means *out*, and the word *kaleo* basically means *to call*. However, when the words *ek* and *kaleo* are combined together to form the compound word *ekklesia*, the meaning changes significantly.

This word *ekklesia* describes *an entire assembly of individuals who are called out, called forth, and separated and who therefore hold a position of honor and privilege.*

The Greek word *ekklesia* has a rich and meaningful history that few understand. The earliest appearance of this word was in ancient Athens, where it was used only in a political context. This early meaning of *ekklesia* is significant because it was still in force when New Testament writers used this particular word to describe the Church of Jesus Christ.

There is no doubt that the writers of the New Testament clearly understood the meaning of the word *ekklesia* — a meaning that was far more profound than the one attributed today to its modern English counterpart, the word "church." Anyone with a superior knowledge of the Greek language in the First Century — and certainly this would include the apostle Paul — would have understood the historical, political, and judicial implications connected to this word. It was therefore no accident that the New Testament writers used *ekklesia* to depict the local church and its role in God's plan. Yet because of this word's strong political implications, to do so constituted a very

Left: This illustration depicts an aerial view of ancient Athens. Athenian citizens would gather for ekklesia *meetings 30 to 40 times a year to discuss and vote on civic matters.*

- Key judicial cases were decided.

- Customs and cultural norms were adapted and changed.

- Officials were appointed.

- State decisions were proclaimed.

- The chief magistrates of the land were elected. (For example, Acts 17:19-34 tells us that the apostle Paul stood before the Areopagus, referring to a group of magistrates elected by Athenian citizens in their *ekklesia*.)

Every Athenian citizen was invited to attend the meeting and participate in this ruling body, regardless of his class or status in society; however, only citizens could attend. Delegates were *called out* from their private lives and *summoned* to take their seats in this distinguished assembly. In many respects, the Athenian *ekklesia* was considered the most prestigious group of people in the land, and people counted it a great privilege and honor to participate in this illustrious body.[10] Its decisions were so far-reaching that they affected every aspect of public and private life.

The meetings of the Athenian *ekklesia* were conducted 30 to 40 times a year. The site where citizens gathered for these meetings was on a small, artificial platform called the Pnyx, located in the southwestern

courageous act at that time. In fact, this act alone could have resulted in charges of treason against the authors of these New Testament epistles and the church members to whom they wrote.

In Classical Greece, the word *ekklesia* denoted an assembly of citizens who were invited to participate in a closed assembly in Athens. At this assembly, a variety of political functions were performed:

- Laws were created.

- Governmental decisions were debated.

- Policies affecting both internal and external affairs were formulated.

district of ancient Athens.[11] After a herald ran throughout the city to announce the meeting, citizens would then begin to gather on this site near the ancient *agora*, which was the city's commercial center. There was no official *ekklesia* building; therefore, the meetings were conducted in the open air. If needed, meetings could be assembled more frequently.

Each session of the Athenian *ekklesia* opened with a prayer and a sacrifice to the gods. The body then proceeded to deal with matters of law and business. The sessions frequently included speakers who made eloquent speeches, taught or debated law, argued for truth, or promoted specific agendas on behalf of the wider population. When meetings concluded, a closing prayer and a final sacrifice were offered to the gods.

The *ekklesia* was such an integral part of Athenian life that famous Greek orators and statesmen — such as Pericles, Aristides, Alcibiades, and Demosthenes — regularly delivered speeches at these meetings. Even Plato referred to events that occurred at Athenian *ekklesia* meetings in his writings.[12]

It is worth noting that political parties and factions were strictly forbidden in this respected assembly. It was a body of equal citizens with equal voices who gathered to assist in the orderly development of society. Thus, the idea that such an illustrious group could degenerate into a group of contentious factions was an intolerable prospect. There was simply too much prestige attributed to the *ekklesia* for Athenian citizens to allow its meetings to deteriorate into ugly fights and divisions.

This idea of a governing body free of factions, strife, and squabbles undoubtedly carried over into the New Testament Church. The apostle Paul's reprimand of

Below: At meetings of the Athenian ekklesia, *citizens were responsible for voting on matters of law and business and for discussing future agendas pertaining to the larger population.*

Above: *The Areopagus (the chief magistrates of ancient Athens) met here on Mars Hill. It is significant to note that the* ekklesia *held such power in ancient Athenian culture that these chief magistrates — the highest judges of the land — were elected by the Athenian citizens attending the meetings.*

the church at Corinth for allowing strife and divisions perfectly fits the model of a faction- and strife-free assembly of people (*see* 1 Corinthians 1:11-15; 3:1-9).

Scholars estimate that the Athenian *ekklesia* meetings were attended by a minimum of 6,000 voting citizens (i.e., adult male citizens). Although this category of citizenship in Athens totaled no more than 20 percent of the city's population,[13] 6,000 people was still a small gathering in comparison to its bustling population at that time. Nevertheless, a meeting of this size required robust leadership and rules to keep it on schedule and to provide order.

As frequently occurs when people become accustomed to privilege and honor, Athenian citizens eventually began to take for granted their right to participate in the *ekklesia* meetings. Over time, attendance at the *ekklesia* dropped substantially, and many citizens would attend meetings only when they were coerced to do so.

The *ekklesia* had different levels of leadership. The council (*boule*) operated when the *ekklesia* was not in session. This council then determined what would be brought before the people (*demos*) at the next general assembly (*ekklesia*).[14] In many respects, the levels of leadership in the

Above: This illustration depicting ancient Athens shows the platform called the Pnyx (upper lefthand corner) where an ekklesia assembly of Athenian citizens met many times each year to make the important decisions pertaining to the city.

Athenian *ekklesia* were similar to the various levels of leadership that later emerged in the New Testament local church.

A herald (*kerux*) made proclamations at the *ekklesia* meetings. During Homer's time, the word *kerux* referred to a spokesman for a king, a prince, or some other superior authority. But in Athens during the Classical Greek period, the *kerux* primarily referred to the person charged with overseeing the official *ekklesia* meetings,[15] which included the following responsibilities:

- Summoning the citizens of Athens to the Pnyx when it was time to conduct an *ekklesia* meeting.

- Opening and closing each session.

- Maintaining order and providing oversight to the assembly.

- Bringing correction to members who were out of order.

- Publicizing the final decisions of the assembly and its leadership.

- Calling soldiers to battle in times of war.

The *kerux* was a chosen spokesman for a higher authority. Consequently, the *kerux* didn't have the authority to negotiate or mitigate issues; rather, his role was to be his superior's voice and to speak on

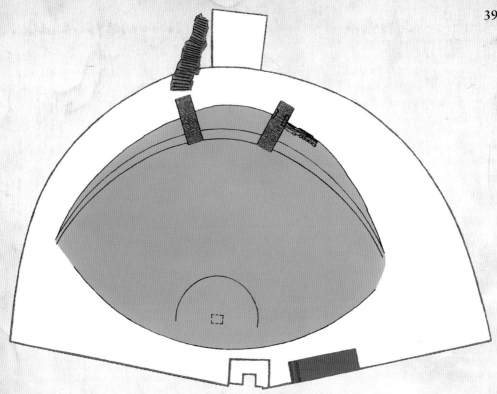

Above: This drawing depicts the Pnyx platform after its second phase of construction in 404-403 BC. Later the platform was enlarged (330-326 BC), as indicated by the red line.[16] The earthen platform was supported by a stone retaining wall and had two stairways leading up to it, with more stairs added later for the enlarged platform. The speaker would stand on the dias to address the ekklesia *assembly.*

behalf of his sender.[17] The *kerux* was to lift his voice loud and clear and to accurately deliver the message that had been entrusted to him, regardless of the crowd's response.

The Greek word *kerux* is another word that may have influenced the thinking of New Testament writers in its connection to the Athenian *ekklesia*. The word *kerux* is the same term used in the New Testament to describe a preacher's responsibility to proclaim the Word of God. In Second Timothy 4:2, where Paul admonishes Timothy to "preach the Word," the word translated "preach" is derived from the Greek word *kerux*.

Paul used this word in reference to the task of a pastor or preacher to speak on behalf of Christ and to accurately represent Him. The minister doesn't have the authority to mitigate the truth or to change the message to satisfy his listeners. Regardless of the people's response, the pastor or preacher must lift his voice loud enough to make the Lord's message clearly heard and to accurately deliver the truth entrusted to him by Jesus Christ.

The Athenian *ekklesia* was a renowned institution throughout the entire Greek-speaking world. The formation of this assembly was one of the key components in the development of democracy, which eventually impacted the entire civilized world. The fame of the Athenian *ekklesia* was so pervasive that any educated writer during the First Century would have understood this word's historical roots and ramifications — including the men who penned the pages of the New Testament.

THE CHURCH

> It is clear why New Testament writers chose the word *ekklesia* to describe God's people. The usage of this word unmistakably means that a local church is a body of individuals who have been called out, called forth, and separated for the purposes of God.

As citizens of God's Kingdom, all believers have the right to participate in the affairs and the life of their church — a right that is at once a joyful privilege, a profound honor, and a sober responsibility. Just as the Athenian *ekklesia* ruled in matters of law, business, society, customs, culture, and judicial matters, God calls upon a local church to exert its influence in every arena of the society in which it exists.

The use of the word *ekklesia* tells us that it was never God's intention for the local church to be a small group of silent, unnoticed people who gather to quietly discuss religious affairs. This power-packed Greek word clearly tells us that

God's original intent was that each local church would have a voice of influence both in private and public life. Just as the Athenian *ekklesia* was a key component in the development of democracy that eventually impacted the entire civilized world, the Lord intends for local churches to have a powerful impact on society. Thus, the scriptural concept of the word *ekklesia* can be described as *a body of believers who are called out of darkness into light to become citizens of Heaven and to apply God's laws in the affairs of the earth.* To be called as members of such a distinguished body is both an *honor* and a *privilege.*

Although the word *ekklesia* is rooted in a political environment, the New Testament Church didn't attempt to invoke a political revolution against the existing government of that day. The early believers understood that the influence and strength of the Church lay in their commitment to keep the principles of God's Word, shine the light of the Gospel into the darkness, live as salt in an unsavory world, and demonstrate the power of the Holy Spirit.

Nevertheless, it was daring and courageous for the New Testament writers to use the word *ekklesia* in describing the local church. A pagan government could have easily perceived the church to be a potential threat, an alternate governing body that might attempt to exert itself in the political realm. Rome had no tolerance for subversion, and everything about this word suggested a desire to influence society. Thus, the use of this word in an epistle to a local church could have been sufficient reason for a charge

APOSTLES' CREED

I believe in God, the Father Almighty, Creator of Heaven and earth. I believe in Jesus Christ, His only Son, our Lord, who was conceived by the power of the Holy Spirit, born of the Virgin Mary, suffered under Pontius Pilate, was crucified, died, and was buried. He descended into hell; on the third day He rose again. He ascended into Heaven and is seated at the right hand of the Father, and He will come again to judge the living and the dead. I believe in the Holy Spirit, the holy catholic Church, the communion of saints, the forgiveness of sins, the resurrection of the body, and life everlasting.

Amen.

NICENE CREED

We believe in one God, the Father Almighty, Maker of Heaven and earth, and of all things visible and invisible; and in one Lord Jesus Christ, the only begotten Son of God, begotten of the Father before all worlds, Light of Light, very God of very God, begotten, not made, being of one substance with the Father, by whom all things were made; who for us men, and for our salvation, came down from Heaven, and was incarnate by the Holy Ghost of the Virgin Mary, and was made man. He was crucified for us under Pontius Pilate, and suffered, and was buried, and the third day He rose again, according to the Scriptures, and ascended into Heaven, and sitteth on the right hand of the Father. From thence He shall come again, with glory, to judge the quick and the dead; whose Kingdom shall have no end. And we believe in the Holy Ghost, the Lord and Giver of life, who proceedeth from the Father, who with the Father and the Son together is worshiped and glorified, who spake by the prophets; and in one holy catholic and apostolic Church. We acknowledge one baptism for the remission of sins, and we look for the resurrection of the dead and the life of the world to come.

Amen.

of treason to be brought against both the author of the epistle and the members of that church. Yet Paul and the other New Testament writers bravely used this word because they believed that God had ordained the local church to be His *ekklesia* on the earth.

In contemporary society, the word "church" is often used to designate a building where religious services are conducted. But the luxury of meeting in or owning a church building didn't exist in the First Century. Churches had no formal meeting places, so they met in homes or in secret locations to avoid being detected by Roman authorities. In the book of Acts, believers met in upper rooms, on streets, in homes, and even in jails. But no matter where the *ekklesia* was conducted, it was always *physical*, *visible*, and *local*.

Many make reference to the universal Church, and certainly there *is* a universal Church. The New Testament Scriptures establish this truth (*see* 1 Corinthians 10:32; Ephesians 3:10,11; 5:23-32). Both the Apostles' Creed (most likely developed in the Second Century) and the later version of the Nicene Creed (written at the First Council of Constantinople in 381 AD) support this concept of a universal Church, referring to it as the holy "catholic church." This term didn't refer to the denomination we call the Catholic Church. Rather, it was a Latin term meaning "universal," used as an early declaration that the Church at large includes *all* those who have received Jesus Christ as their Savior.

However, in the Paul's writings and in the book of Acts, the word *ekklesia* most often refers to a visible church located in a real geographical location. There are many New Testament examples of this, such as in Paul's epistles, where he wrote, "...Unto the church of God which is *at Corinth...*" (*see* 1 Corinthians 1:2; 2 Corinthians 1:1). In these verses, Paul was not writing to a worldwide body of believers; rather, he was addressing a specific congregation with concrete needs and issues, located in a specific city.

Although the truths of New Testament epistles are to be applied to the Church at large, the fact remains that the writers of these epistles weren't addressing the universal Church. Instead, they were writing to specific local churches with real needs and challenges. The New Testament

mentions such churches in many cities, including *Antioch*, *Assos*, *Colossae*, *Derbe*, *Didyma*, *Ephesus*, *Hierapolis*, *Iconium*, *Jerusalem*, *Laodicea*, *Lystra*, *Melitus*, *Perga*, *Pergamum*, *Philadelphia*, *Philippi*, *Pisidian Antioch*, *Rome*, *Sardis*, *Smyrna*, *Thessalonica*, *Thyatira*, and *Troas*. In each city where a church was located, that local church became God's *ekklesia* — a body of individuals whom God had called forth to assemble together and further His Kingdom in the hearts of people and in every arena of life.

'THESE THINGS SAITH HE THAT HOLDETH THE SEVEN STARS IN HIS RIGHT HAND'

In Revelation 2:1, John began to write what he heard Jesus speak to the pastor of the Ephesian church — God's *kerux*.

The church in Ephesus was the largest and most renowned of all New Testament churches. Its pastor was the one called to lead this prestigious and honored group of believers whom God had delivered out of pagan darkness into His glorious light. Jesus said, "Unto the angel of the church of Ephesus write; *These things saith he that holdeth the seven stars in his right hand....*"

This verse states that Christ "holdeth" the seven stars in His right hand. (For an in-depth discussion of the symbolism of these "seven stars," *see* pages 100-113.) The seven stars are symbolic of the seven pastors of the seven churches, and Revelation 2:1

unapologetically states that Jesus "hold-eth" the seven stars in His right hand.

At first, this seems to be a restatement of Revelation 1:16, where John wrote that the exalted Christ whom he saw in his vision "…had in his right hand seven stars…." But when this truth is repeated in Revelation 2:1, John uses a different Greek verb that makes this statement much stronger than the first.

The word "had" in Revelation 1:16 is the Greek word *echo*, which means *to hold tightly* or *to hold in one's firm grasp*, implying Christ's *ownership* of the seven stars, or seven pastors. But the word "holdeth" in Revelation 2:1 is from the Greek word *kratos* — a word that normally denotes *power*. However, as used in this verse, *kratos* refers to Jesus' *control* over the seven stars, or the seven pastors. In the context of this verse, the word *kratos* means *to have power over, to hold fast to*, or *to have a masterful grip on*.

Thus, the word *kratos* expresses the fact that Christ masterfully held the seven pastors in His mighty grip. They were under His control and were constantly in the grip of His authority. The fact that Jesus held these seven stars in His *right* hand is an important point that won't be discussed at length here. Suffice it to say that in Scripture, the right hand represents power and authority. Thus, Jesus was depicted as One who had power and authority over these seven pastors and, through the pastors, over their respective local churches. (For further insight into the reason the seven stars are held in the "right hand" of Christ, *see* pages 104-113, where the symbolism of the "right hand" is dealt with extensively.)

The position of the seven stars in Christ's right hand strongly implies that the seven pastors of the seven churches were *answerable* and *accountable* to the Head of the Church who *controlled* them. They were in Jesus' custodial care, but they were accountable for delivering His message to the churches under their oversight. The seven pastors were Christ's possession (*echo*), and He therefore had the right to direct, correct, and instruct them. Because He held (*kratos*) these seven stars (pastors) in His hand, it is understood that they were responsible to Him. They were called to be the messengers (*angelos*) through which the Head of the Church would speak seven distinct messages to the churches in *Ephesus, Smyrna, Pergamum, Thyatira, Sardis, Philadelphia*, and *Laodicea*. Jesus would hold them accountable for accurately delivering the messages He was about to dictate to them.

It is important to point out that these seven pastors were in the right hand of Christ, *not* in the hands of a board of deacons or a pulpit committee. Of course, it is vital for systems of accountability to be developed and set in place in each local church. But the pastor of each church is called by Jesus Christ and is, first and foremost, answerable to Him. Although God may certainly use deacon boards and pulpit committees, they are not the "seven stars" John saw in his vision. The *under-shepherds* are the ones held in the masterful grip of the Great Shepherd — the Head of the Church — and they will be *answerable* and *accountable* to Him. These seven pastors were expected to deliver with accuracy and precision Jesus' message to their respective churches — seven of the most influential Asia churches that existed at that time.

'WHO WALKETH IN THE MIDST OF THE SEVEN GOLDEN CANDLESTICKS'

In Revelation 2:1, Jesus continued His message to the Ephesian church: "Unto the angel of the church of Ephesus write; These things saith he that holdeth the seven stars in his right hand, *who walketh in the midst of the seven golden candlesticks....*"

The word "walketh" comes from the Greek word *peripatos* — a compound of the words *peri* and *pateo*. The word *peri* means *around*, and the word *pateo* means *to walk*. When these two words are compounded, the new word means *to walk around*. Earlier in Revelation 1:13, John wrote that he saw Christ "in the midst" of the seven candlesticks. But here John described Jesus as *walking* in the midst of the candlesticks. This word *peripateo* reveals how interested Christ was in these seven churches. At the gatherings of these early believers, Jesus walked around them to examine their true spiritual condition

Left: This illustration from an older version of the Catholic Picture Bible, *entitled, "The Revelation of St. John," shows the way the exalted Christ was often depicted by Christian artists through the centuries. Although the drawing shows seven candlesticks, a more accurate rendering of the Greek word* luchnos, *translated "candlesticks" in Revelation 1:20, would be the oil lamp commonly used during the First Century.*

churches, an exterior walk around the churches wasn't sufficient — so He actually entered each church to walk in the "midst" of them. The word "midst" is the Greek word *meson*, which means *in the middle,* describing being *in the very gut of* or *at the very center of* something. So after taking an exterior, preliminary view, Jesus walked right through the center of each congregation to observe, examine, and analyze each of them.

Christ gave His utmost attention to the churches because they were "golden candlesticks." The word "golden" speaks of the great value Jesus Christ places upon the Church. The term "candlesticks" is a reminder of the role God intends for the Church to fulfill in a dark world. The word translated "candlestick" is actually the Greek word *luchnos,* a word that depicts the *oil lamps* used all over the Roman Empire in the First Century. These lamps were designed to give light in darkness, but their ability to produce light came from the oil each lamp contained. Likewise, the Church of Jesus Christ is to be a light in the world, but the ability to shine this light depends on the Holy Spirit who indwells believers both individually and corporately in the Church at

and thereby determine their needs. The Greek tense means Christ didn't simply take a one-time stroll around these congregations; rather, He continually walked around them to inspect, observe, contemplate, probe, and uncover the true condition of each church.

Because Christ was passionately interested in the condition of the seven large. Thus, the fact that these churches are called "candlesticks" reminds us of the honor we have been given as believers to be receptacles of God's glory and presence in the earth (*see* pages 73-77 for more on this subject).

'I KNOW'

In Revelation 2:2, Jesus continued His message by commending the church at Ephesus: "*I know* thy works, and thy labour, and thy patience, and how thou canst not bear them which are evil: and thou hast tried them which say they are apostles, and are not, and hast found them liars."

As we read each of the seven messages, it becomes clear that Jesus was familiar with the specific events and personalities of each church. He knew about each local body's doctrinal problems, challenges, and spiritual climate. This in-depth knowledge of each congregation was clearly the result of Christ's focused attention as He closely examined the condition of His people.

As Jesus walked around each of the congregations and then entered to walk through the "gut" of each church, He was able to authoritatively say, "I *know* thy works...." The word "know" is the Greek word *oida*, which comes from a Greek root that means *to see*. Hence, the word *oida* describes what Jesus had personally seen, not information obtained by any other source. This was *knowledge* based on *personal observation*. Because He walked in the midst of the seven golden candlesticks, Jesus was in a position to *see* everything that happened in these churches.

This Greek word *oida* appears several more times in Revelation 2 and 3 (*see* Revelation 2:9, 2:13, 2:19, 3:1, 3:8, and 3:15), where Jesus emphatically stated that He *knew* all the works of the churches He was addressing. This means that because of Christ's great love for the Church, *nothing* happens in it that escapes His attention. As Head of the Church, it is His responsibility

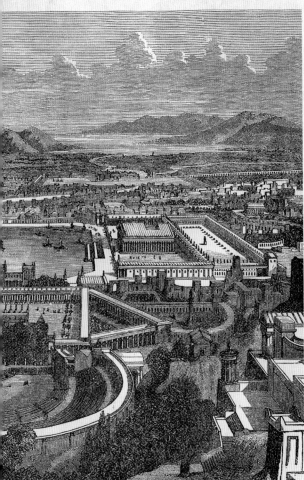

Left: This illustration shows how the city of Ephesus may have looked in the First Century. In the foreground is the Great Theater; in the distance are the Central Marketplace and the Great Harbor of Ephesus. Based on the most recent archeological findings, this illustration is relatively accurate. It was in the midst of this city that Paul started a church that became one of the most prominent and hardworking congregations in all of Asia.

'I KNOW THY WORKS'

> In Revelation 2:2, Jesus continued by saying, "I know *thy works....*"

The word "works" denotes *deeds* or *actions*. But the sentence structure is actually different in Greek. The word "works" is followed by the word "thy" and should therefore be interpreted, "I know the works *of you.*" The emphasis is on that phrase *of you* — in other words, on what Christ implicitly knew about *this* particular church. It lets us know that Christ knew specific details about the works, deeds, and actions that were unique to this local body of believers. A sweeping glance at all the churches in Asia would not have revealed this intimate knowledge. Jesus carefully surveyed and observed everything about each church until He knew the specific details that made it different from all the rest. Thus, He knew that:

- The church of Ephesus had lost its first love (Revelation 2:4).

to see and know everything that is happening in each local body of believers.

We also see that Jesus is not only familiar with large churches, such as the church at Ephesus, but He also knows explicit details about smaller congregations, like the church at Smyrna. Some, like the church at Sardis, are well located; other churches are more remote, such as the church at Thyatira. But regardless of the size or the location of a local church, Jesus has intimate knowledge about the issues and challenges each church faces, and He is familiar with all its works.

- The church of Smyrna was suffering tribulation and poverty (Revelation 2:9).

- The church of Pergamum was confronted with pervasive paganism and demonic strongholds and was facing intense persecution (Revelation 2:13).

- The church of Thyatira was hardworking and charitable but was also being invaded by damnable doctrines (Revelation 2:19,20).

- The church of Sardis was slipping and in danger of dying spiritually (Revelation 3:2).

- The church of Philadelphia had an open door that no man could shut (Revelation 3:8).

- The church of Laodicea was spiritually lukewarm (Revelation 3:16).

The seven pastors and the members of these seven churches must have been stunned when they received these written messages from the apostle John and discovered that Jesus Christ was so intimately acquainted with each of them. Jesus' messages to these seven churches also signaled to all future generations that He is right in the middle of His Church and that *nothing* in the Church goes unseen by Him.

But Jesus didn't stop after saying that He knew generally about the Ephesian believers' works; He proceeded to explain *precisely* what He knew about them. In the rest of Revelation 2:2, Christ spoke words of commendation about their hardworking attitude, their endurance against the many forces arrayed against them, their devotion to ministry, their intolerance for doctrinal impurity, their desire to protect the flock from apostolic pretenders, and their steadfast refusal to give in to fatigue or weariness. In verse 3, Jesus also commended them for having done all of this for "His name's sake." If one only reads Revelation 2:2 and 3, the church at Ephesus sounds like the *ideal* church.

'AND THY LABOUR'

> After Jesus stated that He had firsthand knowledge of the works of the Ephesian church, He then began to cover, point by point, the extraordinary features He knew about it.

Before giving the church a strong rebuke and calling the Ephesian believers to repentance (v. 5), Jesus first commended them for what they were doing correctly. Notice that both here and in Paul's epistles, commendation always precedes correction. As Jesus opened His heart and spoke to His church in Ephesus, He applauded and saluted them for the things they had done correctly. First, He said, "I know thy works, *and thy labour…*" (v. 2).

By naming "labor" as the first item on His list of the Ephesian believers' many commendable works, Jesus drew attention to what might have been the *chief characteristic* of this church: They were a hardworking congregation. The word "labor" in this verse doesn't refer to a normal level of work; rather, it describes

Right: *Pictured here is Curetes Street, the most elegant street in ancient Ephesus. The city was home to the largest and one of the most influential churches in the First Century. In John's vision, Jesus declared that He knew all the works of this productive and longsuffering congregation. Nothing happened in their midst, whether good or bad, that escaped His attention.*

the most difficult, exhausting, and wearisome kind of labor. It is the Greek word *kopos* — a word often used to depict a farmer who works in his field during the hottest season of the year with sweat pouring down his face. Enduring the extreme temperatures of the afternoon sunshine, the farmer strains, struggles, and toils to push that plow through the hardened ground. Although the work is strenuous, the farmer keeps laboring. After he finishes plowing one row, he turns and starts all over again on the next one. By the end of the day, the farmer is physically exhausted, mentally drained, drenched with perspiration, and covered with dirt. His labor (*kopos*) has required his total concentration and devotion.

Jesus' use of this Greek word *kopos* to describe the church of Ephesus lets us know that these believers gave the best physical, mental, and spiritual energies they had to offer. Because this word describes *exhausting* and *wearisome* work, it allows us to see into the life of the Ephesian congregation. These believers gave themselves over to the work of the ministry with no limitations, laboring (*kopos*) to the point of *exhaustion.*

Jesus said, "I know thy *labor.*" Again, the sentence structure in the Greek is

different in a very important way. The word "labor" is followed by the word "thy," and the emphasis is on "thy," or "you." It should literally be interpreted, "I know...the labor *of you*" — implying that this type of labor was a unique characteristic specifically demonstrated by the church of Ephesus.

There were several reasons why the Ephesian congregation labored so intensely. First, it was the largest church of its time. This fact alone demanded a high level of investment from its leadership and its members. However, it must be noted again that Ephesus was the largest city in all of Asia. This brought many visitors to the city, including Christians who were passing through Ephesus en route to other places. Hosting a constant flood of Christian visitors required the highest level of hospitality and organization — which was in itself a very difficult assignment.

Paul himself started the church of Ephesus with the help of Aquila and Priscilla, and people came from across Asia Minor to hear the apostle's teaching, especially during the years he resided there. Ephesus was also the headquarters for the explosive ministry that was expanding throughout Asia — and this,

Left: This is one of the exquisite sidewalk mosaics that decorated the covered colonnades along Curetes Street, where the city's population — including the believers of Ephesus — shopped and went about their daily affairs. One can only imagine the untold multitudes who were saved, healed, and delivered from demonic influence along this very street.

too, attracted Christians to the city. People looked to the church of Ephesus for leadership and direction and considered it to be the center of spiritual oversight for the region. This brought a continual stream of spiritual leaders and believers into the city who were seeking counsel regarding problems they were facing back home.

Even after Paul's departure, Ephesus remained at the forefront of the Early Church, with Timothy presiding as senior pastor and the apostle John eventually settling in the city as the overseer for all Asia churches. It is also probable that many spiritual leaders — including many of the original apostles — traveled to Ephesus to see Mary, who lived on the slopes above the city. Thus, in addition to the hard work required to assist in the growth of the largest congregation in the world at that time and in the ministry of taking care of its own members, the Ephesian church also had to receive the constant influx of visitors into the city. This required organization, teamwork, and an extremely high level of hospitality from the Ephesian congregation, including a continual supply of food and accommodation. The ability of these believers to labor in this capacity and to do it with joy was one of their most outstanding features, and Jesus commended them for it.

The Ephesian congregation was unquestionably a missions-oriented church that sent many Christian workers to assist in the pioneering of other Asia churches during the First Century. For instance, neighboring churches were launched in *Aphrodisias*, *Colossae*, *Hierapolis*, *Laodicea*, *Melitus*, *Pergamum*, *Philadelphia*, *Sardis*, and *Smyrna*, as well as in many other cities of that region. Teachers and workers were dispatched to every part of Asia where churches were being established. The extent of the Ephesian church's outreach is demonstrated in the life of Apollos, who was even sent across the Aegean Sea to serve as pastor of the Corinthian church. Each time workers were dispatched, replacements had to be trained and prepared. Thus, this cycle of preparation and reassignment continued nonstop in the church of Ephesus — requiring a high level of focus, diligence, organization, and manpower in the work of God's Kingdom.

Jesus' use of the word *kopos* clearly depicts a congregation in Ephesus that was extremely hardworking — yet in Revelation 2:2, no hint of complaint can be found. The congregation of Ephesus carried out this work with joy, year after year. Christ *commended* them for their obedience, their willing attitude, and their readiness to do whatever was required for the good of their church and the salvation of the lost.

'AND THY PATIENCE'

Jesus went on to stress the next characteristic that was unique to the church of Ephesus. He said, "I know thy works, and thy labour, and *thy patience*..." (Revelation 2:2).

Although the *King James Version* says, "and thy patience," the Greek sentence structure actually positions the word "patience" first, followed by the word "thy," or "you." In other words, the emphasis is on the *believer's* patience. It should be interpreted to say, "I know… the patience *of you*" — implying a type of patience that was uniquely characteristic of the Ephesian believer.

The word "patience" comes from the Greek word *hupomeno*, which is a compound of the words *hupo* and *meno*. The word *hupo* means *under*, as to be *underneath* something that is very heavy. The word *meno* means *to stay* or *to abide*. It describes *a resolute decision to remain in one's spot*; *to keep a position*; or *to maintain territory that has been gained*. But when the words *hupo* and *meno* are compounded to form the word *hupomeno*, the new word portrays *a person who is under some type of heavy load but who refuses to stray from his position because he is committed to his task*. Regardless of how heavy the load, how fierce the opposition, how intense the stress, or how much weight is thrown against him, this person is inwardly resolved that he is not going to move. He is committed to stay put, and he will never surrender for any reason.

In the earliest years of the Church when believers faced unremitting persecution, they were confronted by a host of hostile powers that were arrayed in opposition against them. The immoral culture, pagan religions, the government, unsaved family and friends — all of these external forces put constant pressure on the early believers to forfeit their faith and return to their old ways. But they firmly believed that if they had *hupomeno*, they would survive and outlast all the opposition. This is why they referred to this spiritual characteristic as the "Queen of all virtues." It was believed that if believers possessed this one virtue, they could survive anything that came against them. Believers understood that if *hupomeno* was operational in their lives, the question was no longer *if* they would overcome their battles — only *when* they would overcome.

The sense of determination inherent in the word *hupomeno* is clearly seen when used in a military sense to portray soldiers who were ordered to maintain their positions, even in the face of fierce combat. Their order was *to stand their ground and defend every inch of territory that had been gained*. To do that, the soldiers had to be resolved to courageously do whatever was required to fulfill that assignment — *no matter how difficult the challenge*. Their goal was to see that they survived every attack and held their position until they had outlasted the resistance. These soldiers had to indefinitely and defiantly stick it out until the enemy, realizing the soldiers couldn't be beaten, therefore decided to give up and retreat. Thus, the word *hupomeno* conveys the idea of being *steadfast, consistent, unwavering,* and *unflinching*.

The *King James Version* translates the Greek word *hupomeno* as "patience" in Revelation 2:2, but a more accurate rendering of this word would be *endurance*. One scholar has described *hupomeno* as *staying power*; another contemporary translator has said it could be described as *hang-in-there power*. Both of these interpretations correctly express the concept behind *hupomeno* because it is the attitude that *hangs in there, never gives up, refuses to surrender to obstacles, and turns down every opportunity to quit.*

If a person has *hupomeno*, it means he is fully committed to standing by his faith, his task, or a principle of truth, regardless of the price to be paid. This person possesses a steadfast, tenacious attitude that refuses to crumble or concede to defeat. Nothing can change his mind or sway his determination to maintain his position — not external circumstances, other people's words, or any other attempt to manipulate or change his stance.

This understanding of the word *hupomeno* was important to the Ephesian believers, considering the fierce opposition their church was facing every day. For instance, these early Christians who lived in Ephesus faced:

Above: Several prominent spiritual leaders of the Early Church — including Paul, Aquila, Priscilla, and Apollos (depicted here preaching in Ephesus) — helped establish a productive, hardworking ministry base in Ephesus that would eventually span its reach throughout the Roman province of Asia.

- Religious intolerance from the Jewish community (*see* Acts 19:9).

- Intense pagan resistance (*see* Acts 19:23-41).

- Persecution of the most horrific forms, including imprisonment and a violent death — even to the point of being forced into the great Stadium of Ephesus to fight lions and other wild beasts (*see* 1 Corinthians 15:32).

Ephesus was the largest and most famous imperial city in Asia and was especially revered by Roman emperors — including Nero and Domitian, two of the most notable rulers who persecuted the Early Church. When the great persecution against Christian believers began under Nero's

Above: Pictured here are the vaulted rooms that served as underpinnings to the Temple of Domitian, located in the center of the city of Ephesus. The temple was seen by Ephesian Christians as an abomination to God, and many believers suffered intense persecution because they refused to show homage to or recognize the deity of this wicked emperor.

regime, it was carried out ruthlessly in every part of the Roman Empire.[18] But because Ephesus was the chief imperial city of the region, it is likely that the city government conducted an even more intense level of persecution to demonstrate to nearby cities how to deal with Christians. Later when Domitian served as emperor, he ordered a large temple to be erected in his honor in the heart of Ephesus' most prestigious district. Those who refused to recognize his deity with a gesture of honor when passing by his statue were punished, imprisoned, or killed. During this time period, the apostle John was arrested and later exiled to Patmos — possibly for committing this very offense.

For believers in this city to survive the unremitting pressure and persecution that was methodically conducted against them, it was essential for them to have an attitude that would sustain them. They needed *hupomeno* — that persistent, steadfast, tenacious spirit which refuses to crumble or concede to defeat. Because they possessed this quality of patience, or endurance, they never surrendered in the face of pressure or capitulated to the forces that attempted to stamp them out.

The Ephesian believers' "patience" was one of their most outstanding features. Although many local churches were also facing intense hostility and persecution, there was something special about the "patience" demonstrated by the church in Ephesus that caused Jesus to pause. This *staying power* was such a unique characteristic among them that Christ commended them for it.

'AND HOW THOU CANST NOT BEAR THEM WHICH ARE EVIL'

As Jesus Christ continued to speak to the Ephesian leadership and church members, He also commended them for their intolerance of religious imposters. He said, "I know thy works, and thy labour, and thy patience, *and how thou canst not bear them which are evil...*" (Revelation 2:2).

The phrase "canst not" is a form of *dunamai*, which is the word for *ability* or *power*. However, in this verse it is used with a negative, which changes the word to mean *intolerance, inability,* or *powerlessness*. Although intolerance would

normally be perceived as a negative quality, this was a correct type of intolerance for which Christ commended them. It was an intolerance of spiritual imposters who attempted to creep into this church for the sake of self-advantage. The church of Ephesus had no tolerance for such false pretenders. This is the reason Christ went on to say, "I know thy works, and thy labor, and thy patience, *and how thou canst not bear them which are evil....*"

The word "bear" comes from the Greek word *bastadzo* — a word that means *to suffer, to carry, to lift up,* or *to bear something* — as in *to bear* a responsibility. It is used 27 times in the New Testament, and in more than half of those instances, the word means *to physically carry something*. An example of this word is found in John 19:17, where Jesus was called upon to bear His own Cross. It is also used in Acts 21:35, where Paul was *carried* by soldiers, and in Luke 11:27, where it describes a mother *carrying* a child in the womb. In each instance, *bastadzo* denotes a person or group of people who are responsible for *carrying* or for *bearing* some type of responsibility.

As used in Revelation 2:2, this word *bastadzo* denotes the Ephesian congregation's absolute intolerance for those who were "evil." These believers emphatically refused *to carry, endorse, bear responsibility for, lift up,* or *publicize* any person they believed to be "evil." The word "evil" is from the Greek word *kakos*, a word that is used 50 times in the New Testament and that always describes something that is *bad, destructive, evil, foul, harmful, hurtful, injurious,* or *vile*.

As noted earlier, Ephesus was referred to as "The Light of Asia" — a term that describes the enormous effect this intellectual and sophisticated city had on all of Asia. For hundreds of years, Ephesus was an attraction for anyone with a new concept, new religion, or new god. If something new found acceptance in Ephesus, it was easy to extend its influence to other parts of Asia via the many roads that led from the city. As a result, Ephesus became a testing ground of new ideas and a magnet for ambitious new thinkers, as well as for pretenders and charlatans. They all descended on the city to try their luck and see if their new ideas could win popular approval. The pagan population had long grown accustomed to the fact that their city was an attraction to these glory-seekers.

After it became clear that the church at Ephesus was the primary spiritual leader in Asia, the city also attracted a wide range of so-called "Godsent" people who attempted to gain notoriety by trying out their new doctrines and revelations in Ephesus. If one could "make it" in Ephesus and receive that church's endorsement, the door was then opened to all of Asia. As a result, false apostles and prophets were constantly descending on the city.[19]

However, the Ephesian leadership and congregation had *no tolerance* for these people who tried to infiltrate the church with hidden and selfish motives. The Ephesian believers understood their church's pivotal role in the entire region; they understood that what they endorsed would be carried into all the other churches. Therefore, they didn't quickly assume responsibility for newcomers.

Instead, Revelation 2:2 implies that the church set up a system whereby they could test new arrivals to see if they were really what they claimed to be. They loved their church so much that they had no tolerance for anyone who twisted the Word to create a new, popular doctrine, nor did they have any stomach for those who selfishly wished to use the Ephesian church for their own self-advantage.

The phrase "...and how thou canst not bear them which are evil..." also gives us insight into how Jesus feels about those who try to use the Church for selfish gain or for self-glory. He said they are "evil." Again, this word for "evil" always describes something that is *bad, destructive, evil, foul, harmful, hurtful, injurious,* or *vile.* It is damaging to true ministry gifts

Above and Right: At the time of John's vision, the church of Ephesus was the primary leader of all the other Asia churches — a prominent position that was sustained for several centuries. This photo shows the ruins of the Church of St. Mary in Ephesus, where several landmark church councils were held over the years to debate, develop, and test the doctrines of the Church.

when false ministers gain a public foothold and stain or ruin the reputation of the ministry. This situation is so destructive to a church that Jesus *commended* the Ephesian congregation for refusing to tolerate or endure them. Their desire to protect the integrity of God's Word and to uphold the honor of public ministry

Above: *The pictures above show gold liquified under extreme heat in order to extract impurities. The church of Ephesus knew how to test the ministers who came into their midst and claimed to be apostles. Like the heat of a blazing fire that brings impurities to the surface of a metal as it is formed, the testing methods of the Ephesian leadership effectively exposed those who were presenting themselves as apostles but were not.*

was one of the characteristics about this local church that made it commendable.

'AND THOU HAST TRIED THEM WHICH SAY THEY ARE APOSTLES, AND ARE NOT'

In Revelation 2:2, Jesus went on to say, "I know thy works, and thy labour, and thy patience, and how thou canst not bear them which are evil: *and thou hast tried them....*"

The word "tried" is the Greek word *peiradzo*, which means *to put to the test; to test in order to prove;* or *to test a person or object in order to expose the truth or to witness concerning the quality of a substance.* It was often used to test people to determine if they really were what they claimed, boasted, or advertised about themselves.

An example of this is how the word *peiradzo* was used to describe the purifying fires placed under metal. As the metal was put through ever-increasing degrees of blazing heat, the fire caused impurities to rise to the surface that otherwise would have remained undetected to the naked eye. The multiple degrees of blazing fire caused all the impurities to rise to the surface. Once exposed, the impurities were scraped off and removed — but without the test of fire, they would have remained undetectable.

But when the word *peiradzo* is used to describe testing individuals, it depicts *a calculated, premeditated test or an investigation that is deliberately designed to expose any deficiency or falsehoods.* The questioner stokes the flames again and again in an attempt to expose the impurities or defects that otherwise are unseen. If the person is free of defects, the fire will reveal nothing and will prove his quality. But if hidden motives are present, the heat of the flames are designed to bring any defects and impurities to the surface.

This is how the word "tried" is used in this case to describe the process by which the church at Ephesus tested those who claimed to be apostles. This church was inundated with people who claimed to be God-sent — particularly those who claimed to be apostles with new and outstanding revelations.

The church leaders were very serious about protecting the reputation of real apostles and about sparing the church from the assault of false pretenders. The use of the word "tried" — the word *peiradzo* — tells us they aggressively tested people who boasted about being apostles, closely examining them to see if they were truly what they claimed to be. During that testing, the leadership applied criteria that enabled them to determine who did and who didn't have a genuine apostolic gift. The word *peiradzo* implies that the recipients of this testing were so thoroughly examined that

they must have felt as if they were being *put through the fire*. During an unspecified amount of time, the flame of examination was turned up again and again until the church leadership was able to obtain an accurate picture of these individuals and determine whether or not they were genuine apostles or deceptive pretenders.

'THEM WHICH SAY THEY ARE APOSTLES'

> Jesus went on to elaborate in Revelation 2:2, saying, "I know thy works, and thy labor, and thy patience, and how thou canst not bear them which are evil: and thou hast tried them *which say they are apostles, and are not....*"

The issue of apostleship was extremely important to the First Century Church and specifically to the seven churches in Asia. This was evident in Ephesus, where the church leadership "tried" those who claimed to be apostles. These leaders clearly believed that the apostolic ministry was crucial and that its role in the church needed to be protected and honored. It is therefore vital that we look thoroughly at the word "apostle" and discover what this word meant in New Testament times — where the word "apostle" came from, how it was viewed in the secular world, and how it was used by the early believers. (*See* the following section, entitled, "The Characteristics of True Apostles," where this topic is thoroughly discussed.)

FALSE APOSTLES, DECEITFUL WORKERS

> Paul described the growing problem of false apostles in Second Corinthians 11:13,14. He said, "For such are false apostles, deceitful workers, transforming themselves into the apostles of Christ. And no marvel; for Satan himself is transformed into an angel of light."

The phrase "false apostles" comes from the Greek word *pseudapostolos*, a compound of *pseudes* and *apostolos*. The word *pseudes* carries the idea of *any type of falsehood*. It can picture *a person who projects a false image of himself; someone who deliberately walks in a pretense that is untrue; or someone who intentionally misrepresents facts or truths.* In every instance where this word is used in the New Testament, it portrays *someone who misrepresents who he is by what he does, by what he says, or by the lie or misrepresentation that he purports to be true.* The second part of the word is *apostolos* — the word for an *apostle*. Therefore, the word *pseudapostolos* actually describes *a pretend apostle or someone who intentionally represents himself to be an apostle even though he knows he is not.*

Paul called these false apostles "deceitful workers." The word "deceitful" comes from the Greek word *dolios*, which is derived from a root word used to describe *bait that is put on a hook to catch fish*. It conveys the idea of *craftiness, cheating, cunning, dishonesty, fraud, guile,* and *trickery intended to entrap someone in an act of deception.* Like a fisherman who carefully camoflauges a hook with bait, these counterfeit apostles lured sincere believers closer and closer until they finally "took the bait." And once the hook was in their victims' mouths, the false apostles set the hook and took congregations — even entire groups of churches — captive. Paul said these individuals were deceitful "workers." This word "workers" is taken from the Greek word *ergates*, a word that denotes *someone who actively works at what he is doing.* This indicates that nothing was accidental about this act of deception and that these false apostles put forth great effort to impersonate real apostolic ministry.

Paul said these deceitful workers were so skilled at the art of deception that they were able to "transform" themselves into the apostles of Christ. The word translated "transform" in this verse is the Greek word *metaschimatidzo*, which means *to disguise oneself, to deliberately change one's outward appearance,* or *to masquerade in clothing that depicts a person as different than he really is.* Paul was referring to individuals who intentionally attempted to pass themselves off as apostles, knowing full well that they were not. He was describing a blatant act of deception.

At that time, such a large number of people were professing to be apostles that the Ephesian church developed criteria — *a paradigm, pattern,* or *model* — to determine

(Continued on page 439)

THE CHARACTERISTICS
OF TRUE APOSTLES

The Greek word for "apostle" is *apostolos*, which is a compound of the words *apo* and *stello*. The preposition *apo* means *away*, and the word *stello* means *to send*. When the two words are combined together, they form the word *apostolos*, meaning *one who is sent away*. This Greek word appears 79 times in the New Testament. The root of *apostolos* is the word *apostello*, a word that appears no less than 131 times in the

Above: This painting, entitled, "The Last Supper," was painted by artist Philippe de Champaigne (1602-1674). The painting depicts Jesus as He shares His last moments of fellowship with His 12 disciples before His arrest and subsequent death on the Cross. These disciples were Jesus' original 12 apostles, although they were not the only ones to be called to the apostolic ministry.

New Testament and more than 700 times in the Greek Septuagint.

At first, it may seem that the definition of this word *apostolos* — *one who is sent away* — denoted one who had been dismissed, set aside, or rejected. However, this word didn't refer to a person sent away in dishonor or disgrace. Rather, the word *apostolos* was a term of great honor that referred to *a person who was personally selected, commissioned, and sent on an assignment on behalf of a very powerful government or individual*. This person wasn't merely sent off; he was *empowered, invested with authority*, and *then dispatched to accomplish a special task*.

THE ADMIRAL OF A FLEET OF SHIPS

During the time of the ancient Greek orator Demosthenes (384-322 BC), the word *apostolos* was a naval term that described *an admiral, the fleet of ships that traveled with him, and the specialized crew who accompanied and assisted the admiral*.[20] The fleet would be sent out to sea on a mission to locate territories where civilization was non-existent. Once an uncivilized region was identified, the admiral — along with his specialized, apostolic crew and all their cargo and belongings — would disembark, settle down, and work as a team to establish a new community. Then they would begin the process of transforming a strange land into a replica of life as they believed it should be. Their purpose was total *colonization* of the uncivilized territory.

Within this special fleet of ships were both the personnel and the cargo required to establish a new culture, a new life, and a new community. When that fleet pulled up to shore, it contained workers trained to build roads, construct buildings, and teach uncivilized natives how to read, write, and function in a new kind of society. Thus, the admiral became the team leader for the construction of a new society. Once the job was completed, the majority of the team members got back on the ships and launched out to sea again to find another uncivilized area and repeat the entire colonization process all over again.

Left: This relief from Trajan's column depicts Roman soldiers sailing to other lands on a fleet of ships. In ancient Greece, the admiral of such a fleet would have been called an apostolos. *The crew often included not only soldiers, but also skilled workers to help construct a new society in uncivilized territory.*

A PASSPORT THAT GUARANTEES RIGHT OF PASSAGE

The word *apostolos* was so closely associated with the idea of traveling that it eventually became synonymous with the idea of *a passport* or *a travel document*.

If a person wanted to exit a country, he had to possess a travel document that was essentially *an export license, an exit visa,* or *a passport.* This legal document was called an *apostolos* — the same word translated "apostle." This document guaranteed *the right of passage and the ability to move freely from one place to another.*

When the word *apostolos* was applied to New Testament individuals, it referred to God-anointed ministers who were called to lead believers to spiritual heights and to depths of revelation that were unattainable without the apostolic ministry. A New Testament apostle was given revelation of truth and deeply spiritual experiences filled with insight. If a person or a group of churches was connected to a particular apostle, they had access to spiritual truths they wouldn't have been able to obtain on their own. In this sense, an apostle was *a spiritual passport* that gave believers *right of passage* into heavenly realms and deep spiritual truths.

A PERSONAL REPRESENTATIVE

The word "apostle" also described *a person who had the authority to act*

Above: This painting by H. M. Herget shows foreign emissaries or ambassadors (the Greek word apostolos*) coming before the Roman emperor with gifts and communication from the leader who had sent them.*

in the stead of the one who sent him in much the same way an ambassador represents his government to another government. This classical and secular meaning of the word *apostolos* meant *an envoy sent to do business on behalf of the one who sent him.* Thus, the apostle served as the sender's *personal representative, emissary, messenger, agent, diplomat, ambassador,* or *charge d'affaires.* Such an apostle possessed the clout and influence to both speak and act in the place of the one who sent him on his assignment. So when the *apostolos* spoke, his words were counted as the words of his sender. When the *apostolos* acted, his actions were interpreted as those of his sender. The connection between the sender and the person who was sent was almost inseparable.

A SPIRITUAL LEADER

In classical times, the word *apostolos* also signified *a person who had been gifted by the gods and sent to the people as the gods' special messenger.*[21] The general population stood in awe of such individuals, for they supposedly possessed supernatural knowledge and insight that was unavailable to the average man. So even before the development of New Testament terminology, the word *apostolos* came to portray a spiritual leader whose insights would take people *from one realm to the next.*

THE WORD 'APOSTLE' IN NEW TESTAMENT TIMES

By the time of the New Testament, the word *apostolos* was already an old word with quite a lengthy history. It carried many shades of meaning — all of which overlapped and interrelated to each other. So when people in the Early Church heard or read the word *apostle*, they understood its meaning very well. In fact, it is likely that the various shades of meaning previously discussed passed through the minds of those who heard this word. They understood that:

- An apostle was *a person who was specially selected, specially commissioned, and specially sent* to represent the Lord.

- An apostle arrived on the scene with a mandate and vision for establishing the Church in new territory. He was *a pioneer, an*

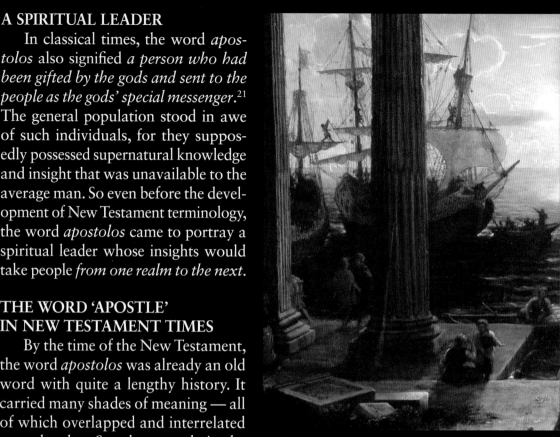

adventurer, an overseer, a coordinator, and *the chief leader* responsible for "colonizing" a new region with the Word of God and the culture of the New Testament Church.

- An apostle provided *passage from one spiritual dimension to another.* An apostolic anointing would literally take a church to new levels in its spiritual growth that it could never reach apart from the apostle's anointing.

- An apostle was authorized to speak and to act on the Lord's behalf, like an ambassador

Left: Claude Gellée painted this beautiful masterpiece depicting Paul embarking on one of his apostolic journeys by sea. In the course of his ministry, Paul traveled countless miles throughout the Roman Empire — sent by God to proclaim "*the power of God unto salvation*" (Romans 1:16) to a world desperate for knowledge of the truth.

WHO IS A TRUE APOSTLE?

Over the centuries, the question "Who is a true apostle?" has been something of a theological conundrum for many Bible scholars. Some insist that only the original 12 were true apostles, whereas others argue that the apostolic ministry has continued since the death of Jesus' original 12 apostles without any distinctions between the foundational apostles and all those called to the apostolic ministry since that time.

The word "apostle" *(apostolos)* is used in both a narrow and a broader sense in the New Testament. In the narrowest sense of the word, it referred to those specifically chosen by Jesus during His time on earth — both the 12 and the 70 (Luke 10:1).

In Luke 6:13, Jesus called together His disciples (those He was mentoring), and from among them, He chose 12 men whom He called apostles, or *sent ones*. Matthew 10:2-4 lists these first 12 apostles:

1. Peter
2. Andrew (Peter's brother)

who represents his government to another government, with the backing of God's Kingdom behind him. As the envoy of the risen Christ, he had the anointing, authority, and spiritual backing to get things accomplished.

- An apostle was *a man of divine revelation*. He wasn't just the implementer of pragmatic ideas and strategies; rather, an apostle carried within him supernatural insight and revelation that was vital for the growth and the building up of the Church.

3. James the son of Zebedee
4. John (James' brother)
5. Philip
6. Bartholomew
7. Thomas
8. Matthew
9. James the son of Alphaeus
10. Thaddaeus
11. Simon the Zealot
12. Judas Iscariot

In Luke 9:1-6, Jesus sent forth these 12 apostles to preach the Gospel, heal the sick, and cast out demons. In the next chapter, Jesus appointed 70 more apostles and "...sent them two by two..." Luke 10:1). These were the "other 70" who were commissioned by Jesus in the flesh to go forth in His name.

With Judas' betrayal of Jesus, Matthias replaced Judas among the original 12 apostles (see Acts 1:15-26). Even Paul recognized Matthias when he referred to the 12 apostles who saw the risen Christ (see 1 Corinthians 15:5). Yet Paul made a bold claim in First Corinthians 9:1 that he, too, had seen the risen Christ and therefore, by implication, had a right to be counted in this group of foundational apostles. Paul didn't receive this appointment in the normal manner; in other words, he wasn't appointed by Jesus during His earthly ministry. Instead, Paul received his call from the resurrected and exalted Christ on the road to Damascus (see Acts 9:1-6).

This is why the apostle Paul stated to the Corinthians that Christ first rose and appeared to Peter and th remainder of the 12 apostles; then H appeared to James and to the othe apostles; then, finally, as Paul states Jesus also appeared to him: "And las of all he was seen of me also, as of on born out of due time" (1 Corinthian 15:8). The phrase "out of due time refers to an abnormal birth, or a birt that didn't occur at the correct time.

The purpose of this foundationa apostolic group was to serve as wit nesses to the resurrection of the Lor Jesus Christ. All of these men — excep the apostle Paul — had been chose while Jesus walked on this earth Paul's words are significant when h states that "...last of all he was see of me..." (v. 8). This seems to indicat that this group is closed, with Pau being the last to be called an apostl in this category.

Yet the word "apostle" is used i a broader sense as well, beyond th foundational group we traditionall think of as apostles. The Greek wor *apostolos* is used in reference to a least 11 other people in the New Testa ment besides the 12, the 70, and Pau

1. Apollos (1 Corinthians 4:6-13)
2. Epaphroditus (Philippians 2:25 "messenger" is *apostolos* in th Greek)
3. James, the Lord's brother (Gala tians 1:19)
4. Barnabas (Acts 14:4,14; 1 Cor inthians 9:5,6)
5. Andronicus (Romans 16:7)

6. Junia (Romans 16:7)
7. Titus (2 Corinthians 8:23; "messenger" is *apostolos* in the Greek)
8. Unnamed brother with Titus (2 Corinthians 8:18,23)
9. Another unnamed brother with Titus (2 Corinthians 8:22,23)
10. Timothy (1 Thessalonians 1:1; 2:6)
11. Silas/Silvanus (1 Thessalonians 1:1; 2:6)

Many theologians have dealt with the question of these other "apostles" by simply claiming that they were among the 70 appointed and sent by Jesus. Yet there is no authoritative or reliable list of the 70 other apostles. Furthermore, Timothy was converted under the ministry of Paul and therefore couldn't be numbered among the 70 apostles. This means apostolic ministry in a broader sense continued in the New Testament Church. Finally, if apostleship were simply limited to the 12, the 70, and Paul, there would have been no need to "try" those who claimed to be apostles

Above: Artist Ludovico Carracci's painting, entitled, "The Conversion of St. Paul," depicts the moment on the road to Damascus when the resurrected Jesus appeared to Paul and called him to the ministry of an apostle as "one born out of due time" (1 Corinthians 15:8).

in order to determine whether or not they were true apostles — one of the very things for which Jesus commended the church of Ephesus (Revelation 2:2). All of these points make it very clear that apostolic ministry has continued beyond the "foundational apostles" — right up to this present day.

So what is the function of a New Testament apostle in the broader sense of the word? It is the same basic function as those who were called as foundational apostles, with this distinction: Those in the original group were sent to lay the foundation of "the universal Church" and to establish apostolic doctrine. Apostles in the broader sense are those called to establish churches and proclaim apostolic doctrine that is already established. Thus, the function is similar, but the scope and authority of the first group was greater.

A VISION OF CHRIST

In First Corinthians 9:1, Paul wrote, "Am I not an apostle? Am I not free? Have I not seen Jesus Christ our Lord? Are not ye my work in the Lord?" There is no evidence that Paul ever physically saw Christ. However, he certainly saw Jesus in a vision on the road to Damascus, and it seems he also had other spiritual encounters with the Lord when he was taught by divine revelation (see Galatians 1:1).

Because of what Paul wrote in First Corinthians 9:1, some suggest that it is

essential for a person to have personally "seen" Jesus in order to be a true apostle. At first, it would seem that this is confirmed by the account in Acts 1:21-26, where the remaining apostles cast lots to choose a replacement for Judas Iscariot. These verses indicate that the person taking the place of Judas Iscariot had to fulfill the requirement of having been with the other apostles from the beginning of Jesus' ministry until the time He ascended into Heaven. However, this requirement was specifically for the one who would join the ranks of the first 12 apostles.

In addition to these 12, the 70, and Paul — the foundational apostles whose role was to serve as witnesses to the resurrection of Jesus and to establish apostolic doctrine — there were the other New Testament people whom the Bible plainly refers to as *apostolos*. If having seen Jesus was a requirement for apostleship, this would present a theological problem, since there is no record of these other apostles having seen Jesus either physically or in a vision. Even if some of the other apostles did have spiritual experiences of this kind, which may be the case, there is no New Testament witness to confirm it. In addition, the broader apostolic office doesn't include the foundational role of being an eyewitness to the resurrected Christ.

Since there were so many in the New Testament called apostles about which no record exists of their having personally experienced divine visitations of Christ, it cannot be assumed that Paul was providing proof of apostleship in First Corinthians 9:1 for anyone but himself. As noted earlier, Paul stated later in his letter to the Corinthians that he was the last of the foundational apostles to see the resurrected Jesus (see 1 Corinthians 15:8).

However, in one sense, each person who carries an apostolic call must have "seen" Christ in the Church. In other words, no apostle can establish the Church if he has not had a personal revelation of the fact that Jesus Christ walks on this earth as manifested through His Body, which is the Church. Every true apostle has grasped the significance of this truth, for it is central to and inseparable from the apostolic call.

CRITERIA FOR APOSTLESHIP

In writing about his own apostolic ministry, Paul said, "Truly the signs of an apostle were wrought among you in all patience, in signs, and wonders, and mighty deeds" (2 Corinthians 12:12). The problem of false apostles was so rampant that Paul felt it necessary to validate his ministry by pointing out the "signs" of an apostle that were evident in his life. In doing so, Paul also asserted that these same signs determine whether or not *any* person's ministry is truly apostolic.

The word "signs" is the Greek word *semeion*. It was used in the vernacular of secular business to describe *the official written notice that announced a court's final verdict*. This word also described *the signature or seal applied to a document to guarantee its authenticity* and *a sign that marked key locations in a city*. This secular word was carried over into New Testament language — as it was used, for instance in Second Corinthians 12:12 by Paul

By using the word *semeion*, Paul declared that certain signs exist as the *final verdict* to prove a person's apostleship. These accompanying activities are like a *signature* or *seal* that *authenticates* and *guarantees* that a person is an apostle. They provide verifiable proof and should accompany every person claiming to carry the apostolic mantle. Thus, Paul was telling us that if the "signs" he listed are evident in a person's ministry, they may be the *announcement*, *guarantee*, or *proof* that this particular person is apostolic

The marks of an apostle that Paul listed in this verse are not all-inclusive However, they serve as a good starting place in describing the signs that point to an apostolic call. Just as a highway sign lets you know you are coming close to a city, these particular signs in a person's ministry may be evidence that you're looking at a person who has a genuine apostolic call on his or her life

In Second Corinthians 12:12, Paul wrote, "Truly the signs of an apostle were wrought among you in all patience, in signs, and wonders, and

mighty deeds." The word "truly" comes from the Greek phrase *ta men*, a phrase that means *emphatically* or *indeed* and could be translated, "*Of a certainty!*" By using this phrase, Paul's message was loud and clear: If a person is apostolic, it is *certain* that he will have these particular signs in his ministry.

Paul first listed "patience" as a sign of true apostleship. It is an attribute that most people overlook, yet it is just as supernatural as healings and miracles. As discussed on pages 407-411, It comes from the Greek word *hupomeno*, which depicts *a person's supernatural ability to hang in there and to stay put no matter what forces try to stop him.*

People with an apostolic call on their lives must often do frontline work in environments that are difficult and even hostile to the Gospel. An example would be the city of Corinth — one of the world's most wicked cities in the First Century — where God called Paul to establish a church. In order to fulfill this divine call, Paul had to resist the demonic powers of that city and all the other forces arrayed against him. This assignment therefore required a special God-given endowment of *patience* — the supernatural ability to *stay put* regardless of the pressure or opposition one encounters. Paul knew that God had given him the supernatural ability to remain steadfast in the midst of the intense resistance that came against him in

Left: Paul stated in First Corinthians 12:12 that the criteria for true apostleship included "signs, and wonders, and mighty deeds." This Fifteenth Century fresco by Alfredo Dagli Orti, located in the St. Benedict Monastery in Subiaco, Italy, depicts the supernatural healing of a lame man at the Gate called Beautiful in Jerusalem — a miraculous sign wrought by God through the apostles Peter and John (see Acts 3:1-10).

Corinth. In fact, Paul was so impacted by the divine grace that enabled him to *stay put* in such a hostile environment that he included it as one of the marks or signs of apostolic ministry.

Such patience is also evidenced in the fact that the apostle is uniquely graced to encompass all five ministerial offices, as needed, in order to establish a church and develop the ministry gifts within believers. Therefore, for a time the apostle will operate prophetically, as an evangelist, in a pastoral capacity, and as a teacher. He may minister consistently as a pastor or teacher, but it will be with a higher level of authority than the pastoral or teaching ministries. That authority is God-ordained and demonstrated in the manner in which the apostle establishes, builds up, and develops the believers — which is why it is crucial for the apostle to recognize and "see" the Lord manifested *in His Church at large* so he can build according to the will and plan of the Lord *for the local church.*

Only a divine endowment of patience and endurance can give a person a sufficient measure of strength and courage to keep him pressing forward when it seems as if all of hell is raging against him. Paul testified that the *hupomeno* ability to *stay put* while laying a foundation and then building upon it — which includes establishing divine order and strengthening the saints, often in the face of potential discouragement or intense opposition — is both remarkable and supernatural. Thus, he listed this attribute as the first sign that always accompanies true apostolic ministry.

As previously noted, Paul began this verse with "truly," which in Greek is *ta men*, meaning *emphatically*, *indeed*, or *of a certainty*. It is as if Paul put an exclamation mark on the indicators that immediately follow. A person's supernatural ability to stand strong and steadfast as he fulfills his divine call to establish the Church, regardless of the opposition that comes against him, is truly — *emphatically* and *undeniably* — one of the signs that will be evident in the life of someone with an apostolic call.

But Paul went on to list more indicators that point to a true apostolic call on a person's life. He continued, "Truly the *signs* of an apostle were wrought among you in all patience, in signs, and wonders, and mighty deeds" (2 Corinthians 12:12). The next criterion Paul mentions is "signs." Paul wrote this verse to the Corinthians, yet there is no clear record in the book of Acts of his working signs and wonders in Corinth (*see* Acts 18). However, because of this statement, we may assume that miraculous signs were wrought through Paul in Corinth similar to the signs God performed through him in other cities — such as:

- Restoring strength to the limbs of the lame (*see* Acts 14:8-10).

- Casting out demons (*see* Acts 16:16-18).

- Transferring God's healing power through aprons or napkins taken from Paul's body to the bedridden who couldn't attend his meetings because of their physical conditions (*see* Acts 19:11,12).

- Raising the dead (*see* Acts 20:9-12).

- Healing the sick (*see* Acts 28:8,9).

People mistakenly get the impression that Paul's ministry was continually visited with miracles of this nature. But if one carefully and honestly examines the book of Acts to determine the regularity in which these types of supernatural signs occurred, you will find that these events did not occur nonstop in Paul's ministry, but rather at pivotal and crucial moments when miracles were needed to open the door for the Gospel even wider. These were supernatural signs intended to grab the attention of listeners and to

Above: "St. Paul," painted by Pompeo Girolamo Batoni, provides the artist's impression of the apostle Paul in action — preaching God's Word by the power and anointing of God.

serve as proof that the Gospel message they were hearing was true.

In addition to these miraculous signs, Paul also listed "wonders" and "mighty deeds" as indicators that a person has an apostolic call on his or her life. The word "wonder" is the Greek word *teras*. The word *teras* was used in classical Greek times to depict the *fright*, *terror*, *shock*, *surprise*, or *astonishment* felt by bystanders who observed events that were contrary to the normal course of nature. Such occurrences were viewed as miracles, and people believed they

could only take place through the intervention of divine power. These miraculous events were so shocking that they left people *speechless*, *shocked*, *astonished*, *bewildered*, *baffled*, *taken aback*, *stunned*, and *awestruck* — and therefore in a state of *wonder*.

This is the reason the word *teras* is most often translated as the word "wonder" in the New Testament. It describes an occurrence so out of the ordinary that people are left in a state of *perplexity*, *amazement*, and *wonder* as a result.

But Paul didn't stop with the word "wonders." He went on to say, "and mighty deeds." The word "and" is the Greek word *kai*, which could — and probably should — be translated *even*, causing the phrase "mighty deeds" to actually *amplify* the word "wonders." Thus, the verse could be translated "wonders, *even mighty deeds*." In other words, Paul was saying that these "wonders" were so amazing, they were truly "mighty deeds."

The phrase "mighty deeds" is a translation of the word *dunamis*, the Greek word for *power*. It is from this word that we derive the English word "dynamite," which is a very appropriate usage of this Greek word. Indeed, *dunamis* power carries the idea of *explosive, superhuman power that comes with enormous energy and produces phenomenal, extraordinary, and unparalleled results.* The word *dunamis* depicts "mighty deeds" that are impressive, incomparable, and beyond human ability to perform. In fact, this very word is used in First Corinthians 12:10 when the apostle Paul lists "the working of miracles" as one of the gifts of the Spirit. Thus, the word *dunamis*, as Paul now uses it in Second Corinthians 12:12, denotes *miraculous power* or *miraculous manifestations*.

Keep in mind that the word "wonders" refers to people being shocked or stunned by events that don't naturally occur in nature, or by experiences that are out of the flow of normal life. Because Paul connected it to the phrase "mighty deeds" — the Greek word *dunamis*, referring to *superhuman or miraculous powers* — we know that he was referring to instances when the laws of nature are overruled or suspended by the supernatural power of God. In some way, God Himself intervenes in the laws of nature and does something that could never occur in the natural realm.

There were many instances of "mighty deeds" in Paul's ministry pertaining to miraculous healings that could never have occurred naturally or with the assistance of medicine. Whenever God's power intervenes to reverse a physical condition that medical science defines as incurable, this can technically be defined as *a miracle.*

But in addition to the supernatural power that flowed from Paul to others to work healing miracles, there were also some truly amazing instances when God's power intervened on *Paul's* behalf. We find an example of this in Acts 16, when Paul was miraculously released from his jail cell in Philippi after a remarkable earthquake shook the prison and set him free.

Acts 16:24 tells us of a time when Paul and Silas were in the "inner prison" and their feet were "fast in stocks." As the two apostles began to pray and sing songs of praise to God in the middle of the night, "...suddenly there was a great earthquake

Above: *This oil painting by Claude-Guy Halle depicts the jailer kneeling before the apostle Paul after God performed a "mighty deed" on Paul's behalf — sending a strong earthquake to shake off the apostle's bonds and deliver him from prison.*

so that the foundations of the prison were shaken: and immediately all the doors were opened, and every one's bands were loosed" (Acts 16:26).

Consider how strange this occurrence was that night. This earthquake shook the prison, opened all the doors, and caused the chains to fall off the prisoners. Yet it seems that not one brick fell, for there is no record of any damage to the actual building. In fact, this appears to have been such a regional earthquake that it affected only one building in the entire city. Only the prison where Paul and Silas were confined apparently felt the impact of this particular earthquake!

When people heard about this landmark event, the news left them in a state of wonder. In other words, they were left *speechless*, *shocked*, *astonished*, *bewildered*, *baffled*, *taken aback*, *stunned*, and *awestruck*. Certainly this earthquake would qualify as a "mighty deed" — a miraculous event — that occurred in the life of the apostle Paul.

Another example of a mighty deed occurring in Paul's life can be found in Acts 28:3, when Paul was shipwrecked and marooned on the island of Melita. On that rainy day as Paul was gathering sticks to build a fire, "...there came a viper out of the heat, and fastened on his hand" (Acts 28:3). When the barbarians saw the deadly, venomous viper hanging from the apostle's hand, they expected Paul to swell up

Left: This Twelfth Century mural, entitled, "St. Paul and the Viper," shows another example of a mighty deed performed by God on the apostle Paul's behalf. It depicts the miraculous moment when Paul was bitten by a poisonous viper while gathering wood on the island of Melita, yet suffered no harm (Acts 28:1-5).

and suddenly fall down dead (*see* v. 6). But instead, verse 5 tells us that Paul "...shook off the beast into the fire, and felt no harm."

The deadly poison of that snake should have killed Paul. But as the powerful venom surged through the apostle's circulatory system, God's power intervened, overruling and nullifying the venom so that it had no adverse effect on Paul whatsoever! On the other hand, this "wonder" had a *huge* impact on those who were standing nearby, watching in amazement. Instead of seeing Paul fall dead, these people saw "...no harm come to him..." (v. 6). They were so shocked by this miraculous event that a major revival erupted, through which many people from every quarter of the island came to Christ. This would therefore definitely qualify as a "mighty deed" occurring in the life of the apostle Paul.

Writing about his many experiences in ministry in Second Corinthians 11, Paul tells of being shipwrecked three times, severely beaten on five different occasions, traveling on dangerous roads and across treacherous rivers, and so forth. If it hadn't been for God's power sustaining Paul and intervening on his behalf, many of these experiences would have ended in the apostle's death. In fact, in Second Corinthians 1:8-10, Paul described an event that was so overwhelmingly difficult, he had to experience a near-resurrection from the dead in order to survive it. This event was apparently so mighty and miraculous that the apostle never forgot it.

Then we must note the time Paul was stoned in Lystra and left for dead. Religious Jews were professionals at stoning people to death. Therefore, it's very significant that Acts 14:19 tells us that certain Jews, "...having stoned Paul, drew him out of the city, supposing he had been dead."

After pummeling Paul's body with stones, these Jews dragged him out of the city and left him to be eaten by animals. But Acts 14:20 goes on to tell us, "...as the disciples stood round about him, he rose up...." This was a *mighty* deed — a special working of God's miraculous power that seems to have actually raised Paul from death itself. This would definitely qualify as a "mighty deed" or a miraculous event occurring in the life of the apostle Paul.

Those who have an apostolic call on their lives serve God on the frontlines of His Kingdom, facing challenges and difficulties beyond what others might encounter. For these individuals to make significant inroads into the enemy's territory, miracles — those undeniable moments when God's power intervenes in the natural course of events — are required. But in addition to impacting those who live in spiritual darkness, miracles are also required to sustain the apostle who is bravely forging his way into territory where no one has dared to go before. Thus, as Paul stated in Second Corinthians 12:12, demonstrations of miraculous power will always be evident in the lives of those whom God has called to be apostles.

WHY WOULD ANYONE CLAIM TO BE AN APOSTLE IF HE WASN'T?

In all fairness, it is possible that some who came to Ephesus claiming to be apostles may have used the term incorrectly out of ignorance. They may have sincerely believed they were apostles because they didn't really understand what it means to occupy that ministry office.

However, many were *not* innocent in this matter. These individuals deliberately claimed to be apostles because they understood the *weight* and *influence* that accompanied this title. They knew that this position held enormous authority and that those who carried this title could obtain leverage in the Church. Therefore, they coveted this title and intentionally claimed it as a way to gain control and exert power over God's people.

What an apostle said carried great weight within a church or even within an entire group of churches. Whoever could lay claim to the apostolic title would be able to influence what happened in the lives of many people. For a genuine apostle, this was a serious responsibility that he exercised with holiness, fear, and prudence. But for a person with impure motives, this position of authority represented an opportunity to obtain power for the sake of selfish gain.

Many imposters therefore moved in on the scene like predators — waiting for the opportunity to seize a fledgling church through deception and then claim it for themselves. This is what the leadership at Ephesus was up against — and that is why they diligently "tried" those who came to Ephesus claiming to be apostles.

False apostles frequently followed Paul from city to city, lying in wait until he left town. Then they would begin implementing their heinous plan of ruining Paul's reputation and claiming the territory for themselves. This is what Paul referred to when he wrote that there was assigned to him "...a thorn in the flesh, the messenger of Satan to buffet me..." (2 Corinthians 12:7).

These deceivers were such a constant hassle to Paul that he called them "the messenger of Satan." Paul endured many afflictions during his ministry, and many of them were a result of these false ministers who fiercely opposed him and constantly tried to displace his position of authority in the local churches. They wanted Paul out of the picture so they could usurp his place of prominence. Therefore, they attempted to discredit the apostle, hoping to shift the spotlight to themselves by boasting that their revelations were superior. Paul alluded to these sheep stealers in Second Corinthians 11:5 (*NIV*) when he sarcastically referred to them as "super apostles" and scoffed at their claims of hyper-spirituality.

APOSTOLIC AUTHORITY IS RELATIONAL

Although spectacular revelation is indeed a facet of genuine apostolic ministry, the fulfillment of the apostolic call is based on *relationships*, not just on spectacular revelations, as the false apostles claimed to possess. For instance, although Paul was universally respected in the Early Church as an apostle, he was *not* an apostle to every First Century believer. He was an apostle only to those with whom he had an *apostolic relationship*.

Churches in other cities and regions acknowledged Paul's apostleship, but he was not *their* apostle. Other believers respected Paul as an excellent minister, a beloved brother in the Lord, and an able leader. But he only had apostolic responsibility for the churches he had helped start and

Above: This Seventeenth Century painting by French artist Philippe de Champaigne depicts Jesus' last meeting with His 12 apostles as He prepared them for His imminent arrest and death on the Cross.

those for whom he served as mentor, teacher, and father in the faith. Thus, Paul's apostleship was limited to those for whom he bore direct spiritual responsibility and with whom he had a unique relationship. This would have included the churches of *Ephesus, Colossae, Corinth, Galatia, Hierapolis, Laodicea, Pergamum, Philadelphia, Philippi, Sardis, Smyrna, Thyatira,* and others. Paul's relationship with these churches is the reason we have the books of First and Second Corinthians, Galatians, Ephesians, Philippians, and Colossians. Paul wrote these letters because he was directly responsible for the spiritual well-being of these believers and because he had a unique apostolic relationship either with them or with their local leadership.

One example of Paul's apostolic relationship with local leadership was the church in Colossae. Although

here is no evidence that Paul personally founded the Colossian church,
we know that he sent Epaphras as
his *personal emissary* to fulfill that
assignment. Under Paul's orders and
spiritual covering, Epaphras traveled
to Colossae and started the church.
Once the Colossian church was established, the congregation received Paul
as the apostle to that church *based on
his relationship to Epaphras.*

Paul was very aware that he wasn't
an apostle to everyone. That's why he
wrote, "Not boasting of things without our measure [or out of our terri-
tory] ...not to boast in another man's
line of things made ready to our hand
i.e., not to take credit for another
person's apostolic work]" (2 Corinthians 10:15,16). Paul was careful not
to cross over into another man's territory if it might produce confusion
about who was supposed to give direction to certain churches or to whom
those churches were accountable (*see
2 Corinthians 10:13,14*). This tells us
that Paul not only *possessed* authority,
but he also *respected* the authority and
territory of others.

This explains why he told the Corinthians, "If I be not an apostle unto
others, yet doubtless I am to you..."
1 Corinthians 9:2). Paul knew that his
apostleship was *limited, geographical,*
and *relational,* so he concentrated on
those with whom he knew he had this
special God-given relationship

APOSTOLIC MINISTRY IS GEOGRAPHICAL AND TERRITORIAL

Paul frequently had to defend his
apostleship because of these deceitful
workers who swarmed in, trying to
exert authority over entire regions of
churches that he and other apostles
had established and to which they had
imparted their lives. Apostleship was
power, so those with impure motives
sought to invade Paul's territory and
claim his fruit, seeing this as an effective way to exploit someone else's
work for themselves.

Interlopers who coveted the apostolic position used every imaginable
method to attract, tempt, lure, entice
and seduce the churches under the
realm of authority of genuine apostles
In Paul's case, the imposters couldn't
find a legitimate reason to accuse the
apostle, so they used slanderous and
even stupid accusations as they tried
to persuade the churches to reject Paul
and submit to *their* authority instead
For example, these false apostles:

- Accused Paul of being unimpres-
  sive in appearance and a poor
  public speaker (*see* 2 Corinthians
  10:10; 11:6).

- Accused him of financially taking advantage of the churches (*see*
  1 Corinthians 9:14,15).

- Endeavored to lure the churches
  back into the noose of legalism by
  accusing Paul of being loose in his

Above: A group of early believers meets together in secret inside a private home, as was often the custom of Christians living within a hostile pagan society. In this illustration, the group is reading a letter from the apostle Paul.

doctrine of grace (*see* Galatians 1:6,7).

• Asserted that Paul's revelations weren't as deep as theirs, prompting Paul to remind his readers that he was the one who actually had a direct revelation of Jesus Himself (*see* 1 Corinthians 9:1).

These usurpers of apostolic authority were after Paul's territory — and in order to get what they were after, they set out to *discredit* Paul. This is why Paul frequently started his letters by saying, "Paul, an apostle of Jesus Christ" (*see* Romans 1:1; 1 Corinthians 1:1; 2 Corinthians 1:1; Galatians 1:1; Ephesians 1:1; Colossians 1:1). He was emphasizing the fact that he was *the* apostle to each of these churches. Paul wrote three letters to churches that don't begin with this apostolic

introduction: Philippians and First and Second Thessalonians. However, Philippi and Thessalonica were the two cities where Paul's apostleship never seemed to be questioned and therefore didn't need to be defended.

Wherever Paul's apostleship was being threatened by false apostles, he rose up like a spiritual father to defend his position. His children in the Lord were in jeopardy, and his relationship with them was at stake. Paul's deep sense of responsibility and his love for the flock wouldn't allow him to remain silent. Rather, it drove him to speak up and wage war if needed against the imposters who were trying to invade his geographical realm of influence. Paul was determined not to allow those deceivers to destroy his credibility so they could steal and ravage the sheep under his care.

who *was* and who *wasn't* an authentic New Testament apostle. The problem was serious in the Ephesian church, and the church was serious about correcting it. This prompted Jesus to tell the Ephesian believers, "...Thou hast tried them which say they are apostles, and are not, and hast found them liars" (Revelation 2:2).

As noted earlier, the word "tried" points to *a thorough and serious investigation*. It means *to try, to examine, to inspect, to investigate, to scrutinize*, or *to put to the test*. The leadership of the church at Ephesus wanted to guard the reputation of the true apostolic gift and protect the members of their congregation from pretenders who sought to lead them astray.

'AND HAST FOUND THEM LIARS'

> The church of Ephesus was birthed in the power of apostolic ministry. The Ephesian believers were noted for their relationship with Paul and his team — and because of that close association, they were very familiar with the signs that should accompany genuine apostles.

It hadn't been long since they had witnessed the supernatural events that distinguished Paul's ministry. Therefore, developing a test — *a series of criteria* — to determine the veracity of people who claimed to be apostles was not a difficult task for these spiritually experienced believers.

We know from Jesus' words in Revelation 2:2 that many of the individuals who came to Ephesus and claimed to be apostles failed the test. Jesus went on to say, "I know thy works, and thy labor, and thy patience, and how thou canst not bear them which are evil: and thou hast tried them which say they are apostles, and are not, *and hast found them liars.*"

The word "found" is from the Greek word *eurisko*. This word *eurisko* can mean *to discover by chance*, but it primarily denotes *to discover as a result of intense research*. There is a sense of exhilaration that accompanies such a discovery, a facet of meaning found in our word *eureka*, which is derived from *eurisko*. The word paints the picture of a researcher who, after a long and diligent search, succeeds in uncovering, digging up, and ferreting out the hidden information he inwardly knew was there all along. In that moment, he strikes it rich as he exposes a rich "mother lode" of information. He exclaims exultantly, "*Eureka, I found it!*"

The use of the word "found" — the Greek word *eurisko* — depicts the great exhilaration the spiritual leadership in Ephesus felt when they exposed a false apostle who had masterfully masqueraded as a real one. Because of the church's strategic location and its leading role in Asia, the Ephesian believers understood their accountability to God regarding the endorsement of ministers. They knew if they got it wrong in this matter, their error in judgment would affect not only their church, but other churches throughout the region as well. Thus, the spiritual leaders of Ephesus made it a priority to carefully test and try people *before* they

Left: *This photo shows a surviving mosaic floor in one of the fabulous terrace houses that have been excavated in the ancient city of Ephesus. Lavish homes adorned the center of this city, which was known as "The Light of Asia" because of its architectural beauty and its sophisticated culture. There is no doubt that the intellectual atmosphere of Ephesus contributed to the Ephesian congregation's love of truth and right doctrine.*

impurity bubbled to the surface and the dishonesty or impurity was exposed. This was a "eureka" moment — the result of a commitment to preserve the integrity of the true apostolic gift and to protect the Church. It was for this steadfast commitment that Jesus commended the leadership at the church of Ephesus.

endorsed them as true apostles and ministers of the Gospel.

The word *eurisko* in verse 2 seems to suggest that the church leaders in Ephesus refused to be swayed by the outward appearance of a person claiming to be an apostle — even if that newcomer looked, sounded, and acted right. If these church leaders inwardly sensed something was amiss, they persistently searched and continued to stoke the flame of questioning higher and higher — until *finally* the

In the phrase, "hast found them liars," the word "liars" is the Greek word *pseudes* — the same word Paul used in Second Corinthians 11:13 to describe *false* apostles. It denotes *a person who misrepresents the truth, twists the facts, projects untrue images, or deliberately misleads others by giving them false information.*

These pretenders were seeking the advantages that might be dishonestly gained — glory, money, control — if they could convince others that they were genuine apostles. But the Ephesian leadership refused to be easily swayed, and their commitment to integrity in ministry helped protect their own church and the churches throughout Asia from being misled by these apostolic charlatans.

'AND HAST BORNE, AND HAST PATIENCE'

> In Revelation 2:3, Jesus further expounded on these points by saying, "And *hast borne*, and hast patience, and for my name's sake hast laboured, and hast not fainted."

The words "hast borne" are a translation of the Greek word *bastadzo*. This word is also used in Revelation 2:2, where it is translated, "canst not *bear* them which are evil." It conveys the idea of the Ephesian believers' *intolerance* or *inability* to endorse or bear responsibility for anyone they found to be questionable or evil. The Greek tense used implies that they *had always been intolerant* of evildoers in the past and *remained intolerant* in the present.

The spiritual leadership in the church of Ephesus had no tolerance for evil, particularly those who falsely called themselves apostles. This had been and continued to be the believers' pattern over the years since the church began. For the second time in two successive verses, Jesus commended them for this important quality, demonstrating the high value He places on integrity in the ministry.

The words "hast patience" are a repetition of what Jesus already said in Revelation 2:2, but the tense used here again implies that *they had been patient in the past* and *they remained consistently patient in the present*. This undoubtedly refers to the continual persecution that assailed the church of Ephesus, as well as the trouble they experienced on account of those pretenders who masqueraded as apostles. The Ephesians' determination to endure trouble and to remain steadfast in the face of difficulties didn't just mark their early years as a church body; this same attitude continued to be a prime feature of this church at the time of John's vision. Thus, Jesus Christ once more commended the Ephesian church for their patience and steadfastness in the midst of great pressure and persecution.

'FOR MY NAME'S SAKE'

> Jesus continued in Revelation 2:3, saying, "And hast borne, and hast patience, *and for my name's sake....*"

The phrase translated "and for my name's sake" actually means *on account of my name*. This is important because it tells us the church of Ephesus endured all their suffering for the right reasons. If they endured all their suffering and trouble for the sake of self-promotion or for any other cause, Jesus would have seen this — for His flaming eyes penetrated every heart and observed each right

Left: This paved street from Ephesus ran along the upper side of the Temple of Domitian in one of the richest neighborhoods of Ephesus. It separated the Temple of Domitian from the Upper Marketplace and led to the road people walked to reach the Gate of Magnesia on the upper side of the city. These are the original stones that existed at the time Paul and his fellow workers established the church of Ephesus.

implies that these believers fervently wanted to bring honor to the name of Jesus and that this heartfelt desire compelled them to maintain excellence and integrity in the work of the ministry.

and wrong motivation within the seven churches. Jesus saw that the Ephesians had done the things for which He had commended them for the right reasons.

As discussed earlier, Acts 19 records that the name of Jesus was marvelously glorified in the city of Ephesus (*see* pages 332-334). The impact of Jesus' name was so great that it brought salvation, healing, deliverance from demonic powers, and freedom to large numbers of pagans who lived in Ephesus. These people never lost their deep appreciation for Jesus' name and what that precious name had accomplished in their lives. This phrase "for my name's sake"

'HAST LABOURED, AND HAST NOT FAINTED'

In Revelation 2:3, Jesus continued to speak to the church of Ephesus, "And hast borne, and hast patience, and for my name's sake *hast laboured, and hast not fainted....*"

The word "labored" comes from the Greek word *kopos*, which was also used in Revelation 2:2 where Jesus told the Ephesian believers that He was aware of the *strenuous labor* they had carried out for the Gospel. In Revelation 2:3, Jesus once again emphasized this quality, revealing the high value He places on those who work hard and consistently for the sake of the Gospel. Just as they *had been* intolerant of evildoers and *remained* intolerant — and just as they *had been* patient in the beginning and *remained* patient — they also *had always been* and *remained* a hardworking church. And regarding all these commendable qualities, Jesus declared that they did everything for the sake of His name.

The Ephesian church had worked extremely hard for many years, bearing continual responsibility in spiritual leadership for all of Asia and enduring many difficulties and afflictions. It is therefore significant that Jesus went on to tell these believers, "And hast borne, and hast patience, and for my name's sake hast laboured, and *hast not fainted*."

The word "fainted" is *kekopiakes*, a form of the word *kopos*, the Greek word for *extreme labor* or *exhausting work*. But the Greek tense used here means that in spite of the difficulties the Ephesian believers had faced, *they never gave in to exhaustion or weariness*. The work they accomplished could have brought any person or congregation to their knees in exhaustion. Yet their spirits remained strong, and they refused to relax their work ethic as they strove to serve their Lord and Savior.

Up to this point, everything Jesus had said to describe the Ephesian congregation made it seem as if it were *the ideal*

Above: In this illustration, Paul is writing from prison to his spiritual son, Timothy, who served as the pastor of the church at Ephesus.

church. Consider what we know so far of this prominent First Century church:

- It had been started by Paul and his team.

- Timothy had been its pastor.

- The apostle John had lived there.

- Mary, the mother of Jesus, was a former member of the church.

- It was the largest and most significant congregation in the entire province of Asia.

- It was the church responsible for starting and overseeing churches throughout the region.

- Most importantly, Jesus commended the congregation multiple times in Revelation 2:2,3 for their outstanding qualities.

But after commending the Ephesian believers for their admirable qualities, Jesus proceeded to tell them of a very serious flaw He had seen in their midst. Although they shone so brightly in the areas He had just described, Jesus made it clear that these believers had to heed His warning and repent; otherwise, one spiritual defect could jeopardize the very future of their church (*see* Revelation 2:5).

'NEVERTHELESS, I HAVE SOMEWHAT AGAINST THEE'

> In Revelation 2:4, Jesus went on to tell the church of Ephesus, "*Nevertheless* I have somewhat against thee, because thou hast left thy first love."

The word "nevertheless" is a translation of the Greek word *alla*, which essentially means "*BUT….*"

Despite all the outstanding commendations Christ had just given to this church, there was one point that was *not* commendable. Jesus was so dismayed and disconcerted by this one serious defect that He told the Ephesian believers, "…*I have* somewhat against thee…."

The words "I have" are a translation of the Greek word *echo*, which means *I have* or *I hold*. In spite of all the remarkable features that made the Ephesian church so outstanding, there was one area where these believers had failed, and it was so bothersome to Christ that He *personally held it against them*. The phrase "against thee" is very personal, informing

us that Christ was *deeply disturbed* by something He knew about this church.

'BECAUSE THOU HAST LEFT THY FIRST LOVE'

> Jesus declared to the Ephesian believers, "Nevertheless I have somewhat against thee, *because thou hast left thy first love*" (Revelation 2:4).

The word "love" in this verse is the Greek word *agape*. This word *agape* is so filled with deep emotion and meaning that it is one of the most difficult words to translate in the New Testament. The task of adequately explaining this word has baffled translators for centuries; nevertheless, an attempt will be made here to clarify the meaning of *agape* and then to apply it to the context of Revelation 2:4.

Agape occurs when an individual *sees, recognizes, understands, and appreciates the value of an object or a person,* causing him to behold this object or person in great esteem, awe, admiration, wonder, and sincere appreciation. Such great respect is awakened in the heart of the observer for the object or person he is beholding that he is *compelled* to love. In fact, his love for that person or object is so strong, it is *irresistible*. This kind of love knows no limits or boundaries in how far, wide, high, and deep it will go to show love to its recipient. If necessary, *agape* love will even sacrifice itself for the sake of that object or person it so deeply cherishes. *Agape* is therefore the *highest*, *finest*, *most noble*, and *most fervent* form of love.

In addition, the Greek sentence structure of this verse is very different from the *King James Version* previously quoted. The original Greek literally states, "*...because your love, the first one, you have left.*" The phrase "the first one" is a clarification of what type of love Jesus was describing. This phrase comes from the Greek words *ten proten*, which modifies *agape* to mean *first love* or *early love*. Jesus used this phrase here to remind the church of Ephesus of the esteem, awe, admiration, wonder, and appreciation that was first awakened in their hearts for Him when they received Him as their Savior many years earlier. Like young people who fall in love, the Ephesians *fell hard* when they first came to Christ. Their hearts were captivated with their love for Jesus. There were no limits to what they would surrender to Him, no boundaries to their obedience. They were willing to sacrifice or leave behind anything to follow Him.

Above: *Artist Eustache Le Sueur entitled this 1649 painting, "The Sermon of St. Paul at Ephesus." It depicts Paul preaching to the Ephesian converts as they throw items from their pagan past into a pile to be burned as an act of public repentance.*

Luke described the Ephesians' early act of public repentance in Acts 19:18 and 19, when they burned their occult fetishes and attempted to amputate every connection to the past that would hinder their new lives in Christ (*see* pages 333-344). The repentance of these new believers was so deeply rooted in their hearts that it produced a radical, far-reaching, profound transformation that completely altered their way of living. They were *fervently* in love with Jesus and completely sold out to Him — with no sorrows, regrets, or reservations.

But by the time John saw the exalted Christ on the island of Patmos, more than

30 years had passed since the Ephesian believers first repented, and, in the vision, Christ issued them this stern warning: "Your love, the first one, you have left." The phrase "you have left" is from the Greek word *aphiemi*, which denotes *the voluntary release of something once held dear* or *to neglect, to ignore*, or *to leave something or someone behind*. Although the Ephesians were still committed to Christ, doing everything "for his name's sake," they no longer had the deep passion and fervency for Him that had once consumed their hearts. Over the years, as they became more doctrinally sophisticated and astute, their simple but profound first love for Jesus had somehow dissipated and slipped away from them, even though they never stopped faithfully serving Him.

After fighting spiritual battles year after year — testing false apostles, training leaders, starting new churches, overseeing entire groups of churches, and dealing with spiritual wolves who were constantly trying to ravage their ministry base — it seems that the Ephesian congregation became so focused on protecting their church that they were no longer able to enjoy their relationship with Jesus as they had many years earlier. This was still a remarkable church, but the spiritual fervency that characterized this body of believers in the past was now missing. It was for this reason that Jesus was so deeply disturbed about what He saw as He walked in their midst. The blazing fire that once characterized the Ephesian believers had gradually waned until it became little more than a smoldering flame.

It often happens that the first generation of Christians during a move of God experiences dramatic salvations as that segment of the Church is born in the power of the Spirit. However, the second generation, raised in a Christian environment, often doesn't experience the same radical deliverance their parents did. Of course, it should be the goal of all believing parents to raise their children in a godly environment; however, it does increase the need to work diligently to retain spiritual passion. As each successive generation becomes more accustomed to a Christian environment — learning to speak the language of the church, sing the songs of the church, and act the way "church" people should act — it becomes easy for the younger generations to slip into a mindset of familiarity. Too often

Left: *The ruins of these intricately carved, ancient graves serve as reminders to us to retain our passion for Jesus and pass on that passion to the next generation. Otherwise, the memories of our early zeal for the Lord will become forgotten and neglected, lost under the overgrowth of life like a neglected grave with no tombstone.*

away, replaced instead by orthodoxy, creeds, and dogmas — a form of religion that lacked the power known by the earlier generation (*see* 2 Timothy 3:5).

If this could happen to the church of Ephesus, it must be taken as a warning for the Church at large in every generation. We must regularly allow the Holy Spirit to search our hearts and reveal whether or not we are still on fire for the Lord as we once were. It may be a painful revelation to realize that we have become doctrinally sophisticated yet powerless. However, if we are willing to remember from whence we have fallen and then to repent, we can be spared the tragedy of becoming irrelevant to our generation.

'REMEMBER'

This is precisely why Jesus said to the Ephesian church, "Remember therefore from whence thou art fallen, and repent, and do the first works; or else I will come unto thee quickly, and will remove thy candlestick out of his place, except thou repent" (Revelation 2:5).

this can produce apathy in people's hearts, ultimately leading them to take the redemptive work of Christ for granted. Therefore, the potential for spiritual fires to grow dimmer increases dangerously with each new generation — *unless* each church and its members become unrelenting in their commitment to retain their spiritual passion for Christ.

There is no clearer example of this vital principle than the illustrious church of Ephesus, which was perhaps the finest congregation that existed in the First Century. Although only 40 years had passed since the birth of this church, the fervency that once gripped these believers' hearts had waned. The spiritual fire that once blazed in their midst was slowly flickering

Notice the three things Jesus urged the congregation in Ephesus to do in order to correct their backslidden condition: 1) *remember*, 2) *repent*, and 3) *do the first works*.

It was essential for the Ephesian believers to recall their place of departure if they were to return to the vibrant relationship they once experienced with Christ. Therefore, He urged them to "remember."

When a church becomes older and more structured, polished, refined, and doctrinally developed, it can become so engaged in ministry business that it runs the risk of forfeiting its zeal and spiritual fire. What was once held as precious often becomes routine. And as the leadership and church members become accustomed to the precious Holy Spirit in their lives, too often they unintentionally begin to simply "traffic" in the things of God. It is difficult to find a single mature Christian who hasn't had to fight this temptation as his or her sinful past gradually becomes a distant memory. It's a subtle backsliding that occurs in the very act of serving God.

The Ephesian congregation had a great deal to remember:

- Their deliverance from idol worship.

- Their liberation from evil spirits.

- The many miraculous healings that occurred in their city.

- The great bonfire where they burned all their occult books and magical incantations.

- Their public act of repentance before a pagan crowd.

From the inception of the Ephesian church, these early believers were renowned for their passion for Jesus, their willingness to sever their new lives in Christ from their pagan past, and their aggressive missionary zeal. All of this was a part of their glorious history.

In its early years, this church burned like a spiritual inferno, and the vibrancy and excitement of these Ephesian believers inspired the same passion in other churches and spiritual leaders. But as the years passed, the zeal the Ephesian church once possessed for the things of God slowly ebbed away. Knowledge increased, but the believers' fiery passion for Jesus diminished. Undoubtedly, as the church grew, so did its members' schedules, routines, habits, customs, and traditions. The subtle backsliding that often occurs when Christians become consumed with serving God began to take hold in this great church. The Ephesians were so busy serving Jesus that they lost their intimacy with Him. It is also likely that they experienced a loss of joy in their service, since joy is impossible to maintain without a vital connection to the Savior.

Revelation 2:4 says the Ephesian believers had lost their "first love" — in other words, the simplicity and passion that marked their early love for Jesus Christ. This tells us how far they had unintentionally drifted from the spiritual zeal that once characterized them. For this reason, Jesus went on to say, "*Remember* therefore from whence thou art fallen..." (v. 5). Christ urged them to stop everything they were doing in order to "remember" the precious fellowship they used to

Above: *Thousands of idols and statues lined the main streets of Ephesus. Pictured here are the bases on which a few of those idols once stood. Acts 19 records that when citizens of Ephesus received the message of the Gospel, they turned from their devotion to pagan idolatry and became passionate about their faith in Jesus.*

enjoy with Him before they became so spiritually sophisticated.

The word "remember" comes from the Greek root *mneia*. In ancient literature, this word denoted *a written record used to memorialize a person's actions*; *a sepulcher*; *a statue*; *a monument*; or *a tombstone*. It is very significant that the word *mneia* can be translated *a sepulcher*. This suggests that the Ephesian believers' early experiences with Christ had become *buried* by 40 years of activity. Thus, Jesus urged them to dig through the clutter of their schedules, routines, and activities so they could "remember" their vibrant beginning. Like dirt on a grave, the busyness of ministry had buried what was once precious to them. Using the word "remember" — the Greek word *mneia* — Jesus implored them to unearth those early memories when their faith was tender and new, to dig deep in order to recall and recover their powerful past. Once they remembered, they would be able to see how far they had drifted from the spiritual fervency that had marked their beginnings.

However, the word in verse 5 translated "remember" (*mneia*) also refers to *a statue* or *a monument*. This tells us that some memories should forever stand tall in our lives and never be forgotten. The purpose of *a statue* or *monument* is to put living people in remembrance of a significant historical event or person. That statue or monument is intended to *memorialize* a historical event or a deceased hero so future generations will never forget.

Most statues, monuments, and tombstones are made of metal or stone; therefore, they endure many years without any human effort or upkeep. Generations can come and go, but because statues and monuments stand tall, it is still possible for present generations to look upon the faces of deceased heroes and read the inscriptions that describe their past actions and contributions. As long as a statue or monument remains in its place, it will stand as a reminder to future generations.

However, memories must be deliberately maintained and cultivated if they are to remain vital in our hearts and minds. And if significant memories are not deliberately passed on to future generations, they become lost under the overgrowth of life, just like a neglected grave with no tombstone. It doesn't take long before the location of such a grave is completely lost. People will walk across it without even knowing that the remains of a precious person lie buried beneath their feet.

Like an unmarked grave, important memories are easily forgotten. Adults forget their childhood; nations forget their heritage; and Christians forget their early beginnings with Jesus. In Revelation 2:5, we discover that churches can forget their past. Years of activity and Christian service can so consume a congregation's energy and strength that they begin to forget the great work of grace God performed in their hearts. Weariness, busy schedules, and a constant stream of new programs to implement all have the ability to wear down a body of believers — turning their activity for God's Kingdom into spiritual drudgery and reducing what was once fresh and exciting into a monotonous, religious routine. Soon their early memories of coming to Christ are buried under an overgrowth of activity and spiritual weeds, and they forget how

Left: This photo shows some of the many graves and tombstones that lined the main road in the ancient city of Hierapolis. These stone sepulchers are indicative of those found in cities all over the Roman Empire, particularly in Asia Minor.

the Ephesian church received from other churches and spiritual leaders throughout the Roman Empire, Jesus could see the true state of this body of believers — and He said they were "fallen."

'FROM WHENCE THOU ART FALLEN'

Jesus continued in His admonition to the Ephesian church: "Remember therefore from *whence* thou art fallen..." (v. 5).

The word "whence" is the Greek *pothen*, which *points back in time to a different place or a different time*. It is intended to draw one's attention back in time to where he came from, to what life was once like, or to a specific moment or experience in the past.

Outwardly, everything looked great in the Ephesian church, but Jesus knew that its leadership and members had lost the spiritual passion that once burned so intensely in their hearts. For this cause, He told them that they were "fallen."

The word "fallen" means *a downfall from a high and lofty position*. The Greek tense doesn't describe the process of falling; rather, it refers to one who has

wonderful God's grace was when it first touched their hearts.

The word translated "remember" in this verse is in the present active imperative, which means Jesus wanted the Ephesian believers *to remain continually mindful* of their past. What God had done in their midst was a wonderful memory that needed to be memorialized among them for all generations. And if they took an honest look at their hearts and compared their present to their past, they would see what Jesus knew about them — that they had *fallen* from the zeal and spiritual passion that had once burned in their hearts. Regardless of the adulation

Above: This photo shows the massive marble cornice that adorned the top rim of the Temple of Serapis in the city of Ephesus. The cornice weighs several tons and was probably produced in the nearby city of Aphrodisias, evidenced by its exquisite Aphrodisias style of carvings. This once-magnificent structure now lies in ruins — a vivid reminder that man's attempts at contriving his own grandeur never last and ultimately result in ruin and decay. Only one's steadfast pursuit of God's truth and grace stands the test of time and lasts into eternity.

already completely fallen and who is now living in *a completely fallen state.*

For the past 40 years, the church at Ephesus had hosted the world's greatest Christian leaders, experienced the power of God, and become more advanced in spiritual knowledge than any other church of that time. The Christian world looked at this congregation as the ideal church. However, we must never forget that what can be carefully hidden from human eyes can never be concealed from Jesus. Hebrews 4:13 tells us that "...all things are naked and opened unto the eyes of him with whom we have to do." Jesus is often

unimpressed with the things that impress us because He sees a different picture than we do. Others may have been impressed with the heritage of the Ephesian church and its roster of famous personalities — but in Jesus' eyes, the church was "fallen."

This is reminiscent of the apostle Paul's words in First Corinthians 10:12, where he said, "Wherefore let him that thinketh he standeth take heed lest he fall." The word "thinketh" comes from the Greek word *dokeo*, which in this context means *to be of the opinion, to reckon, to suppose,* or *to think.* In this verse, the word *dokeo* expresses the idea of what a person *thinks* or *supposes* about himself. There is nothing to verify if that individual's opinion is correct — only that it is the prevailing opinion he has regarding himself.

The word "standeth" comes from the word *istemi*, which simply means *to stand*, *to stand fast*, *to stand firm*, or *to stand upright*. But when the words *dokeo* and *istemi* are combined in the same thought as Paul used them in this verse, the phrase could be read: "*Wherefore let anyone who has the self-imposed opinion of himself that he is standing strong and firm....*" Then Paul added the next critically important words: "...take heed lest he fall."

The words "take heed" are from the Greek word *blepo*, which means *to watch*, *to see*, *to behold*, or *to be aware*. The Greek tense indicates the need not only to watch, but also *to be continually watchful*.

The word "fall" is a form of the same word Jesus used in Revelation 2:5 when He told the believers in Ephesus that they were already fallen. This word in First Corinthians 10:12 describes one who *falls into a terrible predicament* or one who *has fallen into a worse state than he was in before*. It can also depict one who *falls into sin*, *falls into ruin*, or *falls into some type of failure*. In other words, this isn't merely the picture of someone who stumbles a little; it depicts *a downward plummet that causes one to tragically crash*. This verse could therefore be interpreted, "*If anyone has the opinion of himself that he is standing strong and firm, he needs to be continually watchful and always on his guard lest he trip, stumble, and fall from his overly confident position — taking a downward nosedive that leads to a serious crash.*"

Spiritual smugness is an attitude that deceives a person into thinking more highly of himself than he ought to think (*see* Romans 12:3). Often this self-congratulatory attitude emerges among those who "think" they are more advanced, educated, or spiritually sophisticated than others. It is a spiritual pride that blinds one from seeing his own areas of shortcoming and need as he once did and causes him to be overly impressed with himself.

This is a spiritual affliction that the enemy attempts to use against every successful minister or church. It was such a serious problem in the Corinthian church that Paul sternly rebuked them for thinking too highly of themselves. Deeply disturbed by the cocky attitude and spiritual smugness of the Corinthian congregation, the apostle commanded them to repent. Otherwise, he warned them, he would have to come to them with a rod of correction (*see* 1 Corinthians 4:21).

It is vital that we take this as a divine warning that directly pertains to our own walk with God. We must understand that our own opinion of ourselves or the high opinion of others concerning us is not a trustworthy measure. Proverbs 16:2 says, "All the ways of a man are clean in his own eyes; but the Lord weigheth the spirits." According to this verse, flesh is always prone to be self-congratulatory and to excuse its own failures and weaknesses. But there is nothing hidden from Jesus' sight; He sees it all from the beginning to the end. All the public relations in the world will not change what Jesus sees in a person's heart. Therefore, it is what Jesus Christ knows about us that is most important — *not* what we think about ourselves or what others think and say about us.

The church of Ephesus had a glorious past and a famous name. It was large, well known, and recognized by others as a spiritual leader and a model church. Nevertheless, Jesus saw the situation very differently from what human eyes could see.

We must never forget that what can be carefully hidden from human eyes can never be concealed from Jesus' eyes. We already read Hebrews 4:13, which tells us that "...all things are naked and opened unto the eyes of him with whom we have to do." In addition, Psalm 94:9-11 states, "He that planted the ear, shall he not hear? he that formed the eye, shall he not see? He that chastiseth the heathen, shall not he correct? he that teacheth man knowledge, shall not he know? The Lord knoweth the thoughts of man, that they are vanity." As stressed earlier, Christ often sees a different picture than others see. The Ephesian church, with its roster of famous personalities and its spiritual heritage, may have seemed impressive and influential from man's perspective — but in Jesus' eyes, it was "fallen."

If this illustrious ancient church with its list of remarkable accomplishments could be called "fallen" by the Head of the Church, it is clear that any church, regardless of its notable beginning or enduring fame, can also be "fallen." This means one's past is not a guarantee of the future. If an individual or a church is not completely devoted to doing whatever is necessary to retain spiritual passion, it is likely that over time, the initial passion will slowly dissipate, as was the case with the church of Ephesus.

That is why Jesus lovingly pointed the Ephesian believers backward in time, reminding them of the spiritual vibrancy they once possessed but had lost. Then He enjoined them to take action to rekindle their fire. If they would recognize the religious routine into which they had fallen — and allow this knowledge to produce conviction of sin about their backslidden condition — they could repent and turn the situation around.

Repentance demands acknowledgment of sin and agreement with God concerning our condition. *Admitting we have done wrong is the first step in repentance.* That acknowledgment is difficult, but the pain it produces is part of the process that leads us to repentance.

Thus, Christ pleaded with the believers in the Ephesian church to *remember* what they had lost. Once they acknowledged the height from which they had fallen, they would be in a position to take the next step of true repentance.

'AND REPENT'

> Jesus continued to say in Revelation 2:5, "Remember therefore from whence thou art fallen, *and repent....*"

The word "repent" comes from the Greek word *metanoeo*, which is a compound of *meta* and *nous*. The word *meta* means *to turn*, and the word *nous* means one's *mind, intellect, will, frame*

Above: *This photo provides an overview of the ruins of the ancient Theater of Ephesus, a once-magnificent centerpiece of pagan entertainment in this illustrious city that was so prominent during biblical times. In the midst of this beautiful yet pagan environment, a great church was born whose zealous members launched many other churches throughout Asia in the years that followed. Yet approximately 40 years later, Christ spoke to this congregation that once burned so vibrantly with passion for Him and told them to repent.*

of *thinking, opinion,* or *general view of life.* When the words *meta* and *nous* are combined together, the new word depicts *a decision to completely change the way one thinks, lives, or behaves.* This doesn't describe a temporary emotional sorrow for past actions; rather, it is a solid, intellectual decision to turn about-face and take a new direction, to completely alter one's life by discarding an old, destructive pattern and embracing a brand-new one.

As noted earlier, the word *nous* — the second part of the word *metanoeo* — means *the mind.* This is a very important component of the Greek word translated "repent" because it tells us that the

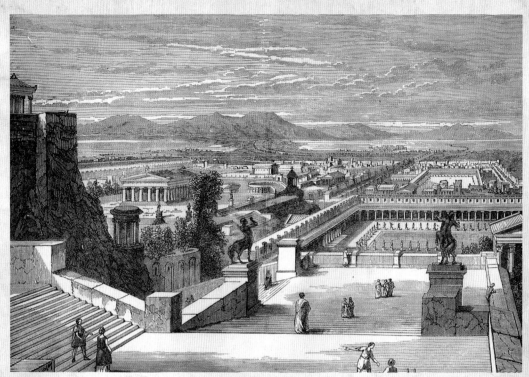

Above: The Apostle Paul had just arrived in Corinth when he wrote his first letter to the Thessalonian believers, in which he commended them for demonstrating true repentance (1 Thessalonians 1:9). The above illustration by an unknown artist gives a glimpse of what the city of Corinth looked like in Paul's day.

decision to repent originates in the mind, not in the emotions. Although emotions may *accompany* repentance, they are not a requirement. True repentance involves a conscious decision both to turn *away from* sin, selfishness, and rebellion and to turn *toward* God with all of one's heart and mind. *It is a complete, 180-degree turn in one's thinking and behaving.*

A prime example of such a *turning* is found in Paul's first letter to the Thessalonian believers when he commended them for the way in which they had "...*turned* to God from idols to serve the living and true God" (1 Thessalonians 1:9). The word "turned" here is the Greek word *epistepho*, which means *to be completely turned around*. The word "serve" is the Greek word *douleuo*, the word for *a slave* or *a servant*. This implies that the Thessalonians had utterly abandoned idolatry and completely dedicated their lives to serving Jesus. By using this word, Paul related that these early believers didn't just claim to have repented; they demonstrated it by the change in the way they *thought*, *lived*, and *served*. The radical change in their outward behavior was the *proof* that true repentance had occurred.

The idea of an across-the-board transformation is intrinsic to the word "repent." If there is no transformation or change of behavior and desire in a person who claims to have repented, it is doubtful that repentance ever truly occurred. *Repentance brings about a conversion to truth so deep that it produces a life change.*

God's demand for "repentance" is an elementary and basic spiritual truth. It is included in "the principles of the doctrine of Christ" listed in Hebrews 6:1,2. The word "principles" comes from the Greek word *arches*, which refers to something that is *elementary* or *from the beginning*. In Hebrews 6:1, this word refers to the *foundational principles* or *doctrines for beginners*. In other words, the principles listed in these two verses are the "ABCs of the Christian faith" — and "repentance" is listed as one of those "ABCs."

In fact, Hebrews 6:1 calls it "the foundation of repentance." The word "foundation" is the Greek word *themelios* — a combination of the Greek words *lithos*, which means *stone*, and *tithimi*, which means *to place*. When combined together, the new word depicts *something that is set in stone*. This indicates that the concept of repentance is so central to the Christian life, it should be *set in stone* in one's thinking. This truth cannot be sidetracked or ignored, for it is the foundation of every area of the Christian life.

Repentance is the starting place for all believers. That's why Hebrews 6:1 lists it as an elementary principle of the doctrines of Christ. If a person's spiritual journey didn't begin with a sincere act of repentance, he hasn't yet entered the Kingdom of God. He may have had a "religious awakening" of some kind. But repentance — acknowledging and deliberately turning *away* from sin — is God's requirement for receiving salvation through Jesus Christ.

THE PAIN OF REPENTANCE

> None of us likes pain, but the role of pain is important because it alerts us whenever something is wrong in our bodies.

When we experience pain, we can either locate and eliminate its source, or we can numb the pain with medication. If we choose the latter, the medication will eventually wear off, and the pain will reemerge because the source was never identified and corrected. The only way to permanently eliminate pain is to identify the problem and then apply the correct treatment.

This principle is also true spiritually, especially for people who are out of fellowship with Christ. For example, a sermon about the Second Coming of Jesus will thrill a Christian's heart and fill him with joy. But that same sermon can create great pain in the heart of an unbeliever or a backslidden Christian. When that person hears about Jesus' soon return, the knowledge may cause him to feel afraid and extremely uncomfortable because he knows he isn't right with God. That unsettled feeling in the pit of his stomach — that pain — signals to him that things are not well in his soul; otherwise, he would rejoice to hear that Jesus is coming again soon.

In this modern age, people want to be comforted and to be told that everything is going to be all right. But the truth is, some things are *not* going to be all right in people's lives unless they make a decision to repent and change. In those cases, it is sometimes up to us to love people enough to be honest with them, no matter how painful it is for them to hear the truth. This type of spiritual pain is good for people to experience because it makes them aware that things are not right between them and God.

Because Christ loves us, He often confronts us with painful truths about ourselves. He identifies the source of backsliding in our lives and then calls on us to repent. At that point, we must make the decision to turn from the sin in our lives and remove every action, attitude, or relationship from our lives that grieves Him and hurts us.

In Revelation 2:5, Jesus didn't mitigate the truth; rather, He had a straightforward confrontation with the Ephesians as He told them that they had allowed their relationship with Him to slip. This congregation was viewed as the model church — an example for churches throughout Asia and other parts of the Roman Empire. Nevertheless, Jesus said its members and leadership were "fallen" compared to what they had experienced earlier with Him. The passionate, on-fire relationship they had once enjoyed with Jesus had slipped away as they became lost in the sophistication of ministry.

When the pastor of the Ephesian church heard this message from Christ, it must have pained his heart; yet it was his responsibility as the *angelos* or *messenger* of the church to pass this message on to the entire congregation. One can only imagine the pain these early believers felt when they heard Jesus' words to them, urging them to put everything on pause and to take the time to remember the intimate relationship they had enjoyed with Him in the past. It must have profoundly affected the Ephesian congregation when they compared their passionate love for Christ in those earlier days to the body of believers they had become — spiritually sophisticated but distant from the Lord in their hearts.

Pain often precedes repentance — yet this is a good thing, for pain can bring us to a place of humility whereby

we cry out for God to forgive and to change us. A good example of this can be found in Acts 2, when the apostle Peter addressed a large crowd on the Day of Pentecost. Peter preached a message that caused such pain in the hearts of his audience that they cried out and asked for help. Acts 2:37 says, "Now when they [the unsaved crowd] heard this, they were *pricked* in their heart, and said unto Peter and to the rest of the apostles, Men and brethren, what shall we do?"

The word "pricked" in this verse is the word *kata-nusso*, a compound of the words *kata* and *nusso*. The word *kata* means *down*; however, in this compound word translated "pricked," *kata* carries the idea of something that is *deep* or *deep down*. The second part of the word is *nusso*, a Greek word that means *to prick*, *to puncture*, *to stab*, *to sting*, *to stun*, or *to pierce*. The only other time this word *nusso* is found in the New Testament is in John 19:34, where John wrote, "But one of the soldiers with a spear pierced (*nusso*) his side, and forthwith came there out blood and water." This word describes how the soldiers took a spear and *pierced*, *punctured*, *stabbed*, or *sliced open* Jesus' side. It was a *deep puncturing* of His side and even His lungs.

When the word *kata* is combined together with the word *nusso* in Acts 2:37, the new word *katanusso* is formed and is translated "pricked." This tells us the people in the crowd that day were *deeply affected* by Peter's words. As they listened to Peter, his message *penetrated* their conscience, *sliced open* their souls, and *pierced* their hearts so *deeply* that they cried out for help. Those anointed words stung their hearts and minds as they became aware of their sinful condition. Suddenly their souls felt a deep ache, and they were filled with anguish as their hearts were *punctured* by the truth Peter preached. And when the people cried out to Peter and the other

Left: On the Day of Pentecost, Peter preached a clear message that included faith in Christ and God's call to repent (Acts 2:38). That divine call to repent has been, is, and always will be God's first requirement for those who come to Him by faith.

apostles, "…Men and brethren, what shall we do?" (Acts 2:37), Peter boldly answered them: *"Repent"* (v. 38).

THE DIFFERENCE BETWEEN REPENTANCE AND REMORSE

To understand the nature of true repentance, it is important to understand the difference between *repentance* and *remorse*.

Left: *After betraying Jesus, Judas regretted but never repented for what he had done. James Jacques Joseph Tissot's illustration shows the moment when Judas unsuccessfully tried to return the blood money he had received for his betrayal.*

The Greek word for "remorse" is *metamelomai*, which expresses the emotions of *sorrow*, *mourning*, or *grief*. A perfect New Testament example of remorse is found in Matthew 27:3-5, where the Bible relates the last hours of Judas Iscariot's life. It says, "Then Judas, which had betrayed him, when he saw that he was condemned, *repented* himself, and brought again the thirty pieces of silver to the chief priests and elders, saying, I have sinned in that I have betrayed the innocent blood. And they said, What is that to us? see thou to that. And he cast down the pieces of silver in the temple, and departed, and went and hanged himself."

Notice the Bible says that Judas "repented" himself. A person who repents doesn't go out and hang himself afterward, so what really happened in this passage of Scripture? The answer lies in the word "repented" (v. 3). This is not the word *metanoeo*, the word most often translated "repent" in the New Testament. Rather, this particular word for "repent" is the Greek word *metamelomai*, which portrays a person who is completely overwhelmed with emotions. This word is used five times in the New Testament, and in each instance, it expresses *sorrow*, *mourning*, or *grief*. The word *metamelomai* rarely depicts someone moved to change but rather refers to a person who is seized with *remorse*, *guilt*, or *regret*.

Right: This illustration by James Jacques Joseph Tissot depicts Judas Iscariot after betraying Jesus to His enemies. Rather than turning to God and deeply repenting for his sin, Judas — filled with remorse and guilt — ran away and hung himself.

- *Metamelomai* can depict *remorse* that grips a person because of an act he committed that he knows is wrong. If he were willing to repent, he could change and be forgiven. But because he has no plans to repent or stop his sinful activities nor to rectify what he has done, he is therefore gripped with remorse. Thus, this emotion produces *no change* in a person's life.

- *Metamelomai* can also express the *guilt* a person feels because he knows that he has done wrong, that he will continue to do wrong, and that he has no plans to change his course of action. He feels shameful about what he is doing but continues to do it anyway, which results in a state of ongoing guilt. This guilt produces *no change* in a person's life or behavior. Yet genuine repentance — turning away from sin and toward God — would eliminate this feeling of guilt completely.

- *Metamelomai* denotes the *regret* a person feels because he got caught doing something wrong. He isn't repentant for committing the sin; instead, he is sorrowful only because he got *caught*. Now he's in trouble and, as a result, has lost an opportunity or some kind of leverage that could have been his. Rather than being repentant, this person is *regretful* that he got caught and must now pay the consequences. Chances are that if he'd never been caught, he would have continued his activities. This kind of regret likewise produces *no change* in a person's conduct.

Because the word *metamelomai* is used in Matthew 27:3, it means Judas Iscariot did not "repent" in the sense of being truly sorry for what he had done and wanting

Left: In this painting, entitled, "The Sorrow of King David," by artist William Brassey Hole, the prophet Nathan confronts King David regarding the sin he had committed with Bathsheba. In that moment, David showed the godly sorrow of true repentance, evidenced by his heart desire to change.

overwhelming sense of loss may have provoked Judas to commit suicide.

Remorse will keep a person perpetually bound and unchanged, enslaving him in sorrow and engulfing him emotionally. It leaves a person feeling depressed, hopeless, and unchanged. It focuses more on one's own personal loss than on the pain or loss caused to others or to the heart of God. Conversely, repentance is indicated by a decision *to change*. And when true repentance occurs in a person's heart and mind, the Holy Spirit releases His divine power to empower that change and to lead that person to freedom.

to make it right with God. Rather, it confirms that he was *remorseful*, seized with *guilt*, and filled with *regret*. Because of his actions, Judas forfeited his opportunity to be a high-ranking member of Jesus' inner circle. Judas was more sorrowful for himself than he was for his participation in Jesus' betrayal. This wasn't a demonstration of repentance that led to salvation, but of sorrow, guilt, and a deep-seated remorse that ultimately led to death. This

Psalm 51 provides a vivid example of genuine repentance and is, in fact, called David's psalm of repentance. In this psalm, one can sense not only David's *sorrow* but also his *decision to change*. In verse 17, he wrote about a heart that is broken over sin: "The sacrifices of God are a broken spirit:

a broken and a contrite heart, O God, thou wilt not despise." The word "contrite" is the Old Testament expression for someone who is genuinely repentant for what he has done. This is a person who has recognized his wrong, decided to change, and now desires to live uprightly.

This was the spiritual condition to which Christ was calling the congregation at Ephesus. He confronted them with the truth: that although they had continued to serve Jesus and to faithfully go through the motions, little by little their spiritual zeal had begun to wane. Then He compelled them to acknowledge — just as He compels us today — that they needed to repent and return to Him, thereby rekindling the fire that once burned so brightly in their hearts.

GOD CALLS ENTIRE CHURCHES TO REPENT

> If necessary, Christ calls entire churches to repent. Besides the seven churches in the book of Revelation, another scriptural example is the Corinthian congregation, to whom Paul brought correction for their many acts of carnality.

When the Corinthian believers received Paul's first letter and recognized that God was speaking to them through the apostle, they were moved with fear to purge themselves of the sin in their midst that had grieved the Holy Spirit. This willingness to change was the *proof* that true repentance had occurred. The indisputable transformation that occurred in the Corinthian church was sufficient evidence for Paul to declare in his second letter that they had cleared themselves in the matters where they had previously been wrong (*see* 2 Corinthians 7:9-11). God's goal in confronting His Church is always to produce cleansing, transformation, and restoration.

Today Jesus is still crying out for the Church to repent of worldliness and carnality. As is true in each generation, today we have a choice: to harden our hearts and turn a deaf ear to the Holy Spirit, or to allow Him to deal deeply with us and produce true repentance in our hearts and souls. Although Christ is always ready to transform His Church, no transformation can occur unless we are willing to hear what His Spirit is saying to us. And once we do hear that divine message, we must be willing to respond with humble obedience, just as the Corinthian church did.

This was the case for the church at Ephesus. Jesus was calling this congregation to recognize their fallen state and to take visible steps to demonstrate that they were sincere about restoring their passion for Him.

'AND DO THE FIRST WORKS'

> Jesus went on to tell the Ephesian church, "Remember therefore from whence thou art fallen, and repent, and *do* the first works..." (Revelation 2:5).

Left: The Great Temple of Artemis in Ephesus played a huge role in the lives of the city's pagan population. Most members of the Ephesian church had once been numbered in that pagan crowd but had willingly severed themselves from their sinful past to commit their lives to Jesus, regardless of the cost.

The word "do" is the Greek word *poieo*, a word that is used 568 times in the New Testament; thus, its meaning is well established in New Testament writings. It literally means *to do*, but it actually conveys much more. This word *poieo* describes all types of *activity*, particularly the idea of *creativity*. For example, the word *poietes* — a form of the word *poieo* — is the source of the word *poet*, which denotes one who has the extraordinary ability to write or create a certain literary form. Thus, this word describes *doing* that produces *results*.

Because the word *poieo* is connected to the creative activity of an author, poet, or painter, let's pause to consider what is required for this type of creative person to produce excellent work. It takes concentration and commitment for a poet to write a poem or for an artist to paint a masterpiece. The person must free himself from all distractions so his mind, emotions, and talent can focus on the specific project before him. When an author or artist can concentrate exclusively on a creative assignment, he is able to put forth an all-out effort and release his full potential to produce a masterful work. Although it may be true that a great work can be produced with intermittent interruptions, the removal of distractions for the purpose of a more concentrated focus enables one to achieve the best results with greater speed.

This is significant in light of Revelation 2:5, where the tense of the word *poieo* calls for *urgent* and *quick* action.

Anything less than a serious response would be found insufficient. Therefore, great effort, prayer, and concentration would be required if the Ephesian believers were to return to their first love and replicate the works that accompanied their early faith. It is obvious that Christ expected the best from them — which would only be achieved if they responded to Him with their best effort. And because the Greek tense demands urgent and quick action, it is also certain that Jesus wasn't willing to wait endlessly for them to respond. If they didn't heed His words, they would lose their position of spiritual leadership in Asia (Revelation 2:5).

But what specifically was Jesus commanding this church to do? He told them in verse 5: "Remember therefore from whence thou art fallen, and repent, and do *the first works....*"

The phrase "first works" comes from the Greek words *prota erga*. The word *prota* means *first* or *early*, and the word *erga* means *works*, *deeds*, or *activity*, conveying the idea of *work that is produced by consistent and tireless effort*. Although the *King James Version* translates this Greek phrase as "first works," it could actually be interpreted, *"the actions that were indicative of you at the first"* or *"the things you did in the very beginning."*

Jesus rebuked the Ephesian believers in Revelation 2:4 for leaving their "first love"; then in verse 5, He commanded them to return to their "first works." He was referring to the words, deeds, and activities that characterized the Ephesian congregation at the beginning of their spiritual journey when they first fell in love with Jesus Christ.

What were these "first works" that once distinguished the church of Ephesus? Scripture reveals several characteristics of this prominent church in its early beginnings:

- They possessed a great spiritual hunger (*see* Acts 18:20).

- They enjoyed rich fellowship among the brethren (*see* Acts 18:27).

- They had an eagerness to repent and to receive what God had for them (*see* Acts 19:1-6).

- They cherished the Word of God (*see* Acts 19:8).

- They sacrificed their religious reputation for Jesus (*see* Acts 19:9).

- They were committed to applying God's Word to their lives (*see* Acts 19:10).

- They were receptive to the power of God and to the gifts of the Spirit (*see* Acts 19:11,12).

- They loved the name of Jesus and the wonder-working power associated with His name (*see* Acts 19:17).

- They were quick to confess their sin and turn from their evil works (*see* Acts 19:18).

- They severed all connections with a pagan past at great personal cost (*see* Acts 19:19).

- They were publicly persecuted for the sake of Christ (*see* 1 Corinthians 15:32).

- They were faith-filled (*see* Ephesians 1:15).

- They were known for their love of the brethren (*see* Ephesians 1:15).

All of the qualities listed above characterized this passionate, vibrant congregation in its early years. The fact that Christ called for them to return to doing these "first works" doesn't necessarily mean they had become completely void of these attributes. However, it is evident that the intensity of their zeal had radically diminished. Thus, Christ urged them *to remember*, *to repent*, and *to do the first works* for these reasons:

- *Remembering how the fire of God once burned in their hearts was essential.* Only by remembering what they used to be could the Ephesian believers realize how far they had drifted.

- *Repentance was God's requirement.* An acknowledgment and confession of sin was the place to begin. If they were willing to humble themselves and repent, it would lead to their restoration and spare them from impending judgment.

- *Repentance demands proof.* A person who confesses his sin with no intention of changing is doing nothing more than admitting his guilt. He is not exhibiting genuine repentance. True repentance is always accompanied by corresponding actions. Regarding the Ephesian believers, Jesus made it clear that the proof of their repentance would be a return to a passionate pursuit of intimately knowing Him.

'OR ELSE I WILL COME UNTO THEE QUICKLY'

In Revelation 2:5, Jesus continued with His message to the Ephesian believers: "Remember therefore from whence thou art fallen, and repent, and do the first works; *or else I will come unto thee quickly....*"

The words "or else" would be better translated, *"and if not."* The Ephesian church had a decision to make, and Christ anticipated that they would do what He asked of them. But *if* they did not, He warned them, "...I will come unto thee quickly...."

The phrase "I will come" is a translation of the Greek word *erchomai*, which describes an event that would indeed take place *if* the Ephesian believers didn't meet Jesus' requirements. If they failed to do what He asked of them, they could expect Him to come to them with judgment, for the issues at hand were far too serious to ignore. The choice had been set before the congregation at Ephesus: They must repent, or Christ would remove them from their place of prominence among the other churches.

In Revelation 2:1, John vividly described Jesus as One who "...walketh in the midst of the seven golden candlesticks." As noted previously, the word "walketh"

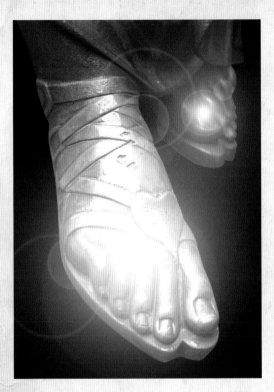

Left: In John's vision, the apostle saw Christ's feet "…like unto fine brass, as if they burned in a furnace…" (Revelation 1:15). Since brass symbolizes judgment in Scripture, this image signifies that Jesus is ready, if necessary, to bring judgment to the Church. However, He is also One who "walketh in the midst of the seven golden candlesticks" — providing ample time for repentance so judgment can be averted and blessing can instead be supplied.

In the apostle John's vision of the exalted Christ, he saw that Jesus' feet were "like unto fine brass" (Revelation 1:15). Brass in Scripture represents judgment, which tells us that Christ was prepared to bring judgment if necessary. But as noted on pages 97-98, brass or bronze is heavy; therefore, it is difficult to quickly move an object made of these metals. The fact that Jesus' feet appeared as brass clearly sends the message that when Christ moves to bring judgment, He does *not* rush. Rather, He moves slowly in that direction, providing ample time for the repentance that will prevent the impending judgment.

Nevertheless, Jesus made it clear to the Ephesian congregation that if they resisted His pleadings, He would have to come to them in judgment. Thus, He warned them, "I will come unto thee quickly." The phrase "unto thee" (or "to you") is the Greek word *soi*, which means *directly to you*. The use of this word *soi* made Christ's warning to the Ephesians extremely *direct* and *personal*. The time allowed for repentance had already been set, and Jesus was walking toward them with His feet of brass. If His voice was

means that Christ literally walked around the seven churches to inspect, observe, contemplate, probe, and uncover the real condition of each congregation. Thus, the potential judgment Jesus spoke of as He addressed the Ephesian church was the result of His contemplative investigation of their spiritual condition. After carefully observing them, Christ gave them a solemn warning: They were to *remember*, *repent*, and *do their first works*, or else He would come "quickly."

There is no Greek word in the original text for this word "quickly"; rather, it was added by the translators to help convey the urgency of the situation. Yet even as Jesus gave the Ephesian church this urgent warning, He also gave them the time frame they needed to respond to His request.

ignored, the outcome would be inevitable: Divine judgment would surely follow.

'AND WILL REMOVE THY CANDLESTICK OUT OF HIS PLACE'

In Revelation 2:5, Christ fore-warned the church of Ephesus: "Remember therefore from whence thou art fallen, and repent, and do the first works; or else I will come unto thee quickly, *and will remove thy candlestick out of his place....*"

The word translated "remove" here can also be translated "move." It can mean *to completely remove*, as to obliterate or to wipe off the face of the earth. It can also mean *to move* or *to relocate* an object from one place to another. In this particular context, Christ wasn't threatening the Ephesian believers with obliteration. Rather, He was telling them in advance that although He wanted this church to continue as the primary "candlestick" in the region, their

Left: By the time Jesus spoke to the seven churches in John's vision, there were many "candlesticks" established throughout Asia — and the "candlestick" of Ephesus was the most prominent of them all. It was a position of stature that was both a privilege and a great responsibility — and as Jesus warned, it was one that could be taken away if the Ephesian congregation didn't heed His call to remember, return to their first love, and do their first works.

position was in jeopardy. If they didn't cooperate with Him and repent, their great influence would be relocated or transferred to another church. Although they might remain an active congregation, they would not retain their prominent stature.

In the original Greek, the word translated "candlestick" is followed by the word for "thy." This could be interpreted, *"your candlestick — yes, even YOUR candlestick!"* To this great, illustrious congregation that had dominated and led the Early Church in Asia for so long, this phrase conveyed the idea, *"It doesn't matter what you have been in the past or how significant you think you are right now. If you don't hear Me and repent, even YOUR influence can be transferred to someone else."* Thus, although the church of Ephesus had been a significant leader for years, *its glorious past was not an automatic guarantee of a glorious future.* Regardless of who they were and what they had accomplished, the Ephesian believers had to heed and respond to Jesus' warning. Otherwise, even this famous church would lose the influential position it held in the world of the First Century, particularly in Asia.

Christ warned them, "...And [I] will remove thy candlestick *out of his place...."* The words "out of" are translated from the Greek word *ek*, which means *out*, as in *to remove.* The Latin word *ex* is derived from this word *ek* and can picture *something that is behind the times, obsolete, outdated, or has fallen into disuse.* For instance, this word can describe an *ex*-friend, *ex*-spouse, *ex*-job, or anything else that is *canceled* or *no longer applicable.* But the word *ex* is also the foundation of the word *exit,* which can depict someone *leaving* or *departing*

from a particular place, as when an actor makes an *exit* from the stage once he has finished playing his role.

The phrase "his place" comes from the Greek word *topos,* which refers to *a specific, marked-off geographical location.* This word conveys the idea of a *territory, province, region, zone,* or *geographical position.* It is from this Greek word *topos* that we derive the word "topographical," as in a topographical map.

This underscores the important role the church of Ephesus had played in the Roman province of Asia. However, if these believers didn't respond properly to Christ, their influential position would become an *"ex*-position" that was no longer applicable to them. Whether or not the church continued to be a strong spiritual leader in the fulfilling of God's purposes in the region depended on one thing: Would they heed and respond to the words of the Master? If not, they would be making a choice that would require God's Spirit to lead them off the center stage of His plan — the position they had occupied for so many years — and raise up another church to take their place.

'EXCEPT THOU REPENT'

At the conclusion of Revelation 2:5, Jesus said, "Remember therefore from whence thou art fallen, and repent, and do the first works; or else I will come unto thee quickly, and will remove thy candlestick out of his place, *except thou repent.*"

Right: *This illustration depicts the first seven deacons of the Early Church, chosen as those qualified to help relieve the apostles' burden of ministry through their practical service to the saints. Many scholars believe that one of these deacons — Nicolas of Antioch — later turned aside from the purity of the truth to propogate erroneous doctrine. Of his followers, the Nicolaitans, Jesus firmly stated that He hated their deeds (Revelation 2:6).*

The grammar used here implies again that Christ rebuked the Ephesian congregation with an expectation that they would repent; however, this outcome wasn't certain. This tells us how far the church of Ephesus had regressed in its spiritual passion. Jesus' warning to these believers was very direct, personal, and clear. Yet they had drifted so far from the fiery love for Him they had once known — and the seeds of institutionalized religion seemed to have already begun to control them so much — that Christ couldn't say with absolute certainty that they would pass this test.

It is worth noting that in Ignatius' Epistle to the Ephesians (written in approximately 110 AD),[22] Ignatius wrote about many of the same commendable characteristics that Jesus used to describe the Ephesian church in Revelation 2.[23] Ignatius' letter provides evidence that the church of Ephesus did indeed heed Christ's message and therefore retained its leadership role in Asia for several hundred years. However, Jesus' warning to this ancient church that its leadership role could be transferred to another church serves as a reminder to every church in each generation that its influence can be retained only if that local body of believers stays in step with the Head of the Church.

'THOU HATEST THE DEEDS OF THE NICOLAITANS, WHICH I ALSO HATE'

In Revelation 2:6, Jesus went on to say, "But this thou hast, that thou hatest the deeds of the Nicolaitans, which I also hate."

The name "Nicolaitans" is derived from the Greek word *nikolaos*, a compound of the words *nikos* and *laos*. The word *nikos* is the Greek word that means *to conquer* or *to subdue*. The word *laos* is the Greek word for *the people*. It is also the word from which *laity* is derived. When these two words are combined into one, they form the name *Nicolas*, which literally means *one who conquers and subdues the people*. This seems to suggest that in some way, the Nicolaitans were conquering and subduing the people of God.

Ireneaus[24] and Hippolytus,[25] two leaders in the Early Church who recorded many of the earliest events of Church history, both wrote that the Nicolaitans were the spiritual descendants of Nicolas of Antioch, who was one of the seven men ordained as deacons in Acts 6:5, which states, "And the saying pleased the whole multitude: and they chose Stephen, a man full of faith and of the Holy Ghost, and Philip, and Prochorus, and Nicanor, and Timon, and Parmenas, and Nicolas a proselyte of Antioch."

We know quite a lot of information about some of these men who were chosen to be the first deacons, whereas little is known of others. Regarding all seven deacons, we know that the chief criteria for their selection was that they were men

"...of honest report, full of the Holy Spirit and wisdom..."(v. 3). Once they had been chosen, they were presented by the people to the apostles, who then laid hands on them to install and officially ordain them into the deaconate (v. 6).

The following presents a brief summary of what we know about each of these seven men:

STEPHEN

Like the other men, Stephen was a man of good report, filled with the Holy Spirit and wisdom. However, Acts 6:5 makes a remark about Stephen that is unique only to him. It says that he was "a man full of faith and of the Holy Ghost." This stronger level of faith may have been a contributing factor to the development

Right: This illustration by William Hatherall depicts the stoning of Stephen, a man full of faith and the Holy Spirit who became the first martyr of the Early Church. Following Stephen's death, countless other Christian martyrs would spill their blood for their faith during the first three centuries of Roman rule.

recorded in Acts 6:8: "And Stephen, full of faith and power, did great wonders and miracles among the people."

Stephen was a God-called evangelist who later became the first martyr in the history of the Church — killed with the full consent of Saul of Tarsus (later known as the apostle Paul; *see* Acts 7:58-8:1). The deaconate ministry was vital proving ground to prepare Stephen for the fivefold office of the evangelist. The name Stephen is from the Greek word *stephanos*, meaning *crown*. This is worth noting, for he was the first to receive a martyr's crown.

PHILIP

Philip was ordained with the other six original deacons. However, Acts 21:8,9 informs us that Philip later stepped in the ministry of the evangelist and that he had four daughters who also prophesied. Just as the deaconate was training and proving ground for Stephen to step into the office of the evangelist, it was also Philip's proving ground to prepare him for the evangelistic ministry that he, too, was called to fulfill. The name Philip means *lover of horses*. This name often symbolized a person who ran with swiftness, as does a horse — a fitting name for the fiery New Testament evangelist Philip later became.

PROCHORUS

The name Prochorus is a compound of the Greek words *pro* and *chorus*. The word *pro* means *before* or *in front of*, as with *a leader*. The word *chorus* is the old Greek word for *the dance* and is where we get the word *choreography*. There is a strong implication that this was a nickname, given to this man because he had been the foremost leader of dance in some school, theater, or musical performance. There is no substantiation for this idea, but his name seems to give credence to the possibility. Strong tradition places Prochorus with John as his assistant in the apostle's latter days, including his time of exile on the island of Patmos. Tradition also states that Prochorus was the first bishop of the Asia city of Nicomedia (*see* pages 22-24).

NICANOR

This unknown brother was found to be of good report, filled with the Holy Spirit and wisdom. Other than this, nothing is known of him. He is never mentioned again in the New Testament after Acts chapter 6. The name Nicanor means *conqueror*.

TIMON

Like Nicanor mentioned above, the deacon named Timon was known to be of good report, filled with the Holy Spirit and wisdom. Nothing more is known of him beyond what is stated in Acts chapter 6. His name means *honorable* or *of great value*.

PARMENAS

We know nothing more of Parmenas other than what is mentioned here in Acts 6. His name is a compound of the word *para* and *meno* — the word *para* meaning *alongside* and *meno* meaning *to remain* or *to abide*. Thus, the name Parmenas came to mean *one who sticks alongside* and conveyed the idea of one who is *devoted*, *loyal*, and *faithful*.

Above: *Pictured are the ruins of the Theater of Pergamum, the First Century capital of Asia. From this wicked center of pagan worship, many decrees were issued to wipe out the illegal Christian "cult." It was also in this city that the Nicolaitan doctrine of compromise gained a foothold among some church members. The church of Pergamum was the only other congregation to which Jesus addressed the doctrinal danger of the Nicolaitans.*

NICOLAS

Acts 6:5 tells us that this Nicolas was "a proselyte of Antioch." The fact that he was a proselyte tells us that he was not born a Jew but had converted from paganism to Judaism. Then he experienced a second conversion, this time turning from Judaism to Christianity. From this information, we know these facts about Nicolas of Antioch:

- He had deep pagan roots, very unlike the other six deacons who came from a pure Hebrew line. Nicolas' pagan background meant he had previously been immersed in the activities of the occult.

- He was not afraid of taking an opposing position, evidenced by his ability to change religions twice. Converting to Judaism would have estranged Nicolas from his pagan family and friends. It would seem to indicate that he was not impressed or concerned about the opinions of other people.

- He was a free thinker and very open to embracing new ideas and concepts. Judaism was very different from the pagan and occult world in which Nicolas had been raised. For him to shift from paganism to Judaism reveals that he was unusually liberal and open-minded in his thinking, because most pagans were offended by Judaism. He was obviously not afraid to entertain or embrace new ways of thinking.

- When Nicolas converted to Christ, it was *at least* the second time he had converted from one religion to another. We don't know if, or how many times, he shifted from one form of paganism to another before he became a Jewish proselyte. His ability to easily change religious "hats" implies that he was not afraid to switch direction in midstream and go in a totally different direction.

According to the writings of the Early Church leaders, Nicolas taught a doctrine of compromise, implying that total separation between Christianity and the practice of occult paganism was not essential.[26] From Early Church records, it seems apparent that this Nicolas of Antioch was so immersed in occultism, Judaism, and Christianity that he had a stomach for all of it. He had no problem intermingling these belief systems in various concoctions and saw no reason why believers couldn't continue to fellowship with those still immersed in the pagan rituals of the Roman empire and its countless mystery cults.

Occultism was a major force that continually warred against the Early Church. In Ephesus, there were many forms of idolatry, but the primary pagan religion was the worship of Diana (Artemis). In the city of Pergamum, numerous dark and sinister forms of occultism existed, causing Pergamum to be one of the most wicked cities in the history of the ancient world. In both of these cities, believers were continually lambasted and fiercely persecuted by adherents of pagan religions.

It was very hard for believers to live separately from all pagan activities in these two cities because paganism and its many religions were their very center of life. Slipping in and out of paganism would have been very easy for young or weak believers to do since most of their families and friends were still pagans. A converted Gentile would have found it very difficult to stay away from all pagan influence.

In light of these facts, note what Jesus declared in Revelation 2:6: "But this thou hast, that thou *hatest* the deeds of the Nicolaitans, *which I also hate*." Both Jesus and the Ephesian believers "hated the deeds" of the Nicolaitans. The word "hate" comes from the Greek word *miseo*, which means *to hate, to abhor*, or *to find utterly repulsive*. It describes a person who has *a deep-seated animosity* or one who is *antagonistic* to something he finds to be *completely objectionable*. He not only *loathes* that object but *rejects it* entirely. This is not just a case of dislike; it is a case of *actual hatred*.

The thing Jesus hated about the Nicolaitans was their "deeds." The word "deeds" is the Greek word *erga*, which means *works*. However, this word is all-encompassing, depicting every aspect of their behavior — including their deeds, actions, beliefs, conduct, and words.

It is significant that the "deeds" and "doctrines" of the Nicolaitans are mentioned only in connection with the churches in these two occultic and pagan cities, Ephesus and Pergamum (Revelation 2:6,15). According to early writings concerning the doctrine of the Nicolaitans, they taught that it was all right to have one foot in both worlds and that one needn't be so strict about separation from the world in order to be a Christian. This was the doctrine of the Nicolaitans that Jesus hated. It led to a weak version of Christianity that was without power and without conviction — a defeated, worldly type of Christianity.

Nicolas' deep roots in paganism produced in him an unacceptable tolerance for occultism and pagan standards. Growing up in this pagan spiritual environment caused him to believe that these belief systems were not so damaging or dangerous. This wrong perception resulted in a liberal viewpoint that encouraged people to stay connected to the world. This is what numerous Bible scholars believe about the Nicolaitans.

This kind of teaching results in defeat, for when believers allow sin and compromise to be in their lives, it drains away the power of the work of the Cross and the power of the Holy Spirit that is resident in a believer's life. This is the reason the name *Nicolas* is so vital to this discussion. The evil fruit of Nicolas' "doctrine" encouraged worldly participation, leading people to indulge in sin and accept a lower godly standard. In this way, he literally *conquered the people.* Compromise with the world always results in a weakened and powerless form of Christianity. Thus, Jesus declared He hated the doctrine and the deeds of the Nicolaitans.

'HE THAT HATH AN EAR, LET HIM HEAR WHAT THE SPIRIT SAITH UNTO THE CHURCHES'

> In Revelation 2:7, Jesus cried out, "He that hath an ear, let him hear what the Spirit saith unto the churches; To him that overcometh will I give to eat of the tree of life, which is in the midst of the paradise of God."

Christ issued an invitation to those with open hearts and with ears to hear, thereby implying that everyone does *not* have ears to hear what the Holy Spirit is saying. Jesus said, "He that hath an ear, *let him hear what the Spirit saith unto the churches….*"

Seven different times in the Synoptic Gospels, Jesus said, "He that hath ears to hear, let him hear" (*see* Matthew 11:15; 13:9,43; Mark 4:9,23; Luke 8:8; 14:35). Thus, this phrase was a familiar one to John — one that he could probably remember hearing Jesus say many years earlier. But this time Jesus added a phrase: "He that hath an ear, let him hear *what the Spirit saith unto the churches….*"

Although Jesus was speaking a specific message to the church at Ephesus, these truths are to be taken as a message from the Holy Spirit to all seven churches in Asia and to the Church at large throughout all history. What church wouldn't benefit from the penetrating statements of commendation, instruction, and rebuke Christ gave to the Ephesian congregation?

Above: This stone relief of Nike, the Greek goddess of victory, is located near Domitian Square on Curetes Street in Ephesus. The celebration of the victorious overcomer — who has achieved that status at the expense of his defeated victims — was a primary feature of Roman culture. However, Jesus introduced a new and higher concept to the Church: that an overcomer in God's eyes is one who overcomes because he chooses to endure all adversity while remaining faithful to Him.

If taken to heart, any local church or believer of any generation will be helped and encouraged by Jesus' words.

'TO HIM THAT OVERCOMETH'

Jesus continued His invitation to the Ephesian church: "He that hath an ear, let him hear what the Spirit saith unto the churches; *To him that overcometh…*" (Revelation 2:7).

The word "overcometh" is the Greek word *nikao*, which denotes *a victor, a champion,* or *one who possesses some type of superiority.* It might also refer to a military victory of one foe over the other. The word *nikao* can be translated *to control, to conquer, to defeat, to master, to overcome, to overwhelm, to surpass,* or *to be victorious.* From this word came the name *Nike,* the Greek goddess of *victory.*

In the context of Revelation 2:7, it is important to understand that the word *nikao* can describe either an *athletic victory* or a *military victory.* This means Jesus was conveying two potential messages to the church of Ephesus. First, He told these early believers that the only way to defeat the foes they faced — foes both *exterior* (false apostles) and *interior* (a cooling of spiritual love and passion) — was for them to maintain the attitude of an athlete. To win the contest before them, the Ephesians had to eliminate all spiritual apathy and prepare for the toughest competition they had ever engaged in. Nothing less than a full commitment would be sufficient to master the exterior adversaries and interior struggles they were facing. Whether Jesus' imagery referred to a runner, wrestler, discus thrower, or any other type of First Century athlete, His message was clear: Only a thoroughly committed believer will win a victor's crown.

Because the word *nikao* was also used militarily to depict the absolute crushing of an enemy, Jesus' words held a second meaning: He was calling the Ephesian believers to rise up like an army to attack and defeat the external and internal enemies that threatened them. Spiritual complacency and the lack of passion were intolerable enemies of their faith that had to be conquered. They were to *wage war* against the weaknesses Christ had brought to their attention. Winning this victory would require the highest level of determination they had ever known, for apathy and complacency are always the most difficult enemies for a person or a church to conquer.

It must also be noted that the tense for "overcometh" in Revelation 2:7 speaks of *a continuous and ongoing victory*. This means Christ wasn't urging the Ephesians to run a temporary race or to fight a short-term battle. He was demanding a commitment to start and to remain in the race until the finish line was reached — to attack and defeat their foes and then to remain victorious over their enemies. Thus, Jesus was actually asking the church of Ephesus — as He asks each of us — *to be permanently and consistently undeterred to overcome and obtain victory in every area of their lives*.

Jesus called each of the seven churches to "overcome." The word is used here in Revelation 2:7, as well as in His messages to the church of Smyrna (Revelation 2:11), Pergamum (Revelation 2:17), Thyatira (Revelation 2:26), Sardis (Revelation 3:5), Philadelphia (Revelation 3:12), and Laodicea (Revelation 3:21). Christ commanded the believers in each of these seven ancient churches — as He commands believers throughout all future generations — to be overcomers. Christians are to make it their continual and unrelenting goal to maintain victory in every possible sphere of life as long as they live on this earth.

'WILL I GIVE TO EAT OF THE TREE OF LIFE'

In Revelation 2:7, the risen Christ made a promise to those who overcome. He said, "He that hath an ear, let him hear what the Spirit saith unto the churches; To him that overcometh *will I give to eat of the tree of life....*"

The words "I will give" are a translation of the word *doso*, a form of the Greek

Above: This detail from a painting by Dutch artist Cornelis van Haarlem illustrates the fateful choice that led to the Fall of all mankind — when Eve "...took of the fruit thereof, and did eat, and gave also unto her husband with her; and he did eat" (Genesis 3:6).

word *didomi*, which means *I give*. In the context of this verse, *doso* could mean *I will allow* or *I will permit*. The use of this word emphatically means that Christ Himself is personally involved in this act. It is His choice *to give*, *to allow*, or *to permit* those who are actively in the process of overcoming "to eat" or "to partake of" the tree of life that is in the midst of the paradise of God. The fact that Jesus *permits*

this means that everyone is not allowed to partake of this promise. It seems that this is a promise available only to overcomers. The phrase "to eat" is a translation of the Greek word *phagein*, which is a form of the word *esthio*, meaning simply *to eat*. This word, of course, describes an essential activity for the maintenance of life.

The phrase "tree of life" refers to the tree located in the Garden of Eden that would impart perpetual life if its fruit were eaten. We know nothing else about the type of fruit this tree produced. We only know that the fruit of the forbidden tree produced spiritual death, whereas the fruit of the tree of life imparted eternal life.

God forbade Adam and Eve to eat of the tree of the knowledge of good and evil, but Genesis chapter 3 tells us that after Eve ate of the forbidden fruit, Adam willfully partook of it along with his wife. According to Genesis 3:7, the moment they ate of that fruit, "...the eyes of them both were opened, and they knew that they were naked; and they sewed fig leaves together, and made themselves aprons."

Genesis 3:8-11 reveals what happened later:

"And they heard the voice of the Lord God walking in the garden in the cool of the day: and Adam and his wife hid themselves from the presence of the Lord God amongst the trees of the garden. And the Lord God called unto Adam, and said unto him, Where art thou? And he said, I heard thy voice in the garden, and I was afraid because I was naked; and I hid myself. And he [God] said, Who told thee that thou wast naked? Hast thou eaten of the tree, whereof I commanded thee that thou shouldest not eat?"

When Adam and Eve disobeyed and ate of that tree, the glory that once adorned them disappeared (*see* Romans 3:23), and they felt utter *shame* — one of the primary fruits of sin. As fallen man always attempts to do, the first man and woman tried to conceal what they had done by covering themselves with aprons made of fig leaves. Ever since that time, lost human beings have been trying to conceal their sin with excuses for their behavior or with good works or religious activities; however, spiritual nakedness is impossible to conceal from the eyes of a holy God.

When God confronted Adam and Eve, they had the opportunity to live up to their sinful failure. But Adam failed to accept responsibility, attempting instead to shift the blame for their disobedience to Eve. Then Eve tried to shift the blame to the serpent for beguiling her (*see* Genesis 3:12,13). Thus, Adam and Eve played the first "blame game" as they both ardently tried to convince God that someone other than themselves should be blamed for their own personal failures. With this first act of disobedience, blameshifting was introduced to the human race as one of the earliest symptoms of sin, and it has remained one of sin's chief characteristics ever since the inexcusable failure that occurred in the Garden of Eden.

If Adam and Eve had eaten from the tree of life after partaking of fruit from the tree of the knowledge of good and evil, they would have been condemned to live eternally in a fallen state. It was for this reason that God mercifully placed cherubim at the entrance of the eastern gate to prohibit them from returning to the enclosure inside the Garden of Eden. God was so committed to keeping Adam and Eve away from the tree of life that He "…drove out the man; and he placed at the east of the garden of Eden Cherubims, and a flaming sword which turned every way, to keep the way of the tree of life" (Genesis 3:24).

It is interesting that God "drove" Adam and Eve from the Garden of Eden. The Hebrew word suggests Adam and Eve didn't want to leave the protection of the Garden and therefore had to be "driven" out by God. It seems likely that

Right: This Gustave Doré illustration depicts one of the cherubim driving out Adam and Eve from the earthly paradise God had created for man. This act of divine mercy kept Adam and Even from partaking of the tree of life after falling into sin — which would have rendered the redemption of mankind impossible, condemning every person born on this earth to live in a fallen state for all eternity.

the Garden of Eden was originally located in what is modern-day northwestern Iran, a geological region that was surrounded with mountains on the north, south, and east, which protected its exquisite, garden-like environment.

Genesis 3:24 also states that when God drove Adam and Eve out of the Garden, He "...placed at the east of the garden of Eden *Cherubims*...." The word "cherubim" refers to an especially powerful category of angels who are strangely and vividly described in Ezekiel 10:3-22. This text states that cherubim have wings and hands; they are full of eyes; they have wheels within wheels; and they can freely move about in any and every direction. Imagining the power and magnificence of these creatures is difficult for our finite minds; however, we know that they are closely associated with the glory of God. Both Psalm 80:1 and Psalm 99:1 state that God dwells between the cherubim. These "cherubim" are the angelic beings God positioned at the eastern gate of Eden to prohibit Adam and Eve from returning and eating of the tree of life (Genesis 3:24).

Left: This 1828 painting, entitled, "Expulsion From the Garden of Eden," by Thomas Cole depicts the contrast between the glory of the Garden that Adam and Eve had to leave behind and the unfamiliar, darker, world that would be their new home. For several thousand years, man would wait for a Savior to come and redeem him from sin, restoring him to the "paradise" of renewed fellowship with God.

recorded in ancient hymns and service books.

In Revelation 2:7, Jesus was speaking to the church of Ephesus, a local body of believers who had already partaken of the life offered through the Cross of Christ. Yet Jesus promised those who *overcame* that He would allow them to eat of the tree of life, "...which is in the midst of the paradise of God" (Revelation 2:7). What could this have possibly meant to these early Christians living in Ephesus, as well as to believers throughout all time?

'WHICH IS IN THE MIDST OF THE PARADISE OF GOD'

As Jesus concluded His message to the church of Ephesus, He declared, "He that hath an ear, let him hear what the Spirit saith unto the churches; To him that overcometh will I give to eat of the tree of life, *which is in the midst of the paradise of God*" (Revelation 2:7).

The Christian view of the "tree of life" has been interpreted in different ways over the centuries. However, historical evidence suggests that leaders in the Eastern Church — the region where these seven ancient churches were located — primarily taught that God set the "tree of life" in the Garden at the beginning of time to foretell the Cross. On that rugged Cross, Jesus' willing sacrifice would provide eternal life for those who partook of God's redemptive plan by faith. In this sense, the Cross of Christ was the ultimate "tree of life" — a belief that was even

The word "paradise" is actually from an ancient Persian word depicting *a garden inside a walled enclosure*. In Hebrew, it is the word *pardes*, which appears in Nehemiah 2:8, Song of Solomon 4:13, and Ecclesiastes 2:5. In each of these scriptures, the word denotes *a pleasure park*, *a garden*, or *an orchard*. In Greek, it is the word *paradeisos*, which is translated "garden" and is the precise word used in the Old Testament Greek Septuagint to describe *the Garden of Eden*.

As the definition of this word translated "paradise" evolved through history, it retained its basic meaning of *a walled estate* or *a royal park carefully concealed behind walls*. It depicted *lush gardens* that lay at the interior of a palace or at the heart of a citadel where royalty resided. Even at the time of John's Revelation, this word translated "paradise" meant *a luxuriant garden at the heart of a palace or royal residence, surrounded by walls to provide privacy and security to those who are within*.

It also cannot be overlooked that on the outskirts of Ephesus was the massive Temple of Artemis, an architectural wonder so magnificent that it was considered one of the Seven Wonders of the World. This complex was surrounded with walls that provided privacy, security, and protection. Its interior grounds included lush gardens with a wide variety of beautiful trees, plants, and animals. Technically, the temple was considered a place of refuge insomuch that those who fled behind the walls of this complex were guaranteed protection as long as they remained inside the temple grounds. For instance, Cleopatra's sister, Arsinoe, fled to the Temple of Artemis at Ephesus for refuge when she discovered her famous sister was planning her death. Arsinoe remained behind the walls of the compound for approximately two years, waiting for the threat to cease. However, in the end, the protection guaranteed to those who sought refuge there didn't save Arsinoe from her sister's deadly plot.[27]

Some scholars conjecture that when Jesus spoke of "paradise" to the church of Ephesus, He used this imagery because it was especially fitting to the people of this city. Since the Ephesian believers lived near this grandiose facility that had such a lush interior park concealed behind walls (a "paradise"), it is possible that the use of this word had a special meaning for the Ephesian congregation. They understood precisely what a "paradise" was because one was located just outside the outskirts of the city.

At a time when Christians were suffering severe persecution, this imagery must have provoked a strong reaction in them. They were facing intense pressures within their society, including the onslaught of a hostile Roman government. Therefore, the prospect of escaping to a place of refuge and protection must have been a very real invitation to "paradise." Jesus Christ, who rules as the King of kings and Lord of lords, invites those who overcome to join Him in His own private quarters.

These believers had already partaken of the eternal life offered in "the tree of

Right: The Cross was the ultimate "tree of life." Through the Cross, Jesus made a way for all who believed in Him to enjoy paradise restored — partaking of intimate fellowship with the Savior in this life and for all eternity.

life" — the Cross of Christ. Now they were invited to walk intimately with the King and to continuously partake of the spiritual sustenance He had made available to them. Certainly this was a promise of reward in the life to come. However, at a time when the believers were suffering so severely, it was also a promise of divine nourishment in the present moment.

The concept of a safe refuge inside a concealed environment was a very important one to these early Christians. To be offered safety and protection in the life to come and divine sustenance in their present circumstances would have been a great encouragement for believers who were suffering the loss of their possessions and severe persecution.

When Adam and Eve failed, they were ejected from the Garden of Eden, and cherubim blocked them from returning to that place of safety and provision. But in Christ, the way to God and to His blessings are restored. The cherubim who once blocked the entrance to the tree of life in the Garden have been removed, and the way has been restored for us to return to Christ and to partake of forgiveness and redemption in all of its aspects. Instead of prohibiting us from entering this holy place, Christ beckons us to come and dwell in this private and secure refuge at the heart of His Kingdom.

Christ concluded His message to the church of Ephesus by extending this invitation of comfort and hope. That same divine invitation is also offered to every one of us who accept His challenge to overcome and to keep our fiery passion for Him burning brightly. Jesus calls us to join Him in His private quarters and to stroll with Him in the cool of the day, just as He once did with Adam and Eve in the Garden of Eden. *This is the promise of paradise restored.*

JESUS' MESSAGE
TO THE CHURCH OF EPHESUS:
SYNOPSIS

In Jesus' message to the church of Ephesus, He commended the believers by acknowledging their strengths (Revelation 2:2,3), but then He followed with a stern reproach: *"Nevertheless, I have somewhat against thee..."* (v. 4). Within the context of this recognition and rebuke, Christ revealed beliefs and behaviors He hates and then stated what is required for His people to receive the reward reserved for those who overcome.

PRIMARY TRUTHS

- Jesus commends devoted service, sound doctrine, endurance, and the disdain of compromise. He demands repentance, however, when His people fall away from the passionate pursuit of a vibrant relationship with Him.

- The pastor is the *angelos,* or the *messenger,* of the local church. He is the one to whom Christ gives direction for the local church and the one from whom He requires stringent accountability. The pastor is called to provide instruction in sound doctrine and to demonstrate a godly lifestyle of consecration that shuns the pollution of worldly affections. Refusal to follow divine direction or to teach and live according to Jesus' instruction will result in judgment.

- Past influence, no matter how far-reaching or enduring, does not assure that a church will maintain God-ordained favor and significance in the future. Refusal to stay in step with the Savior is grounds for one's role to be transferred to another.

- Those who seek their own honor by falsely promoting themselves to be what they are not — such as "false apostles," who claim an authority they don't possess — must not be tolerated. Their deceitfulness is to be exposed, lest they exploit believers and bring many into bondage with their abhorrent tactics and unscriptural revelations designed to detract Christ's followers from a true faith in God.

PRACTICAL APPLICATIONS

- It is entirely possible to lead a large, thriving ministry and yet be backslidden and no longer enraptured with the Lord. Spiritual backsliding occurs when believers lose their focus on Jesus and become preoccupied with other things — including the work of the ministry. A loss of joy in service indicates a lack of intimacy with the Savior and a dire need to return to the fervor of love and heartfelt devotion they experienced when they first repented and yielded to Jesus Christ as Savior and Lord.

- Repentance is more than remorse or regret, which focuses on how a person appears before others as a result of the consequences of his actions. True repentance is focused on the condition of a person's heart in light of the standard and expectation of a holy God.

- People can feel remorse or deep regret without any intention of or action toward change. To repent, however, is to completely change one's position in order to enter into agreement and to align oneself with God. Remorse alone is a feeling based on external circumstances. Repentance is based on an internal choice to hear, receive, and respond to the truth, which in turn leads to a life change that is pleasing to God. Refusal to repent when repentance is required results in a removal of stature in God's eyes. One dare not confuse the praise of man with the approval of God. That is a costly mistake with eternal consequences.

- Tolerance of sin and compromise with ungodly practices drains away and diminishes the power of God working in a believer's life. Doctrines and deeds that indulge sin lower godly standards. Jesus hates such deeds and doctrines because they contend against the work of redemption, ratified by His own blood, and result in a weakened and powerless form of Christianity.

THE CHURCH OF EPHESUS

The church of Ephesus held notable significance in the development of the Early Church. Founded by the apostle Paul as a result of his ministry partnership with Aquila and Priscilla, the Ephesian church wielded tremendous influence in shaping both doctrine and governance in the churches throughout Asia. Consequently, many who aspired to unmerited positions of authority often targeted this church in order to propagate their false doctrines. They knew that if their teaching or ministry gained acceptance in Ephesus, it would secure a position of strength and rapidly spread elsewhere.

The spiritual leadership in the church of Ephesus were known for their rigorous adherence to the doctrine Paul preached, having acknowledged and honored his authentic, earned apostolic leadership over their church. Believers in this church were reputed to be committed to the work of the ministry and completely intolerant of false doctrine, particularly that of the Nicolaitans who promoted spiritual compromise.

The city of Ephesus was referred to as "The Light of Asia" due to its intellectual and cultural sophistication. The pagan population was already accustomed to "glory seekers" pursuing distinction or notoriety. Therefore, when so-called "apostles" sought to infiltrate the church and gain notoriety for their own unscrupulous motives, the Ephesian congregation was quick to scrutinize and stop such false workers, who were a continual irritant to the valid work of the apostle Paul.

CHRIST'S COMMENDATION AND CORRECTION TO THE CHURCH OF EPHESUS

Christ's message to the leadership and members of the church at Ephesus began with a commendation. Stating that He was well acquainted with their works, Jesus' words resounded with approval as He cited the strength of their beliefs and behavior: They were hardworking; they remained patient and endured without fainting, despite persecution; and they were intolerant of false apostles and lying, evil workers. However, when Jesus stated, "Nevertheless, I have somewhat against thee…," it was clear that He reserved His weightiest statement for last: "…Thou hast left thy first love." The seriousness of this violation exposed a breach in the Ephesian congregation so serious that Jesus said, "I have this against you" — meaning their hardness of heart was personally disturbing to Him.

Years of Christian service can so consume the minds and strength of believers that through the passage of time, they can forget the great work of grace that gave them new life. The ongoing, unrelenting work of ministry can reduce what was once fresh and fervent into monotonous, religious routine. Memories of coming to Christ become buried beneath an overgrowth of religious activity until spiritual weeds choke out the gratitude and joy that were once the hallmark of a passionate intimacy with Christ.

Despite its veritable roster of high-profile Christians and an impressive list of accomplishments to its credit, the church of Ephesus was "fallen" in Jesus' eyes. Unintentionally, the believers had drifted from their once-characteristic fire and zeal for the Lord. Sophisticated and impressive in size, influence, and governance, this congregation needed to dig deep to remember from whence they had fallen and repent in order to regain God's approval and retain their stature before Him.

This illustrious church had been the dominant "candle-stick," or influence of light, to the region. Yet its candle-stick would be removed and its influence made void by the Head of the Church Himself if proper priorities were not reestablished. Thus, Jesus' call for this church to repent was issued to prevent the judgment that would assuredly come if they did not — the loss both of favorable stature before God and influence before man.

WHAT THE SPIRIT IS SAYING TO THE CHURCH TODAY

1. Test apostleship according to scriptural criteria.

2. Abhor doctrines that encourage believers to embrace the pollution of unclean or occultist practices and worldly ways.

3. Acknowledge when one is backslidden and out of fellowship with the Lord. To identify the cause: Remember from whence one has fallen, repent, and then return by doing again the first works. Such a return will be evidenced by spiritual hunger for the Word and the presence of God, rich fellowship among the brethren, eagerness to turn from sin, and willingness to sever from an ungodly past, regardless of pain or persecution.

4. God's approval is to be prized far above man's applause.

5. A sure reward awaits those who choose to endure, remain faithful, and overcome the temptation to compromise their standards in order to conform to the world.

He that hath an ear, let him hear
what the Spirit saith unto the churches.
— Revelation 2:29

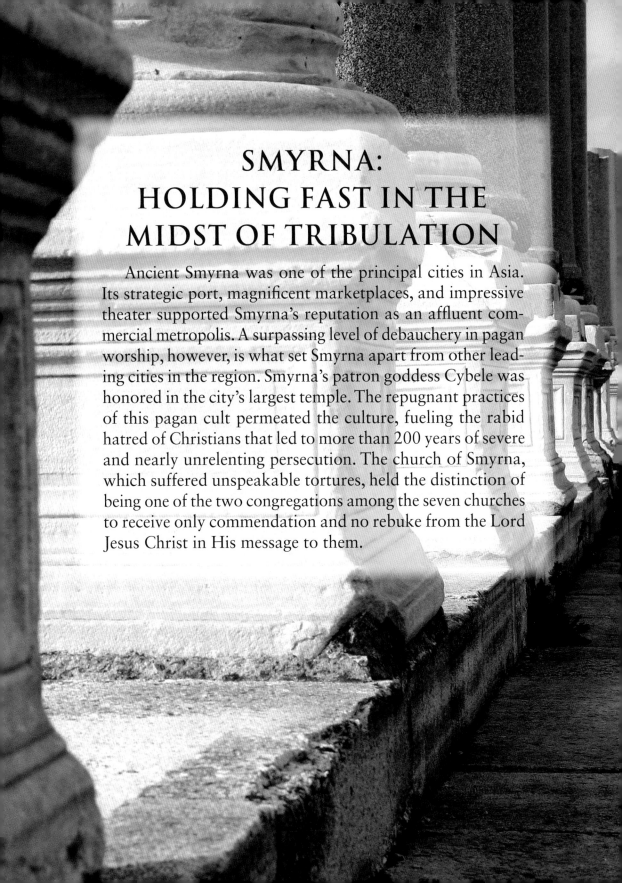

SMYRNA:
HOLDING FAST IN THE
MIDST OF TRIBULATION

Ancient Smyrna was one of the principal cities in Asia. Its strategic port, magnificent marketplaces, and impressive theater supported Smyrna's reputation as an affluent commercial metropolis. A surpassing level of debauchery in pagan worship, however, is what set Smyrna apart from other leading cities in the region. Smyrna's patron goddess Cybele was honored in the city's largest temple. The repugnant practices of this pagan cult permeated the culture, fueling the rabid hatred of Christians that led to more than 200 years of severe and nearly unrelenting persecution. The church of Smyrna, which suffered unspeakable tortures, held the distinction of being one of the two congregations among the seven churches to receive only commendation and no rebuke from the Lord Jesus Christ in His message to them.

Chapter Six

THE CITY OF SMYRNA

First Century Smyrna buzzed with activity as scores of ships arrived every week at its large port. ❶ With roads leading to many other parts of Asia, this ancient seaport was a strategic commercial center, similar to Ephesus' port in many ways. However, the flourishing city of Smyrna that existed during the First Century as the Church was being established was not the original settlement. Rather, it was a newer version rebuilt near a site where a far more ancient metropolis had once stood.

Today it is known that the earliest settlements of Smyrna date back thousands of years. However, its first recorded appearance in history was in the year 688 BC when immigrants from Ionia relocated to the nearby ancient city.[1] After a series of clashes with local authorities, the newly arrived Ionians prevailed and the ruling powers of Smyrna collapsed. Soon after the city fell into the hands of the Ionians, they began to transform it into a glorious city-state of Ionia that boasted a marvelous harbor and an enormous marketplace. Its buildings were decked with stunning marble ornamentations, and pagan temples were scattered throughout every quarter of the city, including the Temple of Athena, ❷ which dated to the Seventh Century BC.[2]

Later in the restored version of ancient Smyrna, the huge Temple of Zeus paled in comparison to the city's largest and most important temple, the Temple of Cybele.[3] Today the Turkish city of Izmir is built directly on the ruins of ancient Smyrna, and these colossal structures are buried deep under modern high-rise buildings. But thousands of years ago, these massive temples were filled with pagan worshipers, fervently committed to their pagan beliefs.

Smyrneans were such devout pagans that it was they — not the Roman government — who eventually instigated persecution against Christians in the First Century. In author Will Durant's book, *The Story*

Left: Massive columns adorned the sides of the Central Marketplace that was constructed in the Second Century in the ancient city of Smyrna. The market ruins pictured here were built on top of an earlier Hellenistic market that some scholars estimate was comprised of more than 400 shops.

of Civilization: Caesar and Christ, he writes: "The opposition to the new religion [Christianity] came rather from the people than from the state. The magistrates were often men of culture and tolerance; but the mass of the pagan population resented the aloofness, superiority, and certainty of the Christians, and called upon the authorities to punish these 'atheists' for insulting the gods...."[4]

Another source of opposition was the large Jewish population of Smyrna. Many Jews resented the new Christian sect and therefore tried to stir up trouble by pinning blame on Christians for every misfortune or calamity that happened. The rage of the Smyrnean population grew to a frenzy by the Second Century — and in approximately 155 AD, the people demanded the death of Polycarp, the bishop of Smyrna. At the age of 86, the elderly Polycarp was led into the Stadium of Smyrna after much cruel treatment, where he died a brave and glorious martyr's death.[5]

All the ancient major cities of Asia were renowned for paganism and occult activities. Ephesus teemed with countless pagan gods and religions but was primarily dominated by the worship of Artemis in the huge Temple of Artemis, located on the outskirts of the city. Pergamum looked like a giant altar rising into the sky, with the smoke of sacrifices swirling into the air above the acropolis every day of the year. This capital city of Asia was especially influenced by the worship of Asklepios and hosted one of the largest Asklepions in the ancient world just outside its perimeters.

Smyrna was no different, for it served as host to one of the world's most foul and vile religions — *the worship of the goddess Cybele*. Just as Ephesus and Pergamum had massive temple complexes beyond their borders, Smyrna did as well. One of the largest religious complexes was built in honor of Cybele outside the main district of Smyrna. And although the beauty of Smyrna's marble structures gleamed brightly in the light of the sun, a dark and ominous spiritual atmosphere hovered over this city — silent testimony to the pervasive, evil influence of Cybele worship.

Then the Gospel arrived in Smyrna, possibly carried there by messengers from Ephesus or perhaps even by the apostle Paul himself. The powers of darkness had held the city captive for centuries, yet darkness quickly began to surrender to the light as the Church of Jesus Christ was established in the power of the Holy Spirit.

(Continued on page 510)

POLYCARP:
SMYRNA'S MOST FAMOUS MARTYR

Throughout the ages, periods of persecution have always arisen against the Church of Jesus Christ. Millions of believers have suffered and endured persecution, and many chose to lay down their lives as martyrs rather than to deny their faith in Christ. These men and women are all remembered as *heroes* of the faith.

The first massive persecution against believers in Jesus Christ occurred during the rule of the Emperor Nero (54-68 AD). An even worse period of persecution later transpired during the reign of the Emperor Domitian (81-96 AD), but this certainly wasn't the end. Since the birth of Christianity more than 2,000 years ago, many

Above: Although Rome was tolerant of most religious ideas, Christians were fiercely persecuted after they were blamed for the Great Fire of Rome in 64 AD. Because they wouldn't recognize the emperor as a god and refused to offer sacrifices and incense in imperial temples, they were looked upon as rebels and as the refuse of the world. This painting illustrates believers huddled together as they prepare to meet death by being mauled and devoured by lions. Many Christians were killed in the Stadium of Smyrna, including Polycarp, the famous bishop of Smyrna.

dictators and evil regimes have tried unsuccessfully to eradicate the glorious light of the Gospel and eliminate the Church (*See* pages 633-651 for an excerpt from *Foxe's Book of Martyrs* on the ten Roman Emperors who were some of history's worst persecutors of believers.) The fact that the Church still remains is itself sufficient proof that the Gospel is a light that cannot be extinguished by demonized leaders and governments.

Persecution was very serious in the First Century. In fact, most New Testament scholars agree that when the writer of Hebrews wrote Hebrews 11:35-38, he ceased to speak of Old Testament saints and switched to the subject of early Christian martyrs. The following words from that passage perfectly describe the difficult plight of believers in the second half of the First Century:

> "...And others were tortured, not accepting deliverance; that they might obtain a better resurrection: and others had trial of cruel mockings and scourgings, yea, moreover of bonds and of imprisonment: they were stoned, they were sawn asunder, were tempted, were slain with the sword: they wandered about in sheepskins and goatskins; being destitute, afflicted, tormented.... They wandered in deserts, and in mountains, and in dens and caves of the earth."

The faithfulness of those who lost their lives because of their courageous stance for Christ will never be forgotten. Although they surely received a martyr's crown for their steadfast witness unto death, most of their names are known only to God except for a few famous cases.

One of the most documented and famous of martyrs from early Christian history is *Polycarp*, who served as bishop of the church at Smyrna in the Second Century. As is true with all early accounts, there is some question as to the exact time of Polycarp's birth. It seems that the likely date is approximately 69 AD — not long after Paul and Peter were martyred in Rome at the order of the Emperor Nero. The exact place of Polycarp's birth is also unknown, but records indicate he was born into a pagan home.

Early tradition states that a wealthy Christian woman by the name of Callistro had a dream in which she was instructed to go to the Ephesian Gate, a gate in Smyrna through which travelers passed as they journeyed to the city of Ephesus. In the dream, Callistro was told she would find a young slave boy at the gate and that she was to redeem him out of slavery. According to tradition, Callistro did as instructed in her dream and found the young slave boy, whose name was *Polycarp*. She purchased the young slave and brought him into her own home, instructing Polycarp in the Christian faith and eventually adopting and raising him as her own legal son.[6]

Early Christian writings state that even at a young age, Polycarp demonstrated a tender heart toward the Spirit of God. He was kind, considerate of others, serious, steadfast in his witness, and intensely committed to the study of the Scriptures.[7] Polycarp's life made an impact on so many that it even drew the attention of the elderly apostle John, who lived 35 miles south of Smyrna, near the city of Ephesus.

Most sources state that the apostle John permanently relocated to Ephesus in the year 67 AD — just two years before Polycarp was most likely born — placing John at an age of approximately 70. At some point before John's death (in approximately 100 AD), he and Polycarp became acquainted with each other and formed a friendship that lasted nearly 20 years. Polycarp's connection to John was recorded by Irenaeus, the bishop of Lyons, who personally knew Polycarp.[8] This means Polycarp was one of the last close contacts with the only surviving original apostle. Polycarp's unique relationship with the apostle John gave the younger man status and importance in the eyes of the Early Church in Asia.

According to tradition, Polycarp first served as a deacon, ministering to the poor and needy people of Smyrna. But when the pastor of the Smyrnean church died, it was a logical choice for Polycarp to be promoted to this vacant position. His many years of intensive study of Scripture had prepared Polycarp to be pastor of this church — a role so important that eventually Polycarp was viewed as bishop to all the churches in the region of Smyrna.

A very old tradition, dating to the Second Century, alleges that Polycarp was ordained to these positions by the apostle John himself. Other early documents show that a bishop of Antioch named Ignatius passed through the city of Smyrna on his way to Rome, where he eventually suffered martyrdom. On his way to Rome, Ignatius stopped in Smyrna to spend time with Polycarp. These ancient sources make it clear that Ignatius and Polycarp were friends and that both of them had known and studied at the feet of the apostle John.[9]

Many apostles passed through Smyrna and ministered there. Polycarp, however, occupies a unique and important place in the history of the Christian Church because he lived and ministered both during and immediately after the age of the apostles. Furthermore, Polycarp's writings are among the earliest Christians writings to survive — namely, his *Epistle to the Philippians* (not to be confused with the New Testament book of Philippians).

But after serving the Lord for most of his life and giving his life selflessly to minister to others, Polycarp was hauled into the Great Stadium of Smyrna, where he died a martyr's death. Although he was respected by many in the community, the significantly large Jewish population of Smyrna resented the new Christian sect and constantly attempted to stir up trouble for Polycarp and for anyone else who claimed to be a member of that group. To turn public opinion against believers, the Smyrnean Jews blamed everything on them — including bad weather, earthquakes, floods, pestilence, and drought. The Jewish community even pointed an accusing finger at Christians because they firmly refused to worship the emperor — even though Jewish law forbade Jews from engaging in idol worship as well!

At the age of 86, Polycarp was attending to the needs of his church when a brazen period of horrific persecution broke out, instigated by the Jewish community of Smyrna and carried out by the frenzied pagan population. During this period of attacks, Christians were dragged into the Great Stadium of Smyrna and fed to wild animals as local citizens cheered with glee. But this didn't satisfy the blood-thirst of the masses, who shouted for the blood of more Christians. As the crowd continued to roar, someone called out for Polycarp to be arrested and killed.

Because Polycarp was deeply loved, leaders from the church of Smyrna pleaded with him to go into hiding to avoid capture by the pagan authorities. At his friends' urging, Polycarp hid in a local farmhouse outside the city and then moved from place to place to conceal his location. However, the police tortured a servant until he finally broke under pressure and revealed Polycarp's secret location.

When the police went to Polycarp's temporary residence to arrest him, the elderly bishop met them at the gate, welcomed them into his hiding place, and offered them food and drink before he surrendered himself to them. After being arrested, he was transported to the massive Stadium of Smyrna, where throngs of people rejoiced that he had been captured. After brutal treatment, Polycarp was put to death. However, this godly man suffered death so gloriously that the story of his martyrdom is one of the most famous accounts of Christian martyrdom ever told.

Early Church historian Eusebius recorded that Polycarp died between 166-167 AD during the reign of the Emperor Marcus Aurelius.[10] Jerome also wrote that Polycarp died during the reign of this emperor.[11] However, other early sources indicate that Polycarp was killed during the time of the proconsul Statius Quadratus. This would place the death of this bishop of Smyrna in 155 or 156 AD.[12]

This latter version is asserted in *The Epistle of the Smyrneans*, a Second Century epistle in which Polycarp's martyrdom is powerfully recorded. The full text of this ancient epistle is included on the following pages.

THE EPISTLE OF THE SMYRNEANS

Translated by J. B. Lightfoot

Prologue: The church of God which sojourneth at Smyrna to the Church of God which sojourneth in Philomelium and to all the brotherhoods of the holy and universal Church sojourning in every place; mercy and peace and love from God the Father and our Lord Jesus Christ be multiplied.

Polycarp 1:1 We write unto you, brethren, an account of what befell those that suffered martyrdom and especially the blessed Polycarp, who stayed the persecution, having as it were set his seal upon it by his martyrdom. For nearly all the foregoing events came to pass that the Lord might show us once more an example of martyrdom which is conformable to the Gospel.

Polycarp 1:2 For he lingered that he might be delivered up, even as the Lord did, to the end that we too might be imitators of him, not looking only to that which concerneth ourselves, but also to that which concerneth our neighbors. For it is the office of true and steadfast love, not only to desire that oneself be saved, but all the brethren also.

Polycarp 2:1 Blessed therefore and noble are all the martyrdoms which have taken place according to the will of God (for it behoveth us to be very scrupulous and to assign to God the power over all things).

Polycarp 2:2 For who could fail to admire their nobleness and patient endurance and loyalty to the Master? Seeing that when they were so torn by lashes that the mechanism of their flesh was visible even as far as the inward veins and arteries, they endured patiently, so that the very bystanders had pity and wept; while they themselves reached such a pitch of bravery that none of them uttered a cry or a groan, thus showing to us all that at that hour the martyrs of Christ being tortured were absent from the flesh, or rather that the Lord was standing by and conversing with them.

Polycarp 2:3 And giving heed unto the grace of Christ they despised the tortures of this world, purchasing at the cost of one hour a release from eternal punishment. And they found the fire of their inhuman torturers cold: for they set before their eyes the escape from the eternal fire which is never quenched; while with the eyes of their heart they gazed upon the good things which are reserved for those that endure patiently, things which neither ear hath heard nor eye hath seen, neither have they entered into the heart of man, but were shown by the Lord to them, for they were no longer men but angels already.

Polycarp 2:4 And in like manner also those that were condemned to the wild beasts endured fearful punishments, being made to lie on sharp shells and buffeted with other forms of manifold tortures, that the devil might, if possible, by the persistence of the punishment bring them to a denial; for he tried many wiles against them.

Polycarp 3:1 But thanks be to God; for He verily prevailed against all. For the right noble Germanicus encouraged their timorousness through the constancy which was in him; and he fought with the wild beasts in a signal way. For when the proconsul wished to prevail upon him and bade him have pity on his youth, he used violence and dragged the wild beast towards him, desiring the more speedily to obtain a release from their unrighteous and lawless life.

Polycarp 3:2 So after this all the multitude, marveling at the bravery of the God-beloved and God-fearing people of the Christians, raised a cry, "Away with the atheists; let search be made for Polycarp."

Polycarp 4:1 But one man, Quintus by name, a Phrygian newly arrived from Phrygia, when he saw the wild beasts, turned coward. He it was who had forced himself and some others to come forward of their own free will. This man the proconsul by much entreaty persuaded to swear the oath and to offer incense. For this cause therefore, brethren, we praise not those who deliver themselves up, since the Gospel doth not so teach us.

Polycarp 5:1 Now the glorious Polycarp at the first, when he heard it, so far from being dismayed, was desirous of remaining in town; but the greater part persuaded him to withdraw. So he withdrew to a farm not far distant from the city; and there he stayed with a few companions, doing nothing else night and day but praying for all men and for the churches throughout the world; for this was his constant habit.

Polycarp 5:2 And while praying he falleth into a trance three days before his apprehension; and he saw his pillow burning with fire. And he turned and said unto those that were with him: "It must needs be that I shall be burned alive."

Polycarp 6:1 And as those that were in search of him persisted, he departed to another farm; and forthwith they that were in search of him came up; and not finding him, they seized two slave lads, one of whom confessed under torture;

Polycarp 6:2 for it was impossible for him to lie concealed, seeing that the very persons who betrayed him were people of his own household. And the captain of the police, who chanced to have the very name, being called Herod, was eager to bring him into the stadium, that he himself might fulfill his appointed lot, being made a partaker with Christ, while they — his betrayers — underwent the punishment of Judas himself.

Polycarp 7:1 So taking the lad with them, on the Friday about the supper hour, the gendarmes and horsemen went forth with their accustomed arms, hastening as against a robber. And coming up in a body late in the evening, they found the man himself in bed in an upper chamber in a certain cottage; and though he might have departed thence to another place, he would not, saying, "The will of God be done."

Polycarp 7:2 So when he heard that they were come, he went down and conversed with them, the bystanders marveling at his age and his constancy, and wondering how there should be so much eagerness for the apprehension of an old man like him. Thereupon forthwith he gave orders that a table should be spread for them to eat and drink at that hour, as much as they desired. And he persuaded them to grant him an hour that he might pray unmolested;

Polycarp 7:3 and on their consenting, he stood up and prayed, being so full of the grace of God, that for two hours he could not hold his peace, and those that heard were amazed, and many repented that they had come against such a venerable old man.

Polycarp 8:1 But when at length he brought his prayer to an end, after remembering all who at any time had come in his way, small and great, high and low, and all the universal Church throughout the world, the hour of departure being come, they seated him on an ass and brought him into the city, it being a high Sabbath.

Polycarp 8:2 And he was met by Herod the captain of police and his father Nicetes, who also removed him to their carriage and tried to prevail upon him, seating themselves by his side and saying, "Why what harm is there in saying, Caesar is Lord, and offering incense," with more to this effect, "and saving thyself?" But he at first gave them no answer. When however they persisted, he said, "I am not going to do what ye counsel me."

Polycarp 8:3 Then they, failing to persuade him, uttered threatening words and made him dismount with speed, so that he bruised his shin, as he got down from the carriage. And without even turning round, he went on his way promptly and with speed, as if nothing had happened to him, being taken to the stadium; there being such a tumult in the stadium that no man's voice could be so much as heard.

Polycarp 9:1 But as Polycarp entered into the stadium, a voice came to him from heaven: "Be strong, Polycarp, and play the man." And no one saw the speaker, but those of our people who were present heard the voice. And at length, when he was brought up, there was a great tumult, for they heard that Polycarp had been apprehended.

Polycarp 9:2 When then he was brought before him, the proconsul inquired whether he were the man. And on his confessing that he was, he tried to persuade him to a denial saying, "Have respect to thine age," and other things in accordance therewith, as it is their wont to say, "Swear by the genius of Caesar; repent and say, Away with the atheists." Then Polycarp with solemn countenance looked upon the whole multitude of lawless heathen that were in the stadium, and waved his hand to them; and groaning and looking up to heaven he said, "Away with the atheists."

Polycarp 9:3 But when the magistrate pressed him hard and said, "Swear the oath, and I will release thee; revile the Christ," Polycarp said, "Fourscore and six years have I been His servant, and He hath done me no wrong. How then can I blaspheme my King who saved me?"

Polycarp 10:1 But on his persisting again and saying, "Swear by the genius of Caesar," he answered, "If thou supposest verily that I will swear by the genius of Caesar, as thou sayest, and feignest that thou art ignorant who I am, hear thou plainly, I am a Christian. But if thou wouldest learn the doctrine of Christianity, assign a day and give me a hearing."

Polycarp 10:2 The proconsul said, "Prevail upon the people." But Polycarp said, "As for thyself, I should have held thee worthy of discourse; for we have been taught to render, as is meet, to princes and authorities appointed by God such honor as does us no harm; but as for these, I do not hold them worthy, that I should defend myself before them."

Polycarp 11:1 Whereupon the proconsul said, "I have wild beasts here and I will throw thee to them, except thou repent." But he said, "Call for them: for the repentance from better to worse is a change not permitted to us; but it is a noble thing to change from untowardness to righteousness."

Polycarp 11:2 Then he said to him again, "I will cause thee to be consumed by fire, if thou despisest the wild beasts, unless thou repent." But Polycarp said, "Thou threatenest that fire which burneth for a season and after a little while is quenched: for thou art ignorant of the fire of the future judgment and eternal punishment, which is reserved for the ungodly. But why delayest thou? Come, do what thou wilt."

Polycarp 12:1 Saying these things and more besides, he was inspired with courage and joy, and his countenance was filled with grace, so that not only did it not drop in dismay at the things which were said to him, but on the contrary the proconsul was astounded and sent his own herald to proclaim three times in the midst of the stadium, "Polycarp hath confessed himself to be a Christian."

Polycarp 12:2 When this was proclaimed by the herald, the whole multitude both of Gentiles and of Jews who dwelt in Smyrna cried out with ungovernable wrath and with a loud shout, "This is the teacher of Asia, the father of the Christians, the puller down of our gods, who teacheth numbers not to sacrifice nor worship." Saying these things, they shouted aloud and asked the Asiarch Philip to let a lion loose upon Polycarp. But he said that it was not lawful for him, since he had brought the sports to a close.

Polycarp 12:3 Then they thought fit to shout out with one accord that Polycarp should be burned alive. For it must needs be that the matter of the vision should be fulfilled, which was shown him concerning his pillow, when he saw it on fire while praying, and turning round he said prophetically to the faithful who were with him, "I must needs be burned alive."

Polycarp 13:1 These things then happened with so great speed, quicker than words could tell, the crowds forthwith collecting from the workshops and baths timber and faggots, and the Jews more especially assisting in this with zeal, as is their wont.

Polycarp 13:2 But when the pile was made ready, divesting himself of all his upper garments and loosing his girdle, he endeavored also to take off his shoes, though not in the habit of doing this before, because all the faithful at all times vied eagerly who should soonest touch his flesh. For he had been treated with all honor for his holy life even before his gray hairs came.

Polycarp 13:3 Forthwith then the instruments that were prepared for the pile were placed about him; and as they were going likewise to nail him to the stake, he said, "Leave me as I am; for He that hath granted me to endure the fire will grant me also to remain at the pile unmoved, even without the security which ye seek from the nails."

Polycarp 14:1 So they did not nail him, but tied him. Then he, placing his hands behind him and being bound to the stake, like a noble ram out of a great flock for an offering, a burnt sacrifice made ready and acceptable to God, looking up to heaven said, "O Lord God Almighty, the Father of Thy beloved and blessed Son Jesus Christ, through whom we have received the knowledge of Thee, the God of angels and powers and of all creation and of the whole race of the righteous, who live in Thy presence;

Polycarp 14:2 I bless Thee for that Thou hast granted me this day and hour, that I might receive a portion amongst the number of martyrs in the cup of [Thy] Christ unto resurrection of eternal life, both of soul and of body, in the incorruptibility of the Holy Spirit. May I be received among these in Thy presence this day, as a rich and acceptable sacrifice, as Thou didst prepare and reveal it beforehand, and hast accomplished it, Thou that art the faithful and true God.

Polycarp 14:3 For this cause, yea and for all things, I praise Thee, I bless Thee, I glorify Thee, through the eternal and heavenly High-priest, Jesus Christ, Thy beloved Son, through whom with Him and the Holy Spirit be glory both now [and ever] and for the ages to come. Amen."

Polycarp 15:1 When he had offered up the Amen and finished his prayer, the firemen lighted the fire. And, a mighty flame flashing forth, we to whom it was given to see, saw a marvel, yea and we were preserved that we might relate to the rest what happened.

Polycarp 15:2 The fire, making the appearance of a vault, like the sail of a vessel filled by the wind, made a wall round about the body of the martyr; and it was there in the midst, not like flesh burning, but like [a loaf in the oven or like] gold and silver refined in a furnace. For we perceived such a fragrant smell, as if it were the wafted odor of frankincense or some other precious spice.

Polycarp 16:1 So at length the lawless men, seeing that his body could not be consumed by the fire, ordered an executioner to go up to him and stab him with a dagger. And when he had done this, there came forth [a dove and] a quantity of blood, so that it extinguished the fire; and all the multitude marveled that there should be so great a difference between the unbelievers and the elect.

Polycarp 16:2 In the number of these was this man, the glorious martyr Polycarp, who was found an apostolic and prophetic teacher in our own time, a bishop of the holy Church which is in Smyrna. For every word which he uttered from his mouth was accomplished and will be accomplished.

Polycarp 17:1 But the jealous and envious Evil One, the adversary of the family of the righteous, having seen the greatness of his martyrdom and his blameless life from the beginning, and how he was crowned with the crown of immortality and had won a reward which none could gainsay, managed that not even his poor body should be taken away by us, although many desired to do this and to touch his holy flesh.

Polycarp 17:2 So he put forward Nicetes, the father of Herod and brother of Alce, to plead with the magistrate not to give up his body, "lest," so it was said, "they should abandon the crucified one and begin to worship this man" — this being done at the instigation and urgent entreaty of the Jews, who also watched when we were about to take it from the fire, not knowing that it will be impossible for us either to forsake at any time the Christ who suffered for the salvation of the whole world of those that are saved — suffered though faultless for sinners — nor to worship any other.

Polycarp 17:3 For Him, being the Son of God, we adore, but the martyrs as disciples and imitators of the Lord we cherish as they deserve for their matchless affection towards their own King and Teacher. May it be our lot also to be found partakers and fellow-disciples with them.

Polycarp 18:1 The centurion therefore, seeing the opposition raised on the part of the Jews, set him in the midst and burnt him after their custom.

Polycarp 18:2 And so we afterwards took up his bones which are more valuable than precious stones and finer than refined gold, and laid them in a suitable place;

Polycarp 18:3 where the Lord will permit us to gather ourselves together, as we are able, in gladness and joy, and to celebrate the birthday of his martyrdom for the commemoration of those that have already fought in the contest, and for the training and preparation of those that shall do so hereafter.

Polycarp 19:1 So it befell the blessed Polycarp, who having with those from Philadelphia suffered martyrdom in Smyrna — twelve in all — is especially remembered more than the others by all men, so that he is talked of even by the heathen in every place: for he showed himself not only a notable teacher, but also a distinguished martyr, whose martyrdom all desire to imitate, seeing that it was after the pattern of the Gospel of Christ.

Polycarp 19:2 Having by his endurance overcome the unrighteous ruler in the conflict and so received the crown of immortality, he rejoiceth in company with the Apostles and all righteous men, and glorifieth the Almighty God and Father, and blesseth our Lord Jesus Christ, the Savior of our souls and Helmsman of our bodies and Shepherd of the universal Church which is throughout the world.

Polycarp 20:1 Ye indeed required that the things which happened should be shown unto you at greater length: but we for the present have certified you as it were in a summary through our brother Marcianus. When then ye have informed yourselves of these things, send the letter about likewise to the brethren which are farther off, that they also may glorify the Lord, who maketh election from His own servants.

Polycarp 20:2 Now unto Him that is able to bring us all by His grace and bounty unto His eternal kingdom, through His only-begotten Son, Jesus Christ, be glory, honor, power, and greatness for ever. Salute all the saints. They that are with us salute you, and Euarestus, who wrote the letter, with his whole house.

Polycarp 21:1 Now the blessed Polycarp was martyred on the second day of the first part of the month Xanthicus, on the seventh before the calends of March, on a great Sabbath, at the eighth hour. He was apprehended by Herodes, when Philip of Tralles was high priest, in the proconsulship of Statius Quadratus, but in the reign of the Eternal King Jesus Christ. To whom be the glory, honor, greatness, and eternal throne, from generation to generation. Amen.

Polycarp 22:1 We bid you God speed, brethren, while ye walk by the word of Jesus Christ which is according to the Gospel; with whom be glory to God for the salvation of His holy elect; even as the blessed Polycarp suffered martyrdom, in whose footsteps may it be our lot to be found in the kingdom of Jesus Christ.

Polycarp 22:2 This account Gaius copied from the papers of Irenaeus, a disciple of Polycarp. The same also lived with Irenaeus.

Polycarp 22:3 And Isocrates wrote it down in Corinth from the copy of Gaius. Grace be with all men.

Polycarp 22:4[13] And I Pionius again wrote it down from the aforementioned copy, having searched it out (for the blessed Polycarp showed me in a revelation, as I will declare in the sequel), gathering it together when it was now well nigh worn out by age, that the Lord Jesus Christ may gather me also with His elect into His heavenly kingdom; to whom be the glory with the Father and the Holy Spirit for ever and ever. Amen.

Polycarp 22:2[14] This account Gaius copied from the papers of Irenaeus. The same lived with Irenaeus who had been a disciple of the holy Polycarp. For this Irenaeus, being in Rome at the time of the martyrdom of the bishop Polycarp, instructed many; and many most excellent and orthodox treatises by him are in circulation. In these he makes mention of Polycarp, saying that he was taught by him. And he ably refuted every heresy, and handed down the catholic rule of the Church just as he had received it from the saint. He mentions this fact also, that when Marcion, after whom the Marcionites are called, met the holy Polycarp on one occasion, and said, "Recognize us, Polycarp," he said in reply to Marcion, "Yes, indeed, I recognize the firstborn of Satan." The following statement also is made in the writings of Irenaeus, that on the very day and hour when Polycarp was martyred in Smyrna, Irenaeus being in the city of the Romans heard a voice as of a trumpet saying, "Polycarp is martyred."

Polycarp 22:3 From these papers of Irenaeus then, as has been stated already, Gaius made a copy, and from the copy of Gaius, Isocrates made another in Corinth.

Polycarp 22:4 And I Pionius again wrote it down from the copy of Isocrates, having searched for it in obedience to a revelation of the holy Polycarp, gathering it together, when it was well nigh worn out by age, that the Lord Jesus Christ may gather me also with His elect into His heavenly kingdom; to whom be the glory with the Father and the Son and the Holy Spirit for ever and ever. Amen.

ALEXANDER THE GREAT
AND THE CITY OF SMYRNA

Smyrna had been one of the most prosperous cities in the region for hundreds of years, exerting political might, intellectual influence, and religious domination over the local coast of Asia, as well as over islands situated close to the mainland.

But the historian Strabo, who is known for his works *History* and *Geography*, records that Smyrna had fallen into complete ruin.[15] Due to a barrage of internal and external conflicts, the city collapsed around the year 600 BC.[16] When this magnificent civilization crumbled, so did its beautiful buildings and temples. The walls of the historic buildings cracked, and the fallen stones tumbled down the slopes of Mount Pagos. From Strabo's report, we can conclude that by the time Alexander the Great arrived to see the legendary city approximately 300 years after Smyrna's destruction, vegetation had overtaken the city, splendid temples had become nothing but collapsed ruins, and the city lay in waste.

According to the Roman historian Pausanias, Alexander the Great ascended the slope to the peak of Mount Pagos ❸ to hunt wildlife among its ruins. On the first night of Alexander's expedition, he camped near a dilapidated temple that, according to Smyrnean legend, had been dedicated to the Nemeses of Smyrna. These two Nemeses were twin goddesses, believed to be daughters of the night who represented righteous anger and vengeance. The temple on Mount Pagos where the Nemeses were once worshiped had fallen into ruins, but it was still considered a holy shrine by people who lived in the region.

The record states that when Alexander slept that night on the ground near the crumbled ruins of this temple, he dreamed that the twin Nemeses hovered over him and instructed him to start the long process of resurrecting Smyrna to its former glory.[17] An ancient connection between Cybele and the goddess Nemesis indicates that Alexander believed these twin Nemeses he saw in his dream were a strange manifestation of the goddess Cybele.[18] Legend states that when Alexander awoke the next morning, he descended from the peak of Mount Pagos to enter the city. There he announced that through the twin Nemeses, Cybele had instructed him to awaken Smyrna from its state of death, digging it from its ashes to bring it back to life again and restore the city's former grandeur.

This legend is so intertwined with Smyrnean history that coins were minted in Smyrna to depict that night when Alexander the Great slept on Mount Pagos. The coin below shows him lying on the ground sleeping, with the twin Nemeses hovering above him and directing him to restore the city.

(Continued on page 520)

ALEXANDER THE GREAT

Alexander the Great is revered as one of the greatest and most important military figures in human history. Although he lived a relatively short life (356-323 BC), his achievements were remarkable, and his might and influence were enormous. During his reign, Alexander had a guiding hand in nearly every aspect of life and cultural development, especially in Greece and Asia Minor. Alexander was ruthless and cruel in many respects; yet he was also an intelligent, imaginative, creative, and a courageous leader.

Alexander was born in 356 BC in Pella, the ancient capital of Macedonia,

as the son of Philip II, King of Macedonia. During Alexander's childhood, he watched his father unify several of the Greek city-states into a powerful military force. As the newly unified Greek army won battle after battle, especially throughout the Balkans, young Alexander gained a unique perspective that would become both the foundation and the motivation for his later military exploits.

To train his son for future leadership, King Philip hired the Greek philosopher Aristotle to teach Alexander when he reached the age of 13.[19] Over the next three years, Aristotle was

Left: This is a detail of the mosaic on pages 514-515 portraying one of the most well-known images ever depicted of Alexander the Great.

the captured fortress *Alexandropolis* after himself.

In 338 BC, King Philip appointed Alexander to a leading military post in the Macedonian army as they prepared to invade Athens and Thebes, two Greek city-states not yet conquered. During the Battle of Chaeronea, Alexander once again proved his aptitude for fighting by utterly defeating the famous Theban Secret Band. Comments from many ancient historians make it clear that Alexander's efforts were viewed as the primary reason for the Macedonian victory.[20]

A nobleman named Pausanias assassinated King Philip in the spring of 336 BC. However, because the relationship between Philip II and Alexander had deteriorated significantly by this time, many historians suggest that Alexander may have required Pausanias to kill his father.[21] If true, this explains why Alexander ordered the swift execution of Pausanias before the man could be brought to trial and interrogated.

With his father dead, Alexander was free to take the throne and rule the Macedonian kingdom. Being a shrewd leader, the young king knew his survival depended on the elimination of his enemies, so he ordered

the primary influence in Alexander's life — teaching him history, literature, philosophy, science, medicine, rhetoric, and the arts, all of which played a major role in Alexander's life when he became ruler of the Greek Empire.

By the time Alexander was 16 years old, King Philip was so impressed with his son's capabilities that he left Alexander to rule in his absence while he invaded Thrace in the year 340 BC. During King Philip's absence, the tribe of Maedi (a region on the edge of northeastern Macedonia) attempted to wage war on his kingdom. In response, young Alexander summoned an army, swiftly defeated the advancing tribe, seized their fortress, and — as a foretaste of the glory he would seek in the future when he became emperor — renamed the execution of all those he believed would try to undermine his leadership. However, when the Illyrians, Thracians, and Greeks learned of Philip's death, they immediately seized the opportunity to try to declare their independence from Macedonia.

Alexander therefore had no choice but to first attack these forces, which he did with great force. By the end of 336 BC, all of Greece had fallen under his control and recognized his uncontested authority. Once Greece had been subjugated, his forces also conquered the Thracians and the Illyrians. These were just the beginning of the many battles that Alexander would fight in his life. Because he had swiftly and abruptly subdued his enemies, his testimony was firmly established from the start that he and his army were a force too mighty to defeat.

After stabilizing Macedonia and Greece, the young 22-year-old king began to make preparations to invade Asia Minor. In the spring of 334 BC, he and his military forces marched to Hellespont, the narrow strait of water between the Balkans and the coast of western Asia Minor, and set sail for the land he had determined to conquer. When Alexander's ship neared the coast, he hurled his spear toward the shore and watched as the spearhead sank into the soil. Then as he stepped off the ship, Alexander vowed that all of Asia would be conquered by the Macedonian spear.[22]

Alexander's chief officers and captains were all of Macedonian descent. In addition, he had approximately 39,000 troops — primarily Macedonians with a mixture of Greeks, Thracians, and Illyrians. Marching together to confront Alexander and his troops was the much larger Persian army of King Darius III, numbering approximately 60,000 soldiers — 20,000 of whom were Greeks who had joined forces with Persia after King Philip II defeated the Greeks at the Battle of Chaeronea.

At the Battle of Granicus, Alexander's military genius was reaffirmed when his army profoundly defeated the Persian army. Thousands of Persians were killed, as well as most of the Greeks who had sided with them. Afterward, Alexander sent the remaining 2,000 Greeks into forced labor as prisoners of war. Through it all, his army lost only 120 men in battle.[23]

Encouraged by this victory, Alexander led his armies into southern Asia Minor, where the coastal cities fiercely resisted him. After a series of battles, Alexander's army completely conquered the region and then turned toward the legendary city of Gordium in central Asia Minor. This city had long held to an ancient legend that the man who untied the ancient knot at Gordium would be able to rule the whole world. Hitherto, no one had ever been able to untie the legendary Gordium knot — but when Alexander

arrived in the city, he cut the knot in half with his sword, declaring it to be "loosed, if not untied." The inhabitants of Gordium took this as a sign that Alexander was indeed the man who would rule the world.[24]

In 333 BC, King Darius III, humiliated by his past defeat, decided to make another attempt at defeating Alexander the Great and his army. At a mountain pass in northwestern Syria, 30,000 renegade Greeks fought alongside Persians to defeat Alexander's troops in the Battle of Issus.

Darius' army outnumbered the Macedonians two to one, but Alexander was far superior at motivating his troops. The young general personally went to the frontlines of battle to rouse his army and exhort them to courageously face their enemy. The Roman historian Curtius related:

...Riding to the front line, Alexander named each soldiers one by one, and they each responded from the places where they were lined up. The Macedonians, who had won so many battles in Europe and set off to invade Asia, were tremendously encouraged

Above: This mosaic, dating back to the First Century BC, depicts Alexander the Great pursuing Darius III (380-330 BC) in the Battle of Issus. Discovered in the ruins of the House of Faun among the ruins of Pompeii, it is a Roman copy of a Greek painting dating back to the Fourth Century BC.

by him, as he reminded them of how great they were. He told them they were the world's liberators...and that together, they would subdue all the races on earth and that even Bactria and India would become provinces of Macedonia. He reminded them that those who were the enemy they were facing had previously provoked war with Greece and burned their temples and cities. As Illyrians and Thracians lived on plunder taken from enemies, he urged his soldiers to look at the enemy as glittering gold to take for plunder.[25]

Although it seemed logistically impossible, Alexander and his Macedonian troops defeated Darius' army and killed tens of thousands of Persians, Greeks, and other nationalities who had all aligned themselves with

Above: This coin depicts Alexander the Great wearing a ram's head, the head-dress of the Egyptian god Amum-Ra, to symbolize his own deity. Although Alexander was ruthless and cruel, he was also an intelligent, imaginative, creative, and courageous leader.

King Darius. History tells us that King Darius fled so quickly that he deserted his own mother, wife, and children. However, Alexander treated Persia's royal family with great respect when he discovered they had been abandoned.

In 332 BC, Alexander began to move his troops southward into Syria and Phoenicia. As word spread regarding the defeat of Darius, nearly all cities voluntarily surrendered to the Macedonian army — all, that is, except the little island city of Tyre. Tyre's rebellion resulted in a seven-month battle that ended when Alexander gave the order for his troops to build a rock bridge from the land to the island so his troops could march directly to the island and seize it for themselves. This was a monumental task requiring Alexander's soldiers to move tons of rock off shore, little by little, as they built a bridge that would eventually connect the two bodies of land and make the island city accessible.

Alexander the Great was determined to finish off the city of Tyre. After the rock bridge was completed, he surrounded the city with his ships, which assaulted Tyre's walls with rocks launched from catapults until the fortifications finally collapsed. The Macedonian army then entered the city and quickly conquered it. Thousands of Tyre's citizens were slaughtered in the mêlée, and the remaining 30,000 were exiled into slavery.[26]

After the Battle of Tyre, Alexander marched south into Egypt, battling through resistance in Gaza along the way. After two months of continuous fighting in Gaza, the region fell to the Macedonian army. With that victory, the entire eastern coast of the Mediterranean Sea was completely under Alexander's rule, and he resumed his march southwestward into Egypt.

In 331 BC, Alexander finally entered Egypt and was welcomed by the Egyptians as their great liberator from Persian rule. In honor of his arrival and of Egypt's surrender, Alexander gave the order for a city to be constructed in his name — the city

THE CITY OF SMYRNA 517

of *Alexandria*, situated at the mouth of the Nile River. Although Alexander didn't live long enough to see the dream of Alexandria fully realized, it eventually became the magnificent new capital of Egypt, one of the most prosperous commercial cities in the entire world.

While traveling throughout Egypt, Alexander — a dedicated pagan believer — made a point to visit many pagan temples. However, a landmark moment occurred at one of these temples when he visited the oracle of *Amum-Ra*, the Egyptian god whom many Greeks associated with the Greek god *Zeus*. This was a very important symbolic act, for Egyptian pharaohs believed that they were the sons of Amum-Ra. Because Alexander had become the undisputed ruler of Egypt, he wanted the gods to acknowledge that he, too, was the son of Amum-Ra and, therefore, *divine*.

After Alexander traveled across dangerous deserts to see this oracle of Amum-Ra, the priests of the oracle welcomed him. At his request, Alexander spoke to the oracle — and as he anticipated, the oracle declared that he was indeed the son of Amum-Ra.[27] This confirmed to Alexander an earlier story he'd been told: that although his mother was human, he was in fact the son of Zeus, the Greek equivalent of Amum-Ra. Feeling empowered by his new belief that he was divine, Alexander returned confidently to the city of

Tyre, where he prepared to contend with King Darius and march all the way into the famous city of Babylon.

A massive Persian army was gathered in the plains of Gaugamela, located near the modern city of Irbil in Iraq. Although it is possible that the recorded size of Darius' army is an exaggeration, ancient writings state that the Persian king assembled an army of *one million men* to face Alexander and his forces.[28] When the Macedonian army saw lights from Persian campfires and realized the immense size of the enemy, Alexander decided to attack at night under cover of darkness. But because he wanted to give Darius a final, decisive defeat in an equally matched battle, he then changed his mind and returned to his initial plan to attack at daylight.

On October 31, 331 BC, the Macedonian and Persian armies faced each other for the long-anticipated confrontation. Alexander's cavalry boldly rode into the midst of the Persian army without showing fear — and again King Darius fled in panic in the midst of the intense battle that ensued.

Alexander the Great then proceeded to invade, conquer, and occupy the city of Babylon, completely subduing Persian territory. When King Darius took flight, Alexander continued pursuing the Persian king until he finally caught up with him. But upon reaching the chariot in which Darius had fled, Alexander found the king already dead, apparently assassinated by Bessus, a commander of Bactria who had proclaimed himself the "king of kings."

Even though King Darius had been a hostile enemy, Alexander honored him in death and gave him a royal funeral. Afterward, Alexander turned his attention to finding Bessus, the commander who had killed the king.

Meanwhile, to show his respect for the newly defeated Persians, Alexander made a political move and began to appoint many Persians as local governors. He also began to dress in Persian clothes for public ceremonies, enlisted Persians in the Macedonian army, and encouraged the men of Macedonian to intermarry with Persian women. In fact, while in the eastern Persian province of Sogdia, Alexander met a beautiful princess named Roxana, with whom he fell in love and married.

All of these policies proved unpopular with most of the Macedonian army, who were proud of their heritage and offended by Alexander's attempt to incorporate Persian customs and culture into his empire. Soon rumors of an assassination plot were uncovered, and many of Alexander's leaders, suspected of instigating the plot, were tortured and executed.

For two years, Alexander's army fought in Bactria against the followers of Bessus. When Bessus was finally captured, Alexander ordered his execution for the murder of King Darius III, and Bactria came under Macedonian control.

Alexander had long proclaimed that he would march into India, and in 327 BC, Alexander and his troops achieved that goal. In 326 BC, his army crossed a river during a violent thunderstorm and defeated the Indian forces that awaited him. However, the Indians were mightily equipped for battle, even using elephants to march against Alexander's men. The Macedonian army had never seen elephants, and for them, it was a terrifying sight. In the end, the enemy was defeated, and Alexander conquered the region — but Alexander's faithful horse Bucephalus, which had been with him since childhood, was wounded in battle and died. Alexander was so stricken with grief at the death of his beloved horse that he founded a new city and named it in honor of Bucephalus.

After a prolonged campaign in India, Alexander's army was physically exhausted. Although he wanted to push farther, his soldiers refused, having heard continual rumors that the armies directly ahead of them were equipped with more elephants. Under pressure from military commanders, Alexander

Right: The famous "Alexander Sarcophagus," now located in the Istanbul Museum, is a masterpiece of Hellenistic sculpture. This detail depicts Alexander routing the Persians in the Battle of Issus (333 BC).

agreed to stop his advance. Instead, he would march the army south to reach the ocean, which was considered to be the southern edge of the world.

En route to the ocean, Alexander the Great was seriously wounded in an attack by an Indian tribe when an armor-piercing arrow pierced his breastplate and entered his chest. However, Alexander recovered and continued to lead his army south to the mouth of the Indus River. Then in 325 BC, he and his army turned toward Persia and began the long trip toward home. However, by the time his army reached the ancient Persian city of Susa, thousands of his men had perished from the scorching summer temperatures in the Gerdosian Desert.

Although Alexander dreamed of a unified army of Macedonians and Persians, he would never see his dream come to pass, for he fell sick with a fever after attending a private party. Day by day, the fever became stronger, until finally he became so weak that he was no longer able to move or even to speak. On June 7, 323 BC, Alexander the Great died at the age of 33 without designating a successor to the Macedonian Empire.

Upon Alexander's death, the generals who had served alongside Alexander for years now fought for control of the empire. Antigonus gained control of the greater part of Asia Minor but was subsequently killed in battle when displeased Macedonian generals formed a coalition against him. Afterward, the Macedonian Empire was divided into four kingdoms: *Seleucus* ruled the eastern regions of Asia Minor; *Ptolemy* ruled Egypt; *Lysimachus* ruled Thrace and western Asia Minor; and *Cassander* ruled Macedonia and Greece. Eventually Cassander murdered Alexander's wife and all of his children. Thus ended the grandiose but short-lived ambitions of the remarkable young ruler named Alexander the Great, still known as one of the greatest military minds of all time.

In obedience to a perceived divine mandate, Alexander the Great initiated and financed the earliest phases of this massive undertaking, but his plan to rebuild Smyrna and add marvelous new sections would take years to accomplish. First, overgrowth had to be removed; then ruins had to be excavated from layers of dirt accumulated over hundreds of years. Thus, the full restoration of Smyrna was completed years later during the rule of Antigonus (316-301 BC) and of Lysimachus (301-281 BC).[29]

THE CITY OF SMYRNA IS REBORN

After many years of excavation and reconstruction, Smyrna emerged far more magnificent and grandiose than the former city. The city had literally risen from the ashes as a resurrected and thriving metropolis. Its appearance was so stunning that coins minted in this city during the First Century included the inscription that Smyrna was the "first in all of Asia" — a claim contested by the powerful neighboring cities of Ephesus and Pergamum, both of which also claimed this coveted title.[30]

A Greek rhetorician and sophist named Aelius Aristides wrote extensively about the city of Smyrna. Aristides studied under Herodes Atticus of Athens, Polemon of Smyrna, and Alexander of Cotyaeum. His writings were so esteemed that they were used as a part of the curriculum in Roman schools, and his insights so revered that writers wrote commentaries about them. Aristides' career as a politician was cut short by an unidentified illness that restricted him to his home in Smyrna for most of his life.[31] Because his affection for Smyrna was so intense, Aristides wrote extensively about the rebuilt city and recorded explicit details about its design and architectural layout. Therefore, although most of the city today lies under the modern city of Izmir, the writings of Aristides give us a remarkable description of the city's physical appearance as it existed at the height of its glory.

According to Aristides, the slopes and neighborhoods of Smyrna were covered with luscious groves of trees. He described Smyrna as a "flower of beauty, such as the earth and sun had never shown to mankind."[32] Aristides also praised Smyrna's "grace that extends over every part like a rainbow, and strains the city like a lyre into tenseness harmonious with itself and with its beautiful surroundings, and the brightness which pervades every part and reaches up to heaven, like the glitter of bronze armour in Homer."[33]

Aristides also suggested that the city had been designed like a great statue, with its feet resting on the shores near the sea, its body gradually rising up the slopes of the mountain, and its mid-section

decorated with beautiful buildings and porticoes. The head of the great statue, according to Aristides, was the rounded peak of Mount Pagos, "crowned" with a mighty fortress that had been constructed during the rule of Lysimachus.[34]

Aristides was not alone in his assessment of Smyrna's design. Apollonius of Tyana (a city in the Cappadocian region of Asia Minor), who was a Greek Pythagorean philosopher and teacher, also alluded to "the crown" of Smyrna in his writings.[35] Similar references by other ancient writers indeed suggest that the entire layout of this city, from the Aegean Sea to the top of Mount Pagos, was intended to reflect the likeness of the goddess Cybele. The city had been rebuilt at the order of Alexander the Great, who believed that Cybele herself had instructed him to do so. Thus, it can be reasonably concluded that the resurrected city of Smyrna was designed to be a giant, symbolic idol of its patron goddess.

THE HISTORY OF CYBELE WORSHIP

Before the earliest written records of Smyrna were recorded, the pagans of this region had worshiped Cybele (or an earlier form of the Great Mother Goddess) for thousands of years. The cult of the Mother Goddess evolved over the centuries into the worship of Cybele in certain regions of Asia Minor[36] (and later in Ephesus, it evolved into the worship of the Ephesian goddess Artemis). This Mother Goddess cult was so archaic that many scholars believe it is the earliest form of pagan worship in human history.[37]

One myth claimed that Cybele originally dwelt near the city of Troy on Mount Ida.[38] Other versions of the legend placed her earliest residence on Mount Dindymus in Phrygia.[39] Regardless of Cybele's mythical place of origin, however, local Smyrnean legend stated that the goddess descended her mountain to take up residency in the region where the city of Smyrna was eventually built. Because this religion was so deeply rooted in the region, Cybele was honored as the patron goddess and guardian of Smyrna, similar to the worship of Artemis as the patron goddess and guardian of Ephesus.

The cult of Cybele became an "official Roman religion" in the year 205 BC,[40] but the worship of the goddess was so despicable that at first it was resisted in most of the empire. However, in time, this depraved, evil religion quickly spread from Asia to

Left: The Fountain of Cybele, located in Madrid, Spain, in which the patron goddess of Smyrna is depicted riding a chariot pulled by lions.

522

Above: *The image on this Second Century plate depicts the goddess Cybele in her chariot, drawn by lions, on the way to a votive sacrifice.*

other regions of the Greek and Roman Empire and later became a religious entity that fiercely and aggressively opposed the Christian faith. Idols, frescoes, and mosaics of Cybele portray her as a queen with a towering crown and two lions at her side. She is either seated on a throne or being pulled in a royal chariot. The Romans called her *Mater Deum Magna Idaea*, which means *the Great Mother of the Gods*. Pagan believers regarded Cybele as the giver of life and the Great Mother to gods, humans, and beasts.

Left: Most images of Cybele depicted her as a queen seated on a throne, with a towering crown on her head and two lions sitting on each side of her.

Early coins minted in Smyrna picture Cybele with a towering crown on her head — a crown that resembled the walls and towers of the fortress on Mount Pagos (*see* images on pages 528-529 and 580). This also lends support to Aristides' suggestion that the city was designed as a giant idol and that the mountaintop fortress was Cybele's towering crown.

Although the goddess Cybele was eventually worshiped throughout the Roman Empire, no population held her in higher regard than the people of Smyrna. Because Cybele was Smyrna's patron goddess and guardian, it would be difficult to overstate the impact this evil, repulsive religion had on the city. The Smyrneans avidly worshiped Cybele with bloody, sensual rituals, attacking any person or group

Above: *According to legend, Attis (depicted here in an ancient fresco) was both the son and lover of Cybele, whose bloody death was commemorated each year on "The Day of Blood."*

who refused to enter into their pagan celebrations that were designed to show their devotion to the goddess.

THE BLOODY RITUALS OF CYBELE WORSHIP

Even from the earliest beginnings in mythology about Cybele, the worship of the goddess was always associated with the shedding of blood and was accompanied by wild, orgiastic celebrations and rituals of self-mutilation. According to one of the primary legends concerning the origin of this cult, Cybele was an offspring of Zeus who was both male and female. When Zeus saw his new child, he was horrified and ordered the male organs to be removed — transforming the creature into the female goddess Cybele.[41]

Because the act of castration was involved in the creation of Cybele, the rituals connected to this pagan worship emphasized the virtues of self-mutilation and self-castration. But stories of castration didn't stop with Cybele's creation. A myth fundamental to Cybele worship stated that Attis, a god who fell in love with Cybele, was brutally castrated and bled to death. Therefore, on March 24 of each year, the chief priestess of Cybele — who was in fact a castrated man made into a "priestess" — came into the temple, slit his arms, drew blood, and offered it to Cybele in memory of Attis' bungled castration. This annual event was called "The Day of Blood."[42]

Celebrations on this high day of Cybele worship included wild music

Above: This is an engraving on a Fifth Century silver Roman shield depicting the goddess Cybele in a lion-drawn chariot. Next to her is her lover Attis, holding a shepherd's crook and a reed pipe.

played by low-level priestesses, while other priestesses and worshipers swirled around the altar in a mad frenzy, sadistically slashing themselves with knives and splattering their blood on the altar. This ghastly ritual was revered as the highest, holiest act of Cybele worship.

For the most part, males served Cybele as eunuch-priests, called *galli*,[43] although some historical writings provide evidence of female priestesses as well.[44] These *galli* had to emasculate themselves and then, from that point on, dress in feminine garments in order to be more closely identified with Cybele and deemed worthy to be called her "priestesses."[45]

Once their male organs had been removed, Cybele's neutered "priestesses" were considered a "third gender" — neither male nor female.[46] The transformation of these men into *galli* was dramatic. They took female names, and their physical appearance became so feminine that they were frequently mistaken for genetically born women when they ventured beyond the temple grounds.

One function of the *galli* was to be a vehicle through which inhabitants of the spirit world could speak to worshipers. In the Bible, such human vehicles are called *mediums*. Today they are often referred to as *channelers*. But in the Greek and Roman world, they were called *oracles* and were widely accepted as the mouthpieces of the gods and spirits. Thus, one of the primary responsibilities of the *galli* was to connect with the spirit world and channel the messages of spirits and pagan gods to those seeking answers. Strangely, it was believed that through the castration of the *galli*, not only were they created in the likeness of Cybele, but their psychic abilities were also increased, enabling them to experience a stronger connection with the spirit world.[47]

People came to the magnificent Temple of Cybele to seek wisdom and supernatural direction. Priestesses used wine and, at times, naturally occurring hallucinogens found in certain plants to open themselves up to the spirit realm so they could yield to spirits; then the spirits would speak through these oracles to give answers to people seeking wisdom.[48]

As the number of people increased who sought help from the goddess Cybele, so did the number of her *galli* eunuch-priests and her priestesses, called *Melissae* (meaning *bees*). The origin of the name *Melissae* may have come from an ancient legend stating that the first priestess of this Mother Goddess was Melissa, the daughter of Melissus, king of Crete.[49] The bee was also a symbol of fertility, a key aspect of Cybele worship.[50] In addition, Greeks may have used this term to depict the swarms of religious workers who filled some temples to overflowing. Certainly as the numbers of the *galli* and the *Melissae* priestesses increased in Asia — and especially in the city of Smyrna — it must have looked as if literal swarms of those in Cybele's service filled the temple grounds of this grotesque religion.

The worship of Cybele became so widespread throughout the empire that temples were built to her in nearly every major city, including especially large temples in the Asia cities of Hierapolis, Sardis, Pergamum, and Ephesus. But the fact that Cybele was the *principal* goddess

Above: This relief depicts a number of the galli *— the eunuch-priests of the goddess Cybele. The* galli *were considered a "third gender" — neither male nor female. As Augustine later described one of the* galli*: "Neither is he changed into a woman nor does he remain a man...."[51] These eunuch-priests served as mediators between the spirit realm and the pagan worshipers.*

of Smyrna is an indicator of how deeply entrenched the people of Smyrna were in the bloody, dark, occult activities that were an integral part of this religion.

(Continued on page 533)

PAGAN DIVINATION

The ancient peoples of Greece and Rome perceived the natural world to be like a small microcosm floating in an ocean of spiritual reality. They believed that spirits permeated every sphere of this physical realm, inhabiting the earth and controlling the forces of nature. Even places such as springs or groves of trees had their own specific spirits, known as nymphs (called *genii* by Romans). Although nymphs were subordinate to the gods in mythology, they were believed to fill the universe like a hand fills a glove. To the Greeks and Romans, the natural world was alive with spiritual vitality as represented by the numerous gods and nymphs.

Therefore, spiritual reality was not distant, either in time or space; rather, the spiritual realm was present in the here and now. In the hearts of the ancients, this knowledge cultivated both fear and desire. Therefore, to calm their own fears of the unknown, people fervently sought to gain knowledge of the spiritual realm and to discover the will of the gods through various means of divination. In addition, people used divination to gain an advantage in the outworking of spiritual reality in their personal lives.

The practice of divination, or the method by which one seeks to gain spiritual insight, was done in diverse places by many distinctive means, depending on the culture and the nature of each specific spirit. Famous oracles, such as the oracles of Apollo at Delphi or Zeus at Dodona, were highly prized and revered. These oracles were the two oldest in the ancient Grecian world.[52] Originally both of these oracles were dedicated to the worship of "Mother Earth," who was identified in Phrygia as Cybele, but they were later transferred to the worship of Zeus and Apollo.

Oracles used many different means to contact the spirit realm, such as the casting of lots, receiving dreams on temple grounds, or entering altered states of consciousness through naturally occurring hallucinogens found in certain herbs or gases. In fact, the female oracle at Delphi, who was called a *pythia*, would be lowered into a cavern or fissure that was likely filled with ethylene gas. The fumes would cause the oracle to hallucinate and enter an altered state of consciousness. In this condition, she would babble unintelligibly, and her utterances would then be recorded and translated by temple priests acting as supposed "interpreters."[53]

Since all of nature was charged with spiritual power, certain oracles and temple priests or priestesses also specialized in observing the flight of birds or the movement of the stars to predict future events or determine the will of the gods. Still others used sacred texts to determine the divine purpose in different situations.

For the Romans, one of the most important methods of divination was the Sibylene books, written by a *sibyl* (female prophet) from the region surrounding ancient Troy. According to legend, these books were originally a set of nine, and the sibyl of Cumae offered them to Tarquinius, the last Roman king, for an exorbitant price. The king — unaware of who the woman was or what she was selling — refused this seemingly outrageous price, and the sibyl burned three of the books in response. She then offered to sell him six books for the same price, and he scorned her again — which caused her to incinerate three more books. Finally recognizing the sibyl's power and ability, the king purchased the remaining three texts. These books were then maintained, preserved, and consulted by 15 individuals specifically assigned to protect and hide them.[54] Only upon the order of the Senate could these prophetic writings be used.

During the invasion of Hannibal, the Senate ordered that the books be reviewed. Conveyed through the text was a message: Victory was assured to the Romans if they would honor the goddess Cybele — "Mother Earth of Ida." Cybele worship thus became an "official religion" of Rome by order of the Senate.[55] This was, in fact, the only religion the Senate specifically mandated.[56]

The ancient Greek and Roman civilizations firmly believed the prophecies of oracles were direct messages from the gods. Thus, words of an oracle often changed the course of history, affecting the lives of entire peoples. One such example occurred during the Dorian invasion of ancient Greece. Seeking counsel, the Dorian leaders called on the oracle at Delphi, and she predicted that their invasion would succeed so long as King Codrus of Athens lived — for either Codrus

or Athens was appointed to die. Upon hearing of this prophecy, Codrus disguised himself as a peasant and slipped into the enemy camp, intending to die to save his city. Unaware that this peasant was the Athenian king, the Dorian soldiers rushed over and killed the intruder — only then to discover Codrus' identity. Heeding the prophecy of the oracle, the Dorian army decided to give up their attempt on the Athenians, and the city-state of Athens was preserved.[57]

Below is an abbreviated list of some of the most common means of divination:

- **Aeromancy** — *the observation of the clouds and sky as a means of divination.* Since many ancient religions believed the most powerful spiritual entity was the god of the sky, the observation of the sky was a very important means of receiving divine insight.

- **Astrology** — *the study of the stars, planets, and other celestial phenomena as a means of divination.* The zodiac, which is the circular formation of the 12 main constellations, was central to many ancient and even modern cultures in discerning divine information.

- **Augury** — *the study of the flight of birds as a means of divination.* Since all of nature was considered to be permeated with "spirit," the flight of birds was considered a key to unlocking supernatural revelation.

- **Bibliomancy** — *the use of books as a means of divination.* The exact methods varied, but the Sibylene books were the most prominent example of this in the Roman world.

Left: Inherent in the pagan religions of ancient Rome was the worshipers' desire to communicate with the gods. Certainly this was true in the cult centered around Cybele, the mother goddess, one of the primary goddesses of Asia Minor during biblical times.

- **Extispicy** — *the inspection of the entrails of sacrificial animals as a means of obtaining divine insight.* Some ancient religions considered sacrificial animals to be a vehicle of communication with the spiritual realm.

- **Heptascopy** — *the examination of the liver of animals set apart for the gods as a means of divination.* The liver is a central organ in both human and animal physical systems and, in many ancient cultures, it was associated with the location of the spirit. Therefore, it was a central tool in divination.

- **Scrying** — *the use of reflective material to determine the future or obtain divine knowledge.* This included mirrors, water, and the now-infamous crystal ball. Staring into such an object would produce an altered state, which allowed the user to see into the spiritual realm.

- **Necromancy** — *divination by means of consulting the dead.* A medium would act as a channel for a departed spirit.

- **Pyromancy** — *the use of fire to seek spiritual revelation.* This was done by either examining the smoke or examining the pattern of cracks left by fire in bones or shells, such as a turtle shell.

The following are two means of divination used both by pagans and Jews:

- **Cleromancy** — *the casting of lots to determine a course of action.* In the highest councils of Athenian democracy, this was the original process used to select leaders. Aristotle approved of this practice, asserting that it was the most "democratic means" for leadership selection. Also, in Jewish culture, this was a biblically accepted means of determining God's will (*see* Proverbs 16:33). In Acts chapter 1, Judas was replaced by the casting of lots. This method is still used today in the jury-selection process.

- **Oneiromancy** — *the interpretation of dreams as a means of receiving divine revelation.* Dreams and visions were a common means of receiving divine insight for pagans, Jews, and Christians. Because receiving the dream was only part of the process, experts were often used to interpret the meaning of dreams, as in the cases of both Joseph and Daniel (*see* Genesis chapters 40 and 41; Daniel chapter 2).

In today's society, people trying to understand the biblical world often read the text of Scripture through a modern, naturalistic worldview. Yet all the ancients were supernaturalists. Pagans, Jews, and Christians alike believed the world was literally brimming over with spiritual substance. The distinction between pagan, Jew, and Christian was not a "secular naturalist" versus a "supernatural" worldview. Rather, the boundary between them was the source of their revelation and the object of their worship. Whereas pagans revered and worshiped a plethora of spirits, demigods, and gods or goddesses, Jews and Christians believed in the one true, transcendent God — and Christians believed that this one true God sent His Son to die for the salvation of mankind. During the First Century when pagan worship was so prevalent, it was this distinction that set Christians apart, causing them to shine like beacons of brilliant light in the midst of an empty, dying world.

Above: These are actual pagan altars from Smyrna on which sacrifices were offered to the gods. Altars like these were common in pagan temples, where priests and worshipers offered sacrifices as they sought supernatural wisdom and direction from the gods.

These gigantic bronze double doors adorn the entryway to a church today, but they were once the original doors to a great pagan temple in the city of Rome. Doors such as these would have been typical entry doors that led to the inner sanctuaries of pagan temples like the giant Temple of Cybele in Smyrna.

THE TEMPLE COMPLEX OF CYBELE IN SMYRNA

The Temple of Cybele ❹ was the largest temple complex in Smyrna. Although this temple has never been excavated, archeologists believe it was situated just beyond the city wall, separated from the rest of the city because it was a "holy" site, not to be contaminated by the daily activities of life. One record indicates that the Temple of Cybele and its many facilities were located at the end of the "Street of Gold." This was a beautifully decorated street that started at the steps of the Temple of Zeus ❺ and twisted through the center of Smyrna until it reached the entrance of the Temple of Cybele.[58]

Based on the examples of other similar temple complexes, it is certain that the Temple of Cybele was enormous in size. It was most likely surrounded with massive columns that were topped with magnificently carved capitals that were either painted or gilded with gold. The interior was adorned with the finest marble, incrustations of precious stones, and numerous large mosaics on its

huge floors. Beautiful frescoes decorated its walls, and ceiling ornaments were gold-gilded or painted with rich colors.

As is customary in such temples, the innermost part of the sanctuary would

---

Below: *Most Greek and Roman temples were covered with marble, decorated with friezes and statues, lined with magnificent columns, and had roofs covered with tiles made of various materials and intricately carved stone ornaments. The temple reliefs were marvelously painted; the doors were made of wood and covered with bronze; and the central sanctuary always housed a great idol. This illustration depicts the inside of the Temple of Athena in Athens, which was very similar in design to the Temple of Cybele in Smyrna. The Smyrnean temple had a mammoth statue of Cybele standing in its sanctuary. This statue has never been discovered because the ancient ruins of Smyrna lie under the modern Turkish city of Izmir.*

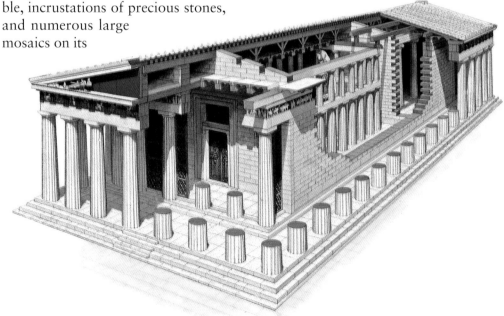

include a room that contained a gigantic idol of Cybele — a crown on her head and two lions at her side — either seated on a throne or being pulled in her royal chariot. Although this particular idol has never been found, similar idols of other gods were first fashioned of wood, then covered with ivory to depict skin and clothed with a meshed material made of pure gold. It isn't known for certain, but it is possible that the idol of Cybele fit this familiar description.

At the entrance of the temple were two massive wooden doors fully covered with decorative bronze. As worshipers passed through those immense doors, they bowed their heads and walked slowly and reverently toward the great idol of Cybele to offer their sacrifices. Peering upward through a haze of sacrificial smoke rising from the altar to look into the goddess's eyes, the people would silently freeze, feeling nearly paralyzed with fear and reverence as Cybele's insidious, black-painted eyes stared down upon them.

THE ANATOMY OF PAGAN SACRIFICES

Sacrificing to the gods was one of the most important acts in Greek and Roman religions. Altars were scattered throughout all Asia Minor cities to make it easier for those who wished to offer a sacrifice. These pagan altars came in a wide variety of sizes and shapes — tall, short, round, square, long, hexagonal, etc. They were placed along the sides of streets and on street corners, as well as in marketplaces, gymnasiums, bathhouses, and every other public building. Temples as large as the Temple of Cybele would include *many* altars in order to accommodate a large crowd of worshipers desiring to offer sacrifices.

The highest form of pagan sacrifice was to offer a bull, but a sheep, goat, or other kind of domestic animal could be used as well. Garlands of flowers, single flowers, cakes, or food could also be offered as sacrifices. Worshipers offered sacrifices to express thanksgiving to the gods or as a means of requesting their help. These were always serious rituals, conducted with respect and reverence.

Pagan sacrifices — including sacrifices offered at the Temple of Cybele — began with a long procession to the altar that was often accompanied with mystical music. The worshiper would first wash his hands with holy water and then shake the droplets of water from his hands onto the sacrificial animal as a sign that it was a holy sacrifice. The animal was then

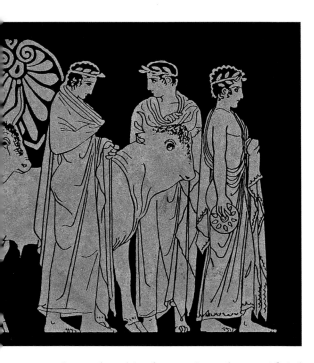

Left: Sacrificial ceremonies, such as the one depicted on this piece of Greek pottery, were central activities in Greek and Roman temples. The most important animal to be offered in these ceremonies was a bull, but people also sacrificed sheep, goats, and other smaller animals. After the animal was sacrificed and burned in fire, the remaining meat was boiled and eaten in a sacrificial meal, which was a very important part of the ceremony.

sheared and its fur put into the sacrificial fire to be burned while the participants prayed. Before the animal was killed, barley was hurled on it. Afterward, its throat was slit, and the blood that poured from its neck was collected in a bowl and poured onto the altar. The animal was then cut into pieces, and the thighbone was burned on the altar. Finally, wine was poured onto the altar and on the ground around the altar, and worshipers drank a portion of the wine as part of the religious ceremony.[59]

In addition to the central temple itself and the many altars that filled its interior and the temple grounds, the Temple of Cybele complex included many other sacred buildings. Tall walls completely surrounded the entire religious complex in order to conceal temple activities from outside observers and to keep it separate from the outside world. Within the walls,

a great host of *galli* and priestesses moved from one altar to the next, serving the needs of the seekers and worshipers. Because the worship of Cybele was the most popular religion in Smyrna, the facilities had to be large enough to accommodate hordes of worshipers who regularly came to the enormous temple complex to participate in its dark and perverted worship rituals.

THE ROMAN PERIOD IN SMYRNA

By the time Lysimachus completed the rebuilding of Smyrna in 281 BC, the city was once again what Strabo later called "the most beautiful of all" cities in Asia Minor.[60] In 188 BC, the city positioned itself as an ally of Rome in the Romans' war against the Seleucid king Antiochus III. After Rome's victory, Asia Minor cities that allied themselves with Antiochus were placed under the rule of Eumenes II (including the city of Ephesus), whereas cities allied with Rome were given independent status — including Smyrna.[61] In the years that followed, this thriving commercial port continued to be enhanced, becoming a frequent

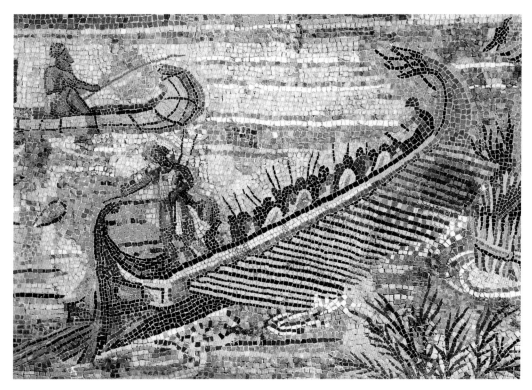

Left: This Roman mosaic, dating to approximately 80 BC, depicts a Roman ship transporting troops down the Nile River. Similar ships once arrived regularly at the Port of Smyrna and then carried soldiers up the Hermus River to the inland regions of Asia Minor.

recipient of Rome's beneficent donations that helped embellish Smyrna with new temples, improve its two harbors, and strengthen its infrastructure. As a result of all these structural improvements, even more people began streaming into Smyrna until it became the second largest city in Asia — second only to Ephesus, located 35 miles to the south.

Later in 133 BC, Attalus III, the last Pergamene ruler, bequeathed his entire kingdom to Rome in order to avoid squabbles over his kingdom after his death. At that time, Smyrna officially came under the jurisdiction of the Roman Senate, along with other cities that fell within the territory of the expansive Pergamene kingdom.[62]

Once the Pergamene kingdom was in the hands of Rome, the influence of Rome quickly began to move eastward into other regions of Asia Minor. Simultaneously, the Seleucid kingdom was moving westward, encroaching on territory close to Smyrna.[63] Because of this threat from the East, Smyrneans felt the need to garner protection against the invaders. As for the Romans, they needed both a port and a military base from which they could repel the Seleucidians' advances.

Right: This relief is of Dea Roma, the goddess of the Roman Empire. The worship of Dea Roma was established later in imperial times and was intended to unify the various peoples, cultures, and religions of the empire. Temples were built to Dea Roma in every major Roman city. The city of Smyrna was the first to construct a temple dedicated to this goddess of Rome.

This mutual threat brought Rome and Smyrna even closer, and together they formed a partnership to withstand the impending menace against Smyrna and the potential assault against Rome's grip on the region.

Rome needed a base and an accessible route for ships to travel up the Hermus River in order to defend the inland regions of Asia Minor. The large, double-harbor Port of Smyrna ❻ was ideal to meet this need. However, although Rome officially ruled the region, this port was still in the Smyrneans' hands. As a result of this alliance, Smyrna opened its port to Rome and gave Roman ships and troops unlimited access. For its part, Smyrna obtained a political ally, gained a strong military presence, and enjoyed onsite protection against the enemy approaching from the East. The deal was especially lucrative for Smyrna because it also meant that ships with thousands of troops and visitors would be regularly traveling to and from the city. This would enhance Smyrna's stature as an Asia Minor seaport and bring a great deal of commerce and riches to the city.

Smyrna's close relationship with Rome had begun in 195 BC when its people constructed the first temple in Asia to the goddess *Dea Roma* — the goddess of Rome created as part of a propaganda campaign to idealize and deify everything Roman. Temples to Dea Roma were later constructed in Ephesus (*see* pages 249-250), Sardis, and Delos, but it was the temple in Smyrna that inaugurated the worship of Dea Roma in the province of Asia.[64] From that point on, the people of

Smyrna willingly and passionately idealized everything "Roman," even to the point of embracing the worship of this goddess of Rome as proof of their absolute devotion.

Smyrna's loyalty to Rome was further proven in 130 BC[65] when the Roman army found itself embattled in a prolonged conflict with the army of Mithridates. The beleaguered Roman troops didn't expect the fight to last so long and were not physically outfitted for the cold temperatures of winter. When the people of Smyrna heard of the Roman army's plight, in one accord they removed clothes from their own bodies and sent the clothing to the troops to help the soldiers withstand the freezing cold.[66]

This act of kindness didn't go unnoticed. Rome never forgot the manner in which the Smyrneans demonstrated their support. Cicero indicated in his writings the esteem Rome had for Smyrna's countless demonstrations of loyalty, calling it "the city of our most faithful and most ancient allies."[67]

In the year 26 AD, the Roman Senate decided to return the favor to the people of Smyrna. When the Senate decided to build a magnificent temple to the Emperor Tiberius in Asia, every large city in Asia competed for the honor of building the temple within its borders. But the Senate chose Smyrna for the site as a way of showing Rome's gratitude for the city's devotion to the empire.[68]

The construction of an imperial temple was significant. It gave Smyrna a political stamp of approval, and it brought more worshipers and tourists to the city. All this meant even more power and riches would be gained for this ancient coastal metropolis.

A POLITICAL 'STOPOVER' FOR THE PROCONSUL OF ASIA

The city of Ephesus was 35 miles to the south; Pergamum was 60 miles to the northeast; and the road that connected these two cities traversed directly through the center of Smyrna. This was very significant.

The proconsul of Rome lived in Ephesus, but his official headquarters were located in Pergamum, which meant he and his entourage had to frequently travel the 95 miles between the two cities. Traveling this distance was a considerable undertaking in the First Century when people traveled primarily by chariot or on horseback. By the time the proconsul and his entourage had traveled the 35 miles from Ephesus to Smyrna, it had already been a long trip. It therefore would have been customary to make Smyrna the "stopover" city.[69] Each time the proconsul, his advisers, and a large attachment of high-ranking military officers made the journey between Ephesus and Pergamum, they would stop and rest, spending the night in Smyrna before continuing on to Pergamum. Consequently, Smyrna could boast of a strong imperial presence, even though it had no imperial officer who actually lived there.

As the proconsul and his large entourage of troops and dignitaries entered Smyrna, they passed through the Ephesian Gate ❼ — a huge city gate built on the south side of the city facing Ephesus. This monumental gate was decorated with sculptural reliefs and inscriptions written

Right: Roman soldiers protected Smyrna from eastern aggressors and monitored traffic traveling on the Royal Road that connected this ancient seaport to the heart of the Persian Empire. In addition, the proconsul of Rome and his high-ranking entourage regularly passed through the city in their travels between the proconsul's headquarters in Pergamum and his home in Ephesus. This Second Century relief depicting high-ranking Roman soldiers is on display in the Louvre in Paris.

in Greek and Latin. Everyone traveling from Ephesus to Smyrna passed through it — including the apostle Paul and his messengers, who may have been responsible for starting the church in Smyrna during Paul's residency in Ephesus. If this was the case, these God-sent preachers passed through this same Ephesian Gate each time they traveled from Ephesus to Smyrna, intent on piercing the oppressive spiritual darkness that pervaded Smyrna with power and authority from on High.

The proconsul was the representative of the Roman emperor, and no political official other than the emperor had more power, might, wealth, or military support in that Roman province. When the proconsul traveled, he was accompanied by many Roman troops for protection. Therefore, during his frequent stops in Smyrna, the city would accommodate these high-ranking soldiers, who were responsible for keeping order in the city to assure the safety of the proconsul and his company. Since these troops were additions to the contingent of soldiers already based in Smyrna, there was an increased presence of the Roman army in the city whenever the proconsul made one of his stopover visits.

Rome kept a relatively low military profile in First Century Asia Minor, allowing local authorities to rule autonomously unless a disturbance erupted.[70] Nevertheless, Smyrna had one of the largest populations of Roman troops in all of Asia, despite the fact that it had no resident imperial officer. The substantial number of soldiers residing in the city was the result of Smyrna's strategic location on the Aegean Sea, the importance of its port, and its use as a frequent "stopover" by the proconsul and other high-ranking delegations of politicians. Any day of the week, splendidly outfitted soldiers walked the streets, protected key buildings, kept guard at the harbor, and watched over the traffic that came and went on the roads that connected Smyrna to other Asia Minor cities, as well as to the eastern kingdoms of Persia and Assyria.

It must be noted that wherever a substantial number of Roman soldiers resided throughout the empire, a large community of prostitutes could also be found. Smyrna was no different in this respect, for its prostitution industry was significant.

Prostitutes could especially be seen at the harbor, in the marketplaces, in the bathhouses, at the theater, and at the stadium, where many men gathered for sporting competitions and other games. When spectators at the games or theater left their seats to walk to the toilets, prostitutes waited for them under the arches of the structure. These prostitutes were there to lure men aside for a moment of pleasure as they walked from the toilets to return to their seats.[71] The word "fornication" actually comes from the word *fornix*, which is the Latin word for the "arches" of a stadium or theater. The word "fornication" literally referred to a brief sexual encounter *under the arches*.

In Roman society, sex with a prostitute was *not* considered adultery. Therefore, pagan men felt no sense of embarrassment

or guilt to restrain them from a cheap moment of carnal pleasure.

In Smyrna, all aspects of the prostitution industry just described were prolific and pervasive. This was largely due to the substantial presence of Roman troops and the steady influx of sailors and visitors to this coastal city.

A HUB FOR TRAVELERS IN ASIA

Smyrna was not only a stopover for high-ranking politicians, but it was also a convergence point for thousands of visitors who arrived by ship at the port or by foot, horseback, or chariot as people

Left: This photo shows the modern-day city of Izmir, Turkey, which is built directly on top of the ancient city of Smyrna. Izmir still has one of the most beautiful harbors in Turkey. However, in the First Century, Smyrna was considered one of the most impressive seaside cities in the world, and visitors and tourists flocked to its beaches from across the Roman Empire.

to function adequately, there had to be an entire work force employed to cook, make breads and pastries, serve tables, and clean up. Food companies had to be developed to make deliveries to stores and restaurants so they could adequately meet the needs of their clientele.

The giant Port of Smyrna was large enough to receive many ships at the same time, and it was continually filled with ships carrying passengers who had come to shop at the massive Lower Marketplace of Smyrna. **8** The Lower Marketplace was one of the largest markets in all of Asia — most likely surpassing even Ephesus' huge Central Marketplace. Merchants traveled from afar to Smyrna's Lower Marketplace to sell their goods, buy products, or offer their services.

The Lower Marketplace of Smyrna was a commercial market, which meant that goods were sold there in large quantities for discounted prices. The deals found at this marketplace were so significant compared to other Asia markets that many visitors traveled to Smyrna for the express purpose of buying products to take back to their cities and towns, where they could then sell those products for a higher price. The Lower Marketplace was truly

traveled between the cities of Ephesus and Pergamum. Smyrna was already the second largest city in Asia with a population of nearly 200,000 people. But it also overflowed with travelers — temporary residents who used Smyrna as a hub in their journeys to other cities.

This meant travelers needed to find lodging where they could spend the night. Furthermore, the hotel industry had to be large enough to accommodate the constant arrival of new visitors. To meet the needs of hungry travelers, the city also required a large number of restaurants and cafes to be built throughout every quarter of the city. For restaurants

Above: *These remarkable reliefs once served as cornice moldings that adorned the exterior of colonnades surrounding a large marketplace in the ancient city of Aphrodisias. It is likely that these moldings are similar in style to those that once graced the Lower Marketplace of Smyrna. Although the Lower Marketplace has never been excavated, many sculptures on display in the Archeological Museum of Izmir once graced this ancient commercial center and give a sense of how magnificent it was in its heyday. It was one of the largest and most elegant marketplaces in all of Asia.*

a shopper's paradise, and the city was a prime location for people who desired to make money. As a result, Smyrna was renowned as a center for both tourism and business in the ancient world.

From the large, open beaches of Smyrna, viewers enjoyed one of the most beautiful, panoramic seaside vistas in all of Asia. The view at sunset was breathtaking as the sun dropped below the edge of the Aegean Sea and the sky changed into pastel shades overhead. The winds that blew across the sea caused Smyrna to feel cool even during its hottest seasons. The westerly breeze, called Zephyrus, helped create ideal temperatures, which attracted even more visitors desiring to flee the scorching temperatures of their various regions. Aristides praised Smyrna's idyllic climate in his writings, declaring that "the winds blow through every part of the town, and make it fresh like a grove of trees."[72]

In addition to all these factors that lent to Smyrna's reputation as a popular destination, there were also untold thousands of religious pilgrims who arrived regularly to worship in the city's ancient temples. Just as modern tourists flock to see ancient sites such as the Pyramids of Egypt, people were also drawn to Smyrna because of its ancient and illustrious history. When one also considers the city's beautiful beaches, temperate climate, large number of hotels and good restaurants, excellent shopping opportunities, and the wide array of options for religious experience, it becomes clear why the First Century city of Smyrna was such a popular tourist attraction and an ideal center for pagan worship and business.

The sizable inflow of traveling dignitaries, Roman troops, sailors, and tourists who regularly arrived in Smyrna caused the city to experience substantial growth at a rapid pace. To assist with the challenges of this growth, the Roman Senate, along with local and foreign investors, authorized and invested significant resources into the expansion of the city's infrastructure. The city needed more local governance; its police forces needed to be enlarged; medical care had to be regularly updated and improved; roads needed to be expanded and upgraded; building facades needed to be regularly repaired

---

Right: The Lower Marketplace of Smyrna was one of the most spectacular marketplaces in the Roman Empire. It was filled with sculptures and was considered an architectural masterpiece in its day. The Archeological Museum of Izmir is filled with relics from the lower part of Smyrna that have survived from the Hellenistic and Roman periods, including the marvelous sculpture pictured to the right.

and refinished. All of this meant that there was a great deal of work available for laborers, which brought even more business and wealth to the city.

It must be noted that an unusually large number of luxurious homes have been excavated from the ruins of ancient Smyrna.[73] These excavations best demonstrate the wealth that the elite of Smyrna possessed as a result of the excellent business opportunities available at that time. Of course, the entire Smyrnean population wasn't rich. Ordinary people lived clustered in multi-storied *insulae* apartments, as they did in other cities throughout the Roman Empire. However, of all the ancient cities excavated to date, it appears that Smyrna had one of the largest numbers of splendid homes of any city in Asia. In fact, one of the oldest multi-roomed private homes ever excavated was discovered in the ruins of ancient Smyrna.

THE ROYAL ROAD

Ancient Smyrna was an outstanding city with enormous potential. But as important as the aforementioned factors were to the city's growth, another crucial factor to Smyrna's amazing prosperity still remained: the kingdoms east of Asia Minor, such as Assyria and Persia, which were major trading partners with Smyrna and the Roman Empire. Assyria and Persia needed access to the Aegean Sea for the back-and-forth transportation of its people, products, and merchandise — and as a result, the *Royal Road* ❾ was constructed in the Fifth Century BC. The road was built at the order of King Darius I of Persia for the purpose of opening a route for commerce between the East and the

West. The road started at the Persian capital city of Susa and continued many miles westward. After the initial construction was completed, the road measured more than 1,500 miles and reached the city of Sardis, the capital of the Lydian kingdom in Asia Minor.[74]

Each successive generation continued to expand and enhance the Royal Road. During Greek and Roman times, the road was greatly expanded until it eventually reached the city of Smyrna on the banks of the Aegean Sea. This access to the Aegean Sea was a significant milestone, opening the way for people and goods to be transported between the eastern kingdoms and the various parts of the Roman Empire.

Beginning at the Port of Smyrna, the Royal Road continued onward to Sardis, capital of the Lydian kingdom. It

Left: The Royal Road began at the city of Susa in the kingdom of Persia and wound westward nearly 2,000 miles through the kingdoms of Assyria and Lydia, finally concluding at the Port of Smyrna. It was one of the longest roads in the ancient world and was considered a feat of human engineering.

and visitors arriving from eastern cities in Assyria and Persia. Consequently, Smyrna's marketplaces and shops were rich with exotic items — herbs, garments, silks, tapestries, carpets, and so forth — that were rare and hard to find in other cities. This exotic element created an oriental atmosphere that became another enticement to the massive influx of visitors traveling to ancient Smyrna.

THE HERMUS RIVER AND THE MELES RIVER

The single most important contributor to the city's prosperity was unquestionably its port, which helped connect the Aegean Sea to the Hermus River ❿ (an ancient name for the second largest river in Asia Minor). The Hermus River emptied into the Gulf of Smyrna north of the ancient city. Its source was located on Mount Dindymus in central Phrygia. As it flowed 250 miles to the Aegean Sea, the river was fed by many small tributaries that increased its depth and width, making it navigable for ships to travel deep into the interior of Asia Minor.[76]

The Hermus River was a very significant river in this Roman province. It twisted and turned through Asia Minor, flowing directly by the city of Sardis. From Sardis, the river remained wide and

then snaked across the harsh terrain of Assyria to the city of Nineveh and onward to Babylon, finally ending at the ancient Persian city of Susa. Because its construction was initially paid for from the king of Persia's treasury and was maintained at his expense, it therefore became known as the Royal Road.[75] By the time it was expanded to reach Smyrna, the road was so long that it normally took almost three months for a traveler to travel its entire length. It was one of the longest roads in the Middle East at that time and considered a great feat of human engineering.

Thus, in addition to the heavy traffic that continually arrived at the Port of Smyrna and the multitudes who regularly stopped in Smyrna during their travels between Ephesus and Pergamum, there was also a steady stream of merchants

deep enough for ships to continue onward to the city of Philadelphia — a city that had been originally built to commemorate the brotherly love between the Pergamene kings Attalus II and Eumenes II.[77]

The river was named in honor of the pagan god Hermus, who was believed to be the god of this river. It is possible that early preachers traveled by ship up the Hermus River to reach cities like Sardis and Philadelphia with the Gospel, since this was the fastest route from the Aegean coast to the inland cities of Asia Minor.

Besides the Hermus River, the Meles River also emptied into the Gulf of Smyrna — a smaller river, yet still important. According to local legend, the writer Homer was born close to the city of Smyrna on the banks of the Meles River[78] and wrote *The Iliad* between 750 and 725 BC[79] while he resided in Smyrna. Homer's birthplace on the Meles River was such a well-known legend that he was even referred to as *Meleigenes*, which translates as *the son of Meles*.[80] Many series of coins minted in Smyrna bear Homer's image as the city's testimony to his time of residence there. The Meles River was minuscule in comparison to the Hermus, but it was rich in Smyrnean history and therefore important to the city's story.

Left: The ancient writer Homer was born on the banks of the Meles River near the city of Smyrna. It is believed that he wrote The Illiad *between 750 and 725 BC at his home near the Meles River, and a Homereium was constructed in Smyrna in memory of his residence there. This statue of Homer dates to the Hellenistic period in the city of Smyrna.*

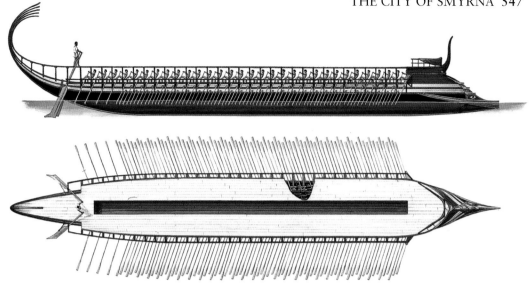

Above: *These illustrations of a Roman ship show the large number of oars used by the rowers who served as the "engine" that moved the ship forward. Rowers were usually condemned criminals who served the remainder of their lives in the bottom galleys of huge shipping vessels. They were trained to move their oars in unison to keep the ship moving at a fast forward speed. Vessels carried many types of cargo — such as wheat and other grains from Egypt — to ports throughout the Roman Empire, including the large, double-harbor Port of Smyrna.*

THE PORT OF SMYRNA

In Greek and Roman times, ships continually arrived at the giant Port of Smyrna with an incalculable number of passengers and tons of cargo. The destination of the ships varied. Some were destined only for Smyrna; others were destined for inland cities located up the Hermus River. The only other port that could compete with Smyrna was the Harbor of Ephesus (*see* pages 143-146). By the latter years of the Roman Empire, Ephesus' harbor had become so full of silt that ships could no longer access the city from the Aegean Sea via the Cayster River.[81] But the Port of Smyrna remained fully functional and ultimately had no rival on the coast of Asia.

Smyrna's port included both an outer and inner harbor. The inner harbor was formed by a natural basin, with a narrow opening that could be closed by a rope if needed. The outer harbor provided a large, offshore mooring ground in the open gulf for larger ships.[82] By the First Century, the Port of Smyrna was one of the largest and most majestic in the Roman Empire, competing with port cities such as Rome, Alexandria, Ephesus, and Caesarea.

As ships slowly glided through the outer harbor to enter the inner harbor, passengers heard the rush of water as oars were shoved deep into the sea to fight the currents and slow the speed of the ship. As ships steered toward the port, they sailed right alongside two long piers of stone that lined both sides of the port entrance. The head of each pier was decked with two large, marvelously carved marble lions that were depicted devouring smaller beasts. The strategic placement of these lions at the entrance to the Port of Smyrna was no accident. They conveyed a clear message to newcomers: Smyrna was a city of immense might and political power with imperial ties, and if anyone dared to challenge it, they would suffer serious consequences. This was a city that was strong enough to attack and devour any foe.

The most spectacular view of Smyrna was undoubtedly seen by those who stood on the decks of ships approaching the city from the sea. The closer the ship came to the port, the more breathtaking was the sight before them. Newcomers must have been struck by the city's beauty, with its gleaming marble structures sprawling up the slopes of Mount Pagos all the way to the peak.

Religious pilgrims who came to worship at the Temple of Cybele must have especially been captivated by the sight of the beautiful city. They had heard the legend that the city had been redesigned and rebuilt at the order of Alexander the Great and that its layout actually reflected the image of the goddess Cybele. Gazing upon the city as their ship approached the port, they might have imagined a statue of their goddess with her feet planted at the sea, her mid-section laced with beautiful buildings, porticoes, and temples, and her head crowned with the ancient fortress on the peak of Mount Pagos. Seeing Smyrna for the first time must have been an awe-inspiring moment for these devoted pagan worshipers. Before their eyes was the symbolic image of Cybele herself, stretched out across the mountain before them, greeting them as they arrived at the port.

THE SIGHTS AND SOUNDS OF SMYRNA

After a newcomer disembarked from his ship, he could travel directly into the heart of the city on one of several wonderful roads. Smyrna was famous for its straight streets that were neatly paved with stones. If the newcomer desired to do so, he could venture immediately up the

---

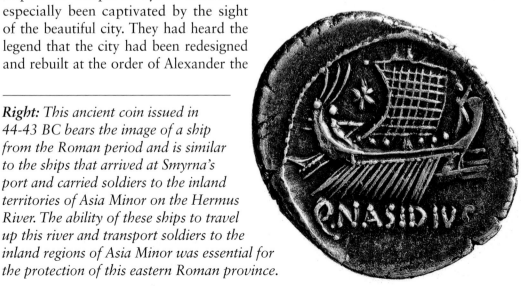

Right: This ancient coin issued in 44-43 BC bears the image of a ship from the Roman period and is similar to the ships that arrived at Smyrna's port and carried soldiers to the inland territories of Asia Minor on the Hermus River. The ability of these ships to travel up this river and transport soldiers to the inland regions of Asia Minor was essential for the protection of this eastern Roman province.

most historical road of the city — a street called the "Sacred Way."  It was a good place to start, because it began immediately at the Harbor Gate and continued all the way up the slopes of the city to the very peak of Mount Pagos. When Alexander the Great himself ascended the slopes of Pagos, it is possible he used this same road, which may have dated back to the city's earliest settlement. In fact, this street was so ancient that even in the First Century, it was considered to be one of the oldest existing roads in the world.

Like other streets in large Asia cities, the Sacred Way was lined with covered colonnades filled with shops and mosaic walkways. Vendors sold specialty items to people who walked up the steep incline, and people could be heard negotiating with sellers working in the small shops under the colonnade roofs. But as the name indicates, it was also a "sacred" street because it was crowded with temples, a seemingly limitless number of idols, and a glut of altars on which the population could make sacrifices to their pagan gods. Sights and sounds truly did abound from every direction for people who had never been to Smyrna.

However, no street in Smyrna was more famous than the Street of Gold. **12** Even Aristides specifically wrote about this celebrated street.[83] Although much of ancient Smyrna remains unexcavated today, it is generally agreed by historians and archeologists that the Street of Gold started at the steps of the Temple of Zeus on the southwestern slope of the city; then it curved around the lower slope of the city until it came to the temple complex of Cybele erected on the northeastern

---

Right: The Sacred Way was considered one of the holiest streets in Smyrna. Leading from the harbor all the way to the peak of Mount Pagos, this road connected several of the city's temples and was lined with altars to many gods, such as these three altars pictured here.

Right: The city of Smyrna had multiple gymnasiums. It is known that one was located at the Ephesian Gate, and it is likely that another significant gymnasium was located near the Harbor Bathhouse at the city's port. The god Asklepios was honored and worshiped in the gymnasiums of Smyrna. The gymnasium in the photo above, constructed in the typical style of First Century gymnasiums, was located in the city of Hierapolis.

side of Mount Pagos. Aristides wrote that this beautiful street ran west to east and connected one temple to the other, one mountain to the next.

Aristides also wrote that from a distance, the street gave the appearance of a lovely necklace wrapped around a neck as it graciously curled around the lower slopes of the city, lined on each side with elegant buildings. The "neck" he referred to, of course, was that of the goddess Cybele, in whose image the entire city was allegedly created.

The sights of the city were almost too numerous to comprehend. Aristides wrote: "Stand on the acropolis: the sea flows beneath you, the suburbs lie about you, the city through three lovely views fills the goblet of your soul.... Everything to the very shore is a shining mass of gymnasia, markets, theaters...baths — so many that you hardly know where to bathe...fountains and public walks, and running water in every home. The abundance of her spectacles, contests, and exhibitions is beyond telling, and the variety of her handicrafts. Of all cities this is best suited for those who like to live at ease...."[84]

If Aristides' words are taken to be literally true, Smyrna had multiple gymnasiums, multiple marketplaces, and multiple theaters. Strabo's report adds more details to this picture. He tells us that the city had large, quadrangular porticoes with lower and upper stories, a library, and a Homereium, which was a shrine to Homer containing a wooden statue of the poet. Strabo noted the harbor was so technologically advanced that it could be closed if needed.[85]

All of these descriptions point to the same conclusion: Smyrna was a sophisticated and cultured city possessing the highest technology available at that time.

THE GYMNASIUMS OF SMYRNA

So what is known about each of the specific sights in Smyrna that Aristides

The historian Strabo implied that one gymnasium was built near the Harbor Bathhouse.[87] This seems plausible, since gymnasiums were often connected to bathhouses during Roman times.

Aristides wrote that one of Smyrna's gymnasiums was so large that it had a special hall for people to worship Asklepios, the god of healing — a god that was dear to Aristides because he constantly battled with illness.[88] This particular gymnasium was said to have a courtyard that was surrounded by 98 marble columns. Since such columns usually supported covered colonnades, we may assume that this gymnasium had an inner courtyard surrounded with a covered colonnade that was supported with marble columns. This would

mentioned in his writings — that is, the gymnasiums, markets, theaters, and bathhouses? Let's begin with a description of the city's gymnasiums.

One gymnasium ⓭ was located near the Ephesian Gate on the road to Ephesus.[86] But in the previous quote, Aristides plainly stated that there were "gymnasia" in Smyrna, indicating that the city had a number of them.

Right: A bronze statue of a fighter, probably created as an adornment for a public bath. This boxer is pictured wearing the heavy boxing gloves associated with boxers who trained in the "palaestra" of a gymnasium. Notice the heavy leather strips in the gloves, which were reinforced with metal and specially designed to deliver a more dangerous, bloody punch.

be a typical design for a Roman gymnasium. This gymnasium may have also been equipped with a special room with a gilded roof that was used for council meetings.[89] Unfortunately, none of the gymnasiums referred to by Strabo or Aristides have ever been located because they are buried deep under the present-day city of Izmir.

THE MARKETPLACES OF SMYRNA

Next, Aristides mentioned the "marketplaces" of Smyrna. It isn't known with certainty, but it can be assumed that many people who arrived at the Smyrnean port made a fast dash to the city's Lower Marketplace, located near the harbor in the lower district. As noted on page 541, this was one of the largest commercial markets in the Roman world, and most products available for purchase in this market were sold in bulk. The opportunity to conduct business in this massive marketplace was the reason that man.y people traveled to Smyrna.

It is remarkable that the Lower Marketplace has never been excavated and its exact location has never been identified. Nevertheless, much is known about its exquisite architectural design because scores of magnificent statues, monuments, and idols that once adorned the market have since been unearthed. Today these treasures are displayed in the Archeological Museum of Izmir in the city of Izmir, Turkey. These relics from antiquity are among the most exemplary sculptures to survive from the Roman world, evidence of the marketplace's splendor in its heyday.

Public marketplaces of that day were surrounded with colonnades covered with

terracotta roofs. Colored marble pillars, crowned with gorgeous, hand-carved capitals, supported the roofs. In the very center of such marketplaces, there was usually a large, circular building called a *tolos*. The *tolos* would include a marble idol and altar where merchants could make a morning sacrifice or burn incense and thereby request the blessings of the gods on that day's business transactions.

Businessmen walked about these public marketplaces, talking to merchants while servants carried their masters' goods. Customers wrangled with vendors, and

Left: Although the Lower Marketplace has never been excavated, the ruins of the massive Central Marketplace still survive from the Second Century AD. Three sides were surrounded with covered colonnades, and the colonnade roofs were supported by 200 enormous marble columns topped with intricately carved capitals.

the Great)[90] has been partially excavated in what was once the middle district of Smyrna. It is one of the best-preserved Roman marketplaces in Asia and gives us a glimpse into what Smyrna's Lower Marketplace — which was far larger and more beautiful than the Central Marketplace 14 that can be seen today — may have looked like in ancient times.

Only two of the Central Marketplace's four sides have been completely exposed; however, this is enough to let archeologists know what the other two sides looked like, even though they are still buried under Izmir neighborhoods. Three sides of the marketplace were surrounded with long, covered colonnades — each 54 feet deep and 225 feet long. Although nearly nothing remains of the original floors, it is known that they were covered with fabulous mosaics and that they were supported from underneath by a complex system of arches. These arches also formed underground corridors that ran the entire length of the market on all four sides.

From the main courtyard, three rows of marble steps led upward to the covered colonnades. As a visitor stepped up three rows of steps into the colonnades, he had to walk between the massive columns — nearly 300 in all — that surrounded all

people traded money at the marketplace bank. Most marketplaces had a "debaters' corner," where new ideas were discussed and people with unpopular ideas were publicly punished. In a city like Smyrna, where Christians were horribly persecuted for their faith, it is probable that believers were punished in the open spaces of the Lower Marketplace and even suffered martyrdom for their faith there.

Although the ruins of the Lower Marketplace have never been discovered, a large, Second Century Central Marketplace (first built in the time of Alexander

four sides of the marketplace, supporting the heavy beams and terracotta roofs of the colonnades.

One side of the Central Marketplace was flanked with a large Basilica, surpassed in size only by Trajan's Basilica in Rome. Used primarily for public debates and political functions, the Basilica was 87 feet deep and 480 feet long. Each of its three floors was open on the side of the marketplace and was lined with columns. Interspersed between the columns were meticulously carved statues of gods, including the impressive sculpture of Poseidon and Amphitrite, which today is exhibited in the Museum of Art and History in the city of Izmir. Columns on

the second and third levels of the Basilica were fashioned from an unusual variegated, rose-beige marble.

The entire Basilica complex was built in honor of the gods with a special tribute to the Emperor Marcus Aurelius (161-180 AD) and his wife Faustina, the patrons of the Central Marketplace. In addition to an altar to Zeus, statues have been unearthed of Cybele, Vesta, Hermes, Dionysus, Eros, Herakles, and many other unidentified entities. These idols, as well as other excavated statues of marble, stone, and terracotta, provide sufficient proof that the Central Marketplace abounded with a lavish display of idols and images of the gods. This made the marketplace itself a

Interspersed between the rose-beige columns on the facade of the Basilica (right) were statues of gods, including the famous sculpture of Poseidon and Amphitrite that is now on display in the Museum of Art and History in Izmir (pictured on page 554).

prominent pagan shrine in the city of Smyrna.

Robin Lane Fox, author of the book *Pagans and Christians*, relates the story of one Christian leader named Pionius who was arrested in this exact marketplace during the reign of the Emperor Decius (249-251 AD) in the year 250 AD.[91] Decius had issued a special edict that required every person to make a sacrifice to the gods. One day Pionius and his friends, all of them committed Christians, walked through the double gate of the Central Marketplace — straight into a pagan celebration. The colonnades lining the marketplace and its stunning Basilica were packed with pagans celebrating, worshiping, and sacrificing to the gods.

At this time, Smyrna's Central Marketplace had just been rebuilt after a recent earthquake, and the new version was magnificent. The east and west sides were lined with high, two-story colonnades and had facades with marvelous marble columns extending approximately 400 feet in length. The colonnades, Basilica, and vast open courtyard were filled with pagan revelers, but Pionius and his Christian friends just walked past them all. As they approached an arch in the west colonnade, they passed busts of the Emperor Marcus Aurelius and his wife Faustina — the patrons of rebuilt Smyrna. The building itself was dedicated to the twin Nemeses, as well as to all the gods and goddesses and to the emperors. But Pionius and his companions ignored all the people making sacrifices and kept walking.

That day the authorities noticed the Christians' lack of reverence for the gods. Pionius was arrested and forcibly taken to the temple of the Nemeses, where officials demanded that he sacrifice to the gods and eat pagan meats. When Pionius refused, a pagan temple official said, "You know, of course, about the emperor's command

Above: The lower part of the Central Marketplace was surrounded by a series of remarkable underground arches that once housed hundreds of shops where merchants and shoppers carried out business transactions. This market was famous in the ancient world and drew visitors from around the Roman Empire.

and how the law requires you sacrifice to the gods."

Pionius replied, "We know the edicts of God, and He bids us to worship Him alone."

Pionius' refusal to sacrifice to the gods and to eat meat that had been offered to idols resulted in his martyrdom in Smyrna soon afterward. This entire event unfolded in the Central Marketplace that still stands in the city of Izmir today. However, this was only one instance of martyrdom that occurred in this famous marketplace. Many believers were publicly paraded and mocked here, and many were ordered to violate their conscience and their faith by

sacrificing to the gods. Those who succumbed to pressure escaped death, but of the large number of brave believers who refused to bow to pressure, many were publicly punished or killed right in the middle of the market among the idols and the pagan worshipers, who stood around celebrating the spectacle.

THE THEATERS IN SMYRNA

Aristides didn't stop with his mention of the "marketplaces" of Smyrna. He continued by mentioning the city's "theaters" — implying that Smyrna had more than one. This is certainly plausible, since Roman cities nearly always had at least one bathhouse and theater. Some cities were privileged to have more than one theater. An example is the city of Laodicea, a city that boasted two exceptionally large theaters. Smyrna may very well be another example, although the only theater that has been found in Smyrna to date is the large one situated on the north slope of Mount Pagos.

The Theater of Smyrna ⑮ was the first to be built in the region[92] and was undoubtedly one of the largest of the ancient world, testifying to the crucial role that entertainment, culture, and luxury played in this ancient city. At a minimum, the theater easily accommodated 20,000 people, but archeologists speculate that it may have been larger than the Great Theater of Ephesus, which seated 24,000 people. To date, only theaters in Pompeii and Rome match the physical proportions of the Theater of Smyrna. It had a diameter of 508 feet, occupied a space of 139,000 square feet, and included a stage that was 180 feet in width — sufficiently large to facilitate the largest known theatrical or musical performances.

Although theater originated with the Greeks, the first Roman theater was constructed of wood in Rome in 179 BC. The first permanent theater, which was constructed of stone at the order of Pompey in 55 BC, was so large that it seated approximately 40,000 spectators.[93] From that point onward, theater became an integral part of Roman culture.

Most Roman theaters were semi-circular in their design, including the Theater of Smyrna. It was composed of three primary sections: the *stage*, the *orchestra*, and *the seats for the audience*. Rows of seats rose sharply to accommodate large numbers of spectators who came to watch a variety of performances. Because the seats rose dramatically, each spectator had an unobstructed view of the performances being carried out on stage.

Romans typically built their theaters into the sides of hills, using the slope of the hill as a platform on which to build the semi-circle foundation for the spectators' seats. If no hill was available, the theater was constructed on massive arches, but the Romans preferred a hill as the base for their theaters. The back wall of the stage was often enclosed within a tall wall equal in height to the top row of seats. This wall had doors through which entertainers entered the stage and was itself a work of art, adorned with highly ornamented pillars and statues of emperors, heroes, and gods.

By the First Century, much of what transpired on the stage was lewd, ill-mannered, and derogatory. Public nudity and male body parts were openly displayed in attempts to make the crowd roar with laughter. The theater became so generally associated with crude behavior that it was one of the places Christians avoided altogether. As noted earlier, some believers were dragged onto theater stages to be mocked by the pagan audience, who scorned their faith in Christ. Theaters were also used for gladiatorial fights and pagan religious ceremonies. Because Dionysus — the god of wine, revelry, and debauchery — was also the god of theater and actors, a temple to the god was almost always located near a Roman theater.

In every part of the Roman Empire, the theater stage was filled with actors and entertainers who performed music,

Above: The Theater of Smyrna was among the largest theaters in the entire Roman Empire. It seated more than 20,000 people, yet only a faint outline remains in Izmir today. Smyrna's theater was similar in style to the theater that still exists in Hierapolis, which is pictured above.

mime, comedy, and tragedy. Theaters were also used for public speeches; however, in time the honorable talent of giving public speeches degenerated into public opportunities to mock, disdain, disparage, ridicule, and scoff at public figures or segments of society who were looked down upon or not accepted.

Sadly, New Testament believers were frequently the brunt of such ridicule. That is why New Testament writers used the word *theatron* — the Greek word for a *theater* — to describe those moments when early Christians felt abused and mocked by the world around them.

An example is found in Hebrews 10:33, where the writer of Hebrews identified with suffering readers and let them know that he was aware of what they had been through for their faith: "Partly, whilst ye were made a gazingstock both by reproaches and afflictions...." The word "gazingstock" comes from the Greek word *theatron* — the word for a *theater* — and the verse could be interpreted, *"You became a show for those who were watching you. In fact, they mocked you with their vulgarities and insults...."*

In his book, *The Story of Civilization: Caesar and Christ*, author Will Durant

states: "From the time of Nero, Roman law seems to have branded the profession of Christianity as a capital offense; but under most of the emperors this ordinance was enforced with deliberate negligence. If accused, a Christian could usually free himself by offering incense to a statue of the emperor; thereafter, he was apparently allowed to resume the quiet practice of his faith. Christians who refused this obeisance might be imprisoned, or flogged, or exiled, or condemned to the mines, or, rarely, put to death.... At Smyrna, the populace demanded of the 'Asiarch' Philip that he enforce the law; he complied by having 11 Christians executed in the amphitheater."[94]

Those 11 Christians were executed in the same theater where Smyrneans regularly gathered for entertainment. This event illustrates the level to which the Roman theater had degenerated by this time: Not only had the eloquence of Greek plays disappeared, but the killing of Christians had become acceptable entertainment. As the crowds sank deeper into depravity, attendance at the theater increased, requiring larger and more elaborate structures to be built. These complexes became the symbol of Rome's claim to sophistication and civilization — but in reality, the crude and depraved practices perpetrated in theaters throughout the Roman Empire were far from civilized.

THE BATHHOUSES OF SMYRNA

Lastly, Aristides referred to the "bathhouses" of Smyrna. Once again, he wrote the plural form, implying that Smyrna had a number of bathhouses.

As in other cities in Asia, Smyrna would have had a Harbor Bathhouse ❶⑥ where newcomers could go to bathe and cleanse directly after disembarking from their ships. People were arriving at this seaport from faraway territories, where unknown sicknesses and diseases were rampant. It was believed that bathing would ensure that newcomers' sicknesses and diseases were cleansed away before they entered the city.

Smyrna's Harbor Bathhouse would have been impressive and large enough to hold hundreds of people at one time. In typical fashion of the day, it is certain that its walls were paneled with beautiful marbles and its niches were graced with statues and idols created from marble and bronze. Altars were stationed in visible locations throughout the entire building so patrons could offer sacrifices to the gods. If desired, patrons could obtain sexual services in private rooms, which was a common practice in the bathhouses of the Roman Empire.

Not everyone participated in the morally decadent activities that were such an integral part of the bathhouse culture. But since Romans considered it socially acceptable to participate in such practices, it isn't surprising that many people from every sphere of society indulged in the sexual immorality that transpired in Roman bathhouses.

The Harbor Bathhouse wasn't the only bathhouse in Smyrna, for Aristides specifically mentioned "baths" in a plural sense when he wrote about the city's bathhouses. In a city as large as Smyrna, it would have been normal to have several bathhouses.

It is likely that a bathhouse ❶⑦ was located at the Ephesian Gate. As noted earlier, a sizable gymnasium was constructed near this huge city gate. It is therefore probable that a bathhouse was also built at that location, since Roman gymnasiums and bathhouses were usually constructed in conjunction with each other.

Although it can't be said with certainty because the area is covered with modern buildings and cannot be excavated, it is also probable that a third large bathhouse ❶⑧ stood near the city gate on the road that led to the city of Pergamum. Roman hygienic rules stated that people entering a city had to bathe before entering the population. Therefore, it seems likely that a bathhouse was located near each entrance to the city: the harbor, the Ephesian Gate, and the gate that led to

Left: Whether exclusive baths for the elite or public baths for the common class, Roman bathhouses were all marvelously decorated and often had floors covered with exquisite mosaics. This mosaic, which once decorated the pool of a bathhouse in Rome, provides a vivid example of the way thousands of pieces of glass or tile were used to create the elaborate designs that adorned the floors of most Roman bathhouses, including those in the city of Smyrna.

Pergamum. This would have enabled people traveling from any direction to bathe before entering Smyrna.

BATHHOUSES IN THE ROMAN EMPIRE

Baths were so central to Roman culture that when a city or town was established, the bathhouses were among the first structures to be erected, regardless of the size of the settlement. In earlier Roman times, bathhouses were small, but over the centuries, they took on a more significant role in society and thus were built larger.

Roman bathhouses were masterpieces of architecture and interior design, lavishly decorated with beautiful marble, mosaics, hand-carved columns, fountains, statues, and monuments. Bathhouse complexes often included gymnasiums, libraries,

meeting rooms for various purposes, and lovely gardens, where patrons strolled when they grew tired of sitting indoors.

The finest baths were in Rome, which boasted approximately 900 bathhouses. The size of these bathhouses varied, with some accommodating only a few people, and others capable of accommodating many hundreds of people, such as the gigantic baths constructed at the order of the Emperor Trajan. In 216 AD, the Emperor Caracalla surpassed all previous Roman bathhouses when he completed the construction of a complex[95] so immense that it covered an area of 33 acres and accommodated 1,600 people at one time.[96]

Most people in Roman cities used the public baths as a daily regimen. Under arched and vaulted ceilings, local people socialized with friends, talked to associates, conducted business transactions, or gave themselves to physical exercise and refreshment. In the book *Baths and Bathing in Classical Antiquity*, we find this description of Roman baths:

> The universal acceptance of bathing as a central event in daily life belongs to the Roman world, and it

is hardly an exaggeration to say that at the height of the empire, the baths embodied the ideal Roman way of urban life. Apart from their normal hygienic functions, they provided facilities for sports and recreation. Their public nature created the proper environment — much like a city club or community center — for social intercourse varying from neighborhood gossip to business discussions. There was even a cultural and intellectual side to the baths, since the truly grand establishments incorporated libraries, lecture halls, colonnades, and promenades and assumed a character like the Greek gymnasium.[97]

Although bathhouses varied in size, nearly all of them had the same four basic rooms: 1) the *apodyterium*, 2) the *frigidarium*, 3) the *tepidarium*, and 4) the *caldarium*. The *apodyterium* was a dressing room where patrons undressed or dressed, depending on whether they were entering or exiting. The walls of the apodyterium often had niches where patrons placed their personal belongings while they were in the bathhouse.

When the bathhouse patrons were undressed and ready to proceed, they next entered the *frigidarium*. The *frigidarium* was a *cold room* where clients bathed in cold temperatures. Roman science taught that cold temperatures were excellent at killing disease, so part of the bathing process was to dip or bathe in frigid waters. The word "frigid" is derived from the *frigidarium*.

Next, patrons entered the *tepidarium*, which was a *warm room* where servants poured expensive oils onto bathers' flesh. Soap was not used in the cleansing process.

Instead, oil was applied, rubbed into the skin in the form of a massage, and then scraped off with metal instruments. When the oil was removed, the dirt and grime were removed as well, thus "cleansing" the client. The room was kept warm to keep the oil hot and malleable. The word "tepid" comes from the word *tepidarium*.

Finally, bathers reached the room called the *caldarium*, the *hottest* room in the bathhouse. It was heated in an underground furnace called the *praefurnium*. Servants worked out of sight, stoking the

Left: Another example of the exquisite mosaics that decorated bathhouses during Roman times.

hot furnace to keep it piping hot so boiling water would continually be carried by the pipes under the floor of the *caldarium*. As heat rose from the underground pipes, it heated the floor and ascended through small pockets of space between the wall and the decorative interior plaster, causing even the walls of the *caldarium* to be hot. The word "cauldron" is derived from the *caldarium*, and the word "furnace" comes from the word *praefurnium*.

If Aristides was correct, the city of Smyrna had several of these bathhouses in different parts of the city. And because Smyrna was a highly pagan city, the immoral practices mentioned in Chapter Three that often occurred in Roman bathhouses would have been ordinary activities in the Smyrnean bathhouses as well.

THE STADIUM OF SMYRNA

If a person's trip began as he exited the Harbor Bathhouse, there were a number of different roads he could follow into various sections of the city. As a fully reconstructed city, Smyrna was one of the first planned cities in the history of the world, very different from most ancient cities whose roads twisted and turned through the various districts. Strabo recorded that Syrmna was divided into right angles with perpendicular streets, paved with stone and constructed mostly in straight lines.[98] Therefore, it wasn't difficult for a newcomer to find his way around this coastal city.

It is certain that many people exiting the Harbor Bathhouse would have headed toward the Stadium of Smyrna, **⑲** which was one of the largest in Asia. Sporting events, chariot races, wild-animal hunts, gladiator fights, and the execution of criminals and undesirables — including Christians — were all exceedingly popular stadium events during the First Century when the Church was being established in Smyrna and in other parts of Asia.

Although the Stadium of Smyrna has completely fallen into ruins, its faint outline can still be seen today close to the peak of Mount Pagos. The history of this stadium is very crucial to the Christian faith, for many believers died for their faith there in the first few centuries of the Church.

Most stadiums were long structures with one rounded end, seating thousands of spectators who came to the stadiums to see horse racing, chariot races, and wild-animal hunts. Near the rounded, semi-circular end, a wall was constructed that divided one-third of the stadium into a smaller viewing area specially reserved for gladiatorial games. Archeologists estimate the Stadium of Smyrna seated approximately 30,000 people, which made it a significantly large stadium — similar in dimension to the Stadiums of Ephesus and of Aphrodisias (*see* photos on pages 177, 566-567).

There is no doubt that some of the most intense persecution against Christians in the Roman Empire occurred in Smyrna and that many of the atrocities occurred in the main arena of the city's stadium. Because of the excessive fanaticism of pagan worshipers in Smyrna, the city was rife with terrible persecutions from the time of Nero onward. As late as 250 AD, the Smyrnean pagans were still viciously persecuting believers in the city.

Robin Lane Fox wrote about what occurred in the year 250 AD when the Emperor Decius sent forth an edict demanding that people everywhere make a special sacrifice to the gods. According to Fox, many Christians appealed to pagan authorities to free them from this requirement and the inevitable punishment of non-compliance. Some pagan authorities felt sorry for the Christians and signed

false affidavits, attesting that the bearer had completed a sacrifice to the gods. Those who were able to produce certificates were saved from harassment, but those who could not do so, and who *would* not sacrifice to the gods, suffered unthinkable consequences. Fox's earlier account of the martyrdom of Pionius (*see* pages 555-556) is a famous example of a believer in Smyrna who refused to obey this imperial edict and paid for it with his life.

In this environment of religious hatred, it can be said with certainty that many acts of persecution against Christians were carried out on the arena floor of Smyrna's huge stadium. Believers were publicly humiliated, forced to fight wild beasts or gladiators unarmed — and many were burned alive, slain with the sword, and sawn in pieces. It was here in this very stadium that the aged Polycarp, bishop of Smyrna, laid down his life for his faith in Christ.

OTHER OLDER FEATURES OF THE CITY

Other older elements in the city dated back to Hellenistic times. One example was the Temple of Zeus, located on the lower slope of the city, closer to the Aegean Sea. An even more ancient structure was the Temple of Athena, which dated back to the Seventh Century BC. At the time Alexander the Great visited Smyrna, the Temple of Athena was already 400 years old.[99]

In recent years, some of the foundation stones of the Temple of Athena were discovered during local construction in the city of Izmir. Although archeologists always believed the temple was

(Continued on page 572)

STADIUMS
IN THE ROMAN EMPIRE

In the Roman Empire, nearly every major city had a stadium in which thousands of people regularly gathered for entertainment. People today often associate the word "stadium" with the magnificent, grandiose Coliseum, which was located in the very heart of Rome. However, in Roman times, the structures known as "stadiums" were actually quite diverse, differing greatly in size and physical appearance based on their respective location. Although most were elongated arenas, these buildings could also be egg-shaped like the Roman Coliseum or shaped as a circle or semi-circle.

Seating tens of thousands of people at each event, these stadiums hosted a variety of games and spectacles, most important of which were the chariot races. The vast amounts of time and money invested into these massive

constructions bear testimony to the great importance Romans placed on public entertainment in the First Century.

The ancient Greeks were the first to build stadiums, using them for public events and athletic competitions as early as 900 BC.[100] In 776 BC, the Greeks held the first Olympic Games in Olympia, Greece, in one of those early stadiums.[101] Most of these Greek stadiums were U-shaped and constructed in geographical locations naturally suited to their purpose. Small dips or valleys in a landscape were most often selected, for many rows of seats could be constructed on the surrounding slopes for hundreds or even thousands of sport-loving spectators.

Ancient Greek stadiums of this type were equipped with dressing rooms and almost always had a pagan temple on or near its grounds. Each day's games commenced with an official religious ceremony that involved a special sacrifice offered to the gods. On days when no games were planned, stadiums were also used for large pagan religious celebrations. In Greece,

Above: Although hardly anything remains of the Stadium of Smyrna today, at one time it was massive in its dimensions. It was built in a similar style to the well-preserved stadium that still exists today in the ancient city of Aphrodisias, located in modern-day Turkey (pictured above). Many Christians were killed for their faith in Smyrna's stadium, including Polycarp, the bishop of Smyrna (see pages 497-509).

Right: This is an artist's rendering of what the Coliseum looked like when it was first opened to the public. This colossal stadium was 165 feet tall and 617 feet long and could accommodate between 50,000 and 70,000 spectators. The middle walkway was paneled with expensive marbles, statues, and idols. Over the top of the stadium seats was a massive canopy made of canvas sails, designed to protect spectators from the heat of the sun during all-day events. The Grand Opening commenced with 100 days of fights, including gladiator fights and wild-beast hunts. The

women were not allowed to attend the games, with the exception of priestesses who presided over religious rituals that might precede the games.

The name "stadium" is actually a Latin derivative of the Greek word *stadion* — an ancient Greek word that describes a specific length of approximately 600 feet. Most stadiums were exactly one *stadion* in length — hence, the reason for their name. Such structures could be larger, but this was an exception to the general rule in the construction of stadiums. If the space for construction was limited, smaller stadiums could also be built, although this was rarely the case.

The earliest stadiums built by the Greeks were used primarily for footraces and, in time, also accommodated chariot races. However, the bloody atrocities that most people now associate with stadiums didn't begin to occur until the rise of the Roman Empire.

Like the Greeks, the Romans were very passionate about athletic competitions. However, holding precedence over their love of sport was the Romans' insatiable desire to see the mighty and powerful take advantage of the weak and powerless. Hence, the activities held in Roman stadiums began to take on a much bloodier tone. Gory and horrific spectacles, such as gladiatorial fights (*see* pages 188-196) and mass public executions of prisoners as a form of entertainment, became immensely popular and widespread during Roman times.

As noted earlier, the city of Rome was home to the Coliseum, an enormous stadium that today is the most

wild animals would often be detained for long periods of time in dark tunnels with no food. Then when the door from the tunnel to the arena was suddenly opened, the hungry, angry beast would charge onto the arena floor to attack its hapless prey. Animals fought animals; animals attacked unarmed men; or animals were hunted and killed by men carrying weapons. Crowds cheered with enthusiasm when lions, tigers, leopards, rhinoceroses, bears, bulls, wild dogs, and crocodiles either killed human victims or were killed by gladiators.

---

well-known structure of the ancient Roman Empire. This marvel of architectural ingenuity was so colossal in size that it took 12 years to build and had a seating capacity of 50,000 people. With 76 entrances and exits, it was designed with such sophistication that it could be completely emptied in only three minutes. In addition, a large canvas canopy could be pulled around the edges of the stadium on hot summer days to protect spectators from the rays of the sun.

Near this Roman stadium stood a colossal statue depicting the Emperor Nero as a mighty god. Towering over the crowds, the statue was more than 100 feet tall. It was in reference to this statue that this particular stadium eventually came to be known as the "Coliseum."

In addition to the thousands of people who were slain in the Coliseum, tens of thousands of animals were also killed there during the years of its heyday. In fact, the Roman historian Dio Cassius recorded that during the grand opening of the stadium, 9,000 wild animals were killed in a 100-day inauguration celebration.[102]

This stadium was used for many different kinds of events and spectacles, including races, wild-animal hunts, gladiator fights, and the killing of criminals or others who had fallen out of favor with the government. Most scholars also believe that the base could even be sealed off and filled with water so crowds could watch actual battleship fights.

The central floor of the Roman Coliseum encompassed 6 acres, or approximately 195,000 square yards. When the Emperor Domitian came to power, he ordered the construction of an underground system of rooms and tunnels.[103] Both intricate and complex, this underground network was comprised of cells that held condemned prisoners; cages that housed wild animals; tunnels through which gladiators, victims, and animals walked from one part of the stadium to another; and special, hidden trapdoors that allowed ferociously hungry, angry beasts to suddenly appear on the floor of the vast arena and take victims by surprise.

Because Rome's dominion stretched over North Africa, many strange and unique animals were brought back to the heart of the empire. Special expeditions captured lions, leopards, elephants, crocodiles, rhinoceroses, hippopotamuses, wild dogs, and other beasts, which were then transported to Rome and other cities to be used in a variety of spectacles.

However, the largest public venue in Rome was not the Coliseum; rather, it was the Circus Maximus, an elongated stadium that could easily seat 100,000 people at a single event. After its initial construction, this latter structure underwent massive additions, until by the reign of Nero, it had been expanded to seat 250,000 people.[104]

Rome had several circuses, including another that seated 30,000 people — but at 700 yards long and 135 yards wide, the Circus Maximus was

the largest in the Roman Empire. It had three tiers of covered seats that surrounded three sides of the structure, as well as one open side that served as the main entrance and the starting point for chariot races. Its central section, called the *spina*, was lined with statues, monuments, and idols of various gods and goddesses.

On the days of the games, both spectators and patrons packed the stadiums, filling the seats to capacity. They watched chariot races, beasts attacking other wild beasts, armed hunters combating ferocious animals, and brutal gladiatorial fights. To the Roman masses, all of these sickening acts were merely part of a day's events.

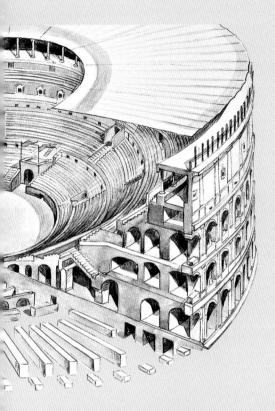

Left: This vivid illustration of the Roman Coliseum shows both an exterior and interior view of the massive stadium. Thousands of Romans packed the Coliseum to attend the public games. As time progressed, the masses grew hungrier for spectacles offering an increasing level of bloodshed and gore.

To spare itself the task of executing prisoners, the Roman government would frequently use criminals and political dissidents to entertain the ruthless crowds. Often the prisoners were thrown into the arena with ravenous wild beasts, and the masses would gleefully shout as the animals tore them to pieces. Other times, prisoners were forced onto the stadium floor without weapons to be brutally hacked to death by heavily armed gladiators. Those who were not killed by animals or gladiators were executed with the sword or even burned alive. As the victims' blood poured onto the sandy floor, the bloodthirsty spectators, watching from their stadium seats, would stomp and shout with exhilaration — relishing the gross displays of human suffering taking place before their eyes.

Stadiums were located in many Asia cities, such as Ephesus, Smyrna, Sardis, and Laodicea. These stadiums became places of dread for Christians and for others who had fallen out of favor with the government. During periods of brutal Christian persecution, the sadistic, malicious crowds watched with delight as misunderstood believers were taken to Roman stadiums to be tortured, burned alive, attacked by armed gladiators, or viciously attacked by ravenous beasts that had been deprived of food so they would readily kill and devour their victims. Although this practice spared the government the trouble of conducting special executions for Christians, it also produced an unexpected result. Even to this day, believers are inspired by the accounts of these brave early Christians who held fast to their faith in the midst of intense persecution and established an enduring legacy of courage in the face of unbearable circumstances.

significantly large, today it's been proven that the Temple of Athena was substantially larger than was previously assumed.

POWER TO WITHSTAND THE FORCES OF DARKNESS

As we've already seen, the illustrious city of Ephesus was very dark spiritually, and Smyrna was no less dark. In fact, because of the evil influence of Cybele worship, the spiritual atmosphere in Smyrna may have seemed even more ominous and oppressive than in Ephesus. Certainly the radically committed pagans of Smyrna demonstrated some of the most extreme behavior during times of Roman persecution, unremitting in their fervor to raise their voices against believers and instigate horrifically violent demonstrations against them.

Christians suffered persecution in nearly all cities of the Roman Empire, but from time to time, reprieves occurred when laws against believers were relaxed and the Church was able to breath a sigh of relief. But this wasn't true in Smyrna. When Christians in other cities and regions were thanking God for a lull in the intense persecution, nearly uninterrupted pressure continued to assail the Smyrnean believers from the pagan population, hostile Jews, and governmental authorities. Nevertheless, despite all the pressures that came against the believers of Smyrna, they didn't break, and eventually the powers of darkness crumbled beneath the light of the Gospel.

If these early believers could survive victoriously in the midst of such utter darkness, committed Christians today can be assured that they, too, can withstand the forces of evil surrounding them and be sustained by the glorious light of truth. The Bible says, "…Where sin abounded, grace did much more abound" (Romans 5:20). This was certainly true in ancient Smyrna, as it will be true in the lives of all believers who will call upon the matchless grace of God to assist them.

Above: Pictured are underground water cisterns built during Roman times to provide water for Smyrna.

THE CITY OF SMYRNA AS IT EXISTED IN THE FIRST CENTURY

The following numbered list corresponds to the sites described in this chapter. In this chapter, we have dealt with buildings, monuments, and religious structures that existed at the time the book of Revelation was written — with the exception of the Central Marketplace of Smyrna, which was constructed during the middle of the Second Century AD. This marketplace is mentioned in this chapter because it gives us a glimpse into what the Lower Marketplace once looked like and because it was a major site where Christians were martyred for their faith in the Second and Third Centuries AD.

1. Port of Smyrna
2. Temple of Athena
3. Mount Pagos
4. Temple of Cybele
5. Temple of Zeus
6. Double Harbor
7. Ephesian Gate
8. Lower Marketplace
9. Royal Road
10. Hermus River
11. Sacred Way
12. Street of Gold
13. Gymnasium at Ephesian Gate
14. Central Marketplace
15. Theater of Smyrna
16. Harbor Bathhouse
17. Bathhouse at Ephesian Gate
18. Third Bathhouse
19. Stadium of Smyrna

Map of Ancient Smyrna

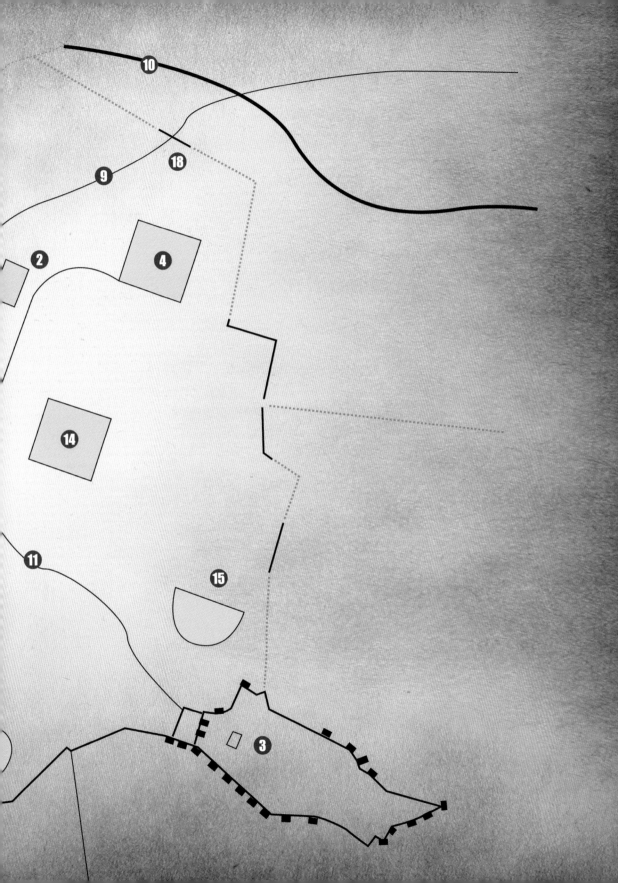

Revelation 2:8-11

8 And unto the angel of the church in Smyrna write; These things saith the first and the last, which was dead, and is alive;

9 I know thy works, and tribulation, and poverty, (but thou art rich) and I know the blasphemy of them which say they are Jews, and are not, but are the synagogue of Satan.

10 Fear none of those things which thou shalt suffer: behold, the devil shall cast some of you into prison, that ye may be tried; and ye shall have tribulation ten days: be thou faithful unto death, and I will give thee a crown of life.

11 He that hath an ear, let him hear what the Spirit saith unto the churches; He that overcometh shall not be hurt of the second death.

Chapter Seven

JESUS' MESSAGE TO THE CHURCH OF SMYRNA

Early writers called the beautiful ancient city of Smyrna "the first in Asia."[1] Yet despite its outward beauty and superb location on the shores of the Aegean Sea, Smyrna was one of the spiritually darkest cities in Asia. This was primarily true because of the widespread paganism that had gripped the city for centuries. In particular, the entire city was devoted to its patron goddess Cybele, which represented one of the most grotesque forms of First Century paganism. This barbarous religion included self-mutilation and frenzied, bloody rituals, which lent to the eerie atmosphere that pervaded Smyrna.

However, Smyrna was dark for many other reasons as well.

- Idols lined the streets of the city, and smoke continuously whirled upward into the air from the many altars where sacrifices were made throughout Smyrna.

- The huge stadium constructed on the slopes of Mount Pagos was the site of multiple massacres of believers who died for their faith. In addition to using the Stadium of Smyrna as a setting to execute believers for entertainment, Smyrnean citizens also customarily packed the stadium seats to watch other human victims being mercilessly slaughtered by gladiators or torn limb from limb by savage beasts.

- Salacious performances were regularly conducted on the public stage for the masses who filled the seats of the sprawling Theater of Smyrna — which, as recent research reveals, may have been the largest public theater in all of Asia.[2]

- Because Smyrna was a port city and a crossroads to many other parts of Asia, it overflowed with sailors, soldiers, and commercial travelers who sought the services of prostitutes, thereby producing a thriving prostitution industry within the city.

- As noted in the previous chapter, Smyrna had at least three major public bathhouses. As in other First Century cities of the Roman Empire, these bathhouses were magnificent architectural structures decorated with the finest marble; however, they were also places where all manner of unrestrained sexual promiscuity was practiced.

- On the basis of unfounded stories created to stir up hatred toward Christians, the Smyrnean Jewish community provoked Roman authorities to turn their vengeance on believers who lived in the city. The hatred this Jewish community stirred up was intense enough to incite uncontrollable riots against the Christian community. As a result of this Jewish propaganda, Roman authorities regularly rooted out believers and viciously killed them.

Because of these and many other factors, Christians in Smyrna were more likely to withdraw from the mainstream of Roman society. In the pages that follow, it will be clearly demonstrated how their need to separate from the godlessness surrounding them frequently led to public suspicion about Christians and their private activities. This often resulted in rumors — primarily fueled by an antagonistic Jewish community — that induced some of the most severe persecution against believers in all of Asia during the First Century. It is often true that people attack what they don't understand or what seems foreign to them, and this was precisely the case in Smyrna. The persecution against believers in this ancient city was extraordinarily intense, and some of the most infamous cases of early Christian martyrdom occurred there.

Just before Jesus went to the Cross, He prayed that those who followed Him would be kept from the evil that is in the world (*see* John 17:15). Thus, to avoid worldly entanglement, early believers deliberately steered clear of places associated with their previous, sinful pagan lifestyles. For example, Christians on the whole refused to attend the theater because of the immoral acts performed on the stage. And although public baths were a fundamental feature of Roman society,

Left: This painting by artist Jan Styka depicts Christians being thrown to hungry, wild animals in the Circus Maximus of Rome, but it portrays what was also occurring regularly in the Stadium of Smyrna at the time of Jesus' message to the Smyrnean church. Of all the cities in Asia, persecution was especially intense in Smyrna. Thus, we know that this bloody scene was replayed countless times in the city's stadium during the ten periods of Roman persecution that afflicted believers throughout the first three centuries of the Church.

most Christians shunned them because of the illicit sexual activities that occurred there. These early believers were truly "in the world" (John 17:11), but they ardently sought to remain free from the evil that surrounded them. In a pagan city like Smyrna where wickedness and temptation abounded, Christians had to withdraw from many activities that other citizens would have considered acceptable.

Paganism was so widespread in Smyrna that every person who lived there had to deal with its influence to some extent. Even the Jewish community had to learn how to navigate their pagan surroundings. On the surface, this beautiful coastal metropolis may have glistened in the sun's golden light, but a deeper look revealed a city infested with evil religions and moral filth.

There were a myriad of pagan cults in Smyrna, but none was as revered as the abominable cult of Cybele. Other cities also had patron gods and goddesses. For example, the city of Athens was dedicated to Athena; Aphrodite was the patron goddess of Corinth; and Ephesus was the center for the worship of Artemis. All these forms of pagan worship were wicked, sensual, and immoral. But the worship of Cybele was vastly different from all the other cults, primarily because of the grotesque self-mutilations that played a major role in its rituals. Even by pagan standards, what transpired during these perverse rituals was a stomach-churning sight.

The cult of Cybele has already been dealt with extensively in the previous chapter, but it must be briefly mentioned again as a reminder of the central role this religion played in the city of Smyrna. It is easy to see why the brutal nature of the

Left: Smyrna was host to one of the world's most foul and vile religions — the worship of the mother goddess Cybele. This marble sculpture represents the head of Cybele, who was also the city's patron goddess. The cult of Cybele was marked by perverse and bloody rituals that made it one of the most brutally violent forms of pagan worship in the entire Roman Empire. By the early Third Century AD, this evil religion had spread throughout the empire, becoming a major source of aggressive opposition to the Christian faith. Throughout this period, Smyrnean believers bore the brunt of the vicious persecution stirred up by the pagan worshipers of this goddess.

Cybele rituals was repulsive to so many in the Roman Empire — even to adherents of other pagan cults. Suffice it to say here that on what was called "The Day of Blood," Cybele's priests and worshipers slashed and mutilated their bodies, splashing their blood onto the altars, walls, and floors of temples dedicated to the goddess. The accompanying music was loud and pulsating, designed to mesmerize worshipers into a trancelike state — until, at the peak of this spirit-induced state, they would begin to violently mutilate their bodies. As disgusting as this sounds, these acts on "The Day of Blood" were considered some of the most "holy" moments in the worship of Cybele. (*See* pages 524-526 for more information on this pagan cult.)

Yet despite the dark spiritual atmosphere that pervaded Smyrna, a very courageous and highly organized church had been established in this ancient city by the time John penned the book of Revelation. It isn't known who first brought the Gospel to Smyrna, but many scholars believe the first Gospel preachers came to the city during the years the apostle Paul resided in Ephesus, located 35 miles to the south. These unknown believers most likely entered Smyrna through the Ephesian Gate on the south side of the city. By the power of the Holy Spirit, they began to bravely proclaim the Cross of Christ in the midst of this grave darkness — and as a result of their Spirit-filled courage, the church of Smyrna was born.

At the time the apostle John received the book of Revelation on Patmos, it is probable that he personally knew the pastor who was leading the church of Smyrna. It is also likely that Polycarp, who eventually became the second bishop

Right: Polycarp holds an important place in Church history as one of the first bishops of Smyrna and as one of the earliest Church leaders whose writings have survived. Early Christian writers assert that Polycarp was a disciple of the apostle John. This relationship with one of the original apostles gave Polycarp credibility in his latter years as a reliable witness of truth within the Early Church — a crucial position to hold after the death of the original apostles when varied interpretations of Jesus' teachings were being widely propagated. The astounding account of Polycarp's martyrdom in the city of Smyrna is well documented in early Christian writings. The date of his death is disputed, but the most likely year was 155 or 156 AD.

© Mary Evans Picture Library

of Smyrna, was already serving in active leadership on some level in the church before John's death. Writings by Early Church fathers imply that the elderly apostle John was a friend and mentor of young Polycarp and that certain apostles ordained Polycarp as bishop of Smyrna.[3] John may very well have been one of those apostles, since he was responsible for the oversight of the Asia churches until his death. Although countless Christians were martyred in Smyrna during the first three centuries of the Church, no martyrdom is better documented than that of Polycarp in approximately 156 AD (*see* pages 497-509).

From the very beginning of the Smyrnean church, Christians faced an onslaught of intense, sustained persecution. In other parts of the Roman Empire, believers were granted periodic reprieves from persecution. However, historical records show that such reprieves didn't extend to Smyrna, where persecution — or the ever-present threat of fresh outbreaks of violence — continued nearly unabated until the early years of the Fourth Century.[4] Christians were regularly massacred as entertainment in the stadium, slaughtered before crowds at the theater, and openly killed in the Central Marketplace, as well as in many other locations throughout the city.

These were the horrifically difficult circumstances Smyrnean believers faced at the time Jesus appeared to John on the island of Patmos and addressed them with a message of comfort, straight from the throne of God. Jesus' words to the believers of Smyrna continue to be a message of divine comfort to believers of every age who suffer persecution for His sake.

'UNTO THE ANGEL'

> Given Smyrna's physical proximity to Ephesus and the close relationship that the Smyrnean church had with the Ephesian leadership, it is logical that Jesus would direct His next message to the church of Smyrna after concluding His message to the Ephesian church.

As John continued to behold the exalted Christ in this divine visitation, the apostle heard these words:

> And unto the angel of the church in Smyrna write; These things saith the first and the last, which was dead, and is alive; I know thy works, and tribulation, and poverty, (but thou art rich) and I know the blasphemy of them which say they are Jews, and are not, but are the synagogue of Satan.
>
> Fear none of those things which thou shalt suffer: behold, the devil shall cast some of you into prison, that ye may be tried; and ye shall have tribulation ten days: be thou faithful unto death, and I will give thee a crown of life. He that hath an ear, let him hear what the Spirit saith unto the churches; He that overcometh shall not be hurt of the second death.
>
> Revelation 2:8-11

Christ began His message to the church of Smyrna in the identical way He began His message to the Ephesian church. He said, "And unto the *angel* of the church in Smyrna write..." (v. 8).

The word "angel" in this verse is the Greek word *angelos*, which can indeed be translated "angel"; however, it can also be translated "messenger" (*see* Luke 7:24, 9:52; James 2:25). As discussed in-depth on pages 371-372, the way *angelos* is translated depends on the context in which it is used. In this context, the word "angel" referred to the *messengers* of the seven churches, or to the *pastors* who had the oversight of the seven congregations.

This is the second time Jesus spoke a specific message to a pastor, whose responsibility was to then deliver the message to the congregation Christ had placed under his care. As discussed earlier, this was a demonstration of divine order in operation. Before the Head of

Left: Christians in Smyrna were severely discriminated against because of their faith. Many lost their jobs and suffered great financial loss. Many others endured beatings and were even put to death in public locations throughout the city. One of the most infamous cases of early martyrdom occurred near the columns of the Central Marketplace, pictured in this photo. Although much of Smyrna lies hidden below the modern city of Izmir, ruins of the Central Marketplace have been excavated and can be visited today.

The pastor's God-given responsibility is to hear and internalize Christ's message and then be the first to accept and respond to His correction, rebuke, or commendation. Afterward, the pastor is responsible for accurately delivering that message in the power of the Holy Spirit to the congregation under his care. This was clearly Christ's expectation for the "angels" — the pastors — of the seven churches in Asia, and this is still His expectation for Christian leaders today.

THE CHURCH AT SMYRNA

In Revelation 2:8, Jesus began His message to the Smyrnean church: "And unto the angel of the *church* in Smyrna...."

In this verse, Jesus once again used the Greek word *ekklesia* (translated "church"), referring to a body of individuals whom God had given the honor and privilege of being *called forth* and separated unto Him to *assemble together*

the Church addresses a local church with a correction, a rebuke, or an exhortation, He *first* addresses its pastor — His messenger to that particular congregation — regarding the issue at hand.

This point is very important, for it reveals that Christ respects and honors those whom He has set in authority and that He doesn't bypass the divine order He has established. Even if a God-appointed messenger refuses to hear, Jesus will nonetheless speak to him *first* by His Spirit; then the pastor has the opportunity to accept, ignore, or reject what the Holy Spirit is saying. But even if Christ already knows that the pastor doesn't have ears to hear, He will not circumvent the chain of authority in the local church.

for the purpose of furthering His Kingdom. He was addressing a particular local body of believers about their specific needs and challenges (*see* pages 372 and 388-398 for an in-depth discussion of the word *ekklesia*). In this case, Christ had strong words of comfort for the believers in Smyrna, who were enduring an unrelenting onslaught of intense persecution because of their faith in Him.

Outside the New Testament, information about the church of Smyrna is very limited, although there is an abundance of historical information about the city itself (*see* Chapter Six). In addition to this local body's mention in Revelation 2:8-11, information about the church of Smyrna can be found in two Second Century letters that Ignatius of Antioch wrote to the church. Eusebius also indicated in his writings that the Smyrnean church — although fiercely persecuted, under constant assault, and smaller than many of the other early churches — was nevertheless a very strong congregation that remained steadfast despite horrendous and unrelenting persecution.[5]

There were many martyrs in Smyrna, but as noted earlier, the most famous was Polycarp. The account of Polycarp's capture and execution was recorded in a Second Century letter written to the church of Philomelium (*see* pages 501-509). Other early writers listed the first bishops of Smyrna, which lets us know that this local church was organizationally developed. Early Smyrnean bishops included: Strataes, Bucolus, Polycarp, Papirius, Camerius, Eudaemon (who succumbed to pressure and denied Christ during the persecution of the Emperor Decius in 250 AD),[6]

and Thraseas of Eumenia (who was also martyred and buried in Smyrna).[7]

Because of Smyrna's pivotal location between Ephesus and Pergamum and its role as a major port for Asia, the city was commercially, religiously, and politically significant. Its influence was also greatly enhanced by the fact that it was the nearest western seaport for the ancient Royal Road that led eastward through Sardis to Susa, Persia. In addition, Smyrna was the primary entrance for Roman troops into Asia and, as a result, had a substantial military presence. Its relationship to Rome was so significant that it became the first city in Asia to be granted the privilege of constructing a temple to Dea Roma, the official goddess of Rome. Smyrna's strong connection to this imperial religion also contributed to the intense persecution against believers, whose faith in Jesus Christ prohibited them from making sacrifices to Dea Roma or any other pagan deity.

Smyrna also had a substantially large Jewish community. In fact, although Asia Minor was primarily pagan, large Jewish communities existed in every city where there was great business potential — such as Ephesus, Smyrna, Sardis, Laodicea, and other cities throughout Asia.

Pagans belittled Jews for their "narrow-minded" religious views; however, they appreciated the Jews' skills in administrating, managing, and conducting successful business ventures. This explains why many Jewish names can be found in connection with markets and business dealings throughout the ancient pagan world.

From the very inception of the Smyrnean church, the Jewish community

Right: This photo shows a detail from a relief on the Column of Antoninus Pius depicting the goddess Dea Roma. Smyrna had strong ties to the Roman imperial authorities and served as a center for the worship of Dea Roma, the goddess of Rome.

within the city maintained an especially malevolent attitude against Christians. It was, in fact, the Jewish community that was largely responsible for the Second Century martyrdom of Polycarp. The book of Revelation was written prior to Polycarp's death (in approximately 96 AD); however, Jesus' words to the pastor of this church make it clear that the Smyrnean Jewish community was already a weapon used by Satan to oppose the message of the Cross. It isn't known how many Christians were martyred in Smyrna because of disturbances incited by local Jews — but historical records indicate that the number was quite large.

'THESE THINGS SAITH THE FIRST AND THE LAST, WHICH WAS DEAD, AND IS ALIVE'

In Revelation 2:8, Jesus continued His message to the church at Smyrna: "And unto the angel of the church of Smyrna write; *These things saith the first and the last, which was dead, and is alive.*"

As was also the case in Revelation 1:17 (*see* pages 132-133), the words "the first" and "the last" have definite articles. This means Jesus doesn't depict Himself merely as *a* beginning; He is *the* beginning. Likewise, He is not just *an* ending; He is *the* end or *the* last.

Thus resounds the triumphant message that Jesus is the *beginning*, the *conclusion*, and *everything in between*. Therefore, He knows the *past*, the *present*, and the *future* — a message that must have meant a great deal to the Smyrnean believers who were undergoing such intense persecution. They would have realized that this means *nothing* happens that Christ isn't aware of. He knows what *has* happened; He knows what *is* happening; and He knows what *will* happen in the future. Because Jesus is Lord of all, nothing escapes His attention or takes Him by surprise.

This message must have been comforting to believers in Smyrna who were suffering severe persecution because of their faith in Christ. These believers were suffering many forms of maltreatment — often instigated by the Jewish community (Revelation 2:9) and implemented by the pagan world around them.

As noted earlier, the persecution against Christians in Smyrna was so intense that it often resulted in their death. Therefore, Christ's next words in Revelation 2:8 — *"which was dead and is alive"* — must have provided an even greater measure of comfort for these believers. By identifying Himself as the One who "was dead," Jesus sent a clear message to the Smyrnean congregation that He understood their situation completely.

© Mary Evans Picture Library

The word "was" in this phrase comes from the Greek word *ginomai*, which means *to become* but also conveys the idea of *an unexpected turn of events*. Who could have ever imagined that God would become flesh and then submit Himself to those who would put Him to death — and not just any death, but the wretched death of a Cross? Yet this is precisely what God endured when Jesus Christ, the Son of God, *became* (*ginomai*)

Left: This wood engraving by Friedrich Overbeck depicts the glory of Jesus' resurrection — the moment in history when death was permanently defeated by the Lord of life. Believers of every age can take comfort in the One "which was dead and is alive." Because Jesus triumphed over the grave, death holds no more power, for eternal life awaits all who have trusted in Him.

The word "dead" comes from the word *nekros*, which is the Greek word for *a dead body* or *a corpse*. This means that Christ's death was not a metaphysical death but a real, physical death. He endured physical death — but as Acts 2:24 tells us, death didn't have the power to hold Him.

The Smyrnean congregation would have received great encouragement from this truth, since many were facing imminent death themselves. Jesus' words reassured them that just as He had been resurrected from death, they, too, would be resurrected. Even if these believers should be required to die for their faith, Christ wanted them to know that death is only a temporary foe that He has permanently defeated. Whether experiencing death by persecution or by natural causes, believers of every age can be assured that Jesus' victory over death has secured a similar victory for *all* who believe in Him (*see* 1 Corinthians 15:20,51-57).

In Revelation 2:8, Christ continued by declaring that He is "alive." The tense of the word used here makes the declaration even stronger, for it means that Christ is *continually alive*. The word "alive" in the original Greek emphatically means that Jesus Christ now lives *perpetually*,

dead. Of course, God always knew that this was the plan, but no human being could have ever conceived this turn of events. The apostle Paul wrote with amazement and wonder that God Himself would humble Himself unto death, even the death of a Cross (*see* Philippians 2:8). Although Christ had existed for eternities past, a moment came when His eternal existence was interrupted, and He temporarily *became* dead.

Above: *Christians were frequently forced to find shelter in caves, catacombs, and other underground settings while enemies of the faith pursued them relentlessly, trying to destroy this new religion that threatened their pagan way of life.*

continuously, and *forever*; His is an *unending life* that will never see death again.

Jesus visited and conquered death, tasting it once for every man (*see* Hebrews 2:9). But death was nothing more than a brief interruption to His endless life. Now it has been permanently put behind Him, and He is alive forevermore — a living Savior who promises eternal life to all those who come to Him in faith. For Smyrnean believers who were confronted with the constant threat of death, this was a

divine promise that would help guide them through deadly times.

Regarding Revelation 2:8, theologian Albert Barnes provided further insight into this powerful verse: "As He [Christ] had Himself triumphed over death in all its forms, and was now alive for ever, it was appropriate that He should promise to His true friends the same protection from the second death. He who was wholly beyond the reach of death could give the assurance that they who put their trust in Him should come off victorious."[8]

Above: This Nineteenth Century engraving entitled, "Christians Hunted Down in the Catacombs" depicts a common scenario in the first several centuries of the Early Church.

'I KNOW THY WORKS'

In Revelation 2:9, Jesus continued to address the Smyrnean congregation, stating, "*I know thy works*, and tribulation, and poverty, (but thou art rich) and I know the blasphemy of them which say they are Jews, and are not, but are the synagogue of Satan."

Notice that after Christ addressed the angel, or pastor, of the church and introduced Himself, He immediately told them, "*I know*...." The word "know" is the Greek word *oida*, which comes from a Greek root that means *to see and therefore to know*. It is the same word Jesus used in Revelation 2:2 when He spoke to the church at Ephesus. As noted on pages 402-403, the word *oida* describes *knowledge* that Jesus *attained through personal observation*. Although the Smyrnean believers may never have seen Jesus with their physical eyes, He was nevertheless walking in

Above: This engraving by German painter and illustrator Carl Offterdinger (1829-1889), portrays how relentlessly Christians were persecuted in the Early Church.

the midst of the seven golden candlesticks and had therefore seen everything that had happened in their congregation.

Jesus continued saying, "I know thy *works*...." The word "works" is the identical word used in Revelation 2:2 and denotes *deeds* or *actions*. But as noted earlier, in the original Greek, the word "works" is followed by the Greek word for "thy" and can literally be interpreted, "*I know the works of you*." This means Christ knew specific details about the works, deeds, and actions that were exclusive to the church of Smyrna.

However, the words "thy works" in Revelation 2:9 are not found in the earliest surviving texts of the New Testament. Some scholars suggest that a copyist who wanted to make Jesus' message to Smyrna consistent with His words to the other churches added the words "thy works." If these words were included in Christ's original message, it indeed added consistency to the seven messages and alerted readers to the fact that He is personally aware of everything that occurs within His Church.

But if these words were *not* included in Jesus' original words to the church of

Smyrna, it means He went straight to the heart of His message to these believers by simply saying, *"I know thy tribulation, and poverty...."* If so, this emphasizes the fact that Christ was very sensitive to the urgent needs pressing against this church. Rather than review their activities, He directly addressed the pain and hardships this congregation was experiencing on a daily basis.

'TRIBULATION AND POVERTY'

In Revelation 2:9, Jesus went on to state, "I know thy works, *and tribulation, and poverty...."*

In the original Greek, the word "tribulation" is followed by the word "thy" and could be literally interpreted, *"I know the tribulation of you...."* Thus, Jesus referred to a tribulation that was specific to the church at Smyrna and different from that which was being experienced by the other churches in Asia. Something about *this* "tribulation" set the Smyrnean congregation apart in a category of difficulty and hardship that superseded what any of the other churches were experiencing. In fact, this was the only church out of the seven where Jesus used the word "tribulation" to describe their plight.

This word "tribulation" comes from the word *thlipsis*, a word that is frequently used in the New Testament, especially in the writings of the apostle Paul when he described *difficult events* that he and his team encountered. This word is so strong that it is impossible to misunderstand the intensity of these difficulties. It conveys the idea of *a heavy-pressure situation.* In fact, the word *thlipsis* was first used to describe the specific act of tying up a victim with a rope, laying him on his back, and then placing a huge boulder on top of him until his body was *crushed.* As time progressed, this word came to describe *any situation that was crushing or debilitating.* In addition, the adjectives *acute, awful, critical, dire, dreadful, grave, grim, humiliating, overpowering, pressing,* and *subduing* would all accurately convey the various nuances of meaning encompassed in the word *thlipsis.*

One of the best examples of the word *thlipsis* is found in Second Corinthians 1:8, where Paul wrote, "For we would not, brethren, have you ignorant of our *trouble* which came to us in Asia...." The word "trouble" is the word *thlipsis.* The verse could be rendered, *"We would not, brethren, have you ignorant of the horribly tight, life-threatening squeeze that came to us in Asia...."*

By using this word *thlipsis,* Paul let his readers know that his time in Asia included some of the most grueling experiences he had ever undergone. If he and his companions hadn't experienced the sustaining power of God, those experiences would have been *unbearable, intolerable,* and *impossible to survive.* Paul used the word *thlipsis* several other times in his epistles to convey a similar message: Over the course of his ministry, he had lived through crushing situations that would have been *devastating* if the power of God had not sustained him.

This word *thlipsis* is also used in the following New Testament scriptures:

592

- In Acts 11:19, where it depicts the *intense pressure* being wielded against the church at Jerusalem.

- In Second Corinthians 1:4, where it is used to describe the *troubles* and *persecution* Paul and his team had experienced in Asia and that other believers in the region were also facing.

- In Second Corinthians 8:2, where it describes *a terrible trial* experienced by the churches in Macedonia.

- In First Thessalonians 1:6, where it depicts the *severe suffering* believers were experiencing in Thessalonica.

- In First Thessalonians 3:3, where it is used again to convey *a burden that would normally crush a person.*

When John was on the island of Patmos, he also suffered horrible hardships. With plenty of time to reflect, the elderly apostle most likely remembered the words Jesus had spoken nearly 60 years earlier: "…In the world ye shall have tribulation: but be of good cheer; I have overcome the world" (John 16:33). In fact, it was John who eventually recorded those words in his gospel, using the word *thlipsis* to describe the "tribulation" Jesus spoke of in John 16:33. As always, this word describes a *distress*, *affliction*, or *trouble* so intense that it is almost unbearable to the soul.

Certainly John had experienced such tribulation on account of his faith; therefore, Jesus' words must have provided

Left: The painting "Paul and Silas in Prison" by William Hatherall shows one of the landmark moments in the apostle Paul's ministry when intense suffering and hardship (thlipsis) *was turned into an even mightier deliverance by the power of God. An earthquake loosened the men's chains, freeing them from prison and ultimately bringing salvation to the jailer and his entire household.*

continual comfort to his own heart. John vividly remembered that Jesus told His disciples to be of "good cheer," and the apostle must have clung to those words through every trial he had endured through the years. The phrase "good cheer" comes from a single Greek word *tharseo*, which literally means *to be courageous.* It is consistently translated "fear not" in the *King James Version*, but a more accurate rendering would be *"take heart!"* It is a word spoken to strengthen someone who is facing a hardship or a difficult trial. Thus, Jesus was literally saying, *"In this world you will go through some distressing times, but take heart and be courageous...."*

Jesus went on to assure His disciples, *"...I have overcome the world."* The word "overcome" comes from the Greek word *nikos*, which can be translated *to overcome* but is also the word for *victory.* However, the grammar used in this verse doesn't imply a single victory; rather, it denotes a continuous, abiding victory both now and in the future. Therefore, the idea presented in Jesus' statement could be interpreted, *"I have overcome the world; I am overcoming the world; and I will always be overcoming the world."*

The memory of these words spoken by the Master must have provided great encouragement and strength for John as he suffered on the island of Patmos. Eventually those same words would become a source of strength for suffering believers everywhere when John recorded these words in his gospel. When it seemed like the entire world was trying to annihilate them, early believers could hold on to the promise that Jesus *had* overcome the world; He *was* overcoming the world; and He *would always overcome* the world.

The word translated "world" in John 16:33 is the Greek word *kosmos*, which describes all the *human systems of the world*, such as the religious bodies and governments that were aligned against those who had found faith in Christ. This same word is used in John 14:30, where Jesus described Satan as the "prince of this world." The word "prince" is the word *archon* and is used here to depict Satan as a *ruler* of worldly systems. This scripture doesn't teach that Satan is the god of the earth itself; rather, he is the *prince* or *ruler* of *human systems* and *human organizations*. These worldly systems were — and they continue to be — used by Satan to attack the Church of Jesus Christ from its inception in the First Century right up to this present day.

This was certainly true in the pagan city of Smyrna. A demonic force was exerting its influence in Smyrna through religious groups, education, entertainment, and the political machine of that time. Satan was using these systems to wage war against the Smyrnean church and to deal crushing blows to its members again and again. This is the reason Jesus specifically stated in Revelation 2:9, "I know thy works, and tribulation...." As stated previously, the emphasis in the original Greek reads, "I know *your* tribulation," which reveals that the church of Smyrna was undergoing a miserable, torturous ordeal. In addition to physical persecution, it seems that the painful trauma these believers were experiencing was also connected to financial suffering — thus, the reason Christ went on to say, "I know thy works, and tribulation, *and poverty*...."

It must be noted that the Greek text has an article before the word "poverty," which means it refers to *a specific or unique kind of poverty* that was wreaking havoc in the lives of the Smyrnean believers. The word customarily used to describe a poor person is *penia*, which describes *a person from a lower class who must perform manual labor to make a living.* If a person fit in the category of *penia*, he was capable of providing a meager income but didn't own land or have investments for his future. However, the word "poverty" in this verse isn't *penia*; rather, it is the word *ptochos*, which is the Greek word for *abject poverty*. This word refers to *total* impoverishment — an appalling and horrifying level of poverty. It depicts a person so destitute that he is deprived of the barest essentials for living. In fact, this word *ptochos* would normally picture a homeless person or someone who has to scrounge to find enough food to eat. It is a person whom society would consider down and out, financially ruined, and poverty-stricken.

In the ancient world, one's ability to accumulate material possessions was often viewed as a sign of divine favor. Likewise,

Right: This scene, painted on an ancient vase, depicts a man painting on the side of just such a vase, as well as a woman painting the handles of a large urn. Greeks and Romans produced vessels made both of clay and of metal, the latter including vessels fashioned of copper, bronze, silver, and gold. Both Greek and Roman cultures established trade guilds for various industries of this type.

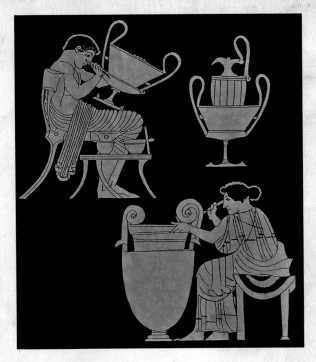

the pagan population viewed impoverishment as a *punishment* inflicted by the gods because of some evil that a person or a group of people had done. Therefore, those who were destitute not only suffered material and financial lack, but they also suffered as social outcasts, which added to their misery. Even if there were understandable reasons explaining why a person or group of people was experiencing poverty, the general view was that the gods were offended and had therefore thrust them into an impoverished state.

It is true that many First Century converts to Christianity were poor slaves (*see* Ephesians 6:5; Colossians 3:22; 1 Timothy 6:1; Titus 2:9; 1 Peter 2:18). However, it is unlikely that this was what Jesus was referring to in Revelation 2:9. The lower classes of the empire knew how to cope with poverty and, for the most part, wouldn't have found it unusual or particularly crushing. But Jesus' words to the Smyrnean church indicate that these believers had experienced something out of the ordinary. They weren't accustomed to such poverty. Furthermore, this wasn't just a situation of experiencing lack; this was *deprivation*. The view of most scholars is that the word "poverty" is an amplification of the word "tribulation." Although the Smyrnean believers were experiencing many forms of hardship, their greatest daily tribulation was their extreme poverty. Something had occurred in Smyrna that plunged believers into dire straits both materially and financially.

This critical situation may be explained by the fact that Roman society had "trade guilds" for various crafts and specialized trades. These trade guilds, known officially as *collegia* in Latin (Greek: *hetaireia*), were somewhat similar to what developed later into workers' unions. There were *collegia* for painters, dyers, weavers, tanners, teachers, doctors, bronze workers, goldsmiths, silversmiths, and idol makers. In some cities, these

Above: This ancient vase painting shows three men working in a bronze smithshop to produce a statue made of bronze. Such statues were abundant in Greek and Roman times and adorned temples, palaces, gymnasiums, and other public places. Consequently, the trade guilds for skilled workers of this craft were often enormous.

trade guilds were so powerful that they were able to determine prices for various services and to regulate their trades within their respective cities.[9] If a person wasn't a member of a trade guild, it was often very difficult for him to find work in his profession.

In some aspects, these *collegia* were similar to clubs where friendships are formed and mutual support is shared. Workers' social lives and occupations were built around their respective guilds. Even pagan worship played a role in these *collegia*. For example, a person began his initiation into a guild by offering a sacrifice to an idol that represented the particular god his group worshiped.

The importance that pagan worship played in these groups cannot be overstated. Pagans believed that staying in good favor with the gods was essential for business to prosper, so worship around an idol was a central part of all *collegia*. At each gathering, members were required to regularly make sacrifices and thereby acknowledge the group's patron god.[10]

There were *collegia* for poorer workers, as well as for workers of a wealthier class. In all of these groups, regardless of their financial status, members would socially interact and corporately celebrate pagan feasts — eating, drinking, and reveling together as a group.[11] However, wealthier people were often attracted to gods of a more taboo nature,[12] the worship of which frequently involved deviant sexual behavior and riotous acts not fit for a public temple setting. Thus, it would be reasonable to conclude that when these wealthier *collegia* held their regular meetings, morally perverse activities often took place behind closed doors.

Above: *The various types of* collegia *groups would regularly gather to celebrate pagan feasts together — events that often included drunken reveling and immoral interaction, especially among the wealthier classes of trade guilds. Because Christians refused to attend these mandatory* collegia *gatherings, they were shut out of the trade guilds and therefore often prevented from working in their respective professions. As a result, many believers were thrust into abject poverty because of their faith in Christ.*

For all these reasons, new believers found it very difficult, if not almost impossible, to retain membership in their *collegia* and at the same time remain faithful to Christ.[13] Believers shunned any setting that involved pagan sacrifices, drunkenness, and sexual promiscuity — all of which occurred within *collegia* gatherings.[14] However, functioning in business outside of one's guild — which operated on a "buddy system" that preferred members above outsiders — was almost impossible. Those who tried to work outside their *collegia* were largely unsuccessful and found little opportunity to earn an income.[15]

Because believers refused to sacrifice to the gods or to participate in drunken gatherings and immoral activities, they either deliberately removed themselves from their *collegia* or their membership was revoked due to lack of participation. This meant believers who were once financially secure and well connected in their various trades often found themselves without a job and with little ability to earn an income. These believers were not just poor — they were *destitute*, all because they refused to compromise their commitment to Christ by following the requirements the pagan world demanded of them.

However, there is yet another factor that probably contributed to the poverty of the Smyrnean church. We are told in Hebrews 10:34 that believers in the Early Church were vandalized by those who opposed their faith. Hebrews 10:34 says, "...[You] took joyfully the spoiling of your goods, knowing in yourselves that ye have in heaven a better and an enduring substance."

The word "spoiling" is the Greek word *harpage*, which means *to seize*, *to carry off*, *to plunder*, or *to confiscate*. Cleon L. Rogers Jr., a well-known modern Greek scholar, states, "The word [spoiling] implies that their own property either had been confiscated by the authorities or plundered in some mob riot."[16] This word *harpage* infers that these believers' homes and businesses had been raided and ransacked and that their "goods" had been pillaged. The word "goods" is *huparcho*, a word that describes *physical possessions*, *financial resources*, or *property*. Hebrews 10:34 doesn't identify the culprits who did the looting. But regardless of who they were, the perpetrators had plundered these believers and walked away with their goods. Yet throughout this difficult ordeal, the believers kept their focus on Heaven, where they had "...a better and an enduring substance."

Some scholars believe that members of the Jewish community in Smyrna raided, looted, and robbed many Smyrnean believers of their possessions.[17] Jesus' words in Revelation 2:9 make it plain that the Jewish community was a menace to believers in the city. Therefore, it stands to reason that the Jews of the city could have been a contributing factor to the poverty that was thrust upon members of the church.

If the Jewish community stole from the Christians, it is logical to conclude that the pagan population also found it easy to do so. According to Roman law, the church was an illegal religious cult, which made it much easier for people to take advantage of its members. Furthermore, the city of Smyrna was a strong ally of Rome and an important base for Roman troops. Therefore, it wouldn't have been difficult to stir up trouble against an illegal group of people who refused to bow their knees in worship to Roman emperors. Christians were already out of favor with the law, so it was nearly impossible for individual church members to appeal for legal help if they were attacked. All of this made Smyrnean believers easy targets for anyone who wanted to plunder their property and rob them of their goods.

In light of these facts, Jesus' next words to the Smyrnean congregation were significant. Although these believers had lost much both materially and financially, He went on to exuberantly declare that they were *rich* in other ways.

'BUT THOU ART RICH'

Jesus continued His message to the church of Smyrna, saying, "I know thy works, and tribulation, and poverty, *(but thou art rich)*..." (Revelation 2:9).

Above: This painting depicts pagans violently attacking a group of early believers, discovered as they met together in the Roman catacombs. Pagans both feared and hated the "upstart" new religion called Christianity and went to great lengths — both vicious and futile — to wipe Christians off the face of the earth. Thus, early Christians were often forced to meet secretly in underground catacombs, caves, and other hidden places to fellowship and worship God together.

The word "rich" is the Greek word *plousios*. It depicts a person who is *extremely wealthy*. In fact, the word "plutocrat" is derived from this word and describes someone in the governing class of a society who is excessively wealthy. A person who is *plousios* isn't merely rich — he is *very* rich. This was the word Jesus used when He told the church of Smyrna, "…(But thou art rich)…."

This is in sharp contrast to Jesus' preceding description of the Smyrnean believers as financially destitute. But riches are not always measured in dollars and cents. In fact, there are many less tangible yet infinitely more valuable forms of riches that cannot be purchased with money — and in regard to those riches, the church of Smyrna was *extremely* wealthy.

A study of the word *plousios* in the New Testament shows that it often does refer to *a superabundance of possessions or finances*. But it can also refer to *spiritual riches*, as in First Corinthians 1:5 where the word *plousios* describes a *wealth* of spiritual gifts in the church of Corinth.

In Ephesians 2:4, *plousios* describes *the riches* of God's mercy, which emphatically means God is *superabundantly wealthy* in terms of mercy.

Jesus had already made it clear in Revelation 2:9 that the church of Smyrna was impoverished materially and financially. Thus, in this context, the word *plousios* refers to *spiritual riches*. Although the Smyrnean believers were materially poor, they were *spiritually very rich*.

In Second Timothy 3:12, the apostle Paul taught that those who "...live godly in Christ Jesus shall suffer persecution." Sometimes when believers faithfully maintain their commitment to Christ, their obedience to God places them "outside" the world's favor. But if a steadfast commitment to Christ puts believers in that difficult position, that is precisely where God wants them to be. In those cases — especially when Christians suffer the loss of revenue or material possessions — God compensates His people with other types of riches that are infinitely more precious.

The Smyrnean believers may have been deprived in terms of worldly goods, but they were rich in many other ways. They had forfeited their creature comforts, and all legal protection had been removed from them, causing them to lean on fellow believers for support. This brought about a rich, meaningful level of fellowship that is less prevalent in countries where believers' rights are protected and the need for close-knit relationships isn't felt as intensely. The love of Christ permeated the Smyrnean church as its members spiritually and emotionally lent encouragement and help to each other during their time of great need.

Words can't describe the tenderness of the Holy Spirit that was present when these early believers gathered in illegal underground meetings to worship Jesus. It is no wonder they greeted each other with a holy kiss every time they met together (*see* Romans 16:16), for whenever they departed from a meeting, they were never certain they would see each other again. The entire congregation lived in a hostile environment where the threat of arrest, seizure, or death was constantly imminent. As they held hands to pray or lifted their hands to worship quietly so they wouldn't be heard and caught, these believers shared a depth of spiritual commitment and covenant relationship rarely experienced in today's world where such concepts are often viewed as radical and strange.

For the Smyrnean congregation, tribulation had come in many forms. Jobs had been lost; property had been seized; and slander had destroyed their reputations. They had been made outcasts by both Jews and pagans. But in the midst of it all, these believers experienced a different kind of richness — one that can't be measured in worldly wealth. It was a richness of the Holy Spirit's presence, a richness of patience, a richness of strength to endure, a richness of faith, a richness of love among the saints, and a richness in spiritual rewards for their steadfastness in the face of adversity. In experiencing a death to self, the church of Smyrna had come to know the power of the resurrected Christ. Although these believers had suffered great tribulation and had been reduced to abject material poverty, they were *plousios* — *magnificently rich* — in all of these other, less tangible ways.

Right: This photo show the main street in ancient Laodicea, once a wealthy commercial center of First Century Asia. Jesus told the church at Laodicea that although they thought they were "rich, and increased with goods, and have need of nothing," spiritually, they were "poor, and blind, and naked" (Revelation 3:17). By contrast, the church of Smyrna was suffering great physical poverty, yet Jesus declared that they were spiritually rich. The Smyrnean and Laodicean congregations stand as an everlasting reminder that a church can be materially poor yet spiritually very rich and that, conversely, a financially wealthy church may actually be spiritually destitute.

We must never forget that some of the poorest churches in history have been *spiritually rich* and some of the wealthiest churches have been *spiritually destitute*. Church buildings may be adorned with gold, silver, and treasures, but they are often vacant of the true riches of the Holy Spirit. A church's coffers may be filled and its congregation may include many wealthy people, but that is no guarantee that the church is truly rich. In God's eyes, many financially prosperous churches are actually spiritually famished.

This principle is evident in an anecdote that has been passed down from the life of St. Thomas Aquinas. As he was visiting the Vatican, Pope Innocent IV invited Aquinas to view the breathtaking treasures that had been amassed by the Church. With great pride, the pope told him, "No longer can the Church say, 'Silver and gold have we none'!" To this, St. Thomas Aquinas answered, "Holy Father, that is very true indeed. But neither can we say to the poor and afflicted, 'Rise, take up your bed and walk.'"[18]

No scripture differentiates between material and spiritual wealth more clearly than Revelation 3:17. In this verse, Jesus told the rich Laodicean church: "...Thou sayest, I am rich, and increased with goods, and have need of nothing;

602

and knowest not that thou art wretched, and miserable, and poor, and blind, and naked." We know from Jesus' words to the church at Laodicea that although the congregation was materially *rich*, it was spiritually *poor*.

But as Jesus walked in the midst of the seven golden candlesticks, He saw that the Smyrnean congregation was truly a rich church, even though they were poor by the world's standards. They were suffering poverty because of their faith in Christ, but they were extremely rich (*plousios*) in the eyes of the Lord. Of the seven churches Jesus addressed in Revelation 2 and 3, Smyrna was the poorest of all — but He acknowledged that these believers were *spiritually rich* despite their financial and material losses.

'I KNOW THE BLASPHEMY OF THEM WHICH SAY THEY ARE JEWS, AND ARE NOT'

Jesus continued to address the church of Smyrna, saying, "I know thy works, and tribulation, and poverty, (but thou art rich) *and I know the blasphemy of them* which say they are Jews, and are not, but are the synagogue of Satan" (Revelation 2:9).

There were large Jewish populations throughout Asia, but it seems that the Jewish community in Smyrna was especially hostile to the Gospel. Of this group of Jews, Jesus stated, "...I know the *blasphemy of them*...."

Left: *"The Stoning of St. Stephen," by Harmensz van Rijn Rembrandt, depicts the first time a New Testament believer gave his life for his faith in Jesus Christ. One of the most zealous enemies of the Christian faith at that time was Saul of Tarsus, who stood nearby as a witness, consenting to Stephen's murder.*

The word "blasphemy" in this verse must be viewed in its context. It is the Greek word *blasphemia* — and it does *not* primarily refer to speaking irreverently about divine matters. Rather, it has a broader meaning that refers to *any type of debasing, derogatory, nasty, shameful, ugly speech or behavior that is intended to humiliate someone else.*

We see this word in First Timothy 1:13, where Paul described himself before his conversion to Christ: "Who was before a *blasphemer*, and a persecutor, and injurious...." Although Paul was a strictly religious Jew before he surrendered his life to Jesus, he declared that he had been guilty of blasphemous behavior.

As a devout Jew, Paul never would have deliberately committed blasphemy against God. But Paul used the word "blasphemer" to describe his own past words and actions when he purposefully *mistreated* and *humiliated* believers for whom he had no tolerance.

Before Paul's conversion to Christ, he was moved with a heartfelt conviction to persecute believers in Jesus Christ with a vengeance. To make sure readers understood how atrocious his treatment of Christians was before his conversion, Paul said he was once a "blasphemer." He then clarified what he meant by that statement, stating that he also used to be a "persecutor" and "injurious."

The word "persecutor" comes from the Greek word *dioko*, which means *to pursue*. This word means *to ardently follow after something until the object of pursuit is apprehended*. It was the very word used to depict a hunter who hunted animals. By using this word *dioko*, Paul revealed that he aggressively pursued Christians to capture or kill them like a relentless hunter tracking the scent of an animal.

Proof of this is found in the book of Acts. For instance, Acts 7:57,58 states that Paul (then called Saul of Tarsus) was present at the stoning of Stephen: "Then they cried out with a loud voice, and stopped their ears, and ran upon him with one accord, and cast him out of the city, and stoned him: and the witnesses laid down their clothes at a young man's feet, whose name was Saul." Also, from Paul's testimony before King Agrippa, we know that he cast his vote for the death of many believers. The apostle told Agrippa, "...Many of the saints did I shut up in prison, having received authority from the chief priests; and when they were put to death, I gave my voice against them" (Acts 26:10).

There is no doubt that before Paul came to Christ and was still known as Saul, he was such a *scourge* to the Church that believers everywhere had heard of his vengeance (*see* Acts 9:21). Saul was obsessed with a sense of duty to eradicate Christians and to cleanse this "filth" from the Jewish community. In fact, when Paul later described his behavior before his conversion in First Timothy 1:13, he dramatically used the word "injurious" to explain the maliciousness of his past behavior.

The word "injurious" is the word *hubristes* — the Greek word for *a sadist*. In *The New Linguistic and Exegetical Key to the Greek New Testament*, Bible scholar Cleon Rogers Jr. states: "The word [*hubristes*] indicates one who in pride and insolence deliberately and contemptuously mistreats, wrongs, and hurts another person just to...humiliate the person. It speaks of treatment which is calculated to publicly insult and openly humiliate the person who suffers it."[19]

Although Paul claimed he had been among the most religious of Jews (*see* Philippians 3:5,6), his use of the word *hubristes* — the word for *a sadist* — in First Timothy 1:13 reveals that hatred once raged in his heart. Paul was acknowledging that his loathing of Christians was once so intense that he derived personal pleasure when *humiliation* and *pain* were inflicted on them. Whereas the word "blasphemer" reveals that he once verbally humiliated believers, the word "injurious" indicates that his physical behavior toward Christians was also shameful — and that he enjoyed doing it. Both his words and actions were intended to *debase, defame, dehumanize, depreciate, drag down, malign, mock, revile, ridicule, scorn, slander, slur, smear,* and *vilify* believers.

It must be noted that God commanded the Israelites to treat the Gentiles or non-Jews who lived among them with respect (*see* Leviticus 19:34). In addition, the teachings of the Torah prohibited:

- Speaking ill of someone with the intention of negatively affecting that person's reputation.

Above: This photo shows a Torah scroll in an ornamental case. The Torah provides the Jewish religion with foundational laws and teachings on how to live right before God. These teachings are in direct contradiction to the hostile actions of certain radical segments of the Jewish community against the early believers — actions that often included vicious slander, looting, and even murder. Certainly all Jews of this time were not guilty of such wicked behavior, but the militant segments of the Jewish community proved to be very effective at stirring up trouble against Christians in many parts of the Roman Empire.

- Making a false accusation against someone that stains his reputation.

- Publicly humiliating another person.

All of these behaviors were prohibited according to Jewish teachings and law. To demonstrate why such behavior was considered blasphemous, it is necessary to consider the commandments of the Torah.

Vicious slander — called *lashon hara* — is a sin strictly forbidden by the Torah. Orthodox Rabbi Joseph Telushkin, one of the leading contemporary scholars of the ethics and commandments of the Torah, wrote about this subject in his work, *A Code of Jewish Ethics*. Telushkin stated, "We often speak *lashon hara* when we are angry at someone and want to do damage to that person's good name. Understandable as a desire for vengeance may be, Jewish law counsels those of us who have a grievance against someone to confront him directly, rather than to

Left: *This photo shows a collection of Torah scrolls. In some traditions, the Torah is housed in an ornamental wooden case and adorned with metal.*

go about speaking ill of him. Many of us, however, lack the courage to do so. Instead we take revenge by denigrating the person and thereby diminishing the person's reputation."[20]

Rabbi Telushkin also made this observation regarding the subject: "*Lashon hara* often does incalculable damage to the good name of the person being discussed. Unlike a physical injury, where the full extent of the trauma is usually obvious, *lashon hara* is likely to be repeated by those who hear it, and they in turn will tell it to others,

thereby causing an ever-expanding circle of harm. Even if the speaker eventually regrets the damage he has done to his victim's reputation, it is usually impossible to undo it by getting in touch with all the people who heard the negative report."[21]

When Paul was still Saul of Tarsus, he violated all of these commandments. Saul discriminated against believers, treated them with hostility, dehumanized them, and even contributed to their deaths (*see* Acts 8:3; 9:1; 26:11). He, along with many others in the Jewish community who felt threatened by the Christian faith, moved with rage to extinguish the spreading flame of Christianity. However, one encounter with Jesus on the road to Damascus was all it took for Saul's heart to be instantly emptied of rage and hatred and filled instead with a deep love for the Church he had so horribly persecuted and humiliated in the past.

All of this is mentioned here to demonstrate that even very religious Jews could be blasphemous in their actions and words toward those whom they didn't tolerate — and there is no better example of this than that of Paul before his conversion to Christ. However, it seems that this type of horrific treatment of believers was also what Jesus referred to when He said to the Smyrnean church: "...I know the blasphemy of them which say they are Jews..." (Revelation 2:9).

Although we don't know exactly what the Jews in Smyrna were saying about believers, we do know that the Jewish community contributed significantly to the intense hatred that arose against Christians in that city. It is therefore logical to conclude that the Jews in Smyrna were involved in *verbally dehumanizing* Christians, thereby committing "blasphemy" against them. In other words, the Jewish community aggressively attempted to publicly embarrass, humiliate, denigrate, and lower the status of believers in Smyrna by attacking their character. In this sense, the Jews committed "blasphemy" as they deliberately spread half-truths, trumped-up charges, lies, slander, and accusations about believers in an attempt to sway the opinions of both the government and society against Christians.

This evil called *lashon hara* — malicious gossip and the spreading of lies — can be devastating in its effects, not only to individuals, but also to entire groups of people. As Rabbi Telushkin wrote, "The difference between those who slander individuals and those who slander groups is that, in the case of groups, the victims can number in the tens and hundreds of thousands."[22]

Such was the case for these Smyrnean believers. By the time of John's vision on the island of Patmos, the rumors the Jewish community had circulated about believers in Smyrna had already done incalculable damage to the local Christian community. Like a blazing fire raging out of control, stories about Christians had swept through both the pagan and Jewish communities, causing widespread panic. Christians were blamed for bad weather, sicknesses, plagues, and all kinds of other disasters.

As is always the case when referring to people groups, it is certain that not all of the Smyrnean Jews participated in this vile behavior. However, the fact remains that the Jewish community was the primary source of vicious attacks that effectively destroyed the reputation of believers in that city.

Rabbi Telushkin commented that when slander is directed at a specific group, "...the damage inflicted can include murder...."[23] Telushkin went on to stress that once a slanderous characterization renders a group of people less than human, they become easy to kill. Whether or not the goal of the Jews' slanderous attacks was to render Christians "easy to kill" is unknown. Nevertheless, it is

indisputable that in many cases, murder was the result of these attacks.

One thing *is* clear: These Jews intended to permanently stain the reputation of Christians and thereby lower their status in the city. The Jewish community understood the power of speech. They knew that if they could ruin the good name of believers, they might be able to turn the tide of public opinion against them. This willingness to publicly humiliate Christians demonstrated that the Smyrnean Jews had wandered so far from the commandments God deems

holy and good that Jesus accused them of "blasphemy."

It is clear from historical records that the Jews of Smyrna had an intense dislike for Christians, whom they viewed as threats — "sheep-stealers" belonging to a deviant Jewish sect. However, according to their own law, this aversion to Christianity didn't give these Jews the right to violate the laws of *lashon hara*. Yet if surviving manuscripts from the first three centuries are correct, the believers living in Smyrna were continually assailed and verbally

Left: This illustration shows Christians during the reign of the Emperor Nero being dipped in pitch, tied to stakes, and burned alive. Polycarp, an early bishop of Smyrna, was one of the most famous of the early Christian martyrs who were tied to stakes to be burned alive. However, ancient writings assert that the fire miraculously didn't touch Polycarp, forcing the executioner to slay him with a sword.

to Polycarp's arrest and, ultimately, to his martyrdom in the Stadium of Smyrna.

When hatred consumes people's hearts, they act irrationally — even to the extent of violating the principles they hold to be holy and true. For example, we know that according to the official record of Polycarp's death:

- The Jewish population joined with the pagans to cry out for Polycarp's arrest, even though the Jews *knew* he had committed no crime. By doing so, they allowed their rage and hatred to override their convictions — thus horribly violating the teachings of the Torah.

- After the Jewish community cried out for Polycarp's arrest, knowing the charges were false, they could have come forward to testify in his defense. In failing to do so, they were thereby guilty of this righteous man's murder according to the teachings of the Torah.

- Polycarp's martyrdom occurred on a Sabbath with the full participation of the Jews who physically gathered wood and carried

assaulted by the Jewish community. These hostile actions directly contributed to the suffering of believers who lost their jobs and were rejected by society, thrust into poverty, and even martyred for their faith.

No account demonstrates this evil behavior better than the historical record of Polycarp, the elderly leader of the Smyrnean church whose death was largely instigated by the local Jewish community (*see* page 499-500). Harboring deep hatred against Christians, certain Jewish leaders helped start a riot that led it into the stadium so he could be burned alive. By gathering wood on the Sabbath to consume and cremate Polycarp's body, these Jews knowingly broke the rules of the Sabbath in violation of the Torah's teachings.

- Although the Jewish community in Smyrna had a divine code of ethics that had guided them for several thousand years, they allowed their passionate hatred of Christians to override their sense of right and wrong, thus defying the teachings of the Torah they claimed to love and revere. As a result, the Jews in Smyrna not only treated Christians unjustly, but they also willfully contributed to the horrific tragedies that afflicted the Smyrnean believers over a period of many years.

This illustration of Jews gathering in a synagogue shows the simplicity of design inherent in most synagogues of the First Century.

'THEM WHICH SAY THEY ARE JEWS'

> Christ continued in His message to the church at Smyrna, saying, "I know thy works, and tribulation, and poverty, (but thou art rich) and I know the blasphemy of them *which say they are Jews, and are not,* but are the synagogue of Satan" (Revelation 2:9).

Jesus described the Jews of Smyrna by stating, "...them which say they are Jews...." The words "which say" could be translated *to assert*, *to claim*, or *to profess*. These people were natural-born Jews and proudly professed themselves to be such. However, Jesus didn't accept their claim simply because they were of Jewish origin. He said, "...I know the blasphemy of them which say they are Jews, *and are not...."*

Although these people were Jewish by birth, their blasphemous behavior didn't coincide with the teachings of the Torah. In fact, their behavior was so offensive to Christ that He called them the "synagogue of Satan." Of these Smyrnean Jews, Albert Barnes noted: "Although they were of Jewish origin, they were not worthy of the name. That spirit of bitter opposition was indeed often manifested in their treatment of Christians...but still it was foreign to the true nature of their religion."[24]

'THE SYNAGOGUE'

To better understand the nature of the tribulation the Smyrnean believers endured, we must consider the significance of the phrase "synagogue of Satan" that Jesus used to describe the Jews of Smyrna.

First, the word "synagogue" comes from the Greek word *sunago*, which is a compound of the Greek words *sun* and *ago*. The word *sun* means *with* and carries the idea of *something done corporately with another*. The word *ago* means *to lead*

and was first used to depict the leading of animals, such as a shepherd leading sheep. But when these words are combined together, the new word depicts *a place of meeting or assemblage where people — not animals — are gathered together*. In Greek, it is the word *sunago*; in Latin, it is *synagoga*; and in English, it is *synagogue*.

Most scholars agree that the system of synagogue worship that emerged all over the Roman Empire first originated in Babylon while the Jews were held in captivity there. The Temple in Jerusalem had been destroyed, so it was important for the Jewish community in Babylon to develop a system whereby they could meet together for the reading of Scripture, for prayer, and for special meetings.[25]

This new system spread so quickly that by the Hellenistic period, synagogues could be found wherever Jews lived and had become the customary meeting places for their worship, religious study, and communal activity. In addition, Jewish elders would gather at the local synagogue to debate and reach decisions on matters that affected the entire Jewish community.

The earliest synagogues were primitive, with simple seating that lined the walls of a rectangular or square meeting hall. During the Roman period, synagogue meetings were sometimes held in the open air because pagan authorities wouldn't permit the construction of a synagogue in some cities and villages. However, this didn't stop the functioning of the synagogue, which was defined as an assembly of at least ten Jews *anywhere*, whether the meeting was held in a building or in the open air. Although it cannot be categorically stated, some archeologists believe that Ephesus may have had an open-air synagogue because the ruins of a Jewish meeting place have never been found (*see* page 282).

For the Jewish community, life revolved around the synagogue. This explains why synagogues are referenced more than 55 times in the New Testament, supporting the evidence that they were widespread throughout the Roman Empire by the First Century. In fact, it is estimated that Jerusalem alone had between 390 and 480 synagogues at the time of its destruction in 70 AD.[26] In addition, various groups of Jews from throughout the Roman Empire who had settled in Jerusalem — such as the Alexandrian, Cilician, and Hellenistic Jews — each had their own separate synagogues as well.[27]

From accounts in the four gospels, we know that many synagogues existed in Galilee, including those mentioned in Nazareth (*see* Matthew 13:54; Mark 6:2; Luke 4:16) and Capernaum (*see* Mark 1:21; Luke 7:5; John 6:59). Cities such as Alexandria and Rome also had a large number of synagogues to accommodate their sizable Jewish populations.

'THE SYNAGOGUE OF SATAN'

Jesus went on to say in Revelation 2:9, "…I know the blasphemy of them which say they are Jews, and are not, but are the synagogue *of Satan*."

We can only imagine how offensive it would have been for members of the Jewish community in Smyrna to hear

that Jesus called them "the synagogue of Satan." The Hebrew word *satan* is derived from the Hebrew verb meaning *to oppose*. When it is used with a definite article, it refers to an actual *literal being* and not merely to a metaphorical personification of evil. The verb form of the word also means *to accuse*, indicating that Satan is the one who *accuses* and *slanders* those whom he *opposes*. The Greek word for Satan is *satana*, which denotes *an adversary*, *an antagonist*, or *a wicked opponent*. But in the New Testament, it always refers to *a spiritual being* that stands in opposition to God — namely, *the devil*.

Jesus' words reveal that Satan operated in the synagogues of Smyrna, causing them to become a breeding ground for adversaries of Christianity. An antagonistic spirit thrived in these synagogues, which were filled with wicked opponents of the Gospel.

The blasphemous behavior of the Smyrnean Jewish community was so offensive to Christ that He referred to them as the "synagogue of Satan" — which is to say, in effect, that they functioned as "a community of accusers" who were inspired by the great accuser himself, Satan. Their inflammatory indictments against Christians were fueled, or so they claimed, by ardent religious devotion. But in reality, this particular group's malicious fervor against believers spewed from baser motivations, made evident by their plundering of believers' material goods.

The book of Acts makes it clear that Smyrna wasn't the only city where Christians met with intense opposition from the Jewish population. In many cities where the apostle Paul preached, he was confronted with people from local synagogues who were antagonistic to his message. Although it is never correct to make sweeping generalizations, it must be noted that for the most part, the Gentile community was more receptive to Paul's message than the Jewish community. Although many Jews did become believers in Christ, Paul was often assaulted by militant Jewish segments who were so enraged by the message of Jesus Christ that they attempted to sabotage any positive results, at times turning entire cities against those who preached the Gospel. Numerous examples of such attacks are found throughout the book of Acts.

DAMASCUS

Acts 9:20-25 relates that after Paul's conversion, he entered the synagogue at Damascus to preach Christ. In response, the Jewish leadership in the synagogue "took counsel to kill him" (v. 23). Paul's life was spared only because he was informed of their intentions and was then able to escape during the night.

These fanatical Jewish zealots in Damascus were so enraged by Paul's message that they were willing to commit murder — an appalling violation of the Torah. As was the case in Smyrna, Satan sought to use this particular group of Jews to thwart the advancement of the

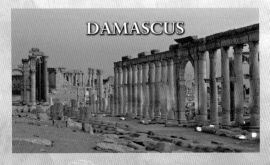

DAMASCUS

Gospel. This small group of angry zealots in Damascus may very well have qualified as another "synagogue of Satan" in God's eyes.

JERUSALEM

Acts 9:29 relates an encounter between the apostle Paul and "the Grecians" in Jerusalem: "And he spake boldly in the name of the Lord Jesus, and disputed against the Grecians: but they went about to slay him." This word "Grecians" refers to the Greek-speaking Jews who lived in Jerusalem. The city had many Hellenistic synagogues, and this text suggests that Paul entered one of them to preach the Gospel of Jesus Christ to the Jews who were there. Why the apostle chose to enter a Hellenistic synagogue isn't known; perhaps he thought they would be more open-minded because of their Greek heritage. Regardless, this verse goes on to say that the Grecian Jews "...went about to slay him." Evidently there was a group of diehard, militant Jews in this Hellenistic synagogue who were extremely antagonistic to the Gospel message.

As was true in the city of Smyrna, Satan attempted to use an isolated group of Jews in Jerusalem to attack those who proclaimed the message of the Gospel. It would be wrong to make a broad generalization that all Hellenistic Jews living in Jerusalem were involved in this wicked plot. Nevertheless, we know that an undetermined number of Grecian Jews in that city were so antagonistic to the Gospel that they were willing to go against their own Jewish law by committing murder. Their evil intent and their actions against Paul were so detestable in God's sight that this group of Jews living in Jerusalem also

JERUSALEM

ANTIOCH IN PISIDIA

Above: This is the Tower of David, an ancient citadel near the city walls of old Jerusalem. Paul's encounter with hostile Grecian Jews in Jerusalem was a part of the persecution believers endured in the city after Stephen's martyrdom, which caused many believers to scatter and to spread the Gospel wherever they went.

Above: Pictured are ruins in the ancient city of Antioch in Pisidia, (a region in modern-day southwestern Turkey) where Paul and Barnabas once proclaimed their mandate to be "a light of the Gentiles" after encountering opposition from a faction of the city's Jewish community (Acts 13:47).

may have qualified as members of a "synagogue of Satan."

ANTIOCH IN PISIDIA

Acts 13:14-51 relates the account of the time Paul and Barnabas traveled to Antioch in Pisidia. The two apostles went to the synagogue to preach the Gospel to the Jews, and many were receptive to Paul's message: "Now when the congregation was broken up, many of the Jews and religious proselytes followed Paul and Barnabas: who, speaking to them, persuaded them to continue in the grace of God" (v. 43). As Paul and Barnabas left the synagogue, the Gentiles of the city asked the apostles to come back and preach to them the following Sabbath. But when that day came and nearly the entire city gathered to hear Paul preach, they encountered intense opposition from a faction of intolerant, jealous Jews: "...When the Jews saw the multitudes, they were filled with envy, and spake against

those things which were spoken by Paul, contradicting and blaspheming" (v. 45). Infuriated with Paul's message, this group of Jews verbally assaulted the apostles, blaspheming them and their message.

Once again, Satan employed the same strategy, attempting to use the fanatical Jews of Antioch in Pisidia to oppose the preaching of the Gospel. The text makes it clear that there were many Jews in that city who had open hearts. However, this radical group hindered Paul and opposed his preaching, behaving in a blasphemous manner — which was a glaring violation of the Torah's teaching. Such intense hatred filled the hearts of this group of Jews that they very well could have qualified as another "synagogue of Satan" in God's eyes.

ICONIUM

In Acts 14:1, we are told that when Paul and Barnabas arrived in the city of Iconium, they entered "...into the synagogue of the Jews, and so spake, that a

Above: *Pictured are the ruins of Eflatun Pinar — a spring rising up from the ground near the ancient city of Iconium (modern-day Konya in Turkey) that served as an oasis for travelers. Paul and Barnabas may have stopped here on their way to Iconium to preach the Gospel.*

Above: *Most of the ancient city of Lystra, once located 19 miles south of Iconium, lies unexcavated beneath the ground near the Turkish town of Klistra. It was in Lystra that Paul was stoned by hostile Jews and left for dead. After being supernaturally raised up, the apostle returned to Lystra to continue his ministry.*

great multitude both of the Jews and also of the Greeks believed." Both Jews and Gentiles heard the apostles' message with receptive hearts, and many were saved. Then Acts 14:2 goes on to say, "…The unbelieving Jews stirred up the Gentiles, and made their minds evil affected against the brethren."

An isolated group of local militant Jews, enraged by the apostles' message, tried to turn the people's opinion against them — and to some extent, these hostile Jews succeeded. Verses 4-6 state what happened next: "But the multitude of the city was divided: and part held with the Jews, and part with the apostles. And when there was an assault made both of the Gentiles, and also of the Jews with their rulers, to use them despitefully, and to stone them, they were ware of it…." Warned about the wicked plans of these venomous Jews, Paul and Barnabas fled to the cities of Lystra and Derbe to avoid being stoned to death.

Satan attempted to use this fanatical segment of the Jewish community in Iconium to oppose the light of the Gospel, even to the point of murdering Paul and Barnabas. Just as was true regarding the hostile groups of Jews in Damascus, Jerusalem, and Antioch in Pisidia, this segment of Jews in Iconium may have also qualified as a "synagogue of Satan."

LYSTRA

In Acts 14:8-10, Paul and Barnabas arrived in Lystra and began to preach with miraculous results: "And there sat a certain man at Lystra, impotent in his feet, being a cripple from his mother's womb, who never had walked: The same heard Paul speak: who stedfastly beholding him, and perceiving that he had faith to be healed, said with a loud voice, Stand upright on thy feet. And he leaped and walked."

After the lame man was miraculously healed, the pagan audience exclaimed that

Above: *These ruins of ancient Thessalonica, located in the northern Greek region of Macedonia, give us a glimpse of the city as it stood when Paul traveled there to preach the Gospel. Today modern Thessalonica remains an influential city of Greece.*

Paul and Barnabas were gods, calling Paul "Jupiter" and Barnabas "Mercury." The pagans were so taken aback by the supernatural power working through the apostles that even the pagan priest at the Temple of Jupiter attempted to make sacrifices to them (v. 13). However, Acts 14:19,20 tells us that this receptiveness soon turned cold when "...there came thither certain Jews from Antioch and Iconium, who persuaded the people, and, having stoned Paul, drew him out of the city, supposing he had been dead. Howbeit, as the disciples stood round about him, he rose up, and came into the city: and the next day he departed with Barnabas to Derbe."

The pagans in Lystra were receptive to the Gospel until radical, anti-Christian Jews arrived from Antioch and Iconium to negatively affect the crowd. These particular Jews were so venomous that they actually stoned Paul and left him for dead. Undoubtedly, the hatred that raged in the

hearts of this faction of Jews qualified them as a "synagogue of Satan."

THESSALONICA

In Acts 17:1, we read that Paul and Silas came to the Macedonian city of Thessalonica. As soon as they arrived, the apostles went straight to the local synagogue. Verse 2 says, "And Paul, as his manner was, went in unto them, and three Sabbath days reasoned with them out of the scriptures." Paul's message bore good fruit, causing some Jews to believe and even to join Paul and Silas as they went about the city, preaching to the Gentiles: "...Some of them believed, and consorted with [joined] Paul and Silas; and of the devout Greeks a great multitude, and of the chief women not a few" (v. 4).

However, this receptive atmosphere didn't last long. We are told in verse 5 that "...the Jews which believed not, moved with envy, took unto them certain lewd fellows of the baser sort, and gathered a company, and set all the city on an uproar, and assaulted the house of Jason [a known associate of Paul], and sought to bring them out to the people." That same night, the brethren in the city "...immediately sent away Paul and Silas by night unto Berea..." (v. 10).

Some Thessalonian Jews responded well to Paul's message; however, this victory was largely spoiled by the attacks of militant Jewish zealots. Although some of the Jews "believed" and "consorted" with Paul, the other group of hostile Jews — many of them from Iconium and Antioch in Pisidia — were used by Satan to attack Paul with horrific and blasphemous behavior. This vile group may well

BEREA

Above: These are the original steps of the synagogue in Berea of Macedonia, from which Paul preached Christ to the Jewish community. Although many Jews believed Paul's message, many more were influenced by a group of hostile Jews opposing the Gospel.

have qualified as a "synagogue of Satan" in the city of Thessalonica.

BEREA

Despite the difficulties Paul and Silas had just experienced in Thessalonica, they remained undeterred in their passion to preach the Gospel to their Jewish brethren. Acts 17:10 states that as soon as the two men arrived in Berea, they immediately "…went into the synagogue of the Jews." Verses 11,12 go on to relate that "these [the Jews at Berea] were more noble than those in Thessalonica, in that they received the word with all readiness of mind, and searched the scriptures daily, whether those things were so. Therefore many of them believed; also of honorable women which were Greeks, and of men, not a few."

Paul and Silas found great receptivity among the Jews in the Berean synagogue. But this receptiveness was spoiled by the blasphemous behavior of a select group of angry Jews who followed them from Thessalonica. Acts 17:13,14 relates, "But when the Jews of Thessalonica had knowledge that the word of God was preached of Paul at Berea, they came thither also, and stirred up the people. And then immediately the brethren sent away Paul to go as it were to the sea…."

This passage of Scripture makes it clear that even though many Jews in Berea were open to the Gospel, some were influenced by the subversive group from Thessalonica whom Satan used to stir up the Bereans against Paul and his message. The record doesn't state the extent to which they were able to turn the city against Paul, but it seems likely that a large number of people were negatively affected. It may well be that Jesus looked upon this small group of fanatical Jews as a "synagogue of Satan."

CORINTH

In Acts 18:4, we are told that when Paul arrived in Corinth, "…he reasoned in the synagogue every sabbath, and persuaded the Jews and Greeks." After Paul preached in the synagogue for an unspecified period of time, a group of hostile Jews began to blaspheme the apostle, his message, and his companions in ministry. The conflict became so severe that Paul declared, "…Your blood be upon your own heads; I am clean: from henceforth I will go unto the Gentiles" (v. 6).

From that moment forward, Paul turned his attention away from the Corinthian synagogue and focused on fulfilling his call to be "a light of the Gentiles" (Acts 13:47) as he preached to the city's pagan population. This resulted in one of the greatest periods of Paul's

CORINTH

Above: Under Roman rule, the thriving city of ancient Corinth was made a seat of government for southern Greece. Paul resided in Corinth for 18 months, preaching the Gospel and establishing the Corinthian congregation.

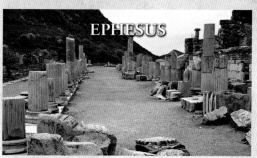

EPHESUS

Above: Pictured here are the marble ruins of the ancient Basilica of Ephesus, located in the city's upper Administrative District. It was in this city that Paul encountered the first wave of opposition from the Jews who resided in Asia.

ministry — although it wasn't long before Satan attempted to use these radical Jews, who were infuriated by Paul's success, to have the apostle prosecuted. However, the pagan deputy of Achaia, a man named Gallio, refused to hear the case because Paul hadn't violated any Roman law.

It isn't known how many Jews were saved before Paul left his ministry in the Corinthian synagogue. But many Jews *did* come to Christ — including many well-known Jews, such as Crispus, the former leader of the synagogue (*see* Acts 18:8).

Nevertheless, within the Corinthian Jewish community was a radical group of Jews who ferociously opposed the Gospel message. These Corinthian Jews were so adamant in their opposition against Christians that Jesus may have also viewed them as another "synagogue of Satan."

EPHESUS

Acts 18:19 relates that when Paul first arrived in Ephesus, he "...entered into the synagogue and reasoned with the Jews

(*see* page 284). However, Paul's first trip to Ephesus was brief because of the Nazarite vow he had made earlier that had to be fulfilled at the Temple in Jerusalem.[28] When Paul returned to Ephesus, "...he went into the synagogue, and spake boldly for the space of three months, disputing and persuading the things concerning the kingdom of God" (Acts 19:8).

It is remarkable that Paul was allowed to speak for three months without interruption before facing opposition from the offended Jewish leadership. However, the favor he enjoyed didn't last. Acts 19:9 (*NKJV*) states, "But when some were hardened and did not believe, but spoke evil of the Way before the multitude, he departed from them...."

Ephesus had a Jewish community of approximately 10,000 people. It is likely that many Jews came to Christ before Paul departed from the synagogue. Acts 19:9 states that the apostle "...separated the disciples, disputing daily in the school of one Tyrannus." The word "disciples" refers to converts won to Christ while Paul was preaching in the Ephesian synagogue. There were probably a large number of such Jewish conversions during the three months Paul taught there.

But there was also a group of Jews who took great offense and publicly took a stand against Paul and his message. They "…spoke evil of the Way before the multitude…" — indicating their intent to denigrate and stain Paul's reputation and to eliminate this new spiritual competitor. This demonstration of *lashon hara* — vicious slander — was a hateful act forbidden by the Torah. It is therefore possible that Jesus looked upon this group as another "synagogue of Satan" — just as He viewed the radical group of Smyrnean Jews who instigated such horrific persecution against the Christians who lived there.

We can see from all these scriptural examples that it wasn't uncommon for Satan to find refuge in synagogues throughout the Roman Empire. The enemy tried to use certain Jews in many communities to oppose the Gospel. But Revelation 2:9 makes it very clear that the persecution and opposition instigated by certain Jews in Smyrna was especially intense. These hostile Jews created such a malignant and destructive atmosphere for the newly emerging church that Jesus unapologetically declared they were "the synagogue of Satan" — a gathering of Jews among whom Satan fostered strife, lies, gossip, hatred, and even murder. Jesus implied that great numbers of the Smyrnean Jewish community were swept into this anti-Christian fervor and caught up in the pandemonium that ensued against believers. The synagogue — a meeting place originally intended to be a house of God — had, in fact, become a habitation for Satan.

'FEAR NONE OF THOSE THINGS WHICH THOU SHALT SUFFER'

In the midst of the Smyrnean believers' great tribulation, Jesus spoke words of both warning and comfort in Revelation 2:10: "Fear none of those things which thou shalt suffer: behold, the devil shall cast some of you into prison, that ye may be tried; and ye shall have tribulation ten days: be thou faithful unto death, and I will give thee a crown of life."

There were many reasons why the believers in Smyrna were tempted to feel fearful or panic-stricken. In addition to what they had already suffered, what they saw in the future looked very bleak. There was no prospect of a reprieve from persecution anywhere in sight. At the moment Jesus was speaking these words to the apostle John on the island of Patmos, afflictions were escalating for believers all over Asia, and the city of Smyrna was the scene of some of the most horrifying persecutions of that time. Nonetheless, Christ declared to them: "Fear none of those things which thou shalt suffer…."

The word "fear" in this verse is the Greek word *phobos*, which can be translated *fear*, *fright*, or *terror*. In fact, the word "phobia" — which describes *a fearful obsession, dread, or terror about something that is either imaginary or real* — is derived from this Greek word. In the case of the church in Smyrna, the *phobos* that was trying to grip their hearts was based on a *very real* threat of impending persecution and tribulation. Yet in spite of the hazardous times that lay ahead of these Christians, Jesus exhorted them to throw back their shoulders, stand fast, and courageously face the ordeal that loomed ahead of them.

In the strongest tone of voice available in the Greek language, Christ commanded these believers to "fear none" of those things that awaited them. The word "none" in Greek is *meden*, a word that demands the *immediate halt of something already in progress*. Like a powerful commander, Jesus lifted His voice and ordered the Smyrnean congregation to immediately halt the operation of fear in their midst. Thus, the Greek could actually be translated, *"Stop fearing!"* Christ didn't condemn these believers for being fearful, but neither did He allow them to coddle their fear.

The command to "fear not" was a very familiar phrase in Jesus' ministry. He regularly confronted fear and commanded people to stop allowing it to control their lives. The New Testament is replete with examples of this (*see* Matthew 14:25-27; 17:1-7; Mark 5:35,36; 6:47-50; Luke 5:1-10; 8:41-50; Acts 18:4-9; 27:19-24). The Greek wording may vary a little in these scriptures, and the people in each instance had a variety of reasons for feeling fearful. But in each situation, Jesus' message was the same: He ordered His listeners to *halt the operation of fear* and *to terminate its*

mastery over them. Christ still speaks these same words to His people today whenever they are tempted to become engulfed with fearful thoughts and emotions.

We live in a day when people long to be comforted and told that everything will be all right — that they can somehow escape all forms of suffering. But as Jesus spoke His message to the church of Smyrna, He knew that for them, suffering was *inescapable*. Therefore, He lovingly forewarned them so they might be prepared. The difficult and burdensome trials they had already borne were only a foretaste of the tribulations that lay ahead of them — and because Jesus loved them, He told them the truth.

The purpose of this truth was not to make the Smyrnean believers fearful about the future that lay ahead of them; rather, Christ desired to equip them mentally and spiritually so they could be prepared and make the decision to conquer any form of fear that might attempt to grip their hearts and minds. Like a military commander who prepares his troops for battle, Christ sounded the alarm and warned these believers that they would endure intense opposition, conflicts, and suffering in the days to come as they pressed forward to gain territory for the Kingdom of God.

Because these believers had already suffered unimaginable difficulties, it might have been difficult for them to conceive how things could grow worse. But Jesus solemnly told them, "...Thou *shalt* suffer..." — pointing to *future events* that hadn't occurred yet. The word "shalt" is the word *mello*, which sets forth the idea of *events that have yet to occur* — as opposed to events that have already occurred in the

© Mary Evans Picture Library

Left: In this illustration, Jesus stills the storm that is raging as He and His disciples sail across the Sea of Galilee, firmly commanding His disciples to "Fear not!"

be negatively affected by something. These believers had already experienced discrimination, the deprivation of jobs, the loss of income, and even death. But the word *pascho* in this verse pointed to a future suffering with devastating consequences on their lives beyond anything they had already endured.

Jesus loved these believers so fervently that He told them of the trouble He saw in their future. This wasn't a lack of faith; it was an act of love. From His exalted position at the right hand of the Father, Christ could see what awaited the Smyrnean believers, and He recognized the need to warn them so they could be spiritually, mentally, and emotionally prepared for the struggles that awaited them.

This congregation may have mistakenly believed the worst was already behind them, yet Christ knew the worst actually lay ahead. Therefore, His love compelled Him to forewarn His people about the coming danger in order to *forearm* them for the challenging times that awaited them.

past or that are presently taking place. Christ was warning the Smyrnean congregation of future events still awaiting them. In John 16:33, Jesus taught that a part of the Holy Spirit's ministry is to show believers things to come. In Christ's message to Smyrna, a spirit of revelation was at work to unveil the future to God's people so they could be prepared to courageously walk through the challenges that lay ahead as overcomers in Christ.

Jesus plainly told the congregation in Smyrna that they would "suffer." This is the Greek word *pascho*, meaning *to*

Not only was this a message from Jesus to the church of Smyrna; it is also a message to the Church today as we look ahead to the serious challenges we may face in the coming days. The turbulent waters that lie ahead are uncharted. Therefore, it is vital that we open our spiritual ears to hear what Christ has to say to the Church *today*.

Jesus doesn't want His Church to be taken off-guard or by surprise. Regardless of what lies in the future, He has already seen all that will transpire on this earth. Even if what He sees is grim or hard for us to hear, Jesus' love for us is so great that He will warn us in advance of impending difficulties — *if* our hearts are open to hear and heed what He has to say. Thus, we can be assured that just as Jesus spoke to the seven Asia churches in the First Century, He remains available to forewarn and forearm us concerning every challenge we might face in the days to come.

'BEHOLD, THE DEVIL SHALL CAST SOME OF YOU INTO PRISON'

Concerning the tribulation yet to come for the Smyrnean church, Jesus continued: "Fear none of those things which thou shalt suffer: *behold, the devil shall cast some of you into prison*." (Revelation 2:10).

The word "behold" is the Greek word *idou*, a word that is very difficult to translate. The *King James Version* translates it as *behold*, but in our contemporary world, this ancient Greek word might be better rendered, "*Wow!*" It conveys a sense of *amazement*, *shock*, and *wonder*. Although not a literal translation, it carries the idea: "*Wow — if you could see what I see! What is about to happen to you nearly leaves Me speechless. Yes, I am the One who knows the end from the beginning — but even I am amazed to see what you are about to endure....*"

There was only one reason the word "behold" would be used, and that was to dramatize a point so the Smyrnean believers wouldn't underestimate what they were about to hear. By using the word "behold,"

Left: Christians faced brutal persecution from both pagans and hostile Jews throughout the Roman Empire. Often they were thrown into stadium arenas with wild beasts as a form of public entertainment.

by *mudslinging*, *smearing*, and *vilifying* in order to ruin a person's reputation. But the word "devil" in Revelation 2:10 has a definite article, which emphatically means this referred to Satan himself and *his* attempts to accuse and to slander.

Jesus warned the Smyrnean church that a devilish attack would be waged against them in the coming days. Although the attack might seem to come from pagans or the Jewish community, the devil himself would be the one orchestrating these attacks, as confirmed by Paul's words in Ephesians 6:12: "For we wrestle not against flesh and blood, but against principalities, against powers, against the rulers of the darkness of this world, against spiritual wickedness in high places." Those who attacked the Smyrnean Christians would merely be weapons in the hands of a diabolical spiritual enemy.

The list of devilish accusations and slander leveled against First Century believers throughout the Roman Empire is so long that an entire book could be devoted to this subject alone. Because believers lived in a manner so contrary to the pagan world around them, they were misunderstood — and whatever people misunderstand, they are prone to attack. In addition, many in the Jewish community both despised and feared the growing Christian movement, so in defense, they instigated a growing swell of false allegations against believers in Christ.

Christ reached out to grip His listeners and make them realize the severity of what He was about to describe. He continued to tell them, "...*Behold, the devil shall cast some of you into prison....*"

The word "devil" is the Greek word *diabalos*, a word used 61 times in the New Testament. It paints the picture of *one who repetitiously throws accusations at someone, striking again and again.* It depicts the activity of *one who incessantly accuses and slanders someone* or *one who continually brings allegations, assertions, charges, claims, or indictments against someone.* The purpose of the accusations is to carry out a *character assassination*

The following is a sample of the false accusations brought against Christians in the Roman Empire:

- Christians were accused of *propagating anti-government rhetoric* because they spoke of another king and kingdom.[29] Of course, we understand that they were speaking of Christ and the Kingdom of God. But according to the Roman mindset, a reference to another king and kingdom was considered both dangerous and subversive. Consequently, rumors abounded that Christians were subverters of the Roman government.

- Christians were accused of *being rebellious to authority* because they refused to bow to idols of the Emperor Domitian.[30] Believers also refused to call Domitian "lord" as was demanded of people throughout the entire Roman Empire, including Roman senators and nobility. Few people had the courage to disobey this imperial order to worship the emperor; thus, the Christians' refusal to bow to pressure caused a pagan world to view them as rebels in Roman society.

- Christians were accused of *being law-breakers* because they gathered together in meetings, even though they didn't have permission to do so.[31] It was illegal to congregate without the approval of the Roman government; therefore, every time Christians met to pray or worship, it was a violation of Roman law. Christians were already held in suspicion because they spoke of another king and kingdom. Add to this the fact that Christians violated pagan law in order to merely congregate, and it gave the pagan world the impression that Christians were meeting in illegal, underground meetings to discuss subversive plans against the government.

- Christians were accused of *being anti-societal* because they wouldn't attend the public games where human beings were slaughtered, nor would they frequent the theater, where godlessness was paraded on the public stage.[32] To a pagan world, it seemed that Christians had withdrawn into a suspicious subculture in which they refused to participate in the normal affairs of life. This commitment on the part of believers to live holy and separate lives from the godless world around them produced great misunderstanding and resulted in many rumors that they were an anti-societal group.

- Christians were accused of *being atheists* because they had no idols in their homes and didn't attend pagan temples for worship.[33] The homes and businesses of pagans were adorned with many idols. Furthermore, it was a common practice for people to go to their pagan temples to worship and make sacrifices. Therefore, in a society filled with idolatry, the Christians' lack of any idols and their refusal to go to pagan temples meant they were without "gods" and were therefore atheists.

- Christians were accused of *being sexually loose* because they celebrated an event called a "love feast" in their illegal meetings.[34] This referred to a time of fellowship between the saints that included the celebration of Communion and a communal meal. But in a pagan world where perversion was commonplace, this Christian event was misconstrued to be a feast where participants indulged in sex of every kind. One can only imagine how horrible the rumors must have been, considering they were created by morally loose pagans who possessed very few taboos.

- Christians were accused of *practicing cannibalism* because they celebrated Communion, which, of course, is a celebration of the shed blood and broken body of Jesus.[35] It was rumored that Christians were eating flesh and drinking blood in their illegal underground meetings. Although it seems almost unbelievable that such a charge could be considered serious, this speculation about Christians practicing cannibalism continued for several centuries.[36]

- Christians were accused of *being arsonists* after the great fire of Rome in 67 AD. The Emperor Nero was responsible for the blaze that destroyed much of Rome and caused great loss of life. But when he saw that he was going to be blamed for this devastating fire, Nero searched for a scapegoat. He found that Christians were a convenient choice because they publicly preached that judgment and eternal fire awaited the unrighteous.[37] This Christian message was very unpopular with the pagan Roman population, so it was easy for Nero to blame the inferno on those who preached about the fires of hell. It was this very charge that initiated the first brutal, large-scale wave of persecution against believers in Jesus Christ.

Above: Pictured are the arched ruins of Smyrna's Central Marketplace. Once this was a huge, four-sided structure that included a magnificent marble Basilica on one side and two-story, covered colonnades filled with shops on the other three sides. It is a well-documented fact that many Christians were publicly killed within the confines of this famous marketplace — often after refusing to pay homage to pagan gods.

By the time Jesus spoke to John in the vision on the island of Patmos, the church of Smyrna had already endured years of intense persecution. So when Jesus said to these believers, "…The *devil* shall cast some of you into prison…" (Revelation 2:10), His use of the word "devil" emphatically meant that Satan himself was preparing to unleash all his fury against the Smyrnean Christians. The devil's strategy would be to stir up local residents with lies and false allegations about the church and to coax people to believe the worst about its Christian members. Jesus' words indicated that at least for a time, the enemy's strategy would succeed and many believers would suffer discrimination, imprisonment, and death — dying for their faith in Christ in the stadium, the theater, the marketplaces, and other locations throughout the city.

In verse 10, Christ continued by giving the church of Smyrna specific details regarding the persecution to come: "Fear

Above: *Pictured is the lower chamber of the Mamertine Prison (formerly called the Tullianum), where the apostles Peter and Paul were both likely confined. Once this was a horrifying, dark dungeon where prisoners languished amidst the stench of death and decay. Today the chamber is open to the public and includes an altar where visiting believers can pause to worship.*

none of those things which thou shalt suffer: behold, the devil *shall cast some of you into prison...*" (v. 10).

The words "shall cast" show the fury with which this attack will occur. These words come from a form of the word *ballo*, which means *to hurl* or *to throw*. It unquestionably means that once the attack against believers in Smyrna began, it would be intensely ferocious — to the extent that believers would be literally *hurled*, *slammed*, or *thrown* into prison.

The word "prison" is the Greek word *phulake*, a word that describes *a Roman prison*, which was one of the most dreadful, fearsome places in the Roman world of the First Century.

Roman prisons were nothing more than miserable holes in the earth that served as holding tanks for condemned criminals until their appointed time to die. Wealthier citizens were often kept under house arrest or banished as a form of punishment. However, poorer people

Top Right: From the upper chamber of the Mamertine Prison (pictured here), prisoners were lowered through a hole in the floor to the dreaded underground chamber. Later this upper chamber was made into a church to honor the two apostles who, according to tradition, were once imprisoned in the chamber below.

lacked any means of defense — so when they were sent to prison, they had little hope of ever seeing freedom again.

People in Roman prisons were frequently tortured or killed according to their crime. For example, those accused with arson were often burned alive.[38] This explains why so many Christians were burned to death after Nero accused them of starting the great fire of Rome in 67 AD.

One of the most famous Roman prisons — one that can still be visited today — is located at the bottom of Capitoline Hill in Rome, beneath what was once the imperial palace. In the First Century, it was commonly referred to as the *Tullianum*, although it was later renamed the *Mamertine Prison*. Early Christian tradition states that both Paul and Peter were incarcerated in this horrifying place on separate occasions. When the Roman historian Sallust described this prison, he wrote, "…When you have gone up a little way towards the left, there is a place called the Tullianum, about 12 feet below the surface of the ground. It is enclosed on all sides by walls, and above it is a chamber with a vaulted roof of stone. Neglect, darkness, and stench make it hideous and fearsome to behold."[39]

The Tullianum was built to be a cistern for spring water but eventually was used for the collection of palace sewage.[40] Later it became one of the most dreaded prisons in the Roman Empire.[41] Prisoners were forcibly hurled into this underground chamber — and when the door slammed shut, they were plunged into utter darkness, to be kept there in isolation until they were either executed or died of torture or starvation. Only rarely was a prisoner ever

Bottom Left: This illustration shows the underground chamber of the Mamertine Prison — the ultimate nightmare for Roman prisoners. Pitched into this place of utter darkness and filth, the hapless prisoners were left to either await their execution or to die of starvation.

who died in this prison were cast through this very door into the Tiber[44] after their corpses had been displayed for several days on the steps leading into the upper chamber of the prison.[45] Rats roamed through the prison, feeding on sewage and dead bodies not yet thrown into the Tiber River. Chained to the chamber walls, the prisoners couldn't defend themselves against the rats that would often chew on their arms, fingers, legs, and feet. It was a grim, disgusting, and brutally painful place. This was the condition of a Roman prison.

Because imprisonment usually meant an imminent death sentence had been given, it was considered unprofitable to feed, care for, or tend to the needs of prisoners. The general official attitude was not to waste public funds on those who were awaiting execution and wouldn't be alive much longer anyway. Bible scholar James Burton Coffman wrote, "Those seized by the government and awaiting trial and execution were held in prison, which in that ancient culture was only an anteroom to death."[46]

This is important to understand in light of Christ's words to the church at Smyrna: "...The devil *shall cast* some of you *into prison*...." This statement must be understood in the context of Roman imprisonment, which in the First Century was, more often than not, the equivalent of a death sentence.

released and given his freedom again. If tradition is correct, both Paul and Peter were confined in this prison at different times, and it is remarkable that they both survived this detestable pit.[42]

The roof of the Tullianum was 6-1/2 feet high, and the room itself was about 30 feet long and 22 feet wide. Most prisoners held here died by either strangulation, torture, or starvation.[43] An ancient door is still visible through which sewage emptied into the Tiber River. It is believed that those

'THAT YE MAY BE TRIED'

> In Revelation 2:10, Jesus continued, "Fear none of those things which thou shalt suffer: behold, the devil shall cast some of you into prison, *that ye may be tried....*"

Being put in prison is a great ordeal under any circumstance. But to be thrown into a Roman prison was a horrid prospect to contemplate. Thus, with great love, Christ forewarned the church of Smyrna that the devil was going to use this experience to test their commitment and the steadfastness of their faith.

The word "tried" is the Greek word *peiradzo*, which is the same word used in Revelation 2:2. It describes *a calculated test deliberately designed to expose any deficiency*. By using this word, Christ made it clear that the hardships these Christians would endure were intended to test them to see if their faith was genuine. They had confessed Jesus as Lord, and soon Satan would "try" them to discover if their commitment to Christ's Lordship was truly sincere. Just as the devil tempted Jesus in the wilderness (*see* Matthew 4:1-11; Luke 4:1-13), the enemy was now preparing to tempt these believers with persecutions beyond anything they had ever endured or imagined.

Believers throughout the Roman Empire were undergoing persecution as well. When the apostle Peter wrote to the believers in Pontus, Galatia, Cappadocia, Asia, and Bithynia, he referred to the fiery trials that were testing *their* faith: "That the trial of your faith, being much more precious than of gold that perisheth, though it be tried with fire, might be found unto praise and honour and glory at the appearing of Jesus Christ" (1 Peter 1:7).

Both Scripture and experience confirm that a declaration of faith often triggers a devilish attack. Satan's purpose was to test the sincerity of the Smyrnean believers' faith — to see if they would break under pressure. Therefore, Christ warned the church of Smyrna that these present and imminent attacks would verify whether or not they were really committed to the faith they had publicly declared. If there was any deficiency in their faith, those fiery trials would expose it, for the devil would design this calculated test to break them. Some would succumb to his attacks and recant their faith — but the majority of those who were to be "tried" would endure and prove themselves faithful, even unto death.

'AND YE SHALL HAVE TRIBULATION'

> Jesus had more to say to the Smyrnean church about what was to come: "Fear none of those things which thou shalt suffer: behold, the devil shall cast some of you into prison, that ye may be tried; *and ye shall have tribulation...*" (Revelation 2:10).

The word "tribulation" reveals how intense these fires of testing would be for the believers in Smyrna. It is the Greek word *thlipsis*, which is the same word used in Revelation 2:9 when Jesus said, "I know thy works, and *tribulation*, and poverty...." As noted on pages 591-592, the word *thlipsis* conveys the idea of *a burden that is crushing, debilitating, or overpowering*. Most often, the word *thlipsis* was used in connection with *displays of extreme hostility* or *torture*. The word was used by Christ again in verse 10 to forecast *a time of distress, oppression, pressure, and stress*. This word "tribulation" may be understood as a clarification of the word "tried." The tests the church of Smyrna was about to endure would be *crushing, debilitating*, and *overpowering*, resulting in *great distress, oppression, pressure*, and *stress*.

It is interesting that although Christ told these believers, "Fear none of those things which thou shalt suffer...," He didn't hesitate to tell them that very difficult times awaited them. Jesus knew that Satan was about to unleash a horrendous onslaught to attack the faith of these believers — but He also knew they could endure this test because their faith was indeed genuine.

'TEN DAYS'

> Jesus then went on to promise the Smyrnean church that this time of tribulation would last only for a limited period. He said, "Fear none of those things which thou shalt suffer: behold, the devil shall cast some of you into prison, that ye may be tried; and ye shall have tribulation *ten days*...."

Jesus knew that the intense bombardment yet to come would seem unending to the congregation in Smyrna. So when He asserted, "...Ye shall have tribulation *ten days*...," the phrase "ten days" was meant to give encouragement and hope to the suffering church — letting the believers know that their hardships wouldn't endure forever.

The meaning of the words "ten days" is an enigma that many theologians and writers have tried to understand, explain, and interpret throughout the ages. Theologian Albert Barnes noted that the reference to "ten days" refers to "a short time; a brief period; a few days."[47] Bible scholar Henry Alford suggested, "The expression is probably used to signify a short and limited time."[48] But it must be taken into account that the persecution against Christians that raged in Smyrna lasted much longer than ten literal days. Therefore, it is generally believed that the meaning of "ten days" must be symbolic.

The persecutions in Smyrna actually lasted for more than two centuries, and persecution throughout the Roman Empire continued into the Third Century. In light of this fact, one author wrote, "This cannot mean a literal ten days, but rather to the ten persecutors, the number of which is historically factual."[49] A noted theologian stated, "The number ten is of special interest, for history informs us that there were just ten persecutions of Christians by the Roman emperors."[50] Finally, Bible scholar W. A. Spurgeon wrote: "...The 'ten days' of persecution must refer to the ten persecutions of secular history during which great numbers of Christians were imprisoned and slain."[51]

One thing is certain regarding Jesus' statement of tribulation lasting "ten days": He was offering hope that this time of intense adversity would eventually come to an end. However, because many theologians strongly suggest that this was a prophetic statement corresponding to ten specific Roman persecutions against the Church, an adapted excerpt (entitled "Ten Periods of Roman Persecution") from the ancient classic *Foxe's Book of Martyrs* has been included on the following pages. Much insight can be gained by the study of this material regarding the ten periods of intense persecution against believers that occurred throughout the Roman Empire.

As promised by Christ, this time of tribulation and persecution did come to an end. As it happened, it concluded after ten periods of persecution — perhaps what Jesus was referring to in Revelation 2:10 when He used the phrase "ten days."

Hard times are inescapable in this life, but God's power *always has* and *will continue* to sustain those who are determined to be faithful to Him. Even if the fires of adversity rage and it seems as if they will never cease, those trials are temporary and will eventually come to an end. In addition, the fires that Satan uses to test, God simultaneously uses to purify. Almost 2,000 years of Church history have proven that the persecuted Church always comes forth purer than gold and mightier in the Spirit. The spiritual darkness may seem overpowering at times as Satan fiercely attempts to blot out the light of truth. But as John 1:5 promises, the light cannot be held perpetually under the domain of darkness. Victory belongs

to those who endure to the end (*see* Matthew 10:22).

History bears witness that the Spirit of God always warns His people in advance when difficult times are coming. There are abundant historical records that relate accounts of believers in hostile nations throughout the world who were forewarned by the Holy Spirit of future hardships. Such divine warnings prepare believers to face the impending challenges, *if* they will hear and heed the voice of the Spirit.

In Jesus' message to the church at Smyrna, we find a scriptural record of this type of divine warning. Jesus was lovingly preparing His people for the turbulent times that awaited them.

'BE THOU FAITHFUL UNTO DEATH'

As Jesus continued speaking to the church of Smyrna in Revelation 2:10, He added a strong exhortation: "Fear none of those things which thou shalt suffer: behold, the devil shall cast some of you into prison, that ye may be tried; and ye shall have tribulation ten days: *be thou faithful unto death....*"

The words "be thou" is the Greek word *ginou*, a form of the word *ginomai*, which describes *a process of becoming*. Thus, the phrase "be thou faithful" could

(Continued on page 652)

(**Author's Note:** The following is an adapted excerpt from *The Book of Martyrs* by John Foxe, which was first published in 1563. Commonly known as *Foxe's Book of Martyrs*, the work's original full title was *Actes and Monuments of These Latter and Perillous Days, Touching Matters of the Church*. The first part of the book deals with the martyrdom of early Christians. Much of Foxe's material was borrowed from early Christian writers. Throughout the course of his life, Foxe collected additional material on this subject, which resulted in three revised editions.)

Pictured Right: John Foxe

TEN PERIODS OF ROMAN PERSECUTION

THE FIRST PERSECUTION, UNDER NERO, 67 AD

The first persecution of the Church took place in the year 67, under Nero, the sixth emperor of Rome. This monarch reigned for the space of five years, with tolerable credit to himself, but then gave way to the greatest extravagancy of temper and to the most atrocious barbarities. Among other diabolical whims, he ordered that the city of Rome should be set on fire, which order was executed by his officers, guards, and servants. While the imperial city was in flames, he went up to the tower of Macænas, played upon his harp, sung the song of the burning of Troy, and openly declared that "he wished the ruin

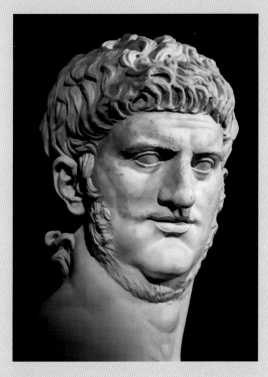

NERO

of all things before his death." Besides the noble pile, called the Circus, many other palaces and houses were consumed; several thousands perished in the flames, were smothered in the smoke, or buried beneath the ruins.

This dreadful conflagration continued nine days; when Nero, finding that his conduct was greatly blamed and a severe odium cast upon him, determined to lay the whole upon the Christians, at once to excuse himself and have an opportunity of glutting his sight with new cruelties. This was the occasion of the first persecution, and the barbarities exercised on the Christians were such as even excited the commiseration of the Romans themselves. Nero even refined upon cruelty, and contrived all manner of punishments for the Christians that the most infernal imagination could design. In particular, he had some sewed up in the skins of wild beasts and then worried by dogs till they expired; and others dressed in shirts made stiff with wax, fixed to axletrees, and set on fire in his gardens, in order to illuminate them.

This persecution was general throughout the whole Roman Empire; but it rather increased than diminished the spirit of Christianity. In the course of it, St. Paul and St. Peter were martyred. To their names may be added, Erastus, chamberlain of Corinth; Aristarchus, the Macedonian; and Trophimus, an Ephesian, converted by St. Paul, and fellow-laborer with him; Joseph, commonly called Barsabas, and Ananias, bishop of Damascus; each of the Seventy.

THE SECOND PERSECUTION, UNDER DOMITIAN, 81 AD

The Emperor Domitian, who was naturally inclined to cruelty, first slew his brother, and then raised the second persecution against the Christians. In his rage he put to death some of the Roman senators, some through malice and others to confiscate their estates. He then commanded all the lineage of David be put to death.

Among the numerous martyrs that suffered during this persecution was Simeon, bishop of Jerusalem, who was crucified; and St. John, who was boiled in oil and afterward banished to Patmos.

A variety of fabricated tales were, during this time, composed in order to injure the Christians. Such was the infatuation of the pagans that if famine, pestilence, or earthquakes afflicted any of the Roman provinces, it was laid upon the Christians. These persecutions among the Christians increased the number of informers and many, for the sake of gain, swore away the lives of the innocent.

A law was made that "no Christian, once brought before the tribunal, should be exempted from punishment without renouncing his religion." Further, when any Christians were brought before the magistrates, a test oath was proposed, when, if they refused to take it, death was pronounced against them; and if they confessed themselves Christians, the sentence was the same.

Timothy was the celebrated disciple of the Apostle Paul, and bishop of Ephesus, where he zealously governed the church until 97 AD. At this period, as the pagans were about to celebrate a feast, Timothy, meeting the procession, severely reproved them for their ridiculous idolatry, which so exasperated the people that they fell upon him with their clubs and beat him in so dreadful a manner that he expired of the bruises two days later.

DOMITIAN

THE THIRD PERSECUTION,
UNDER TRAJAN, 108 AD

Nerva, succeeding Domitian, gave a respite to the sufferings of the Christians; but reigning only 13 months, his successor Trajan, in the tenth year of his reign, 108 AD, began the third persecution against the Christians. While the persecution raged, Pliny the Second, a man learned and famous, seeing the lamentable slaughter of Christians, and moved therewith to pity, wrote to Trajan, certifying him that there were many thousands of them daily put to death, of which none did any thing contrary to the Roman laws worthy of persecution; to whose epistle Trajan returned this indecisive answer: "They are not to be sought out; if they are denounced and proved guilty, they are to be punished...." Trajan, however, soon after wrote to Jerusalem and gave orders to his officers to exterminate the stock of David; in consequence of which, all that could be found of that race were put to death.

Symphorsa, a widow, and her seven sons, were commanded by the emperor to sacrifice to the heathen deities. Refusing to comply with the impious request, she was carried to the temple of Hercules, scourged, and hung up, for some time, by the hair of her head: then being taken down, a large stone was fastened to her neck, and she was thrown into the river, where she expired. With respect to the sons, they were fastened to seven posts, and being drawn up by pullies, their limbs were dislocated: these tortures, not affecting their resolution, they were martyred by stabbing, except Eugenius, the youngest, who was sawed asunder.

Phocas, bishop of Pontus, refusing to sacrifice to Neptune, was, by the immediate order of Trajan, cast first into a hot lime-kiln, and being drawn from thence, was thrown into a scalding bath till he expired.

In this persecution suffered the blessed martyr, Ignatius, who is held in famous reverence among very many. This Ignatius was appointed to the bishopric of Antioch next after Peter in succession. He boldly vindicated the faith of Christ before the emperor, for which he was cast into prison and tormented in a cruel manner; for after being dreadfully scourged, he was compelled to hold fire in his hands, and at the same time, papers clipped in oil were put to his sides and set alight. His flesh was then torn with red hot pincers, and at last he was dispatched by being torn to pieces by wild beasts.

Trajan being succeeded by Hadrian, the latter continued this third persecution with as much severity as his predecessor. About this time Alexander, bishop of Rome, with his two deacons, were martyred, as were about 10,000 other Christians. Many in Ararat were crucified, crowned with thorns, and spears run into their sides in imitation of Christ's passion.

Many other similar cruelties and rigors were exercised against the Christians until Quadratus, bishop of Athens, made a learned apology in their favor before the emperor and Aristides, a philosopher of the same city, wrote an elegant epistle, which caused Hadrian to relax in his severities and relent in their favor.

Hadrian died in the year 138 AD and was succeeded by Antoninus Pius, so amiable a monarch that his people gave him the title of "The Father of Virtues." Immediately upon his accession to the throne, he published an edict, forbidding any further persecution against the Christians.

TRAJAN

THE FOURTH PERSECUTION, UNDER MARCUS AURELIUS ANTONINUS, 162 AD

Antoninus Pius was succeeded by Marcus Aurelius Antoninus Verus, who began the fourth persecution in 162 AD, in which many Christians were martyred, particularly in several parts of Asia and in France.

Such were the cruelties used in this persecution that many spectators shuddered with horror at the sight, and were astonished at the intrepidity of the sufferers. Some of the martyrs were obliged to pass, with their already wounded feet, over thorns, nails, sharp shells, etc., upon their points; others were scourged until their sinews and veins lay bare; and after suffering the most excruciating tortures that could be devised, they were destroyed by the most terrible deaths.

Germanicus, a young and true Christian, being delivered to the wild beasts on account of his faith, behaved with such astonishing courage that several pagans became converts to a faith which inspired such fortitude. This enraged others so much that they cried he merited death, as they did also of Polycarp, the pious and venerable bishop of Smyrna.

The circumstances attending the execution of this venerable old man were of no common nature. It was observed by the spectators that, after finishing his prayer at the stake — to which he was only tied, but not nailed as usual, as he assured them he should stand immovable — the flames, on their kindling the fagots, encircled his body, like an arch, without touching him; and the executioner, on seeing this, was ordered to pierce him with a sword, when so great a quantity of blood flowed out as extinguished the fire.

Soon after persecution raged in France, particularly at Lyons, where the tortures, to which many of the Christians were put, almost exceed the power of description.

MARCUS AURELIUS

Blandina, a Christian lady of a weak constitution, on the day when she and three other champions were first brought into the amphitheater, was suspended on a piece of wood fixed in the ground and exposed as food for the wild beasts; at which time, by her earnest prayers, she encouraged others. But none of the wild beasts would touch her, so that she was remanded to prison. When she was again produced for the third and last time, she was accompanied by Ponticus, a youth of 15, and the constancy of their faith so enraged the multitude that neither the sex of the one nor the youth of the other was respected, being exposed to all manner of punishments and tortures. Being strengthened by Blandina, he persevered unto death; and she, after enduring all the torments heretofore mentioned, was at length slain with the sword.

Martyrs were compelled to sit in red-hot iron chairs till their flesh broiled. Some were sewn up in nets and thrown on the horns of wild bulls; and the carcasses of those who died in prison, previous to the appointed time of execution, were thrown to dogs. Indeed, so far did the malice of the pagans proceed that they set guards over the bodies while the beasts were devouring them, lest the friends of the deceased should get them away by stealth; and the offals left by the dogs were ordered to be burnt.

THE FIFTH PERSECUTION, COMMENCING WITH SEVERUS, 192 AD

Severus became emperor in 192 AD. When he had been recovered from a severe fit of sickness by the prayers of a Christian, he became a great favorer of the Christians in general. But the prejudice and fury of the ignorant multitude again prevailed, and the obsolete laws were put in execution against the Christians. The pagans were alarmed at the progress of Christianity, and they revived the stale calumny of placing accidental misfortunes to the account of its professors. Fire, sword, wild beasts, and imprisonments were resorted to, and even the dead bodies of Christians were torn from their graves and submitted to every insult; yet the Gospel withstood the attacks of its boisterous enemies. Tertullian, who lived in this age, informs us that if the Christians had collectively withdrawn themselves from the Roman territories, the empire would have been greatly depopulated.

Victor, bishop of Rome, suffered martyrdom in the first year of the Third Century, 201 AD. Leonidus, the father of the celebrated Origen, was beheaded for being a Christian. Many of Origen's hearers likewise suffered martyrdom; particularly two brothers, named Plutarchus and Serenus: another Serenus, Heron, and Heraclides were beheaded; Rhais had boiling pitch poured upon her head and was then burnt, as was Marcella her mother.

Irenaeus, bishop of Lyons, ruled his diocese with great propriety. He was a zealous opposer of heresies in general. This zeal, in favor of Christianity, pointed him out as an object of resentment to the emperor; and in 202 AD, he was beheaded.

The persecutions now extending to Africa, many were martyred in that quarter of the globe; the most particular of whom was Perpetua, a married lady of about 26 years of age, with a

SEVERUS

young child at her breast. Several other persons were to be executed with her; among these, Felicitas, a married lady, was big with child at the time of her trial. Revocatus was a catechumen of Carthage and a slave. The names of the other prisoners destined to suffer upon this occasion were Saturninus, Secundulus, and Satur. On the day appointed for their execution, they were led to the amphitheater. Satur, Saturninus, and Revocatus were ordered to run the gauntlet between the hunters, or such as had the care of the wild beasts. The hunters being drawn up in two ranks, they ran between and were severely lashed as they passed. Felicitas and Perpetua were stripped, in order to be thrown to a mad bull, which made his first attack upon Perpetua and stunned her; he then darted at Felicitas and gored her dreadfully; but not killing them, the executioner did that office with a sword. Revocatus and Satur were destroyed by wild beasts; Saturninus was beheaded; and Secundulus died in prison. These executions occurred in the year 205, on the 8th day of March.

The crimes and false accusations objected against the Christians at this time were sedition and rebellion against the emperor, sacrilege, murdering of infants, incestuous pollution, and eating raw flesh. It was also objected against them that they worshiped the head of an ass, which was propagated by the Jews. They were charged also with worshiping the sun, because before the sun rose, they met together singing their morning hymns to the Lord, or else because they prayed towards the east, but particularly because they would not with them worship their idolatrous gods.

Calistus, bishop of Rome, was martyred in 224 AD, but the manner of his death is not recorded; and in 232 AD, Urban, bishop of Rome, met the same fate.

THE SIXTH PERSECUTION, UNDER MAXIMINUS, 235 AD

MAXIMINUS

Maximinus, who was emperor in 235 AD, raised a persecution against the Christians.

The principal persons who perished under this reign were Pontianus, bishop of Rome; Anteros, a Grecian, his successor, who gave offense to the government by collecting the acts of the martyrs; Pammachius and Quintus, Roman senators, with all their families and many other Christians; Simplicius, senator; Calepodius, a Christian minister, thrown into the Tiber; Martina, a noble and beautiful virgin; and Hippolytus, a Christian prelate, tied to a wild horse and dragged until he expired.

During this persecution, raised by Maximinus, numberless Christians were slain without trial and buried indiscriminately in heaps, sometimes 50 or 60 being cast into a pit together, without the least decency.

The tyrant Maximinus died in 238 AD and was succeeded by Gordian, during whose reign, and that of his successor Philip, the Church was free from persecution for the space of more than ten years.

THE SEVENTH PERSECUTION, UNDER DECIUS, 249 AD

In the year 249 AD, Decius being emperor, a dreadful persecution was begun against Christians. This was occasioned partly by the hatred he bore to his predecessor Philip, who was deemed a Christian, and partly to his jealousy concerning the amazing increase of Christianity; for the heathen temples were almost forsaken, and the Christian churches crowded with proselytes.

These reasons stimulated Decius to attempt the very extirpation of the name of Christian, and it was unfortunate for the Gospel that many errors had, about this time, crept into the Church; the Christians were at variance with each other; self-interest divided those whom social love ought to have united, and the virulence of pride occasioned a variety of factions. The heathens in general were ambitious to enforce the imperial decrees upon this occasion and looked upon the murder of a Christian as a merit to themselves. The martyrs, upon this occasion, were innumerable; but the principal we shall give some account of.

Fabian, the bishop of Rome, was the first person of eminence who felt the severity of this persecution. He was accordingly seized, and on January 20, 250 AD, he suffered decapitation. Julian, a native of Cilicia, was also seized upon for being a Christian. He was put into a leather bag, together with a number of serpents and scorpions, and in that condition thrown into the sea.

Agatha, a Sicilian lady, was not more remarkable for her personal and acquired endowments than her piety: her beauty was such that Quintian, governor of Sicily, became enamored of her and made many attempts upon her chastity without success. In order to gratify his passions with the greater conveniency, he put the virtuous lady into the hands of Aphrodica, a very infamous and licentious woman. This wretch tried every artifice to win her to the desired prostitution but found all her efforts were vain, for her chastity was

DECIUS

impregnable, and she well knew that virtue alone could procure true happiness. Aphrodica acquainted Quintian with the inefficacy of her endeavors, who, enraged to be foiled in his designs, changed his lust into resentment. On her confessing that she was a Christian, he determined to gratify his revenge, as he could not his passion. Pursuant to his orders, she was scourged, burnt with red-hot irons, and torn with sharp hooks. Having borne these torments with admirable fortitude, she was next laid naked upon live coals, intermingled with glass, and then being carried back to prison, she there expired on February 5, 251 AD.

The persecution raged in no place more than the island of Crete; for the governor, being exceedingly active in executing the imperial decrees, that place streamed with pious blood. Babylas became bishop of Antioch in 237 AD. He acted with inimitable zeal and governed the church with admirable prudence during the most tempestuous times. In the reign of Decius, that emperor came to Antioch, where, having a desire to visit an assembly of Christians, Babylas opposed him, and absolutely refused to let him come in. The emperor dissembled his anger at that time; but soon sending for the bishop, he sharply reproved him for his insolence and then ordered him to sacrifice to the pagan deities as an expiation for his offense. This being refused, he was committed to prison, loaded with chains, treated with great severities, and then beheaded in 251 AD, together with three young men who had been his pupils.

Origen, the celebrated presbyter and catechist of Alexandria, at the age of 64, was seized, thrown into a loathsome prison, laden with fetters, his feet placed in the stocks, and his legs extended to the utmost for several successive days. He was threatened with fire, and tormented by every lingering means the most infernal imaginations could suggest. During thus cruel temporizing, the Emperor Decius died, and with Gallus, who succeeded him, engaging in a war with the Goths, the Christians met with a respite. In this interim, Origen obtained his enlargement, and retiring to Tyre, he there remained till his death, which happened when he was in the sixty-ninth year of his age.

The Emperor Gallus, having concluded his wars, a plague broke out in the empire; and sacrifices to the pagan deities were ordered by the emperor to appease their wrath. On the Christians refusing to comply to these rites, they were charged with being the authors of the calamity, and thus the persecution spread from the interior to the extreme parts of the empire. Many fell martyr to the impetuosity of the rabble, as well as the prejudice of the magistrates. Among these were Cornelius, the Christian bishop of Rome, and Lucius, his successor, who was martyred in 253 AD.

THE EIGHTH PERSECUTION, UNDER VALERIAN, 257 AD

This persecution began under the Emperor Valerian in the month of April, 257 AD, and continued for three years and six months. The martyrs that fell in this persecution were innumerable, and their tortures and deaths as various and painful. The most eminent martyrs were the following, though neither rank, sex, nor age were regarded.

Stephen, bishop of Rome, was beheaded in the same year, and about that time Saturnius, the pious orthodox bishop of Thoulouse, refusing to sacrifice to idols, was treated with all the barbarous indignities imaginable, and fastened by the feet to the tail of a bull. Upon a signal given, the enraged animal was driven down the steps of the temple, by which the worthy martyr's brains were dashed out.

Sextus succeeded Stephen as bishop of Rome. His great fidelity, singular wisdom, and uncommon courage distinguished him upon many occasions. In the year 258 AD, Marcianus, who had the management of the Roman government, procured an order from the emperor Valerian to put to death all the Christian clergy in Rome, and hence the bishop with six of his deacons suffered martyrdom in 258.

Laurentius, generally called St. Laurence, the principal of the deacons, who taught and preached under Sextus, followed him to the place of execution; when Sextus predicted that he should, three days after, meet him in heaven. Laurentius, looking upon this as a certain indication of his own approaching martyrdom, at his return gathered together all the Christian poor and distributed the treasures of the church, which had been committed to his care, among them.

VALERIAN

This liberality alarmed the persecutors, who commanded him to give an immediate account to the emperor of the church treasures. This he promised to do in three days, during which interval, he collected together a great number of aged, helpless, and impotent poor; he repaired to the magistrate, and presenting them to him, said, "These are the true treasures of the church." Incensed at the disappointment, and fancying the matter meant in ridicule, the governor ordered him to be immediately scourged. He was then beaten with iron rods, set upon a wooden horse, and had his limbs dislocated. These tortures he endured with fortitude and perseverance; then he was ordered to be fastened to a large gridiron, with a slow fire under it, that his death might be the more lingering. His astonishing constancy during these trials, and serenity of countenance while under such excruciating torments, gave the spectators so exalted an idea of the dignity and truth of the Christian religion that many became converts upon the occasion, of whom was Romanus, a soldier.

In Africa the persecution raged with peculiar violence; many thousands received the crown of martyrdom, among whom the following were the most distinguished characters:

Cyprian, bishop of Carthage, who was an eminent leader of the church, was martyred during this time. The brightness of his genius was tempered by the solidity of his judgment; and with all the accomplishments of the gentleman, he blended the virtues of a Christian. In 257 AD, Cyprian was brought before the proconsul Aspasius Paturnus, who exiled him to a little city on the Lybian sea. On the death of this proconsul, he returned to Carthage, but was soon after seized and carried before the now governor, who condemned him to be beheaded, which sentence was executed on the 14th of September, 258 AD. The disciples of Cyprian, martyred in this persecution, were Lucius, Flavian, Victoricus, Remus, Montanus, Julian, Primelus, and Donatian.

At Utica, a most terrible tragedy was exhibited; 300 Christians were, by order of the proconsul, placed around a burning limekiln. A pan of coals and incense being prepared, they were commanded either to sacrifice to Jupiter or to be thrown into the kiln. Unanimously refusing, they bravely jumped into the pit and were immediately suffocated.

It is here proper to take notice of the singular but miserable fate of the Emperor Valerian, who had so long and so terribly persecuted the Christians. This tyrant, by a stratagem, was taken prisoner by Sapor, emperor of Persia, who carried him into his own country and treated him with the most unexampled indignity, making him kneel down as the meanest slave and treading upon him as a footstool when he mounted his horse.

After having kept him for the space of seven years in this abject state of slavery, he caused his eyes to be put out, though he was then 83 years of age. This not satiating his desire of revenge, he soon after ordered his body to be flayed alive and rubbed with salt, under which torments he expired; and thus fell one of the most tyrannical emperors of Rome, and one of the greatest persecutors of the Christians.

In 260 AD, Gallienus, the son of Valerian, succeeded him, and during his reign (a few martyrs excepted) the church enjoyed peace for some years.

THE NINTH PERSECUTION, COMMENCING WITH AURELIAN, 274 AD

In the year 274 AD, the Emperor Aurelian commenced a persecution against the Christians. The principal of the sufferers was Felix, bishop of Rome. He was the first martyr to Aurelian's petulancy, being beheaded on the 22nd of December in the same year.

Agapetus, a young gentleman, who sold his estate and gave the money to the poor, was seized as a Christian, tortured, and then brought to Præneste, a city within a day's journey of Rome, where he was beheaded.

These are the only martyrs left upon record during this reign, as it was soon put a stop to by the emperor's being murdered by his own domestics at Byzantium.

Aurelian was succeeded by Tacitus, who was followed by Probus, as the latter was by Carus. This emperor being killed by a thunderstorm, his sons, Carnious and Numerian, succeeded him, and during all these reigns the Church had peace.

Diocletian mounted the imperial throne in 284 AD; at first he showed great favor to the Christians. In the year 286, he associated Maximian with him in the empire, and some Christians were put to death before any general persecution broke out.

AURELIAN

Marcus and Marcellianus were twins, natives of Rome and of noble descent. Their parents were heathens, but the tutors to whom the education of the children was entrusted brought them up as Christians. Their constancy at length subdued those who wished them to become pagans, and their parents and whole family became converts to a faith they had before reprobated. They were martyred by being tied to posts and having their feet pierced with nails. After remaining in this situation for a day and a night, their sufferings were put to an end by thrusting lances through their bodies.

Zoe, the wife of the jailer, who had the care of the before-mentioned martyrs, was converted by them, and hung upon a tree with a fire of straw lighted under her. When her body was taken down, it was thrown into a river, with a large stone tied to in it order to sink it.

In the year of Christ 286 AD, a most remarkable affair occurred; a legion of soldiers, consisting of 6,666 men, contained none but Christians. This legion was called the Theban Legion, because the men had been raised in Thebias: they were quartered in the east till the emperor Maximian ordered them to march to Gaul, to assist him against the rebels of Burgundy. They passed the Alps into Gaul, under the command of Mauritius, Candidus, and Exupernis, their worthy commanders, and at length joined the emperor. Maximian, about this time, ordered a general sacrifice, at which the whole army was to assist; and likewise he commanded that they should take the oath of allegiance and swear, at the same time, to assist in the extirpation of Christianity in Gaul.

Alarmed at these orders, each individual of the Theban legion absolutely refused either to sacrifice or take the oaths prescribed. This so greatly enraged Maximian that he ordered the legion to be decimated, that is, every tenth man to be selected from the rest and put to the sword. This bloody order having been put in execution, those who remained alive were still inflexible, when a second decimation took place, and every tenth man of those living were put to death.

This second severity made no more impression than the first had done; the soldiers preserved their fortitude and their principles, but by the advice of their officers they drew up a loyal remonstrance to the emperor. This, it might have been presumed, would have softened the emperor, but it had a contrary effect; for, enraged at their perseverance and unanimity, he commanded that the whole legion should be put to death, which was accordingly executed by the other troops, who cut them to pieces with their swords on September 22, 286 AD.

Alban, from whom St. Alban's, in Hertfordshire, received its name, was the first British martyr. Great Britain had received the Gospel of Christ from Lucius, the first Christian king, but did not suffer from the rage of persecution for many years after. He was originally a pagan but converted by a Christian ecclesiastic, named Amphibalus, whom he sheltered on account of his religion. The enemies of Amphibalus, having intelligence of the place where he was secreted, came to the house of Alban; in order to facilitate his escape, when the soldiers came, he offered himself up as the person they were seeking for. The deceit being detected, the governor ordered him to be scourged, and then he was sentenced to be beheaded, June 22, 287 AD. Upon this occasion, the executioner suddenly became a convert to Christianity and entreated permission to die for Alban, or with him. Obtaining the latter request, they were beheaded by a soldier, who voluntarily undertook the task of executioner.

Faith, a Christian female of Acquitain in France, was ordered to be broiled upon a gridiron and then beheaded in 287 AD. Quintin was a Christian and native of Rome, but determined to attempt the propagation of the Gospel in Gaul; with one Lucian, they preached in Amiens; after which Lucian went to Beaumaris, where he was martyred. Quintin remained in Picardy and was very zealous in his ministry. Being seized upon as a Christian, he was stretched with pullies until his joints were dislocated; his body was then torn with wire scourges, and boiling oil and pitch poured on his naked flesh; lighted torches were applied to his sides and armpits, and after he had been thus tortured, he was remanded back to prison and died of the barbarities he had suffered October 31, 287 AD. His body was sunk in the Somme.

THE TENTH PERSECUTION, UNDER DIOCLETIAN, 303 AD

Under the Roman Emperors, commonly called the Era of the Martyrs, was occasioned partly by the increasing number and luxury of the Christians and the hatred of Galerius, the adopted son of Diocletian, who, being stimulated by his mother, a bigoted pagan, never ceased persuading the emperor to enter upon the persecution until he had accomplished his purpose. The fatal day fixed upon to commence the bloody work was the 23rd of February, 303 AD, that being the day in which the Terminalia were celebrated, and on which, as the cruel pagans boasted, they hoped to put a termination to Christianity.

On the appointed day, the persecution began in Nicomedia, on the morning of which the prefect of that city repaired, with a great number of officers and assistants, to the church of the Christians, where, having forced open the doors, they seized upon all the sacred books and committed them to the flames. The whole of this transaction was in the presence of Diocletian and Galerius, who, not contented with burning the books, had the church levelled with the ground. This was followed by a severe edict, commanding the destruction of all other Christian churches and books; and an order soon succeeded to render Christians of all denominations outlawed.

The publication of this edict occasioned an immediate martyrdom, for a bold Christian not only tore it down from the place to which it was affixed, but execrated the name of the emperor for his injustice. A provocation like this was sufficient to call down pagan vengeance upon his head; he was accordingly seized, severely tortured, and then burned alive. All the Christians were apprehended and imprisoned; and Galerius privately ordered the imperial palace to be set on fire, that the Christians might be charged as the incendiaries and a plausible pretence given for carrying on the persecution with the greatest severities.

A general sacrifice was commenced, which occasioned various martyrdoms. No distinction was made of age or sex; the name of Christian was so obnoxious to the pagans that all indiscriminately fell sacrifices to their opinions. Many houses were set on fire, and whole Christian families perished in the flames; and others had stones fastened about their necks, and being tied together were driven into the sea. The persecution became general in all the Roman provinces, but more particularly in the east; and as it lasted ten years, it is impossible to ascertain the numbers martyred or to enumerate the various modes of martyrdom. Racks, scourges, swords, daggers, crosses, poison, and famine were made use of in various parts to dispatch the Christians; and invention was exhausted to devise tortures against such as had no crime, but thinking differently from the votaries of superstition.

Maximus, governor of Cilicia, being at Tarsus, three Christians were brought before him; their names were Tarachus, an aged man, Probus, and Andronicus. After repeated tortures and exhortations to recant, they, at length, were ordered for execution. Being brought to the amphitheater, several beasts were let loose upon them; but none of the animals, though hungry, would touch them. The keeper then brought out a large bear, that had that very day destroyed three men; but this voracious creature and a fierce lioness both refused to touch the prisoners. Finding the design of destroying them by the means of wild beasts ineffectual, Maximus ordered them to be slain by the sword on October 11, 303 AD.

A city of Phrygia, consisting entirely of Christians, was burnt, and all the inhabitants perished in the flames.

Tired with slaughter, at length, several governors of provinces represented to the imperial court, the impropriety of such conduct. Hence many were respited from execution, but though they were not put to death, as much as possible was done to render their lives miserable, many of them having their ears cut off, their noses slit, their right eyes put out, their limbs rendered useless by dreadful disloca-

DIOCLETIAN

tions, and their flesh seared in conspicuous places with red-hot irons.

It is necessary now to particularize the most conspicuous persons who laid down their lives in martyrdom in this bloody persecution.

Sebastian, a celebrated martyr, born in Gaul, who instructed the principles of Christianity at Milan, and afterward became an officer of the emperor's guard at Rome. He remained a true Christian in the midst of idolatry; unallured by the splendors of a court, untainted by evil examples, and uncontaminated by the hopes of preferment. Refusing to be a pagan, Sebastian was ordered to be taken to a field near the city, and there to be shot to death with arrows; which sentence was executed accordingly.

Some pious Christians coming to the place of execution in order to give his body burial, perceived signs of life in him, and immediately moving him to a place of security, they, in a short time effected his recovery, and prepared him for a second martyrdom. As soon as he was able to go out, he placed himself intentionally in the emperor's way as he was going to the temple and reprehended him for his various cruelties and unreasonable prejudices against Christianity. As soon as Diocletian had overcome his surprise, he ordered Sebastian to be seized and carried to a place near the palace and beaten to death; and, that the Christians should not either use means again to recover or bury his body, he ordered that it should be thrown into the common sewer. Nevertheless, a Christian lady, named Lucina, found means to remove it from the sewer and bury it in the catacombs, or repositories of the dead.

Romanus, a native of Palestine, was deacon of the church of Cæsarea at the time of the commencement of Diocletian's persecution. Being condemned for his faith at Antioch, he was scourged, put to the rack, his body torn with hooks, his flesh cut with knives, his face scarified, his teeth beaten from their sockets, and his hair plucked up by the roots. Soon after he was ordered to be strangled on November 17, 303 AD.

In the year 304 AD, when the persecution reached Spain, the governor of Terragona ordered Valerius the bishop, and Vincent the deacon, to be seized, loaded with irons, and imprisoned. The prisoners being firm in their resolution, Valerius was banished, and Vincent was racked, his limbs dislocated, his flesh torn with hooks, and he was laid on a gridiron, which had not only a fire placed under it, but spikes at the top, which ran into his flesh. These torments neither destroying him, nor changing his resolutions, he was remanded to prison and confined in a small, loathsome, dark dungeon, strewn with sharp flints, and pieces of broken glass, where he died, January 22, 304 AD. His body was thrown into the river.

In 304 AD, the persecution under Diocletian began particularly to rage, and that is when many Christians were put to cruel tortures and the most painful and ignominious deaths. Marcellinus, bishop of Rome, having strongly opposed paying divine honors to Diocletian, suffered martyrdom by a variety of tortures in the year 304 AD. Victorius, Carpophorus, Severus, and Severianus were brothers, and all four employed in places of great trust and honor in the city of Rome. Having exclaimed against the worship of idols, they were apprehended and scourged with the plumbetae, or scourges, to the ends of which were fastened leaden balls. This punishment was exercised with such excess of cruelty that the pious brothers fell martyrs to its severity.

It now happened that, weary of the farce of state and public business, the Emperors Diocletian and Maximillian resigned the imperial diadem and were succeeded by Constantius and Galerius; the former a prince of the most mild and humane disposition and the latter equally remarkable for his cruelty and tyranny. These divided the empire into two equal governments, Galerius ruling in the east and Constantius in the west; and the people in the two governments felt the effects of the dispositions of the two emperors; for those in the west were governed in the mildest manner, but such as resided in the east felt all the miseries of oppression and lengthened tortures.

As Galerius bore a prejudiced and implacable hatred to Christians, we are informed that "he not only condemned them to tortures, but to burn in slow fires in this horrible manner: They were first chained to a post, then a gentle fire put to the soles of their feet, which contracted the callus till it fell off from the bone; then flambeaux just extinguished were put to all parts of their bodies so that they might be tortured all over; and care was taken to keep them alive by throwing cold water in their faces and giving them some to wash their mouths. Thus their miseries were lengthened out whole days, till, at last, and they were just ready to expire, their bodies were thrown into a great fire, after which their ashes were thrown into some river."

Among the many martyred by the order of Galerius, Amphianus was a gentleman of eminence in Lucia and a scholar of Eusebius; Julitta, a Lycaonian of royal descent, was more celebrated for her virtues than noble blood. While on the rack, her child was killed before her face. Julitta, of Cappadocia, was a lady of distinguished capacity, great virtue, and uncommon courage. To complete the execution, Julitta had boiling pitch poured on her feet, her sides torn with hooks, and received the conclusion of her martyrdom by being beheaded, April 16, 305 AD.

Later Galerius was visited by an incurable and intolerable disease, began with an ulcer in his secret parts, that spread progressively to his inmost bowels, and baffled all the skill of physicians and surgeons. By a dropsy also his body was grossly disfigured; for although his upper parts were exhausted and dried to a skeleton, covered only with dead skin, the lower parts were swelled up like bladders, and the shape of his feet could scarcely be perceived.

Torments and pains insupportable, greater than those he had inflicted upon the Christians, accompanied these visitations, and he bellowed out like a wounded bull, often endeavoring to kill himself and destroying several physicians for the inefficacy of their medicines. These torments kept him in a languishing state a full year, and his conscience was awakened at length, so that he was compelled to acknowledge the God of the Christians and to promise, in the intervals of his paroxysms, that he would rebuild the churches and repair the mischief done to them. An edict in his last agonies was published in his name, and the joint names of Constantine and Licinius, to permit the Christians to have the free use of religion and to supplicate their God for his health and the good of the empire, on which many prisoners were liberated. At length, Constantine the Great was determined to redress the grievances of the Christians, and in the end, a law was published in favor of the Christians. Thus concluded the tenth and last general persecution.

literally be interpreted *"become faithful."* In *The New Linguistic and Exegetical Key to the Greek New Testament*, the author quoted Bible scholar Henry Barclay Swete's comments on the words "be thou": "prove yourself loyal and true, to the extent of being ready to die for my sake."[52] Theologian A. T. Robertson said this phrase could be rendered, *"keep on becoming faithful"* or *"keep on proving faithful unto death."*[53] Thus, the idea conveyed in this verse could read, *"…Give it your best effort, putting all your energies into the goal of progressively becoming more and more faithful…."*

The word "faithful" is the Greek word *pistos*, which is the most common New Testament word for *faith*. It conveys the idea of people who are *faithful, reliable, loyal,* and *steadfast*. No matter what assails them or how hot the fires of persecution blaze, they remain unwavering in their commitment to Jesus Christ. Thus, Jesus was requiring His people in Smyrna to remain *devoted, trustworthy, dependable, dedicated, constant,* and *unwavering,* even in the face of the worst circumstances imaginable. Breaking their commitment to Him under the weight of external pressures, no matter how extreme, was not an acceptable option. Christ expects faithfulness "unto death" from His people.

The word "unto" is *archi,* which means *unto, up to,* or *including.* In other words, the Smyrnean believers were *never* to renege on their commitment to Christ. This divine call to commitment — regardless of the price that had to be paid — was so serious that, if necessary, Christ expected them to be faithful *unto, up to,* or even *to the point of* death itself.

A faith that remains steadfast only when times are good is unacceptable. The Savior endured the Cross in order to experience His resurrection and exaltation — and now He calls on us to endure to the end. Just as the Holy Spirit enabled Jesus to run His race to the end, the Spirit of God will enable us to endure any affliction, hardship, pressure, problem, trial, or tribulation that we encounter as we prove the authenticity and sincerity of our faith.

We are called to pick up our cross and follow Christ, regardless of the price we are required to pay. That may not be pleasant to consider, but it is a fact nonetheless. Scripture never teaches that we are to draw back from our faith when hardships approach. Rather, Jesus Christ demands commitment and faithfulness, even unto the point of death, if that's what is required as a part of our journey in Him.

Believers who live in parts of the world that are hostile to the Christian faith understand this type of commitment very well. Those who have come to Christ in a non-hostile environment often don't comprehend the life-and-death type of commitment others have been required to make. Yet throughout the centuries of Church history, Christians have often given their very lives for what they believed. And this isn't just a past reality. It is a statistical fact that in the past century, more believers died for their faith than in all the previous centuries of accumulated Christian history combined.[54] Believers have suffered "unto death" for Jesus' sake in the past, and they still are doing so today.

The word "death" in this verse is the Greek word *thanatos,* which is a word that is used more than 120 times in the New Testament. It describes *the physical state of death* or *extinction of life*. But in the New Testament, it also depicts *a mortal danger*, *a dangerous circumstance*, or *something that is fatal*. In the Roman legal system, it described *the death penalty*. Jesus had already told this pastor and his church that they would be falsely accused, thrown into prison, and intensely tested by the devil. In addition, He forewarned them in a most straightforward manner that mortal dangers were coming — and that for many who followed Christ in Smyrna, the danger would prove to be fatal. For these believers, a death penalty would be issued against them and carried out with great cruelty. Yet regardless of what they might have to endure, Christ urged them to "be faithful unto death."

'I WILL GIVE THEE A CROWN OF LIFE'

> As Jesus continued in Revelation 2:10, He told the Smyrnean church, "Fear none of those things which thou shalt suffer: behold, the devil shall cast some of you into prison, that ye may be tried; and ye shall have tribulation ten days: be thou faithful unto death, *and I will give thee a crown of life*."

The words "I will give thee" are a translation of the Greek word *doso* — a future form of the word *didomi*, which means *I give* but in this verse could mean *I allow* or *I permit*. The use of this word *doso* emphatically means that Christ Himself will be personally involved in this act of bestowing "a crown of life" to those who faithfully endure unto the end. However, the word "crown" here is not the word for a royal diadem, as a king would wear. Rather, it is the Greek word *stephanos*, which describes *the crown given to athletes — most notably, runners — after they had run their race or finished their contest victoriously*.

At the conclusion of a contest or race, a winner was declared and a crown placed on the champion's brow made of pine or olive branches and leaves. Although the crown wasn't made of expensive material, it was highly valued as a public recognition of the skill, commitment, discipline, endurance, self-control, self-mastery, and training that had enabled the athlete to win the competition. Being awarded the victor's crown brought a person great acclaim, honor, and respect in the eyes of an adoring public. Therefore, it was every athlete's chief aim to obtain this crown.

This is precisely the word used in Revelation 2:10 when Jesus said, "...Be thou faithful unto death, and I will give thee *a crown of life*." This *crown of life* is one specifically given to those who are *faithful unto death*. And because the word *doso* is used, meaning *I will give*, we know that Christ Himself will be personally involved in bestowing "a crown of life" to those who have faithfully endured unto the end.

There could be no greater reward than Jesus Christ Himself personally placing this victor's crown on the brow of Christians who have endured to the end and victoriously finished their race of faith. This is the

Above: The art on this ancient Greek vase depicts an athlete who has won a competition. A victor's crown made of interlocking leaves rests on his brow — a public testament to his skill, endurance, commitment, training, and mastery of his sport. It was an athlete's most desired achievement in both Greek and Roman cultures to win the victor's crown, for it brought honor and respect to the one who attained such a prize.

promise Jesus gave to the Smyrnean believers. He emphatically announced that a day was coming when He would step forward, dressed in the regal splendor of the exalted King of kings, and place a crown of life upon the heads of those who had faithfully run their race to the very end. The Savior Himself would be personally involved in the giving of this priceless reward.

It should be noted here that there are five different types of crowns mentioned in the New Testament. Each of these crowns is to be viewed as a reward for Christians who have faithfully fulfilled God's call on their lives.

- The *crown of incorruption* is referred to in First Corinthians 9:25. Paul describes this as a

special crown that will be given to believers who practiced *physical self-governance* and therefore ran a successful race in life.

- The *crown of rejoicing* is found in First Thessalonians 2:19. This is often referred to as the *soulwinner's crown*.

- The *crown of righteousness* is mentioned in Second Timothy 4:8. This crown is specially designated for those who longed for Jesus' appearing and lived holy lives in anticipation of His return.

- The *crown of glory* is referred to in First Peter 5:4. This is often called the *pastor's crown* because it is a special reward that will be given to shepherds who faithfully pastored and taught God's people.

- The *crown of life* is found both in James 1:12 and Revelation 2:10. This particular crown is often referred to as the *martyr's crown* because it is given to those who suffered for their faith, those who died for Christ, or those who were committed to finishing their race of faith, regardless of the difficulties they encountered in this life.

The imagery of a crown of life was very pertinent for believers who lived in Smyrna, for this city was the site of great athletic competitions, as was the case in many cities throughout Asia. According to the Greek geographer Pausanias, public games were an important part of life in Smyrna.[55] Therefore, the image of placing a garland crown (*stephanos*) on the head of a champion was a very familiar one to every resident of the city.

Athletes who prepared, trained, and won their competitions were highly regarded. Likewise, Christ would give special honor to those in Smyrna who victoriously fought their fight of faith to the end, even at the cost of their own lives. These believers were still in that fight, and their struggle had already been great. But the King of kings Himself reassured them that a time would come when He placed a crown of life on the heads of all those who remained faithful, even if it meant paying the ultimate price.

As a final note, some Bible scholars have suggested the "crown of life" was an allusion to the "crown of Cybele" that crested the peak of Mount Pagos above the city of Smyrna. F. F. Bruce was among those who hold this opinion. He stated, "…The imagery here is suggested by 'the crown of Smyrna,' the circle of colonnaded buildings on the crest on Mount Pagos."[56] (For more about the "crown" that adorned the peak of Mount Pagos, *see* page 521, 548).

'HE THAT HATH AN EAR, LET HIM HEAR WHAT THE SPIRIT SAITH UNTO THE CHURCHES'

> In Revelation 2:11, Jesus cried out to the church of Smyrna: "He that hath an ear, let him hear what the Spirit saith unto the churches; He that overcometh shall not be hurt of the second death."

Just as Jesus did when speaking to the church of Ephesus (Revelation 2:7), He again issued an invitation to those who have ears to hear. The implication is that everyone does *not* have ears to hear what the Holy Spirit is saying. But to those who have open hearts and open ears, Jesus urges, "He that hath an ear, *let him hear what the Spirit saith unto the churches….*"

As noted earlier in Chapter Five, this exhortation was a familiar one to John. The Synoptic Gospels record seven different times when Jesus said, "He that hath ears to hear, let him hear" (*see* Matthew 11:15; 13:9,43; Mark 4:9,23; Luke 8:8;

14:35). Once again, however, Jesus added a significant phrase: "He that hath an ear to hear, *let him hear what the Spirit saith unto the churches....*" Although Christ was speaking a specific message to the church of Smyrna, these truths are to be taken as a message from the Holy Spirit to all seven churches in Asia and to the Church at large throughout all history.

'HE THAT OVERCOMETH'

Once again in Revelation 2:11, Jesus sent out a divine call to His people to *overcome* in the midst of the difficult challenges they were facing. He said, "He that hath an ear, let him hear what the Spirit saith unto the churches; *He that overcometh....*"

The word "overcometh" is the Greek word *nikao* — the same word used in Revelation 2:7 when Christ concluded His message to the angel at the church at Ephesus. This word denotes *a victor* who has gained the mastery of his competition and ultimately reigns supreme as the champion in the game. It can be translated *to control, to conquer, to defeat, to master, to overcome, to overwhelm, to surpass,* or *to be victorious.*

The use of this word is important in the context of Revelation 2:11 because it carries the image of *an athletic victory.* To win the contest before them, the congregation in Smyrna had to be prepared for the toughest competition they had ever faced. As was true with the Ephesian church,

no attitude less than a full commitment would be sufficient for the Smyrnean believers to master the external adversaries and internal struggles they were facing. Only those who were thoroughly committed would win a victor's crown.

Just as in Revelation 2:7, the Greek tense used here speaks of *a continuous and ongoing victory.* This means Christ was asking these believers to get in the race and *remain* in the race until the goal was reached and to stay in the fight until their enemies were permanently overcome.

Left: A wreath of laurel leaves forming a victor's crown has long been symbolic of outstanding achievement and endurance. Originally horseshoe in shape but later becoming circular, laurel wreaths are said to be the forerunner of the crown itself. The golden laurel wreath shown here is a vivid illustration of what Jesus was referring to in John's vision when He promised the crown of life as a reward to believers who remain steadfast in their faith to the end.

'SHALL NOT BE HURT OF THE SECOND DEATH'

Concluding His message to the church of Smyrna, Jesus declared, "He that hath an ear, let him hear what the Spirit saith unto the churches; He that overcometh *shall not be hurt of the second death*" (Revelation 2:11).

The word "hurt" is the Greek word *adikeo*, meaning *to harm, to hurt,* or *to injure.* The phrase "second death" comes from the Greek phrase *thanatou tou deuterou,* which literally means *death of the second kind.* It refers to eternal punishment for those who did not accept Jesus Christ as their Savior in this life.

Someone once stated that if *a person is born once* (natural birth), *he dies twice* (natural and spiritual death). However, *when a person is born twice* (natural birth and spiritual rebirth), *he dies only once* (physical death). Those who have been born twice — once naturally and a second time spiritually — will never be harmed,

Since these goals are never fully reached in this life, Jesus was asking the congregation in Smyrna to be *permanently consistent and undeterred in their determination to overcome and obtain victory in every area of their lives.*

As mentioned earlier, Jesus called each of the seven churches — and He calls believers throughout all future generations — to be overcomers (*see* Revelation 2:7,11,17,26; 3:5,12,21). Christians are to make it their unceasing goal to maintain victory in every possible sphere of life.

hurt, injured, or even touched by the *second death*, which is *eternal punishment*.

It is inescapable for every person to experience "death of the first kind" when his or her physical body fails and dies. But *death of the second kind* — which includes eternal punishment and banishment from the presence of God — is reserved only for those who die without Christ. On the other hand, when believers in Jesus Christ pass on from this life, they are immediately ushered into the presence of Christ and will not taste any further death. This was Jesus' message to the believers in Smyrna: Even if they died physically for their faith, He joyfully promised that eternal death would never touch them.

Finally, it must be noted that Christ had *no rebuke* for the Smyrnean church. These believers had already suffered tribulation in many forms. Scandal, false

accusations, slanderous stories, the loss of jobs and income, discrimination, and death were already present realities. But Christ's message was loud and clear: Hard times still lay ahead of them; however, they could be assured that their faith would withstand the onslaught. Those who stayed faithful unto death would be specially rewarded with a crown of life. If physical death was the price they had to pay to be faithful, they could be assured

Above: These are the ruins of a mighty fortress on the rounded peak of Mount Pagos above the city of Smyrna. The original fortress was constructed during the reign of Lysimachus (301-281 BC). Ancient writers called this fortress "the crown of Cybele."

that the second death would never touch them and that they would rest eternally safe in the arms of the Savior.

JESUS' MESSAGE TO THE CHURCH OF SMYRNA: SYNOPSIS

In Jesus' message to the church of Smyrna, He offered commendation and encouragement to these believers who had endured unrelenting suffering yet remained steadfast in their faith. Acknowledging their patience through severe persecution and abject poverty, Jesus declared the believers in the church of Smyrna to be truly rich (Revelation 2:9). He did not chastise or rebuke this church; rather, He identified with their sufferings and then described the difficulties they would continue to suffer for His name's sake. Jesus assured the Smyrnean believers that they would not be touched by the second death, promising them the eternal reward of a crown of life, which is reserved for those who remain faithful (Revelation 2:10,11).

PRIMARY TRUTHS

- Jesus identifies with believers who patiently endure tribulations because of their faith in Him. Those who suffer scandal, false accusations, slander, loss of jobs and income, discrimination, and death for Christ's sake prove the fervency of their love for Him. Therefore, Jesus will demonstrate His love for *them* by publicly crowning them with honor and life for eternity. Those who experience the loss of their material goods, reputation, and potential livelihood because of their uncompromising commitment to Christ are highly esteemed by Him as being truly rich.

- Hard times are inescapable, but God's power unfailingly sustains those who are determined to be faithful to Him. Even if the fires of adversity rage until it seems they will never cease, trials are *always* temporary. Satan uses fires to test, but God allows those same fires to purify. Church history has proven that the persecuted Church always emerges purer than gold and mightier in Spirit, not weaker. *Always.*

- Jesus does not take it lightly when a person takes on the attribute of Satan, the great accuser. Evil speaking with the intent to cause harm, raise suspicion, or slander is defined by the Head of the Church as being in league with darkness and is a practice that Christ hates.

PRACTICAL APPLICATIONS

- The Spirit of God always warns His people in advance when difficult times are coming. When God issues such divine warnings, they are intended to prepare believers to face the impending challenges and to assure them of His ever-present grace and a future reward.

- To bend or break one's commitment to Christ under the weight of external pressure, no matter how extreme, is not an acceptable option. Jesus expects His followers to remain faithful unto death — just as He was faithful unto death for all who would be His.

- Material goods are temporal and fleeting. Christians are to pursue and treasure the value of enduring riches, which are the Holy Spirit's presence, patience, strength to endure, faith, love between the saints, and spiritual rewards for steadfastness in the face of adversity.

THE CHURCH OF SMYRNA

The ancient port city of Smyrna held a position of prominence in its superb location along the shores of the Aegean Sea. Many called this beautiful coastal metropolis "the first of Asia," yet its spiritual climate reeked with rampant depravity from the vilest of pagan perversions. The most grotesque of those rituals were attributed to the patron goddess of the city, Cybele.

The church of Smyrna was small yet spiritually strong. Their steadfast devotion to Christ and His doctrine literally cost them everything. All familiar ties were disrupted and ultimately severed in order for them to maintain pure devotion to Christ. The bond of fellowship between believers in Smyrna was extremely close-knit, since their connection to Christ and to one another was essentially all they had left.

Christians in Smyrna refused to participate in the pagan practices they had once celebrated prior to their conversion; therefore, they were accused of being atheists and anarchists. As a result of such slander, believers fell under the suspicion of the pagan community and the government. In addition, slanderous accusation from the Jewish community of Smyrna heightened suspicion about Christians and led to horrendous persecution against them.

The blasphemous behavior of the Smyrnean Jews toward believers reflected nothing of the core beliefs of Judaism and was far removed from ethics espoused by their own religious heritage. In fact, their behavior was so offensive to Christ that He called them the "synagogue of Satan" because of the malicious, false accusations they hurled at believers. They claimed to oppose Christians because of their own religious zeal, yet it was clear that the viciousness from a malevolent sector in that particular Jewish community was fueled strictly by self-interest and greed. Their accusations instigated the rage of the pagan culture against Christians, escalating the persecution against the church of Smyrna. This not only blocked believers from participation in the professional groups that ensured their livelihood, but also resulted in the constant threat of being arrested and murdered as a form of entertainment for the masses in Smyrna's stadium or theater.

CHRIST'S COMMENDATION AND CORRECTION TO THE CHURCH OF SMYRNA

The violence perpetrated against Christians was so widespread in Smyrna that believers faced death on a daily basis. It was common for believers to be mobbed and put to death in the city's streets, markets, theater, and stadium while onlookers not only approved but encouraged the fatal attacks, as was the case in the martyrdom of Polycarp. Therefore, when Jesus referred to Himself as One "which was dead, and is alive" (Revelation 2:8), He fully identified with the Smyrnean believers' plight while indicating that they, too, would put death behind them and become like their Savior: beyond the reach of death and alive forevermore.

Jesus went on to say He understood the scope and extent of their tribulation and poverty, emphasizing that their hardship and pain was personally known to Him. Although the believers in Smyrna lived under constant duress and were inescapably destitute, Jesus called them rich. This laudatory description clearly signifies that the Smyrnean congregation experienced an abundance of riches that could not be measured in worldly wealth.

In Revelation 2:10, Jesus gave specific details of the persecutions to come as He spoke words of warning and comfort: "Fear none of those things which thou shalt suffer…be thou faithful unto death, and I will give thee a crown of life." The persecutions in Smyrna lasted for more than two centuries, and persecution throughout the Roman Empire continued into the Third Century. A demonic force was exerting its influence in Smyrna through religious groups, education, entertainment, and the political machine of that time. Satan was using these systems to wage war against the church of Smyrna and to deal a crushing blow to its members. But the fires of adversity only caused this church to emerge stronger, purer, and honored as precious in the Lord's sight.

WHAT THE SPIRIT IS SAYING TO THE CHURCH TODAY

1. Temporal goods can be accumulated by those who are impoverished spiritually. However, true riches — that which is not measured in monetary or material wealth — are reserved for those who prize faithfulness to Christ above all else, even if it means the loss of all worldly goods. Pursue eternal riches, which cannot be stolen or plundered by man, and the eternal favor that God alone can bestow.

2. Refuse to compromise your faith in Christ with worldly practices, no matter the cost.

3. Fear not! Christ forewarns His people — not to frighten them but to forearm and to call them to a focused preparation. There will be intense opposition, conflicts, and suffering as believers press forward to gain territory for the Kingdom of God. But Christ will equip His people with courage, patience, and peace — and, in the end, impart an incorruptible great reward.

4. Jesus laid down His life for His Church. Thus, when members of His Church are willing to lay down their lives for Him, He will personally comfort them in tribulation and will publicly (and eternally) acknowledge and honor their faithfulness as precious to Him.

He that hath an ear, let him hear
what the Spirit saith unto the churches.
— Revelation 2:29

CONCLUSION

The early believers who lived in ancient Ephesus and Smyrna (as well as in the cities of the other five churches Jesus addressed in John's vision) were assaulted on every side by pagans, a plethora of intolerant religions, and wicked rulers. But no matter how intensely the opposition waged against the Church, the spiritual darkness that had long ruled the province of Asia and the rest of the Roman Empire eventually succumbed to the light of the Gospel. So has it been throughout the centuries since those early days of the Church. When believers remain steadfast in their faith, regardless of the price that must be paid or how long it may take, the glorious light of truth will ultimately pierce through the darkness as God calls the lost out of Satan's kingdom and into the Kingdom of God's Son.

Much has transpired throughout the pages that precede. We have seen:

- The apostle Paul's departure from Corinth and his arrival in Ephesus with Aquila and Priscilla.
- The dramatic events that transpired in the early days of the church of Ephesus as recorded in Acts 19.
- The role of the church at Ephesus in establishing churches all over Asia.
- The key roles the apostle John held in the region of Asia.
- John's arrest and exile to the island of Patmos during the reign of the Emperor Domitian.

This leads us to the main theme of this book, which focuses on the first two chapters of John's vision. All 22 chapters of the book of Revelation are filled with spectacular sights and sounds, but the entire message begins with that moment when John's world was invaded by God's presence, and the apostle saw a vision of the exalted Christ and heard His messages to the seven churches located in Ephesus, Smyrna, Pergamum, Thyatira, Sardis, Philadelphia, and Laodicea. Because it wasn't possible to do justice to all seven of those messages in one volume, this first volume has focused primarily on the image of the resurrected Jesus that John beheld in his vision and Jesus' first two messages to the churches of Ephesus and Smyrna.

Almost 2,000 years have passed since the apostle John first saw his vision, yet Jesus' words to the seven churches are just as relevant today as when they were first spoken. Christ addressed current problems and trends of the First Century Church, but it is clear that these were prophetic messages that still speak to the problems and trends in the Church today. The names of nations, regions, and cities have changed; emperors and governments have come and gone; and church leadership has been replaced by the next generation of leaders countless times. However, the challenges and problems facing the modern Church at the end of the age are nearly identical to those faced by early believers almost 2,000 years ago when Jesus' messages were first spoken.

As the last days unfold before us and we draw near to the Lord's return, the powers of darkness are putting forth their best efforts to throw the world into an ever-deepening downward spiral of spiritual darkness and confusion. The enemy is aggressively working to set the stage for an earthly, wicked leader who will one day exercise control at the end of the age. This "mystery of lawlessness" has been working for 2,000 years, preparing the unsaved world to receive the "man of lawlessness," who Paul foretold would be revealed in the immediate years preceding Christ's Second Coming (see 2 Thessalonians 2:7,8).

One generation ago, it would have been almost impossible to imagine how a "man of lawlessness" could emerge on the world scene with a worldwide reception. But the spiritual temperature of the world has changed. It is no secret that as modern society has turned from God, it has become increasingly tolerant of what

was once viewed as sinful or wrong. Yet in its effort to become accommodating and defensive of everyone's individual rights, society has increasingly become intolerant of those who hold beliefs or opinions that differ from the mainstream culture. As time passes, the degeneration of society will only worsen. This makes Christ's messages to the seven churches even more crucial and relevant, for the Early Church confronted many of the problems that are reemerging at the end of this age.

Before each chapter of this book that teaches Christ's message to the pastors and churches of Ephesus and Smyrna, a historical chapter was deliberately included to give readers a glimpse into what life was like for those who lived in these ancient cities. Having read these chapters, you can better understand the social environment that confronted the Early Church and recognize that these same challenges are unfolding again in these last days before Christ's return. It is a mistake to assume that Jesus' words in Revelation 2 and 3 are merely historical messages to past congregations. On the contrary, these are prophetic words that continue to give us insight into God's perspective of modern society, a glimpse forward into what the future holds, and precise direction to guide us through the difficulties of the present hour.

Parallels between today's world and the Roman world of the First Century are shockingly similar. Deviant and morally decadent activities that were once carried out in the privacy of Roman bathhouses are now common scenes on the Internet, television, movies, and other forms of media. What used to be taboo only one generation ago is now accepted and often promoted, even to elementary school children. Whereas the Greek and Roman worlds were inundated with an array of different religions that seemed to all blend together, the present trend is to blend all religions together and to make one's faith nothing more than a matter of personal preference.

Those who believe their faith exclusively represents the only means for man's salvation — and who hold fast to fixed moral standards and beliefs — are considered primitive and closed-minded and are ridiculed by those who claim to possess superior intelligence. Believers who are committed to living by the teachings of the Bible are scorned by the world — very similar to the way Christians were once scorned by a loose Roman world that rejected moral absolutes. Society doesn't participate in outright idolatry as was true in the First Century; instead, a more subtle and even more dangerous form of idolatry exists today. Modern society has placed man and the pursuit of his pleasure as its central focus. The "rights" of mankind have become supreme and are worshiped at the expense of absolute biblical principles and truths.

If we want to know where society is headed, all we need to do is to look back at the past, for what once existed only in textbooks is reappearing before our eyes as society continues to turn from God. This deterioration will continue as time passes but at a faster rate of speed. Before a "man of lawlessness" can be revealed, the world must first become a place where lawlessness abounds, for a world guided by God's Word would never tolerate a lawless leader. Therefore, the moral temperature of society must continue to decrease dramatically if the bulk of the population is ever to embrace a man of lawlessness. As time slips away and the deterioration of modern society accelerates, this will be a clear signal that Christ's return is at hand.

The similarities between the Church at the end of the First Century and the Church that exists today are remarkable. Back then the Church struggled with tolerance of sin, false doctrine, a falling away from one's first love, passionless spiritual routines, and spiritual cold-heartedness. The Church today struggles with these same issues. However, the answers to these problems are also similar. Just as Jesus cried out to His Church in the First Century, His voice is still crying out to His people today, calling on them to repent of their waywardness — to return to Him and do their first works. What the Head of the Church said in the past to His people is what He continues to say in the present. His remedies for the spiritual maladies afflicting the modern Church are no different than those He prescribed for the Church almost 2,000 years ago.

Just as He did then, Christ is still calling His Church to shine as a light in the darkness. If we will open our hearts to listen, we will hear Jesus speaking to us through His messages to the pastors and congregations of Ephesus and Smyrna and the other churches of Revelation. We will still hear His clarion call of divine authority: "He that hath an ear, let him hear what the Spirit saith unto the churches…" (Revelation 2:11). And as we respond to His voice in humble obedience, we will rise up to be the glorious Church He has called us to be on this earth, just as was prophesied by the prophet Isaiah:

For, behold, the darkness shall cover the earth,
and gross darkness the people:
but the Lord shall arise upon thee,
and his glory shall be seen upon thee.
And the Gentiles shall come to thy light,
and kings to the brightness of thy rising.
— Isaiah 60:2,3

A LIGHT IN DARKNESS
VOLUME ONE

ENDNOTES

BIOGRAPHIES

BIBLIOGRAPHIES

RICK RENNER: Author

TURKEY RESEARCH TEAM

Rick Renner was born in 1958 in the city of Tulsa, Oklahoma. A love for the Bible directed his studies toward the Greek language, the lands of the New Testament, and Christian theology. An avid student of history, Rick developed a specialized interest in Greco-Roman culture.

Rick has devoted his life to the study of the New Testament — especially the writings of the apostle Paul and the churches and cities addressed in the book of Revelation. Over the years, Rick's studies have led him to travel extensively to explore historical sites of the First Century Church throughout Greece, Turkey, Italy, Egypt, and Israel. Additionally, he has conducted extensive research trips to museums, archives, and archeological sites in various nations to further inform his study.

Rick's love of the Bible, biblical languages, and history is evident in the engaging style of his teaching. Weaving doctrine and vivid background details like a master storyteller, Rick's teaching brings to life the human experience while addressing the divine expectation in the context of history and contemporary life. *A Light in Darkness* is the culmination of these decades of devoted study and research. Rick is also the author of more than 30 other books that have collectively sold in the millions, including the best-selling *Sparkling Gems From the Greek 1* and 2, and *Dressed To Kill: A Biblical Approach to Spiritual Warfare*.

During the course of more than 30 years of teaching and pastoral ministry, Rick, along with his wife and lifelong ministry partner Denise, founded a thriving ministry in the former Soviet Union. Rick and Denise reside in Moscow, Russia, with their three adult sons and their families, where they pastor the Moscow Good News Church and continue to lead the many aspects of their international ministry.

ASIL TUNÇER
Historian and Professional Tour Guide

Asil Tunçer was born in 1966 in Izmir, Turkey — the modern-day city built on the site of ancient Smyrna and the port city nearest to the ancient city of Ephesus. As a local resident growing up near Ephesus, Asil developed a lifelong love for the ancient city and has dedicated his life to the study of Ephesus and the other ancient cities of Asia Minor. Asil graduated from Dokuz Eylul University in Izmir. Later he graduated from the same university with a Masters Degree in History. He has given lectures on the ancient cities of Turkey in several influential universities, with a special emphasis on the seven cities in the book of Revelation.

Asil has more than three decades of experience as a professional guide and is licensed by the Turkish Ministry of Culture and Tourism. His primary focus as a guide has been to assist teachers, professors, students of advanced studies, and those whose field of expertise is connected to ancient history and archaeology. Throughout his work as a guide, Asil has maintained and developed his academic research and writings, specifically a manuscript on the ancient city of Ephesus (not yet published). *Asil worked alongside the Turkey research team during multiple trips to pertinent ancient sites, providing invaluable assistance in the accumulation of facts and details provided in this book and in the other volumes of* Seven Messages to the Seven Churches *series.* For further information, visit www.asiltuncer.com.

MAXIM MYASNIKOV
Executive Assistant

Maxim Myasnikov was born in 1973 in the Soviet Union in the city of Volgograd, Russia — the city formerly known to the world as Stalingrad, which was devastated by Nazi attacks in World War II. Raised in a prestigious Communist home with parents who were avowed atheists, Maxim never had a thought about God until, as a young man, he visited a Protestant church that had been started by a former pastoral student of Rick Renner and ultimately came to Christ. In 1995, Maxim graduated from River Transportation College with a degree in economics. Today Maxim serves as personal assistant and interpreter for Rick Renner. Together with his wife Olga, Maxim also leads the senior citizen outreach of the Moscow Good News Church, which ministers to thousands of senior citizens each month. Maxim and Olga have a daughter, Anastasia, and a son, Matthew. *Maxim was responsible for the transportation and logistical coordination of the Turkey research team.*

CINDY HANSEN
Editor

Cindy Hansen was born in Yakima, Washington, in 1955. She was raised in cities along the Rocky Mountains of Montana, Wyoming, and Colorado, where she cultivated a passionate interest in history and a love for adventure and travel. Cindy graduated in 1979 from Colorado State University with a degree in English and a minor in Political Science. Her love of history and her studies in these combined disciplines continued to inform her approach in observing and recording significant spiritual and global events and in articulating their significance in a contemporary context via the printed page. Cindy also graduated from Bible schools in Alaska and in Oklahoma and has edited or written more than 75 books for various Christian authors and ministers, with Rick Renner among them. Cindy is the Editorial Director in the U.S. office of RENNER Ministries. *As a key member of the research team for this book project, Cindy devoted countless hours to the preparation and finalization of this volume, poring over multiple drafts and editing hundreds of pages as she helped Rick shape the content and presentation of this material.*

ERIC HANSEN
Editorial Assistant

Eric Hansen was born in Anchorage, Alaska, in 1986 and lived in a log cabin near Mt. McKinley during his early years, later moving with his family to Oklahoma. Years later, Eric graduated from the University of Oklahoma with honors for outstanding scholarship and academic excellence. Today an opthamologist, Eric was a medical student during the research for this book. His medical training and his passion for helping the oppressed has led him to travel on medical mission trips to such places as India, Cambodia, and Papua New Guinea, working in field clinics in remote areas. Eric's strong interest in cross-cultural studies focused his keen eye for detail during the research team's field excursions in Turkey. *As editorial assistant for the Turkey team, Eric assisted in research and in chronicling the many hours of fact-finding in support of this project.*

ALEXANDER GLADILOV
Photographer

Alexander Gladilov was born in 1964 in the city of Sumi, which was located in what was then known as the Ukrainian Republic of the USSR. Alexander's avid interest in photography began during those early years growing up as he made full use of his simple Soviet "Smena 8" camera and developed his skill in capturing real life as a photographic art form.

After military service, Alexander studied at Sumi State University in Ukraine and graduated with a degree in chemistry and engineering. After graduation, he worked at that same university as a chemist and engineer.

In 1996, Alexander came to Christ and has been employed by RENNER Ministries since 2002. Along with other duties, today Alexander holds the position of official photographer for RENNER Ministries in Moscow, Russia. *Alexander was the Turkey team's photographer and is responsible for the majority of photos used in this book that are accredited to our own photography staff.*

ENDNOTES

CHAPTER ONE

1. William M. Ramsay, *The Letters to the Seven Churches* (Whitefish, MT: Kessinger Publishing, 2004), p. 85.

2. Ibid.

3. Fatih Cimok, *A Guide to the Seven Churches* (Istanbul: A Turizm Yayinlari, 2007), p. 17.

4. Michael Grant, *Constantine the Great: The Man and His Times* (New York: Charles Scribner's Sons, 1993), pp. 202-207.

5. Samuel Fallows, ed., *The Popular and Critical Bible Encyclopedia and Scriptural Dictionary, Vol. 2* (Chicago: The Howard-Severance Co., 1907), p. 1121.

6. Paul Trebilco, *The Early Christians in Ephesus From Paul to Ignatius* (Grand Rapids, MI: Wm. B. Eerdmans Publishing Co., 2007), pp. 252-253. *See also* Eusebius, *Church History*, III.xxxi.2-3.

7. Eusebius, *Church History*, V.viii.4.

8. Irenaeus, *Against Heresies*, III.iii.3-4; V.xxxiii.4.

9. Clive Foss, *Ephesus After Antiquity: A Late Antique, Byzantine, and Turkish City* (Cambridge, England: Cambridge University Press, 1979), p. 33.

10. A. R. Fausset, *Bible Cyclopedia* (Hartford, CT: S. S. Scranton Co., 1910), pp. 689-690.

11. Procopius, *Buildings*, V.i.4-6.

12. John Foxe, *Foxe's Book of Martyrs* (Old Tappan, NJ: Fleming H. Revell Co., 1980), p. 13.

13. Jerome, *Lives of Illustrious Men*, IX; Eusebius, *Church History*, III.xviii.1-3.

14. Brian W. Jones, *The Emperor Domitian* (New York: Routledge, 1992), pp. 106-107.

15. Suetonius, *Lives of the Twelve Caesars*, Domitian, X.

16. Pliny, *Letters*, III.xi.3., trans. B. Radice.

17. Eutropius, 7.23.

18. Suetonius, *Lives of the Twelve Caesars*, Domitian, XVII.

19. Tertullian, *Prescription Against Heretics*, c. 36.

20. Annoula, *Patmos: Island With a Halo* (Brigitte Hurdalek, 2000), p. 65.

21. Cimok, p. 18.

22. Irenaeus, *Against Heresies*, I.xxvi.3; III.xi.1.

23. Hippolytus, *The Refutation of All Heresies*, VII.26.

24. Sabine Baring-Gould, *The Lives of the Saints* (London: John Hodges, 1880), p. 130.

25. Cimok, p. 17.

26. Irenaeus, *Against Heresies*, III.iii.4.

27. Cassius Dio, *Dio's Roman History*, LXVIII.3.

28. Pliny, *Letters*, X.96-97.

29. Galen, *De Methodo Medendi*, IX.8.

30. Cassius Dio, *Dio's Roman History*, LXVIII.32.

31. Cassius Dio, *Dio's Roman History*, LXVIII.33.

32. Pliny, *Letters*, X.96-97.

33. "The Bollandists (24 Jan.) give two lives of St. Timothy, one ascribed to Polycrates (an early Bishop of Ephesus, and a contemporary of St. Irenaeus) and the other by Metaphrastes, which is merely an expansion of the former. The first states that during the Neronian persecution St. John arrived at Ephesus, where he lived with St. Timothy until he was exiled to Patmos under Domitian." "Epistles to Timothy and Titus," *The Catholic Encyclopedia, Vol. 14* (New York: Robert Appleton Co., 1912; Online Edition, K. Knight, 2003).

34. William Barclay, *New Testament Words* (Philadelphia, PA: The Westminster Press, 1974), pp. 144-145.

35. Cassius Dio, *Dio's Roman History*, LXVIII.1.

36. Eusebius, *Church History*, III.xx.10-11.

37. Alexander Roberts and James Donaldson, eds., *The Ante-Nicene Fathers: Translations of the Writings of the Fathers Down to AD 325, Vol. 7*, "Commentary on the Apocalypse" by Victorinus, trans. Robert Ernest Wallis (Grand Rapids, MI: Wm. B. Eerdmans Publishing Co., 1950), p. 353.

38. Eusebius, *Church History*, II.ix.2-3.

39. Eusebius, *Church History*, III.i.1.

40. Gregory of Nazianzus, *Oration* 33.XI.

41. Jerome, *Ep. ad Marcell.*, XXII.

42. Theodoret, *On the Psalms*, CXVI.

43. Nicephorus, *Short History*, II.39.

44. Eusebius, *Church History*, V.x.3.

45. Eusebius, *Church History*, III.xxiv.6.

46. Nicephorus, *Ecclesiastical History*, II.40.

47. Eusebius, *Church History*, II.xv.1-2.

48. Irenaeus, *Against Heresies*, III.i.1

49. Clement of Rome, *Letter to the Corinthians*, V.

50. Ignatius, *Letter to the Romans*, IV.3.

51. Eusebius, *Church History*, II.xxv.8.

52. Tertullian, *Scorpiace*, XV.

53. Eusebius, *Church History*, II.xxv.5-7.

54. Eusebius, *Church History*, II, xxv.5.

55. Arthur Stapylton Barnes, *St. Peter in Rome and His Tomb on the Vatican Hill* (London: Swan Sonnenschein and Co., 1900), p. 26.

56. Moses of Chorene, *History of Armenia*, IX.

57. G. Adolf Deissmann, *Bible Studies*, trans. Alexander Grieve (Edinburgh: T. & T. Clark, 1901), pp. 217-219.

Chapter Two

1. William M. Ramsay, *The Letters to the Seven Churches* (Whitefish, MT: Kessinger Publishing, 2004), pp. 178-181.

2. Ibid.

3. Albert Barnes, *Notes, Explanatory and Practical on the Book of Revelation* (London: Knight and Son, 1853), p. 75.

4. Fatih Cimok, *A Guide to the Seven Churches* (Istanbul: A Turizm Yayinlari, 2007), p. 23.

5. Mary G. Houston and Florence S. Hornblower, *Ancient Egyptian, Assyrian, and Persian Costumes Decorations* (London: A. & C. Black, 1920), pp. 50-53, 80-81.

6. Douglas Schar (author of *The Backyard Medicine Chest: an Herbal Primer*, Washington DC: Elliott and Clark Publishing, 1995), "Frankincense," planetbotanic.ca/fact_sheets/frankincense_fs2.html.

7. Ibid.

8. Much of this information about stars was obtained from the following articles on the NASA website: "Stars," https://science.nasa.gov/astrophysics/focus-areas; Paul J. Green, "Star," World Book Online Reference Center, 2005, World Book, Inc., nasa.gov/worldbook/star_worldbook.html.

9. John F. Walvoord, *The Revelation of Jesus Christ* (Chicago: Moody Press, 1966), pp. 26, 45.

10. Suetonius, *Lives of the Caesars, Domitian* (Cambridge, MA: Harvard University, Loeb Classical Library, 1992), p. 351.

11. Ibid., p. 385.

12. Ernest Janzen, "The Jesus of the Apocalypse Wears the Emperor's Clothes" (Atlanta: Scholars, *Seminar Papers*, 1994), footnote 55.

13. Suetonius, *Domitian*, p. 345.

14. Janzen, pp. 645-647.

15. Engelbert Stauffer, *Christ and the Caesars* (Hamburg: Friedrich Wittig Publishers, 1952), p. 152.

16. Janzen, ibid.

17. Brian W. Jones, *The Emperor Domitian* (London: Routledge, 1992), p. 75.

CHAPTER THREE

1. Fatih Cimok, *Journeys of Paul: From Tarsus to the Ends of the Earth* (Istanbul: A Turizm Yayinlari, 2004), p. 159.

2. Jerome Murphy-O'Connor, *Paul's Ephesus: Texts and Archeology* (Collegeville, MN: Liturgical Press, 1971), pp. 26-27.

3. John C. Kraft, Helmut Buckner, Ilhan Kayan, and Helmut Engelmann, "The Geographies of Ancient Ephesus and the Artemesion in Anatolia," *Geoarcheology: An International Journal, Vol. 22, No. 1* (Hoboken, NJ: Wiley Interscience, 2007), p. 135.

4. Ibid., p. 140.

5. Murphy-O'Conner, pp. 54-57.

6. Strabo, *Geography*, XIV.i.24.

7. Trudy Ring, Robert M. Salkin, and Sharon La Boda, eds., *International Dictionary of Historic Places, Vol. 3: Southern Europe* (Chicago: Fitzroy Dearborn Publishers, 1995), p. 216.

8. Dennis E. Smith, ed., *Chalice Introduction to the New Testament* (Atlanta: Chalice Press, 2004), p. 108.

9. William Barclay, *The New Daily Study Bible: The Revelation of John, Vol. 1, 3rd ed.* (Louisville, KY: Westminster John Knox Press, 2004), p. 65.

10. Ibid.

11. Diana E. E. Kleiner, *Cleopatra and Rome* (Cambridge, MA: Harvard University Press, 2005), p. 112.

12. Sadan Gökovali, *Ephesus*, trans. Altan Erguvan (Istanbul: Net Turistik Yayinlar A. S.), p. 31.

13. Robin Waterfield, *Athens: A History, From Ancient Ideal to Modern City* (New York: Basic Books, 2004), pp. 168-169.

14. This ratio is reflected in both the *Iliad* and the *Odyssey*, written by the ancient Greek poet Homer, where the majority of slaves mentioned are women taken as booty from war.

15. Glenn R. Marrow, *Plato's Law of Slavery in Relation to Greek Law* (Urbana, IL: University of Illinois Press, 1939), pp. 73-78.

16. Yvon Garlan, *Slavery in Ancient Greece*, trans. Janet Lloyd (Ithaca, NY: Cornell University Press, 1988), p. 79.

17. Peter Garnsey, *Ideas of Slavery From Aristotle to Augustine* (New York: Cambridge University Press, 1996), p. 9.

18. Ibid., p. 108.

19. Ibid., p. 109.

20. Ibid.

21. Matthew Dillon and Lynda Garland, *Ancient Rome: From the Early Republic to the Assassination of Julius Caesar* (New York: Routledge, 2005), p. 299.

22. Keith Hopkins, *Conquerors and Slaves* (New York: Cambridge University Press, 1978), p. 8 (footnote).

23. William Smith, ed., *A Dictionary of Greek and Roman Antiquities* (New York: Harper and Brothers, 1886), p. 887.

24. Gauis, *Institutes*, I.52.

25. Walter Scheidel, ed., *Debating Roman Demography* (Leiden, Netherlands: Koninklijke Brill NV, 2001), p. 29, footnote 113.

26. Junius P. Rodriguez, *The Historical Encyclopedia of World Slavery, Vol. 1* (Santa Barbara, CA: ABC-CLIO, Inc., 1997), p. xvi.

27. Richard Ross Watkins, *Slavery: Bondage Throughout History* (New York: Houghton Mifflin, 2001), pp. 35-36.

28. William Linn Westermann, *The Slave Systems of Greek and Roman Anti-quity* (Philadelphia, PA: The American Philosophical Society, 1955), p. 99.

29. Frank Richard Cowell, *Life in Ancient Rome* (New York: The Berkley Publishing Group, 1961), p. 97.

30. Seneca, *Essays, Book I, On Anger*, III.32.

31. Florence Dupot, *Daily Life in Ancient Rome* (Cornwall, England: International Ltd., 1993), p. 62.

32. Westermann, p. 87.

33. Clive Foss, *Ephesus After Antiquity: A Late Antique, Byzantine, and Turkish City* (Cambridge, England: Cambridge University Press, 1979), p. 56.

34. Dennis E. Smith, p. 108.

35. Tacitus, *Annals*, XV.44.

36. William D. Halsey and Bernard Johnston, eds., *Collier's Encyclopedia, Vol. 5* (New York: Macmillan Educational Co., 1991), p. 704.

37. Livy, *History of Rome*, I.35.

38. Alexander Petrovich Kazhdan and Giles Constable, *People and Power in Byzantium: An Introduction to Modern Byzantium Studies* (Washington DC: Dumbarton Oaks, 1982), pp. 66-67.

39. Suetonius, *Lives of the Twelve Caesars, Domitian*, VII.

40. Pliny the Elder, *The Natural History of Pliny*, trans. John Bostock and H. T. Riley (London: George Bell and Sons, 1890), pp. 324, 326.

41. J. A. Simpson and E. S. C. Weiner, eds., *The Oxford English Dictionary* (Oxford: Oxford University Press, 1989). *Vol. 6* ("furor"), p. 282; *Vol. 3* ("circensian"), p. 226.

42. Tertullian wrote eloquently about the passion of the spectators at Roman chariot races in his treatise entitled, *Of the Games* (Latin: *De Spectaculis*). Tertullian wrote this treatise in an effort to help early Christians understand the biblical perspective regarding their attending Roman games or theatrical performances. He stated: "Then since passion [*furor*] is forbidden to us Christians, we are warned to hold aloof from every public entertainment, even from the Circus, because passion holds sway there. See how the people rush to the racecourse with frantic enthusiasm, a disorderly mob, blind and already in a fury of anxiety about their bets. The praetor seems to them to be wasting time; every eye is turned on him as he shakes in the urn the lots for the draw for stations. Thus they wait in desperate eagerness for the start. Then they go mad and roar as one man; you can tell they are mad because of their sheer silliness. The praetor drops the white cloth, and they all call out 'They're off,' telling one another what everyone can see for himself. This shows how blind they are; they do not see what he has dropped. They think it is a white cloth; in fact it is a symbol of the devil thrown out of Heaven...." Tertullian, *Of the Games*, XVI.

43. Alexander P. Kazhdan and Alice-Mary Talbot, eds., *The Oxford Dictionary of Byzantium, Vol. 2* (Oxford: Oxford University Press, 1991), p. 1473.

44. Sarah B. Pomeroy and Stanley Mayer Burstein, eds., *Ancient History* (Princeton, NJ: Markus Wiener Publishing, Inc., 1984), p. 160.

45. David Stone Potter and D. J. Mattingly, eds., *Life, Death, and Entertainment in the Roman Empire* (Ann Arbor, MI: University of Michigan Press, 1999), p. 289.

46. David Matz, *Daily Life of Ancient Romans* (Westport, CN: Greenwood Press, 2002), p. 101.

47. Lesley A. DuTemple, *The Colosseum* (Minneapolis, MN: Lerner Publications, 2003), p. 11.

48. Ibid., p. 12.

49. Tertullian, *Of the Games*, XII.

50. Thomas E. J. Wiedemann, *Emperors and Gladiators* (New York: Routledge, 1992), p. 5.

51. Jackson J. Spielvogel, *Western Civilization, Vol. A: To 1500, 7th ed.* (Belmont, CA: Thomson Wadsworth, 2006), p. 164.

52. Cassius Dio, *Dio's Roman History*, XLVIII.xxxiii.4; LVI.xxv.7-8; LI.xxii.4.

53. Thomas George Tucker, *Life in the Roman World of Nero and St. Paul* (New York: The Macmillan Company, 1910), p. 282.

54. Lawrence Richardson, *A New Topographical Dictionary of Ancient Rome* (Baltimore, MD: John Hopkins University Press, 1992), p. 236.

55. Potter, p. 317.

56. Reader's Digest Association, Inc., *The Truth About History: How New Evidence Is Transforming the Story of the Past* (London: Planet Three Publishing, 2003), p. 71.

57. Cassius Dio, *Roman History*, LXVI.25.

58. Thomas Wiedemann, *Emperors and Gladiators* (New York: Routledge, 1992), p. 57.

59. Ibid., p. 55.

60. Alan Baker, *The Gladiator: The Secret History of Rome's Warrior Slaves* (New York: St. Martin's Press, 2000), p. 84.

61. James Chidester Egbert, *Introduction to the Study of Latin Inscriptions* (New York: American Book Co., 1906), p. 237.

62. Dennis E. Smith, p. 108.

63. Fik Meijer, *The Gladiators: History's Most Deadly Sport* (New York: St. Martin's Press, 2003), p. 56.

64. Philip H. Towner, *The Letters to Timothy and Titus* (Grand Rapids, MI: Wm. B. Eerdmans Publishing Co., 2006), p. 37.

65. Debra Bruch, "The Prejudice Against Theater," *The Journal of Religion and Theater, Vol. 3, No. 1* (Houghton, MI: Michigan Technological University, 2004), pp. 2-4.

66. Cimok, *Journeys of Paul*, pp. 173-174.

67. Tacitus, *Annals*, XII.64-69.

68 Christine Thomas, trans., *Ephesus* (Istanbul: Do Gu Yayinlari), pp. 62-63.

69. Gökovali, p. 31.

70. Chris Scarre, *The Penguin Historical Atlas of Ancient Rome* (New York: Penguin Group, 1995), p. 76.

71. Josephus, *Antiquities of the Jews*, XV.4.

72. Patricia Turner and Charles Russell Coulter, *Dictionary of Ancient Deities* (Oxford: Oxford University Press, 2000), p. 136.

73. John Foxe, *Foxe's Book of Martyrs*, Chapter II, "Ten Primitive Persecutions."

74. Clyde E. Fant and Mitchell Glenn Reddish, *A Guide to Biblical Sites in Greece and Turkey* (Oxford: Oxford University Press, 2003), p. 191.

75. Matthew Kuefler, *The Manly Eunuch: Masculinity, Gender Ambiguity, and Christian Ideology in Late Antiquity* (Chicago: University of Chicago Press, 2001), p. 87.

76. Tertullian, *Prescription Against Heretics*, c. 36.

77. Pat Southern, *Domitian: Tragic Tyrant* (Bloomington, IN: Indiana University Press, 1997), p. 118.

78. Gökovali, p. 13.

79. Alan M. Fildes and Dr. Joann Fletcher, "Alexander the Great in Egypt," arabworldbooks.com/new/alexander.html.

80. Robert Turcan, *The Cults of the Roman Empire*, trans. Antonia Nevill (Cambridge, MA: Blackwell Publishers, 1996), pp. 114-116.

81. Ibid., pp. 116-118.

82. Selahattin Erdemgil, *Ephesus Ruins and Museum* (Istanbul: Net Turistik Yayinlar, 1986), p. 52.

83. William Barclay, *Letters to the Seven Churches* (Nashville: Abingdon Press, 1957), pp. 28-29.

84. *Ephesus* (Istanbul: Do-Gu Press), p. 19.

85. Robert M. Grant, *Gods and the One God* (Philadelphia, PA: Westminster Press, 1986), p. 45.

86. Lyman Abbott, *The Life and Letters of the Apostle Paul* (Boston: Houghton, Mifflin & Co., 1898), p. 46.

87. William Stearns Davis, *A Day in Old Athens: A Picture of Athenian Life* (Needham Heights, MA: Allyn & Bacon, 1914), p. 204.

88. B. J. Beitzel, ed., "The Third Journey of Paul," *Biblica: The Bible Atlas* (Sydney: Global Book Publishing, 2006), p. 478.

89. Murphy-O'Connor, p. 7.

90. Ibid., p. 98.

91. Pat Yale, Jean-Bernard Carillet, and Virginia Maxwell, *Turkey, 9th ed.* (Lonely Planet, 2005), p. 225.

92. H. B. Collier, "Meteorites," *The Journal of the Royal Astronomical Society of Canada, Vol. 7, No. 5* (Toronto, September-October, 1913), p. 315.

93. Henry Barclay Swete, *The Apocalypse of St. John* (London: Macmillan and Co., 1906), p. 57.

94. Plutarch, *Parallel Lives, Life of Alexander*, I.iii.5-6.

95. Charles Anthon, *A Classical Dictionary: Containing an Account of the Principal Proper Names Mentioned in Ancient Authors* (New York: Harper and Brothers, 1891), p. 476.

96. Archibald Henry Sayce, *The Hittites: The Story of a Forgotten Empire* (New York: F. H. Revell Co., 1888), pp. 78-79.

97. Hilda M. Ransome, *The Sacred Bee in Ancient Times and Folklore* (London: George Allen & Unwin, 1937), pp. 56-61.

98. Antipater, *Greek Anthology*, IX.58.

99. Otto F. A. Meinardus, *St. Paul in Ephesus and the Cities of Galatia and Cyprus* (New Rochelle, NY: Caratzas Brothers Publishers, 1979), p. 51.

100. Clinton E. Arnold, *Ephesians: Power and Magic, The Concept of Power in Ephesians in Light of Its Historical Setting* (Cambridge, England: Cambridge University Press, 1989), pp. 15-16.

101. Richard Belward Rackham, *The Acts of the Apostles: An Exposition* (London: Methuen and Co., 1901), p. 338.

102. Murphy-O'Connor, pp. 105-106.

103. G. L. Borchert, "Ephesus," *International Standard Bible Encyclopedia,Vol. 2* (Grand Rapids, MI: Wm. B. Eerdmans Publishing Co., 1979), pp. 115-117.

104. F. Randall, "The Pauline Collection for the Saints," *Christian Literature and Review of the Churches, Vol. 10, No. 2* (New York: Christian Literature Co., 1893), p. 44a.

CHAPTER FOUR

1. F. F. Bruce, *The Acts of the Apostles* (Grand Rapids, MI: Wm. B. Eerdmans Publishing Co., 1951), pp. 348-349.

2. Plutarch, *The Lives of the Noble Grecians and Romans*, trans. John Dryden (New York: Random House, 1932), p. 819.

3. Richard Watson and Nathan Bangs, *A Biblical and Theological Dictionary: Explanatory of the History of the Jews and Neighboring Nations* (New York: B. Waugh and T. Mason, 1832), p. 37.

4. Strabo, *The Geography of Strabo*, trans. Horace Leonard Jones (Cambridge, MA: Harvard University Press, 1959), pp. 23-29.

5. Peter D'Epiro and Mary Desmond Pinkowish, *What Are the Seven Great Wonders of the World?* (New York: Random House, 1998), pp. 186-187.

6. Josephus Flavius, *Jewish Antiquities*, XII.11.

7. *The Letter of Aristeas*, trans. H. St. J. Thackeray (New York: The Macmillan Co., 1917), p. vii.

8. Edward Alexander Parsons, *The Alexandrian Library: Glory of the Hellenistic World* (Amsterdam, Netherlands: The Elsevier Press, 1952), pp. 93-103.

9. John Calvin, *Commentary on Acts, Vol. 2*, Acts 18:24-28.

10. A. T. Robertson, *Word Pictures in the New Testament, Vol. 3, The Acts of the Apostles* (Nashville: Broadman Press, 1930), p. 307.

11. William Barclay, *The Acts of the Apostles* (Philadelphia, PA: The Westminster Press, 1976), p. 139.

12. Regarding the statement in Acts 18:27 that says, "Then he [Apollos] was disposed to pass into Achaia…," Bible scholar Adam Clarke writes this: "There is a very long and important addition here in the Codex Bezae, of which the following is a translation: 'But certain Corinthians, who sojourned at Ephesus, and heard him, entreated him to pass over with them to their own country. Then, when he had given his consent, the Ephesians wrote to the disciples at Corinth, that they should receive this man. Who, when he was come, etc.' The same addition is found in the later Syriac, and in the Itala version in the Codex Bezae." *Adam Clarke's Commentary*, Electronic Database, Biblesoft, 1996.

13. Fatih Cimok, *Journeys of Paul: From Tarsus to the Ends of the Earth* (Istanbul: A Turizm Yayinlari, 2004), p. 177.

14. James Hastings, John Alexander Selbie, Andrew Bruce Davidson, Samuel Rolles Driver, and Henry Barclay Swete, eds., *A Dictionary of the Bible: Pleroma-Zuzim* (New York: Charles Scribner's Sons, 1902), p. 822.

15. F. F. Bruce, *The Book of Acts* (Grand Rapids, MI: Wm. B Eerdmans Publishing Co., 1988), p. 366.

16. Cimok, ibid.

17. Paul Trebilco, *The Early Christians in Ephesus From Paul to Ignatius* (Grand Rapids, MI: Wm. B. Eerdmans Publishing Co., 2007), p. 195.

18. Cimok, p. 14.

19. Bruce, *The Book of Acts*, p. 366.

20. Albert Barnes, *Barnes' Notes on the New Testament: Acts* (Grand Rapids, MI: Baker Book House, 1985), p. 279.

21. Bruce, *The Book of Acts*, p. 368. It was a popular Jewish belief that Solomon had been given the power of expelling demons and that he had passed on certain formulae that were effective in exorcism. *See also* Josephus, *Jewish Antiquities*, VIII.ii.5.

22. Bruce, *The Acts of the Apostles*, p. 358.

23. J. A. Alexander, *The Acts of the Apostles Explained, Vol. 2* (New York: Charles Scribner, 1857), p. 196.

24. Trebilco, p. 150, footnote 206.

25. F. F. Bruce, *The New International Commentary on the New Testament: Commentary on the Book of Acts* (Grand Rapids, MI: Wm. B. Eerdmans Publishing Co., 1954), pp. 391-392.

26. Edward Falkener, *Ephesus, and the Temple of Diana* (London: Day and Son, 1862), p. 288.

27. Martin J. Price, *The Seven Wonders of the Ancient World* (London: Routledge, 1988), p. 86.

28. Charles Anthon, *A Classical Dictionary: Containing an Account of the Principal Proper Names Mentioned in Ancient Authors* (New York: Harper and Brothers, 1891), p. 476.

29. William Smith, ed., *A Dictionary of Greek and Roman Antiquities* (London: John Murray, 1878), p. 142.

30. Trebilco, pp. 83-85.

31. James Hastings, et al., pp. 800-801.

CHAPTER FIVE

1. Eusebius, *Church History*, II.xxv.5.

2. Charles G. Herbermann, Edward A. Pace, Condé B. Pallen, Thomas J. Shanan, and John J. Wynne, eds., *The Catholic Encyclopedia, Vol. 9* (New York: The Universal Knowledge Foundation, Inc., 1910), p. 422.

3. An example of scholarly discussion regarding Christian leaders' traveling to Ephesus to see John and Mary — in this case, the travels of Luke — can

be found in Edward Clapton's book, *The Life of Saint Luke* (London: J. & A. Churchill, 1902), pp. 52-53.

4. B. Rohner, *Illustrated Life of the Blessed Virgin* (New York: Benziger Brothers, 1871), pp. 340-347.

5. Eusebius, *Church History*, V.xxii.

6. Eusebius, *Church History*, IV.xvi.1-9; IV.xviii.6.

7. John Walvoord, *The Revelation of Jesus Christ* (Chicago: Moody Press, 1966), p. 53.

8. Craig S. Keener, *The IVP Bible Background Commentary: New Testament* (Downers Grove, IL: InterVarsity Press, 1993), p. 577.

9. Josephus Flavius, *Jewish Antiquities*, XIX.viii.2.

10. John Boardman, Jasper Griffin, and Oswyn Murray, *The Oxford History of Greece and the Hellenistic World* (New York: Oxford University Press, 1986), p. 157. A pertinent point is made regarding the popular sovereignty of the *ekklesia*, which was "...best illustrated by the power which the people retained — and used — to depose and punish its servants...."

11. Josiah Ober, *Mass and Elite in Democratic Athens: Rhetoric, Ideology, and the Power of the People* (Princeton, NJ: Princeton University Press, 1989), p. 132.

12. Mogens Herman Hansen, *The Athenian Ecclesia II: A Collection of Articles, 1983-1989* (Copenhagen: Museum Tusculanum Press, 1989), p. 199.

13. Eric W. Robinson, *Ancient Greek Democracy: Readings and Sources* (Hoboken, NJ: Blackwell Publishing, 2003), pp. 301-302.

14. Anton Powell, *Athens and Sparta: Constructing Greek Political and Social History from 478 BC* (New York: Routledge, 1988), pp. 300-301.

15. Joint Association of Classical Teachers, *The World of Athens: An Introduction to Classical Athenian Culture* (Cambridge, England: Cambridge University Press, 1984), p. 214.

16. Christopher Lyle Johnstone, *Theory, Text, Context: Issues in Greek Rhetoric and Oratory* (Albany, NY: State University of New York Press, 1996), pp. 112-114.

17. Ibid.

18. Moses Stuart, *A Commentary on the Apocalypse, Vol. 1* (New York: Van Nostrand and Terrett, 1851), pp. 224-226.

19. Charles Foster Kent, *The Historical Bible: The Work and Teachings of the Apostles* (New York: Charles Scribner's Sons, 1916), pp. 178-179.

20. David Francis Bacon, *Lives of the Apostles of Jesus Christ* (New Haven, CT: L. H. Young, 1836), p. 8.

21. Joel B. Green, Scot McKnight, and I. Howard Marshall, eds., *Dictionary of Jesus and the Gospels* (Downers Grove, IL: InterVarsity Press, 1992), p. 27.

22. Handley Carr Glyn Moule, *The Epistle to the Ephesians, Vol. 41* (London: Cambridge University Press, 1891), p. 27.

23. Ignatius, *Epistle to the Ephesians*, c. 8-9.

24. Irenaeus, *Against Heresies*, I.xxvi.3.

25. Hippolytus, *The Refutation of All Heresies*, VII.24.

26. Irenaeus, ibid.; Hippolytus, ibid.

27. Jerome Murphy-O'Connor, *Paul's Ephesus: Texts and Archaeology* (Collegeville, MN: Liturgical Press, 1971), p. 45.

CHAPTER SIX

1. Trudy Ring, Robert M. Salkin, and Sharon La Boda, eds., *International Dictionary of Historic Places: Southern Europe* (Chicago: Fitzroy Dearborn Publishers, 1995), p. 348.

2. Ibid.

3. Philip Schaff, ed., *A Dictionary of the Bible: Including Biography, Natural History, Geography, Topography, Archeology, and Literature* (Philadelphia, PA: American Sunday-School Union, 1880), p. 814.

4. Will Durant, *The Story of Civilization, Part 3: Caesar and Christ* (New York: Simon and Schuster, 1972), p. 647.

5. Philip Francis Esler, ed., *The Early Christian World, Vols. 1-2* (New York: Routledge, 2002), pp. 519-520.

6. J. B. Lightfoot, ed., *The Apostolic Fathers: Clement, Ignatius, and Polycarp, Part 2, Vol. 1* (Peabody, MA: Hendrickson Publishers, 1989), p. 433.

7. Ibid. pp. 433-435.

8. Irenaeus, *Against Heresies*, III.iii.4.

9. Lightfoot, pp. 442-443.

10. Eusebius, *Church History*, IV.xiv.10; IV.xv.1.

11. Lightfoot, p. 649.

12. Edgar J. Goodspeed, *The Apostolic Fathers* (London: Independent Press, 1950), p. 255.

13. Robin Lane Fox, *Pagans and Christians* (New York: Alfred A. Knopf, Inc., 1987), pp. 472-473. The final copyist of this epistle, who gives his name as Pionius, was the very man who would later stand in the Central Marketplace of Smyrna, refusing to offer sacrifices to pagan gods and who was ultimately martyred for his faith in Jesus Christ (*see* pages 391-392).

14. J. B. Lightfoot, the translator of this version of *The Epistle of the Smyrneans*, stated that this second version of verses 22.2-22.4 represents an alternate rendering as found in what is known as "the Moscow manuscript."

15. Strabo, *Geography*, XIV.i.37.

16. John Boardman and N. G. L. Hammond, *The Expansion of the Greek World, Eighth to Sixth Centuries BC* (Cambridge, England: Cambridge University Press, 1982), p. 197.

17. Pausanias, *Description of Greece*, VII.v.1-3.

18. Lewis Richard Farnell, *The Cults of the Greek States, Vol. 2* (Oxford: Clarendon Press, 1896), pp. 499-500.

19. Paul Cartledge, *Alexander the Great: The Hunt for a New Past* (Woodstock, NY: The Overlook Press, 2004), p. 84.

20. Plutarch, *The Age of Alexander*, trans. Ian Scott-Kilvert (London: Penguin Books, 1973), pp. 260-261.

21. Marcus Junianus Justinus, *Justin: Epitome of the Philippic History of Pompeius Trogus*, trans. J. C. Yardley (New York: Oxford University Press, 1997), p. 328.

22. N. G. L. Hammond, *The Genius of Alexander the Great* (London: Gerald Duckworth & Co. Ltd., 1997), pp. 62-64.

23. J. F. C. Fuller, *The Generalship of Alexander the Great* (London: Butler & Tanner, Ltd., 1958), p. 154.

24. Robin Lane Fox, *Alexander the Great* (New York: Allen Lane, 1973), pp. 149-151.

25. Q. Curtius Rufus, *History of Alexander*, III.x.4-10.

26. John Warner Barber, *Elements of General History: Embracing All the Leading Events in the World's History* (New Haven, CT: Horace C. Peck, 1866), pp. 58-59.

27. J. R. Hamilton, *Alexander the Great* (London: Hutchinson & Co. Ltd, 1973), pp. 74-78.

28. Fuller, p. 164.

29. Strabo, *Geography*, XIV.i.37.

30. Richard S. Ascough, ed., *Religious Rivalries and the Struggle for Success in Sardis and Smyrna* (Waterloo, Ontario: Wilfrid Laurier University Press, 2005), p. 8.

31. Aelius Aristides, *The Complete Works: Orations I-XVI*, trans. Charles Allison Behr (Leiden, Netherlands: E. J. Brill, 1986), pp. 1-4.

32. William M. Ramsay, *The Letters to the Seven Churches* (Whitefish, MT: Kessinger Publishing, 2004), p. 257.

33. Ibid., p. 261.

34. Ibid., p. 258.

35. Ascough, ibid.

36. Hilda M. Ransome, *The Sacred Bee in Ancient Times and Folklore* (London: George Allen & Unwin, 1937), p. 56.

37. Walter Burkert and John Raffan, *Greek Religion: Archaic and Classical* (Oxford: Blackwell Publishing, 1986), p. 12.

38. Erich S. Gruen, *Studies in Greek Culture and Roman Policy* (Berkeley, CA: University of California Press, 1990), p. 18.

39. Gaius Valerius Catullus, *Catullus* (Boston: Ginn and Co., 1893), p. 119.

40. Alan K. Bowman, Peter Garnsey, and Dominic Rathbone, eds., *The Cambridge Ancient History: The High Empire, A.D. 70-192* (Cambridge, England: Cambridge University Press, 2000), p. 994.

41. Michael Grant and John Hazel, *Who's Who in Classical Mythology* (New York: Routledge, 2002), p. 152.

42. James Hastings, John Alexander Selbie, and John Chisholm Lambert, eds., *Dictionary of the Apostolic Church, Volume 2* (New York: Charles Scribner's Sons, 1918), p. 58.

43. John Gresham Machan, *The Origin of Paul's Religion* (New York: The MacMillan Co., 1921), pp. 228-229.

44. James Hastings, ed., *Encyclopedia of Religion and Ethics, Part 10* (Whitefish, MT: Kessinger Publishing, 2003), pp. 581-582.

45. Ibid.

46. Martti Nissinen and Kirsi Stjerna, *Homoeroticism in the Biblical World: A Historical Perspective* (Minneapolis, MN: Augsburg Fortress, 1998), pp. 31-32.

47   Stephen Benko, *The Virgin Goddess: Studies in the Pagan and Christian Roots of Mariology* (Leiden, Netherlands: Koninklijke Brill, 2004), p. 78.

48. Yulia Ustinova, *Caves and the Ancient Greek Mind: Descending Underground in the Search for Ultimate Truth* (Oxford: Oxford University Press, 2009), p. 86.

49. Lactantius, *Divine Institutes*, I.xxii.19-21.

50. "Cybele is associated with bees, swarming with life, another symbol coming from Crete. Her priestesses, like those of Artemis and Persephone, were called Melissae, or bees." Gillian Alban, *Melusine the Serpent Goddess in A.S. Byatt's Possession and in Mythology* (Oxford: Lexington Books, 2003), p. 147.

51. Augustine, *De Civitate Dei*, VII.24.

52. Sarah Iles Johnston, *Ancient Greek Divination* (West Sussex, England: John Wiley and Sons, 2008), p. 62.

53. Ibid., p. 33.

54. Eric M. Orlin, *Temples, Religion and Politics* (Leiden, Netherlands: E. J. Brill, 1997), pp. 76-77, 81.

55. Lynn E. Roller, *In Search of God the Mother: The Cult of Anatolian Cybele* (Berkeley, CA: University of California Press, 1999), pp. 284-285.

56. Titus Livius (Livy), *The History of Rome, Vol. 2*, trans. D. Spillan and Cyrus Edmonds (New York: Harper and Brothers, 1895), pp. 580-581.

57. Emma Willard, *Universal History in Perspective* (New York: A. S. Barnes and Co., 1854), pp. 50-51.

58. James Hastings, John Alexander Selbie, Andrew Bruce Davidson, Samuel Rolles Driver, and Henry Barclay Swete, eds., *A Dictionary of the Bible: Pleroma-Zuzim* (New York: Charles Scribner's Sons, 1902), p. 554.

59. Jeffrey Carter, *Understanding Religious Sacrifice: A Reader* (New York: Continuum, 2003), pp. 214-215.

60. Strabo, *Geography*, XIV.i.37.

61. David Magie, *Roman Rule in Asia Minor: To the End of the Third Century After Christ* (Salem, NH: Ayer Co., 1988), p. 108.

62. Ring, et al., p. 350.

63. Ramsay, p. 254.

64. Erich S. Gruen, *The Hellenistic World and the Coming of Rome, Vol. 1* (Los Angeles: University of California Press, 1984), p. 178.

65. Michael Dumper and Bruce E. Stanley, eds., *Cities of the Middle East and North Africa: A Historical Encyclopedia* (Santa Barbara, CA: ABC-CLIO, Inc., 2007), p. 189.

66. Tacitus, *Annals*, IV.56.

67. Ramsay, p. 254.

68 Ibid.

69. Fox, *Pagans and Christians*, p. 490.

70 Stephen Mitchell, *Anatolia: Land, Men and Gods in Asia Minor* (Oxford: Oxford University Press, 2001), p. 9.

71. William Smith, *A Dictionary of Greek and Roman Antiquities, Vol. 1* (London: John Murray, 1890), pp. 873-874.

72. Ramsay, p. 261.

73. George M. A. Hanfmann, *From Croesus to Constantine: The Cities of Western Asia Minor and Their Arts in Greek and Roman Times* (Ann Arbor, MI: University of Michigan Press, 1975), p. 9.

74. Robert B. Strassler, ed., *The Landmark Herodotus: The Histories*, trans. Andrea L. Purvis (New York: Pantheon Books, 2007), pp. 388-389. *See also* Herodotus, *Histories*, V.52-54; VIII.98.

75. M. G. Lay and James E. Vance, *Ways of the World: A History of the World's Roads and of the Vehicles That Used Them* (Piscataway, NJ: Rutgers University Press, 1992), p. 46.

76. John Lemprière, *A Classical Dictionary* (New York: G. and C. and H. Carvill Broadway, 1831), p. 672.

77. Colin J. Hemer, *The Letters to the Seven Churches of Asia in Their Local Settings* (Cambridge, England: Wm. B Eerdmans Publishing Co., 2001), pp. 154-155.

78. Lemprière, p. 359.

79. Aaron Shurin, *The Illiad* (New York: Barron's Educational Series, Inc.), pp. 1-2.

80. William Mitchell Ramsay and Agnes Margaret Ramsay, *Studies in the History and Art of the Eastern Provinces of the Roman Empire* (Aberdeen, Scotland: University of Aberdeen Press, 1898), pp. 98-99.

81. John C. Kraft, Helmut Buckner, Ilhan Kayan, and Helmut Engelmann, "The Geographies of Ancient Ephesus and the Artemesion in Anatolia," *Geoarcheology: An International Journal, Vol. 22, No. 1* (Hoboken: NJ: Wiley Interscience, 2007), pp. 141-146.

82. Ramsay, *The Letters to the Seven Churches in Asia*, p. 253.

83. Ibid., pp. 259-260.

84. Will Durant, p. 515.

85. Strabo, *Geography*, XIV.i.37.

86. *The Encyclopedia Brittanica: A Dictionary of Arts, Sciences, and General Literature* (New York: Henry G. Allen Co., 1890), p. 186.

87. Strabo, *Geography,* XIV.i.37.

88. Aristides, *Orations,* XLVII.17.

89. Cecil John Cadoux, *Ancient Smyrna* (Oxford: Basil Blackwell, 1938), p. 181.

90. Ascough, p. 9.

91. Fox, *Pagans and Christians,* pp. 460-465, 472-473.

92. Ömer Özyigit, "Recent Work at Phokaia in the Light of Akurgal's Excavations" (Izmir: Ege Üniversitesi, 2003), p. 10.

93. George Freedly and John A. Reeves, *A History of the Theatre* (New York: Crown Publishers, 1941), pp. 35-36.

94. Durant, pp. 647-648.

95. Janet DeLaine, *The Baths of Caracalla* (Portsmouth, RI: Journal of Roman Archaeology, 1997), p. 15.

96. Leland M. Roth, *Understanding Architecture Its Elements, History, and Meaning* (New York: Harper Collins Publishers, 1993), pp. 233-234.

97. Fikret Yegul, *Baths and Bathing in Classical Antiquity* (New York: The Architectural History Foundation, 1992), p. 30.

98. Strabo, *Geography,* XIV.i.37.

99. Ring, et al., p. 348.

100. Christopher Thomas Gaffney, *Temples of the Earthbound Gods: Stadiums in the Culture of Rio Grande and Buenos Aires* (Austin, TX: University of Texas Press, 2008), p. 5.

101. William D. Halsey and Bernard Johnston, eds., *Collier's Encyclopedia, Vol. 18* (New York: Macmillan Educational Co., 1991), p. 120.

102. Cassius Dio, *Roman History,* LXVI.25.

103. D. L. Bomgardner, *The Story of the Roman Amphitheatre* (New York: Routledge, 2000), p. 21.

104. John Clark Ridpath, *Ridpath's Universal History* (Cincinnati, OH: The Jones Brothers Publishing Co., 1899), p. 809.

CHAPTER SEVEN

1. Richard S. Ascough, ed., *Religious Rivalries and the Struggle for Success in Sardis and Smyrna* (Waterloo, Ontario: Wilfrid Laurier University Press, 2005), p. 8.

2. Frank Sear, *Roman Theatres: An Architectural Study* (Oxford: Oxford University Press, 2006), p. 113.

3. Irenaeus, *Against Heresies*, III.4.

4. Noted theologian and historian William Barclay stated, "Nowhere can life have been more dangerous for a Christian than in Smyrna…. For a man to become a Christian anywhere was to become an outlaw. In Smyrna, above all places, for a man to enter the Christian Church was literally to take his life in his hands. In Smyrna the Church was a place for heroes." William Barclay, *Letters to the Seven Churches* (Louisville, KY: Westminster John Knox Press, 2001), p. 19.

5. Eusebius, *Church History*, IV.xv.4,45-47.

6. Charles George Herbermann, Edward A. Pace, Conde B. Pallen, and Thomas J. Shahan, eds. *The Catholic Encyclopedia, Vol. 14* (New York: Universal Knowledge Foundation, Inc., 1912), p. 60.

7. Eusebius, *Church History*, V.xxiv.4.

8. Albert Barnes, *Notes, Explanatory and Practical, on the Book of Revelation* (New York: Harper and Brothers Publishers, 1859), p. 90.

9. Records of an ancient Egyptian salt-dealer trade guild provide us with a rare glimpse into the economic organization of some of the *collegia* of that time. Jinyu Liu, *Collegia Centonariorum: The Guilds of Textile Dealers in the Roman West* (Netherlands: Brill, 2009), p. 15.

10. E. A. Judge and James R. Harrison, *The First Christians in the Roman World: Augustan and New Testament Essays* (Tübingen, Germany: Mohr Siebeck, 2008), p. 636.

11. Liu, pp. 248-250.

12. Stanley E. Porter, ed., *Paul and His Opponents* (Danvers, MA: Brill, 2005), p. 55.

13. Colin Hemer, *The Letters to the Seven Churches of Asia in Their Local Setting* (Grand Rapids, MI: Wm. B. Eerdmans Publishing Co., 2001), p. 123.

14. In his defense of Christian *"agape* feasts" against the slander propagated by the pagan population, Tertullian also revealed the early Christians' view of the pagan *collegia* feasts: "…You abuse also our humble feasts, on the ground that they are extravagant as well as infamously wicked. To us, it seems, applies the saying of Diogenes: 'The people of Megara feast as though they were going to die on the morrow; they build as though they were never to die!' But one sees more readily the mote in another's eye than the beam in his own. Why, the very air is soured with the eructations of so many tribes, and *curiæ*, and *decuriæ*. The Salii cannot have their feast without going into debt; you must get the accountants to tell you what the tenths of Hercules and the sacrificial banquets cost; the choicest cook is appointed for the Apaturia, the Dionysia, the Attic mysteries; the smoke from the banquet of Serapis will call out the firemen. Yet about the modest supper-room of the Christians alone a great ado is made. Our feast explains itself by its name. The Greeks call it *agapè*, i.e., affection. Whatever it costs, our outlay in the name of piety is gain, since with the good things of the feast we benefit the needy; not as it is with you, do parasites aspire to the glory of satisfying their licentious propensities, selling themselves for a belly-feast to all disgraceful treatment…." Tertullian, *Apology*, c. 39.

15. Hemer, pp. 68, 91.

16. Cleon L. Rogers Jr., *The New Linguistic and Exegetical Key to the Greek New Testament* (Grand Rapids, MI: Zondervan Publishing House, 1998), p. 541.

17. George Bradford Caird, *The Revelation of Saint John* (Peabody, MA: Hendrickson Publishers, 1993), p. 35.

18. William Seward, *Anecdotes of Distinguished Persons: Chiefly of the Present and Two Preceding Centuries* (London: T. Cadwell Jun. and W. Davies, 1798), pp. 5-6.

19. Rogers, p. 488.

20. Joseph Telushkin, *A Code of Jewish Ethics, Vol. 1: You Shall Be Holy* (New York: Crown Publishing, 2006), p. 365.

21. Ibid., p. 337.

22. Ibid., p. 376.

23. Ibid., p. 422.

24. Barnes, pp. 90-91.

25. *The Encyclopedia Americana: a Library of Universal Knowledge, Vol. 16* (New York: The Encyclopedia Americana Corporation, 1919), p. 109.

26. Joel B. Green, Scot McKnight, and I. Howard Marshall, eds., *Dictionary of Jesus and the Gospels* (Downers Grove, IL: InterVarsity Press, 1992), p. 782.

27. *The Encyclopedia Americana*, p. 109.

28. F. F. Bruce, *Acts of the Apostles: The Greek Text With Introduction and Commentary* (London: Tyndale Press, 1951), p. 398.

29. J. A. Hammerton, *Illustrated Encyclopedia of World History, Vol. 4* (New Delhi: Mittal Publications, 1992), pp. 2181-2183.

30. John Foxe, *History of Christian Martyrdom: From the Commencement of Christianity, to the Latest Periods of Pagan and Popish Persecution* (New York: J. P. Peaslee, 1836), pp. 17-18.

31. James William Ermatinger, *Daily Life of Christians in Ancient Rome* (Westport, CT: Greenwood Press, 2007), p. 71.

32. D. Ayerst and A. S. T. Fisher, *Records of Christianity, Vol. 1* (Oxford: Basil Blackwell, 1971), p. 98.

33. Ermatinger, pp. 66-67.

34. Robin Lane Fox, *Pagans and Christians* (New York: Alfred A. Knopf, Inc., 1987), p. 427.

35. Ibid.

36. The views stated by the Roman named Caecilius in the following dialogue written by a Christian apologist reflect the common Roman view of the "deviant" Christian sect (Minucius Felix, *Octavius*, IX): "I hear that they adore the head of an ass, that basest of creatures, consecrated by I know not what silly persuasion — a worthy and appropriate religion for such manners. Some say that they worship the virilia of their pontiff and priest, and adore the nature, as it were, of their common parent. I know not whether these things are false; certainly suspicion is applicable to secret and nocturnal rites; and he who explains their ceremonies by reference to a man punished by extreme suffering for his wickedness, and to the deadly wood of the cross, appropriates fitting altars for reprobate and wicked men, that they may worship what they deserve. Now the story about the initiation of young novices is as much to be detested as it is well known. An infant covered over with meal, that it may deceive the unwary, is placed before him who is to be stained with their rites: this infant

is slain by the young pupil, who has been urged on as if to harmless blows on the surface of the meal, with dark and secret wounds. Thirstily — O horror! — they lick up its blood; eagerly they divide its limbs. By this victim they are pledged together; with this consciousness of wickedness they are covenanted to mutual silence. Such sacred rites as these are more foul than any sacrileges. And of their banqueting it is well known all men speak of it everywhere; even the speech of our Cirtensian testifies to it. On a solemn day they assemble at the feast, with all their children, sisters, mothers, people of every sex and of every age. There, after much feasting, when the fellowship has grown warm, and the fervour of incestuous lust has grown hot with drunkenness, a dog that has been tied to the chandelier is provoked, by throwing a small piece of offal beyond the length of a line by which he is bound, to rush and spring; and thus the conscious light being overturned and extinguished in the shameless darkness, the connections of abominable lust involve them in the uncertainty of fate. Although not all in fact, yet in consciousness all are alike incestuous, since by the desire of all of them everything is sought for which can happen in the act of each individual."

37. Tacitus, *Annals*, XV.38-44.

38. Ralph Martin Novak, *Christianity and the Roman Empire: Background Texts* (Harrisburg, PA: Trinity Press, 2001), p. 29.

39. Sallust, *Catiline*, 55.3-4.

40. John Henry Middleton, *The Remains of Ancient Rome, Vol. 1* (London: Adam and Charles Black, 1892), pp. 153-154.

41. Isabel Lovell, *Stories in Stone From the Roman Forum* (New York: The Mac-Millan Co., 1904), pp. 23-24.

42. Fr. Lohr, *A Day in Ancient Rome* (Boston: D. C. Heath and Co., Publishers, 1897), p. 23.

43. Lovell, p. 23.

44. Frank J. Korn, *A Catholic's Guide to Rome: Discovering the Soul of the Eternal City* (Mahwah, NJ: Paulist Press, 2000), p. 160.

45. Middleton, pp. 154-155.

46. James Burton Coffman, *Commentaries on the Old and New Testament* (reproduced by permission of Abilene Christian University Press, Abilene, TX), searchgodsword.org.

47. Barnes, p. 92.

48. Henry Alford, *The Greek Testament: Vol. 4* (Boston: Lee and Shephard, Publishers, 1878), p. 567.

49. Foy E. Wallace, Jr., *The Book of Revelation* (Nashville: Foy E. Wallace, Jr., Publications, 1966), p. 90.

50. Arno C. Gaebelein, *The Revelation* (Glasgow, Scotland: Pickering and Inglis, 1915), p. 36.

51. W. A. Spurgeon, *The Conquering Christ* (Muncie, IN: Scott Printing Co., 1936), p. 28.

52. Rogers, p. 616.

53. A. T. Robertson, *Word Pictures in the New Testament, Vol. 6* (Grand Rapids, MI: Baker Book House, 1933), p. 303.

54. John Foxe, *Foxe: Voices of the Martyrs* (Alachua, FL: Voice of the Martyrs, 2007), p. xiv.

55. Pausanias, *Description of Greece*, VI.xiv.2-3.

56. F. F. Bruce, *The International Bible Commentary* (Grand Rapids, MI: Zondervan, 1986), p. 1602.

SELECTED BIBLIOGRAPHY

(**Note:** Much of the historical material presented in this book was obtained through original, on-site research in Turkey with the help of historian and guide, Asil Tunçer.)

Abbott, Lyman. *The Life and Letters of the Apostle Paul*. Boston: Houghton, Mifflin & Co., 1898.

Abbot, T. K. *A Critical and Exegetical Commentary of the Epistles to the Ephesians and to the Colossians*. Edinburgh: T. & T. Clark, 1985.

Akrugal, Ekrem. *Ancient Civilizations and Ruins of Turkey*. Istanbul: Net Turistik Yayinlar San. Tc. A. S., 2007.

Alban, Gillian. *Melusine the Serpent Goddess in A. S. Byatt's Possession and in Mythology*. Oxford: Lexington Books, 2003.

Alexander, J. A. *The Acts of the Apostles Explained, Vol. 2*. New York: Charles Scribner, 1857.

Alford, Henry. *The Greek Testament: Vol. 4*. Boston: Lee and Shephard Publishers, 1878.

Anemodoura, Katerina. (ed.). *The Acropolis*. Athens: Orfeas Publications, 2009.

Anthon, Charles. *A Classical Dictionary: Containing an Account of the Principal Proper Names Mentioned in Ancient Authors*. New York: Harper and Brothers, 1891.

Antipater, *Greek Anthology*.

Aristides, Aelius. *The Complete Works: Orations I-XVI*. Translated by Charles Allison Behr (Leiden, Netherlands: E. J. Brill, 1986.

Arnold, Clinton E. *Ephesians: Power and Magic, The Concept of Power in Ephesians in Light of Its Historical Setting*. Cambridge, England: Cambridge University Press, 1989.

Ascough, Richard S. (ed.). *Religious Rivalries and the Struggle for Success in Sardis and Smyrna*. Waterloo, Ontario: Wilfrid Laurier University Press, 2005.

Ashworth, Leon. *Gods and Goddesses of Ancient Rome*. London: Cherrytree Books, 2001.

The Athenian Acropolis. Athens: Hellenic Ministry of Culture, Archeological Receipts Fund, 2006.

Athenon, Ekdone. *Philip of Macedon.* Athens: Ekdotike Athenon, 1992.

Augustine. *De Civitate Dei.*

Ayerst, D., and A. S. T. Fisher. *Records of Christianity, Vol. 1.* Oxford: Basil Blackwell, 1971.

Bacon, David Francis. *Lives of the Apostles of Jesus Christ.* New Haven, CT: L. H. Young, 1836.

Baines, John, and Jaromir Malek. *Ancient Egypt.* Cairo: The American University in Cairo Press, 2005.

Baker, Alan. *The Gladiator: The Secret History of Rome's Warrior Slaves.* New York: St. Martin's Press, 2000.

Baker, Warren, Tim Rake, and David Kemp. (eds.). *The Complete Word Study: Old Testament.* Chattanooga, TN: AMG Publishers, 1994.

Barber, John Warner. *Elements of General History: Embracing All the Leading Events in the World's History.* New Haven, CT: Horace C. Peck, 1866.

Barclay, William. *The Acts of the Apostles.* Philadelphia, PA: The Westminster Press, 1976.

———. *Letters to the Seven Churches.* Nashville: Abingdon Press, 1957.

———. *The New Daily Study Bible: The Revelation of John, Vol. 1, 3rd ed.* Louisville, KY: Westminster John Knox Press, 2004.

———. *New Testament Words.* Philadelphia, PA: The Westminster Press, 1974.

Baring-Gould, Sabine. *The Lives of the Saints.* London: John Hodges, 1880.

Barnes, Albert. *Barnes' Notes on the New Testament: Acts.* Grand Rapids, MI: Baker Book House, 1985.

———. *Notes, Explanatory and Practical, on the Book of Revelation.* London: Knight and Son, 1853.

Barnes, Arthur Stapylton. *St. Peter in Rome and His Tomb on the Vatican Hill.* London: Swan Sonnenschein and Co., 1900.

Barnett, Mary. *Gods and Myths of Ancient Greece.* New York: Smithmark Publishers, Inc., 1996.

Bayraktar, Vehbi. *Pergamon.* Istanbul: Net Turistik Yayinlar, 1987.

Beitzel, B. J. (ed.). *Biblica: The Bible Atlas.* "The Third Journey of Paul." Sydney: Global Book Publishing, 2006.

Belozerskaya, Marina, and Kenneth Lapatin. *Ancient Greece.* London: The British Museum Press, 2004.

Benko, Stephen. *The Virgin Goddess: Studies in the Pagan and Christian Roots of Mariology.* Leiden, Netherlands: Koninklijke Brill, 2004.

Bingham, Jane, et al. *Encyclopedia of the Ancient Rome.* London: Usborne Publishing Ltd., 2002.

Boardman, John, and N. G. L. Hammond. *The Expansion of the Greek World, Eighth to Sixth Centuries BC.* Cambridge, England: Cambridge University Press, 1982.

Boardman, John, Jasper Griffin, and Oswyn Murray. *The Oxford History of Greece and the Hellenistic World.* New York: Oxford University Press, 1986.

Bohec, Yann Le. *The Imperial Roman Army.* London: B. T. Batsford Ltd., 1994.

Bomgardner, D. L. *The Story of the Roman Amphitheatre.* New York: Routledge, 2000.

Bouquet, A. C. *Everyday Life in New Testament Times.* New York: Charles Scribner's Sons, 1953.

Bowman, Alan K., Peter Garnsey, and Dominic Rathbone. (eds.). *The Cambridge Ancient History: The High Empire, A.D. 70-192.* Cambridge, England: Cambridge University Press, 2000.

Bromiley, Geoffrey W. (ed.). *International Standard Bible Encyclopedia, Vol. 2.* "Ephesus" by G. L. Borchert. Grand Rapids, MI: Wm. B. Eerdmans Publishing Co., 1979.

———. *Theological Dictionary of the New Testament.* Grand Rapids, MI: Wm. B. Eerdmans Publishing Co., 1985.

Brouskari, Maria. *The Monuments of the Acropolis.* Athens: Archeological Receipts Fund, 2001.

Browne, Colin. (ed.). *New International Dictionary of New Testament Theology.* Grand Rapids, MI: Zondervan, 1971.

Bruce, F. F. *The Acts of the Apostles.* Grand Rapids, MI: Wm. B. Eerdmans Publishing Co., 1951.

———. *The Book of Acts.* Grand Rapids, MI: Wm. B. Eerdmans Publishing Co., 1988.

———. *The Books and the Parchments.* Old Tappan, NJ: Fleming H. Revell Co.

———. *The International Bible Commentary.* Grand Rapids, MI: Zondervan, 1986.

———. *A Mind for What Matters.* Grand Rapids, MI: Wm. B. Eerdmans Publishing Co., 1990.

———. *The New International Commentary on the New Testament: Commentary on the Book of Acts.* Grand Rapids, MI: Wm. B. Eerdmans Publishing Co., 1954.

Burckhardt, Jacob. *The Greeks and Greek Civilization.* Translated by Sheila Stern. New York: St. Martin's Press, 1998.

Burkert, Walter, and John Raffan. *Greek Religion: Archaic and Classical.* Oxford: Blackwell Publishing, 1986.

Butler, Alban. *Lives of The Saints.* Michael Walsh (ed.). New York: Harper One, 1956.

Buxton, Richard. *The Complete World of Greek Mythology.* London: Thames & Hudson, 2004.

Cadoux, Cecil John. *Ancient Smyrna.* Oxford: Basil Blackwell, 1938.

Caird, George Bradford. (ed.). *The Revelation of Saint John.* Peabody, MA: Hendrickson Publishers, 1993.

Calvin, John. *Commentary on Acts, Vol. 2.*

Camp, John M. *The Athenian Agora.* New York: Thames and Hudson, 1986.

Cantor, Norman F., and Dee Ranieri. *Alexander the Great.* New York: HarperCollins Publishers, 2005.

Cartledge, Paul. *Alexander the Great: The Hunt for a New Past.* Woodstock, NY: The Overlook Press, 2004.

Carter, Jeffrey. *Understanding Religious Sacrifice: A Reader*. New York: Continuum, 2003.

Catullus, Gaius Valerius. *Catullus*. Boston: Ginn and Co., 1893.

Cimok, Fatih. *A Guide to the Seven Churches*. Istanbul: A Turizm Yayinlari, 2007.

———. *Journeys of Paul: From Tarsus to the Ends of the Earth*. Istanbul: A Turizm Yayinlari, 2004.

Clapton, Edward. *The Life of Saint Luke*. London: J. & A. Churchill, 1902.

Clayton, Peter. *Great Figures of Mythology*. New York: Crescent Books, 1990.

———. *Treasures of Ancient Rome*. New York: Crescent Books, 1995.

Clement of Rome. *Letter to the Corinthians*.

Coffman, James Burton. *Commentaries on the Old and New Testament*. Reproduced by permission of Abilene Christian University Press, Abilene, Texas. searchgodsword.org.

Connolly, Peter. *Greece and Rome at War*. London: Greenhill Books, 1998.

———. *Pompeii*. Oxford: Oxford University Press, 1990.

Conti, Flavio. *A Profile of Ancient Rome*. Los Angeles: Getty Publications, 2003.

Cornel, Tim, and John Matthews. *Atlas of the Roman World*. Oxford: Andromeda Oxford Ltd., 1982.

Cowell, Frank Richard. *Life in Ancient Rome*. New York: The Berkley Publishing Group, 1961.

D'Epiro, Peter, and Mary Desmond Pinkowish. *What Are the Seven Great Wonders of the World?* New York: Random House, 1998.

D'Orazio, Federica. *Rome: Then and Now*. San Diego, CA: Thunder Bay Press, 2004.

Davis, William Stearns. *A Day in Old Athens: A Picture of Athenian Life*. Needham Heights, MA: Allyn & Bacon, 1914.

Deissmann, G. Adolf. *Bible Studies*. Translated by Alexander Grieve. Edinburgh: T. & T. Clark, 1901.

DeLaine, Janet. *The Baths of Caracalla*. Portsmouth, RI: Journal of Roman Archaeology, 1997.

Delaney, John, J. *Dictionary of Saints*. New York: Image Doubleday, 2004.

Detzler, Wayne A. *New Testament Words in Today's Language*. Wheaton, IL: Victor Books, 1986.

Dillon, Matthew, and Lynda Garland. *Ancient Rome: From the Early Republic to the Assassination of Julius Caesar*. New York: Routledge, 2005.

Dio, Cassius. *Dio's Roman History*.

Dumper, Michael, and Bruce E. Stanley. (eds.). *Cities of the Middle East and North Africa: A Historical Encyclopedia*. Santa Barbara, CA: ABC-CLIO, Inc., 2007.

Dupot, Florence. *Daily Life in Ancient Rome*. Cornwall, England: International Ltd., 1993.

Durando, Furio. (ed.). *Ancient Italy*. Vercelli, Italy: White Star Publishers.

Durant, Will. *The Story of Civilization, Part III: Caesar and Christ*. New York: Simon and Schuster, 1972.

DuTemple, Lesley A. *The Colosseum*. Minneapolis, MN: Lerner Publications, 2003.

Egbert, James Chidester. *Introduction to the Study of Latin Inscriptions*. New York: American Book Co., 1906.

Encyclopedia Americana: A Library of Universal Knowledge, Vol. 16. New York: The Encyclopedia Americana Corp., 1919.

Encyclopedia Brittanica: A Dictionary of Arts, Sciences, and General Literature. New York: Henry G. Allen Co., 1890.

Ephesus. Istanbul: Rehber Basim Yayin Dağitim Reklamcilik ve. Tic. A.S.

Erarslan, Ali. *Pamukale Hierapolis*. Denzili, Turkey: Eris Turizm Tc. Pazarlama, 2006.

Erdemgil, Selahattin. *Ephesus: Ruins and Museum*. Istanbul: Net Turistik Yayinlar, 1986.

Erdemgil, S., et al. *Ephesus*. Translated by Dr. Christine Thomas. Istanbul: DO-GU Press.

Erin, Kenan T. *Aphrodisias*. Istanbul: Net Turistik Yayinlar, 2006.

Ermatinger, James William, *Daily Life of Christians in Ancient Rome*. Westport, CT: Greenwood Press, 2007.

Esler, Philip Francis. (ed.). *The Early Christian World, Vols. 1-2.* New York: Routledge, 2002.

Eusebius, *Church History.*

Falkener, Edward. *Ephesus, and the Temple of Diana.* London: Day and Son, 1862.

Fallows, Samuel. (ed.). *The Popular and Critical Bible Encyclopedia and Scriptural Dictionary, Vol. 2.* Chicago: The Howard-Severance Co., 1907.

Fant, Clyde E., and Mitchell Glenn Reddish. *A Guide to Biblical Sites in Greece and Turkey.* Oxford: Oxford University Press, 2003.

Farnell, Lewis Richard. *The Cults of the Greek States, Vol. 2.* Oxford: Clarendon Press, 1896.

Fausset, A. R. *Bible Cyclopedia.* Hartford, CT: S. S. Scranton Co., 1910.

Felix, Minucius. *Octavius.*

Ferguson, Everett. *Backgrounds of Early Christianity.* Grand Rapids, MI: Wm. B. Eerdmans Publishing Co., 1987.

Ferguson, John. *The Religions of the Roman Empire.* Ithaca, NY: Cornel University Press, 1991.

Flavius, Josephus. *Jewish Antiquities.*

Foss, Clive. *Ephesus After Antiquity: A Late Antique, Byzantine, and Turkish City.* Cambridge, England: Cambridge University Press, 1979.

Fox, Robin Lane. *Alexander the Great.* New York: Allen Lane, 1973.

———. *Pagans and Christians.* New York: Alfred A. Knopf, Inc., 1987.

Foxe, John. *Foxe's Book of Martyrs.* Old Tappan, NJ: Fleming H. Revell Co., 1980.

Freedly, George, and John A. Reeves. *A History of the Theatre.* New York: Crown Publishers, 1941.

Frend, W. H. C. *The Rise of Christianity.* Philadelphia, PA: Fortress Press, 1984.

Fuller, J. F. C. *The Generalship of Alexander the Great.* London: Butler & Tanner, Ltd., 1958.

Gaebelein, Arno C. *The Revelation.* Glasgow, Scotland: Pickering and Inglis, 1915.

Gaffney, Christopher Thomas. *Temples of the Earthbound Gods: Stadiums in the Culture of Rio Grande and Buenos Aires.* Austin, TX: University of Texas Press, 2008.

Gaius. *Institutes.*

Galen. *De Methodo Medendi.*

Garlan, Yvon. *Slavery in Ancient Greece.* Translated by Janet Lloyd. Ithaca, NY: Cornell University Press, 1988.

Garnsey, Peter. *Ideas of Slavery From Aristotle to Augustine.* New York: Cambridge University Press, 1996.

Giorgi, Rosa. *Saints.* New York: Abrams, 2005.

Gökovali, Sadan. *Ephesus.* Translated by Altan Erguvan. Istanbul: Net Turistik Yayinlar A. S.

Golden, Mark. *Sport in the Ancient World From A to Z.* New York: Routledge, 2004.

Goodspeed, Edgar J. *The Apostolic Fathers.* London: Independent Press, 1950.

Grant, Michael. *A Guide to the Ancient World.* New York: Barnes & Noble, 1986.

———. *Constantine the Great: The Man and His Times.* New York: Charles Scribner's Sons, 1993.

Grant, Michael, and John Hazel. *Who's Who in Classical Mythology.* New York: Routledge, 2002.

Grant, Robert M. *Gods and the One God.* Philadelphia, PA: Westminster Press, 1986.

Green, Joel B., Scott McKnight, and I. Howard Marshall. (eds.). *Dictionary of Jesus and the Gospels.* Downers Grove, IL: InterVarsity Press, 1992.

Gregory of Nazianzus. *Oration.*

Gruen, Erich S. *Studies in Greek Culture and Roman Policy.* Berkeley, CA: University of California Press, 1990.

———. *The Hellenistic World and the Coming of Rome, Vol. 1.* Los Angeles: University of California Press, 1984.

Guhl, E., and W. Koner. *Everyday Life of the Greeks and Romans.* New York: Crescent Books, 1989.

Hadziaslani, Cornelia. *Parthenon Promenades*. Greece: Melina Mercouri Foundation, 2001.

Hales, Shelley. *The Roman House and Social Identity*. Cambridge, England: Cambridge University Press, 2003.

Halsey, William D., and Bernard Johnston. (eds.). *Collier's Encyclopedia, Vol. 5*. New York: Macmillan Educational Co., 1991.

Hamilton, J. R. *Alexander the Great*. London: Hutchinson & Co. Ltd., 1973.

Hammerton, J. A. *Illustrated Encyclopedia of World History, Vol. 4*. New Delhi: Mittal Publications, 1992.

Hammond, N. G. L. *The Genius of Alexander the Great*. London: Gerald Duckworth & Co. Ltd., 1997.

Hanfmann, George M. A. *From Croesus to Constantine: The Cities of Western Asia Minor and Their Arts in Greek and Roman Times*. Ann Arbor, MI: University of Michigan Press, 1975.

Hansen, Mogens Herman. *The Athenian Ecclesia II: A Collection of Articles, 1983-1989*. Copenhagen: Museum Tusculanum Press, 1989.

Hastings, James. (ed.). *Encyclopedia of Religion and Ethics, Part 10*. Whitefish, MT: Kessinger Publishing, 2003.

Hastings, James, et al. (eds.). *A Dictionary of the Bible: Pleroma-Zuzim*. New York: Charles Scribner's Sons, 1902.

Hastings, James, John Alexander Selbie, and John Chisholm Lambert. (eds.). *Dictionary of the Apostolic Church, Vol. 2*. New York: Charles Scribner's Sons, 1918.

Hemer, Colin J. *The Book of Acts in the Setting of Hellenistic History*. Winona Lake, IN: Eisenbrauns, 1990.

———. *The Letters to the Seven Churches of Asia in Their Local Settings*. Cambridge, England: Wm. B. Eerdmans Publishing Co., 2001.

Herbermann, Charles G., et al. (eds.). *The Catholic Encyclopedia, Vol. 9*. New York: Universal Knowledge Foundation, Inc., 1910.

———. *The Catholic Encyclopedia, Vol. 14*. New York: Universal Knowledge Foundation, Inc., 1912.

Herodotus. *Histories*.

Hippolytus. *The Refutation of All Heresies*.

Homer, *The Illiad*.

Homer, *The Odyssey*.

Hopkins, Keith. *Conquerors and Slaves*. New York: Cambridge University Press, 1978.

Houston, Mary G., and Florence S. Hornblower. *Ancient Egyptian, Assyrian, and Persian Costumes and Decorations*. London: A. & C. Black, 1920.

Ignatius. *Epistle to the Ephesians*.

———. *Letter to the Romans*.

Irenaeus. *Against Heresies*.

Jerome. *Ep. ad Marcell*.

———. *Lives of Illustrious Men*.

Johns, Catherine. *Sex or Symbol: Erotic Images of Greece and Rome*. London: The British Museum Press, 1989.

Johnston, Sarah Iles. *Ancient Greek Divination*. West Sussex, England: John Wiley and Sons, 2008.

Johnstone, Christopher Lyle. *Theory, Text, Context: Issues in Greek Rhetoric and Oratory*. Albany, NY: State University of New York Press, 1996.

Joint Association of Classical Teachers. *The World of Athens: An Introduction to Classical Athenian Culture*. Cambridge, England: Cambridge University Press, 1984.

Jones, Brian W. *The Emperor Domitian*. New York: Routledge, 1992.

Judge, E. A., and James R. Harrison. *The First Christians in the Roman World: Augustan and New Testament Essays*. Tubingen, Germany: Mohr Siebeck, 2008.

Justinus, Marcus Junianus. *Justin: Epitome of the Philippic History of Pompeius Trogus*. Translated by J. C. Yardley. New York: Oxford University Press, 1997.

Kazhdan, Alexander Petrovich, and Giles Constable. *People and Power in Byzantium: An Introduction to Modern Byzantium Studies.* Washington DC: Dumbarton Oaks, 1982.

Kazhdan Alexander P., and Alice-Mary Talbot. (eds.). *The Oxford Dictionary of Byzantium, Vol. 2.* Oxford: Oxford University Press, 1991.

Keener, Craig S. *The IVP Bible Background Commentary: New Testament.* Downers Grove, IL: InterVarsity Press, 1993.

Kekeç, Tevhit. *Pamukale Hierapolis.* Istanbul: Hitit Color.

Kent, Charles Foster. *The Historical Bible: The Work and Teachings of the Apostles*, New York: Charles Scribner's Sons, 1916.

Kerenyi, C. *The Gods of the Greeks.* London: Thames & Hudson, 2002.

Keskin, Naci. *Ephesus.* Istanbul: Keskin Color, 2007.

Kleiner, Diana E. E. *Cleopatra and Rome.* Cambridge, MA: Harvard University Press, 2005.

Korn, Frank J. A. *Catholic's Guide to Rome: Discovering the Soul of the Eternal City.* Mahwah, NJ: Paulist Press, 2000.

Kraft, John C., Helmut Buckner, Ilhan Kayan, and Helmut Engelmann. *Geoarcheology: An International Journal*, Vol. 22, No. 1. "The Geographies of Ancient Ephesus and the Artemesion in Anatolia." Hoboken: NJ: Wiley Interscience, 2007.

Kubo, Sakac. *A Reader's Greek-English Lexicon on the New Testament.* Grand Rapids, MI: Zondervan, 1975.

Kuefler, Matthew. *The Manly Eunuch: Masculinity, Gender Ambiguity, and Christian Ideology in Late Antiquity.* Chicago: University of Chicago Press, 2001.

Lactantius. *Divine Institutes.*

Lay, M. G., and James E. Vance. *Ways of the World: A History of the World's Roads and of the Vehicles That Used Them.* Piscataway, NJ: Rutgers University Press, 1992.

Leberati, Anna Maria, and Fabio Bourbon. *Ancient Rome.* New York: Barnes & Noble, 2004.

Lemprière, John. *A Classical Dictionary*. New York: G. and C. and H. Carvill Broadway, 1831.

The Letter of Aristeas. Translated by H. St. J. Thackeray. New York: The Macmillan Co., 1917.

Lightfoot, J. B. (ed.). *The Apostolic Fathers: Clement, Ignatius, and Polycarp, Part Two, Vol. 1*. Peabody, MA: Hendrickson Publishers, 1989.

Livius, Titus (Livy). *The History of Rome, Vol. 2*. Translated by Spillan and Cyrus Edmonds. New York: Harper and Brothers, 1895.

Liu, Jinyu. *Collegia Centonariorum: The Guilds of Textile Dealers in the Roman West*. Netherlands: Brill, 2009.

Lohr, Fr. *A Day in Ancient Rome*. Boston: D. C. Heath and Co., Publishers, 1897.

Lovell, Isabel. *Stories in Stone From the Roman Forum*. New York: The MacMillan Co., 1904.

Machan, John Gresham. *The Origin of Paul's Religion*. New York: The MacMillan Co., 1921.

MacMullen, Ramsey. *Christianizing the Roman Empire*. New Haven, CT: Yale University Press, 1984.

Magie, David. *Roman Rule in Asia Minor: To the End of the Third Century After Christ*. Salem, NH: Ayer Co., 1988.

Marrow, Glenn R. *Plato's Law of Slavery in Relation to Greek Law*. Urbana, IL: University of Illinois Press, 1939.

Matyszak, Philip. *Chronicle of the Roman Republic*. London: Thames & Hudson, 2003.

Matz, David. *Daily Life of Ancient Romans*. Westport, CT: Greenwood Press, 2002.

McCarty, Nick. *Rome*. London: Carlton Books, 2005.

Meijer, Fik. *The Gladiators: History's Most Deadly Sport*. New York: St. Martin's Press, 2003.

Meinardus, Otto, F. A. *St. Paul in Ephesus and the Cities of Galatia and Cyprus*. New Rochelle, NY: Caratzas Brothers Publishers, 1979.

Middleton, John Henry. *The Remains of Ancient Rome, Vol. 1*. London: Adam and Charles Black, 1892.

Mitchell, Stephen. *Anatolia: Land, Men and Gods in Asia Minor*. Oxford: Oxford University Press, 2001.

More, Daisy, and John Bowman. *Aegean Rivals*. Boston: Boston Publishing Co., 1986.

Morris, Leon. (ed.). *Revelation*. Downers Grove, IL: InterVarsity Press, 1987.

Morton, H.V. *In the Steps of St. Paul*. London: Methuen & Co. Ltd., 1937.

Moses of Chorene. *History of Armenia*.

Moule, Handley Carr Glyn. *The Epistle to the Ephesians, Vol. 41*. London: Cambridge University Press, 1891.

Mounce, Robert H. *The New International Commentary on the New Testament: The Book of Revelation*. Grand Rapids, MI: Wm. B. Eerdmans Publishing Co., 1998.

Murphy-O'Connor, Jerome. *Paul's Ephesus: Texts and Archeology*. Collegeville, MN: Liturgical Press, 1971.

Nicephorus. *Ecclesiastical History*.

———. *Short History*.

Novak, Ralph Martin. *Christianity and the Roman Empire: Background Texts*. Harrisburg, PA: Trinity Press, 2001.

Ober, Josiah. *Mass and Elite in Democratic Athens: Rhetoric, Ideology, and the Power of the People*. Princeton, NJ: Princeton University Press, 1989.

Onen, Helga-Ulgur. *Ephesus*. Istanbul: Ulgur Onen, 1989.

Orlin, Eric M. *Temples, Religion and Politics*. Leiden, Netherlands: E. J. Brill, 1997.

Özyigit, Ömer. "Recent Work at Phokaia in the Light of Akurgal's Excavations." Izmir, Turkey: Ege Üniversitesi, 2003.

Packer, James E. *The Forum of Trajan in Rome*. Los Angeles: University of California Press, 2001.

Paoli, Enrico Ugo. *Rome: Its People, Life, and Customs*. Translated by R. D. Macnaghten. London: Longman Green Co. Ltd., 1973.

Papadogeorgos, Georgios. *Prominent Greeks of Antiquity*. Athens: Michael Toubis Publication, 2003.

Papahatzis, Nicos. *Ancient Corinth*. Athens: Ekdotike Athenon, 2005.

Papathanassopoulos, G. *The Acropolis*. Athens: Krene Editions, 2006.

Parsons, Edward Alexander. *The Alexandrian Library: Glory of the Hellenistic World*. Amsterdam, Netherlands: The Elsevier Press, 1952.

Patmos. Attiki, Greece: Michael Toubis Publications, 2006.

Pausanias. *Description of Greece*.

Pliny the Younger. *Letters*. Translated by B. Radice.

Pliny the Elder. *The Natural History of Pliny*. Translated by John Bostock and H. T. Riley. London: George Bell and Sons, 1890.

Plutarch. *Parallel Lives: Life of Alexander*.

———. *The Age of Alexander*. Translated by Ian Scott-Kilvert. London: Penguin Books, 1973.

———. *The Lives of the Noble Grecians and Romans*. Translated by John Dryden. New York: Random House, 1932.

Poliakoff, Michael B. *Combat Sports in the Ancient World*. New Haven, CT: Yale University Press, 1987.

Pollitt, J. J. *Art and Experience in Classical Greek*. Cambridge, England: Cambridge University Press, 1972.

Pomeroy, Sarah B., and Stanley Mayer Burstein. (eds.). *Ancient History*. Princeton, NJ: Markus Wiener Publishing, Inc., 1984.

Porter, Stanley E. (ed.). *Paul and His Opponents*. Danvers, MA: Brill, 2005.

Potter, David Stone, and D. J. Mattingly. (eds.). *Life, Death, and Entertainment in the Roman Empire*. Ann Arbor, MI: University of Michigan Press, 1999.

Powell, Anton. *Athens and Sparta: Constructing Greek Political and Social History From 478 BC*. New York: Routledge, 1988.

Price, Martin J. *The Seven Wonders of the Ancient World*. London: Routledge, 1988.

Procopius. *Buildings*.

Rackham, Richard Belward. *The Acts of the Apostles: An Exposition*. London: Methuen and Co., 1901.

Ramsay, William Mitchell. *The Church in the Roman Empire Before A.D. 170.* New York: G. P. Putman's Sons, 1893.

———. *The Letters to the Seven Churches of Asia.* Whitefish, MT: Kessinger Publishing, 2004.

Ramsay, William Mitchell, and Agnes Margaret Ramsay. *Studies in the History and Art of the Eastern Provinces of the Roman Empire.* Aberdeen, Scotland: University of Aberdeen Press, 1898.

Ransome, Hilda M. *The Sacred Bee in Ancient Times and Folklore.* London: George Allen & Unwin, 1937.

Reader's Digest Association, Inc. *The Truth About History: How New Evidence Is Transforming the Story of the Past.* London: Planet Three Publishing, 2003.

Researchers of Ephesus Museum. *The Terrace Houses in Ephesus.* Istanbul: Hitit Color.

Renatus, Flavius Vegetius. *The Military Institutions of the Romans.* Translated by John Clark. Westpost, CT: Greenwood Press, 1985.

Richardson, Lawrence. *A New Topographical Dictionary of Ancient Rome.* Baltimore, MD: John Hopkins University Press, 1992.

Ridpath, John Clark. *Ridpath's Universal History.* Cincinnati, OH: The Jones Brothers Publishing Co., 1899.

Ring, Trudy, Robert M. Salkin, and Sharon La Boda. (eds.). *International Dictionary of Historic Places, Vol. 3: Southern Europe.* Chicago: Fitzroy Dearborn Publishers, 1995.

Robertson, A. T. *Word Pictures in the New Testament, Vol. 3: The Acts of the Apostles.* Nashville: Broadman Press, 1930.

———. *Word Pictures in the New Testament, Vol. 6.* Grand Rapids, MI: Baker Book House, 1933.

Robinson, Eric W. *Ancient Greek Democracy: Readings and Sources.* Hoboken, NJ: Blackwell Publishing, 2003.

Rodriguez, Junius P. *The Historical Encyclopedia of World Slavery, Vol. 1.* Santa Barbara, CA: ABC-CLIO, Inc., 1997.

Rogers Jr., Cleon L. *The New Linguistic and Exegetical Key to the Greek New Testament.* Grand Rapids, MI: Zondervan Publishing House, 1998.

Rohner, B. *Illustrated Life of the Blessed Virgin*. New York: Benziger Brothers, 1871.

Roller, Lynn E. *In Search of God the Mother: The Cult of Anatolian Cybele*. Berkeley, CA: University of California Press, 1999.

Roth, Leland M. *Understanding Architecture: Its Elements, History, and Meaning*. New York: Harper Collins Publishers, 1993.

Rufus, Q. Curtius. *History of Alexander*.

Sacks, David. *A Dictionary of the Ancient Greek World*. Oxford: Oxford University Press, 1996.

Sallust. *Catiline*.

Sayce, Archibald Henry. *The Hittites: The Story of a Forgotten Empire*. New York: F. H. Revell Co., 1888.

Scarre, Chris. *The Penguin Historical Atlas of Ancient Rome*. New York: Penguin Group, 1995.

Schaff, Philip. (ed.). *A Dictionary of the Bible: Including Biography, Natural History, Geography, Topography, Archeology, and Literature*. Philadelphia, PA: American Sunday-School Union, 1880.

Scheidel, Walter. (ed.). *Debating Roman Demography*. Leiden, Netherlands: Koninklijke Brill NV, 2001.

Scherrer, Peter. (ed.). *Ephesus*. Translated by Lionel Bier and George M. Luxon. Ege Yayinlari: Zero Prod. Ltd., 2000.

Sear, Frank. *Roman Theatres: An Architectural Study*. Oxford: Oxford University Press, 2006.

Seneca. *Essays, Book I, On Anger*.

Seward, William. *Anecdotes of Distinguished Persons: Chiefly of the Present and Two Preceding Centuries*. London: T. Cadwell Jun. and W. Davies, 1798.

Shelly, Bruce L. *Church History in Plain Language*. Dallas, TX: Word Publishing, 1995.

Simpson, J. A., and E. S. C. Weiner. (eds.). *The Oxford English Dictionary*. Oxford: Oxford University Press, 1989.

Smith, Dennis E. (ed.). *Chalice Introduction to the New Testament*. Atlanta: Chalice Press, 2004.

Smith, William. (ed.). *A Dictionary of Greek and Roman Antiquities*. New York: Harper and Brothers, 1886.

Souli, Sofia A. *Love Life of the Ancient Greeks*. Attiki, Greece: Michael Toubis Publications, 2006.

Southern, Pat. *Domitian: Tragic Tyrant*. Bloomington, IN: Indiana University Press, 1997.

Spicq, Ceslas. *Theological Lexicon of the New Testament*. Translated and edited by James D. Ernst. Peabody, MA: Hendrickson Publishers, Inc., 1994.

Spielvogel, Jackson J. *Western Civilization, Vol. A: To 1500, 7th ed.* Belmont, CA: Thomson Wadsworth, 2006.

Spurgeon, W. A. *The Conquering Christ*. Muncie, IN: Scott Printing Co., 1936.

Staccioli, Romolo Augusto. *The Roads of the Romans*. Los Angeles: The J. Paul Getty Museum, 2003.

Stambaugh, John E. *The Ancient Roman City*. London: The John's Hopkins University Press, 1988.

Stauffer, Engelbert. *Christ and the Caesars*. Hamburg: Friedrich Wittig Publishers, 1952.

Stephens, William H. *The New Testament World in Pictures*. Nashville: Broadman Press, 1987.

Strabo. *The Geography of Strabo*. Translated by Horace Leonard Jones. Cambridge, MA: Harvard University Press, 1959.

Strassler, Robert B. (ed.). *The Landmark Herodotus: The Histories*. Translated by Andrea L. Purvis. New York: Pantheon Books, 2007.

Stuart, Moses. *A Commentary on the Apocalypse, Vol. 1*. New York: Van Nostrand and Terrett, 1851.

Suetonius. *Lives of the Caesars*. Cambridge, MA: Harvard University, Loeb Classical Library, 1992.

Swaddling, Judith. *The Ancient Olympic Games*. Austin, TX: University of Texas Press, 1988.

Swete, Henry Barclay. *The Apocalypse of St. John*. London: Macmillan and Co, 1906.

Tacitus. *Annals*.

Telushkin, Joseph. *A Code of Jewish Ethics, Vol. 1: You Shall Be Holy*. New York: Crown Publishing, 2006.

———. *A Code of Jewish Ethics, Vol. 2: Love Your Neighbor as Yourself*. New York: Crown Publishing, 2009.

Tenney, Merril C. *New Testament Survey*. Grand Rapids, MI: Wm. B. Eerdmans Publishing Co., 1985.

———. *New Testament Times*. Grand Rapids, MI: Baker Books, 2002.

Tertullian. *Apology*.

———. *Of the Games*.

———. *Prescription Against Heretics*.

———. *Scorpiace*.

Theodoret. *On the Psalms*.

Torrance, David W., and Thomas F. Torrance. (eds.). *The Acts of the Apostles*. Grand Rapids, MI: Wm. B. Eerdmans Publishing Co., 1977.

Towner, Philip H. *The Letters to Timothy and Titus*. Grand Rapids, MI: Wm. B. Eerdmans Publishing Co., 2006.

Trebilco, Paul. *The Early Christians in Ephesus From Paul to Ignatius*. Grand Rapids, MI: Wm. B. Eerdmans Publishing Co., 2007.

Trench, R.C. *Synonyms of the New Testament*. Peabody, MA: Hendrickson Publishers, 1989.

Tsakos, Konstantine. *The Acropolis*. Athens: Hesperos Editions, 2005.

Tucker, Thomas George. *Life in the Roman World of Nero and St. Paul*. New York: The Macmillan Co., 1910.

Turcan, Robert. *The Cults of the Roman Empire*. Translated by Antonia Nevill. Cambridge, MA: Blackwell Publishers, 1996.

Turner, Patricia, and Charles Russell Coulter. *Dictionary of Ancient Deities*. Oxford: Oxford University Press, 2000.

Ustinova, Yulia. *Caves and the Ancient Greek Mind: Descending Underground in the Search for Ultimate Truth*. Oxford: Oxford University Press, 2009.

Verbugge, Verlyn D. (ed.). *The NIV Theological Dictionary of New Testament Words*. Grand Rapids, MI: Zondervan Corporation, 2000.

Veyne, Paul. (ed.). *A History of Private Life*. Translated by Arthur Goldhammer. Cambridge, MA: Harvard University Press, 1987.

Victorinus. Translated by Robert Ernest Wallis. Grand Rapids, MI: Wm. B. Eerdmans Publishing Co., 1950.

Wallace Jr., Foy E. *The Book of Revelation*. Nashville: Foy E. Wallace, Jr., Publications, 1966.

Walsh, Michael. *Roots of Christianity*. London: Grafton Books, 1986.

Walvoord, John F. *The Revelation of Jesus Christ*. Chicago: Moody Press, 1966.

Water, Mark (ed.). *The New Encyclopedia of Christian Martyrs*. Grand Rapids, MI: Baker Books, 2001.

Waterfield, Robin. *Athens: A History, From Ancient Ideal to Modern City*. New York: Basic Books, 2004.

Watkins, Richard Ross. *Slavery: Bondage Throughout History*. New York: Houghton Mifflin, 2001.

Watson, Richard, and Nathan Bangs. *A Biblical and Theological Dictionary: Explanatory of the History of the Jews and Neighboring Nations*. New York: B. Waugh and T. Mason, 1832.

Westermann, William Linn. *The Slave Systems of Greek and Roman Antiquity*. Philadelphia, PA: The American Philosophical Society, 1955.

Wiedemann, Thomas E. J. *Emperors and Gladiators*. New York: Routledge, 1992.

Willard, Emma. *Universal History in Perspective*. New York: A. S. Barnes and Co., 1854.

Writings of the Fathers Down to AD 325, Vol. 7. "Commentary on the Apocalypse" by Victorinus. Translated by Robert Ernest Wallis. Grand Rapids, MI: Wm. B. Eerdmans Publishing Co., 1950.

Yale, Pat, et al. *Turkey, 9th ed*. Lonely Planet, 2005.

Yamauchi, Edwin M. *New Testament Cities in Western Asia Minor*. Eugene, OR: Wipf and Stock Publishers, 2003.

Yegul, Fikret. *Baths and Bathing in Classical Antiquity*. New York: The Architectural History Foundation, 1992.

Zerwick, Max, and Mary Grosvenor. *A Grammatical Analysis of the Greek New Testament*. Rome: Biblical Institute Press, 1981.

STUDY REFERENCE BOOK LIST

1. *How To Use New Testament Greek Study Aids* by Walter Jerry Clark (Loizeaux Brothers).

2. *Strong's Exhaustive Concordance of the Bible* by James H. Strong.

3. *The Interlinear Greek-English New Testament* by George Ricker Berry (Baker Book House).

4. *The Englishman's Greek Concordance of the New Testament* by George Wigram (Hendrickson).

5. *New Thayer's Greek-English Lexicon of the New Testament* by Joseph Thayer (Hendrickson).

6. *The Expanded Vine's Expository Dictionary of New Testament Words* by W. E. Vine (Bethany).

7. *Theological Dictionary of the New Testament* by Geoffrey Bromiley; Gephard Kittle, ed. (Eerdmans).

8. *The New Analytical Greek Lexicon*; Wesley Perschbacher, ed. (Hendrickson).

9. *The New Linguistic and Exegetical Key to the Greek New Testament* by Cleon Rogers Jr. (Zondervan).

10. *Word Studies in the Greek New Testament* by Kenneth Wuest, 4 Volumes (Eerdmans).

11. *New Testament Words* by William Barclay (Westminster Press).

12. *Word Meanings* by Ralph Earle (Hendrickson).

13. *International Critical Commentary Series*; J. A. Emerton, C. E. B. Cranfield, and G. N. Stanton, eds. (T. & T. Clark International).

14. *Vincent's Word Studies of the New Testament* by Marvin R. Vincent, 4 Volumes (Hendrickson).

15. *New International Dictionary of New Testament Theology*; Verlyn D. Verbrugge, ed. (Zondervan).

ILLUSTRATION AND PHOTO CREDIT ACKNOWLEDGMENTS

The Publisher would like to thank the following picture libraries as well as individual copyright owners for permission to reproduce their images. Copyright inquiries should be directed to Rick Renner Ministries, graphics@renner.org.

Many photographs were shot on-site by photographer Alexander Gladilov and/or Rick Renner during various research trips to Turkey. Such photos are credited as Private Collection — Renner.

Photo credits are listed by chapter and page. On pages where more than one photo appears, the following abbreviations are applied: T=top; B=bottom; L=Left; R=right; M=middle (either horizontally or vertically).

COVER / DUST COVER:

Cover Art: *Oil Lamps* © Private Collection — Renner.

Dustcover: *Ephesus Ruins* © Olena Talberg / 123rf.com; Parchment Background © Selahattin BAYRAM / istockphoto.com.

FRONT MATTER:

Private Collection — Renner

i, ii-iii, xiv, xv, xvi, xvii, xviii, xix, xx-xi, xxi, xxxvii © Private Collection — Renner.

Royalty Free

v *Greek Vector Art* © vectorstock.com; **xiv-xxi, xxxvii-xxxviii** *Parchment Background* © Selahattin BAYRAM / istockphoto.com; **xxxix** *Parchment Background With Oil Lamp* © John Said, Selahattin BAYRAM / istockphoto.com; **xx (top)** *Smyrna*

Underground Arches © creatista / Stock.Adobe.com; **xl** *Celsus Library,* (Ephesus, Turkey) © muratart / Stock.Adobe.com.

CHAPTER 1:

Alamy

7 Listed under Royalty Free.

Art Resource

45 *Saint John on the Island of Patmos* © Gianni Dagli Orti / The Art Archive at Art Resource, NY.

Glow Images

47 *Aerial View of Patmos* © Glow Images / Tips Images North America / Guido Alberto Rossi.

Royalty Free

1 *Celsus Library,* (Ephesus, Turkey) © muratart / Stock.Adobe.com; **1** *Greek Design Element* © Vectorstock;

CHAPTER 2:

Akg-images

114-115 *Dacian Warrior,* Detail from a series of reliefs depicting scenes of Trajan's Dacian Wars, first war, third campaign (102 AD) / Museo della Civiltà Romana (No. 3074), Rome, Italy / photo: akg-images; 138-139 *St. John the Evangelist,* (1691) Artist: Tichon Filatyev / Tretjakov Gallery (Inv. No. 15271), Moscow, Russia / photo: akg-images.

Art Resource

85 *Phoenician Gold Belt* © Album / Art Resource, NY / Museo Arqueológico Nacional (National Archaeological Museum of Spain), Madrid, Spain.

Bridgeman Art Library

76 *Oil Lamp Depicting a Chariot Team* (ceramic), Roman (1st Century AD) / Ancient Art and Architecture Collection Ltd. / Bridgeman Images; 80 *Christ Seated on the Throne,* Icon, 17th Century / De Agostini Picture Library / G. Dagli Orti / Bridgeman Images; 86 *Gold and Silver Alloy Belt With Fastening at Rear and Attached Apron Frame* / Werner Forman Archive / Bridgeman Images; 120 *Saul on the Road to Damascus,* 2002 (w/c on paper), Harlin, Greg (b. 1957) / Private Collection / Wood Ronsaville Harlin, Inc. USA / Bridgeman Images; 134 *The Rich Man in Hell,* illustration for "The Life of Christ," c. 1886-94 (w/c & gouache on paperboard), Tissot, James Jacques Joseph (1836-1902) / Brooklyn Museum of Art, New York, USA / Bridgeman Images.

Mary Evans Picture Library

75 *Golden Candlestick* © Mary Evans Picture Library; 94 *Judaism Burnt Offering* © Mary Evans Pictures Library; 135 *Hell* © Mary Evans Pictures Library; 137 *Jesus Christ the Resurrection Easter* © Mary Evans Picture Library / Classic Stock / H. Armstrong Roberts.

Royalty Free

60-126, 128-139 *Parchment Background* © Selahattin BAYRAM / istockphoto.com; 60 *Parchment* © mammuth / istockphoto.com; 61-138 *Greek Design Element* © Vectorstock; 62 *The Last Supper,* 19th Century painting, Saint Michael's Church (Michelskerk), Leuven, Belgium © Renáta Sedmáková / DPC; 64 (1st photo) *Ephesus Ruins* © Terraxplorer / istockphoto.com; 64 (3rd photo) *Pergamum Ruins* © WorldWideImages / istockphoto.com; 64 (5th photo) *Sardis Ruins* © bogdb / istockphoto.com; 64 (7th photo) *Laodicea* © tunart / istockphoto.com; 71 *Molten Gold* © Falcor / istockphoto.com; 73, 78-79 *Oil Lamp* © Yosef Erpert / Fotolia.com; 74 *Ancient Lamp* © Clifford Shirley / Fotomedia / istockphoto.com; 76-77 *Standing Oil Lamp* © Erica Guilane-Nachex / DPC; 78 *Jesus* © Carl Heinrich Block / Restored Traditions; 83 *Enthroned Christ* © Netfalls / Fotolia.com; 91 *Transfiguration of Jesus* © Renáta Sedmáková / DPC 93 *Flames* © MilesPhotos / Fotolia.com; 97L *Frankincense Tree* © mahroch / istockphoto.com; 97R *Dried Frankincense* © fp-pixpics / Stock.Adobe.com; 119 *Jesus Coming* © joshblack /

(3rd Century CE) / Museo Nazionale Romano (Palazzo Massimo alle Terme), Rome, Italy / Image by Marie-Lan Nguyen (Jastrow); Public Domain / Source: Wikimedia Commons (Mosaic Blue Charioteero); **200** *Tragedy and Comedy Theatrical Masks Roman Mosaic*, Capitoline Museums / Public Domain / Source: Wikipedia.org (Google Art Project Theatrical Masks); **231T** *The Baths of Caracalla*, by Sir Lawrence Alma-Tadema (1836-1912) / Public Domain / Source: WikiArt (Sir Lawrence Alma-Tadema).

Special Permissions

171B *Harbour Bath Reconstruction*, Niemann (1902) / Austrian Archaeological Institute (used by permission); **271, 278-279** *Font in maps: Taggettes* © Dr. Marianne Steinbauer (used by permission), www.pia-frauss.de/fonts/fonts.htm.

Private Collection — Renner

140-141 Curetes Street in Ephesus; **153** Brothel Advertisement; **166** Harbor Boulevard (Arcadiane); **168-169** Arcadiane; **170** Altars at Domitian Harbor Bathhouse; **171T** Domitian's Harbor Bathhouse; **172** Steps to Theater; **174** Plateia in Coressus Street; **176** Stadium Entrance; **177TL** Stadium Wall; **177TR** Stadium Seats; **177BL** Gladiator Entrance; **177BR** Gladiator Graves; **194B** Gladiator on Gravestone; **195** Gladiator on Gravestone; **197** Great Theater; **201** Theater Seats; **202** Columns of Ephesus Central Marketplace; **204-205** Ephesus Central Marketplace; **206B** Ephesus Central Market Ruins; **207** Hall of Nero; **208-209** Temple of Serapis; **210-211** Gate of Mazeus and Mithridates; **212-213** Celsus Library; **214-215** Site of School of Tyrannus; **216** Walkway to Brothel; **218-219** Curetes Street; **223** Marble Room Terrace House; **224** Terrace House; **225** Frescoes in Terrace House; **226-227** Mosaic Walkway; **229** Public Toilets; **230** Columns in Central Bathhouse; **231B** Steps to Central Bathhouse; **234** Steps to Temple of Domitian; **234-235M** Domitian Square; **235** Fountain of Domitian; **238T** Head and Hand of Domitian Statue; **238-239B** Altar of Temple of Domitian; **239T** Temple of Domitian Decorated Column; **240** Ephesus Basilica Columns; **241** Basilica Column Top; **244** Ephesus Upper Marketplace; **245** Temple of Isis Ruins; **248** Prythaneum, **249** Temple of Dea Roma; **250-251** Upper Bouleterion/Odeion; **252-253** Upper Bathhouse and Gymnasium; **254** South Road; **255** Magnesia Gate; **263** Artemis Idol; **269** Artemis Idol; **271** Map of Asia Minor Map; **278-279** Map of Ancient Ephesus.

CHAPTER 4:

Akg-Images

297 *The Sermon of the Apostle Paul,* Jacopo da Ponte Bassano, Called Bassano del Grappa c. 1510/18 – 1592 / Padua, Musei Civici / photo: akg-images / Cameraphoto.

Balage Balogh / Archaeology Illustrated

283 *Library of Celsus, Ephesus* (2nd Century AD) © Balage Balogh

Public Domain

299 *The Pentecost*, c. 1604-14 (oil on canvas), by El Greco (Domenico Theotocopuli) (1541-1614) / Prado, Madrid, Spain / Public Domain / Courtesy of: Direct Media, Germany / Source: Wikimedia (Pentecostés) / Permission: Yorck Project (https://commons.wikimedia.org/wiki/Commons:10,000_paintings_from_Directmedia); **310** *Healings*, by Christoph Weigel (1654-1725) / Public Domain, Image courtesy of the Digital Image Archive, Pitts Theology Library, Candler School of Theology, Emory University; **324** *The Sons of Sceva*, by Christoph Weigel (1654-1725) / Public Domain, Image courtesy of the Digital Image Archive, Pitts Theology Library, Candler School of Theology, Emory University; **327** *Jesus Healing the Lunatic*, by Gustave Doré (1832-1883) / Public Domain / Image courtesy of Dover Publications; **328** *Jesus Healing the Man Possessed With a Devil*, by Gustave Doré (1832-1883) / Public Domain / Image courtesy of Dover Publications; **336** *St. Paul at Ephesus*, by Gustave Doré (1832-1883) / Public Domain / Image courtesy of Dover Publications; **341** *Book Burning*, by Tommaso Agostino Ricchini (1675-1762) / Public Domain, Image courtesy of the Digital Image Archive, Pitts Theology Library, Candler School of Theology, Emory University; **356** *Paul Rescued From the Multitudes,* by Gustave Doré (1832-1883) / Public Domain / Image courtesy of Dover Publications.

Private Collection — Renner

280 *Curetes Street*; **282** *Celsus Library*; **284-285** *Harbor of Cenchrea*; **290-291** *Celsus Library*; **292-293** *Marble Street*; **294** *Ruins of Road in Ancient Corinth*; **301** *Hall of Nero*; **302-303** *Steps to Site of School of Tyrannus*; **304-305** *Capital Detail*; **318** *Columns*; **342** *Ephesus Theater and Arcadiane*; **348-349** *Temple of Artemis Model*; **351** *Temple of Artemis Ruins*; **353** *Theater Seats*; **354-355** *Stage of Theater of Ephesus*; **358** *Ruins of Hellenistic Barracks*; **361** *Marble Fragments, Theater Back Stage*; **362-363** *Plateia in Coressus*; **365** *Ephesus Central Marketplace Columns*.

CHAPTER 5:

Akg-images

390-391 *Athens in the Mid-Fourth Century BC*, photo: akg-images / Peter Connolly; **392** *Athenian Citizens Vote*, photo: akg-images / Peter Connolly; **394** *Illustration of Ancient Athens* (Athens, Greece), photo: akg-images / Peter Connolly; **395** *Pnyx Drawing*, photo: akg-images / Peter Connolly.

Alamy

368-369 Listed under Royalty Free.

Bridgeman

373 *Central Panel From the Threshold of Paradise*, 1885-96 (oil on canvas), Vasnetsov, Victor Mikhailovich (1848-1926) / Tretyakov Gallery, Moscow, Russia / Bridgeman Images; **385** *Mary Magdalene and the Holy Women at the Tomb*, illustration from "The Life of

Edition of the Revised New Testament With a History of Revision (1881) / National Publishing Company / Public Domain / Private Collection; **379L** *The Liberation of St. Peter From Prison* (oil on canvas), Augustiner Chorherrenstift, St. Florian, Austria / by Gerard van Honthorst (1592 – 1656) / Public Domain; **379R** *Peter Delivered From Prison* (Acts 12), Illustration From Our Day in the Light of Prophecy (1917), W. A. Spicer / Public Domain / Private Collection; **380-381** *The Annunciation*, engraving by Gustave Doré (1832-1883), Published in the Illustrated Edition of the Revised New Testament With a History of Revision (1881) / National Publishing Company / Public Domain / Private Collection; **387** *The First Vial Angel Pouring His Vial on the Earth*, Published in Forty Coming Wonders (1880) / Fourth Edition, Enlarged With Fifty Illustrations / Christian Herald / Public Domain / Private Collection; **399, 400-401,** *The Revelation of St. John*, by Julius Schnorr von Carolsfeld (1794-1874), Treasury of Bible Illustrations / Public Domain / Image Courtesy of Dover Publications; **402-403** *Ephesus in the Time of St. Paul* (engraving by unknown artist), Published in the Illustrated Edition of the Revised New Testament With a History of Revision (1881) / National Publishing Company / Public Domain / Private Collection; **417** *The Last Supper,* called "The Little Last Supper," by Philippe de Champaigne (1602-1674) / Public Domain (Wikimedia.org > Philippe de Champaigne) / Photo Credit: Rama / Courtesy of Museum of Fine Arts of Lyon; **438** *Gathered Believers Reading a Letter From the Apostle Paul*, Engraving From Treasures of the Bible (1894), Public Domain / Private Collection; **443** *Paul Writing to Timothy From Rome* (engraving by unknown artist), Published in Our Day in the Light of Prophecy (1917) / W. A. Spicer / Pacific Press Publishing Association / Public Domain / Private Collection; **456** *Corinth in the Time of St. Paul* (engraving by unknown artist), Published in the Illustrated Edition of the Revised New Testament With a History of Revision (1881) / National Publishing Company / Public Domain / Private Collection; **458-459** *St. Peter Preaching in Jerusalem* (Oil on Canvas), by Charles Poërson (France, Vic-sur-Seille, 1609-1667) / Public Domain / Source: Los Angeles County Museum of Art (http://collections. lacma.org/node/246454); **464** *Temple of Artemis Engraving*, by Andre Castaigne (1897) / Public Domain / Private Collection; **478** *The Fall of Man* (1592), by Cornelis van Haarlem (1562-1638) / Public Domain / Image Courtesy of Rijksmuseum (English: Imperial Museum), Amsterdam, Netherlands; **479** *Banished From the Garden of Eden*, Engraving by Gustave Dore (1832-1883), Public Domain / Image Courtesy of Dover Publications.

Private Collection — Renner

393 *The Areopagus in Athens;* **405** *Columns on Curetes Street,* **406** *Mosaic Walkway on Curetes Street,* **410** *Temple of Domitian Ruins,* **440** *Terrace House*

Walters Art Museum (Baltimore, USA); **511** *Alexander the Great Founding Alexandria*, by Placido Costanzi (1702-1759) / CC0: The Walters Museum of Art (Baltimore, USA) / Acquired by Henry Walters; **512** *Alexander Fighting King Darius III of Persia* (mosaic), National Archaeological Museum, Naples / CC BY-SA 3.0: Berthold Werner (Photographer) / Source: Wikipedia.org (History of Anatolia); **519** *Alexander Routs Persians* (Relief on Alexander Sarcophagus) / Istanbul Archaeological Museums / CC BY-SA 3.0: Ronald Slabke / Source: Wikipedia (Alexander Sarcophagus); **560-561** *Mosaic From 1st Century BC Roman Bathhouse*, CC BY-SA 2.0: Carole Raddato (Flikr: carolemage).

Public Domain

523 *Plate Depicting Cybele, a Votive Sacrifice, and the Sun God* (2nd Century BCE), Musée Guimet, Ai Khanoum, Afghanistan / Public Domain / Source: Wikipedia (Cybele); **528-529** *Statue of a Seated Cybele With the Portrait Head of her Priestess*, Courtesy of the J. Paul Getty Museum Open Content Program (Los Angeles); **551** *Thermae Boxer Massimo*, National Museum of Rome / Public Domain / Photographer: Marie-Lan Ngugen / Source: Wikimedia (Palazzo Massimo alle Terme > Statues and reliefs).

Special Permissions

525 *Cybele and Attis in a Chariot Drawn by Four Lions*, Detail from the Parabiago plate (embossed silver, c. 200-400 CE) / Archaeological Museum of Milan, Italy /

© Photographer: Giovanni Dall'Orto / Source: Wikipedia (Cybele) / Color Correction DP; **537** *Defaced Dea Roma* / Bardo Museum in Tunis © Giovanni Dall'Orto / Source: Wikipedia (Religion in ancient Rome > Later Republic to Principate); **544-545, 574-575** *Font used in map: Taggettes*, © Dr. Marianne Steinbauer (used by permission), www.pia-frauss.de/fonts/fonts.htm.

Private Collection — Renner

492-493 *Ruins of Central Marketplace, Smyrna*; **494** *Smyrna Central Marketplace Columns*; **522** *Cybele Idol*; **531** *Altars, Smyrna*; **540-541** *Izmir, Turkey*; **542** *Ancient Cornice Moldings, Aphrodisias*; **543** *Goddess of Health, Smyrna Lower Marketplace*; **544-545** *Map of Royal Road*; **546** *Statue of Homer*; **549** *Three Ancient Altars*; **550-551** *Gymnasium Ruin, Hierapolis*; **552-553** *Ruins of Central Marketplace, Smyrna*; **554** *Basilica Sculpture of Poseidon and Amphitrite, Smyrna*; **555** *Basilica Columns, Smyrna*; **556** *Underground Arches, Smyrna Central Marketplace*; **558-559** *Panorama of Theater of Hierapolis*; **566-567** *Ancient Stadium, Aphrodisias*; **572** *Cisterns on Mount Pagos*; **574-575** *Map of Ancient Smyrna*.

CHAPTER 7:

Akg-images

585 *Marble Base Relief of Dea Roma*, from the Honorary Column for Antonius Pius / (Roman, after 161 AD) Cortile della Pigna (Inv. No. 5115) / Vatican Museums, Rome, Italy /

photo: akg-images / Pirozzi; 595 *Vase Painting*, photo: akg-images / Peter Connolly; 596 *Vase Painting*, photo: akg-images / Peter Connolly; 597 *Reconstruction of a House*, photo: akg-images / Peter Connolly; 627 *Mamertine Prison* (Carcere Mamertinus), Rome, Italy / photo: akg-images / Hilbich.

Bridgeman

578-579 *Postcard Depicting the Bloody Games in the Arena in Rome*, illustration from "Quo Vadis," 1910 (colour litho), Styka, Jan (1858-1925) / Private Collection / Archives Charmet / Bridgeman Images; 588 *The Kiss of Peace in the Catacombs* (oil on canvas), Coubertin, Charles Louis Fredy de (1822-1908) / Musee des Beaux-Arts, Rouen, France / Bridgeman Images; 592-593 *Paul and Silas in Prison*, Hatherell, William (1855-1928) / Private Collection / © Look and Learn / Bridgeman Images; 599 *The First Christians in Rome*, 1869 (oil on canvas), Otto, Karl (1830-1902) / Neue Galerie, Kassel, Germany / Bridgeman Images; 602-603 *Stoning of St. Stephen* (pen & ink on paper), Rembrandt Harmensz. van Rijn (1606-69) / Leeds Museums and Galleries (Leeds Art Gallery) UK / Bridgeman Images; 622-623 *Roman Gladiators in the Arena With Animals*, Colosseum (engraving), Italian School, (19th Century) / Private Collection / Ancient Art and Architecture Collection Ltd. / Bridgeman Images; 642 *Head of Trajanus Decius* (201-251) from Samisegetuza, Romania (bronze),

Roman (3rd Century AD) / Museum of Dacian and Roman Civilisation, Deva, Romania / Bridgeman Images; 644 *Valerian* (193/195/200 260 or 264), also known as Valerian the Elder (Roman Emperor from 253 to 260), Marble Bust / Head from a colossal statue probably from Asia Minor / Carlsberg Glyptotek Museum (Copenhagen, Denmark) / Photo © Tarker / Bridgeman Images; 646 *Bust of Roman Emperor Lucius Domitius Aurelianus* / De Agostini Picture Library / A. Dagli Orti / Bridgeman Images.

DK images

610-611 *Jews Gather in the Synagogue*, DKimages.com, Peter Dennis © Dorling Kindersly; 628-629 *Two Drawings of Mamertine Prison*, DKimages.com © Dorling Kindersly.

Mary Evans Picture Library

581 *Polycarp, Bishop of Smyrna* © Mary Evans Picture Library; 586-587 *Jesus Is Resurrected* © Mary Evans Picture Library; 621 *Jesus Calms a Storm*, Artist: William Hole "Life of Jesus" (circa 1890) plate 33 © Mary Evans Picture Library.

Royalty Free

576 *Parchment*, mammuth / istockphoto.com; 576-632, 652-664 *Parchment Background*, Selahattin BAYRAM / istockphoto.com; 577-632, 652-664 *Greek Design Element* © Vectorstock; 582-583 *Smyrna Columns*, BrunoStock.com; 589 *Christians Hunted Down in*

Courtesy of Photographer: Andreas Praefcke / Source: Wikipedia (Laurel Wreath).

Special Permissions

615R *Lystra* © Holy Land Photos, Image courtesy of Dr. Carl Rassmussen (www.HolyLandPhotos.org) used by permission; **616** *Thessalonica Ruins* © courtesy of Tony Cooke; **617** *Ancient Steps Tribute to St. Paul*, Berea (Verria), Greece © Holy Land Photos, Image courtesy of Dr. Carl Rassmussen (www.HolyLandPhotos.org) used by permission.

Private Collection — Renner

601 *Ancient Laodicea*; **618L** *Corinth Ruins*; **618R** *Basilica, Ephesus*; **626** *Underground Arches of Central Marketplace, Smyrna*; **658-659** *Ruins on Mount Pagos*; **666** *Ancient Oil Lamps*.

Back Matter:

Private Collection — Renner

699-703 *Turkey Research Team Photos*.

A LIGHT IN DARKNESS
VOLUME ONE

GENERAL INDEX

C

D

ascension to Heaven 383

authority over demons 325-6, 330-1

betrayal of 422, 460-2

birth of 10, 96-7, 133, 381

blood of 36, 85

dedication of as an infant 117-8

endured the Cross 113, 124-6, 411, 459, 578, 586-7

entrusted care of Mary to John 8

40-day fast in the wilderness 374-5, 630

in the Garden of Gethsemane 375-6

Lordship of 331-5

name of 322, 325-6, 331, 367, 441-2

parables and teachings in the synoptic gospels 75-6, 388, 475, 592-3, 655

resurrection of 87, 97, 292-3, 383, 586-7, 652

Second Coming of 374, 457

taught in Jewish synagogues 283

transfiguration on Mount Tabor 90-1

see also: miracles; of Jesus

Jesus, the exalted Christ 123-4

Alpha and Omega 57, 62, 132

Ancient of Days 81, 87-8, 90

appeared to Paul on the road to Damascus 119-123, 422-4, 607

eyes as a flame of fire 92-3, 121

Great High Priest, The 83-4, 94, 98, 118, 122

Great "I AM," The 130-2

Great Judge, The 97, 114-5, 118, 466-8

Great Refiner, The 72

hated the deeds of the Nicolaitans 23, 470-1, 474-5, 488

Humble Servant 124-6

intimately knew the works of the seven churches 78-9, 402-5, 489, 589

"like unto the Son of Man" 79-82

loves His Church 72, 77, 115

messages to the seven churches 3, 57, 62-3, 66-7, 76-7, 84, 92, 99-100, 115, 117, 138, 141, 234, 277, 369-70, 381, 386, 399, 404, 467, 601, 622

Prince of the kings of the earth 81-2, 86, 112

standing in Heaven 87-9

Victor over death 133-7, 587

see also: church of Ephesus; Jesus' message to

see also: church of Smyrna; Jesus' message to

see also: John; vision of the exalted Christ

Jewish communities 584, 602, 604, 612

in Alexandria 288-9, 612

in Antioch in Pisidia 283, 614-5

in Berea 283, 617

in Corinth 283, 617-8

in Damascus 613

in Ephesus 214-5, 271, 281-4, 300-3, 361, 409, 612, 618-9

in Iconium 283, 614-5

in Rome 612

in Smyrna 496, 500, 578, 584-5, 601-12, 619, 662

in Thessalonica 283, 616-7

Jezebel (destructive member of the church of Thyatira) 79

John, apostle 124, 472

arrest by Emperor Domitian 15, 18, 47, 112, 368

K

L

M

S

T

ENGLISH TO GREEK INDEX

A

B

C

D

GREEK TO ENGLISH INDEX

A

B

C

D

dunamis (mighty deeds) 430

dunamis (miracles) 308

dunamis (strength) 119

dunatos (mighty) 290

E

echo (had) 101

echo (I have) 444

ego (I) 30

ego eimi (I am) 130, 132

eis (into) 282

ek (out) 319, 331, 334, 372, 388, 390

ek (out of) 469

ekklesia (church) 372, 388, 390-8, 583

ekpheugo (fled) 331

ekporeuomai (went out) 319

en (in) 375

en pneumatic (in the spirit) 56, 61

enduo (clothed) 82

enduo (endued) 82-3

enischuo (strengthen) 375

enopion (before) 472

ephallomai (leaped) 330

epistamai (know) 329

epistrepho (turned) 62, 456

erchomai (I will come) 466

erga (deeds) 465, 474

erga (works) 465

ergos (work) 39

ergos (works) 335

erotao (desired) 285

esthio (to eat) 478

euporia (wealth) 346

eurisko (found) 439

exomologeo (confessed) 334

exorkidzo (exorcists) 322

G

ginomai (became) 586, 632

ginomai (was) 45, 56, 61, 134, 586

ginosko (know) 329

ginou (be thou) 632

grammateus (town clerk) 362

gumnos (naked) 331

H

Hades (hell) 136

harpage (spoiling) 598

helios (sun) 118

hetaireia (trade guilds) 595

homoios (like unto) 80

homologeo (to confess) 334

horao (saw) 120

hubristes (injurious) 604

huparcho (goods) 598

hupo (under) 43, 408

hupomene (patience) 43

hupomeno (patience) 408-10, 426, 428

I

idou (behold) 622

ischuos (prevail) 330

ischuos (strength) 330, 375

istemi (standeth) 453

K

kai (and) 430

kakolegeo (spake evil) 302

kakos (evil) 302, 411

kaleo (to call) 388, 390

kata (dominating) 82, 261, 330

O

P

R

S

ABOUT THE AUTHOR

 Rick Renner is a highly respected Bible teacher and leader in the international Christian community. He is the author of a long list of books, including the bestsellers *Dressed To Kill* and *Sparkling Gems From the Greek 1 and 2*, which have sold millions of copies in multiple languages worldwide. Rick's understanding of the Greek language and biblical history opens up the Scriptures in a unique way that enables his audience to gain wisdom and insight while learning something brand new from the Word of God. Rick and his wife Denise have cumulatively authored more than 40 books that have been distributed worldwide.

Rick is the overseer of the Good News Association of Churches, founder of the Moscow Good News Church, pastor of the Internet Good News Church, and founder of Media Mir. He is the president of GNC (Good News Channel) — the largest Russian-speaking Christian satellite network in the world, which broadcasts the Gospel 24/7 to countless Russian- and Ukrainian-speaking viewers worldwide via multiple satellites and the Internet. Rick is the founder and president of RENNER Ministries in Broken Arrow, Oklahoma, and host to his TV program, also seen around the world in multiple languages. Rick leads this amazing work with Denise — his wife and lifelong ministry partner — along with their sons and committed leadership team.

CONTACT RENNER MINISTRIES

For further information
about RENNER Ministries,
please contact the office nearest you,
or visit the ministry website at:
www.renner.org

**ALL USA
CORRESPONDENCE:**
RENNER Ministries
1814 W. Tacoma St.
Broken Arrow, OK 74012
(918) 496-3213
Or 1-800-RICK-593
Email: renner@renner.org
Website: www.renner.org

MOSCOW OFFICE:
RENNER Ministries
P. O. Box 789
101000, Moscow, Russia
+7 (495) 727-1470
Email: blagayavestonline@ignc.org
Website: www.ignc.org

RIGA OFFICE:
RENNER Ministries
Unijas 99
Riga LV-1084, Latvia
+371 67802150
Email: info@goodnews.lv

KIEV OFFICE:
RENNER Ministries
P. O. Box 300
01001, Kiev, Ukraine
+38 (044) 451-8315
Email: blagayavestonline@ignc.org

OXFORD OFFICE:
RENNER Ministries
Box 7, 266 Banbury Road
Oxford OX2 7DL, England
+44 1865 521024
Email: europe@renner.org

BOOKS BY RICK RENNER

Apostles & Prophets
Build Your Foundation*
Christmas — The Rest of the Story
Chosen by God*
Dream Thieves*
Dressed To Kill*
The Holy Spirit and You*
How To Keep Your Head on Straight in a World Gone Crazy*
How To Receive Answers From Heaven!*
Insights on Successful Leadership*
Last-Days Survival Guide*
A Life Ablaze*
Life in the Combat Zone*
A Light in Darkness, Volume One,
    Seven Messages to the Seven Churches series
The Love Test*
No Room for Compromise, Volume Two,
    Seven Messages to the Seven Churches series
Paid in Full*
The Point of No Return*
Repentance*
Signs You'll See Just Before Jesus Comes*
Sparkling Gems From the Greek Daily Devotional 1*
Sparkling Gems From the Greek Daily Devotional 2*
Spiritual Weapons To Defeat the Enemy*
Ten Guidelines To Help You Achieve Your Long-Awaited Promotion!*
Testing the Supernatural
365 Days of Increase
365 Days of Power
Turn Your God-Given Dreams Into Reality*
Unlikely — Our Faith-Filled Journey to the Ends of the Earth*
Why We Need the Gifts of the Spirit*
The Will of God — The Key to Your Success*
You Can Get Over It*

*Digital version available for Kindle, Nook, and/or iBook.

Note: Books by Rick Renner are available for purchase at:
www.renner.org

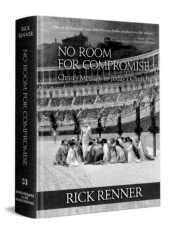

NO ROOM FOR COMPROMISE
VOLUME TWO

No Room for Compromise: Jesus' Message to Today's Church is Volume Two of the *Seven Messages to the Seven Churches* series. It presents an engaging exploration of the pagan culture of the First Century Church, with an emphasis on the city of Pergamum. Against this historical backdrop, Rick Renner highlights Jesus' message to the church of Pergamum when He appeared in a vision during the apostle John's imprisonment on the island of Patmos.

With superb photographs, many of which were shot on location in Turkey, Rick guides readers through a fascinating, detailed explanation of Jesus' message to the Pergamene church as he prophetically declares the critical significance of this message to the Church in these last days before Jesus returns. Rick also gives the reader a larger context within which to frame the pivotal moment when Jesus appeared to John on that isolated island. Rick takes the reader through a revealing overview of the first three centuries AD in which the infant Church grew amidst much opposition within a pagan world, demonstrating that darkness can never overcome the light, life, and power that the truth of Jesus Christ offers all those who believe.

Volume Two is a comprehensive, completely indexed reference book and provides:

- In-depth scriptural teaching that makes the New Testament come alive.
- Nearly 400 images — including more than 100 photos taken on location — classic artwork, artifacts, illustrations, and maps.
- A beautifully bound full-color edition.

SPARKLING GEMS® FROM THE GREEK 1

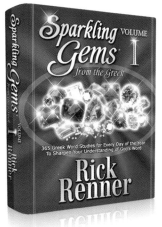

1,048 pages
(Hardback)

In 2003, Rick Renner's *Sparkling Gems® From the Greek 1* quickly gained widespread recognition for its unique illumination of the New Testament through more than 1,000 Greek word studies in a 365-day devotional format. Today *Sparkling Gems® 1* remains a beloved resource that has spiritually strengthened believers worldwide. As many have testified, the wealth of truths within its pages never grows old. Year after year, *Sparkling Gems® 1* continues to deepen readers' understanding of the Bible.

SPARKLING GEMS® FROM THE GREEK 2

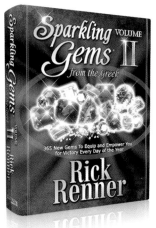

1,280 pages
(Hardback)

Rick infuses into *Sparkling Gems® From the Greek 2* the added strength and richness of many more years of his own personal study and growth in God — expanding this devotional series to impact the reader's heart on a deeper level than ever before. This remarkable study tool helps unlock new hidden treasures from God's Word that will draw readers into an ever more passionate pursuit of Him.

DRESSED TO KILL

A BIBLICAL APPROACH
TO SPIRITUAL WARFARE AND ARMOR

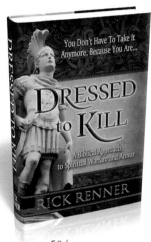

504 pages
(Hardback)

Rick Renner's book **Dressed To Kill** is considered by many to be a true classic on the subject of spiritual warfare. The original version, which sold more than 400,000 copies, is a curriculum staple in Bible schools worldwide. In this beautiful volume, you will find:

- 504 pages of reedited text
- 16 pages of full-color illustrations
- Questions at the end of each chapter to guide you into deeper study

In **Dressed To Kill**, Rick explains with exacting detail the purpose and function of each piece of Roman armor. In the process, he describes the significance of our *spiritual* armor not only to withstand the onslaughts of the enemy, but also to overturn the tendencies of the carnal mind. Furthermore, Rick delivers a clear, scriptural presentation on the biblical definition of spiritual warfare — what it is and what it is not.

When you walk with God in deliberate, continual fellowship, He will enrobe you with Himself. Armed with the knowledge of who you are in Him, you will be dressed and dangerous to the works of darkness, unflinching in the face of conflict, and fully equipped to take the offensive and gain mastery over any opposition from your spiritual foe. You don't have to accept defeat anymore once you are *dressed to kill*!

SIGNS YOU'LL SEE JUST BEFORE JESUS COMES

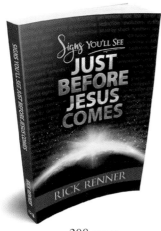

208 pages
(Paperback)

As we advance toward the golden moment of Christ's return for His Church, there are signs on the road we're traveling to let us know where we are in time. Jesus Himself foretold the types of events that will surely take place as we watch for His return.

In his book **Signs You'll See Just Before Jesus Comes**, Rick Renner explores the signs in Matthew 24:3-12, expounding on each one from the Greek text with his unique style of teaching. Each chapter is written to *prepare* and *embolden* a last-days generation of believers, not send them running for the hills!

The signs on the road are appearing closer together. We are on the precipice of something new. Soon we'll see the final sign at the edge of our destination as we enter the territory of the last days, hours, and minutes *just before Jesus comes*.

HOW TO KEEP YOUR HEAD ON STRAIGHT IN A WORLD GONE CRAZY

DEVELOPING DISCERNMENT FOR THESE LAST DAYS

400 pages
(Paperback)

The world is changing. In fact, it's more than changing — it has *gone crazy*.

We are living in a world where faith is questioned and sin is welcomed — where people seem to have lost their minds about what is right and wrong. It seems truth has been turned *upside down*.

In Rick Renner's book ***How To Keep Your Head on Straight in a World Gone Crazy***, he reveals the disastrous consequences of a society in spiritual and moral collapse. In this book, you'll discover what Christians need to be doing to stay out of the chaos and remain anchored to truth. You'll learn how to stay sensitive to the Holy Spirit, how to discern right and wrong teaching, how to be grounded in prayer, and how to be spiritually prepared for living in victory in these last days.

Leading ministers from around the world are calling this book essential for every believer. Topics include:

- Contending for the Faith in the Last Days
- How To Pray for Leaders Who Are in Error
- How To Judge if a Teaching Is Good or Bad
- Seducing Spirits and Doctrines of Demons
- How To Be a Good Minister of Jesus Christ

To order, visit us online at: **www.renner.org**

Book Resellers: Contact Harrison House at 800-722-6774
or visit **www.HarrisonHouse.com** for quantity discounts.

LAST-DAYS SURVIVAL GUIDE

A SCRIPTURAL HANDBOOK
TO PREPARE YOU FOR THESE PERILOUS TIMES

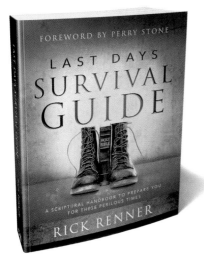

472 pages
(Paperback)

In his book *Last-Days Survival Guide*, Rick Renner thoroughly expands on Second Timothy 3 concerning the last-days signs to expect in society as one age draws to a close before another age begins.

Topics include:

- What the word "perilous" really means and why God is alerting you.

- What exact characteristics will mark society in the very last days.

- What actions to take to protect yourself and those you love.

- Strategies to stop the devil from attacking you and your loved ones.

Rick also explains how not to just *survive* the times, but to *thrive* in their midst. God wants you as a believer to be equipped — *outfitted* — to withstand end-time storms, to navigate wind-tossed seas, and to sail with His grace and power to fulfill your divine destiny on earth!

If you're concerned about what you're witnessing in society today — and even in certain sectors of the church — the answers you need in order to keep your gaze focused on Christ and maintain your victory are in this book!

UNLIKELY

Our Faith-Filled Journey to the Ends of the Earth

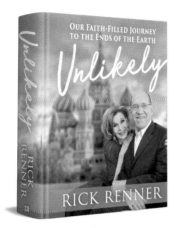

1,116 pages
(Hardback)

Rick Renner shares his life story in detail in his autobiography *Unlikely — Our Faith-Filled Journey to the Ends of the Earth*. In this book, you'll see how our smallest decisions can lead to something *big* if we'll determine to stay the course and follow God's plan for our lives wholeheartedly.

Rick and Denise Renner's lives are "proof positive" that this is true. From their humble upbringings in small Oklahoma towns, a lack of understanding from their peers growing up, and evil assaults from the enemy that threatened to undermine God's plan, the Lord drew Rick and Denise together and sent them, with their three young sons, to live in the former Soviet Union. Rick and Denise live and minister powerfully in the former USSR to this day — and not one of their hurtful, *harrowing* experiences was wasted!

You'll enjoy reading about Rick's adventures of flying in unsafe planes across 11 time zones in the former USSR, of circumventing criminal opportunists, and of dealing with deficits of food, fuel, and heat during harsh winters just after the fall of the Iron Curtain. Rick and his family were gloriously, and, at times, *hilariously* delivered so they could deliver the message of restoration and hope God sent them to give.

You have an unlikely story too. Life is not a game of chance. It can be a thrilling adventure when you give God your *yes* and "buckle up" to receive Heaven's directive for your life. This book can show you how!

To order, visit us online at: **www.renner.org**

Book Resellers: Contact Harrison House at 800-722-6774
or visit **www.HarrisonHouse.com** for quantity discounts.

CHRISTMAS
THE REST OF THE STORY

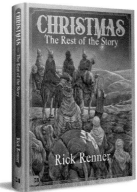

304 pages
(Hardback)

In this storybook of biblical history, Rick takes you on the "magical" journey of Christ's coming to earth in a way you've probably never heard it before. Featuring full-color, original illustrations, *Christmas — The Rest of the Story* gives the spellbinding account of God's masterful plan to redeem mankind, and vividly portrays the wonder of the Savior's birth and His "ordinary" life marked by God's *extraordinary* plan.

If you want to be taken back in your imagination to this earth-shaking course of events that changed the history of the whole world, this book is a *must-have* not just for the Christmas season, but for all time. *Topics include:*

- Why God chose Mary and Joseph.

- The significance of the *manger* and *swaddling clothes.*

- Why angels viewed *God in the flesh* with such wonderment.

- Why King Herod was so troubled by this historical birth.

- How we can prepare for Christ's *next* coming.

Christmas — The Rest of the Story is sure to be a favorite in your family for generations to come! Jesus' birth is truly *the greatest story on earth* — perhaps never more uniquely told than in the pages of this book.

Equipping Believers to Walk in the Abundant Life

John 10:10b

Connect with us for fresh content and news about forthcoming books from your favorite authors...

Facebook @ HarrisonHousePublishers

Instagram @ HarrisonHousePublishing

www.harrisonhouse.com